The Book of
MATRICULATIONS
and
DEGREES

T0381601

The Book of MATRICULATIONS
and DEGREES: a Catalogue of
those who have been Matriculated
or admitted to any Degree in the
UNIVERSITY of CAMBRIDGE from
1901 to 1912

Cambridge :
at the University Press
1915

CAMBRIDGE
UNIVERSITY PRESS

University Printing House, Cambridge CB2 8BS, United Kingdom

Cambridge University Press is part of the University of Cambridge.

It furthers the University's mission by disseminating knowledge in the pursuit of education, learning and research at the highest international levels of excellence.

www.cambridge.org
Information on this title: www.cambridge.org/9781107511934

© Cambridge University Press 1915

First published 1915
First paperback edition 2015

A catalogue record for this publication is available from the British Library

ISBN 978-1-107-51193-4 Paperback

PREFACE

IN the Preface to the Book of Matriculations and Degrees from 1851 to 1900 it was pointed out that lists of persons proceeding to Degrees in the University of Cambridge had already been published covering the period from 1659 to 1884. A Book of Matriculations and Degrees in the University from 1544 to 1659, edited by Dr J. Venn and Mr J. A. Venn, M.A., of Trinity College, has since been published by the University Press. With the present volume, therefore, the period covered, so far as Degrees are concerned, is from 1544 to 1912.

The volume now issued contains the names of all who were matriculated or who completed Degrees from 1 January 1901 to 31 December 1912. Tables of abbreviations of proper names, and of the letters used to designate the various degrees conferred, are printed after this preface. It should be noted that no account is taken of titles of Ordinary Degrees of Master or Doctor to which persons were admitted in the Michaelmas Term of 1912, since these Degrees were not completed until the Easter Term of 1913. It should also be noted that in the year 1908 the day for the Inauguration of Bachelors of Medicine and Surgery was altered from June to December, bringing these Degrees into line with Bachelor's Degrees in Arts, Law, and Music. Hence in the case of all Degrees below that of Master all who have been admitted to a Degree in the civil year are now included. It should be added that there is no separate ceremony of inauguration or creation in the case of Bachelors of Divinity or of complete Degrees conferred *honoris causa*. Honorary titles of Degrees conferred from 1901 to 1912 are included in the volume; in their case the question of the completion of the Degree does not arise.

The present volume has been prepared for the press by Mr B. Benham, M.A., of Corpus Christi College, the Assistant Registrary, and Mr C. J. Stonebridge, the Registrary's Clerk, and I have reason to know that every possible care has been taken by them in the discharge of their duties. My warmest thanks are due to them.

It can hardly be anticipated that no errors are contained in the volume. I shall be grateful for any corrections that may be sent to me.

JOHN NEVILLE KEYNES,
Registrary.

THE REGISTRY OF THE UNIVERSITY, CAMBRIDGE,
16 *August* 1915.

TABLE OF ABBREVIATIONS

CHRISTIAN NAMES

Abbr.	Name	Abbr.	Name	Abbr.	Name
Abr.	Abraham	Ern.	Ernest	Nich.	Nicholas
Alb.	Albert	Fra.	Francis	Pat.	Patrick
Alex.	Alexander	Fre.	Frederick	Pet.	Peter
Alf.	Alfred	Geo.	George	Phil.	Philip
And.	Andrew	Gilb.	Gilbert	Reg.	Reginald
Anth.	Anthony	Hen.	Henry	Rich.	Richard
Archib.	Archibald	Herb.	Herbert	Rob.	Robert
Art.	Arthur	Hor.	Horace	Sam.	Samuel
Barth.	Bartholomew	Hub.	Hubert	Sept.	Septimus
Benj.	Benjamin	Ja.	James	Sid.	Sidney
Bern.	Bernard	Jerem.	Jeremiah	Steph.	Stephen
Cha.	Charles	Jonat.	Jonathan	Syd.	Sydney
Chris.	Christopher	Jos.	Joseph	Theoph.	Theophilus
Clem.	Clement	Leon.	Leonard	Tho.	Thomas
Dan.	Daniel	Matth.	Matthew	Tim.	Timothy
Dav.	David	Maur.	Maurice	Walt.	Walter
Edm.	Edmund	Mich.	Michael	Will.	William
Edw.	Edward	Nath.	Nathaniel		

DEGREES, ETC.

A.B.	Bachelor of Arts	Mus.D.	Doctor of Music
A.M.	Master of Arts	Sc.D.	Doctor of Science
B.C.	Bachelor of Surgery	Dubl. incorp.	By incorporation from Dublin
B.D.	Bachelor of Divinity		
D.D.	Doctor of Divinity	Oxf. incorp.	By incorporation from Oxford
LL.B.	Bachelor of Laws		
LL.M.	Master of Laws	M	Michaelmas Term
LL.D.	Doctor of Laws	L	Lent Term
Litt.D.	Doctor of Letters	E	Easter Term
M.B.	Bachelor of Medicine	*	Fellow of
M.C.	Master of Surgery	†	Conferred in absence
M.D.	Doctor of Medicine	1884 (2)	Inaugurated 19 Dec. 1884
Mus.B.	Bachelor of Music	1908 (2)	„ 19 Dec. 1908
Mus.M.	Master of Music		

Titles of degrees conferred *honoris causa* are denoted by italics.

ERRATA. Vol. 1851—1900

{*For* A'Court, Herb. Holmes ...... Trin.	M 1870	
{*read* à'Court, Herb. Holmes ...... Trin.	M 1870	
{*For* Agar-Ellis, Jacques .... Trin.	M 1881	
{*read* Agar-Ellis, Jacques .... Trin.	M 1881 A.B. 1884 (2). Ja. A.M. 1891	
{*For* Aickin, Edw. ....*Jes.	M 1852 A.B. 1856. A.M. 1859	
{*read* Aikin, Edw. ....*Jes.	M 1852 A.B. 1856. A.M. 1859	
{*For* Aitken, Rob. Mempes ...... Trin.	M 1898	
{*read* Aitken, Rob. Menpes ...... Trin.	M 1898	
{*For* Aitkin, Cha. Edm. .... Trin.	M 1864	
{*read* Aikin, Cha. Edm. .... Trin.	M 1864	
{*For* Alison, Laughton .... Trin.	M 1857 A.B. 1861. A.M. 1864	
{*read* Alison, Loughton .... Trin.	M 1857 A.B. 1861. A.M. 1864	
For Allen, Art. Watts .... H. Sel.	E 1898 *read* Allen, Art. Watts, Joh. E 1898	
{*For* Anant, Ram .... Chr.	M 1893	
{*read* Anant, Ram .... Chr.	M 1893 A.B. 1896	
{*For* Atherley, Syd. Kerr Bulley Trin.	M 1855	
{*read* Atherley, Syd. Kerr Buller Trin.	M 1855	
{*For* Baker, Hen. John Tyack ... Jes.	M 1884 A.B. 1887	
{*read* Bake, Hen. John Tyack ... Jes.	M 1884 A.B. 1887	
{*For* Barrett, Harold Slater ...... Trin.	M 1895 A.B. 1898	
{*read* Barrett, Harold Salter ...... Trin.	M 1895 A.B. 1898	
{*For* Barrington, Cecil Vivian ... Trin.	M 1884 A.B., LL.B. 1897	
{*read* Barrington, Cecil Vivian ... Trin.	M 1884 A.B., LL.B. 1887	
Insert Barrow, Geo. Shuldham Malet Jes.	M 1880	
Omit Barton, Tho. Sept. .... Cai.	M 1852	
Insert Batcheler, Fre. Alb. .... Pet.	M 1859	
{*For* Baxendale, Lloyd Salisbury Down.	M 1848	
{*read* Baxendale, Lloyd Salisbury Trin.	M 1848 Down. LL.B. 1854	
Omit Bellamy, Geo. Tho. .... Cai.	M 1870	
For Benstead, Phil. .... Qu.	M 1899 *read* Bensted, Phil., Qu. M 1899	
{*For* Beresford-Hope, Cha. Tho. Trin.	M 1874	
{*read* Beresford-Hope, Cha. Tho. Trin.	M 1874 A.B. 1878. A.M. 1881	
For Birch, Harold Lee .... Trin.	M 1899 *read* Birch, Harold Lea, M 1899	
{*For* Blair, Forbes Cromartie Hunter } Trin.	M 1877	
{*read* Blair, Forbes Cromartie Hunter } Trin.	M 1877 A.B. 1881. LL.B. 1884	
Omit Blundell, Hen. Seymour Moss Joh.	M 1890	
„ Boswall, Will. Houstoun ... Trin.	M 1868	
„ Bowcher, Alf. Herb. .... Trin.	M 1875	
{*For* Bowes-Watson, Geo. .... Trin.	M 1859	
{*read* Bowes-Watson, Geo. .... Trin.	M 1859 A.B. 1863. A.M. 1866	
{*For* Bowring, John Fredrick Edw. Trin.	M 1885 A.B. 1888	
{*read* Bowring, John Fre. Edw. ... Trin.	M 1885 A.B. 1888	
{*For* Bowyer-Smijth, Edw. ...... Trin.	M 1864	
{*read* Bowyer-Smijth, Edw. ...... Trin.	M 1864 A.B. 1868	
{*For* Boynten, Hen. Somerville ... Mag.	L 1864	
{*read* Boynton, Hen. Somerville ... Mag.	L 1864	
For Bradbury, John Cecil Openshaw } Cla.	M 1891 {*read* Bradbury, John Cecil Openshaw, Cla. M 1892	
{*For* Bridgeman, Frederic Sid. ... Sid.	M 1900	
{*read* Bridgman, Frederic Sid. ... Sid.	M 1900	
{*For* Bridgeman, John Rob. Orlando Trin.	M 1850 A.B. 1853	
{*read* Bridgeman, John Rob. Orlando Trin.	M 1850 A.M. 1853	

{*For*	Brown, Ern. Will.	Trin.	M 1875	
{*read*	Brown, Ern. Will.	Trin.	M 1875 A.B. 1879. A.M. 1893	
To	Browne, Alf. John	Joh.	M 1870 *add* Jukes-Browne, Alf. John,	
			[A.B. 1874	
Add	Buckinghamshire (7th *Earl of*)		*See* Hobart, Sid. Carre (*Lord*)	
{*For*	Budgett, Ja. Herb.	Trin.	M 1866 A.B. 1899	
{*read*	Budgett, Ja. Herb.	Trin.	M 1886 A.B. 1889	
{*For*	Bullock, Art. Hen.	Trin.	M 1849 A.B. 1853. A.M. 1856	
{*read*	Bullock, Art. Hen.	Trin.	M 1849 Down. A.B. 1853. A.M. 1856	
{*For*	Bullock-Webster, Geo. Russell	Trin.	M 1876 A.B. 1880. A.M. 1888	
{*read*	Bullock-Webster, Geo. Russell	Joh.	M 1876 A.B. 1880. A.M. 1888	
Omit	Bulwer-Lytton, Victor Alex.} Geo. Rob.	Trin.	M 1895	
{*For*	Bunbury, Rob. Clem. Seonce	Trin.	M 1866	
{*read*	Bunbury, Rob. Clem. Sconce	Trin.	M 1866	
To	Bund Willis, John Will. ...	Cai.	M 1861 *add* Willis Bund, John Will. Bund,	
{*For*	Burnand, Cha. Fra.	Jes.	M 1894 [A.B., LL.B. 1865. A.M. 1868	
{*read*	Burnard, Cha. Fra.	Jes.	M 1894	
{*For*	Burrow, Geo. Shuldham Malet	Jes.	M 1880	
{*read*	Barrow, Geo. Shuldham Malet	Jes.	M 1880	
Omit	Cake, Wenman	Trin.	M 1875	
{*For*	Calvert, Alex. Colton	Trin.	M 1888	
{*read*	Calvert, Alex. Colton	Trin.	M 1889	
Omit	Candy, Tho. Elger	Trin.	M 1878	
{*For*	Cannon, Frank John	Trin.	M 1870 {A.B. 1874. Fra. A.M. 1877. Fra. John M.B. 1882	
{*read*	Cannon, Fra. John	Trin.	M 1870 A.B. 1874. A.M. 1877. M.B. 1882	
{*For*	Carter, Fra. Hen. Benham	Trin.	M 1872	
{*read*	Carter, Fra. Hen. Bonham	Trin.	M 1872 [A.B. 1864. A.M. 1867	
To	Catt, Edm. Austen	Trin.	M 1860 *add* post Willett, Edm. Austen,	
{*For*	Chand, Diwan Tek	Chr.	M 1891	
{*read*	Chand, Diwan Tek	Chr.	M 1891 A.B. 1895	
{*For*	Chanler, Louis Stuyvesant	Trin.	M 1894	
{*read*	Chanler, Lewis Stuyvesant	Trin.	M 1894	
{*For*	Cheese, Geo. Rooper	Trin.	M 1853	
{*read*	Cheere, Geo. Rooper	Trin.	M 1853	
{*For*	Clifford, Will. Kingdom ...	Trin.	M 1863	
{*read*	Clifford, Will. Kingdon ...	Trin.	M 1863	
{*For*	Clode, Cha. Mathew	Cla.	M 1871	
{*read*	Clode, Cha. Mathew	Pem.	M 1871	
Insert	Cockburn-Hood		*See* Hood, John Shapland Elliot	
„	Coke, Wenman	Trin.	M 1875	
To	Colby, Edm. Reynolds	Em.	M 1852 *add* A.M. Oxf. ad eund. 1863	
Omit	Colby, Edm. Reynolds		A.M. Oxf. ad eund. 1863	
{*For*	Colebrook, Rich. Ern.	Sid.	L 1883	
{*read*	Colebrook, Rich. Ern.	Sid.	L 1893	
{*For*	Colville-Wallis, Will.	Em.	L 1877	
{*read*	Colville-Wallis, Will.	Em.	L 1877 A.B. 1880. A.M. 1883	
{*For*	Compton-Smith, Will.	Trin.	M 1878	
{*read*	Compton-Smith, Will.	Trin.	M 1878 A.B., LL.B. 1882	
Omit	Copeman, Geo. Will. Bazett	Trin. H.	M 1893	
{*For*	Corrie, Tho. Greenway	Trin.	M 1847 A.B. 1851. A.M. 1854	
{*read*	Corrie, Tho. Greenway	Pem.	M 1847 Trin. A.B. 1851. A.M. 1854	
{*For*	Courage, Rob. Michael	Trin.	L 1873	
{*read*	Courage, Rob. Michell	Trin.	L 1873	
{*For*	Courtauld, Will. Julian ...	Trin.	M 1889	
{*read*	Courtauld, Will. Julien ...	Trin.	M 1889	
{*For*	Crafer, Tho. Wilfrid	Chr.	E 1889 A.B. 1892. A.M. 1896	
{*read*	Crafer, Tho. Wilfrid	Chr.	E 1889 A.B. 1892. Jes. A.M. 1896	
{*For*	Creak, Alb. Shelley	Trin.	M 1870	
{*read*	Creak, Alb. Shelly	Trin.	M 1870	

For Crooke, Walt. Barry	Trin.	M 1854	
read Crooke, Walt. Parry	Trin.	M 1854	
Omit Crossley, Fre. Petrus	Chr.	M 1896	
For Davies, Edw. Tho.	Joh.	M 1873 A.B. 1877. A.M. 1880	
read Davies, Edw. Tho.	Joh.	M 1873 Trin. A.B. 1877. A.M. 1880	
To Davies, Ern. Reuter John Wyatt	Trin.	M 1885 *add* Wyatt-Davies, Ern. Reuter John, A.B. 1888. A.M. 1892	
Omit Dawson, Geo. Malcolm	Trin.	M 1849	
For Dearden, Hen. Woodhouse		A.B. Dubl. ad eund. 1858	
read Dearden, Hen. Woodhouse		A.M. Dubl. ad eund. 1858	
For Deck, Hen. Leigh Richmond	C. C.	M 1872 A.B. 1877. A.M. 1880	
read Deck, Hen. Legh Richmond	C. C.	M 1872 A.B. 1877. A.M. 1880	
For De Hochepied Larpent, Lionel Gerrard Harrison	Pem.	M 1883	
read De Hochepied Larpent, Lionel Gerrard Harrison	Pem.	M 1883 A.B. 1886	
For De Kiran Chandra	Joh.	M 1892	
read Dè, Kiran Chandra	Joh.	M 1892	
For De Wet, John Victor Douglas	Joh.	M 1862 A.B., LL.B. 1866. A.M.† 1869. LL.M. 1873	
read De Wet, John Victor Douglas	Joh.	M 1862 Down. A.B., LL.B. 1866. A.M.† 1869. LL.M. 1873	
For Dixon, Tho. Featherston ...	Chr.	M 1853 A.B. 1863. A.M. 1867	
read Dixon, Tho. Featherston ...	Chr.	M 1859 A.B. 1863. A.M. 1867	
For Dobede, Hen. Gerald Farman	Trin.	M 1879	
read Dobede, Hen. Gerald Fairman	Trin.	M 1879	
For Doddrell, Curling Finzell ...	Chr.	M 1893 A.B. 1899	
read Doddrell, Curling Finzel ...	Chr.	M 1893 A.B. 1899	
For Driver, Fre. John	N. C.	M 1873 A.B. 1877. M.B., A.M. 1883	
read Driver, Fre. John	N. C.	M 1873 Chr. A.B. 1877. M.B., A.M. 1883	
For Du Port, Cha. Durrell	Cai.	M 1855	
read Du Port, Cha. Durell	Cai.	M 1855	
For Earle, Sid.	Trin.	M 1883	
read Earle, Syd.	Trin.	M 1883	
For Edmonds, Art. Jonat.	Joh.	M 1862 A.B. 1866. A.M. 1869	
read Edmonds, Art. Jonat.	Joh.	M 1862 Cla. A.B. 1866. A.M. 1869	
For Elder, Harry Montagu	Trin.	M 1880 A.B. 1884. A.M. 1887	
read Elder, Harry Montague	Trin.	M 1880 A.B. 1884. A.M. 1887	
To Elliot, Geo. Fra. Scott	Trin.	M 1879 *add* Scott-Elliot, Geo. Fra., A.B.	
For Ellis, Fre. Geo.	Trin.	M 1848 A.B. 1851 [1883. A.M. 1886	
read Ellis, Fre. Geo.	Trin.	M 1848 A.M. 1851	
For Ellis-Jervoise, Rob. Purefoy	Pem.	M 1876	
read Ellis-Jervoise, Rob. Purefoy	Pem.	M 1876 A.B. 1881	
For Ellison, Douglas	N. C.	M 1882 A.B. 1885. A.M. 1890	
read Ellison, Douglas	N. C.	M 1882 H. Sel. A.B. 1885. A.M. 1890	
For Erskine, Gratney Rodolph Zwilchenbart	Trin. H.	M 1900	
read Erskine, Gratney Rodolph Zwilchenbart	Trin. H.	M 1890	
For Evelegh, Will. Geo.	Pet.	E 1887	
read Eveleigh, Will. Geo.	Pet.	E 1887	
For Facey, Will. Edwin	Joh.	M 1880 A.B. 1884. A.M. 1886	
read Facey, Will. Edwin	Joh.	M 1880 A.B. 1884. M.B. 1886	
For Feilding, Cha. Will. Alex.	Trin.	M 1853 A.B. 1856	
read Feilding, Cha. Will. Alex.	Trin.	M 1853 A.M. 1856	
Omit Fellows, Rob. Bruce	Chr.	M 1850	
For Fiddes, Art. Elphinstone ...	Cla.	M 1856	
read Fiddes, Rob. Elphinstone ...	Cla.	M 1856	
Omit Fisher, Art. Cuthbert Jeddere	Trin. H.	L 1872	
For Fitz Herbert, Sam. Tho. ...	Trin.	M 1865 A.B. 1869. A.M. 1890	
read Fitzherbert, Sam. Tho.	Trin.	M 1865 A.B. 1869. A.M. 1890	

{*For*	Fitzjohn, Tutor	N. C.	M 1896 Cai.
{*read*	Fitzjohn, Tudor	N. C.	M 1896
{*For*	Fletcher, Cha. Art.	Trin.	M 1891
{*read*	Fletcher, Cha. Art.	Trin. H.	M 1891
{*For*	Folkes, Geo. Howe Browne	Trin.	M 1852 A.B. 1856. A.M. 1859
{*read*	ffolkes, Geo. Howe Browne	Trin.	M 1852 A.B. 1856. A.M. 1859
{*For*	Folkes, Will. Hovel Browne	Trin.	M 1866 A.B. 1870. A.M. 1874
{*read*	ffolkes, Will. Hovel Browne	Trin.	M 1866 A.B. 1870. A.M. 1874
To	Fontaine, Will.	Joh.	M 1859 *add* la Fontaine, A.B. 1865. A.M.
{*For*	Fox, Edw. Storrs	Joh.	M 1873 A.B. 1877. A.M. 1891 [1879
{*read*	Fox, Edw. Storrs	Joh.	M 1873 C. C. A.B. 1877. A.M. 1891
{*For*	Fuchs, Hermann Heinrich	Qu.	M 1874 A.B. 1878
{*read*	Fuchs, Hermann Heinrich	Qu.	M 1874 Hermann Hen., A.B. 1878
For	Gald (*page* 239)		*read* Gold
{*For*	Gale, Art. Curwen McClaine	Pem.	M 1889
{*read*	Gale, Alb. Curwen Macclaine	Pem.	M 1889
{*For*	Garbett, Colin Campbell ...	Jes.	M 1890
{*read*	Garbett, Colin Campbell ...	Jes.	M 1900
{*For*	Gardorn, Benj. Will.	Joh.	M 1866 A.B. 1870. A.M. 1874
{*read*	Gardom, Benj. Will.	Joh.	M 1866 A.B. 1870. A.M. 1874
{*For*	Gaskoin, Cha. Jacinth Bellairs	Jes.	M 1895 N. C. A.B. 1898
{*read*	Gaskoin, Cha. Jacinth Bellairs	N. C.	M 1895 A.B. 1898
{*For*	Glenn, Cecil Howard	Pem.	M 1893 A.B. 1896
{*read*	Glenn, Cecil Hayward	Pem.	M 1893 A.B. 1896
{*For*	Goodrich, Alf. Tho. Scrape	Joh.	M 1874
{*read*	Goodrick, Alf. Tho. Scrape	Joh.	M 1874
{*For*	Gour, Harpasad Sing	Down.	M 1889 A.B. 1892
{*read*	Gour, Harpasad Sing	Down.	M 1889 N. C. Harprasad Singh, A.B.1892.
{*For*	Grant, Geo. Randolph }	Trin.	M 1885
	Symons Ogilvie }		[A.M.† 1896
{*read*	Grant, Geo. Randolph }	Trin.	M 1885
	Seymour Ogilvie }		
{*For*	Green, Sid. Sleath	Trin.	M 1886
{*read*	Green, Syd. Sleath	Trin.	M 1886
{*For*	Greene, Geo. Walters	Down.	M 1895 A.B. 1899
{*read*	Greene, Geo. Watters	Down.	M 1895 A.B. 1899
{*For*	Grütering, Carl Anton }	King's	L 1895
	Joseph Marie }		
{*read*	Grütering, Carl Anton }	King's	L 1895
	Jos. Maria }		
{*For*	Guillebaud, Erneste de la }	Trin.	M 1879 A.B. 1881
	Bere }		
{*read*	Guillebaud, Erneste Delabere	Trin.	M 1879 A.B. 1881
To	Hall, Ern. Rich. Bradley ...	Mag.	M 1884 *add* post Hall Watt, Ern. Rich.
			[Bradley, A.B. 1888. A.M. 1892
{*For*	Hall-Watt		*See* Watt, E. R. B. H.
{*read*	Hall Watt		*See* Hall, E. R. B.
Omit	Har, Kishan Singh	Joh.	M 1900
Omit	Hargrave, Wilfrid	Trin.	A.B. 1863
Add	Hargrave		*See* Savory
Omit	Harkie, Fra. Chamberlain }	Trin. H.	L 1883
	Le Gendre }		
To	Harrison, Edw. Ewer	Jes.	M 1867 *add* post Ward, Edw. Ewer, A.B.
			[1872
{*For*	Haselwood, Cha. Geo. Dering	H. Aye.	M 1886
{*read*	Haslewood, Cha. Geo. Dering	H. Aye.	M 1886
{*For*	Haslewood, Chris. Fra. Beevor	H. Aye.	M 1891 A.B. 1894. Cla. A.M. 1899
{*read*	Haslewood, Chris. Fra. Beevor	H. Aye.	E 1891 A.B. 1894. Cla. A.M. 1899
Omit	Hatfield, Heywood Geo. ...	Cai.	M 1890
For	Hatten, Nigel	Trin. H.	L 1894 *read* Hatton, Nigel, Trin.H. L1894
,,	Hausberg, Eric Fra.	Trin.	M 1896 ,, Hausburg, Eric Fra., Trin.
			[M 1896

For	Hausberg, Leslie Leopold } Rudolph	Trin.	M 1891	{ A.B.1894. *read* Hausburg, Leslie Leopold Rudolph, Trin. M 1891. A.B. 1894
„	Haynes, Geo. Secretan	King's	M 1899	*read* Haynes, Geo. Secretan,
{*For*	Hesmondhalgh, Will.	N. C.	M 1898	Cath. [King's L 1899
{*read*	Hesmondhalgh, Will.	N. C.	E 1898	
For	Hewitt, John Wilfrid	Trin.	M 1895	A.B. 1899. *read* Hewitt, John [Wilfred, Trin. M 1895. A.B. 1899
{*For*	Hill, Rob. Greene	Qu.	M 1896	
{*read*	Hill, Rob. Greene	Qu.	L 1896	
For	Hill, Will. Ja. Montague ...	Trin.	M 1895	*read* Hill, Will. Ja. Montagu,
{*For*	Hind, Alf. Ern.	Trin.	M 1897	[Trin. M 1895
{*read*	Hind, Alf. Ern.	Trin. H.	M 1897	
Omit	Hoare, Rich. Hen.	Sid.	M 1898	
Insert	Hobday, Rich. Hen.	Sid.	M 1898	[Trin. M 1894
For	Hoffmann, Geo. Spencer ...	Trin.	M 1894	„ Hoffman, Geo. Spencer,
„	Hoffmann, Harry Drummond	Trin.	M 1895	„ Hoffman,Harry Drummond, [Trin. M 1895
„	Hoffmann, Hen. Westwood	Trin.	M 1855	„ Hoffman, Hen. Westwood, [Trin. M 1855
Insert	Houstoun-Boswall, Will. ...	Trin.	M 1868	A.B. 1872. A.M. 1875
{*For*	Hughes, Art. Amesbury ...	Cla.	M 1891	A.B. 1893
{*read*	Hughes, Art. Amesbury ...	Cla.	M 1891	A.B. 1895
{*For*	Hughes, Will. Hen.	Joh.	E 1898	
{*read*	Hughes, Will. Hen.	Joh.	E 1875	
Omit	Hukam Chand	N. C.	M 1897	
„	Hulton, Tho.	Cai.	M 1897	[Trin. L 1871
For	Humphrey, Hen. John	Trin.	L 1871	*read* Humphery, Hen. John,
„	Humphrey, Hen. Milbourn	Trin.	M 1893	„ Humphery, Hen. Milbourn, [Trin. M 1893
{*For*	Humphrys, Hugh	Trin.	M 1856	A.B. 1856. A.M. 1860
{*read*	Humphrys, Hugh	Trin.	M 1856	A.B. 1860
For	Hunt, Geo. Hen.	Cla.	M 1878	*read* Hunt, Geo. Hen., Cla. M 1887
„	Jallard, Alf. Ern.	Joh.	M 1877	A.B. 1881. A.M. 1884. *read* Jal- [land, Alf. Ern., Joh. M 1877. [A.B. 1881. A.M. 1884
{*For*	Jallard, Alf. Gibson	Sid.	M 1879	
{*read*	Jalland, Alf. Gibson	Sid.	M 1879	
{*For*	James, Hen. Alf.	Qu.	M 1847	A.B. 1851. A.M. 1888
{*read*	James, Hen. Alf.	Trin.	M 1847	Qu. A.B. 1851. A.M. 1888
{*For*	Jenkyn, Cyril Walford Osborn	Trin. H.	M 1892	A.B. 1895. A.M. 1900
{*read*	Jenkyn, Cyril Walford Osborn	Trin.	M 1892	A.B. 1895. A.M. 1900 [M 1873
For	Jennings, Cha. Edm.	Trin.	M 1873	*read* Jenings, Cha. Edm., Trin.
„	Keating, Louis Harold	N. C.	E 1884	„ Keay, Louis Harold, N. C.
Omit	Khan, Mohiuddin Syed Ali	Trin.	E 1888	[E 1884
{*For*	Kindersley, Edw. Leigh ...	Trin.	M 1847	A.B. 1852. A.M. 1856
{*read*	Kindersley, Edw. Leigh ...	Trin.	M 1846	A.B. 1852. A.M. 1856
{*For*	Kirkham, Art. Walt. Mac- } donald	Trin.	M 1871	A.M. 1875. LL.M. 1879
{*read*	Kirkham, Art. Walt. Mac- } donald	Trin.	M 1871	A.B. 1875. LL.M. 1879
For	Kuhn, Oscar Jacob	Trin. H.	M 1894	*read* Kuhn, Oscar Jacob, Trin. [M 1894
„	Lang, Basil Thorne	Trin.	M 1899	„ Lang, Basil Thorn, Trin. [M 1899
„	Langton, John Montague Ellis	Trin.	M 1892	„ Langton, John Montagu [Ellis, Trin. M. 1892
„	Laurence, Cha. Hen.	Trin.	M 1899	„ Lawrence, Cha. Hen., Trin. [M 1899
{*For*	Lawson, Hen. Cyril	Trin.	M 1882	A.B. 1896
{*read*	Lawson, Hen. Cyril	Trin.	M 1882	A.B. 1886

{*For*	Le Brocq, Cha. Noble	...... Pem.	M 1897 A.M. 1900	
{*read*	Le Brocq, Cha. Noble	...... Pem.	M 1897 A.B. 1900	
{*For*	Leigh, Ja. Wentworth	...... Trin.	M 1857 A.B. 1860. D.D. 1896	
{*read*	Leigh, Ja. Wentworth	...... Trin.	M 1857 A.M. 1860. D.D. 1896	
{*For*	Leigh (2nd *Baron*)	.... Trin.	LL.D. 1864	
{*read*	Leigh, Will. Hen. (2nd *Baron*) Trin.		L 1843 LL.D. 1864	[M 1864
For	Lewis, Ja. Dawes	.... Trin.	M 1864 *read* Lewis, Ja. Dawson, Trin.	
„	Lewis, Lewis Fra. Gustave	Chr.	M 1900 „ Lewis, Lewis Fra. Gurslave,	
			[Chr. M 1900	
{*For*	Lingard, Roger Bonson	......	A.M. Oxf. ad eund. 1861	
{*read*	Lingard, Roger Rowson	...	A.M. Oxf. ad eund. 1861	
{*For*	Lloyd, Rob. Lewis	.... Trin.	M 1855 A.B. 1859. A.M. 1862	
{*read*	Lloyd, Rob. Lewis	.... Trin.	M 1855 Mag. A.B. 1859. A.M. 1862	
Omit	Logan	....	*See* Dobinson, Frank	
{*For*	Lorimer, John Horn	.... Trin.	M 1859 A.B. 1863. A.M. 1880	
{*read*	Lorimer, John Horn	.... Joh.	M 1859 A.B. 1863. A.M. 1880	[M 1867
For	Lowe, Art. Ballantine	...... Trin.	M 1867 *read* Lowe, Alf. Ballantine, Trin.	
„	Lowndes, Alan Herb. War-} lington	Trin.	L 1878 {*read* Lowndes, Alan Herb. Watlington, Trin. L 1878	
{*For*	Lüling, Theodore Will.	...... N. C.	M 1887 Trin. H. A.B. 1900	
{*read*	Lüling, Theodore Will.	...... N. C.	M 1887 Trin. H. A.B. 1890	
To	Lunn, Will. Craven	.... Jes.	M 1867 *add* post Rockliffe, Will. Craven,	
			[A.B. 1871. A.M. 1874. M.B. 1877	
Add	Lytton, Victor Alex. Geo.} Rob. (*Earl of*)	Trin.	M 1895 A.B. 1898	
For	Mac Cormick, John Macmill Trin.		L 1863 *read* Mac Cormick, John Macneill,	
{*For*	MacGregor, Alex. Mair	...... Trin.	M 1854 A.B. 1859	[Trin. L 1863
{*read*	MacGregor, Alex. Mair	...... Trin.	M 1854 Trin. H. A.B. 1859	
For	Macpherson, John Featherstonhaugh }	Trin.	M 1892 { A.B. 1895. *read* Macpherson, John Fetherstonhaugh, Trin. M 1892. A.B. 1895	
„	Majoribanks, Norman Edw.	Trin. H.	M 1891 *read* Marjoribanks, Norman Edw.,	
			[Trin. H. M 1891	
„	Mansel, John Colville Morton Trin.		M 1870 „ Mansel, John Colvile Morton,	
			[Trin. M 1870	
{*For*	Mansfield, Cha.	.... C. C.	M 1891 A.B. 1894. A.M. 1900	
{*read*	Mansfield, Cha.	.... C. C.	M 1890 A.B. 1894. A.M. 1900	
For	Marchant, Ja.	.... N. C.	E 1890 *read* Marchant, Ja., N. C. E 1900	
{*For*	Marriner, Edwin Tho. Ja.	Qu.	M 1848 A.B. 1853	
{*read*	Marriner, Edwin Tho. Ja.	Qu.	M 1848 Chr. A.B. 1853	
For	Maxwell, Edw. Hen. Harington }	Trin.	M 1891 { A.B. 1894. *read* Maxwell, Edw. Hen. Harrington, Trin. M 1891. A.B. 1894	
{*For*	Meister, Gerald Carl Quintus King's		M 1890 A.B. 1898	
{*read*	Meister, Gerald Carl Quintus King's		M 1895 A.B. 1898	
Omit	Meulen, Geo. Allen Vander	Trin.	M 1863	
For	Michael, John	.... Trin.	L 1867 *read* Michell, John, Trin. L 1867	
„	Mittra, Raj Naram	.... N. C.	M 1872 Cath. LL.B. 1876. *read* Mittra, Raj [Narain, N. C. M 1872. Cath. [LL.B. 1876	
{*For*	Mohiuddin, Syed Ali Khan	Trin.	M 1888 A.B. 1892	
{*read*	Mohiuddin, Syed Ali Khan	Trin.	E 1888 A.B. 1892	[Trin. M 1886
For	Monro-Ferguson, Rob. Harry Trin.		M 1886 *read* Munro-Ferguson, Rob. Harry,	
„	Moor, Hatherly Geo.	...... Trin.	M 1888 „ Moor, Hatherley Geo., Trin.	
Insert	Moore, Austin	.... H. Aye.	E 1894	[M 1888
For	Moore, Rob. Garrett	.... Trin.	M 1870 „ Moore, Rob. Garret, Trin.	
			[M 1870	
„	Moore, Sam.	.... Cai.	M 1897 „ Moorhouse, Sam., Cai. M	
Omit	Morley, Rich. John	.... Trin.	M 1898	[1897
Add	Morrice, Rich. John	.... Trin.	M 1898	

{*For* Nair, Chettur Ramunni ... N. C.   E 1891

{*read* Nair, Chettur Ramunni ... N. C.   M 1891   [Em. M 1900

For   Neil, John Reg. Jewsbury   Em.   M 1900 *read* Neild, John Reg. Jewsbury,

„   Newman, Walt. Peake ...... Trin.   M 1892 A.B., LL.B. 1895. *read* Newman,
                                           [Walt. Peeke, Trin. M 1892.
                                           [A.B., LL.B. 1895

„   Newmann, Fre. Hen. Cha.   Jes.   M 1899 *read* Newman, Fre. Hen. Cha.,

{*For* Newton, John Raphael ...... Trin. H.   M 1900   [Jes. M 1899

{*read* Newton, John Raphael ...... Trin.   M 1900

For   O'Regan, Art. Rowland Tho. Trin.   M 1874 „   O'Regan, Art. Roland Tho.,
                                           [Trin. M 1874

{*For* Owen, Cha. Maynard ...... Em.   M 1867 A.B. 1870. LL.M. 1874

{*read* Owen, Cha. Maynard ...... Em.   M 1867 A.B. 1871. LL.M. 1874

For   Page, Cecil Herb. Winton   C. C.   M 1896 *read* Page, Cecil Herb. Winter,

{*For* Pain, Barry Eric Odell ...... C. C.   M 1883 A.B. 1896   [C. C. M 1896

{*read* Pain, Barry Eric Odell ...... C. C.   M 1883 A.B. 1886

For   Palmer, Reg. .... Trin.   M 1898 *read* Palmer, Reg., C. C. M 1898

„   Parkin, Hugh Dynely Goodeve Mag.   M 1892 „   Parkin,   Hugh   Dynely
                                       [Goodere, Mag. M 1892

„   Pearce, Sid. Harrison ...... Cla.   M 1891 „   Pearless, Sid. Harrison, Cla.
                                           [M 1891

„   Penball, Will. .... Trin.   M 1877 A.B. 1881. *read* Penhall, Will.,
                                           [Trin. M 1877. A.B. 1881

{*For* Pennington, Ja. Burn ...... Trin.   M 1859 LL.B. 1863

{*read* Pennington, Ja. Burn ...... Joh.   M 1859 Pet. LL.B. 1863

{*For* Penny, Ja. John .... Qu.   M 1872 A.B. 1876

{*read* Penny, Ja. John .... Qu.   M 1872 Joh. A.B. 1876

{*For* Perfect, Will. Hampden ... Pet.   M 1846 LL.B. 1854

{*read* Perfect, Will. Hampden ... Cai.   M 1846 LL.B. 1854

For   Phillips-Conn, Tho. Harry } Cla.   M 1899 {*read* Phillips-Conn, Tho. Harry
      Meredith }   { Meredeth, Cla. M 1899

{*For* Pitcairn, Dav. .... Pet.   M 1854 A.B. 1858

{*read* Pitcairn, Dav. .... Pet.   M 1854 Jes. A.B. 1858

{*For* Platt, Fre. Walt. .... Trin. H.   M 1891 A.B. 1894

{*read* Platt, Fre. Walt. .... Trin.   M 1891 A.B. 1894

For   Pollock, Ralph Geo. Geoffrey Trin.   M 1900 *read* Pollock, Ralph Cha. Geoffrey,

{*For* Poore, Edw. Wright .... H. Sel.   M 1888 A.B. 1891   [Trin. M 1900

{*read* Poore, Edw. Wright .... H. Sel.   M 1888 Chr. A.B. 1891

{*For* Powell, Fra. Edw. .... N. C.   M 1882 A.B. 1885. A.M. 1889

{*read* Powell, Fra. Edw. .... N. C.   M 1882 Chr. A.B. 1885. A.M. 1889

{*For* Powell, Ja. John .... Cla.   M 1883 A.B. 1886. A.B. 1892. M.B., B.C.
                                           [1895

{*read* Powell, Ja. John .... Cla.   M 1883 A.B. 1886. A.M. 1892. M.B., B.C.
                                           [1895

For   Price, Edw. Alan .... Trin.   M 1892 A.B. 1895. *read* Price, Edw. Allan,
                                           [Trin. M 1892. A.B. 1895

„   Procter, Ronald Edwin ...... Cai.   L 1881 *read* Prodgers, Ronald Edwin,
                                           [Cai. L 1881

„   Raby, John Baldwin .... Joh.   M 1884 „   Roby, John Baldwin, Joh.
                                           [M 1884

{*For* Rendle, Anstruther Cardew N. C.   M 1882 Chr. A.B. 1887. M.B., B.C. 1900

{*read* Rendle, Anstruther Cardew N. C.   M 1882 Chr. A.B. 1887. M.B., B.C. 1890

{*For* Reynolds, Edw. .... Qu.   M 1894 A.B. 1897

{*read* Reynolds, Edw. .... Qu.   E 1894 A.B. 1897

For   Rivett-Carnac, Geo. Clennell Trin.   M 1870 A.B. 1874. *read* Rivett-Carnac,
                                           [Geo. Clennel, Trin. M 1870. A.B.

{*For* Robinson, Art. Dalgarno ... Joh.   M 1852 A.B. 1856. A.M. 1860   [1874

{*read* Robinson, Art. Dalgarno ... Joh.   M 1852 Trin. H. A.B. 1856. A.M. 1860

{*For* Roderick, Hen. Buckley ... Em.   M 1891 A.B. 1894. M.B., B.C. 1899

{*read* Roderick, Hen. Buckley ... N. C.   M 1891 Em. A.B. 1894. M.B., B.C. 1899

xiv

Errata

For	Romneys, John Orde .... Joh.	M 1872 *read* Romney, John Orde, Joh.

For   Romneys, John Orde .... Joh.   M 1872 *read* Romney, John Orde, Joh.
[M 1872

„   Rowley, Geo. Fyddell ...... Trin.   M 1869 „ Rowley, Geo. Fydell, Trin.

{*For* Royston (*Viscount*) .... Trin.   M 1855 A.B. 1858   [M 1869

{*read* Royston (*Viscount*) .... Trin.   M 1855 A.M. 1858

For   Royston-Piggott, Walt. Mytton } Trin.   M 1899 {*read* Royston-Pigott, Walt. Mytton, Trin. M 1899

„   Ruggles-Brise, Archib. Wayland } Trin.   M 1872 {*read* Ruggles-Brise, Archib. Weyland, Trin. M 1872

„   Sadiq, Muhammad Gholam Chr.   E 1894 A.B., LL.B. 1887. *read* Sadiq, [Muhammad Gholam, Chr. [E 1894. A.B., LL.B. 1897

„   Safford, Will. Chartres ...... C. C.   M 1848 A.B.1852. A.M.1855. *read* Safford, [Will. Chartres, Cai. M 1848. [A.B. 1852. A.M. 1855

„   Saher, Manabhai Nasarvanji Cath.   M 1892 A.B., LL.B. 1896. *read* Saher, [Nanabhai Nasarvanji, Cath. [M 1892. A.B., LL.B. 1896

„   Salisbury, Edw. Lister ...... Trin. H. M 1849 *read* Salisbury, Edw. Lister, Trin. [M 1849

„   Sanderson, Rich.Withington Bromily } Trin.   M 1869 {*read* Sanderson, Rich. Withing-ton Bromilev, Trin. M 1869

Omit Sanderson, Tho. Geo. Wills Trin. H. M 1899 *add* Sandford, Tho. Geo. Wills, [Trin. H. M 1899

{*For* Sargant, Walt. Lee .... Trin.   M 1886 A.B. 1888. A.M. 1892

{*read* Sargant, Walt. Lee .... Trin.   M 1885 A.B. 1888. A.M. 1892

For   Schuyler, Adoniah Graham Joh.   M 1871 *read* Schuyler, Adoniah Graham, [Joh. M 1871

{*For* Scudamore, Theodore Fre. John } Jes.   M 1875 A.B. 1879

{*read* Scudamore, Theodore Fre. John } Chr.   M 1875 A.B. 1879

{*For* Sears, Lynford Cha. .... H. Sel.   M 1886 A.B. 1900

{*read* Sears, Lynford Cha. .... H. Sel.   M 1896 A.B. 1900

For   Shipman, Geo. Alf. Cargill Trin.   M 1894 A.B. 1897. *read* Shipman, Geo. [Alf. Cargil, Trin. M 1894. A.B. 1897

{*For* Shrubbs, Edw. Alb. .... C. C.   M 1896 A.B. 1899

{*read* Shrubbs, Edw. Alb. .... N. C.   M 1896 A.B. 1899

For   Sinclair, Walter Montgomery N. C.   E 1891 Down. A.B. 1894. *read* Sinclair, [Waller Montgomery, N. C. E 1891. [Down. A.B. 1894

{*For* Skene, Will. Hen. .... Joh.   L 1890 A.B. 1893. A.M. 1897

{*read* Skene, Will. Hen. .... Joh..   M 1890 A.B. 1893. A.M. 1897

{*For* Smith, Alex. Murray .... King's M 1866

{*read* Smith, Alex. Murray .... King's M 1886

Add Starkie, Fra. Chamberlain Le Gendre } Trin. H. L 1883 [King's M 1899

For   Statham, Hen. Purefoy ...... King's M 1899 *read* Statham, Herb. Purefoy,

„   Stawell, Jonas Will. Adcock Trin. M 1867 „ Stawell, Jonas Will. Alcock, [Trin. M 1867

{*For* Stone, Will. Hen. .... Trin.   M 1858 A.B. 1862. A.M. 1887

{*read* Stone, Will. Hen. .... Trin.   M 1858 A.B. 1862

To   Stone, Will. Hen. .... Trin.   M 1880 A.B. 1884. *add* A.M. 1887

{*For* Stoney, Walt. Cha. .... Joh.   M 1865 Cha. Butler, A.B. 1869

{*read* Stoney, Walt. Cha. .... Joh.   M 1865 Butler-Stoney, Cha., A.B. 1869

Omit Stutton, Cha. Rob. Arnold Cla.   M 1884   [M 1867

For   Style, Hen. Winter .... Joh.   M 1867 *read* Syle, Hen. Winter, Joh.

„   Sucherland, Rob. .... Trin.   M 1864 „ Sutherland, Rob., Trin. [M 1864

„   Suermonat, Otto Emil ...... King's M 1884 „ Suermondt, Otto Emil, [King's M 1884

For	Surgey, Herb. Hen.	Joh.	M 1883 A.B. 1886. A.M. 1890
read	Surgey, Herb. Hen.	Joh.	M 1883 Chr. A.B. 1886. A.M. 1890
For	Swann, Linton Hall	Trin. H.	M 1890
read	Swann, Linton Hall	Trin. H.	M 1893
For	Swanvich, Fre. Tertius	Trin.	M 1870 A.B. 1874. A.M. 1877. *read* Swanwick, Fre. Tertius, Trin. M [1870. A.B. 1874. A.M. 1877
For	Taylor, Art. Ern.	Down.	M 1880 A.B. 1898
read	Taylor, Art. Ern.	Down.	M 1880
For	Taylor, Art. Ern.	N. C.	E 1895 Down.
read	Taylor, Art. Ern.	N. C.	E 1895 Down. A.B. 1898
For	Tennon, Will.	King's	L 1882 *read* Tennon, Will., King's L 1882
Omit	Thatchell, Frank	Trin.	M 1891 [Trin. M 1868
For	Thompson, Rich. Heyward	Trin.	M 1868 „ Thompson, Rich. Heywood,
For	Thompson, Will. Hen.	Cai.	M 1852 A.B. 1863. A.M. 1869
read	Thompson, Will. Hen.	Cai.	M 1852
Omit	Thorman, Art. John Webster	Joh.	M 1872
For	Thorold, Will. Lionel De Buckenhuld	Trin.	M 1891 {A.B. 1894. *read* Thorold, Wilfrid Lionel de Buckenhuld, Trin. M 1891. A.B. 1894
For	Thrupp, Jos. Fra. ....*Trin.		M 1838 A.B. 1849. A.M. 1852
read	Thrupp, Jos. Fra. ....*Trin.		M 1845 A.B. 1849. A.M. 1852
For	Tiffany, Edw. Kenrick Bunbury	Trin.	M 1880 {*read* Tighe, Edw. Kenrick Bunbury, Trin. M 1880
„	Todd, Rich. Hutton	Trin.	M 1856 A.B. 1860. A.M. 1863. *read* Todd, [Rich. Utten, Trin. M 1856. [A.B. 1860. A.M. 1863
For	Torr, Will. Geo.	Down.	A.B. Oxf. incorp. 1889
read	Torr, Will. Geo.	Down.	M 1889 A.B. Oxf. incorp. 1889
Omit	Torrs, Will. Geo.	Down.	M 1889
For	Tovey, Symonds Sympson	Trin.	M 1877 A.B. 1881. *read* Tovey, Symons [Sympson, Trin. M 1877. A.B. [1881
„	Tregoning, Geoffry Norris	Trin.	M 1900 *read* Tregoning, Geoffrey Norris, [Trin. M 1900
For	Trewby, Wilfrid Rich.	C. C.	M 1898
read	Trickett, Wilfrid Rich.	C. C.	M 1898
For	Tweedie, Archib. Geo.	Chr.	M 1875 A.B. 1879. A.M. 1882
read	Tweedie, Archib. Geo.	Chr.	M 1875 Cai. A.B. 1879. A.M. 1882
For	Tyser, Edw. Jarratt	Trin.	M 1873 A.B. 1877. A.M. 1880. *read* Tyser, [Edw. Jarrett, Trin. M 1873. [A.B. 1877. A.M. 1880
„	Udney, John Hen. Fullarton	Trin. H.	L 1873 *read* Udny, John Hen. Fullarton, [Trin. H. L 1873
„	Udney, Rich.	Trin.	M 1866 „ Udny, Rich., Trin. M 1866
For	Upcher, Abbot Rowland ...	Trin.	M 1868 A. Roland A.B. 1872. A.M. 1875
read	Upcher, Abbot Roland ...	Trin.	M 1868 A.B. 1872. A.M. 1875
For	Verma, Hirabal	Chr.	L 1900 *read* Verma, Hiralal, Chr. L 1900
„	Vikers, Edw.	Trin. H.	M 1882 „ Vickers, Edw., Trin. H. M 1882
„	Wade, Edw. Bruce Herschell	Trin.	M 1891 A.B. 1894. A.M. 1899. *read* Wade, [Edw. Bruce Herschel, Trin. M [1891. A.B. 1894. A.M. 1899
„	Wade, Herb. Blaney	Trin.	M 1872 LL.B. 1876. *read* Wade, Herb. [Blany, Trin. M 1872. LL.B. 1876
For	Wade, Tho. Fra.		*Litt.D.* 1887. A.M. 1888. *King's [1889
read	Wade, Tho. Fra.	Trin.	M 1837 *Litt.D.* 1887. A.M. 1888. *King's [1889
Omit	Wallis, Will. Colville	Em.	L 1877 A.B. 1880. A.M. 1883
For	Walsham, Cha.	Chr.	M 1857 A.B. 1861. A.M. 1864
read	Walsham, Cha.	Chr.	M 1857 Mag. A.B. 1861. A.M. 1864
Omit	Warick, Rich.	Trin. H.	M 1863

For	Warr, Geo. Cha. Winter ...	Chr.	L 1865 A.B. 1869. A.M. 1872
read	Warr, Geo. Cha. Winter ...	Chr.	M 1865 Trin. A.B. 1869. A.M. 1872
For	Waugh, Geo. Ern.	Down.	M 1894 A.M. 1897
read	Waugh, Geo. Ern.	Down.	M 1894 A.B. 1897 [Trin. M 1885
For	Webb-Ware, Fra. Cooke ...	Trin.	M 1885 *read* Webb-Ware, Frank Cooke,
„	Wesley, Will. Kerr	Trin.	M 1866 „ Wesley, Will. Ken, Trin. M
			[1866
Omit	Wilkins, Will. John	Em.	M 1881
For	Williams, Rich. Davies Garnon	} Trin.	M 1874 { *read* Williams, Rich. Davies { Garnons, Trin. M 1874
„	Witby, Art. Edw.	Trin.	M 1884 A.B. 1887. A.M. 1891. *read* Withy, [Art. Edw., Trin. M 1884. A.B. [1887. A.M. 1891
„	Wroughtson, Edw. Norris	Mag.	M 1866 *read* Wroughton, Edw. Norris, Mag. M 1866.

ERRATA. Vol. 1901—1912

Delete	Barrow, Geo. Shuldham Malet	} Jes.	M 1880
For	Fernando, Cha. Hub. Zuleski	} Joh.	E 1910
read	Fernando, Cha. Hub. Zaleski	} Joh.	E 1910
For	Ginistelli, Edouard Plançon		*See* Plançon, E.
read	Ginistrelli, Edouard Plançon		*See* Plançon, E.
For	Griffin, Frederic Will. Wandby	} King's	M 1900 A.B. 1903. M.B., B.C., A.M. 1908
read	Griffin, Frederic Will. Waudby	} King's	M 1900 A.B. 1903. M.B., B.C., A.M. 1908

MATRICULATIONS AND DEGREES
1901—1912

A

à-Ababrelton,	Rob. Relton de Relton	Down.	M 1910
Abaza,	Mohamed Nagati ...	Trin. H.	M 1909
—	Mohamed Saad Eldin	Trin. H.	M 1908
Abbey,	Ja. Phillips	H. Sel.	M 1901 A.B. 1904. A.M. 1908
Abbott,	Herb. Alldridge ...,..	N. C.	M 1901 Qu. A.B. 1904. A.M. 1908
—	John Cha.	Cath.	E 1899 A.B. 1906
Abdoolcader,	Hoosein Hasanally ...	Chr.	M 1908
Abe,	Riozo	N. C.	M 1904
Abel,	Hen. Geo.	Chr.	M 1894 A.B. 1897. A.M. 1909
Abel Smith,	Desmond	Trin.	M 1911
—	Reg.	Trin.	M 1908
Abercrombie,	Douglas Murray ...	Sid.	M 1904
—	Rodolph Geo.	Cai.	M 1891 A.B. 1894. M.B. 1902. M.D. 1910
Abid,	Syed Hasan	Pet.	L 1902 A.B. 1904
Abraham,	Lionel Martyn	Pem.	M 1912
Abrahams,	Adolphe	Em.	M 1903 A.B. 1906. M.B., B.C. 1911
—	Israel		A.M. 1902
—	Solomon	Em.	M 1902 A.B., LL.B. 1906
Abrahamson,	Isaac	Cla.	M 1910
Abrams,	Lawrence Golding ...	Pet.	E 1902 A.B. 1906
Acharyya,	Maharaj Kumar ⎱ Shoshi Kanta ⎰	Down.	M 1907
Acheson-Gray,	Cha. Gerald Acheson	Trin.	M 1907 A.B. 1910
Ackland,	Bryan Middleton ...	Trin. H.	M 1904 A.B. 1907
Ackroyd,	Harold	Cai.	M 1896 A.B. 1899. B.C. 1903. M.B., A.M.
Acland,	Herb. Art. Dyke ...	King's	M 1905 A.B. 1908 [1904. M.D. 1910
—	Theodore Will. Gull	King's	M 1909 A.B. 1912
Acton,	Hen.	Joh.	M 1909 A.B. 1912
Acworth,	Cecil	Trin.	M 1906 A.B. 1909
—	Will.	Em.	M 1900 A.B. 1903. A.M. 1907
Adair,	Edw. Rob.	Pet.	M 1911
—	John Valintine ...,..	Trin.	M 1907
Adam,	Alan Gordon Acheson	H. Sel.	M 1904 A.B. 1907 [Litt.D. 1903
—	Ja.	Cai.	M 1880 A.B. 1884 (2). *Em. A.M. 1888.
—	Ja. Ronald Glennie	Trin.	M 1894 A.B. 1899. A.M. 1903
—	Neil Kensington ...,..	Trin.	M 1910
—	Will. Arrol	N. C.	L 1901 A.B. 1905
Adams,	Art. Botwell	Em.	M 1905 A.B. 1908
—	Bern. Norton	H. Sel.	M 1898 A.B. 1901
—	Bishop Trerice ,..,..	Cath.	M 1900 A.B. 1903. A.M. 1907
—	Cha. Wilfrid	Trin.	M 1901 A.B. 1904. A.M. 1908
—	Edwin Plimpton	Trin.	M 1902

Adams,	Eustace Victor	Cai.	M 1910
—	Fra. Norris	Chr.	M 1900 A.B. 1903
—	Frank	Joh.	M 1904 A.B. 1907. A.M. 1911
—	Frank Shirley	Chr.	M 1903 A.B. 1906
—	Frederic Bradford ...	Cla.	M 1902 A.B. 1905
—	Harold	Cla.	M 1908 A.B. 1911
—	Hen. Packwood	Trin.	M 1904 A.B. 1907. A.M. 1911
—	Ja. Wilmot	Cai.	M 1903 A.B. 1906
—	John	Joh.	M 1897 A.B. 1900. A.M. 1904
—	John Bern. Pye	Joh.	M 1909 A.B. 1912
—	John Ern. Cocks ...	N. C.	M 1912
—	John Keith	H. Sel.	M 1911
—	Lestock Handley ...	Qu.	M 1906 A.B. 1909
—	Newsham Peers	C. C.	E 1895 A.B. 1899. A.M. 1904
—	Noel Percy	Trin. H.	M 1901 A.B. 1904. A.M. 1908
—	Oliver John	Sid.	M 1900 A.B. 1903. A.M. 1907
—	Reg. Art.	Pem.	M 1884 A.B. 1887. A.M. 1901
—	Rob. Sefton	Trin. H.	M 1908 A.B. 1912
—	Sam. Trerice	Cath.	M 1898 A.B. 1903. A.M. 1906
Adamson,	Edw. Blythman	Joh.	M 1908 A.B. 1911
—	Fra. Douglas	Joh.	M 1910
—	Hen. Bardell	H. Sel.	M 1901 A.B. 1904. A.M. 1908
—	Rob. Randolph	Trin.	M 1902
—	Rob. Step.	Em.	M 1907 A.B. 1910
—	Will.	Trin.	M 1904 A.B. 1907. A.M. 1911
—	Will. Campbell	Trin. H.	M 1905
Adcock,	Frank Ezra ....*King's		M 1905 A.B. 1908. A.M. 1912
—	Harold Meredyth ...	Chr.	M 1909 A.B. 1912
—	Jos. Mould	Cath.	M 1895 A.B. 1898. A.M.† 1903
—	Will. Rob. Colquhoun	Pet.	M 1902 A.B. 1905
Adderley,	Alf. Fra.	Cath.	E 1912
Addy,	Ja. Carlton	Trin.	M 1910
—	Roland	Jes.	M 1910
Ade,	Frank Cha.	Trin.	M 1911
Adeney,	Eric Leon.	Joh.	M 1906 A.B. 1910
Adie,	Clem. Ja. Mellish ...	Trin.	M 1895 A.B. 1898. A.M. 1906
Adkin,	Benaiah Colson	Em.	M 1911
—	Walt. Kenrick Knight	N. C.	L 1901
Adler,	August Ludwig Wilhelm	H. Sel.	M 1894 A.B. 1898. A.M. 1902
—	Fritz Baumann	Cla.	M 1901 A.B. 1904
—	Herb. Marcus	Joh.	M 1894 A.B. 1897. LL.B. 1898. A.M.,
Adrian,	Edgar Douglas	Trin.	M 1908 A.B. 1911 [LL.M. 1901
Adshead,	Art. Roy	Pet.	M 1911
—	Harold Edw.	Chr.	M 1908 A.B. 1911
Affleck,	Rob.	Trin. H.	M 1907 A.B. 1910
Aga Khan,	(The Agha Khan) ...		*LL.D.* 1911
Agar,	Wilfred Eade ....*King's		M 1900 A.B. 1903. A.M. 1907
Agar-Robartes,	(*Hon.*) Cecil Edw.	Mag.	M 1911
Agate,	Leon. Dendy	Pet.	M 1906 A.B. 1910
Ager,	Art. Douglas	Chr.	M 1906 A.B. 1909
Agius,	Edgar Gordon Emmanuel	Trin.	M 1907 E. E. G., A.B. 1910
—	Tancred Ambrose ...	Chr.	M 1910
Agnew,	Alan Graeme	Trin. H.	M 1906
—	Andr. Cha. Eric	Trin.	M 1904
—	Cha. Gerald	Trin.	M 1901
—	Geo. Colin	King's	M 1901
—	Stair Carnegie	Trin.	M 1890 A.B. 1893. LL.B. 1894. A.M. 1901
—	Victor Cha. Walt. ...	Trin.	M 1906 A.B. 1911
Ahlo,	Anth. Lee	N. C.	M 1897 Tr. H. A.B. 1901. post Ahlo,
Ahmad,	Abdul Majid	Down.	M 1910 [Lee-fong, A.M. 1911
—	Bashir-ud-Din	Pet.	M 1906 Bashiruddin, A.B. 1908

Ahmad,	Syed Manzoor	Down.	M 1907 A.B. 1910
—	Zia Uddin	Trin.	M 1901 A.B. 1903. A.M. +1909
Ahmed,	Khabeeruddin	Mag.	L 1905
Aickin,	Geo. Ellis	Joh.	M 1888 A.B. 1891. A.M. 1902
Aikman,	Kenneth Blackie	Cla.	M 1907 A.B. 1910
—	Rob. Blackie	Cla.	M 1902 A.B. 1905
Ailinger,	Alb.	N. C.	M 1906
Ainger,	Tho. Edw.	King's	M 1903 A.B. 1906
Ainley,	John Art. Gibson ...	Jes.	M 1911
—	Will. Preston	Jes.	M 1906 A.B. 1909
Ainsley,	Alan Colpitts	Cai.	M 1909 A.B. 1912
Ainsworth,	Alf. Rich.	King's	M 1898 A.B. 1902
—	Cyrus Gerald	Down.	M 1907 A.B. 1910
—	Ja. Maurice	Em.	M 1912
	Tho.	Trin.	M 1904 A.B. 1907
Airey,	John Robinson	Joh.	M 1903 A.B. 1906. A.M. 1910
Airy,	Bern. John	Trin.	M 1892 A.B. 1895. A.M. 1905
—	Reg.	Trin.	M 1896 A.B. 1899. A.M. 1911
Aitchison,	Irvine Geo.	Pem.	M 1906 A.B., LL.B. 1909
—	John Cha.	Cla.	M 1900 A.B. 1904. A.M. 1911
Aitken,	John	Chr.	M 1903 A.B., LL.B. 1906
—	Rob. Menpes	Trin.	M 1898 A.B. 1901
Aitkens,	Alf. Gamelius	H. Aye.	L 1896 N.C. A.B. 1902
Ajrekar,	Shripad Lakshman ...	N. C.	M 1905 A.B. 1908
Akam,	John Will.	Chr.	M 1912
Akbar,	Mass Thajoon	Em.	M 1900 A.B. 1903. LL.B. 1904
—	Syed Ali	Pet.	M 1912
Akerman,	Conrad	Cai.	M 1897 A.B. 1900. M.B., B.C., A.M. 1906
—	Edw. Ja. Board	Chr.	M 1904 A.B. 1907
Akhurst,	Algernon Frederic ...	Jes.	M 1912
Akroyd,	Reg.	Trin. H.	L 1905
Alam,	Syed Majid	Down.	M 1911
—	Syed Sayid	Down.	M 1907 A.B. 1910. LL.B. 1911
—	Syed Wahid	Down.	M 1907
Albino,	Harry Hurlbutt	Chr.	M 1909 A.B. 1912
Albright,	Martin Chicheley ...	Trin.	M 1905 A.B. 1908
Albu,	Walt. Geo.	Trin. H.	M 1910
Alcock,	Norman Alex.	Qu.	M 1903 A.B. 1906. A.M. 1910
—	Will. Broughton	Trin. H.	M 1906 A.B. 1909. post. Broughton-[Alcock, W., M.B. 1912
Alder,	Wilfrid	Trin.	M 1895 A.B. 1898. A.M. +1902
Aldersey,	Hugh	Trin.	M 1907 A.B. 1910
Alderson,	Alb. Evelyn	Jes.	M 1902 A.B. 1905
—	Gerald Graham	Cai.	M 1903 A.B. 1906. M.B., B.C. 1910
—	John Hen.	H. Sel.	M 1893 A.B. 1896. A.M. 1905
—	Ralph Edw.	Trin.	M 1896 A.B. 1900. A.M. 1905
Alderton,	Colin Fre.	H. Sel.	M 1908
Aldis,	Art. Cyril Webb ......*Trin. H.		M 1897 A.B. 1900. A.M. 1904
—	Harry Gidney		A.M. 1905
Aldous,	Alan Edw.	Jes.	M 1911
—	Arnold Chevalier ...	Jes.	M 1902
—	Frederic Clem.	Jes.	M 1898 A.B. 1901
Aldridge,	Cha. Braxton Mooring	Chr.	M 1896 A.B. 1899. A.M. 1903
—	Cha. Travers	Trin. H.	M 1907
—	Harold Whitchurch Mooring	Chr.	M 1894 A.B. 1897. A.M. 1901
Aldworth,	Herb. John	Qu.	M 1887 A.B. 1891. A.M. 1909
Alexander,	Aaron	Joh.	M 1908 A.B., LL.B. 1912
—	Cyril Wilson	Trin.	M 1898 A.B. 1901. LL.B. 1904
—	Dudley Hallam Wallace	Mag.	M 1908 A.B. 1911
—	Edw.	Cai.	M 1905 A.B. 1908

Alexander,	Ern. Will.	Em.	M 1900 A.B. 1903
—	Frank Dav.	Trin.	M 1897 A.B. 1901
—	Geo. Glover	Down.	M 1884 A.B. 1887. A.M. 1891. LL.M. 1905
—	Gervase Disney	Cai.	M 1898 A.B. 1901. B.C. 1908
—	Hor. Gundry	King's	M 1909 A.B. 1912
—	Ja. Finlay	Trin.	M 1895 A.B. 1898. B.C., A.M. 1902. M.B. [1903. M.D. 1906
—	Ja. Graham	Cla.	M 1899 A.B., LL.B. 1902
—	Ja. Will.	Cla.	M 1905
—	John Bennett	Em.	M 1900 A.B. 1903. A.M. 1907
—	John Hen. Rushbrooke	N. C.	M 1905 Cath. A.B. 1908. A.M. 1912
—	Morris	Joh.	M 1897 A.B., LL.B. 1900. A.M. †1904
—	Phil. Geo.	Joh.	M 1905 A.B. 1908
—	Ralph Cleave	Joh.	M 1905 A.B. 1908
—	Rob. Middleton	Cla.	M 1903 A.B. 1906
—	Tho. Cecil	Cla.	M 1902 A.B. 1905
—	Wilfrid Backhouse ...	King's	M 1906 A.B. 1909
—	Will. Art.	Cai.	M 1899 A.B. 1902
—	Will. Gemmell	Cla.	M 1909 A.B. 1912
—	Will. Lindsay	Cla.	M 1910
Alexander-Katz,	Ernst Moritz Art.	Em.	E 1910
Alford,	Cha. Egerton	Trin. H.	M 1904
—	Cha. Symes Leslie ...	C. C.	M 1903 A.B. 1907. A.M. 1910
—	Edw. John Gregory	King's	M 1909 A.B. 1912
Ali,	Abbas	Down.	M 1910
—	Hamid	Down.	M 1910
—	Imtiaz		*See* Khan
—	Jabir Abdul	N. C.	M 1906 A.B. 1909
—	Mohammad	Chr.	M 1911
—	Syed Ameer		*LL.D.* 1910
Alington,	Julius Hugh	Trin. H.	M 1910
Alison,	Laughton Hassard ...	Pem.	M 1909 A.B. 1912
Alken,	Hen. Seffrien	Qu.	M 1883 A.B. 1887. A.M. 1901
Allan,	Alex. Caldwell	Trin.	M 1912
—	Douglas	Joh.	M 1901 A.B. 1904
—	Fre. Leon.	Em.	M 1912
—	John Botcherby	Cla.	M 1909 A.B. 1912
—	Phil. Bertram Murray	Cla.	M 1903
—	Rob. Geo.	Pem.	M 1899 A.B. 1902. A.M. 1907
Allason,	Hen. Will.	Trin. H.	M 1891 A.B. 1895. A.M. 1902
Allcard,	Rupert	Trin.	M 1903 A.B. 1906
Allcock,	Egerton	Trin. H.	M 1897 A.B. 1901
Allden,	John Eric	Trin.	M 1904
Allen,	Alb. Will.	N. C.	M 1900 Joh. A.B. 1903. A.M. 1907
—	Alex. Drake	Joh.	M 1905 A.B. 1908
—	Alex. Radway	Joh.	M 1896 A.B. 1899. A.M. 1903
—	Art. Watts	Joh.	E 1898 A.B. 1902. A.M. 1910
—	Cecil Conrad	H. Sel.	M 1904 A.B. 1907
—	Cha. Richards	Joh.	M 1906
—	Claude Alb. Blomfield	Down.	M 1906 A.B. 1909
—	Fra.	Joh.	M 1912
—	Fra. Burton	Em.	M 1906 A.B. 1909
—	Fra. Williams	Joh.	M 1900 A.B. 1903
—	Fre. Denison Campbell	Cai.	M 1911
—	Fre. Ja.	Joh.	M 1888 A.B. 1891. A.M. 1905
—	Geoffrey Austin	Joh.	M 1905 A.B. 1908
—	Geo. Cantrell	Joh.	M 1874 A.B. 1878. A.M. 1881. B.D. 1904.
—	Geo. Kendall	Trin.	M 1901 A.B. 1904. A.M. 1908 [D.D. '06
—	Harold Gwynne	Trin.	M 1892 A.B. 1895. A.M. 1911
—	Herb.	N. C.	M 1907 Cath. A.B. 1910
—	Ja.	Joh.	M 1874 A.B. 1878. A.M. 1904.

Allen,	Ja. Edmond Percival	Joh.	M 1901 A.B. 1904. LL.B. 1905
—	John Edric Russell	Trin.	M 1909 A.B. 1912
—	John Hugh	Jes.	M 1907 A.B., LL.B. 1910
—	John Mylrea	Em.	M 1907 A.B. 1910
—	John Stanley	Chr.	M 1910
—	Lancelot John	Trin.	M 1904 A.B. 1907. A.M. 1911
—	Leon. Spencer	H. Sel.	M 1900 A.B. 1907
—	Lucien Art.	Joh.	M 1907 A.B. 1910
—	Maur. Tyrone	Trin.	M 1903 A.B. 1906. A.M. 1910
—	Melville Rich. Hovell Agnew	Trin.	M 1910
—	Norman Percy	C. C.	M 1898 A.B. 1901
—	Paul Hen.	Pem.	M 1909 A.B. 1912
—	Percy Herman Cha.	Cai.	M 1909 A.B. 1912
—	Reg. Clifford	Pet.	M 1908 A.B. 1911
—	Rich. Gerrard Ross	Jes.	M 1908 A.B. 1912
—	Rob. Candlish	Chr.	M 1899 A.B. 1902. A.M. †1906
—	Stanley Edw.	Trin. H.	M 1903
—	Steph. Shepherd	Pem.	M 1901 A.B. 1904. LL.B. 1905. A.M.† '08
—	Will.	Joh.	M 1877 A.B. 1881. A.M. 1902
—	Will.	Cla.	M 1908
—	Will. Hen.	Trin.	M 1892 A.B. 1895. A.M. 1903
—	Will. Howard	Joh.	M 1896 A.B. 1899. A.M. 1903
—	Will. Louis	N. C.	L 1905 Down. A.B. 1909
Alley,	Shujath	Trin. H.	M 1905
Allgood,	Guy Hunter	Trin.	M 1911
Allhusen,	Ormsby	Trin.	M 1907 A.B. 1910
—	Rupert	Trin.	M 1912
Allin,	Harold Wyse	Mag.	M 1908
Allison,	Hazlett Sam.	Jes.	M 1911
Allott,	Cecil Bertram Scott	Joh.	M 1905 A.B. 1908
Allport,	Herb. Ja.	Sid.	M 1895 A.B. 1898. A.M. 1904
Allpress,	Herb. Geo.	N. C.	M 1909
Allshorn,	Lionel	Cath.	M 1905 A.B. 1909
Allworthy,	Edw. Fitzgerald	N. C.	L 1895 A.B. Dubl. incorp. 1895. A.M.
—	Tho. Bateson	Chr.	M 1896 A.B. 1899. A.M. 1903 [1912
Almond,	Ja.	Em.	M 1910
Alsagoff,	Syed Mohamed	Chr.	M 1910
Alston,	Cedric Rowland	Jes.	M 1912
—	Garwood Keningale	H. Sel.	M 1912
—	Leon.	N. C.	M 1901 Chr. A.B. 1903. A.M. 1908
Althorp,	(*Viscount*) Alb. Edw.⎰ John Spencer ⎱	Trin.	M 1910
Alton,	C. K. Tijou		*See* Tijou, C. K.
Altounyan,	Ern. Haik Riddall ...	Em.	M 1908
Ambler,	Geo.	Pem.	M 1912
Ambridge,	Leon. Hinds	Qu.	L 1902
Ambrózy			*See* de Ambrozy
Ames,	Edw. Fra. Welldon ...	Pem.	M 1905 A.B. 1908. A.M. 1912
Amos,	Art. ....*Down.		M 1901 A.B. 1904. A.M. 1912
—	Percy Maur. Mclar-⎰ die Sheldon ⎱	Trin.	M 1891 ⎰P. M. McLardie S., A.B. 1895. ⎱ A.M. †1904
Amps,	Leon. Williamson ...	King's	M 1910
Amyes,	Cha.	Cath.	M 1911
Anderson,	Alan Seymour Moore	Pem.	M 1894 A.B. 1897. A.M. 1901
—	Alex. Cha.	Down.	M 1902 A.B. 1905
—	Art. Emilius Dav. ...	Trin.	M 1905 A.B. 1908
—	Art. Ponsonby Moore	Trin.	M 1892 A.B. 1895. B.C., A.M. 1901
—	Cha. Alex. Kenneth	Pem.	M 1911
—	Cha. Graham Overbeck	Pet.	M 1911
—	Claudius Will. Rob.⎰ John ⎱	N. C.	M 1900 A.B. 1903. A.M. 1912

Anderson,	Dav.	Chr.	M 1907 A.B. 1909
—	Ern. Deane	Pem.	M 1898 A.B. 1901. B.C. 1906. M.B. 1908
—	Harry	Chr.	M 1910
—	Herb. Will.	Chr.	M 1903
—	[1] Hugh Kerr ....*Cai.		M 1884 A.B. 1887. M.B., B.C., A.M. 1891.
—	Ja. Carew O'Gorman	Cla.	M 1912 [M.D. 1898
—	Ja. Drummond	Cai.	A.M. 1909
—	Ja. Rich.	H. Sel.	M 1906 A.B. 1909
—.	John	Trin. H.	M 1901
—	John Ja.	Chr.	M 1899 A.B. 1902
—	John Ja. Moon	Jes.	M 1910
—	Keith	Pem.	M 1906 A.B. 1910
—	Kenneth Belben	Cla.	M 1900 A.B. 1904. A.M. 1909
—	Laurence Allfrey Pelham	Em.	M 1906 A.B. 1909. B.C. 1912
—	Laurence Rob. Dacre	Joh.	M 1905 A.B. 1908
—	Matth. Edm. Moore	Qu.	M 1899 A.B. 1902
—	Ralph Norman	Qu.	M 1906 A.B. 1909
—	Roger Cha.	Cla.	M 1902 A.B. 1905. A.M. 1909
—	Will.	Em.	M 1898 A.B. 1901
—	Will. Art.	Cla.	M 1903 A.B. 1906
—	Will. Blair	Trin.	M 1899 A.B. 1903. A.M. 1908
—	Will. Louis	Cai.	M 1911
Andrade,	Edw. Neville da Costa	Em.	L 1912
Andras,	John Bertram	Trin.	M 1910
Andrew,	Geo. Herb.	Cla.	M 1895 A.B. 1898. A.M. 1902
—	Geo. Will. Macbeath	Em.	M 1904 G. W. Macbeth, A.B. 1907
—	Rich. Hynman	Jes.	M 1903 LL.B. 1906
Andrewes,	Cyril Kingston Floyd	Trin.	M 1901 C. Kingstone F., A.B. 1905
Andrewes-Uthwatt, Hen.		Trin.	M 1904 A.B. 1907
—	Will.	Trin.	M 1900 A.B. 1903
Andrews,	Clem. Osborne	H. Sel.	M 1897 A.B. 1900. A.M. 1904
—	Egbert Art.	Pet.	M 1908 A.B. 1911
—	Eric Leicester	Qu.	M 1905 A.B. 1909. A.M. 1912
—	Ja. Alford	Joh.	M 1895 A.B. 1898. M.B., B.C., A.M. 1902
—	Ja. Collingwood	Joh.	M 1909 A.B. 1912
—	John Lancelot	Pet.	M 1912
—	Keble Theodore	Trin.	M 1912
—	Leon. Martin	Qu.	M 1906 A.B. 1909
—	Sealy Highmore	Cai.	M 1897 A.B. 1901
—	Tho. Ern.	H. Sel.	M 1898 A.B. 1901
—	Walt.	Joh.	M 1874 A.B. 1878. A.M.† 1883. D.D. 1909
—	Walt. Scott	Cai.	M 1905
—	Walt. Thornton	C. C.	M 1898 A.B. 1902
Angas,	Dudley Theyer	Em.	M 1912
Angell,	Cha. Cyril	Joh.	M 1892 A.B. 1895. A.M. 1907
—	Harold Fre.	H. Sel.	M 1893 A.B. 1905
Angrave,	Tho. Cooper	Pet.	M 1880 A.B. 1884. A.M. 1911
Angus,	Cha. Franklin	Trin.	M 1899 A.B. 1902. *Trin. H. A.M. 1906
—	Dav. Ja.	Trin.	M 1895 A.B. 1899. A.M. 1902
—	Geo. Herb. Chris. ...	Chr.	M 1908 A.B. 1911
—	Ronald Mathwin	Pem.	M 1902
—	Will. Brodie Gurney	Chr.	M 1903 A.B. 1906. B.C., A.M. 1910
Anklesaria,	Nasservanjee Navrojee	N. C.	M 1902
Annan,	Ja. Gilroy	King's	M 1905 A.B. 1908. A.M. 1912
Annand,	Archib. Walt.	Pem.	M 1901 A.B. 1904
Annesley,	Will. Monckton	Pet.	L 1900 A.B. 1903. A.M. 1909
Ansari,	Mazherali	Down.	L 1910
Ansbacher,	Sid. Sam.	Trin.	M 1912
Ansdell,	Rich. Carrol	Trin. H.	M 1907 A.B. 1910

[1] Master of Gonville and Caius College, 1912.

[1] Master of Selwyn College Public Hostel, 1907.

Armitage,	Vernon Hay	Pem.	M 1907 A.B. 1911
—	Walt. Alex.	Cla.	M 1898 A.B. 1903
Armour,	John	N. C.	M 1910
Armstrong,	Brian Desmond	Trin. H.	M 1909 A.B. 1912
—	Chris.	Jes.	M 1907
—	Edw. Will.	King's	M 1911
—	Fre. Will.	Joh.	M 1898 A.B. 1901. A.M. 1905
—	Geo. Fre.	Cla.	M 1901 A.B. 1904
—	Hen. Maxwell	Magd.	M 1909
—	Herb. Benj. John ...	H. Sel.	M 1897 A.B. 1900. A.M. 1908
—	Herb. Rowse	Cath.	M 1887 A.B. 1891. A.M. 1902
—	Ja. Rob. Bargrave ...	Trin.	M 1911
—	John Cardew	Cai.	M 1906 A.B. 1910
—	John Leon.	Cath.	M 1911
—	Martin Donisthorpe	Pem.	M 1902 A.B. 1905
—	Michael Rich. Leader	Trin.	M 1908 A.B. 1911
—	Rich. Robins	Trin.	M 1903 A.B. 1906. B.C. 1909. M.B. 1912
—	Vincent	Pem.	M 1904 A.B. 1907
—	Wilfred Ja. Carnsew	Qu.	M 1906 A.B. 1909
—	Will. Herb. Fletcher	Down.	M 1910
Arndt,	Geo. Edw. Hub.	Em.	M 1903 A.B. 1906
Arnell,	Oliver Roach	Cai.	M 1907 A.B. 1910
Arnfield,	Gordon	Cai.	M 1906 A.B. 1909
Arnison,	Geo. Wright	Pem.	M 1894 A.B. 1897. A.M. 1901
Arnold,	Alban Cha. Phidias	Magd.	M 1911
—	Bening Mourant	Jes.	M 1903 A.B. 1906
—	Ern. Hen.	H. Sel.	M 1912
—	Fre. Octavius	Trin.	E 1901 A.B. 1904. M.B., B.C., A.M. 1908
—	Geo. Wilfred	Qu.	M 1908 A.B. 1911
—	John Corry	Joh.	M 1900 A.B. 1903
—	John Hen.	Joh.	M 1905 A.B. 1908. A.M. 1912
—	Leslie Mayhew	Cla.	M 1908
—	Tho. Walker	Mag.	M 1883 A.B. 1886. A.M. 1905
Arnold-Bemrose			*See* Bemrose
Arnold-Wallinger,	Geoffrey Seldon	Trin.	M 1908 A.B. 1911
Arnot,	Dav. Will.	Cai.	M 1903 A.B. 1906
Arnott,	Edw. Winstone	Joh.	M 1902 E. Whiston, A.B. 1905. E. Whin-
—	John	Trin. H.	M 1904 [stone, A.M. 1912
Aron,	Eustace Mars	Jes.	M 1910
—	Fre. Adolph	Cai.	M 1906 A.B. 1910
Arrhenius,	Svante Augustus		*Sc.D.* 1908
Arrowsmith,	Geo. Ern.	Cai.	M 1908 A.B. 1911
—	Leighton Macdonald	Trin.	M 1910
—	Rob.	Em.	M 1912
—	Walt. Gordon	Cai.	M 1908 A.B. 1911
Arthur,	(*Prince*)		*LL.D.* 1903
—	Walt. Lawrence	Chr.	M 1902
Arundale,	Geo. Syd.	N. C.	E 1895 Joh. A.B. 1898. LL.B. 1899. A.M.
Arundel,	Frank Drew	Em.	M 1908 [1902
Asal,	Mohammad	N. C.	M 1906 Pemb. A.B. 1910. A.M. 1911
Aschaffenburg,	Wilhelm Art.	Joh.	E 1908
Ascherson,	Will. Lawrence	Pem.	M 1889 N. C. B.C. 1900. M.B. 1901. M.D.
Ascoli,	Geo. Hugh Dan.	Cai.	M 1906 A.B. 1910 [1907
Asghar,	Mohamad	Down.	M 1902
Ash,	Fra. Hen.	Trin.	M 1912
—	Gerald Beaumont ...	Trin.	M 1901 A.B. 1904
—	Harry Arnold	Pem.	M 1902 A.B. 1905
Ashburner,	Geo. Barrington	Chr.	M 1907 A.B. 1910
—	John Croudson	Chr.	M 1906 A.B. 1909
Ashby,	Hugh Tuke	Em.	M 1900 A.B. 1903. M.B., B.C. 1908
—	Kenneth Harold	Em.	M 1910

Ashby,	Leon.	Chr.	M 1895 A.B. 1898. A.M. 1904
—	Leon. Beauclerk	Trin.	M 1894 A.B. 1897. A.M. 1906
—	Marcus Warner	Trin. H.	M 1900 A.B. 1903. A.M. 1907
—	Norman	Joh.	M 1902 A.B. 1907. A.M. 1910
Ashcroft,	Alec Hutchinson ...	Cai.	M 1906 A.B. 1909
—	Frederic	Em.	M 1905 A.B. 1908
—	Harold	Cai.	M 1904 A.B. 1907. A.M. 1911
—	John Myddleton	Cai.	M 1902 A.B. 1905
—	Rob. Leslie	Cai.	M 1911
—	Will.	Cai.	M 1900 A.B. 1903. A.M. 1908
Ashe,	Geo. Hamilton	Joh.	M 1899 A.B. 1902. A.M. 1909
Asher,	Alb. Hen. Robinson	Qu.	M 1897 A.B. 1905. A.M. 1912
Ashington,	Hen. Sherard Osborn	King's	M 1910
Ashlin,	Spencer Cocking	Cla.	M 1905 A.B. 1910
Ashman,	Edw. Harold Williams	Qu.	M 1908 A.B. 1911
Ashraf,	Syed Sayeed uddin ...	Cath.	M 1911
Ashton,	Alex. Angus Graham	Pet.	M 1909 A.B. 1912
—	Harry	Cai.	E 1911
Ashton Smith,	Gervase	Em.	M 1903 A.B. 1906. A.M. 1911
Ashwin,	Manley Frederic	Pem.	M 1906 A.B. 1909
Ashworth,	Frank	Pet.	M 1895 A.B. 1898. A.M. 1902
—	Fre. Lionel	H. Sel.	M 1903 A.B. 1906
—	John	Chr.	M 1908
Askew,	Edm. Joscelyne Percy	Trin.	M 1905 A.B. 1911
—	Tom Barrick	Chr.	M 1909 A.B. 1912
Askey,	Step. Grange	Joh.	M 1907 A.B. 1910
Askwith,	Edw. Harrison	Trin.	M 1883 A.B. 1886. A.M. 1890. B.D. 1900.
—	Geo.	Qu.	M 1894 A.B. 1897. A.M. 1901 [D.D. '02
—	Wilfred Marcus	C. C.	M 1909 A.B. 1912
Aspin,	Alb.	Joh.	M 1900 A.B. 1903. A.M. 1907
Aspinall,	Geoffrey	Trin.	M 1903 A.B. 1906
Aspinwall,	Cha. Fre.	Chr.	M 1901 A.B. 1904. A.M. 1908
—	Guy Richmond	Cla.	M 1911
Asquith,	Herb. Hen.		*LL.D.* 1908
Astbury,	Frank Llewellyn Davies	N. C.	M 1899 Chr. A.B. 1902. A.M. 1906
—	Harold Stanley	Chr.	M 1909 A.B. 1912
Astley,	Aylmer Anth.	C. C.	L 1870 Anth. Aylmer, Trin. A.B. 1876.
—	Walt.	Chr.	M 1900 A.B. 1903 [A.M. 1901
Aston,	Art. Neville	Trin.	M 1902 A.B. 1905
—	Cyril Thornton	Em.	M 1896 A.B. 1899. A.M. 1907
—	Fra. Will. ....*Trin.		L 1910 A.B. 1912
—	Randolph Littleton	Cai.	M 1888 A.B. 1891. A.M. 1905
—	Walt. Douglas ....*Down.		M 1901 A.B., LL.B. 1905. LL.M. 1908
Atchison,	Geo. Turnour	Chr.	M 1896 A.B., LL.B. 1900. A.M. 1903
Atchley,	Cha. Hor. Tracy	Sid.	M 1901 A.B. 1904. A.M. 1909
Atkey,	Freeman Archib. Haynes	Pem.	M 1901 A.B. 1904. A.M. 1908
Atkin,	Cha. Syd.	Cai.	M 1906 A.B. 1909
—	Eric Edwin	Cai.	M 1899 A.B. 1902. M.B. 1907
—	Keyser	Jes.	M 1911
—	Reg. Will.	N. C.	M 1898 A.B. 1902
Atkins,	Basil Syd.	Cai.	M 1903
—	Edw. Maur.	Cath.	M 1909 A.B. 1912
—	Gordon Richmond ...	Sid.	M 1910
—	Hen. Ern.	Pet.	M 1890 A.B. 1893. A.M. 1901
—	Hugh Leslie	Joh.	M 1900 A.B. 1903
—	John Will. Hey ......*Joh.		M 1898 A.B. 1901. A.M. 1906
Atkinson,	Alex. Victor	Mag.	M 1905 A.B. 1908
—	Art. Geo.	Trin.	M 1900 A.B. 1905. M.B., B.C. 1911
—	Carleton Rich. Buckby	Pem.	L 1912
—	Cha. Gerard	Pem.	M 1902 A.B. 1905
—	Edw. Will.	Cai.	M 1900 A.B. 1903

Avory,	Douglas Hen.	Trin. H.	M 1905 A.B. 1908
—	Hor. Edm.	C. C.	M 1870 LL.B. 1874. [1] LL.D. 1911
Awati,	Pralhad Raoji	N. C.	M 1909 A.B. 1911
Aydon,	John	Cla.	M 1906 A.B. 1911
Ayles,	Herb. Hen. Baker ...	Joh.	M 1882 A.B. 1885. A.M. 1889. B.D. 1899.
Ayliff,	Jonat.	Trin. H.	M 1909 A.B. 1912 [D.D. 1905
Ayre,	Bern. Pitts	Jes.	M 1911
Ayton,	Will. Alf.	Trin.	M 1899 A.B. 1902
Aytoun,	Rob. Alex.	Em.	M 1899 A.B. 1902. A.M. 1910
Azam,	Syed Mahomed	Jes.	M 1912
Aziz,	Abdul	Pet.	M 1904 A.B. 1907
—	Abdul	Down.	M 1908 Syed A., A.B. 1912

B

Babb,	Hugh Webster	Chr.	M 1911
Baber,	John Barton	Trin.	M 1911
Babington,	John Cyril	Pem.	M 1899 A.B., LL.B. 1902. A.M. 1906
Baboneau,	Cha. Alf.	Sid.	M 1910
Bacharach,	Alf. Louis	Cla.	M 1909 A.B. 1912
Bache,	Harold Godfrey	Cai.	M 1908 A.B. 1912
—	Hen. Norman	H. Sel.	M 1903 A.B. 1906
Bachert,	Louis Rich. Art.	Joh.	M 1900 A.B. 1903
Back,	Gilb. Alf.	Cai.	M 1910
—	Hatfield Art. Will. ...	Cai.	M 1909 Hatfeild A. W., A.B. 1912
—	Ivor Gordon	Trin. H.	M 1898 A.B. 1901. M.B., B.C., A.M. 1907
—	Nich.	Down.	M 1910
—	Percy Rob. Hatfield	Cai.	M 1908 P. R. Hatfeild A.B. 1911
Backhouse,	Basil Hen.	Trin.	M 1901 A.B. 1904
—	Hub. Edm.	Trin.	M 1901 A.B. 1904
—	John	Joh.	M 1886 A.B. 1889. A.M. 1903
—	Will. Ormston	Trin. H.	M 1905 A.B. 1909
Backlund,	Johan Oscar		*Sc.D.* 1904
Backwell,	Hen. Fleming	King's	M 1903 A.B. 1906
Bacon,	Fra. Rimington	Trin.	M 1910
—	Frederic	Trin.	M 1899 A.B. 1902. A.M. 1907
Badcock,	Gerald Eliot	Pem.	M 1901
—	Will. Cornish	Qu.	M 1897 A.B. 1900. A.M. 1904
Badger,	Ern. Sam. Tho.	Cath.	M 1884 A.B. 1887. A.M. 1903
Baerlein,	Edgar Maximilian ...	Trin.	M 1898 A.B. 1902
—	Oswald Felix	Trin.	M 1911
Bagchi,	Jnanendra Chandra	Em.	M 1903 A.B. 1906
—	Satis Chandra	Joh.	M 1901 A.B. 1904. LL.B. 1906
Bagenal,	Nich. Beauchamp ...	King's	M 1910
Baggallay,	Mervyn Eric Claude	Trin.	M 1907 A.B. 1911
Bagge,	Hen. Percy	Cla.	M 1898 A.B. 1901
Baggley,	Aubrey Cha.	Em.	M 1907 A.B. 1910
Baggott,	Louis John	Qu.	M 1911
Bagley,	Art. Bracton	Pem.	M 1909
Bagnall,	Fre. Percy Dunn ...	Mag.	M 1908
—	Geo. Barry	Pem.	M 1905 A.B. 1908
—	Reg. Oscar	Mag.	M 1912

---

[1] Honoris causa under Stat. A. Chap. II, Sect. 18, p. 1.

Baguley,	John Minty	Pem.	M 1899 A.B. 1902
Bahr,	Phil. Heinrich	Trin.	M 1900 A.B. 1903. M.B., B.C., A.M. 1908
Baikie,	Rob.	Cla.	M 1910
Bailes,	Hen.	Em.	M 1907 A.B. 1910
Bailey,	Bern. Fra.	Cla.	M 1909 A.B. 1912
—	Cha.	Cla.	M 1897 A.B. 1900. A.M. 1904
—	Edw. Battersby	Cla.	M 1899 A.B. 1902
—	Geo. Fre. Selborne ...	Cai.	M 1900 A.B. 1903. M.B., B.C. 1907. M.D.
—	Harry Reuben	Jes.	L 1909 A.B. 1911 [1910
—	Howard Sinclair	Qu.	M 1908 A.B. 1911
—	John Hen.	Jes.	M 1908
—	John Hewett	H. Sel.	M 1898 A.B. 1901
—	Maur. Armand	Cla.	M 1908 A.B. 1911
—	Phil. Gerald	Cla.	M 1905 A.B. 1908. A.M. 1912
—	Rich. Fitzroy	King's	E 1903 A.B. 1906
—	Tho. Burton	Cai.	M 1909
—	Tom Esmond Geoffrey	Cla.	M 1902 A.B. 1905
—	Victor Tho.	N. C.	E 1896 A.B. 1900. A.M. 1912
—	Walt.	Qu.	M 1911
—	Walt. Douglas	Trin. H.	M 1903
—	Wilfrid Norman	Trin.	M 1912
Baillie,	Ja. Black	Trin.	M 1897 A.B. 1899. A.M. 1904
Baillieu,	Harry Latham	Jes.	M 1911
Baily,	Rob. Edw. Hartwell	Pem.	M 1904 A.B. 1908
Bain,	Donald Kenneth Dove	Trin.	M 1896 A.B. 1899. A.M. 1903
—	Graham Ward	Joh.	M 1910
—	Norman Kerr	Sid.	M 1902 A.B. 1905
—	Percy Will.	Mag.	M 1905 A.B. 1908
Bainbridge,	Fra. Art.	Trin.	M 1893 A.B. 1896. M.B., A.M. 1901. M.D.
—	Geo. Herb.	H. Sel.	M 1894 A.B. 1897. A.M. 1904 [1904
—	Will. Art.	Trin. H.	M 1905 A.B. 1911
Bainbridge-Bell, W. D.			*See* Bell, W. D.
—	Labouchere Hillyer	Em.	M 1912
Bainbrigge,	Phil. Gillespie	Trin.	M 1909 A.B. 1912
Baines,	Athelstan Basil	Chr.	M 1907 A.B. 1911
—	Dennis Lynch	Chr.	M 1900 A.B. 1903
—	Matth. Talbot	Trin. H.	M 1912
—	Walt.	Down.	M 1906 A.B. 1909
Baker,	Alb. Edw.	Trin.	M 1903 A.B. 1906
—	Alex.	Down.	L 1908
—	Art. Forbes Wilfrid	Trin. H.	M 1909
—	Art. Ponsford	Chr.	M 1892 A.B. 1904. A.M. 1907
—	Aubrey	Em.	M 1911
—	Cha. Morton	Chr.	M 1890 A.B., LL.B. 1894. LL.M. 1898.
—	Cha. Will. Evelyn ...	Cla.	M 1902 [A.M., LL.D. 1904
—	Donald	N. C.	M 1909 A.B. 1912
—	Edgar Art. Cha. Ballantine	Chr.	M 1900 A.B. 1904
—	Edw. Conrad	Cath.	M 1911
—	Fra. Barrington	Pet.	M 1911
—	Frank Rob.	Cai.	M 1897 A.B. 1901
—	Gerald Percival	Trin.	M 1898 LL.B. 1901. A.B. 1904
—	Hen. Fre.	*Joh.	M 1884 A.B. 1887. A.M. 1891. Sc.D. 1902
—	[1]Ja. Franklin	*Pem.	M 1881 Bethune-Baker, J. F., A.B.
			[1884 (2). A.M. 1888. B.D. 1901.
—	John Edgar	Trin. H.	M 1907 A.B., LL.B. 1910 [D.D. 1912
—	John Percy	Em.	M 1890 A.B. 1893. A.M. 1907
—	Leon. Tilsley	Sid.	M 1902 [1912
—	Martyn Wilfred	Joh.	M 1902 A.B. 1905. B.C. 1909. M.B., A.M.

[1] Lady Margaret's Professor of Divinity, 1911.

Baker,	Percy	N. C.	L 1909 Cath. A.B. 1911
—	Phil. John	King's	M 1908 A.B. 1912
—	Sid. Ellis	Sid.	M 1909 A.B. 1912
—	Stanley	Cai.	M 1909 A.B. 1912
—	Wilfrid Erwood	Trin.	M 1908 A.B. 1911
—	Will.	Joh.	M 1894 A.B. 1897. post Lambert-Baker,
Bakewell,	Brian	Chr.	M 1909 A.B. 1912 [W., A.M. 1901
—	Geo. Victor	Cla.	M 1906 A.B. 1909. B.C. 1912
Bakhuyzen,	Henricus Gerardus van de Sande }		*Sc.D.* 1904
Balcomb,	Herb. Fra. Geo.	Joh.	M 1902 A.B. 1905
Baldock,	Frank Reg.	H. Sel.	M 1901 A.B. 1904
Baldwin,	Alex. Bertie	Joh.	M 1886 A.B. 1890. A.M. 1908
—	Cecil Will.	Sid.	M 1910
—	Horatio John	Em.	M 1899 J. H. A.B. 1902. A.M. 1906
—	Phil. Fre.	Em.	M 1912
Bale,	Ronald Frank	Qu.	M 1908 A.B.. 1911
Bales,	Percy Geo.	Pet.	M 1906 A.B. 1909
Balfour,	Archib. Edw.	Trin.	M 1888 LL.B. 1892. LL.M. 1906
—	Claud Malcolm	Trin.	M 1909 A.B. 1912
—	Douglas Hastings ...	Em.	L 1905 A.B. 1907
—	Graham		*A.M.* 1907
—	John	Trin.	M 1907 Jack, A.B. 1910
—	Reg. ....*King's		M 1894 A.B. 1897. A.M. 1901
Balgarnie,	Will. Hen.	Trin.	M 1894 A.B. 1897. A.M. 1901
Ball,	Alb. Edw.	Qu.	M 1909 A.B. 1912
—	Cyril Fra.	Cai.	M 1910
—	Edw. Foley	Jes.	M 1902 A.B. 1905. A.M. 1910
—	Geo. Randle	Down.	M 1910
---	Hen. Fre.	Sid.	M 1909 A.B. 1912
—	Will. Alb. Rich.	Em.	M 1904 A.B. 1907. A.M. 1911
Ballamy,	Harold Will.	Trin.	M 1912
Ballance,	Herb. Cecil	Em.	L 1891 A.B. 1901
—	Leslie Art.	Trin.	M 1907 A.B. 1910
Ballard,	Edw.	Cai.	M 1907 A.B. 1910
—	Phil.	Cath.	M 1904
—	Tho.	Cla.	M 1894 A.B. 1897. A.M. 1901
Ballingall,	Dav. Cha. Gordon ...	Em.	M 1907 A.B. 1910
Balls,	Will. Lawrence .....*Joh.		E 1900 A.B. 1903. A.M.† 1907
Balmford,	Alf. Bickerton	Em.	M 1907 Sid. A.B. 1910
Balston,	Fra. Will.	Trin.	M 1899 A.B. 1903
—	Maur. Edw.	Trin.	M 1902 A.B. 1906. A.M. 1909
Baly,	Art. Lionel	Em.	M 1898 A.B. 1901. A.M. 1905
Balzarotti,	Giuseppe Pippo	Trin.	M 1909 A.B. 1912
Bamber,	Fre. Trevor	Down.	E 1892 A.B. 1895. A.M. 1902
—	Fre. Trevor	Jes.	M 1910
Bamford,	Alec Joscelyne	Em.	M 1904 A.B. 1907
Bampfield,	John McWilliams ...	Pem.	M 1888 A.B. 1891. A.M. 1905
—	Lewis Adolphus	Em.	M 1901 A.B. 1904
Bampton-Taylor, Reg. John		N. C.	L 1905
Banbury,	Fra. Edw.	Trin.	M 1912
—	Geo. Chay	Trin. H.	M 1895
—	Ralph Edgar	Trin.	M 1898 A.B. 1901
Bancroft,	Claude Keith	Trin.	M 1905 A.B. 1908. A.M.† 1912
—	Oswald Lawrance ...	Trin.	M 1906 A.B. 1909
Band,	Edw.	Qu.	M 1905 A.B. 1908
Banerjee,	Probhat Nath	Trin.	M 1905 A.B. 1908
—	Sudhindranath	Down.	M 1907 A.B. 1910
Banerji,	Jamini Mohan	Down.	M 1908
—	Khettre Chandra ...	Chr.	M 1901
—	Sureshnath	N. C.	M 1907

Banham,	Hen. Ulric Bower ...	Em.	M 1899 A.B. 1902. A.M. 1906
—	John Clifford	Trin.	M 1900 A.B. 1903. A.M. 1907
—	Vivian Greaves	King's	M 1900 A.B. 1903. A.M. 1908
Banister,	Cha. Gonville	Trin.	M 1908 A.B. 1911
—	Cha. Wilfred	Jes.	M 1911
—	Howard	Jes.	M 1906 A.B. 1910 [M.D. 1910
—	John Bright	Jes.	M 1898 A.B. 1901. A.M. 1905. B.C. 1908.
—	Marmaduke Haddon	Trin.	M 1900 A.B. 1903. A.M. 1907
—	Tho. Roger	Joh.	M 1909 A.B. 1912
—	Thurstan Edm.	Chr.	M 1905 A.B. 1908
Bankart,	Art. Syd. Blundell ...	Trin.	M 1898 A.B. 1901. B.C., A.M. 1908. M.C.
Bankes-Williams, Will.		Qu.	L 1897 A.B. 1901 [1910
Banks,	Ern. Hen.	Em.	M 1903 A.B., LL.B. 1906
—	Leslie	Chr.	E 1909 A.B., LL.B. 1912
—	Reg. Alf.	Chr.	M 1909 A.B. 1912
—	Rob. Geo.	Pem.	M 1901
Bannatyne,	Art. Gordon	King's	M 1904 A.B. 1907
—	Edgar Ja.	Cai.	M 1910
Bannerman,	Dav. Armitage	Pem.	M 1905 A.B. 1909
Banning,	Hen. Burton Smeed ..	Jes.	L 1898 A.B. 1901
Bansall,	Walt. Hen.	Joh.	M 1877 A.B. 1881. A.M. 1901
Banyard,	Fra. Edwin	N. C.	M 1911
—	Ja. Hirst	N. C.	L 1906 Chr. A.B. 1908
Bapanna,	Garimella	N. C.	M 1909
Baptie,	Norman	Chr.	M 1907 A.B. 1910
Barber,	Cha. Alf.	Chr.	M 1884 A.B. 1888. A.M.† 1892. Sc.D. 1908
—	Cyril Art.	Joh.	M 1904 A.B. 1909
—	Harold Wordsworth	Cla.	M 1905 A.B. 1908. B.C. 1911. M.B., A.M.
—	Hor. Hansard	Qu.	M 1891 A.B. 1894. A.M. 1908 [1912
—	John	Trin.	M 1900 A.B. 1903. A.M. 1908
—	Lewis Chris.	King's	M 1905 A.B. 1908
—	Will. Edm.	Chr.	M 1903 A.B. 1906
Barber-Starkey, Cha. Cecil		Mag.	M 1909
—	Fra. Waugh Gordon	Trin.	M 1903 A.B. 1907
—	Roger John Kinloch..	Trin.	M 1902
Barbour,	Geo. Brown	Joh.	M 1912
—	Ralph Hen.	Trin.	M 1902 A.B. 1905. A.M. 1911
—	Rob.	Trin.	M 1894 A.B. 1897. A.M. 1903
Barcikowski, Janusz Witold		Trin.	M 1912
Barclay,	Alf. Ern.	Chr.	M 1894 A.B. 1897. A.M. 1903. B.C. 1904.
—	Art. Victor	Trin.	M 1906 A.B. 1909 [M.D. 1912
--	Cyril Cha.	Trin.	M 1904 A.B. 1907. A.M. 1911
—	Dav. Buxton	Trin.	M 1895 A.B. 1898. A.M. 1902
—	Fra. Hub.	Trin. H.	M 1888 A.B. 1891. A.M. 1904
—	Geoffrey Will.	Trin. H.	M 1910
—	Gilb. Art.	Trin.	M 1900 A.B. 1903. A.M. 1907
—	John Art.	Pem.	M 1911
—	Jos. Fra.	Trin. H.	M 1902
—	Jos. Gurney	Trin.	M 1897 A.B. 1900. A.M. 1904
—	Maur. Edw.	Trin. H.	M 1905 A.B. 1909
—	Tho. Hub.	Trin.	M 1902 A.B. 1906
—	Will. Edm. Alan ...	Down.	M 1906 A.B. 1909
Bardwell,	Tho. Garnett Newman	Jes.	L 1903
Barff,	Fre. Rob.	Chr.	M 1907 A.B. 1910
Barger,	Geo. ....*King's		M 1897 A.B. 1901. A.M. 1904
Barham,	Guy Foster	Cai.	M 1892 A.B. 1895. B.C. 1902. M.B. 1904.
			[A.M., M.D. 1912
Bark,	Geoffrey Mentor	Em.	M 1901 A.B. 1904. LL.B. 1905. A.M. 1910
Barker,	Alan Walt.	H. Sel.	M 1900 A.B. 1904. A.M. 1908
—	Aubrey	Trin.	M 1901 A.B. 1904. B.C. 1909
—	Bertie Tho. Percival	Cai.	M 1895 A.B. 1899. A.M. 1902

Barker,	Cha. Hen. .... Sid.	M 1901 A.B. 1904. A.M. 1911
—	Dalgairns Arundel ... Trin.	M 1900 A.B. 1903
—	Edw. Walt. .... Qu.	M 1907 A.B. 1910
—	Fra. Worsley .... Trin.	M 1907
—	Fre. .... H. Sel.	M 1912
—	Frederic Allan .... Em.	M 1900 A.B. 1903. B.C. 1907. M.B. 1908
—	Geoffrey Palgrave ... King's	M 1906 A.B. 1909
—	Geo. Tho. .... H. Sel.	M 1911
—	Gilb. Dav. .... N. C.	M 1901 Pet. A.B. 1904. A.M. 1908
—	Hen. .... Trin.	M 1894 A.B. 1897. A.M. 1901
—	Hen. Arundel Keith Qu.	M 1911
—	Hor. .... Cla.	M 1910
—	Leon. Emilius Harman⎱ Cai. Ross ⎰	M 1895 A.B. 1898. M.B., B.C. 1903
—	Raymond Inglis Palgrave King's	M 1908 A.B. 1911
—	Rob. Lewis .... Cai.	M 1903 A.B. 1906. B.C. 1911
—	Roland Auriol .... Sid.	M 1910
—	Ronald Will. .... Cai.	M 1901 A.B. 1904
—	Tho. Geo. Ridgwell Cath.	M 1903 A.B. 1906
—	Tho. Will. .... H. Sel.	M 1910
Barkla,	Cha. Glover .... Trin.	M 1899 King's A.B. 1903. A.M. 1907
Barkway,	Ja. Lumsden .... N. C.	L 1901 A.B. 1903. A.M. 1912
Barley,	Ja. Spencer Granville N. C.	M 1890 A.B. 1895. A.M. 1903
Barlow,	Alex. Will. Lancashire Trin.	M 1910
—	Cha. Will. .... Em.	M 1898 A.B. 1901. A.M. 1905
—	Chris. Neild .... Pem.	M 1912
—	Clem. Anderson Montague King's	M 1886 A.B. 1889. LL.B. 1890. A.M. 1893. [LL.M. 1894. LL.D. 1901
—	Edw. Maur. .... Pem.	M 1910
—	Ja. Jardine .... Trin.	M 1904 A.B. 1907. A.M. 1911
—	Lancelot White ...... Cai.	M 1906 A.B. 1910
—	Percival Smith ...... Joh.	M 1902 A.B. 1905. A.M.† 1909
—	Rob. Geo. .... Chr.	M 1911
—	Tho. Dalmahoy ...... Trin.	M 1900 A.B. 1904. A.M. 1909
Barltrop,	Eric Art. .... Qu.	M 1909
—	Ivan Cha. .... Qu.	M 1911
Barnard,	Dennis Chris. .... Trin. H.	M 1899 A.B. 1902. LL.B. 1903
—	Edm. Cha. .... Down.	M 1907
—	Fra. Art. Buchanan King's	M 1911
—	Geo. Will. .... Jes.	M 1904 A.B. 1907
—	Humfrey Denzil ...... Jes.	M 1911
—	John Douglas .... Jes.	M 1904 A.B. 1907. A.M. 1911
—	Keppel Harcourt ... Chr.	M 1905 A.B. 1908
—	Percy Mordaunt ...... Chr.	M 1887 A.B. 1890. A.M. 1894. B.D. 1901
Barnardo,	Will. Stuart Elmslie Pem.	M 1893 A.B. 1897. A.M. 1902
Barnato,	Jack Hen. Woolf ...... Trin. H.	M 1912
Barnes,	Art. Stapylton ...... Trin.	M 1903. A.M Oxf. incorp. 1904
—	Ern. Will. ....*Trin.	M 1893 A.B. 1896. A.M. 1900. Sc.D. 1907
—	Frank .... H. Sel.	M 1905 A.B. 1908. A.M. 1912
—	Geoffrey Geo. .... Joh.	M 1905 A.B. 1908
—	Geo. Le Maire ...... Trin.	M 1905 A.B. 1908
—	Harold Alf. .... Trin.	M 1875 A.B. 1888. A.M. 1908
—	Herb. Sedgwick ...... Jes.	M 1898 A.B. 1901. A.M. 1905
—	Howell Wood .... Jes.	M 1905 A.B. 1908
—	Ja. Edwin .... Cla.	M 1910
—	Ja. Sid. .... Trin.	M 1900 A.B. 1903
—	Percy Earle .... N. C.	M 1898 Chr. A.B. 1901. A.M. 1907
—	Theodore Art. Rich. Trin.	M 1911 [D.D. 1897
—	¹ Will. Emery ....*Pet.	M 1877 A.B. 1881. A.M. 1884. B.D. 1891.
—	Will. Hen. .... Joh.	M 1894 A.B. 1897. A.M. 1907

¹ Hulsean Professor of Divinity, 1901.

Barnett,	Bertram Leeds Tho.	Joh.	M 1893 A.B. 1896. A.M. 1901. M.B., B.C.
—	Frank Steph. Gilmore	Em.	M 1910 [1902
—	John Herb.	Jes.	M 1909
—	Reg. Walt.	Pem.	M 1911
—	Sam. Hen. Gilmore	Em.	M 1903 A.B. 1906
—	Syd. Herb.	Cai.	M 1910
Barney,	John	C. C.	M 1908
Barnicoat,	Guy Humphry	H. Sel.	M 1906 A.B. 1909
Barnicot,	Harry	Pem.	M 1901 A.B. 1904. A.M. 1908
—-	Jos.	Pem.	M 1893 A.B. 1896. M.B., B.C. 1902. M.D.
Barnicott,	Art. Warren	Chr.	M 1898 A.B. 1901 [1905
Barningham,	Ern.	Trin.	M 1911
—	Vincent	Pem.	M 1910
Barnsley,	Donald Gordon	Trin.	M 1902 A.B. 1905
—	Rob. Eric	Trin.	M 1905 A.B. 1908
—	Tho. Kenneth	Trin.	M 1911
Baron,	Spencer Bardsley ...	Qu.	M 1909 A.B. 1912
—	Will. Russell Needham	Chr.	M 1897 A.B. 1900. A.M. 1904
Barr,	Guy	Chr.	M 1904 A.B. 1907
—	John Hen.	Chr.	L 1906 A.B. 1908
Barraclough,	Augustus	H. Cav.	M 1889 Pet. A.B. 1892. A.M. 1907
—	Jack Norman	Cai.	M 1909
—	Rob. Fell	Trin.	M 1903 A.B. 1906
Barradell-Smith,	Syd.	Joh.	M 1898 A.B. 1901. M.B., B.C. 1906
—	Walt.	Joh.	M 1900 A.B. 1903
Barran,	Claude Roulston	Trin.	M 1904 A.B. 1907
—	Colin Adair	Cla.	M 1912
—	Hugh Bradley	Pem.	M 1908 A.B. 1911
Barratt,	Will. Donald	Trin.	M 1902 A.B. 1905
Barraud,	Victor Hugo Alexandre	N. C.	M 1910
Barrell,	Fra. Maxwell	Pem.	M 1911
Barrett,	Cha. Brace Gooden	H. Sel.	M 1905 A.B. 1909
—	Fre. Bertram Johnson	C. C.	M 1905 A.B. 1908
—	Fre. Gamble	Em.	M 1906 A.B. 1909
—	Harold Salter	Trin.	M 1895 A.B. 1898. A.M. 1902
—	Hugh Scott	Joh.	M 1906 A.B. 1909
—	Jack Hardy	Trin. H.	M 1910
—	Lawrence Theodore Salter	Chr.	M 1905 A.B. 1908
—	Lucas	Chr.	M 1910
—	Percy Parker	Sid.	L 1906 A.B. 1908
—	Reg. Octavius	N. C.	M 1911
—	Rollo Sam.	Cai.	M 1902 A.B. 1905
—-	Syd. Tho.	Trin.	M 1912
—	Will. Edw. Colvile ...	Pem.	M 1898 A.B. 1901. A.M. 1905
Barringer,	Rob. Eric	Trin. H.	M 1911
Barrington,	Fra. Edw. Phil.	Cai.	M 1911
Barris,	John Davis	Cai.	M 1898 A.B. 1901. M.B., B.C. 1910
Barritt,	Jos. Luther	Em.	M 1911
—	Newton Wood	Em.	M 1907 A.B. 1910
—	Will. Vernon	Joh.	M 1903 A.B. 1906. A.M. 1910
Barron,	Edw. Alphonsus Winston	Trin.	M 1901
—	Geo. Desmond	Cai.	M 1910
Barrow,	Alf. Ja.	Mag.	M 1902 A.B. 1906
—	Eric Burton Pat. ...	Trin.	M 1909
—	Geo. Shuldham Malet	Jes.	M 1880
—	Ja. Hen. Martyn ...	Qu.	M 1912
—	John Rothney	Qu.	M 1900 A.B. 1903
—	Pat. Lindsay	Pem.	M 1911
—-	Reg. Lousada	Pem.	M 1907 A.B. 1910
—	Rich. Martin	King's	M 1912
Barry,	Art. Gordon	Pem.	M 1905

Barry,	Cha. Bissell	Pem.	M 1905 A.B. 1908
—	Cha. Ja.	C. C.	M 1901 A.B. 1904. A.M. 1908
—	Eric Gordon Wolfe	Trin.	M 1904 A.B. 1909
—	Geo. Duncan	Cai.	M 1883 A.B. 1886. A.M. 1891. B.D. 1911
—	Tom	Trin.	M 1909
—	Will. Hen.	Trin.	M 1895 A.B. 1898. A.M. 1902
Barstow,	John Nelson	Mag.	M 1909 A.B. 1912
Barter,	Elder Gaul	Sid.	M 1910
Bartholomew,	Augustus Theodore	Pet.	M 1901 A.B. 1904. A.M. 1908
—	Graham Topley	King's	M 1900 A.B. 1903. A.M. 1907
Barthropp,	Sid. Alf. Nath. Shafto	Trin.	M 1910
Bartlam,	Eric Walt.	Chr.	M 1910
—	Frank Harold	Chr.	M 1903 A.B. 1906
Bartlett,	Alb. Cha.	Em.	M 1912
—	Alb. Will.	N. C.	M 1901 Chr. A.B. 1903. A.M. 1909
—	Alf. Cyril	N. C.	L 1899 A.B. 1902
—	Donald Mackenzie Maynard	Cla.	M 1892 A.B. 1895. A.M. 1911
—	Edw. Morton	Pem.	M 1897 A.B. 1900. A.M. 1904
—	Frederic Cha.	Joh.	M 1912
—	Geo. Bertram	Sid.	M 1899 A.B. 1902
—	Gilb. Harrison	C. C.	M 1900 A.B. 1903
—	Harold Sloan	Cai.	M 1906
—	Lionel Art.	Cath.	M 1903
Barton,	Art. Kingsley	Cath.	M 1910
—	Bertie Bowman	Trin. H.	M 1905 A.B., LL.B. 1908
—	Bertram	Trin.	M 1904 A.B. 1907
—	Cecil Edw.	Trin. H.	L 1888 A.B. 1890. A.M. 1906
—	Cecil Ja. Juxon Talbot	Down.	M 1910
—	Cha. Geoffrey	Pem.	M 1909 A.B. 1912
—	Cha. Godfrey	Qu.	M 1897 A.B. 1900. A.M. 1904
—	Cha. Ja.	Mag.	M 1893 A.B. 1896. A.M. 1910
—	Conrad Hen.	Cath.	M 1898 A.B. 1901. A.M. 1907
—	Edw. Ja.	Sid.	M 1910
—	Edw. John	Sid.	M 1898 A.B. 1902. A.M. 1910
—	Guy Douglas :.......	Pem.	M 1894 A.B. 1897. M.B., B.C. 1903
—	Harry	H. Sel.	M 1896 A.B. 1899. A.M. 1911
—	John Fra.	Qu.	M 1904 A.B. 1907
—	Tho. Eyre	Trin. H.	M 1906
Bartram,	Harold	Trin. H.	M 1903
Barwell,	Harry Barrington ...	Cath.	M 1912
—	Noël Fre.	Trin.	M 1897 A.B. 1900. A.M. 1910
Bashford,	Alf. Myddleton	Jes.	M 1900 A.B. 1903. A.M. 1908
—	Percy Fre. Rob.	Chr.	M 1904 A.B. 1907
Basit,	Ali Khan	Pet.	M 1909 A.B. 1912
Bass,	Roger Art.	Joh.	M 1904
—	Victor Abram	Cla.	M 1907
Bassett,	Harold Llewellyn ...	Trin. H.	M 1908 A.B. 1912
Bassett Smith,	Will. Rodolph ...	N. C.	M 1906 A.B. 1909
Bastow,	Frank	Cla.	M 1912
Basu,	Birendra Kumar	Em.	M 1909 A.B. 1911
—	Kasi Prosad	N. C.	M 1897 Down. A.B., LL.B. 1901
—	Manmathanath	Em.	L 1902 A.B. 1905. A.M.† 1908
—	Sisir Kumar	N. C.	M 1899 A.B. 1902. A.M.† 1906
Bate,	Art.	Trin.	M 1908 A.B. 1911
—	Art. Geoffrey	King's	M 1894 A.B. 1897. B.C. 1902. M.B. 1903
Bateman,	Eustace	Em.	M 1900 A.B. 1903. A.M. 1907
—	Fra. John Harvey ...	Pem.	M 1887 A.B. 1890. A.M. 1901
—	Harry ....*Trin.		M 1900 A.B. 1903. A.M. 1907
—	Rich. John Sacheverell	King's	M 1901 A.B. 1904
—	Will.	Em.	M 1902 A.B. 1905. A.M. 1909
Bateman-Champain,	John Norman	Cai.	M 1898 A.B. 1902. A.M. 1907

Bates,	Frederic Alan	Trin.	M 1903
—	Geo. Newton	Sid.	M 1891 A.B. 1894. A.M. 1903
—	Guy Lockington	Trin. H.	M 1890 A.B. 1891. A.M. 1902
—	Harold Rob.	Em.	M 1900 A.B. 1903
—	Harry Stuart	Cath.	M 1912
—	John Vincent	Pem.	M 1910
—	Percy Vernon	C. C.	M 1900 A.B. 1903. A.M. 1907
—	Reg. Will.	Pem.	M 1900 A.B. 1903
Bateson,	1 Will. ....*Joh.		M 1879 A.B. 1883. A.M. 1886
—			*See* de Yarburgh Bateson
Bather,	Edw. John	Cla.	M 1907 A.B. 1910
Bathurst,	Cha. Rob.	Em.	M 1898 A.B. 1901. A.M. 1906
—	Hen. Cha.	Qu.	M 1906 A.B. 1909
—	Herb. Addington ...	Pem.	M 1901 A.B. 1904
—	Phil. Lancelot	Mag.	M 1911
Batley,	Ja. Yorke	Trin.	M 1902 A.B. 1906. A.M. 1909
—	John	Trin. H.	M 1911
Batra,	Atar Chand	King's	M 1912
Batstone,	John	Qu.	M 1909
Batten,	Herb. Copeland Cary	Trin. H.	M 1903 A.B. 1907
—	Lindsey Willett	Sid.	M 1908 A.B. 1911
—	Will. Douglas Grant	Cai.	M 1909 A.B. 1912
Battenberg,	(*H.H. Prince*) Leopold Art. Louis of	Mag.	M 1907
Batterbury,	Geoffrey Rich.	Cai.	M 1903 A.B. 1906. A.M. 1911
Batterby,	Tho.	C. C.	M 1904 A.B. 1907
Batterham,	Douglas John	Cai.	M 1912
Battersby,	Rich.	Cath.	M 1894 A.B. 1897. A.M. 1904
Battiscombe,	Geo. Chris.	Trin.	M 1879 N. C. A.B. 1890. A.M. 1901
—	John Will. Harold ...	Sid.	M 1899 A.B. 1902
Batty,	Archib. Douglas Geo. Staunton	Mag.	M 1907 A.B. 1910
—	Will. Reg.	Jes.	M 1907 A.B. 1910
Batty-Smith,	Syd. Harry	Cai.	M 1909 A.B. 1912
Baty,	Tho.	Trin.	M 1894 A.B. Oxf. incorp. 1894. LL.M.
Ba U,	Maung	Trin. H.	M 1908 A.B. 1911 [1901. LL.D. 1907
Baugh,	Harold Ryle	Qu.	M 1900 A.B. 1903. A.M. 1907
Baumann,	Herb. Will.	C. C.	M 1898 A.B. 1901. A.M. 1905
Bausor,	Harold Will.	Cla.	M 1895 A.B. 1898. A.M. 1903
Bawdon,	Will. Satterley	Em.	M 1910
Bax,	Harold Edm. Ironside	Pem.	M 1901
Baxandall,	Archib.	H. Sel.	M 1912
Baxter,	Art. Harold Young	Joh.	M 1900 A.B. 1903. A.M. 1907
—	Godfrey Fleming ...	Em.	M 1898 A.B. 1901. A.M. 1905
—	Hen. Arnold	H. Sel.	M 1908 A.B. 1911
—	Tho. Harold	King's	M 1904 A.B. 1907
—	Tho. Vincent Torry	C. C.	M 1899 A.B. 1902. A.M. 1909
—	Will. Hedley Bruce	Pem.	M 1911
Bayer,	Sid. Fra.	Cai.	M 1901 A.B. 1904. A.M. 1912
Bayley,	Edmond Leslie	Cla.	M 1908
Bayliss,	Bertram Harold	Mag.	M 1907
—	Ern. Clapham	Em.	M 1886 A.B. 1889. A.M. 1904
—	Reg. Wyke	Pet.	M 1886 A.B. 1889. A.M. 1909
Bayly,	Bern. Martin	Trin.	M 1906 A.B. 1909
Baynes,	Denman Lambert Hen.	Cla.	M 1904 A.B. 1907. A.M. 1911
—	Frederic Will. Wilberforce	Cai.	M 1908 A.B. 1911
—	Helton Godwin	Trin.	M 1904 A.B. 1907. M.B., B.C. 1912
—	Hen. Arden Kennett	Trin.	M 1906 A.B. 1909
—	Humphrey	Trin.	M 1901

---

1 Professor of Biology, 1908.

Baynes,	John Bern.	Trin.	M 1897 A.B. 1900. A.M. 1911
—	Keith Stuart	Trin.	M 1906
—	Will. Edw. Colston	Trin.	M 1894 A.B., LL.B. 1897. A.M., LL.M.
Baynham,	Cuthbert Theodore	Jes.	M 1908 A.B. 1911 [1903
—	John Herb.	Jes.	M 1893 A.B. 1896. A.M. 1902
—	Wilfrid Gordon	Jes.	M 1912
Beacall,	Tho.	Joh.	M, 1900 A.B. 1904
Beach,	Dav. Westbrook	N. C.	M 1902 A.B. 1905
—	Geo. Cope	Mag.	M 1897 A.B. 1900. A.M. 1912
Beacock,	Geo. Ashton	Em.	M 1904 A.B. 1907. A.M. 1912
Beal,	Stuart Edw.	Trin. H.	M 1904
Beale,	Clifford Will.	Cai.	M 1911
—	Cyril	Joh.	M 1907 A.B. 1910
—	Edgar	Pet.	M 1911
—	Eric Victor	King's	M 1912
—	Harold Lansdown ...	Trin.	M 1897 H. Lansdowne, A.B. 1900. A.M.
—	Hub. Kenrick	Trin.	M 1888 A.B. 1891. A.M. 1902 [1904
—	Jos. Rich.	Cla.	M 1898 A.B. 1901. A.M. 1905
—	Sam. Rich.	Trin.	M 1899 A.B. 1903
Beall,	Gilb. Claridge	Trin.	M 1909 A.B. 1912
Beament,	Will. Oliver	H, Sel.	M 1912
Beamish,	Cha. Noel Bern.	Em.	M 1896 A.B. 1900. A.M. 1911
—	Rich. de Beaumont	Cai.	M 1896 A.B. 1901
—	St John Hungerford	C. C.	M 1896 A.B. 1902
Bean,	Basil Clarence Lahey	H. Sel.	M 1905 A.B. 1908
—	John Willoughby Butler	H. Sel.	M 1898 A.B. 1901. M.B., B.C. 1909
Beard,	Art. John	Joh.	M 1912
—	Branscombe Arderne	Trin.	M 1898 A.B. 1901
—	Cyril Godfrey	Cai.	M 1908
---	Edwin Cyril	Joh.	M 1909 A.B. 1912
—	Hugh Spencer Gascoyen	H. Sel.	M 1905 A.B. 1910
—	Walt. Fra.	Cai.	M 1888 A.B. 1891. A.M. 1903
Beardall,	John	Joh.	M 1876 A.B. 1880. A.M. 1905
Beaton,	Edwin	Cai.	M 1899 A.B. 1902. M.B., B.C. 1909
Beatty,	Rich. Terence	Em.	M 1908 A.B. 1910
Beauchamp,	Edw. Archib.	Trin. H.	M 1909
Beaufoy,	Geo. Maur.	Mag.	M 1912
—	Hen. Mark	Trin.	M 1906
Beaumont,	Bertrand Fre.	N. C.	M 1905 Down. A.B. 1908
—	Douglas Cha.	Chr.	M 1912
—	Hor. Fre.	Trin.	M 1902 A.B. 1905
—	John Lionel	Trin.	M 1904 LL.B. 1907
—	John Will. Fisher ...	Pem.	M 1896 A.B. 1899. A.M. 1904
—	Owen Alb.	Chr.	M 1909 A.B. 1912
—	Percy Ja.	N. C.	M 1903 A.B. 1906
—	Rich.	Jes.	M 1910
—	(*Hon.*) Wentworth Hen. } Canning	Trin.	M 1909 A.B. 1912
Beaumont James,	Ja. Lyne	Mag.	M 1906 A.B. 1909
Beaven,	Victor	H. Sel.	M 1909
Beazley,	Cha. Murray	Trin.	M 1909
Becher,	Cha. Leon. Routh ...	Cla.	M 1911
—	Godfrey Geo.	Trin.	M 1905 A.B. 1909. A.M. 1912
—	Maur. And. Noel ...	Trin.	M 1903
Beck,	Bern. Redin	Cla.	M 1898 A.B. 1901. A.M. 1905
—	Cha. Broughton Harrop	Pem.	M 1910
—	[1] Edw. Anth.	*Trin. H.	M 1867 A.B. 1871. A.M. 1874 [M.P. 1904
—	Edw. Ashton Anth.	Cla.	M 1895 A.B. 1898. A.M. 1902. B.C. 1903.
—	Edwyn Walt. Tyrrell	Cla.	M 1905 A.B., LL.B. 1908. A.M. 1912

[1] Master of Trinity Hall, 1902.

Beck,	Egerton Will. Townsend	Sid.	M 1877 N. C. A.B. 1898. Jes. A.M. 1901
—	Fre. Geo. Meeson ...*Cla.		M 1901 A.B. 1904. A.M. 1908
Becke,	Cha. Rob.	Trin. H.	M 1904
Becker,	Wilfred Trevor Leigh	Pem.	M 1910
Beckett,	Cha. Murray	Cai.	M 1912
—	Fra. Hen. Mears Allden	H. Sel.	M 1894 A.B. 1897. M.B., B.C. 1902
—	Harold Ambrose	Pem.	M 1908 A.B. 1911
—	John Norton	Joh.	M 1901 A.B. 1904
—	Victor Louis Syd. ...	Chr.	M 1901
—	Phil. Art.	Cla.	M 1911
Beckton,	Hen.	Cla.	M 1889 A.B. 1892. A.M. 1898. M.D. 1908
Becquerel,	Antoine Henri		Sc.D. 1904
Bedale,	Cha. Lees	Cla.	M 1898 A.B. 1901. A.M. 1905
—	Fre. Stanley	Cla.	M 1905 A.B. 1908. A.M. 1912
Beddow,	Harold Josiah	Chr.	M 1897 A.B. 1900. A.M. 1907
Bedell-Sivright, Dav. Revell		Trin.	M 1899 A.B. 1902
Bedford,	Harry	N. C.	M 1909 A.B. 1912
—	Seaton Hall	Cai.	M 1907 A.B., LL.B. 1910
—	Tho. Geo.	Sid.	M 1894 A.B. 1897. A.M. 1901
Bee,	John Matthias	Cath.	M 1906 A.B. 1909
Beech,	John	Cai.	M 1906 A.B. 1909
Beecroft,	Art. Edw.	Chr.	M 1906 A.B., LL.B. 1910
Beer,	Stanley Geo. King ...	H. Sel.	M 1909 A.B. 1912
Beesley,	Lawrence	Cai.	M 1900 A.B. 1903
Beevor,	John Hare	Pem.	M 1879 A.B. 1883. A.M. 1903
Beg,	Mirza Abbas	Down.	M 1908
Bein,	Alb. Baruch	King's	M 1911
Beith,	Benj. Dav. Fleming	Pem.	M 1903 A.B. 1906
—	Gilb.	Joh.	M 1901 A.B. 1904
—	John Hay	Joh.	M 1895 A.B. 1898. A.M. 1902
Békássy,	Ferenc István Dénes} Gyula }	King's	M 1911
Beken,	Cha. Jos.	N. C.	M 1907 A.B. 1910
Belcher,	Gordon	Cath.	M 1904 A.B. 1907
—	Hen. Cha. Penoyre	N. C.	M 1898 Joh. A.B. 1901. A.M. 1905
Belfield,	Stafford St George } Conway }	Cai.	M 1906 A.B. 1909
Belgrave,	Art. Cyril	Joh.	M 1903 A.B. 1906
—	Norman Will. Cummins	Joh.	M 1909
Bell,	Alan Carstairs	Jes.	M 1911
—	Alan Thorp	Pem.	M 1909 A.B. 1912
—	Art. Clive Heward	Trin.	M 1899 A.B. 1902. A.M. 1907
—	Aubrey Parker	Cai.	M 1907
—	Bern. Humphrey ...	Trin.	M 1903 A.B. 1906
—	Cha. Hen.	Chr.	M 1907 A.B. 1910
—	Cheviot Wellington Dillon	Trin.	M 1911
—	Dav. Wellesley	Cla.	M 1905
—	Elliott	Cla.	M 1898 A.B. 1901
—	Frank	Jes.	M 1896 A.B. 1899. A.M. 1909
—	Geo. Gordon	Cath.	M 1911
—	Harold Rob.	H. Sel.	M 1903 A.B. 1906
—	Howard Alex.	Jes.	M 1906 A.B. 1910
—	Ja. Art. Herb.	Chr.	M 1908 A.B. 1911
—	John Dobrée	Cai.	M 1909 A.B. 1912
—	John Hen.	Cla.	M 1905
—	Norman Murray	Trin.	M 1909 A.B. 1912
—	Randal	Cla.	M 1896 A.B. 1900. A.M. 1904
—	Rich. Eardley Tho.	Joh.	M 1902 A.B. 1905. A.M. 1909
—	Rob.		Sc.D. 1903
—	Rob. Duncan	Trin.	M 1901
—	Rob. Harman	C. C.	M 1906 A.B. 1909

Bell,	Rob. Will.	Jes.	M 1896 A.B. 1899. A.M. 1903
—	Syd. Pyman	King's	M 1894 A.B., LL.B. 1898. A.M. 1902
—	Tho. Osmond	Joh.	M 1905 A.B. 1908
—	Will. Archib. Juxon	Trin. H.	M 1902 A.B. 1905
—	Will. Godfrey	N. C.	M 1900 Pet. A.B. 1903. A.M. 1909
---	Will. Hen. Dillon ...	Trin.	M 1902 A.B., LL.B. 1905
—	Will. Stanley	Pet.	M 1903 A.B. 1906
—	Winthrop Pickard ...	Em.	M 1909
Bellamy,	John	Jes.	M 1903 A.B. 1906
—	Reg. Leopold	Cath.	M 1903
Bellars,	Alb. Ern.	Mag.	M 1899 A.B. 1902. A.M. 1906
—	Art. Rob.	Pem.	M 1908 A.B. 1911
Bellerby,	Alf. Courthope Benson	Em.	M 1907 A.B. 1910
Bellew,	Bryan Bertram	Trin. H.	M 1909
—	Edw. Hen.	Trin. H.	M 1908
Bellman,	Alex. Fre.	Joh.	M 1909 A.B. 1912
Bellward,	Geoffrey Will. Frank	Em.	M 1910
Bellwood,	Kenneth Benson	Pem.	M 1909 A.B. 1912
Beloe,	John Seppings	Cla.	M 1899 A.B. 1902
Belshaw,	Pet.	Joh.	M 1895 A.B. 1898. A.M. 1904
Bemrose,	Hen. Howe	Cla.	M 1875 A.B. 1879. Arnold-Bemrose, [A.M. 1882. Sc.D. 1908. post [Bemrose, H. H.
Benbow,	Herb. Clifton	Trin.	M 1880 A.B. 1884. A.M. 1910
Bence,	Ern. Geo. Will.	H. Sel.	E 1891 A.B. 1894. A.M. 1903
Bendall,	¹ Cecil	Trin.	M 1875 *Cai. A.B. 1879. A.M. 1882
—	Frederic Will. Duffield	H. Sel.	M 1901 A.B. 1904
Benest,	Edw. Ern.	Cai.	M 1910
Beney,	Cha. Clem.	Jes.	M 1911
Benfield,	Fra. John Barker ...	Trin.	M 1884 A.B. 1887. A.M. 1906
Bengough,	John Crosbie	Em.	M 1908 A.B. 1911
Benham,	John Hen. Findlay	Jes.	M 1903
Benians,	Ern. Alf. ....*Joh.		M 1899 A.B. 1902. A.M. 1906
Benjamin,	John Alf.	Cla.	M 1911
—	Roy Neville	Cla.	M 1912
Benn,	Cha. Anth.	Trin. H.	M 1887 A.B. 1890. A.M. 1906
Bennell,	Ja. Cha.	N. C.	M 1911
Bennett,	Alb. Ern.	N. C.	M 1906
—	Art. Russell	Cai.	M 1904 A.B. 1907
—	Basil Gordon	Sid.	M 1910
—	Bern. Callender	H. Sel.	M 1897 A.B. 1900. A.M. 1905
—	Cha. Will.	Joh.	M 1898 A.B. 1901. A.M. 1905
—	Chris. Llewellin	Cla.	M 1900 A.B. 1903. A.M. 1907
—	Clem. Art.	Jes.	M 1901 A.B. 1904
---	Douglas	Trin. H.	M 1905 A.B. 1908
—	Edw. Bailey	Chr.	M 1909
—	Eric	Trin.	M 1911
—	Ern. Fre.	Trin. H.	M 1904
—	Geoffrey Neville	Trin. H.	M 1908 A.B. 1911
—	Geo.	Em.	M 1906 A.B. 1909
—	Geo. Anselm	Joh.	M 1900 A.B. 1903. A.M. 1907
—	Geo. Melvill	Trin. H.	M 1896 A.B., LL.B. 1899. A.M.† 1903
—	Geo. Trenery	Cla.	M 1909 A.B. 1912
—	Harry Herb. Gladstone	Em.	M 1910
—	Hen. Cecil Llewellin	Cla.	M 1909 A.B. 1912
—	Hen. Ryan	Cai.	M 1912
—	John Gordon	King's	M 1904 A.B. 1907
—	Keith Llewellin	Cla.	M 1902 K. Llewellyn, A.B. 1906
—	Reg. Thorne	Cath.	M 1903 A.B. 1906

¹ Professor of Sanskrit, 1903.

Bennett,	Risdon	Trin. H.	M 1901 A.B. 1904
—	Sam. Lowe	Pem.	M 1910
—	Syd. Garner	Down.	M 1907
—	Tho. Claude	H. Sel.	M 1911
—	Tho. Lawrence	Trin.	M 1901 A.B. 1904. A.M. 1909
—	Will. Ern.	Sid.	M 1911
—	Will. Hen. ....*Joh.		M 1878 A.B.1882. A.M.1885. Litt.D.1902
—	Will. Porter	Em.	M 1909 A.B., LL.B. 1912
Bennett-Evans,	Geo. Lewis	Down.	M 1905
Bennion,	Art. Topham	Trin.	M 1900 A.B. 1903. A.M. 1907
—	Cha. Fawcett	Pem.	M 1903 A.B. 1907
—	Claud	Pem.	M 1904 A.B., LL.B. 1907
—	John Menlove	Joh.	M 1895 A.B. 1898. M.B., B.C., A.M. 1903.
Bennison,	John Jennings	C. C.	M 1911 [M.D. 1907
Benny,	Leon. Berger	Chr.	M 1906 A.B. 1909
Benoist,	René Théodule Eugéne	Down.	M 1908
Benoly,	Herb. John	Chr.	M 1909 A.B. 1912
Benskin,	Ern.	Down.	M 1906
—	Jos. Pugh	Chr.	M 1903 A.B. 1906
Benson,	Art. Chris.	King's	M 1881 A.B. 1884(2). A.M. 1888. *Mag.
—	Cha. Thornton Vere	King's	M 1901 A.B. 1904
—	Edw. Ern. McGowan..	Trin.	M 1892 A.B. 1895. A.M.† 1908
—	Ern. Moore	Joh.	M 1894 A.B. 1897. A.M. 1901
—	Herb. Walt.	Em.	M 1910
—	John	H. Sel.	M 1896 A.B. 1899. A.M. 1908
—	Will. Noël	Em.	M 1911
Bensted,	Phil.	Qu.	M 1899 A.B. 1903
Bensted Smith,	Will. Fra.	Pem.	M 1906 A.B. 1909
Bentall,	Cha. Edw.	Cai.	M 1904
Benthall,	Edw. Cha.	King's	M 1912
—	Will. Louis	Joh.	M 1887 A.B. 1890. A.M. 1904
Bentinck,	Art. Will. Douglas ...	Trin.	M 1906 A.B. 1909
—	Hen. Duncan Aldenburg	Trin.	M 1899 A.B. 1902. post H. D.
Bentley,	Art. Ja.	Joh.	M 1907 A.B. 1910
—	Frank	Cla.	M 1904 A.B. 1907
—	John Dalrymple	Em.	M 1910
—	John Hen.	Joh.	M 1903 A.B. 1906. A.M. 1910
—	Jos. Reg.	Em.	M 1892 M.B., B.C. 1904
—	Reg. Art.	Joh.	M 1908 A.B. 1911
—	Ronald Cameron	Qu.	M 1910
—	Will. Wallace	Qu.	M 1903 A.B. 1906. A.M. 1911
Bentliff,	Hub. Dav.	Trin.	M 1910
Bently,	Fra. Middleton	Qu.	M 1895 A.B. 1898. A.M. 1902
Benton,	Donald	Em.	M 1910
—	Gerald Montagu	N. C.	L 1906 A.B. 1910
Bentwich,	Norman De Mattos	Trin.	M 1901 A.B. 1905. A.M. 1908
Benyon,	Hen. Art.	Trin. H.	M 1903
Berens,	Herb. Art.	Sid.	M 1908 A.B. 1911
Beresford,	Fitzherbert	Joh.	M 1897 A.B. 1900. A.M. 1904
—	Gilb. Adrien	Joh.	L 1907 G. Adrian, A.B. 1910
—	Hans Aden	Joh.	M 1903 A.B. 1907. A.M. 1911
—	John Baldwyn	King's	M 1907 A.B. 1910
—	Sam.	N. C.	E 1912
—	Tristram de la Poer..	Trin. H.	M 1906
Berg,	Axel Will.	Trin.	M 1903 A.B. 1906
Berger,	Sam. Hen.	Trin.	M 1904
Bergheim,	Pet.	Em.	E 1904
Beridge,	Basil Ja. Goodeve Sparrow	Mag.	E 1902
Berkeley,	Geo. Harold Art. Comyns	Cai.	M 1883 A.B. 1887. M.B., B.C. 1892. A.M.,
—	Maur. Kenneth Fitzhardinge	Pem.	M 1912 [M.D. 1911
—	Roger Mowbray	Em.	M 1899 A.B. 1903

Berlein,	Leslie Herman	Mag.	M 1912	
Bernard,	Brian Edw. Vivian ...	Trin.	M 1909	
—	Geo. Hen. Brian	Joh.	M 1900 A.B. 1903	
—	Hen. Claude	Joh.	M 1912	
—	John Gerald Mortimer	Trin.	M 1908	
Berney,	(*Sir*) Tho. Reedham (*Bart.*)	Trin. H.	M 1912	
Berney-Ficklin,	Hor. Pettus McKin- tosh	Jes.	M 1911	
Berrington,	Kenneth Clunes	Pem.	M 1902 A.B. 1905. LL.B. 1906	
—	Leslie Geo.	Cai.	M 1904	
Berry,	Alex. Geo.	Sid.	M 1904 A.B. 1907	
—	Art. John	Trin.	M 1906 A.B. 1909	
—	Ern. Edw.	Chr.	M 1902 A.B. 1905. A.M. 1909	
—	Frank Norman	Trin.	M 1898 A.B. 1901. A.M. 1905	
—	Hen. Vaughan	Cai.	M 1910	
—	Hor. Simeon	Cla.	M 1900 A.B. 1903. A.M. 1907. B.C. 1908	
—	Leon. Will.	Sid.	M 1909 A.B. 1912	
—	Leslie Lionel	Chr.	M 1905	
—	Percy Haycraft	King's	M 1907 A.B. 1910	
—	Sid. Malcolm	Cla.	M 1900 A.B. 1903	
—	Will.	King's	M 1902 A.B. 1905	
Berwick,	Will. Edw. Hodgson	Cla.	M 1906 A.B. 1909	
Bescoby,	Art. Cecil	Em.	M 1905 A.B. 1908. A.M. 1912	
Besley,	Walt. Phil.	King's	M 1889 A.B. 1895. A.M. 1901	
Besly,	Edw. Maur.	Cai.	M 1907 A.B. 1910	
Best,	Isaac Ja.	Joh.	M 1902 A.B. 1906	
—	John Kenneth	Qu.	M 1907 A.B. 1910	
—	Oswald Herb.	Qu.	M 1912	
—	Ronald Will. Glennie	Pet.	M 1911	
—	Tho. Will.	Trin.	M 1912	
Bestelmeyer,	Christoph Wilhelm Adolf	Trin.	M 1903	
Beswick,	Wilfrid Tho.	Trin. H.	M 1911	
Bethell,	Alex. Duke	Joh.	M 1911	
—	Chris.	Trin.	M 1904 A.B. 1907. LL.B. 1908	
—	Dav. Jardine	Trin.	M 1911	
—	Hugh Wood	Joh.	M 1895 A.B. 1902	
Bethune,	Frank Pogson	H. Sel.	M 1901 A.B. 1905. A.M.† 1909	
—	John Walt.	H. Sel.	M 1901 A.B. 1904. A.M.† 1909	
Bethune-Baker			*See* Baker, Ja. Franklin	
Bethway,	Walt. Sid.	Trin.	M 1910	
Betteridge,	Benj. Fairthorne	Chr.	M 1912	
—	Cyril Deane	Jes.	M 1910	
—	John Edw. Hen.	Jes.	M 1909	
Betton,	Edw. Guy Betton Bright	H. Sel.	M 1903 A.B. 1906. A.M. 1912	
—	Harold Rich. Bright	H. Sel.	M 1911	
Betts,	Harold Sid.	Qu.	M 1909 A.B. 1912	
Beuttler,	John Cecil Oakley ...	Qu.	M 1908	
Bevan,	Alb. Edw.	King's	M 1911	
—	Alf. Edw.	Joh.	M 1895 A.B. 1899. A.M.† 1909	
—	Clem. Beckford	Cla.	M 1912	
—	Guy Theodore Molesworth	Joh.	M 1909 A.B. 1912	
—	Hub. Woodall	Em.	M 1902 A.B. 1905	
—	John	Jes.	M 1911	
—	John Maybery	Cai.	M 1905 A.B. 1908	
—	Maur.	Trin.	M 1904	
—	Penry Vaughan	*Trin.	M 1896 A.B. 1899. A.M. 1903. Sc.D. 1911	
—	Tho. Rich.	Trin.	M 1909	
Bevan Brown,	Cha. Maur.	Em.	M 1909 A.B. 1912	
—	Rob. Eldred	King's	E 1911	
Beven,	Fra. Lorenz	Chr.	M 1891 A.B. 1894. A.M.† 1902	

Beven,	John Junius Osmund	Chr.	M 1908 A.B. 1912
Beveridge,	Dav. Alex.	Pem.	M 1905 A.B. 1908
—	Geo.	Cla.	M 1910
—	Rob. Barrie	Pet.	M 1909
Beverley,	Rob. Berthold	Trin. H.	M 1907
—	Russell	Qu.	M 1908 A.B. 1912
Beves,	Cameron Howard ...	Trin.	M 1905 A.B. 1908. A.M. 1912
Bevington,	Alistair de Horne ...	Pet.	M 1909
Bevir,	Cyril Edw. Felix ...	Pem.	M 1909 A.B. 1912
—	Will.	Mag.	M 1898 A.B. 1901
Bevis,	Ronald Alf.	Qu.	M 1907 A.B. 1910
Bewes,	Cha. Tho. Anstis ...	Trin. H.	M 1905
Bewicke-Copley,	Rob. Godfrey ⎱ Wolsey ⎰	Trin.	M 1911
Bewley,	Edw. Neville	Cai.	M 1903 A.B., LL.B. 1906
Bewoor,	Gurunāth Venkatesh	Sid.	M 1909 A.B. 1911
Bhandari,	Diwan Chand	N. C.	M 1909
Bhargava,	Panna Lal	N. C.	M 1911
Bharucha,	Navroji Maneckji ...	Cai.	M 1910
Bhate,	Bhaskar Kashinath	N. C.	M 1910
Bhatia,	Sohan Lal	Pet.	M 1910
Bhatt,	Pranshanker Jeyshanker	N. C.	M 1907
Bhide,	Mahadeo Vishnu ...	Joh.	M 1904 A.B. 1907
Bhidé,	Vithal Shivaram	N. C.	M 1912
Bhose,	Nripendra Nath	Down.	M 1908 A.B. 1911
Bibby,	Edw. Ern.	Pet.	M 1906 A.B. 1909
—	Rob. Edw.	Pem.	M 1904
Bickerdike,	Rob. Brian	Cai.	M 1902 A.B. 1905
Bickers,	Hor. Algernon Sykes	Trin.	M 1902
Bicket,	Tho. Barrett	Cla.	M 1910
Bickford,	Will.	Cla.	M 1901 A.B. 1904. W. Pennington, A.M.
Bickford-Smith,	John Clifford ...	Cai.	M 1900 A.B. 1905 [1908
—	Will. Nugent Venning	Pem.	M 1911
Bickley,	Geo. Howard	Pem.	M 1911
Bicknell,	Cha. Dion	Cath.	M 1909 A.B. 1912
—	Phil. Wimberley	Trin.	M 1902 A.B. 1907
Biddell,	Herman Masterman	Cath.	M 1896 A.B. 1899. A.M. 1908
Bidder,	Harold Fra.	Trin.	M 1894 A.B. 1897. A.M. 1910
Biddle,	Fre. Arnold	Trin.	M 1896 A.B., LL.B. 1899. A.M. 1903
Bidgood,	Geo. John Bunce ...	Cath.	M 1910
Bidlake,	Art. Danvers Melancthon	Pem.	M 1901 A.B. 1905. A.M. 1909
Bidwell,	Fre. Will.	H. Sel.	M 1892 A.B. 1895. A.M. 1904
—	Reg. Alf.	Trin.	M 1903 A.B. 1906. A.M. 1911
Biedermann,	Cecil Clare Reg.	Cai.	M 1901
—	Elek	Jes.	M 1908
Bienemann,	Gustav Adolph Jo-⎱ hannes ⎰	Em.	M 1909 A.B. 1912 [*Cath.
Biffen,	[1] Rowland Harry	Em.	M 1893 A.B. 1896. Cai. Em. A.M. 1902,
Bigby,	Will. Scott	Trin. H.	M 1890 A.B. 1893. LL.M.† 1902
Bigg,	Edw.	Cai.	M 1893 A.B. 1897. A.M. 1903. B.C. 1904
Biggar,	Cha. Leslie Pinckard	Chr.	M 1912
Bigge,	Hub.	Trin.	M 1907 H. John, A.B. 1910
Bigger,	Walt. Grimshaw	Qu.	M 1907 A.B. 1910
—	Will. Kenneth	Em.	M 1909 A.B. 1912
Biggs,	Edw. Kenneth	Cla.	M 1901
—	Harold	King's	M 1899 A.B. 1903. A.M. 1906
—	Hen. Fra.	King's	M 1906 B.A. incorp. Dubl. 1906
Bigg-Wither,	Harold Steph.	Chr.	M 1907 A.B. 1910
—	Ralph Woodgate ...	King's	M 1908 A.B. 1911

---

[1] Professor of Agricultural Botany, 1908.

Bigland,	Alf. Douglas	Cai.	M 1905 A.B. 1908
Bignold,	Cecil Sam.	Cla.	M 1907 A.B. 1910
Bikaner,	(Ganga Singh) *Maha-* *raja of*		*LL.D.* 1911
Bilderbeck,	Alured Cha. Lowther O'Shee	Chr.	M 1907 A.B. 1910
Bilgrami,	Syed Ali		A.M. 1904
Bill,	Syd. Alf.	Trin.	M 1902 A.B. 1905. A.M. 1909
Billing,	Edw.	Cai.	M 1903 A.B. 1906
Billinger,	Hector Fussell	Joh.	M 1911
Bilney,	Alwyn Alf. Hope ...	Trin.	M 1906
Bilsborough,	Ja. Herb.	H. Sel.	M 1907 A.B. 1910
Bilsland,	Alex. Steven	Joh.	M 1910
—	Ja. Alex.	Joh.	M 1906 A.B. 1909
—	Will. Blair	Joh.	M 1908
Bilton,	Claude Herb. Evelyn	Cla.	M 1908 A.B. 1911
—	Edw. Barnard	Cla.	M 1906 A.B. 1909
Bindloss,	Allan Kell	Cla.	M 1906
Bindon,	Will. Fra. Vereker ...	Sid.	M 1897 A.B. 1901
Bingham,	Hen. Carrington Fanshawe	Sid.	M 1901 A.B. 1904
Bingham Newland,	Roger Frankland	Jes.	M 1909
Bingley,	Edw. Fanshawe	H. Sel.	M 1887 A.B. 1890. A.M. 1904
--	Gerald Art.	Joh.	M 1911
Binks,	Basil Hen.	Qu.	M 1906 A.B. 1909
—	Benj. Bern.	Chr.	M 1908 A.B. 1912
Binney,	Rich. Creighton	Em.	M 1895 A.B. 1898. A.M. 1902
Binning,	Stevenson	Cai.	M 1900 A.B. 1903
Binnion,	Sam.	Em.	M 1905 A.B. 1908
Binns,	Art. Lennon	Joh.	M 1911
—	Cuthbert Cha. Harber	Cai.	L 1903 A.B. 1905. B.C. 1911. A.M. 1912
—	Leon. Elliott	Em.	M 1908 A.B. 1911
Binyon,	Basil	Trin.	M 1904 A.B. 1907
Bion,	Rupert Euston	Trin.	M 1910
Birbeck,	Reg. Jos.	Trin.	M 1892 A.B. 1895. A.M.† 1910
Birch,	Alan Grant	Trin.	M 1900 A.B. 1903
—	Art. Clarkson	King's	M 1908 A.B. 1911
—	Cecil Percival Lea ...	Chr.	M 1903
—	Cha. Victor	Trin.	M 1902
—	Fra. Lyall	King's	M 1909 A.B. 1912
—	Geo. Cha.	Trin.	M 1905 A.B. 1908
—	Harold Lea	Trin.	M 1899 A.B. 1902. A.M. 1907
—	Ja. Ragland	Cla.	M 1902 A.B. 1905
—	Will. Colet	King's	M 1904 A.B. 1907
Birchall,	Walt. Raymond	Trin.	M 1907 A.B. 1910
Birchenough,	Rich. Peacock	Trin. H.	M 1904
Bird,	Alan Lance	N. C.	M 1904 Pet. A.B. 1907
—	Angus Kidman	Em.	M 1912
—	Bertram Hugh	Jes.	M 1899 A.B. 1902. A.M. 1908
—	Cha. Barnard	Pem.	M 1912
—	Cha. Tho. Grant	Em.	M 1901 A.B. 1904. A.M. 1908
—	Colin Kidman	King's	M 1911
—	Edw. Gwynne	N. C.	L 1900 A.B. 1902
—	Gerald Fra.	Trin.	M 1897 A.B. 1900. B.C., A.M. 1905. M.B. [1906
—	Herb. John	Em.	M 1899 A.B. 1902
—	Lawrence Wilfred ...	Trin.	M 1901
—	Martin Wright Kidman	Em.	M 1908 A.B. 1911
—	Maur. Bonner	Cath.	M 1910
—	Percy Cha. Hilton ...	Cath.	M 1911
—	Steph.	Cla.	M 1906 A.B. 1909

Atkinson,	Will.	Chr.	p	M 1627	(?same as above)
Atkys,	Hen.	Trin.	s	M 1566	
—	John	Joh.	s	L 1579–80	
Atley,	Rich.	[Trin.		E 1644]	
—	W[ill.]	Cai.	p	E 1586	[Atlee]
Atlee,	Will.	Qu.	s	E 1633	A.B. 1636–7
Atmear	....	[Sid.	p	E 1600]	
Atsloe,	Edw.	[Pet.	p	E 1616]	
Atterbery,	Steph.	Joh.	p	E 1609	
Atterbie,	Tho.	Chr.	p	M 1572	A.B. 1576–7; A.M. 1580
Attersall,	Will.	Pet.	p	M 1579	A.B. (Cla.)1582–3,Attersold; A.M. [(Pet.) 1586
Attersoll,	Will.	Pet.	p	E 1608	A.B. 1611–2; A.M. 1615
Aterton,	(John)				A.B. 1539–40; A.M. 1545; *Trin.
Atterton,	Tho.				A.B. (Cai.) 1588–9 [Atharton]
Attlesey,	Phil.	Pet.	s	E 1627	A.B. 1629–30; A.M. 1638
Attewell *v.* also Otwell					
Atwell,	Geo.	Chr.	s	E 1658	
Atewell,	Ralph				A.B. (King's) 1578–9
Atwell	....	[Em.	s	E 1628]	
Atwood,	Ja.	[C. C.		1624]	
—	John	Qu.	p	E 1615	
—	John	*Em.	s	L 1647–8	A.B.1649–50;A.M.1653;S.T.B.'60
—	Walt..........	Qu.	p	E 1618	A.B. 1621–2; A.M. 1625 (Matr.
Atwoode,	Will.	Qu.	p	E 1614	[Alwood)
Atwood,	Will.	Trin.H.	p	M 1647	
Atwood	....	[C. C.	f-c	1553]	
Aubrey *v.* Awbery					
Aubie,	Andr..........	Trin.	p	E 1634	A.B. 1638, ?Anbie
Aubigny,	Geo. (Brother of Duke of Lennox)				A.M. 1634
Auborne,	Matth.	Em.	s	E 1625	A.B. 1628–9; A.M. 1633
Auburne,	Will.	Joh.	p	E 1648	
Aubye,	Geo.	Sid.	f-c	E 1618	[Awnby]
Aucher,	Anth..........	Cla.	f-c	E 1633	
—	Anth..........	Trin.	p	E 1636	[Adm. Pet. 1636]
—	Anth..........	King's	f-c	E 1655	
—	Edwin	Trin. [schol.		E 1608]	A.B. 1608–9
—	Hatton	*Cla.	p	M 1654	A.B. 1660; A.M. (*Trin. H.) 1664
—	John	C. C.	p	L 1634–5	A.B. 1637–8; A.M. (*Pet.) 1641; [S.T.P. (*Lit. Reg.*) 1660
Auckerson *v.* Anckerson					
Auder,	Will.				(?A.B.); A.M. (Chr.) 1606
Audian,	Rich.	Trin.	s	E 1550	A.B. 1550–1; A.M. 1559
Awdleye,	Edm.	Chr.	p	E 1554	
Audley,	Hen.	Chr.	p	E 1607	A.B. 1610–11
Awdley,	John	Mag.	p	E 1544	
Audlye,	John	Chr.	p	E 1560	
Audley,	John	Joh.	p	c. 1596	
—	John	Chr.	s	E 1621	A.B. 1624–5; A.M. 1628
—	John	Cath.	s	M 1622	A.B. 1627
—	John	Chr.	p	M 1649	A.B. 1652–3; A.M. 1656
—	John	Qu.	s	E 1656	A.B. 1659–60; A.M. 1663
—	Lewis.........				A.B. (King's) 1637–8; A.M. 1641
Awdeley,	Phil.	Joh.	p	M 1555	
Awdley,	Rob.	Cla.	p	E 1553	
Audley,	Rob.	Pem.	p	E 1579	
Awdley,	Rob.	Pem.	p	M 1585	
Audley,	Rob.	C. C.	p	E 1611	A.B. 1615–6; A.M. 1619
—	Rob.	Trin.	p	E 1641	
Awdley,	Tho.	Mag.	p	E 1544	
Audley,	Tho.	Pem.	p	L 1577–8	
Awdley,	Tho.	Pem.	p	M 1585	

Audley,	Tho.	Pem.	s	E	1626	A.B. 1628–9; A.M. 1632
—	Will.	C. C.	p	E	1611	A.B. 1614–5; A.M. 1618; M.D.
Awdry,	John	Mag.	p	M	1567	[1631–2? (On King's visit)
Audry,	Will.	Cla.	s	c.	1590	A.B. 1593–4
Audsley,	Roger.........					A.B. (Trin. H.) 1621; A.M. 1632
Aufyld,	Tho.	*King's	p	M	1568	A.B. 1572–3
Aufield,	Will.	*King's	p	E	1618	(A.B. 1620–1); A.M. 1625
Auger *v.* also Anger						
Auger,	John	Pet.	s	M	1633	
Augar,	Nich.					A.B. (Joh.) 1608–9; A.M. 1612
Augars,	Nath..........	[Em.	s	E	1600]	
Aulabye *v.* Anlabye						
Auldin,	Hen.	Sid.	s	E	1634	A.B. 1637–8; A.M. 1641
Aumant,	Rob.					A.B. (Pet.) 1595–6; A.M. 1599
Austen,	Benj.	Joh.	p	M	1586	A.B. 1590–1; A.M. 1594
—	Edw.	Trin.	f-c	M	1626	
Asten,	Fra.	Joh.	p	E	1585	A.B. 1588–9; A.M. 1592
Austen,	Fra.					A.B. (Cath.) 1609
Austin,	John	Joh.	s	E	1631	
Austen,	John	[Pet.			1645]	
Austin,	Pet.	[Joh.	s	E	1655]	
—	Ralph					A.M. 1622 (Incorp. fr. Oxf.)
—	Rich.	Qu.	[p	M	1644]	A.B. 1644–5 (prev. at Oxf.)
Austen,	Rob.	*King's	p	E	1612	(A.B. 1615–6); A.M. 1619; S.T.B.
Austin,	Rob.	Trin.	s	E	1628	[1626; S.T.P. 1639
Austen,	Rob.	*King's	p	M	1647	A.B. 1651
—	Sam.	King's	p	c.	1593	
Austyne,	Tho.	Qu.	s	E	1567	A.B. 1570–1, Austen; A.M. 1574
Austin,	Tho.	C. C.	s	E	1637	A.B. 1639–40; A.M. 1643
Awsten,	Walt..........	Chr.	p	M	1551	
Austen,	Will.	C. C.	p	E	1578	A.B. 1582–3; A.M. 1586
Austin,	Will.	Cla.	p	c.	1597	
—	Will.	[Trin. H. schol.		E	1599 : the above ?]	
Austen,	Will.	Joh.	f-c	E	1603	
Austin,	Will.	Em.	p	E	1626	
—	Will.	Joh.	p	E	1637	A.B. 1639–40
Austen,	Will.	Pet.	p	L	1645–6	M.B. 1653
Austin,	Will.	Chr.	f-c	E	1647	A.B. 1648–9
Awston ?	....	Trin.	p	c.	1592	
Austin	....	[Trin.	f-c		1656]	
—	....	[Trin.	f-c		1656]	
Austria,	Dan.	Trin.	p	E	1629	
Avarell	....	[C. C.	f-c		1579]	
Avenand,	Alex. (*imp.*)	Qu.	p	L	1557–8	A.B. 1563–4
Avery,	Dudley	Cath.	p	E	1641	[(Leonard in *grace*)
—	Rich.					A.B. (Trin.) 1624–5; A.M. 1628
Avis,	Will.	Sid.	s	E	1621	A.B. 1624–5; A.M. 1628
Awbery,	Art.					A.M. 1583 (Incorp. fr. Oxf.)
Awford,	Edw. *v.* Hawford					
Awlforde,	Fra.					A.B. 1548–9, Alford
Awnby,	Geo. *v.* Aubye					
Awnshame,	Rich. *v.* Ansam					
Awstell,	Edw.	Chr.	s	E	1579	A.B. 1582–3, Astell
Awstrup,	Will.	Joh.	p	M	1547	
Axbye,	Rob.	Trin.	p	M	1555	
Axtell,	Will.	[Chr.	p	E	1643]	A.B. (Qu.) 1646–7
Axton,	Hugh..........	Qu.	p	M	1571	A.B. 1575–6, Acson
—	Will.	*Trin.	p	M	1566	A.B. 1570–1; A.M. 1574; S.T.B.
Axup *v.* Haxup						[1598, Haxton
Ayenson,	Sam.	Trin.	s	E	1606	
Ayerton,	John	Trin.	p	E	1567	

Blew,	Cha. Leslie	Cai.	M 1900 A.B. 1904. A.M. 1911
—	Kynnersley	Pem.	M 1912
Bligh,	Edw. Hen. Swinburne	Pem.	M 1903 A.B. 1906
Blinkhorn,	Rob. Howard	Cla.	M 1905
Bliss,	Art. Edw. Drummond	Pem.	M 1910
—	Ern. Will.	Chr.	M 1908 A.B. 1911
—	Fra. Kennard	King's	M 1911
Blockey,	Hartley Sanders	Cla.	M 1904 A.B. 1907
Blois,	Gervase Vanneck ...	Trin.	M 1900 A.B. 1903. A.M. 1907
Blom,	Alf. Hogarth	Trin.	M 1909 A.B. 1912
Blomefield,	Hen. Art. Gilb.	C. C.	M 1894 A.B. 1897. A.M. 1907
Bloom,	Edw. Fra. Dandridge	Joh.	M 1896 A.B. 1899. A.M. 1903
Blower,	Lester Cha.	Chr.	M 1904 A.B. 1907
Bluett,	Duncan Campbell ...	Em.	M 1902
—	Tho. Lovell Chapman	Em.	M 1903 A.B. 1906
Blumenfeld,	Franz	Trin.	M 1911
Blumhardt,	Edw. Hen. Fenwick ..	Joh.	M 1910
Blundell,	Edm. Keith	H. Sel.	M 1905 A.B. 1908
Blunt,	Denzil Layton	King's	M 1909 A.B. 1912
Blyth,	Art. Cecil	Chr.	M 1909 A.B. 1912
—	Douglas	Trin. H.	M 1910
—	Ern. Will.	Chr.	M 1906 A.B. 1909
—	Maur. McAuslane ...	H. Sel.	M 1894 A.B. 1897. A.M. 1905
—	Nisbet Duncan	Cla.	M 1902
—	Phil. Gledstanes	Qu.	M 1894 A.B. 1897. A.M. 1901
—	Sam. Fra. Pet.	Chr.	M 1901 A.B. 1904
Boag,	Geo. Townsend	Trin.	M 1903 A.B. 1906
Board,	Douglas Leon.	Qu.	M 1907 A.B. 1910
—	John Hen.	Pem.	M 1900 A.B. 1903. M.B. 1908(2)
—	Jos. Hen.	N. C.	M 1912
Boardman,	John Hopwood	Cai.	M 1910
—	Tho. Hen.	N. C.	M 1894 Pet. A.B. 1897. A.M. 1903
Bock,	Ern. Norman	Cai.	M 1911
Bocking,	John Child	Pet.	M 1886 A.B. 1889. A.M. 1911
Boddam-Whetham, Gerald Avery		Cai.	M 1907 A.B. 1911
Boddington,	Oswald Will.	Em.	M 1907 A.B. 1910
—	Reg. Edgar	Jes.	M 1905
—	Vincent Coke	Joh.	M 1905 A.B. 1908
Bode,	John Ern. Victor ...	H. Sel.	M 1907 A.B. 1910
Boden,	Alf. Ern.	Joh.	M 1886 A.B. 1890. A.M. 1904
—	John Fra. Worsley	Jes.	M 1905 A.B. 1908. A.M. 1912
Bodger,	Fre. Will.	N. C.	M 1894 A.B. 1900. A.M. 1903
Bodington,	Art. Eaton	Cai.	M 1883 A.B. 1887. A.M. 1892. B.C. 1900.
—	Cecil Herb.	Pet.	M 1899 A.B. 1902 [M.D. 1903
Bodkin,	Art. Malcolm	King's	M 1904 A.B. 1907. M.B., B.C. 1912
—	Gilb. Edwin	Jes.	M 1905 A.B. 1908
—	Will. Theodore Douglas	King's	M 1897 A.B. 1900. A.M. 1904
Bodley,	Alf. Lang	Cla.	M 1909 A.B. 1912
—	Douglas Hoskyns ...	Pem.	M 1911
Bodmer,	Harold Siemens	Em.	M 1909
Body,	Lawrence Ambrose	Joh.	M 1892 A.B. 1895. A.M. 1912
Boggis,	John Edm.	H. Sel.	M 1910
—	Rob. Ja. Edm.	Pet.	M 1882 A.B. 1885. A.M. 1889. B.D. 1901
Bohr,	Niels Henrik Dav. ...	Trin.	M 1911
Bolden,	Art.	Trin.	M 1899 A.B. 1902
Bolderston,	Will. Northcott	Joh.	M 1904 A.B. 1907. A.M. 1911
Bolingbroke,	Cha. Bensly	Em.	M 1909 A.B. 1912
Bolitho,	Geoffrey Rich.	Trin.	M 1911
—	Tho. Gerald Glynn	Trin.	M 1908 A.B. 1911
Bolland,	Bern. Godfrey Clarke	Pem.	M 1907 A.B. 1910
Bolton,	Alf. Bern.	Chr.	M 1909 A.B. 1912

Bolton,	Dav. Cheney	Trin.	M 1902
—	Lyndon	Cla.	M 1880 A.B. 1884. A.M. 1907
—	Maur. Baldwin	Pem.	M 1912
—	Mich. Alf.	Chr.	M 1902 A.B. 1906
—	Percy	King's	M 1908 A.B. 1911
—	Tho.	N. C.	M 1897 A.B. 1901. A.M. 1906
—	Will. Sproule	Trin.	M 1904 A.B. 1907
Bomanji,	Jal Kursaidji Ruttonji	Trin.	M 1905 A.B., LL.B. 1908
Bombal,	Domingo Lucas	N. C.	M 1911
Bompas,	Hugh Steele	Pem.	M 1900 A.B. 1904
Bonaparte,	Roland		Sc.D. 1909
Bonar,	Tho. Lonsdale	Cai.	M 1909
Bonas,	Gordon Jonah	Chr.	M 1907 A.B. 1910
Bond,	Cha. Eric	Cai.	M 1911
—	Denys	Mag.	M 1899 A.B. 1902. A.M. 1906
—	Edw. Vines	Trin.	M 1889 A.B. 1892. A.M. 1902
—	Fra. Godolphin	Pem.	M 1901
—	John Stuart	Em.	M 1905 A.B. 1908
—	Raymond Alured	Trin. H.	M 1892 A.B. 1895. A.M. 1901
—	Will. Schuyler Studdert	King's	M 1907
Bonham-Carter,	Fra. Hugh	Trin.	M 1898 A.B. 1901
Bonham Christie,	Rob. Art.	Trin. H.	M 1911
Bonhote,	Edw. Frederic	Cla.	M 1907 A.B. 1910
—	John Lewis Ja.	Trin.	M 1893 A.B. 1897. A.M. 1901
—	Tho. Edw.	Cai.	M 1904 A.B. 1907
Bonnaud,	Cyril Alf.	Down.	M 1912
Bonne,	Tho. Will.	Down.	M 1907 A.B. 1910
Bonner,	Cecil Art. Ja.	Em.	M 1905 A.B. 1908
—	Cha. Bradlaugh	Trin.	M 1909 A.B. 1912
Bonnor,	Ern. John	N. C.	L 1896 Jes. A.B. 1898. A.M. 1902
Bonny,	Art. Edw.	Sid.	M 1899 B.C. 1912
Bonser,	Geoffrey Alwyn Gershom	Joh.	M 1907 A.B. 1910
—	Winfield Joyce	Chr.	M 1904 A.B. 1907
Bonsey,	Rich. Yerburgh	Joh.	M 1893 A.B. 1897. A.M. 1909
—	Will. Hen.	Joh.	M 1892 A.B. 1898. A.M. 1909
Bonvalot,	Edw. St Laurent	Trin.	M 1910
Booker,	Edw.	Joh.	M 1900 A.B. 1903. A.M. 1912
—	Geo. Hen.	Mag.	M 1912
Boon,	Ja. Newson Matthews	Em.	M 1909 A.B. 1912
Boone,	Art. Pearson	Jes.	M 1900 A.B. 1903
Boot,	John Campbell	Jes.	M 1907
Boote,	Cha. Will.	Em.	M 1908 A.B., LL.B. 1911
Booth,	Arnold Fre.	Chr.	M 1912
—	Cha. Zachary Macaulay	Trin.	M 1905 A.B. 1909
—	Claude Hebden Barker	King's	M 1905 A.B. 1908
—	Harris	Trin.	M 1903 A.B. 1906
—	Herb. Hen. de l'Isle	Pet.	M 1883 A.B. 1903. A.M. 1906
—	Hor. Fearne	Cath.	M 1895 A.B. 1898. A.M. 1902
—	Lancelot Hedley	Trin.	M 1892 A.B., LL.B. 1895. A.M., LL.M. [1902
—	Lionel Barton	Chr.	M 1902 A.B. 1905
—	Syd. Russell	Trin.	M 1898 A.B. 1901
—	Tho. Edw.	N. C.	M 1905 A.B. 1911
—	Walt. Reynolds	C. C.	M 1910
Boothroyd,	Eric Edw.	Trin.	M 1902 A.B. 1905. A.M. 1912
—	Herb. Evan	Sid.	M 1896 A.B. 1899. A.M. 1903
Booty,	Maur. Gordon Reece	Chr.	M 1904 A.B. 1907. A.M. 1911
Borlase,	John Jennings Dingle	Sid.	M 1897 A.B. 1900. LL.B. 1901
Born,	Maximilian	Cai.	E 1907
Borough,	Roland Fre.	Cla.	M 1896 A.B. 1899. A.M. 1903
Borrett,	Percy Rygate	Mag.	M 1908 A.B. 1911
Borrows,	John Cha. Abr.	Cath.	M 1894 A.B. 1897. A.M. 1908. LL.B. 1911

Borthwick,	Cecil Hamilton	Sid.	M 1906 A.B. 1909
—	Lionel Clements	Sid.	M 1910
Bosanquet,	Art. Rivers	Trin.	M 1909
—	Geoffrey Courthope	King's	E 1896 A.B. 1899. A.M. 1907
—	Will. Syd. Bence ...	King's	M 1911
Boscawen, (*Hon.*)	Evelyn Hugh John	Trin.	M 1905 A.B. 1908
—	(*Hon.*) Mildmay Tho.	Trin.	M 1910
—	Vere Douglas	Trin.	M 1909
Bose,	Alf.	N. C.	L 1900 A.B. 1902
—	Arabinda Mohan ...	Pem.	M 1912
—	Debendra Mohan ...	Chr.	M 1907
—	Jibon Mohan	N. C.	M 1907
—	Kiran Chandra	N. C.	M 1912
—	Lal Mohun Vivian ...	Pem.	M 1910
—	Sailendra Krishna ...	Down.	M 1904 A.B., LL.B. 1907
—	Satyendra Nath	Chr.	M 1907
—	Sudhansu Mohan ...	Chr.	M 1897 A.B. 1899. LL.B. 1902. A.M.†1903
Bossier,	Alf. Geo. Alwin Heinrich	Pet.	M 1910
Bostock,	Sam. Cha.	Trin.	M 1912
Boston,	Lawrence	Cla.	M 1911
Boswell,	Arnold	C. C.	M 1912
—	Denis St George Knox	Pem.	M 1912
—	Phil. Rutherford ...	Qu.	M 1908 A.B. 1911
Bosworth,	Tho. Owen	Joh.	M 1903 A.B. 1906
Bosworth Smith,	Nevil Digby ...	Pem.	M 1904 A.B. 1907
Botha,	Louis		*LL.D.* 1911
Botham,	Art. Fre.	Cla.	M 1908 A.B. 1911
Bott,	Will. Ern.	H. Sel.	M 1912
Botterill,	Art.	Pem.	M 1897 A.B. 1900. A.M. 1904
Botting,	Cecil Geo.	Em.	M 1889 A.B. 1892. A.M. 1904
Bottome,	Geo. McDonald	Chr.	M 1906 A.B. 1909
Bottomley,	Art. Cousen	Cla.	M 1904 A.B. 1907
—	Cha. Cookson	Cai.	M 1898 A.B. 1901
Botwood,	Sid. Benson	N. C.	M 1902
Boucher,	Scott	Trin.	M 1892 A.B. 1896. A.M. 1902
Boughey,	Cha. Lovell Fletcher	Trin.	M 1905 A.B. 1908. A.M. 1912
—	Geo. Menteth	Trin.	M 1898 A.B. 1902
—	Percy Fletcher	Pem.	M 1901 A.B. 1904. A.M. 1908
Boulderson,	Geo. Hen. Carne	Cla.	M 1908 A.B. 1911
Boulenger,	Cha. Leopold	King's	M 1903 A.B. 1906. A.M. 1910
Boultbee,	Harold Dalton	Qu.	M 1905 A.B. 1908
—	Horace Townsend ...	Chr.	M 1904 A.B. 1907. A.M. 1911
Boulton,	Guy Fra. Pelham ...	King's	M 1908 A.B. 1911
—	Harold	Cla.	M 1891 A.B. 1894. M.B., B.C. 1906
—	Rich. John	Cla.	M 1911
Boumphrey,	Donald	Qu.	M 1912
Bouquet,	Alan Coates	Trin.	M 1902 A.B. 1905. Jes. A.M. 1910
Bourchier,	Basil Graham	Qu.	M 1899 A.B. 1903. A.M. 1906
—	Le Gendre Claude ...	Trin.	M 1906 A.B. 1909
Bourdillon,	Gerard Leigh	H. Sel.	M 1905 A.B. 1908
Bourne,	Aleck Will.	Down.	M 1905 A.B. 1908. B.C. 1911. M.B. 1912
—	Austin Spencer	H. Sel.	M 1910
—	Cyprian	H. Sel.	M 1907 A.B. 1910
—	Harry Ralph	Jes.	M 1907 A.B. 1912
—	John Gilb.	Pem.	M 1902 A.B. 1905
Bourner,	Art. Cha. Nicholson	Cla.	M 1903 A.B. 1906
Bousfield,	Hen. Tho. Wishart	Chr.	M 1909 A.B. 1912
—	John Keith	Cai.	M 1912 [M.D. 1907
—	Leon.	Pem.	M 1894 A.B. 1897. M.B., B.C. 1903. A.M.,
—	Rob. Bruce	Cai.	M 1905 A.B. 1908 [1901. M.D. 1910
—	Stanley	Cai.	M 1889 A.B. 1892. A.M. 1900. M.B., B.C.

Bousfield,	Will. Eric	Cai.	M 1900 A.B. 1903
Boutflower,	Cha.	Trin.	M 1897 A.B. 1900. A.M. 1905
Bouwens,	Bethell Godefroy ...	Trin.	M 1902 A.B. 1906. A.M. 1909
Bovey,	Fra. Hen. Wilfrid ...	Trin. H.	M 1903 LL.B. 1906
Bovill,	Edw. Hen.	Pem.	M 1906 A.B. 1910
—	Edw. Will.	Trin.	M 1911
Bowden,	Edw. Ratcliffe	Pem.	M 1907 A.B. 1910
—	Geo. Cha.	N. C.	M 1897 King's A.B. 1902
—	Will. Geo.	C. C.	M 1905 A.B. 1908
Bowdler,	Archib. Penrhyn ...	Sid.	M 1895 A.B. 1898. M.B., B.C., A.M. 1902
Bowdon,	Walt. Syd.	N. C.	L 1897 Joh. A.B. 1899. A.M. 1912
Bowe,	Ja. Hodgson	Jes.	M 1900 A.B. 1903. A.M. 1907
Bowen,	Fra. Goding	Cai.	M 1892 A.B. 1895. B.C. 1902
—	Geo.	Chr.	M 1901 A.B. 1904. A.M. 1909
—	Ja. Bevan	Trin.	M 1902
—	John Edmund	Trin.	M 1911
—	Leslie Harold	Joh.	M 1907 A.B. 1910
—	Tho. Steph.	Cla.	M 1910
Bowen-Colthurst,	Rob. MacGregor	Trin.	M 1902 A.B. 1905
Bower,	Cedric Will.	Cai.	M 1908
—	Cha. Fra.	C. C.	M 1910
—	Geo. Noel	C. C.	M 1903 A.B. 1906
—	Harold Ja.	Em.	M 1907 A.B. 1910
—	Norman Dow	Chr.	M 1896 A.B. 1899. A.M. 1903
Bowers,	John Philips Allcot	Joh.	M 1873 A.B. 1877. J. Phillips A., A.M.
Bowker,	Rob. Cha. Stancer ...	Em.	M 1911 [1880. D.D. 1903
Bowlby,	Russell Frank	Trin.	M 1909
Bowle,	Cha. Will.	Trin.	M 1898 A.B. 1901
—	Hor. Edgar	Pem.	M 1905 A.B. 1908
Bowler,	Syd.	N. C.	M 1911
Bowles,	Geo. Frederic Stewart	Trin.	M 1897 A.B. 1901. A.M. 1905
—	Reg. Julian Albany	Cla.	M 1910
—	Walt. Cullen	C. C.	M 1896 A.B. 1899. A.M.† 1907
Bowley,	Alex.	Sid.	M 1906
Bowman,	Frank	Trin.	M 1911
—	Geoffrey Hilton	Trin.	M 1910
—	Kenneth Ja.	Qu.	M 1912
—	Tho. Favell	Cath.	M 1903 A.B., LL.B. 1906
Bown,	Percy Hen.	N. C.	L 1896 Joh. A.B. 1898. A.M. 1904
Bowring,	Cha. Stuart	Trin.	M 1898 A.B. 1902
—	Harold	King's	M 1901 A.B. 1904. M.B., B.C. 1912
Boxall,	Will. Percival Gratwicke	Em.	M 1905 A.B. 1909
Boyall,	Art. Vincent	Trin.	M 1905 A.B. 1908
Boyce,	Art. St John	Qu.	M 1903 A.B. 1906
Boycott,	Art. Godfrey	H. Sel.	M 1907 A.B. 1910
Boyd,	Cha. Will.	Cath.	M 1909 A.B. 1912
—	Edgar Ja.	Sid.	M 1907 A.B. 1910
—	Halbert Johnston ...	Em.	M 1895 A.B. 1898. A.M. 1907
—	Ja.	Trin.	M 1910 A.B. 1912
—	Rob. Hen.	C. C.	M 1894 A.B. 1898. A.M. 1901
—	Tho. Kenneth	Trin.	M 1903 A.B. 1906 [1907
Boyde,	Alf. Caine	Joh.	M 1894 N. C. A.B. 1898. LL.B. 1899. A.M.
Boyes,	Will. Osborn	Joh.	M 1863 LL.B. 1867. LL.M. 1895. LL.D.
Boyle,	Dav. Harrop	N. C.	M 1901 Joh. A.B. 1904. A.M. 1908 [1901
—	Geo. Frederic	Trin.	M 1912
—	Gerald Egerton	H. Sel.	M 1903 A.B. 1906. A.M. 1910
—	Ja.	C. C.	M 1898 A.B. 1901. A.M. 1906
—	Rich. Fre. Rob. Pochin	Trin. H.	M 1906
Boys,	Justin Cha. Edm. ...	Em.	M 1908 A.B. 1911
Boyson,	Hugh Alex.	Cai.	M 1912
—	John Cha.	Cai.	M 1906

Boys-Stones,	Will.	Cai.	M 1901 A.B. 1904
Boyt,	Jos. Ern.	Joh.	M 1895 A.B. 1898. A.M. 1902
Boyton,	Hen. Ja.	Jes.	M 1910
Braby,	Herb. Wilson	Sid.	M 1907 A.B. 1910
Bracecamp,	Frank Will.	Jes.	M 1910
Brachi,	Cha. Clarence	Cath.	M 1900 A.B. 1903. A.M. 1907
Brackenbury,	Basil Vyvian Fabian	Qu.	M 1909
—	Cecil Fabian	H. Sel.	M 1899 A.B. 1902 [A.M. 1905
—	Gerald Harry	Cai.	M 1896 G. H. Prendergast, A.B. 1899.
Bradburne,	Tho. Will.	Pem.	M 1893 A.B. 1896. A.M. 1904
Bradbury,	John Fowler	King's	M 1903 A.B. 1906. LL.B. 1907
—	Lyle Art.	Em.	M 1902 A.B. 1905. A.M. 1911
—	Norman	Cai.	M 1910
—	Rich.	Cath.	M 1901 A.B. 1904. A.M. 1908
Braddon,	Will. Vaudrey	Trin. H.	M 1892 M.B., B.C. 1905
Bradfield,	Linden Gordon	Cai.	M 1905 A.B. 1908
—	Rich.	Cai.	M 1905 A.B. 1908
Bradford,	Ern. Cordley	Pem.	M 1907 A.B. 1910
—	John	Em.	E 1891 A.B. 1895. M.B., B.C. 1902
Bradley,	Art. Frederic	Chr.	M 1904 A.B. 1907
—	Art. Sylvester	Cai.	M 1895 A.B. 1898. B.C. 1902. M.B., A.M.
—	Edwin John	Jes.	M 1908 A.B. 1911 [1904
—	Eric Jatinga	Pem.	M 1911
—	Geoffrey Montagu ...	Jes.	M 1911
—	Gilb. Leslie	Jes.	M 1897 A.B. 1900. A.M. 1909
—	Hub. Penrose	Cai.	M 1892 A.B. 1895. B.C. 1900. M.B., A.M.
—	Hugh Lionel	H. Sel.	M 1903 A.B. 1906 [1902
—	Leon.	H. Sel.	M 1902 A.B. 1905
—	Micah Gedling	Trin.	M 1901 A.B. 1904
—	Stanley Blackall ...	Cai.	M 1910
—	Walt. de Winton Herb.	Jes.	M 1907 A.B. 1911
—	Walt. Eliot	N. C.	M 1898 W. Elliot, A.B. 1901. A.M. 1905
Bradney,	Jos. Alf.	Trin.	M 1877 A.B. 1881. A.M. 1912
Bradshaw,	John Horsley	Joh.	M 1899 A.B. 1902
—	Theodore Edw. Ja. ...	Trin.	M 1906 A.B. 1909
Bradstock,	Geo.	Jes.	M 1907
Brady,	Frank	Joh.	M 1903
—	Lionel Fra.	Cath.	M 1899 A.B. 1902. A.M.† 1912
Bragg,	Rob. Cha.	Trin.	M 1912
—	Will. Lawrence	Trin.	M 1909 A.B. 1912
Braham,	Phil. Edw.	Cla.	M 1900 A.B. 1903 [1904. M.C. 1905
Brailey,	Art. Robertson	Down.	M 1896 A.B. 1899. A.M. 1903. M.B., B.C.
—	Will. Herb.	Qu.	E 1893 A.B. 1896. M.B., B.C., A.M. 1903.
			[M.D. 1910
Brailsford,	Will.	H. Aye.	M 1886 Qu. A.B. 1889. A.M.† 1912
Braimbridge,	Clifford Viney	Down.	M 1911
Brain,	Fra. Syd.	Trin. H.	M 1912
Braithwaite,	Cha. Fre.	Cai.	M 1898 A.B. 1901
—	Phil. Pipon	Cai.	M 1899 A.B. 1902
—	Tho. Miles	Cla.	M 1899 A.B., LL.B. 1902. A.M. 1909
Braley,	Evelyn Foley	Down.	M 1907 A.B., LL.B. 1910
Bramall,	Edm. Haselden	Pem.	M 1908
Brameld,	Art. John Masterman	Cath.	M 1903 A.B. 1906
Bramley-Moore,	Leslie	Trin.	M 1895 A.B. 1908
Bramwell,	John Crighton	Trin.	M 1907 A.B. 1910
—	John Nicholson	Pem.	M 1898 A.B. 1901
Brand,	Harold Geo.	Qu.	M 1908 A.B. 1911
Brandau,	Hermann Hugo Fried-} rich Julius }	N. C.	M 1911
Brandon,	Alf. de Bathe	Trin. H.	M 1902 A.B. 1905. LL.B. 1906
Brandram,	John Bulkeley	Qu.	M 1911

Brandram,	Rich. And.	....	Chr.	M 1893 A.B. 1897. A.M. 1905
Brandreth,	Roland Hen.	....	H. Sel.	M 1896 A.B. 1899. A.M. 1909
Brandt,	Edm. Hub.	....	King's	M 1903 Qu. A.B. 1906
—	Will. Rob.	....	King's	M 1902
Branson,	Will. Phil. Sutcliffe		Trin.	M 1893 A.B. 1896. M.B., B.C. 1900. M.D.
Branston				*See* Brantsen [1904
Brantsen,	Carlo Alberto	....	Trin.	M 1904 Cha. Alb. A.B. 1908. A.M. 1911.
				[post Branston, LL.M. 1912
Brash,	Edw. John Yelverton		Joh.	M 1907 A.B. 1910
—	Ja. Basset	....	Qu.	M 1909
Brasnett,	Tho. John Grose	...	Chr.	M 1912
Brass,	Will.	....	Trin.	M 1904
Bratton,	Allen Basil	....	Cai.	M 1909 A.B. 1912
Braun,	Geoffrey Cha. Phillip		Trin.	M 1908
Braunholtz,	Eugen Julius Karl	...	King's	M 1909 A.B. 1912
—	Gustav Ernst Karl	...	Em.	M 1906 A.B. 1909
—	Hermann Justus	......	Joh.	M 1908 A.B. 1911
Brawn,	John Art.	....	Chr.	M 1912
Bray,	Alf. Cha.	....	N. C.	M 1904 Jes. A.B. 1907. A.M. 1911
—	Archie Leslie	....	Down.	M 1906 A.B. 1909
—	Fra. Edmond	....	Trin.	M 1901 A.B. 1904. A.M. 1911
Brayn,	Rich. Fysher	....	Joh.	M 1899 A.B. 1903. A.M. 1912
Brayne,	Art. Hen.	....	Pem.	M 1900 A.B. 1904
—	Frank Lugard	....	Pem.	M 1900 A.B. 1903
Brayshaw,	Edm. Leon.	....	Trin. H.	M 1903 A.B. 1907
Brayshay,	Sid.	....	Joh.	M 1903 A.B. 1906
—	Stanley	....	Cath.	M 1902 A.B. 1905
Breach,	Wilfred Norman	...	Cai.	M 1906 A.B. 1910
Brearley,	Art. Jos.	....	Em.	M 1909 A.B. 1912
Breay,	Cyril	....	C. C.	M 1911
—	Wilfrid	....	H. Sel.	M 1910
Bree,	Herb. Reg. Stapylton		H. Sel.	M 1904 A.B. 1908
Breese,	Will. Lawrence	......	Trin.	M 1902
Breffit,	Hor. Edgar Yorke		H. Sel.	M 1894 A.B. 1897. A.M. 1903
Brehaut,	Alf. Hocart		H. Sel.	M 1893 A.B. 1896. M.B., B.C. 1901. M.D.
Bremner,	Fra. Donald Holden		Trin.	M 1911 [1908
Brenan,	Alex. Rich. Micklethwait	Trin.	M 1893 A.B. 1896. M.B., B.C., A.M. 1901.
—	Herb. Eustace	....	Pem.	M 1893 A.B. 1896. A.M. 1901 [M.D. 1904
Brend,	Will. Alf.	....	Sid.	M 1892 A.B. 1895 A.M. 1901
Brennan,	Ja. Ward	....	Pem.	M 1901 A.B. 1904. A.M. 1908
—	Jos.	....	Chr.	M 1907 A.B. 1910
Brenton,	Hen. Courtier	....	C. C.	M 1901 A.B. 1904. A.M. 1909
Brereton,	John Lancelot	......	Trin	M 1906
—	Phil. Harington Lloyd	Chr.	M 1895 A.B. 1898. A.M. 1902
Bretherton,	Humphrey	....	Trin.	M 1908 A.B. 1911
Brett,	Jos. Herb.		Cai.	M 1911
—	Sid. Reed	....	Cath.	M 1912
Breul, Ern. Damian Eugen Theodore			Trin.	M 1907 E. D. T. E. A.B. 1910
—	[1] Karl Hermann	......		A.M. 1886 King's, Litt.D. 1896
Brewer,	Cecil Harold	....	Cla.	M 1903 A.B. 1906. A.M. 1910
—	Fra. Geo.	....	Cai.	M 1912
—	Jos.	....	Em.	M 1906 A.B. 1910
Brewis,	Cha. Carrick	....	Down.	M 1908 A.B. 1911
Brewster,	Geo. Will.	....	King's	M 1899 A.B. 1902. A.M. 1907
Breymann,	Will. Hans	....	N. C.	E 1905
Brian,	Fre. Reg. Hugh	......	Joh.	M 1912
Brice-Smith,	Harold Fra.		Joh.	M 1908 A.B. 1911
—	Hugh Middleton	......	Qu.	M 1903 A.B. 1906
—	Rollo	....	Joh.	M 1905 A.B. 1908. A.M. 1912
Bridell,	Leon. Tho.	....	Down.	M 1911

[1] Schröder Professor of German, 1910.

Bridge,	Donald	Qu.	M 1892 A.B. 1895. A.M. 1901
—	John	Down.	M 1908 A.B. 1911
—	Joshua	Down.	M 1908 A.B. 1911
Bridgeman,	Orlando	Trin.	M 1893 A.B. 1896. A.M. 1903
—	Roger Orlando	Trin.	M 1908 A.B. 1911
Bridger,	Will. Reg. Pritchett	Cath.	M 1903 A.B. 1906. A.M.† 1909
Bridges,	Fra. Llewellyn	C. C.	M 1904 A.B. 1907. A.M.† 1911
—	Jos. Sam.	Em.	M 1909
—	Leslie Walt.	H. Sel.	M 1909 A.B. 1912
Bridgman,	Frederic Sid. ...＾.....	Sid.	M 1900 A.B. 1903
Bridson,	Phil. Syd.	Em.	M 1912
Brierley,	Cha. Geo. Gordon ...	Qu.	M 1912
—	John	Trin.	M 1906 A.B. 1909
—	Will. Bertie	Chr.	M 1905 A.B. 1908
Briggs,	Cha. Edw.	Sid.	M 1906 A.B. 1909
—	Geoffrey Rawdon ...	Jes.	M 1908
—	Geo. Edw.	Joh.	M 1912
—	Geo. Wallace	Em.	M 1894 A.B. 1897. A.M. 1901
—	Milton	Sid.	M 1906 A.B. 1909
—	Percy Ja.	Chr.	M 1912
—	Waldo Raven	Chr.	M 1901 A.B. 1904. LL.B. 1906. A.M. 1908
—	Will.	N. C.	M 1887 Jes. A.B. 1890. LL.B. 1891. A.M. [1894. LL.M. 1895. LL.D. 1902
—	Will. Art.	Joh.	M 1900 A.B. 1903. A.M. 1909
—	Will. Robertson	Trin.	M 1904
Bright,	Frank Ransom	Trin.	M 1911
—	Frank Tho.	N. C.	M 1907 A.B. 1910
—	Hen. Augustus	Cath.	M 1904 A.B. 1907
—	Wilfred Ja.	N. C.	L 1911
—	Will. Art.	Cai.	M 1898 A.B. 1901
Brightman,	Eustace Webster	Trin.	M 1906 A.B. 1909
Brind,	Walt. Hinde	C. C.	M 1893 A.B. 1896. A.M. 1907
Brinton,	Cecil Cha.	Cai.	M 1901 A.B. 1904. A.M. 1909
Briscoe,	Fra. Edw.	Qu.	M 1912
—	Ja. Rynd	H. Sel.	M 1896 A.B. 1902. M.B., B.C. 1910
—	Ralph Angus Nugent	H. Sel.	M 1905 A.B. 1908
Brisley,	Cuthbert Everard ...	Cai.	M 1905 A.B. 1910
—	Gerald Gehagan Vivian	Cai.	M 1908
Bristow,	Cha. Holditch	Chr.	M 1906 A.B. 1909
—	Ern.	Joh.	M 1893 A.B. 1897. A.M. 1904
—	Ronald Victor	H. Sel.	M 1911
Brittain,	Alb. Will.	Chr.	M 1909
—	Edw. Sam.	Cai.	M 1910
—	Harold Meigh	Cla.	M 1896 A.B. 1899. A.M. 1904
—	Reg.	Cla.	M 1896 A.B. 1899. A.M. 1912
Britton,	John	C. C.	M 1905 A.B. 1908
—	Will. Hub.	H. Sel.	M 1910
Broad,	Cha. Noel Frank	Pem.	M 1903
—	Charlie Dunbar ......*Trin.	M 1906 A.B. 1910
—	Fre. Horwood	Pem.	M 1910
—	Percival Gordon	Joh.	M 1901 A.B. 1904. A.M. 1910
Broadbent,	Cecil Hoyle	Trin.	M 1900 A.B. 1903. A.M. 1912
—	Frank	Cath.	M 1907 A.B. 1910. LL.B. 1911
—	Hen. Geoffry	Qu.	M 1911
—	John Will.	N. C.	M 1896 A.B. 1899. A.M. 1903˙
Broadhead,	Hen. Dan	Trin.	M 1911
—	Tho. Wright	N. C.	M 1895 Cath. A.B. 1898. A.M. 1902
Broadmead,	Harold Hamilton ...	Cai.	M 1907 A.B. 1910
Broadrick,	Hen. Crewdson	Trin.	M 1894 A.B. 1897. A.M. 1901
Brochner,	Theodor Carl Craven	Jes.	M 1910
Brock,	Art. Gordon	Pem.	M 1905 A.B. 1908

Brock,	Eric Geo.	Joh.	M 1911	
Brockbank,	Birkett	Joh.	M 1903 A.B. 1906. A.M. 1910	
Brocklehurst, Cha.		Trin. H.	M 1902	
—	Edw. Howard	Trin. H.	M 1895 A.B. 1898. LL.B., A.M. 1903	
—	(*Sir*) Philip Lee	Trin. H.	M 1904	
—	Tho. Pownall	Trin. H.	M 1905 A.B., LL.B. 1908	
Brockman,	Ralph St Leger	Cai.	M 1907 A.B. 1910	
—	Will. Dominic	Cai.	M 1910	
Brocksopp,	Will. Ern.	C. C.	M 1900 A.B. 1903. A.M. 1907	
Brode,	Reg. Tho.	Chr.	M 1911	
Brodetsky,	Selig	Trin.	M 1906 A.B. 1909	
Brodhurst,	Hugh	Pem.	M 1893 A.B. 1896. A.M. 1901	
Brodie,	Pat.	Cla.	M 1899 A.B. 1902	
Brodsky,	Grigori Alexandrovitch	Trin.	E 1906	
Brogden,	Ingram Rich. Rhodes	Cla.	M 1910	
Brögger,	Waldemar Christofer		*Sc.D.* 1907	
Bromet,	John Neville	Cla.	M 1911	
Bromfield,	Jos. Dicken	Joh.	M 1911	
Bromhead,	John Paul	Sid.	M 1912	
Bromley,	Hen. Victor Rob. ...	Em.	M 1904 A.B. 1907. A.M. 1912	
—	Lancelot	Cai.	M 1903 A.B. 1906. M.B., B.C. 1911	
—	Nath. Ern.	H. Sel.	M 1901 A.B. 1904	
Bromwich,	Tho. John I'Anson	*Joh.	M 1892 A.B. 1895. A.M. 1899. Sc.D. 1909	
Brook,	Cha. Augustine	Down.	M 1908 A.B. 1911	
—	Fre. Benj.	Sid.	M 1899 A.B. 1902. LL.B. 1903	
Brooke,	Fra. Norman	Pem.	M 1912	
—	Geo. Cyril	C. C.	M 1903 A.B. 1906	
—	Gilb. Edw.	Pem.	M 1891 A.B. 1894. A.M. 1902	
—	John Callaghan	Cai.	M 1912	
—	Justin	Em.	M 1904 A.B., LL.B. 1908	
—	Nevile John	C. C.	M 1910	
—	Rupert Chawner	King's	M 1906 A.B. 1909	
—	Will. Alf. Cotterill	King's	M 1909 A.B. 1912	
—	Zachary Nugent ...	Joh.	M 1902 A.B. 1905. *Cai. A.M. 1909	
Brooker,	Reg. Hugh Godfrey	Pem.	M 1910	
Brookes,	Alb.	N. C.	M 1907 A.B. 1911	
—	Frank Meridyth	Trin. H.	M 1902	
—	Tho. Cannon	Trin. H.	M 1894 A.B. 1897. A.M. 1907	
Brooking,	Granville Fra.	Trin.	M 1870 Cath. A.B. 1901	
Brooks,	Cha. Davis	King's	M 1905 A.B. 1908. A.M. 1912	
—	Fre. Tom	Em.	M 1902 A.B. 1905. A.M. 1909	
—	Harry Cribb	Cath.	M 1893 A.B. 1896. A.M. 1902	
—	Herb. Reg. Graham	Trin.	M 1912	
—	Jos. Rayner	Trin. H.	L 1903	
—	Kenneth Howard ...	Trin.	M 1912	
—	Leon.	N. C.	M 1907 A.B. 1910	
—	Leslie Walt.	Cla.	M 1911	
Brooksbank, Stamp		Trin. H.	M 1905 A.B. 1908	
Brooman-White, Cha. Ja.		Trin. H.	L 1904	
Broome,	Rob. Reeves	Chr.	M 1906 A.B. 1909. Mus.B. 1911	
Broomfield,	Rob. Stonehouse	Chr.	M 1901 A.B. 1904	
Brophy,	Gerald Mary	Mag.	M 1910	
Broster,	Edw. Davenport	Chr.	M 1910	
Brothers,	John Malam	Trin. H.	M 1900 A.B. 1904	
—	Malam	Cla.	M 1901 A.B. 1904. LL.B. 1905	
Brough,	Ja. Stanley Bromfield	Em.	M 1897 A.B. 1900. A.M. 1911	
Broughton,	Alf. Delves	Cai.	M 1910	
Broughton-Alcock, W. *See* Alcock, W. B.				
Brown,	Alex.	Cai.	M 1898 A.B. 1901. A.M. 1912	
—	Alf. Reg. ....*Trin.		M 1902 A.B. 1905. A.M. 1909	
—	Anth. Will. Scudamore	Cai.	M 1900 A.B. 1903. A.M. 1907	

Brown,	Art.	Trin. H.	M 1911
—	Art. Anth.	Cai.	M 1905
—	Art. Edw.	Joh.	M 1903 A.B. 1906. LL.B. 1907. A.M. 1912
—	Art. Edw.	Chr.	M 1907 A.B. 1911
—	Art. Ern.	Trin. H.	M 1901 A.B. 1904. A.M.† 1908
—	Art. Macdonald	Joh.	M 1877 A.B. 1881. post MacDonald, A.
—	Austin Cha.	King's	M 1902 A.B. 1905　　　[A.M. 1911
—	Bertram Goulding ...	Trin.	M 1900 A.B. 1903. A.M. 1907
—	Cedric Clifton	Trin.	M 1906 A.B. 1909
—	Cha. Barrington	Cai.	M 1906 A.B. 1909
—	Cha. Cuthbert	Trin.	M 1907 A.B. 1910
—	Chris. Wilkinson ...	Joh.	M 1911
—	Cyril Roberts	Pet.	M 1909 A.B. 1912
—	Douglas Clifton	Trin.	M 1898 A.B. 1901. A.M. 1905
—	Edw. Middleton	Pem.	M 1897 A.B. 1900. B.C. 1904. M.B. 1905
—	Eric Barlow	Cai.	M 1912
—	Eric Metcalfe	Joh.	M 1912
—	Ern. Will.	N. C.	L 1906 A.B. 1909
—	Eugene Will.	H. Sel.	M 1892 N. C. A.B. 1900. A.M. 1904
—	Fra. Cyril	Trin.	M 1900 A.B., LL.B. 1904
—	Frank Rich.	Cath.	M 1909
—	Geoffrey Manwaring	King's	M 1910
—	Geoffrey Will.	Chr.	M 1912
—	Geo. Leon.	Jes.	M 1910
—	Geo. Matthews	Trin.	M 1898 A.B. 1900. A.M. 1908
—	Geo. Miller	Jes.	M 1907 A.B. 1910
—	Geo. Syd. Rob. Johnston	Cla.	M 1909
—	Gerald Burdon	King's	M 1905 A.B. 1908. A.M. 1912
—	Harold	Jes.	M 1899 A.B. 1902
—	Harold Arrowsmith	Cai.	M 1898 A.B. 1901
—	Harold Cuthbert Brooksbank	Trin.	M 1911
—	Harold Ethelwald ...	Jes.	M 1908
—	Harold Montagu ...	Cai.	M 1906 A.B. 1909
—	Hen. Coddington	Em.	M 1895 A.B. 1898. M.B., B.C. 1902
—	Hen. Forester	Trin. H.	M 1911
—	Hen. Noel	Trin. H.	M 1912
—	Hub.	Pem.	M 1898 A.B. 1901. A.M. 1905
—	Hub. Horan	Cai.	M 1904 A.B. 1907
—	Ian Macdonald	Down.	M 1907 A.B. 1910
—	Ja. Cartmell Dennison	Pem.	M 1912
—	John	Sid.	M 1906 A.B. 1909
—	John Duncan	Cla.	M 1903 A.B. 1906
—	John Rob.	N. C.	M 1896 Joh. A.B. 1899. A.M. 1903
—	John Topham	Trin.	M 1903 A.B. 1906
—	John Will. Harold ...	Pem.	M 1898 A.B. 1901. A.M. 1905
—	Kenneth Ashby	Jes.	M 1905
—	Lionel Dudley	Cath.	M 1911
—	Mathew Hugh	Jes.	M 1905
—	Nevill Dallison	Pem.	M 1902 A.B. 1907
—	Osbert Harold	Pem.	M 1910
—	Percy Barrington ...	Pem.	M 1900 P. Rich. B. A.B. 1903. A.M. 1907
—	Percy Houghton	Joh.	M 1886 A.B., LL.B. 1889. A.M., LL.M.
—	Regin. Art.	Trin.	M 1908 A.B. 1911　　[1893. LL.D. 1902
—	Rob. Branston	H. Sel.	M 1892 A.B. 1895. A.M. 1901
—	Rob. Cha.		*A.M.* 1912
—	Russell Edw.	C. C.	M 1897 A.B. 1900. A.M. 1904
—	Sam. Edw.	Chr.	M 1897 A.B. 1900. A.M. 1904
—	Sam. Ralph	Joh.	M 1899 A.B. 1902. A.M. 1906
—	Sam Vernon	Down.	M 1909 A.B. 1912
—	Stuart Kelson	King's	M 1904 A.B. 1907
—	Tho.	Cai.	M 1908 A.B. 1911

Brown,	Tho. Bolney	Trin.	M 1902 A.B. 1905
—	Tho. Cocker	N. C.	M 1905
—	Vernon Syd.	Jes.	M 1907 A.B. 1910
—	Walt. Hargreaves ...	Trin.	M 1900 A.B. 1903. A.M. 1907
—	Walt. Langdon	Joh.	M 1889 A.B. 1892. A.M. 1896. M.B., B.C.
—	Wilfrid Stephenson	Cai.	M 1911 [1897. M.D. 1901
—	Will. Barrowclough	King's	M 1912
—	Will. Edw. Leighton	Trin.	M 1912
—	Will. Jethro	Joh.	M 1887 A.B., LL.B. 1890. A.M.† 1894.
—	Will. Rob. Railston...	H. Sel.	M 1910 [LL.M. 1899. LL.D. 1905
Brown Douglas,	Fra. Campbell ...	Trin.	M 1912
Browne,	Archib. Douglas	Qu.	M 1908 A.B. 1911
—	Art. Edw.	N. C.	M 1894 Cath. A.B. 1904. A.M. 1908
—	Barrington	Joh.	M 1910
—	Barry Mathew Cha. Sleater	Chr.	M 1890 A.B. 1893. A.M. 1902
—	Cha. Percival	Trin.	M 1905
—	Cha. Will. Hemson	N. C.	M 1876 Cai. A.B. 1882. A.M. 1910
—	Cyril Ross	Em.	M 1912
—	[1] Edw. Granville ......*Pem.		M 1879 A.B. 1883. A.M. 1886. M.B. 1887
—	Edwin Brooshooft ...	H. Aye.	L 1891 N. C. A.B. 1894. Brown, E. B.
—	Elmitt Raithby	Sid.	M 1884 A.B. 1887. A.M. 1905 [A.M. 1904
—	Fra. Deshon	Jes.	M 1889 A.B. 1892. A.M. 1902
—	Fre. Maur.	Pet.	M 1900 A.B. 1903
—	Harrie Spencer Dav..	Trin.	M 1894 A.B. 1897. Harry S. D. M.B. 1904
—	Laurence Edw.	Sid.	M 1906 A.B. 1909
—	Lindsay Foster	Qu.	M 1909 A.B. 1912
—	Maur. Anth.	Chr.	M 1904 A.B. 1907
—	Meyrick Gouldesbery	Trin.	M 1907 M. Gouldsbury, LL.B. 1910
—	Noel Gordon Monod	Sid.	M 1903 A.B. 1906
—	Rob. Hen.	H. Aye.	L 1895 H. Sel. A.B. 1897. A.M. 1904
—	Walt. Marshall	Chr.	M 1904 A.B. 1907. A.M. 1911
—	Will.	N. C.	M 1896 Joh. A.B. 1899. A.M. 1903
—	Will. Cha. Denis ...	Cla.	M 1907 A.B. 1910. Mus.B. 1912
—	Will. Edw. Clifford	Em.	M 1907 A.B. 1910
Browning,	Guy Arrott	Joh.	M 1896 A.B. 1899. A.M. 1903
—	Herb. Acland	Joh.	M 1898 A.B. 1901. A.M. 1906
—	Kendall Colin	Joh.	M 1894 A.B. 1897. A.M. 1901
—	Percy Triquet	Trin.	M 1901 A.B. 1904. A.M. 1909
—	Will. Frank	H. Sel.	M 1908 A.B. 1911
Brownlee,	Wilfred Methven	C. C.	M 1912
Brownrigg,	Fre. Kingsmill	Qu.	M 1905 A.B. 1908
Brownscombe,	Alf.	Joh.	M 1896 A.B. 1899. A.M. 1903
Brownson,	Roger Dawson Dawson-} Duffield }	Joh.	M 1902 A.B. 1905. M.B., B.C. 1911
—	Tho. Kerfoot	Joh.	M 1908 A.B. 1912
Brownsword,	Douglas Anderson ...	Cai.	M 1909
Browse,	Geo.	Cla.	M 1892 A.B. 1895. B.C. 1900. M.B. 1908
Bruce,	Alex. Bannerman ...	Pet.	M 1886 A.B. 1889. A.M. 1909
—	Cha. Edw. Hovel } Thurlow Cumming}	Trin.	M 1888 A.B. 1891. A.M. 1905
—	Cha. Gordon	Em.	M 1905 A.B. 1908
—	Cha. Matthewes	Em.	M 1894 A.B. 1897. C. Mathewes A.M. 1908
—	Frederic Donnison ...	Trin. H.	M 1898 A.B., LL.B. 1901. A.M., LL.M.
—	John Collingwood Gainsford	Trin. H.	M 1895 A.B. 1901. A.M. 1904 [1905
—	John Synnot	Trin.	M 1898 A.B. 1901
—	Michael Victor Stuart	C. C.	M 1905
—	Oswald	Joh.	M 1901
—	Pat. Alex.	Trin.	M 1907 A.B. 1910
—	Stanley Melbourne	Trin. H.	L 1903 A.B. 1905

[1] Sir Thomas Adams' Professor of Arabic, 1902.

Bruce Adam,	Douglas	C. C.	M 1911
Bruce-Payne,	Orlebar Dav.	Cai.	M 1895 A.B. 1898. A.M. 1902
Bruck,	Gerhard	Chr.	M 1903
Brudenell Bruce, Ja. Ern. John ...		Trin.	M 1897 A.B., LL.B. 1900. A.M. 1906
Bruford,	Walt. Horace	Joh.	M 1912
Brühl,	Julius Wilhelm		*Sc.D.* 1904
Brundrit,	Percy Wright	King's	M 1894 A.B. 1897. LL.B. 1898. A.M. 1901
Brunner,	Egon	Chr.	M 1910
—	Frederic Ern.	Cai.	M 1892 A.B. 1895. M.B., B.C. 1901
Brunt,	Dav.	Trin.	M 1908 A.B. 1910
Brunton,	Archib.	Cla.	M 1901
—	Edw. Hen. Pollock	Trin.	M 1907 A.B. 1910
Brunwin,	Alan Deed	Trin.	M 1897 A.B. 1900. A.M. 1904. M.B., B.C.
Brunwin-Hales, Greville Oxley ...		Jes.	M 1907 [1906. M.D. 1909
Brutton,	Hen. Lionel	Trin.	M 1899 A.B. 1904
Bryan,	Frank	King's	M 1895 A.B. 1898. B.C. 1903. M.B. 1904
Bryan-Brown, Douglas Steph.		Down.	M 1905 A.B. 1908
—	Guy Spencer	Down.	M 1904 A.B. 1907. A.M. 1911
—	Willoughby	Down.	M 1903 A.B. 1906
Bryant,	Cha. Leslie	Down.	M 1900 A.B. 1903. A.M. 1907
—	Geo. Will.	Em.	M 1906 A.B. 1909
—	Rolf Leatherland ...	Jes.	M 1905
—	Vernon Seymour ...	Down.	M 1897 A.B. 1900. A.M. 1910
Bryce,	Dav. Lawrence	Em.	M 1899 A.B. 1902. A.M. 1909
—	Will. Theodore Percival	Trin.	M 1910
Brydon,	Ja. Herb.	Pem.	M 1900 A.B. 1903
Brydone,	Ja. Marr	Jes.	M 1893 M.B., B.C. 1902
Bryers,	John Shaw	Joh.	M 1894 A.B. 1897. A.M.† 1906
Buchanan,	Alan	Down.	M 1910
—	Art. Noel	Trin.	M 1903
—	Douglas Mudie	Trin.	M 1898 A.B. 1901. A.M.† 1905
—	Ebenezer John		*LL.D.* 1906
—	Fraser Campbell	Pem.	M 1912
—	Hugh	Trin. H.	M 1910
—	John Nevile	Trin.	M 1905 A.B., LL.B. 1908
Buchheister, Athos Jürgen		N. C.	M 1907
Buck,	Geo. Reg.	C. C.	M 1909 A.B. 1912
—	Rich. Vivian Stukely	Pem.	M 1911
Buckell,	Edw. Ronald	Cai.	M 1908 A.B. 1911
Buckingham, Stanley Heard		N. C.	M 1908
Buckland,	Tho. Adrian	Trin.	M 1911
Buckle,	Cuthbert Lyons	King's	M 1904 A.B. 1907
—	Geo. Walt.	Trin.	M 1904 A.B. 1907
—	Will. Fre.	Cai.	M 1894 A.B. 1898. M.B., B.C. 1903. A.M.,
Buckler,	Fra. Will.	Trin. H.	M 1910 [M.D. 1909
Buckley,	Alb. St David	N. C.	M 1910
—	Bryan Burton	King's	M 1909 A.B. 1912
—	Donald Finnimore ...	Chr.	M 1906 A.B. 1909
—	Edw.	Cath.	M 1905 A.B. 1908
—	Horace Hen. Clem.	Mag.	M 1907 A.B. 1912 [M.D. 1912
—	John Phil.	Trin.	M 1901 A.B. 1904. A.M. 1908. B.C.† 1909.
—	Rich.	Em.	M 1898 A.B. 1901. LL.B. 1902. A.M. 1905
Bucknell,	Will. Hen.	Chr.	M 1911
Buckney,	Frank	Sid.	M 1902 A.B. 1905
Bucknill,	John Cha.	Em.	M 1898 A.B. 1901
Buckston,	Geo. Moreton	Trin.	M 1900 A.B. 1903
Budd,	Walt.	Trin. H.	M 1909 A.B. 1912
Buddell,	Ja. Leon.	N. C.	M 1905 A.B. 1908
Buddin,	Walt.	Sid.	M 1909 A.B. 1912
Budenberg,	Christian Fre.	Trin.	M 1912
Budge,	Hen. Lionel Beaufort	Pem.	M 1899 A.B. 1902

Budgett,	Hub. Maitland	Trin.	M 1900 A.B. 1903
—	John Sam.	Trin.	M 1894 A.B. 1898. A.M. 1901
Budibent,	Geo. Bryan	Cath.	M 1896 A.B. 1899. A.M. 1908
Bugeja,	Vincent	Sid.	M 1911
Buissinné,	Templer	Pem.	M 1898 A.B. 1902. A.M.† 1905
Bulcraig,	Herb. Hen.	Cai.	M 1899 A.B., LL.B. 1902
Bull,	Archib. Will. Major ..	Trin. H.	M 1907
—	Cha. Ravenscroft ...	Cath.	M 1897 A.B. 1900. A.M. 1907
—	Douglas Will. Anderson	Cai.	M 1898 A.B. 1901. M.B., B.C. 1908
—	Edw. Leon.	H. Sel.	M 1884 A.B. 1887. A.M. 1906
—	Geo. Vernon	Cai.	M 1890 A.B. 1893. M.B., B.C. 1901
—	Godfrey John Oswald	Mag.	M 1908 A.B. 1911
—	Harold Rob.	Qu.	M 1907 A.B. 1910
—	Hen. Cecil Herb. ...	Cai.	M 1909 A.B. 1912
—	Hen. Martin	Cath.	M 1896 A.B. 1899. A.M. 1903
—·	Hugh Farquharson	Jes.	M 1911
—	Ja. Chris.	Cath.	M 1900 A.B. 1903
—	Oswin Boys	Jes.	M 1901 A.B. 1904
—	Reg. Cha. Theodore	C. C.	M 1908
—	Will. Edw. Hugh ...	Cai.	M 1908 A.B. 1911
Bullard,	Reader Will.	Qu.	E 1906
Bulleid,	Cha. Hen.	Trin.	M 1901 A.B. 1904. A.M. 1908
Bullen,	Fre. John	Joh.	M 1911
—	Hor. Braithwaite ...	Cla.	M 1910
—	Roy Evans	Jes.	M 1911
Bullen-Smith,	Cecil Ja.	Trin.	M 1899 A.B. 1902
Buller,	Mowbray Louis	Trin.	M 1912
Bulley,	Felix Marshall	Em.	M 1896 A.B. 1899. A.M. 1903. M.B., B.C.
Bullivant,	Ritchie Pelham	Trin.	M 1902 A.B. 1906. A.M. 1909 [1907
—	Trevor	Trin. H.	M 1909
Bulloch,	Ja. Howell	Trin.	M 1894 A.B. 1897. J. Howel A.M. 1902
Bullock,	Chris. Llewellyn	Trin.	M 1910
—	Fra. Geo.	N. C.	M 1896 A.B. 1900. A.M. 1905
—	Geo. Godfrey Ashwin	Pem.	M 1896 A.B. 1899. A.M. 1904
—	Harold Malcolm	Trin.	M 1909 A.B. 1912
—	John Cecil	Cai.	M 1911
—	Reg. Wilton	Pem.	M 1894 A.B. 1897. A.M. 1901
Bullough,	Edw.	Trin.	M 1899 A.B. 1902. A.M. 1906. *Cai.
—	Harold	Sid.	M 1897 A.B. 1900. A.M. 1904
—	John Leodius	Jes.	M 1912
Bulmer,	Alan Campbell	Jes.	M 1909
—	Dav. Geo.	Cai.	M 1905 A.B. 1908
—	Phil. Hen.	Cath.	M 1908 A.B. 1911 [1904. M.D. 1910
Bulstrode,	Chris. Victor	Trin.	M 1894 A.B. 1897. B.C., A.M. 1902. M.B.
—	Roger	Pem.	M 1897 A.B. 1900. A.M. 1904
Bulteel,	John Phil. Ern.	King's	M 1895 A.B. 1898. A.M. 1902
Bunbury,	Cha. Hen. Napier ...	Trin.	M 1905
—	Hen. Will.	Trin. H.	M 1907
—	Percy St Pierre	Cath.	M 1899 A.B. 1903. A.M. 1906
—	Walt. Shirley Gibson	Cath.	M 1901 A.B. 1904
Buncombe,	Gerald Fra.	H. Sel.	M 1905
Bunn,	Cha. Grinling	Em.	M 1903 A.B. 1907
—	Frederic Art.	H. Sel.	M 1910
Bunny,	Hen. Southcomb	C. C.	M 1903 A.B. 1906. A.M. 1910
—	Jos.	Em.	M 1904
Bunt,	Art. Percival	Joh.	M 1910
Bunting,	Sheldon Art. Steward	Chr.	M 1901 A.B. 1904
—	Will. Louis	Trin. H.	M 1893 A.B. 1896. A.M. 1901
Burbery,	Rob. Jackson Peyton	Chr.	M 1901 A.B. 1906
Burbidge,	Fra. Will.	Chr.	M 1892 A.B. 1895. A.M. 1902
—	Tho. Harold	Em.	M 1893 A.B. 1896. A.M. 1906

Burch,	Fre. Leopold	Cath.	M 1898 A.B. 1901
—	Raymond Sanderson	Em.	M 1911
Burchard,	Christian Conrad ...	N. C.	E 1906
—	Johann Heinrich ...	N. C.	M 1902
Burchell,	Frank Bruce	N. C.	M 1902 King's. A.B., LL.B. 1905
—	Ja. Melvill	Trin.	M 1904 A.B. 1908
Burden,	Harry Archib.	Trin.	M 1902 A.B. 1905
Burder,	Gordon Eustace Lennox	Trin.	M 1904 A.B. 1907
Burdett,	Osbert Hen.	King's	M 1903 A.B. 1907
—	Tho. Frederic	Pem.	M 1902 A.B. 1905. A.M. 1909
Burdon,	Edw. Russell	Sid.	M 1899 A.B. 1902. A.M. 1906
—	John Alder	C. C.	M 1885 A.B. 1888. Chr. A.M. 1901
—	Will. Wharton	Trin. H.	M 1909
Burfield,	Stanley Tho.	H. Sel.	M 1908 A.B. 1911
Burgess,	Alec Rigby	Trin.	M 1900 A.B. 1903. A.M. 1907
—	Art. Savell	Cai.	M 1898 A.B. 1901. A.M. 1907. M.B., B.C.
—	Fred	Cath.	M 1905 A.B. 1908 [1909
—	Hen. Norman	Joh.	M 1896 A.B. 1899. A.M. 1907
—	Oliver Ireland	Trin.	M 1912
—	Leslie Ern.	Chr.	M 1905 A.B. 1908
—	Rob.	Cai.	M 1899 A.B. 1902. B.C. 1908. M.B. 1910
—	Wilfrid Cha.	Down.	M 1909 A.B. 1912
Burgoyne,	Lennox Stuart	Trin.	L 1910
Burgoyne Johnson, Fra. Wise		Cai.	M 1911
—	Luther Vincent	King's	M 1909 A.B. 1912
Burgum,	Geo. Alb.	Qu.	M 1907 A.B. 1910
Burke,	Harold French	King's	M 1902 A.B. 1905
—	John Benj. Butler ...	Trin.	M 1898 (a. s.) A.B. 1900. A.M. 1906
—	Michael Lawrence ...	King's	M 1907 A.B. 1910
—	Rudolph Edm. Maur.	Trin. H.	M 1910
Burkitt,	[1]Fra. Crawford	Trin.	M 1883 A.B. 1886. A.M. 1890
—	Fre. Tho.	Chr.	M 1911
—	Miles Crawford	Trin.	M 1909 A.B. 1912
Burleigh, Leon. Tekenika Will. Gilb.		Qu.	M 1910
Burlend,	Edw. Ern.	Chr.	M 1902 A.B. 1905. A.M. 1909
—	Tho. Harold	Chr.	M 1901 A.B. 1904. A.M. 1908
Burles,	Art. Claude Perrin	H. Sel.	M 1906 A.B. 1909
Burling,	Edw. Ja. Poynter ...	Joh.	M 1912
Burlingham, Ralph Ellis	....	Cai.	M 1895 A.B. 1898. A.M. 1902
Burlton,	Rich. Ferrer	C. C.	M 1908
Burn,	And. Ewbank	Trin.	M 1882 A.B. 1885. A.M. 1889. B.D. 1898.
—	Cuthbert John	Cai.	M 1912 [D.D. 1904
—	Fra. Will.	Trin.	M 1905
—	Herb. Southerden ...	Pem.	M 1902 A.B. 1905
—	John Southerden ...	Trin.	M 1903 A.B. 1906. M.B., B.C. 1912
—	Joshua Harold	Em.	M 1909 A.B. 1912
—	Percy Edgar	H. Sel.	M 1901 A.B. 1904
—	Rob. Christie	N. C.	M 1899 Trin. H. A.B. 1902. A.M. 1906
Burnaby,	Hen. Beaumont Fowke	Trin.	M 1893 A.B. 1899. A.M. 1904
—	Hugh	Jes.	M 1909 A.B. 1912
—	John	Trin.	M 1910
Burnand,	Cyril Fra.	Trin.	M 1909 A.B. 1912
—	Geoffrey Chasemore	Cla.	M 1901 A.B. 1904
Burn Callander, Fra.	....	Cla.	M 1907
Burne,	Benj.	Cai.	M 1898 A.B. 1901. A.M. 1911
—	Sambrooke Art. Higgins	Pet.	M 1898 A.B. 1901. A.M. 1905
Burnell,	Ern. Will.	Cai.	M 1898 A.B. 1901
Burness,	John Alf.	Qu.	M 1910
Burnet,	John Rudolph Wardlaw	Cai.	M 1905 A.B. 1908

[1] Norrisian Professor of Divinity, 1905.

Burnett,	John Edw. Parry ...	H. Sel.	M 1907 A.B. 1910
Burn-Murdoch, Alex.		Trin.	M 1905 A.B., LL.B. 1908
Burn Murdoch, Hector		Trin.	M 1899 A.B. 1902. LL.B. 1903
Burns,	Cecil Delisle	N. C.	M 1897 A.B. 1900. A.M. 1906
—	Emile Bern. Vivian	Trin.	M 1909 A.B. 1912
—	Ja. Thompson	H. Sel.	M 1892 A.B. 1896. A.M. 1901
Burnside,	Bruce	Cla.	E 1909 A.B. 1912
—	John Harold	Pet.	M 1894 A.B. 1897. A.M. 1902
—	Walt. Fletcher	Pem.	M 1892 A.B. 1895. A.M. 1902
Burnup,	Herb. Watson	Cla.	M 1895 A.B. 1898. A.M. 1906
Burr,	Alb. Lionel	King's	M 1909 A.B. 1912
—	Fre. Godfrey	Joh.	M 1908 A.B. 1911
—	Herb. Frank	Cath.	M 1904 A.B. 1907
Burrell,	Ellis Morgan	Cla.	M 1911
—	John Hugh	Joh.	M 1912
—	Lancelot Steph. Topham	Trin.	M 1901 A.B. 1904. A.M. 1908. M.B., B.C.
—	Raymond Fra. Topham	Trin.	M 1908 [1910
—	Rob. Eric	Trin. H.	M 1908 A.B., LL.B. 1911
Burrill,	Will. Robinson	Cla.	M 1903 A.B. 1906
Burroughes,	Hen. Neville	Trin.	M 1896 A.B. 1899. M.B., B.C., A.M. 1906
Burrow,	Sid. Geo.	Pet.	M 1904
—	Will. Ja. Atkinson ...	Chr.	M 1902 A.B. 1906
Burrowes,	Rob. Vivian	H. Sel.	M 1912
Burrows,	Arnold Hayes	Sid.	M 1903 A.B. 1906
—	Cresswell	N. C.	M 1893 Em. A.B. 1896. M.B., B.C. 1904.
—	Harold Alban	Cath.	M 1907 A.B. 1910 [A.M. 1909. M.D. 1911
—	Roland	Trin. H.	M 1903 A.B. 1906. A.M. 1910
—	Sterndale	N. C.	E 1893 Trin. H. A.B. 1896. A.M. 1901
Burt-Marshall, Ja.		Cla.	M 1905
Burton,	Alf. Hen. Wellesley	Pem.	M 1911
—	Art. Fre.	Chr.	M 1899 A.B. 1902
—	Art. Pelham	Qu.	M 1909 A.B. 1912
—	Bede Carlisle	H. Sel.	M 1910
—	Bunnell Lewis Earnshaw	Trin.	M 1909 A.B. 1912
—	Cha. Kingsley	C. C.	M 1910
—	Dav. Cecil Fowler ...	Jes.	M 1906
—	Donald Fraser	Em. .	M 1906 A.B. 1910
—	Eli Franklin	Em.	M 1904 A.B. 1906
—	Geoffrey Duke	Qu.	M 1912
—	Gordon Ern.	Cla.	M 1911
—	Harold Gustavus ...	Trin.	M 1875 A.B. 1879. A.M. 1904
—	Harold John Chandos	Mag.	M 1897 A.B. 1900. A.M. 1904
—	Humphrey Phillipps Walcot	Joh.	M 1907 A.B. 1910
—	John Ashton	Qu.	M 1909 A.B. 1912
—	Maur. Geo. Walt. ...	Trin.	M 1912
—	Rob. Will. Westbrooke	Trin. H.	M 1902
—	Will.	Chr.	M 1903 A.B. 1906
—	Will.	Em.	M 1904 A.B. 1906. A.M. 1910
Burwell,	Rob. Parmenter	Sid.	M 1910
—	Will. Keith	Cai.	M 1901 A.B. 1904
Bury,	And.	Em.	M 1909 A.B. 1912
—	Edmond Will.	Trin. H.	L 1904
—	Edw. Basil	King's	M 1909
—	Ern.	Trin.	M 1903
—	[1]John Bagnell ....*King's		A.M. 1903
—	Lindsay Edw.	Trin.	M 1901 A.B. 1904
—	Phil. Entwisle	Cla.	M 1903
—	Rob. Gregg	Trin.	M 1886 A.B.1889. A.M. 1893. Litt.D. 1910
Bush,	Fra. Rob.	Cai.	M 1895 A.B. 1899. A.M. 1903

---

[1] Regius Professor of Modern History, 1902.

Bush,	Gilb. Bremridge	Pem.	M 1911
—	Rich. Eldon	Joh.	M 1909
—	Whittington Bremridge	Pem.	M 1908 A.B. 1911
Bushe-Fox,	Loftus Hen. Kendal	*Joh.	M 1882 A.B. 1885. LL.B. 1886. A.M. 1889.
Bushell,	Herb. Donald	Joh.	M 1912 [LL.M. 1912
—	Warin Foster	King's	M 1903 A.B. 1906. A.M. 1912
Busk,	Edm. Westly	Trin. H.	M 1911
—	Edw. Teshmaker	King's	M 1904 A.B. 1907
—	Hans Acworth	King's	M 1912
—	Hen. Gould	King's	M 1909 A.B. 1912
Buss,	Harold Alf. Woodward	Em.	M 1899 A.B. 1902
—	Leslie Caron	Pem.	M 1908 A.B. 1911
Buswell,	Hen. Leslie Farmer	Cai.	M 1905 A.B. 1908
Buszard,	Stanley Geo.	Chr.	M 1908
Butcher,	Art. Douglas Deane	Chr.	M 1903 A.B. 1906
—	[1] Sam. Hen.	*Trin.	M 1869 A.B. 1873. A.M. 1876. *Litt.D.* 1907
—	Trevor Aveling	Qu.	M 1912
—	Will. Guy Deane ...	Trin.	M 1910
Butler,	Alf. Ja. Agard	Trin.	M 1894 A.B. 1898. A.M. 1902
—	Algernon Salisbury ...	Trin.	M 1900 A.B. 1903.
—	Archib. John Salisbury	Pem.	M 1906 A.B. 1909
—	Art. Fra.	Pem.	M 1894 A.B. 1897. A.M. 1905
—	Edm. Pierce	Pem.	M 1905 A.B. 1908
—	Edw. Cuthbert	Chr.	M 1896 A.B. 1898. A.M. 1903
—	Edw. Haskell	H. Sel.	M 1911
—	Eustace Norman	Cla.	M 1907 A.B. 1910
—	Frank Gregory	Pet.	M 1906 A.B. 1909
—	Geo. Geoffrey Gilb.	Trin.	M 1906 A.B. 1909, *C. C.
—	Geo. Guy	Em.	M 1899 A.B. 1902. M.B., B.C. 1911
—	Geo. Herb. Cuming	Trin.	M 1893 A.B. 1896. A.M. 1902
—	Gordon Kerr Montagu	Trin.	M 1910
—	Hedley Ormonde	Em.	M 1894 A.B. 1897. M.B., B.C. 1902
—	Herb. Paul	Jes.	M 1903 A.B. 1906. A.M. 1911
—	Hilton Cawood	Trin.	M 1910
—	Hugh Montagu	Mag.	M 1908 A.B. 1911
—	Ja. Ramsay Montagu	Trin.	M 1907 A.B. 1910
—	Julian Ja.	Jes.	M 1912
—	Nevile Montagu	Trin.	M 1912
—	Nich. Murray		*LL.D.* 1907
—	Ralph Lewis Giberne	Trin.	M 1902 A.B. 1905. A.M. 1909
—	Reg. Cha. Salisbury	King's	M 1907 A.B. 1910
—	Tho. Dacres	Trin. H.	M 1902 A.B. 1905
—	Walt. Gasking	Qu.	M 1905 A.B. 1908
—	Will. Martin	Trin.	M 1901 A.B. 1904
Butlin,	Hen. Guy Trentham	Trin.	M 1911
—	Tho. Herb.	Em.	M 1909 A.B. 1912
Bütschli,	Otto		*Sc.D.* 1909
Butt,	Geo. Holden	Jes.	M 1851 A.B. 1855. A.M. 1901
—	Geo. Malleson	Trin.	M 1898 A.B. 1901
—	Harold Tho. Hayward	Chr.	M 1902 A.B. 1905
—	John Eede	Trin.	M 1902
—	Sam	Joh.	M 1907
Buttanshaw,	Cyril	Cla.	M 1910
Buttemer,	Rob. Will.	Em.	M 1890 A.B. 1893. A.M. 1902
Butterwick,	Ja. Cyril	Chr.	M 1909 A.B. 1912
Butterworth,	Art. Bern.	Pet.	M 1906 A.B. 1909
—	Rupert	Chr.	M 1889 A.B. 1892. B.C. 1903. M.B. 1904
—	Walt.	C. C.	M 1909 A.B. 1912
Buttery,	Harold Rob.	Chr.	M 1906 A.B. 1909

[1] Representative in Parliament, 1906.

Buttle,	Will. Fra.	Down.	E 1911
Button,	Arnold Elliot	Joh.	M 1908 A.B. 1911
Bux,	Hafiz Mohamed	Down.	M 1908
Buxton,	Alf. Barclay	Trin.	M 1909 A.B. 1912
—	And. Rich.	Trin.	M 1898 A.B. 1901
—	Anth.	Trin.	M 1901 A.B. 1904
—	Art.	Trin.	M 1901 A.B. 1904. A.M. 1909
—	Cha. Roden	Trin.	M 1894 A.B. 1898. A.M. 1901
—	Clarence Edw. Victor	Trin.	M 1911
—	Edw. North	Trin.	M 1912
—	Guy	Trin.	M 1906
—	Harold Jocelyn	Trin.	M 1898 A.B. 1901. A.M. 1905
—	Ivor	Trin.	M 1903 A.B. 1907
—	Leland Will. Wilberforce	Trin.	M 1902 A.B. 1905. A.M.† 1911
—	Murray Barclay	Trin.	M 1908 A.B. 1911
—	Pat. Alf.	Trin.	M 1911
—	Rich. Gurney	Trin.	M 1905
—	Tho. Fowell	Trin.	M 1908 A.B. 1911
Byatt,	Harry Vivian Byatt	Cla.	M 1901 A.B. 1904
—	Rich. Noël Byatt ...	Cla.	M 1907 A.B. 1910
Byers,	John	Pem.	M 1899 A.B., LL.B. 1902
Bygrave,	Will.	Chr.	M 1901 A.B. 1904. A.M.† 1911
Byng,	Ern. Gustav	Pem.	M 1905
Byrde,	Evelyn Hook	Down.	M 1903 A.B. 1906
Byrne,	John Hen.	N. C.	M 1912
—	Martin Geo. McLeavy Cahill	Cla.	M 1912
Byrne-Johnson,	John Vivian	Cla.	M 1912
Byron-Scott,	Wallace	Joh.	M 1904 A.B. 1908. A.M. 1911
Bythway,	Montague Hayes	King's	M 1899 A.B. 1902
Bywaters,	Fre. Ja.	N. C.	M 1911

C

Cable,	John Alex.	Trin.	M 1899 A.B. 1902. LL.B. 1903
Cadbury,	Egbert	Trin.	M 1912
—	Geo. Norman	Trin.	M 1909
—	Hen. Tylor	Cla.	M 1901 A.B. 1904. A.M. 1908
—	Laurence John	Trin.	M 1907 A.B. 1910
Caddick,	Syd. Dav.	Joh.	M 1900 A.B. 1903. Sid. A.M. 1908
Cader,	Mohamad Bacha Abdul	Down.	M 1909 A.B., LL.B. 1912
Cadman,	Cuthbert Will. Montagu	Trin.	M 1907 A.B. 1910
—	Hal	King's	M 1904 A.B. 1907
—	Hub. Smelter	Chr.	M 1896 A.B. 1899. A.M. 1905
Cæsar,	Harold Douglass	Em.	M 1907 A.B. 1910
Cahn,	Heinz	Trin. H.	M 1911
Cahusac,	Stuart Douglas Nugent	Trin. H.	M 1905 A.B. 1910
Caiger,	Steph. Langrishe ...	Chr.	M 1905 S. Langrish, A.B. 1908
Cain,	Ern.	Trin. H.	M 1911
—	Will. Nicholas	Jes.	M 1903
Caine,	Rich. Claude	Cath.	M 1910
—	Tho.	Pem.	M 1895 A.B. 1898. A.M. 1903
Calderbank,	John	H. Sel.	M 1910
Calderwood,	John Lindow	Cai.	M 1906 A.B., LL.B. 1909
Caldwell,	Herb. Fre. Hay	Trin.	M 1900 A.B. 1903. A.M. 1907

Caldwell, Keith Farquhar Townley Trin. H. M 1906 A.B. 1909
— [1] Rob. Townley .... *C. C. M 1861 A.B. 1865. A.M. 1868. LL.M. 1875.
Caldwell Smith, Eric Lauder ...... Trin. M 1910 [LL.D. 1911
Caledon, (*Earl of*) Eric Ja. } Trin. M 1905
  Desmond Alex. }
Caley, Fre. Goodman .... Pem. M 1902 A.B. 1905. M.B., B.C., A.M. 1911
— Hugh Will. .... Pem. M 1904 A.B. 1908
Calkin, John Bern. .... Jes. M 1911
Callaghan, Kenneth Ford ...... Cai. M 1908 A.B. 1911. LL.B. 1912
Callender, Reg. .... Chr. M 1887 A.B. 1890. A.M. 1903
— Reg. Hen. .... N. C. M 1911
Calligas, Paul Pet. .... Trin. M 1902 A.B. 1905
Callinan, Tho. Will. .... Qu. M 1902 A.B. 1905
Callingham, Laurence Fre. .... Trin. M 1906 A.B., LL.B. 1909
Callis, Montagu Clare ...... Pet. M 1912
Calvert, Edw. .... Joh. L 1907 A.B. 1909
— Herb. Edw. .... H. Sel. M 1896 A.B. 1899. A.M. 1903
— Lawrence Morrice ... Pem. M 1912
— Will. John Rawson .. Trin. M 1904 A.B. 1907. A.M. 1912
Calvert-Jones, Hugh Fra. .... Jes. M 1912
Cam, Walt. Holcroft ...... Cai. M 1902 A.B. 1906. M.B., B.C. 1912
Cama, Byramji Navroji ...... Joh. M 1898 A.B. 1901
— Camajee Navrojee ... Joh. M 1898 A.B. 1901. C. Byramjee N. LL.B.
Cambon, Pierre Paul .... *LL.D.* 1906 [1903
Camenisch, Frank .... King's M 1900 A.B. 1903
Cameron, Cha. Lovett .... Trin. M 1903 A.B. 1906
— Colin .... H. Sel. M 1906 A.B. 1910
— Dav. Wilkie .... Cai. M 1912 [1907. M.D. 1910
— Hector Cha. .... Joh. M 1898 A.B. 1901. B.C., A.M. 1906. M.B.
— Ian Grant .... H. Sel. M 1898 A.B. 1901. A.M. 1908
— John .... Trin. M 1901 A.B. 1904
— John Forbes ....*Cai. M 1895 A.B. 1898. A.M. 1902
— Sid. .... Joh. E 1899 A.B. 1902
Cammell, Cha. Rich. .... Trin. H. M 1909
Campbell, Allan .... Trin. M 1898 A.B. 1902. A.M. 1905
— Archib. Douglas Pitcairn Trin. M 1899 A.B. 1902
— Archib. Ean .... Cla. M 1876 A.B. 1880. A.M. 1883. D.D. 1904
— Archib. Young ......*Joh. M 1904 A.B. 1907. A.M. 1911
— Basil Pat. .... Cla. M 1900 A.B. 1903. B.C. 1908. M.B. 1909
— Bruce Atta .... Trin. H. L 1908
— Colin Guy Hirst ...... Joh. M 1905 A.B. 1908
— Donald Neil .... Trin. H. M 1904 A.B. 1907
— Donald Swinton ...... Trin. M 1910
— Edw. Maitland ...... Trin. M 1909 A.B. 1912
— Evan Roland ...... Trin. M 1906 A.B. 1909
— Fre. Rob. Maxwell ... Jes. M 1902
— Geo. Augustus ...... Trin. M 1892 A.B. 1895. A.M. 1902
— Gerald .... Trin. M 1898 A.B. 1901
— Hen. .... Trin. M 1854 A.B. 1858. A.M. 1861. post Camp-
  [bell Bannerman. *LL.D.* 1907
— Ian Malcolm .... Trin. M 1902 A.B. 1906
— John Douglas Sutherland *See* Lorne (*Marquis of*)
— John Graham .... Trin. M 1906
— Keir Art. .... Trin. M 1911 [Campbell-Douglas, L.C.H.D.
— Leopold Colin Hen. Douglas Trin. M 1899 A.B. 1903. A.M. 1906. post
— Norman Rob. ....*Trin. M 1899 A.B. 1902. A.M. 1906. Sc.D. 1912
— Rob. Cha. Cowburn . King's M 1907 A.B. 1910
— Roderick Hugh ...... Trin. M 1899 A.B. 1902
— Ronald Walker Fra. . Pem. M 1906 A.B. 1909. LL.B. 1910

[1] Master of Corpus Christi College, 1906.

Campbell,	Sid. Geo. ....*Chr.	M 1898 A.B. 1901. A.M. 1905	
—	Will. Gordon .... Trin.	M 1910	
—	Will. Hastings ...... Cai.	M 1905 A.B. 1908	
Campbell-Bannerman, Hen.		*See* Campbell, H.	
Campbell-Douglas		*See* Campbell, L. C. H. D.	
Campbell-Johnstone, John Augustus Jes.		M 1906	
Campbell Jones, Owen .... King's		M 1912	
Campling,	Will. Cha. .... Trin.	M 1909 A.B. 1912	
Candeth,	Madhavan Arathil ... King's	M 1907 A.B. 1910. LL.B. 1911	
Candler,	John Pycock .... C. C.	M 1892 A.B. 1895. M.B., B.C., A.M. 1901.	
Candy,	Edw. Townshend ... Cai.	*A.M.* 1906. A.M. 1908 [M.D. 1908	
—	Kenneth Edgerley ... Cai.	M 1910	
Cane,	Art. Skelding .... King's	M 1903 A.B. 1906. A.M. 1911	
—	Edw. Geoffrey Stayner Jes.	M 1904 A.B. 1907	
—	Howard Ja. Barrell Cai.	M 1901 A.B. 1904	
—	Leon. Buckell .... King's	M 1900 A.B. 1903. M.B., B.C. 1908. M.D.	
—	Leon. Dobbie .... Sid.	M 1901 A.B. 1904. A.M. 1909 [1911	
—	Maur. Hereward ...... King's	M 1906 A.B. 1909	
Canham,	Edwin Dillon Frank Joh.	M 1900 A.B. 1905	
Cann,	Basil Claude .... Cath.	M 1909	
Cannan,	Gilb. Eric .... King's	M 1902 A.B. 1905	
Canney,	Ja. Robertson Campbell Chr.	M 1901 A.B. 1905. M.B., B.C. 1909. A.M.	
Cannington,	Art. Shelmerdine ... Cai.	M 1905 [1911	
Cannon,	Geo. Harry Franklyn Down.	M 1909	
Canny,	Gerald Bain .... Qu.	M 1900 A.B. 1903	
Cant,	Fre. Vaudrey .... Cai.	M 1909 A.B. 1912	
Cantagalli,	Laurence Rob. ...... Trin.	M 1902 A.B. 1907	
Canti,	Ronald Geo. .... King's	M 1902 A.B. 1905	
Cantrell-Hubbersty, Geo. Alb. ⎱ Jessop ⎰	Trin.	M 1900 A.B. 1903	
Caporn,	Art. Cecil .... Trin. H.	M 1903 A.B., LL.B. 1906	
Cappel,	Norman Louis ...... Trin.	M 1904 A.B. 1907. A.M. 1911	
Capper,	Tho. .... Trin.	M 1875 A.B. 1879. A.M. 1910	
Capron,	John Wynyard ...... King's	M 1902 A.B. 1905. A.M. 1910	
—	Maur. Athol .... King's	M 1909 A.B. 1912	
—	Norman Hugh ...... Pem.	M 1903 A.B. 1906. A.M. 1910	
Carbery,	(*Lord*) John Evans-Freke Trin.	M 1910	
Card,	Fre. Will. Farmer ... Jes.	M 1909	
Cardall,	Hugh Hamilton ...... Trin.	M 1903 A.B. 1906	
Cardew,	Hen. Jameson .... Cla.	M 1892 A.B. 1898. A.M. 1905. B.C. 1908.	
Cardwell,	Alf. Geo. .... Joh.	M 1908 A.B. 1912 [M.B. 1908 (2)	
—	Cyril Rowland ...... Cai.	M 1907 A.B. 1910	
—	Howard Elliott ...... Chr.	M 1898 A.B. 1901	
—	Will. .... Cai.	M 1901 A.B. 1906. A.M. 1909	
Care,	Hen. Clifford .... Joh.	M 1911	
Carew,	Pet. Gawen .... Trin.	M 1912	
Carey,	Conrad de Lisle ...... Em.	M 1894 A.B. 1897. B.C. 1902. M.B. 1903	
—	Dav. Sausmarez ...... Mag.	M 1900 A.B. 1903. A.M. 1907	
—	Douglas Falkland ... Trin. H.	M 1895 A.B. 1898. A.M. 1902	
—	Fra. Clive Savill ... Cla.	M 1901 A.B. 1904. Mus.B. 1906	
—	Gordon Vero .... Cai.	M 1906 A.B. 1909	
—	Rich. Stocker .... C. C.	M 1901 A.B. 1905	
Carkeek,	Bern. Morgan .... Sid.	M 1908 A.B. 1911	
Carlile,	Chris. .... Mag.	M 1897 A.B. 1902	
—	Edw. Hildred Hanbury Trin.	M 1899 A.B. 1904. A.M. 1907	
—	Reg. Clifford .... Pem.	M 1903 A.B. 1906	
Carlill,	Harold Flamank ...... Trin.	M 1894 A.B. 1897. A.M. 1901	
—	Hildred Bertram ...	*See* Carlyll	
Carlisle,	Fre. Montague Methven Pem.	M 1908 A.B. 1911	
—	Hen. Barry .... King's	M 1910	
—	John Cha. Denton ... Trin.	M 1906 A.B. 1909	

Carlton,	Sam. John		*See* Deutschberger
Carlton Williams, Erith Walt.	...	Chr.	M 1909 A.B. 1912
Carlyll,	Hildred Bertram	Joh.	M 1900 A.B. 1903. M.B., B.C., A.M. 1909.
Carlyon,	Ern. Tristrem Rupert	Pem.	M 1912 [post Carlill, H. B.
Carmichael,	Douglas	Jes.	M 1911
—	Douglas Will. Winn	Chr.	M 1898 A.B. 1901. A.M. 1905
—	Edw. Wilson	N. C.	M 1902 A.B. 1905
—	Hor. Montague	Pem.	M 1905
—	Pet. Maur. Stewart	Chr.	M 1901 A.B. 1904
Carnegie,	Cha. Edw.	N. C.	E 1881 H. Cav. A.B. 1884 (2). N.C., A.M.
Carnley,	Will. Birch	Qu.	M 1903 A.B. 1906 [1906
Carnoy,	Alb. Jos.	N. C.	L 1903
Caröe,	Will.	Trin.	M 1875 A.B. 1879. A.M. 1882. post W.
Carpenter,	Cha. Gordon	Joh.	M 1908 A.B. 1911 [Douglas
—	Edw. Harry Osmund	King's	M 1906 A.B. 1909
—	Fre. Will.	Cla.	M 1900 A.B. 1904. A.M. 1911
—	Geo. Ern.	N. C.	M 1898 A.B. 1901. A.M. 1905
—	Spencer Cecil	Cai.	M 1896 A.B. 1899. A.M. 1907
—	Will. Harold	Qu.	M 1901 A.B. 1904
Carpmael,	Will. Percy	Jes.	M 1883 A.B. 1886. A.M. 1903
Carr,	Alan Ingold	Cath.	M 1907 A.B. 1910
—	Anth. Laurence	Trin.	M 1911
—	Art. Perronet	Em.	M 1892 A.B. 1895. A.M. 1907
—	Basil Alderson	H. Sel.	M 1898 A.B. 1901. A.M. 1910 [LL.M.1907
—	Cecil Tho.	Trin.	M 1897 A.B. 1900. LL.B. 1901. A.M. 1904.
—	Donald Will.	Trin.	M 1886 A.B. 1889. M.B., B.C. 1893. M.D.
—	Edw. Hallett	Trin.	M 1911 [1907
—	Frank	Trin. H.	M 1890 A.B., LL.B. 1893. LL.M. 1899.
—	Frederic Geo. Procter	H. Sel.	M 1901 A.B.1904. A.M.1908 [LL.D. 1905
—	Geo. D'Rastricke ...	Cai.	M 1908 A.B. 1911
—	Jos. Will.	H. Sel.	M 1906
—	Paton Richards	Pem.	M 1911
—	Will. Ja.	Trin.	M 1901 A.B. 1904
Carran,	Walt.	Em.	M 1900 A.B. 1903. A.M. 1909
Carr Forster,	Edw. Will.	Cla.	M 1912
Carrie,	Will. Harvie Bisset	Em.	M 1901 A.B. 1904. A.M. 1908
Carrington,	Cha. Walt.	N. C.	L 1886 A.B. 1888. A.M. 1903
—	Edm. Alf.	Chr.	M 1911
Carroll,	Fra. Radcliffe	Trin.	M 1894 A.B. 1897. M.B., B.C., A.M. 1904
—	Herb. Edw.	Trin.	M 1902 A.B. 1905
Carrow,	Rich. Boddam	King's	M 1911
Carruthers,	Geo. Simpson	H. Sel.	M 1898 A.B. 1901
—	Kenneth St Clare ...	N. C.	M 1908 Joh. A.B. 1911
—	Tho.	Cla.	M 1906
Carruthers-Johnstone,	Banner	Trin.	M 1902 A.B. 1907
Carsberg,	Alf. Ern.	Cai.	M 1891 A.B. 1894. M.B., B.C., A.M. 1899.
Carse,	Geo. Alex.	Em.	M 1904 [M.D. 1912
—	Ja. Will.	Em.	M 1903
Carslake,	Will. Bampfield	*Pem.	M 1912
Carslaw,	Horatio Scott ....*Em.		M 1891 A.B. 1894. A.M. 1898. Sc.D. 1908
Carson,	John Justin Godfrey	King's	M 1894 A.B. 1897. A.M. 1902
Carstairs,	Ja. Leslie	Chr.	M 1901 A.B. 1904
Carter,	Art. Burnell	Jes.	M 1890 A.B. 1893. M.B., B.C. 1910
—	Cha. Chris.	Joh.	M 1902 A.B. 1905
—	Cha. Noel	Trin.	M 1911
—	Edw. Hen.	Jes.	M 1897 A.B. 1901
—	Frank Lutton	Cai.	M 1894 A.B. 1897. A.M. 1902
—	Geo. Leslie Lewis ...	Chr.	M 1910
—	Geo. Stuart	Cai.	M 1912
—	Harold Gordon	Trin.	M 1901 A.B. 1904
—	Hen. Child	Chr.	M 1910 A.M. Oxf. Incorp. 1910

Carter,	Hen. Gordon	Mag.	M 1912	
—	Hen. Robison	Joh.	M 1911	
—	Humphrey Gilb.	N. C.	M 1910	
—	Ja. Shuckburgh	King's	M 1900 A.B. 1903	
—	Jesse	Cath.	M 1911	
—	John Fra.	Pem.	M 1896 A.B. 1899. A.M. 1906	
—	Ken Oliver	Cla.	M 1901 A.B. 1904. A.M. 1911	
—	Rich. Hen. Archib.	Trin.	M 1906 A.B. 1909	
—	Theodore Reg. Geo.	H. Sel.	M 1907 A.B. 1911	
—	Will. Edw.	Trin.	M 1904 A.B. 1907. A.M. 1912	
—	Will. Herb.	Joh.	M 1908 A.B. 1911	
—	Will. Jos.	N. C.	M 1891 A.B. 1894. A.M. 1903	
Carthigasen,	Sinnatamby Thambiah	Chr.	M 1906 A.B. 1909	
Cartwright,	Cha.	Cath.	M 1904	
—	Cha. Johnson	Pem.	M 1891 A.B. 1894. A.M. 1903	
—	Edm. Bruce Willoughby	Trin. H.	M 1890 A.B. 1893. A.M. 1901	
—	Edw.	Jes.	M 1904	
—	Fra. Geoffrey	H. Sel.	M 1900 A.B. 1903	
—	Geo. Fre.	Pem.	L 1895 A.B. 1897. A.M. 1901	
—	Walt. Perry	Qu.	M 1898 A.B. 1901	
—	Will.	Cla.	M 1899 A.B. 1902. A.M.† 1906	
Carus,	Edw. Hegeler	Trin.	M 1912	
Carus-Wilson,	Cecil Caradoc	Trin.	M 1911	
—	Eric	Trin.	M 1908 A.B. 1911	
Carver,	Alf. Edw. Art.	Cai.	M 1902 A.B. 1905. M.B., B.C., A.M. 1910	
—	Art. Edm.	Cla.	M 1891 A.B. 1894. M.B., B.C. 1901. M.D.	
—	Bern. Nash	H. Sel.	M 1908 A.B. 1911	[1904
—	Chris. Fitzjames	Qu.	M 1907 A.B. 1910	
—	Edm. Tucker	Pem.	M 1903 A.B. 1906	
—	Guy Armitage	Trin.	M 1906	
—	Hugh	Cla.	M 1902 A.B. 1905	
—	Lionel Hen. Liptrap	Jes.	M 1902 A.B. 1905	
—	Norman Clifton	King's	M 1895 A.B. 1898. B.C. 1904. M.B. 1906	
—	Oswald Armitage ...	Trin.	M 1905 A.B. 1908	
Case,	John	Mag.	M 1906 A.B. 1909	
Casey,	Hen. Ja.	Cla.	M 1903 A.B., LL.B. 1906	
—	Rich. Gardiner	Trin.	M 1910	
Cash,	Caleb Howard	Pet.	M 1912	
Caslaw,	John McConnell	Trin. H.	M 1911	
Casley,	Reg. de Chastelai ...	Sid.	M 1905 A.B. 1908. A.M. 1912	
Casper,	Art. Emil	Chr.	M 1900 A.B. 1903	
Cassan,	Art. Will. Marshall	N. C.	M 1903 A.B. 1906	
Cassels,	John Sam. de Oleveira	Joh.	M 1907	
Cassidi,	Fra. Laird	C. C.	M 1907 A.B. 1910	
Cassidy,	Colin	Sid.	M 1899 A.B. 1903. M.B., B.C., A.M. 1907	
—	Maur. Alan	Cla.	M 1898 A.B. 1901. M.B., B.C., A.M. 1906.	
				[M.D. 1909
Castellain,	Herménégilde Geo. Pourtalès	Trin.	M 1903 A.M. Oxf. Incorp. 1903, Her- [ménégild G. P. B.C. 1911	
—	John Graham	Trin.	M 1894 A.B. 1901	
Castello-Child,	Fre. Cha.	Jes.	M 1891 A.B. 1894. A.M. 1902	
Castle,	Graham Hunt	Joh.	M 1903 A.B. 1906. A.M. 1910	
—	Tudor Ralph	Trin.	M 1901 A.B. 1904	
Castleden,	Geo. Douglas	Pem.	M 1894 A.B. 1897. A.M. 1901	
Castlehow,	John Allan Scott ...	H. Sel.	M 1909 A.B. 1912	
Castlerosse,	(*Viscount*) Valentine Edw. Cha.	Trin.	M 1909	
Castley,	Cuthbert Cha.	Sid.	M 1897 A.B. 1900. A.M. 1908	
—	Reg. John	Sid.	M 1893 A.B. 1896. A.M. 1908	
Catford,	Rob. Coleridge	Pem.	M 1902	

Catling,	Harry Debron	N. C.	M 1888 Joh. A.B. 1892. A.M. 1904
Catmur,	Harry Alb. Fre. Valentine	Qu.	M 1911
Cator,	Geoffrey Edm.	H. Sel.	M 1903 A.B. 1906
Cattell,	McKeen	Chr.	M 1912
—	Tho. Edw.	Down.	M 1910
Catton,	Theodore	C. C.	M 1896 A.B. 1899. A.M. 1909
Catty,	Frank Bovill	Chr.	M 1911
Cautley,	Proby Fra. Lister ...	Trin.	M 1901 A.B. 1904. A.M. 1909
Cavalier,	Fra. Bern.	Joh.	M 1909
—	Harold Omer	Trin.	M 1900 A.B. 1903
Cave,	Edm. Howard	Cla.	M 1906 A.B. 1909
—	Harvard Wells	Cai.	M 1910
—	Hen. Cha. Fra.	Chr.	M 1912
—	Tho. Storrar	C. C.	M 1910
—	Will. Tho. Cha.	Cai.	M 1901 A.B., LL.B. 1904
Cave-Moyles,	Geo. Edw. Phil.	Cai.	M 1894 A.B. 1898. A.M. 1903
Cavendish,	Victor Christian Will.	Trin.	M 1887 A.B. 1891. post Devonshire, *Duke*
Cavendish Butler,	Hen. Halpin ...	Pem.	M 1903 A.B. 1906 [*of. LL.D.* 1911
Cawston,	Edw. Percy	Pem.	M 1901 A.B., LL.B. 1904
—	Fre. Gordon	Cai.	M 1903 A.B. 1906. M.B., B.C. 1910
Cawthra,	John Jos.	Cla.	M 1897 A.B. 1901. A.M. 1905
Cay,	Alb. Jaffray	Trin.	M 1898 A.B. 1902
Cazalet,	Guy Langston	Jes.	M 1909 A.B. 1912
—	Rob. Geo.	Cla.	M 1909 A.B. 1912
Cecil,	Fre. Rotheram	Down.	M 1912
Chadha,	Tirjogi Narayan	Down.	M 1906 A.B. 1911
Chadwick,	Brian Lloyd	Joh.	M 1910
—	Cha. Egerton	C. C.	M 1905 A.B. 1909
—	Cha. Rob.	Pem.	M 1906 A.B. 1909
—	Dav. Tho.	Sid.	M 1895 A.B. 1898. A.M. 1911
—	Harold	Trin.	M 1910
—	Ja. Fra.	Trin.	M 1908 A.B. 1911
—	Ja. Hen.	Trin.	M 1907 A.B. 1910
—	John	Pem.	M 1897 A.B. 1900. LL.B. 1902. A.M. 1904
—	Morley	Joh.	M 1908 A.B. 1911 [LL.M. 1905
—	Rob. Agar	Joh.	M 1896 A.B. 1899. LL.B. 1900. A.M.,
—	Tho. Lionel	Mag.	M 1892 A.B. 1895. A.M. 1901
—	Will. Edw.	Jes.	M 1877 A.B. 1881. A.M. 1884. B.D. 1906.
Chaffer,	Clifford	Pet.	M 1903 A.B. 1906. A.M. 1910 [D.D. 1908
Chaffey,	Lionel Bethell Trenchard	Chr.	E 1894 A.B. 1897. A.M. 1905
Chafy,	Ralph Evelyn Westwood	Trin.	L 1907
Chakrabarti,	Praphulla Kumar ...	Chr.	M 1905 A.B. 1908
Chalk,	Hub. Gaster	Trin. H.	M 1905
—	Will. Ja.	Cai.	M 1895 A.B. 1903. A.M. 1906
Challands,	Rob. Syd.	Em.	M 1899 A.B. 1902. A.M. 1906
Challenor,	Will.	N. C.	E 1878 A.B. 1881. A.M. 1901
Challinor,	Will. Fra.	Trin.	M 1900 A.B. 1903. A.M. 1907
Challis,	John Fre.	Cath.	M 1908 A.B. 1911
Challoner,	Alan Crawhall	Cai.	M 1911
Chalmers,	Cha. Hugh Lindsay } Henderson }	Trin.	M 1901
—	Ian Pat. Honyman	Trin.	M 1906
—	Rob.	Pet.	M 1911
Chaloner,	Tho. Weston Peel Long	Trin.	M 1908
Chamberlain,	Durie Avery	Cai.	M 1898 A.B. 1901. A.M. 1912
—	Eric Dunstan	Trin.	M 1912
—	Hen. Maxwell	King's	M 1897 A.B. 1900. A.M. 1909
—	Percy Garratt	Cai.	M 1899 A.B. 1902. A.M. 1906
—	Tho. Art.	Cla.	M 1899 A.B. 1902
—	Walt. Basil	Trin.	M 1901 A.B. 1905
Chambers,	Art.	King's	M 1905 A.B. 1908

Chambers,	Bertram Fra.	Trin.	M 1905
—	Eric Holland	Trin. H.	M 1909
—	Ern. Leon.	Em.	M 1901 A.B. 1904
—	Frederic Walt.	Cla.	M 1900 A.B. 1906
Champion,	Art. Beresford	Jes.	M 1903 A.B. 1906. A.M. 1911
—	Art. Cecil	Qu.	M 1908 A.B. 1911
—	Cha. Coverley	Pem.	M 1906 A.B. 1909
—	Herb.	N. C.	M 1904 Down. A.B. 1907
—	Hub. Hayward	King's	M 1892 A.B. 1895. A.M. 1908
—	Raymond Everard ...	Jes.	M 1910
Champneys,	Mich. Weldon	Trin.	M 1903 A.B. 1906. A.M. 1910
Chan,	Sze Jin	Down.	M 1904 A.B., LL.B. 1907
—	Sze Pong	Cai.	M 1901 A.B. 1906. B.C. 1907. M.B. 1908
Chance,	Clinton Fre.	Trin.	M 1901 A.B. 1904. A.M. 1909
—	Edgar Percival	Trin.	M 1901 A.B. 1904. A.M. 1908
—	Geoffrey Rob. Lucas	Trin.	M 1904 A.B. 1907. A.M. 1911
—	Kenneth Macomb ...	Trin.	M 1898 A.B. 1901. A.M. 1905
—	Rob. Chris.	Trin.	M 1901 A.B. 1904
—	Roger Ja. Ferguson	Trin.	M 1912
Chand,	Bakhshi Mehr	Sid.	M 1908 A.B. 1911
—	Diwan Khem	Chr.	M 1906
Chandanani,	Thanwardas Pritamdas	N. C.	M 1911
Chandavarkar,	Vithal Narayan ...	King's	M 1908 A.B. 1911
Chandler,	Bertram Geo.	Qu.	M 1908
—	Frederic Geo.	Jes.	M 1905 A.B. 1908. M.B., B.C. 1912
—	Hugh Elphinstone ...	Qu.	M 1912
—	Rob. Alan	Jes.	M 1910
—	Will. Kelman	Trin. H.	M 1902 A.B. 1905. LL.B. 1906
Chandless,	Cecil Tho. Chandless	Trin.	M 1906 A.B. 1909
Chandra,	Brij Bhan	Down.	M 1910
—	Ram	Trin.	M 1910
Chang,	Showbin Wei	N. C.	M 1907 Pem. A.B.† 1911
Chaning-Pearce,	Wilfrid Tho.	Em.	M 1904 A.B. 1907
Channell,	Herb. Mitford Trevelyan	Trin.	M 1905 A.B. 1909
Channon,	Fra. Granville ....*C. C.		M 1894 A.B. 1897. A.M. 1901
Chaplin,	Alan	Trin.	M 1895 A.B. 1899. A.M. 1902
—	Cha. Alf.	Trin. H.	M 1906
—	Lindsay Lennox	Trin. H.	M 1901 A.B. 1904. A.M. 1911
—	Percy Frank Plunkett	Cai.	M 1902 A.B. 1905
—	Rob. Hen.	H. Aye.	M 1894 Cath. A.B. 1899. A.M. 1911
Chapman,	Alb. Ern.	Trin.	M 1904 A.B. 1907
—	Art. d'Arcy Eugene ..	N. C.	E 1909 King's A.B. 1912
—	Art. Frederic	Em.	M 1905 A.B. 1908
—	Art. Greig	Joh.	M 1879 A.B. 1884 (2). A.M. 1908
—	Benj. Burgoyne	Trin.	M 1910 A.B. 1912
—	Cha. Sydney	Chr.	M 1907 A.B. 1910
—	Ern. Hall	Down.	M 1905 A.B. 1908. A.M. 1912
—	Geo.	N. C.	M 1896 A.B. 1899. A.M. 1903
—	Geo. Gibson	Pet.	M 1900 A.B. 1903
—	Geo. Martin	Cai.	M 1907 A.B. 1910
—	Harold John Colston	Cla.	M 1908 A.B. 1911
—	Harry	Chr.	M 1905 A.B. 1908
—	Hen.	Sid.	M 1910
—	Henry Arburn		*A.M.* 1906
—	Ja. Crosby	Cai.	M 1910
—	John Fotherley Dale	Qu.	M 1901
—	Jos.	Cla.	M 1893 A.B. 1897. A.M. 1903
—	Jos. Crawhall	Trin.	M 1871
—	Macklin Cha.	N. C.	E 1908 Pet. A.B. 1911
—	Percival Dav.	Sid.	M 1911
—	Syd.	Trin.	M 1908 A.B. 1911

Chapman,	Syd. John	Trin.	M 1895 A.B. 1898. A.M. 1903
—	Tho. Musgrave Gray	Trin.	M 1909 A.B. 1912
—	Vincent	Trin.	M 1904 A.B. 1907
—	Wilfrid Hub.	Trin.	M 1898 A.B. 1903
—	Will. Dan.	C. C.	M 1889 A.B. 1892. M.B., B.C., A.M. 1903
Chappell,	Fre. Edmondson	C. C.	M 1900 A.B. 1903
—	Harold Stanley	Cla.	M 1906
Chapple,	Alf.	Joh.	M 1895 A.B. 1897. A.M. 1906
—	Alf. Geo.	N. C.	M 1907 A.B. 1910
—	Ern.	Jes.	M 1906 A.B. 1908
—	Harold	Joh.	M 1901 A.B. 1904. A.M. 1909. B.C. 1910.
Charles, Art. de Courcey Cranstoun		Mag.	M 1900 A.B. 1903 [M.B. 1911. M.C. 1912
—	Ja. Art. Merriman ...	Trin.	M 1908 A.B. 1912
—	John Roger	Cai.	M 1891 A.B. 1894. M.B., B.C. 1898. A.M.,
—	Rich. Dudley Stafford	Pem.	M 1908 A.B. 1911 [M.D. 1901
—	Will. Bern.	Sid.	M 1902 A.B. 1905
Charlesworth, Eric Barff		Trin.	M 1904 A.B. 1907. A.M. 1911
—	John Caradoc	Cath.	M 1907
—	Will. Hen.	Mag.	L 1903
Charleton,	Geo. Hen.	Cath.	M 1907 A.B. 1911
Charlewood, Will. Hen.		H. Sel.	M 1912
Charley,	Leslie Will.	N. C.	M 1908 A.B. 1911
Charlton,	Geoffrey Dav.	H. Sel.	M 1909 A.B. 1912
—	Roderick Lindsay Murray	Qu.	M 1898 A.B. 1901. LL.B. 1902
—	Wilfrid Edw.	Em.	M 1905 A.B. 1908
Charter,	Herb. Reg.	Em.	M 1909 A.B. 1912
Chase,	Cha. Allen	Qu.	M 1902 A.B. 1905. A.M. 1909
—	Corrie Denew	Sid.	M 1897 A.B. 1900. A.M. 1904
—	Cyril Fra.	Pem.	M 1903 A.B. 1906
—	Frederic Alliston ...	Pem.	M 1898 A.B. 1901. A.M. 1905
—	Geo. Armitage	Qu.	M 1905 A.B. 1908. A.M. 1912
—	Rob. Godwin	Trin.	M 1902 A.B. 1905. M.B., B.C. 1908
Chasemore,	Phil. Alec	Trin. H.	M 1903 A.B. 1906. A.M. 1912
Chastel de Boinville, Aubrey		C. C.	M 1886 A.B. 1889. A.M. 1906
—	Basil Will.	H. Aye.	M 1884 C. C. A.B. 1888. A.M. 1904
Chasteney,	Howard Everson	Joh.	M 1907 A.B. 1910
Chater,	Cecil Herb.	H. Sel.	M 1906 A.B. 1909
Chatfield,	John Kyrle	Trin.	M 1893 A.B. 1896. LL.B. 1897. A.M. 1901
Chatra,	Mom Chow	Pem.	M 1905
Chatterji,	Amulya Kumar	Joh.	M 1909
—	Jagadish Chandra ...	Trin.	E 1906 A.B.† 1909
Chatterton,	Geo.	Em.	M 1905 A.B. 1909
Chau,	Sin Kok	Cath.	M 1912
Chaudhry,	Girdhari Lall	Joh.	M 1910
Chaudhuri,	Amiya Nath	Trin. H.	E 1898 A.B., LL.B. 1901
—	Arya Kumar	Down.	M 1909
—	Aswini Kumar	Down.	M 1909
—	Sushil Chandra	N. C.	M 1910 A.B. 1912
Chavasse,	Fra. Ja.		*LL.D.* 1908
Chawner,	Will. Rupert	Em.	M 1908 A.B. 1911
Che,	Hin Shing	Chr.	E 1912
Chéah,	Hee Ngan	Chr.	M 1911
Checkland, Montmorency Beaumont		Joh.	M 1902 A.B. 1907
Chee,	Khoo Soon	Pet.	M 1912
Cheese,	Will. Gerard	Joh.	M 1902 A.B. 1905
Cheetham,	Cha. Ern.	Em.	M 1899 A.B. 1903
—	Ern. Mark	Joh.	M 1912
—	Frederic Phil.	Joh.	M 1909 A.B. 1912
Cheffaud,	Paul Harry Martin ..	Cai.	M 1910
Chell,	Harold	Joh.	M 1908
Chenalloy,	Edm. Hub.	Chr.	M 1910

Cherrington,	Douglas Geo.	Trin.	M 1903 A.B. 1907
Cheshire,	Fra. Moreton	Joh.	M 1906 A.B. 1909
—	Ralph Waldo	Trin.	M 1907 A.B. 1910
Chesterman,	Hugh	Cath.	M 1902 A.B. 1905
Chester-Master,	Archie Geo.	Pem.	M 1909
Chetwynd-Stapylton,	Phil. Miles ..	Pem.	M 1907 A.B. 1910
Chevalier,	Will. Hen. Cha.	Joh.	M 1888 A.B. 1904. A.M. 1909
Chevassût,	Fre. Geo.	Trin.	M 1909 A.B. 1912
Chew,	Ja. Edgar	H. Sel.	M 1905 A.B. 1908
Cheyne,	Will. Hunter Watson	Trin.	M 1907 A.B. 1910
Chhatrapati,	Shahu		*LL.D.* 1902
Chibnall,	Alb. Cha.	Cla.	M 1912
Chichester,	Art. O'Neill Cubitt ..	Trin.	M 1908 A.B. 1911
—	Gerald Hen. Crofton	Trin.	M 1906
—	Shane Randolph	Pem.	M 1902 A.B. 1905
—	Will. Geo. Cubitt ...	Trin.	M 1911
Chick,	Herb. Geo.	Cai.	M 1903
Chignell,	Norman Ja.	Cla.	M 1902 A.B. 1905
Child,	Cha. Ja. Napoleon ...	N. C.	E 1894 Chr. A.B. 1897. A.M. 1901
—	Fra. Jos.	Chr.	M 1893 A.B. 1896. A.M. 1900. M.B., B.C.
—	Gerald Julius	Cai.	M 1911 [1901. M.D. 1905
—	Harrison Bird	Trin.	M 1910
—	Stanley	Pem.	M 1894 A.B. 1897. M.B., B.C., A.M. 1905
—	Will. Noël	Chr.	M 1901 A.B. 1904. A.M. 1909
Childers,	Hugh Rob. Eardley	King's	M 1881 A.B. 1884 (2). A.M. 1904
Chipp,	Rob. Edm. Oliver ...	Jes.	M 1905 A.B. 1910
Chippindall,	Will. Syd.	Cai.	M 1912
Chirnside,	Cha. Rothwell	Cla.	M 1904
—	Rob. Gordon	Trin. H.	E 1902
Chisholm,	Colin John	Trin.	M 1911
Chittick,	Hub. Stanley	Cai.	M 1904 A.B. 1908. A.M. 1911
Chittock,	Craufurd	Trin.	M 1901 A.B. 1904. A.M. 1908
Chitty,	Geo. Jameson	King's	M 1895 A.B. 1898. A.M. 1905
Chivers,	John Stanley	Jes.	M 1911
—	Will. Batterson	Chr.	M 1912
Chodat,	Rob. Hippolyte		*Sc.D.* 1909
Cholerton,	Alf. Thornton	King's	M 1911
Chom,	Nai	King's	M 1905
Chope,	Will. Bern.	Pet.	M 1909 A.B. 1912
Chopra,	Ram Nath	Down.	E 1903 A.B. 1905. B.C. 1908 (2). A.M.
Chowdhury,	Satyendra Narayan ..	Down.	M 1906 [1909
Chowlá,	Gopal Singh	Pet.	M 1907 A.B.† 1909
Choyce,	John Coley	Em.	M 1901 A.B. 1904
Christie,	Harold Alf. Hunter ..	Trin. H.	M 1903 A.B. 1906
—	Ja. Fra. Alex.	Cai.	M 1909
—	John	Trin.	M 1902 A.B. 1905
—	John Fairfax	Cai.	M 1911
—	Louis Desmond	Trin.	M 1909 A.B. 1912
—	Syd. Orme Kingscote	Cai.	M 1911
Christmas,	Dudley Vyvyan	Pem.	M 1905 A.B. 1908
Christoffelsz,	Art. Eric	Qu.	L 1912
Christopher,	Cha. Mordaunt de } Aguilar	Pem.	M 1907 A.B. 1910
Chrouschoff,	Ivan	Trin.	M 1909 A.B. 1912
Chrystall,	Harvey Maitland ...	Em.	M 1912
Chuan,	Nai	King's	M 1903 A.B., LL.B. 1906
Chubb,	Cecil Herb. Edw. ...	Chr.	M 1901 A.B. 1904. LL.B. 1905. A.M. 1908
—.	Clifford	Em.	M 1903 A.B. 1906
—	Fra. John MacLardie	King's	M 1912
—	Hub. Parry Brockman	H. Sel.	M 1887 A.B. 1890. A.M. 1904
—	John Fre.	Chr.	M 1906 A.B. 1909

Chubb,	Ralph Nich.	H. Sel.	M 1910
Chubildas,	Jaumayjay	Chr.	M 1909 A.B. 1912
Chudadhuj,	(*H.R.H. Prince*)	Mag.	M 1912
Chudleigh,	Cuthbert Augustine Edw.	Jes.	M 1908 A.B. 1911
Chujo,	Sēichiro	N. C.	M 1904
Chun,	Ja. Wing-cham	Trin.	M 1906
—	John Wing Hon	Trin.	M 1906 A.B. 1909. M.B., B.C. 1912
Churcher,	Walt. Donald	Cai.	M 1912
Churchill,	Arnold	Trin.	M 1903 A.B. 1906
—	Arnold Robertson ...	Cai.	M 1902 A.B., LL.B. 1905
—	Augustus Will.	Trin.	M 1892 A.B. 1895. A.M. 1902
—	Cha. Montague Salisbury	Trin.	M 1898 A.B. 1902
—	Fre. Herb. John Salisbury	Cla.	M 1898 A.B. 1901. A.M. 1905
—	Gordon Seton	C. C.	M 1898 A.B. 1901
—	Harold Edwin	C. C.	M 1912
—	John	Trin.	M 1900 A.B. 1903. A.M. 1909
—	Spencer	Trin.	M 1899 A.B. 1902. M.B., B.C., A.M. 1908
—	Wandril Maur.	Trin.	M 1901
Churchward,	Art. Cyril	N. C.	L 1905 Joh. A.B. 1907. A.M. 1912
—	Basil	C. C.	M 1908 A.B. 1911
—	Hub. Alan	C. C.	M 1911
Circuit,	Edw. Frank	Cath.	M 1908 A.B. 1911
Civil,	Hen. Geo. Victor ...	H. Sel.	M 1906 A.B. 1909
Clabburn,	Tom Cha. Goold	C. C.	M 1908
Clague,	Cyril Kingston	Trin.	M 1895 A.B. 1898. A.M. 1902
—	John	Pet.	M 1901 A.B. 1904
Clapham,	Roderic Art.	Em.	M 1894 A.B. 1897. B.C. 1904. M.B., A.M.
Clapton,	Art.	Mag.	M 1912 [1905. M.D. 1909
Clarabut,	Edm. Alban	C. C.	M 1909 A.B. 1912
Clare,	Frank Conquest	Qu.	M 1908 A.B. 1911
—	Mervyn Joshua	Em.	M 1892 A.B. 1895. A.M. 1902
Clarence Smith,	Kenneth Will. ...	Cai.	M 1909
Clark,	Alan Gordon	Jes.	M 1909
—	Alf. Jos.	King's	M 1903 A.B. 1907. M.E. 1910
—	Cecil Reg.	Sid.	M 1901 A.B. 1904
—	Claude Stanley	Pem.	M 1911
—	Edwin Dowsett	Trin.	M 1906 A.B. 1909
—	Edwin Fowler	Trin.	M 1908 A.B. 1910
—	Fra. Hartley Hall ...	Trin.	M 1904 A.B. 1908. A.M. 1911
—	Frank Kynoch	Qu.	M 1904 A.B. 1908. A.M. 1912
—	Fre. John	Down.	M 1900 A.B. 1904
—	Garnet Leslie	Jes.	M 1910
—	Geo. Ern.	Trin.	M 1904 A.B. 1907
—	Geo. Wingfield	Cai.	M 1896 A.B. 1901. A.M. 1910
—	Gerard Hen. Wake ..	H. Sel.	M 1906 A.B. 1910
—	Gerald Maitland	Cath.	M 1899 A.B. 1902. A.M. 1906
—	Hen. Douglas	Trin.	M 1906 A.B. 1911
—	Hen. John	Cla.	M 1911
—	Hen. Rob. Ern.	Joh.	M 1910
—	Ja. Hen. Maur.	Trin.	M 1910
—	Leon. Seymour	Cath.	M 1900 A.B. 1903. A.M. 1907
—	Noel Mories	Jes.	M 1910
—	Paul Newbury	Pet.	E 1888 King's A.B. 1891. A.M. 1907
—	Ralph Erskine	Cath.	M 1900 A.B. 1903. A.M. 1907
—	Ralph Neville	Trin.	M 1908 A.B. 1912
—	Roderic Kendall	King's	M 1903 A.B. 1906
—	Will.	Cla.	M 1911
—	Will. Hen.	Trin.	M 1894 A.B. 1897. A.M. 1901
—	Will. Hen.	N. C.	M 1909
—	Will. Mories	King's	M 1903 A.B. 1906. A.M. 1910
—	Wyndham Damer ...	Trin.	M 1901 A.B. 1904. A.M. 1909

Clarke,	Alan Strafford	....	Cla.	M 1900 A.B. 1904. A.M. 1907
—	Allan Johnston	......	Em.	M 1895 A.B. 1898. post Fairlie-Clarke.
				[M.B., B.C. 1902. A.M., M.C. 1906
—	Art. Edw.	....	N. C.	L 1881 Chr. A.B. 1884. A.M. 1904
—	Cecil Herb.	....	King's	M 1906 A.B. 1909
—	Cha. Edw.	....	Em.	M 1906 A.B. 1908
—	Denys Harcourt	......	King's	M 1898 A.B. 1901. A.M. 1911
—	Edm. Stephenson	...	Trin.	M 1912
—	Edw. Booth	....	Em.	M 1907
—	Edw. Fra. Routh	...	Pem.	M 1901 A.B. 1904
—	Edw. Revely	....	Joh.	M 1894 A.B. 1897. M.B. 1902
—	Edw. Rudland	....	Sid.	M 1911
—	Edw. Tho.	....	Sid.	M 1903 A.B. 1905. A.M. 1912
—	Ern. Wilson	....	Qu.	E 1904 A.B. 1907
—	Ern. Wrangham	......	Cath.	M 1893 A.B. 1896. A.M. 1906
—	Fra. Will.	....	Jes.	M 1894 A.B. 1897. A.M. 1901
—	Fra. Will.	....	Pem.	M 1898 A.B. 1901. A.M. 1905
—	Frank	....	Em.	M 1899 A.B. 1902. A.M. 1906
—	Fre. Will.	....	Pet.	M 1896 A.B. 1899. A.M. 1906
—	Geo. Trevor Kellner		Pem.	M 1898 A.B. 1901
—	Gilb. Alf. Cha.	......	Down.	M 1909 A.B. 1912
—	Guy Cuthbert	....	Cai.	M 1907 A.B. 1910
—	Harold Martin	......	Cla.	M 1907 A.B. 1910
—	Harold Tho.	....	C. C.	M 1904 A.B. 1907
—	Hen. Douglas	....	Jes.	M 1906 [1905. M.D. 1909
—	Hen. Herb.	....	Trin.	M 1894 A.B. 1897. B.C., A.M. 1904. M.B.
—	Hen. Joy	....	Trin.	M 1900 A.B. 1903. M.B., B.C., A.M. 1907
—	Hen. Lowther	....	Joh.	M 1870 A.B. 1874. A.M. 1877. D.D. 1902
—	Hen. Milford	....	Cla.	M 1897 A.B. 1900. B.C. 1905. M.B. 1907
—	Hen. Sid. Stanton	...	Em.	M 1895 A.B. 1898. A.M. 1905
—	Herb. Lovell	....	Joh.	M 1901 A.B. 1904. A.M. 1908
—	Ja. Bertram	....	Cai.	M 1902
—	John Harrison	......	Joh.	M 1912
—	John Hen.	....	Trin.	M 1909 A.B. 1912
—	John Percy Dalzell	..	C. C.	M 1910 [M.B. 1902
—	John Stephenson	...	Cai.	M 1892 A.B. 1896. A.M. 1900. B.C. 1901.
—	John Will.	....	N. C.	M 1902 A.B. 1905. A.M. 1909
—	Jos. Douglas	....	Sid.	M 1906 A.B. 1909
—	Jos. Spottiswoode	...	Mag.	M 1907 A.B. 1911
—	Kenneth	....	Joh.	M 1893 A.B. 1896. A.M. 1902
—	Lionel Beale	....	Em.	M 1905 A.B. 1908. A.M. 1912
—	Louis Colvill Grey	...	Trin. H.	M 1899 A.B. 1903
—	Maur. Tredway	......	Cath.	M 1902 A.B. 1905
—	Noel Leicester	....	Chr.	M 1904 A.B. 1907. B.C. 1910
—	Percy Geo. Fre.	......	Down.	M 1908 A.B. 1911
—	Ralph Stephenson	...	King's	M 1911
—	Rob. Barton	....	Cath.	M 1911
—	Rob. Bruce	....	Trin.	M 1906 Will. R. B. A.B. 1909
—	Rob. Shuttleworth	...	Joh.	M 1909 A.B. 1912
—	Roger Heine	....	Cai.	M 1908 A.B. 1911
—	Sept. John Childs	...	Sid.	M 1895 A.B. 1899. A.M. 1902
—	Sid. Herb.	....	Cai.	M 1897 A.B. 1900. M.B., B.C., A.M. 1906.
—	Syd.	....	Trin.	M 1911 [M.D. 1910
—	Syd. Herb.	....	Trin.	M 1912
—	Tho. Benj.	....	N. C.	E 1896 A.B. 1900. A.M. 1908
—	Will. Fairlie	....	Joh.	M 1894 A.B. 1897. A.M. 1902
—	Will. Gerald	....	Trin. H.	M 1912
—	Will. Kemp Lowther	*Jes.	M 1899 A.B. 1902. A.M. 1906
—	Will. Pet. Dunham	..	King's	L 1908 A.B. 1911
—	Will. Sefton	....	N. C.	M 1887 Chr. A.B. 1890. A.M. 1907
Clark Kennedy, Archib. Cha.	......	H. Sel.	M 1899 A.B. 1902. A.M. 1906

Clark Kennedy,	Archib. Edm. ...	C. C.	M 1911
Clarkson,	Randolph Norman MacGregor	Em.	M 1908 A.B. 1911
—	Wilfrid Bairstow ...	Trin.	M 1909 LL.B. 1912
Clark-Turner,	Frank	Sid.	M 1912
Clatworthy,	Hugh Edw.	C. C.	M 1891 A.B. 1895. A.M. 1902
Claudet,	Frederic Herb. Bontemps	Cai.	M 1908 A.B. 1911
Claughton,	Ian Drummond	King's	M 1909 A.B. 1912
Clawson,	John Wentworth ...	Qu.	M 1901 A.B. 1904
Claxton,	Alb. Narcisse	Qu.	M 1905 A.B. 1908. A.M. 1912
—	Ecroyde Ihler	King's	M 1895 A.B. 1898. M.B., B.C., A.M. 1902
—	Josiah Art.	Qu.	M 1892 A.B. 1895. A.M. 1905
Clay,	Bern. Augustine	Trin.	M 1904
—	Frederic Harden	Trin.	M 1895 A.B. 1898. LL.B. 1908
—	Hugh Travis	Trin.	M 1894 A.B. 1897. A.M. 1902
—	John Hamblin	Trin.	M 1902 A.B. 1905. A.M. 1909
—	Will. Keatinge	Joh.	M 1899 A.B. 1902
Clayden,	Hen. King	Jes.	M 1905 A.B. 1908. A.M. 1912
Claye,	Geoffrey Woolley ...	Cla.	M 1912
—	Hugh	Cai.	M 1907 A.B. 1910
Clayton,	Edw. Bellis	Cai.	M 1900 A.B. 1903. M.B., B.C. 1910
—	Frank	Trin.	M 1900 A.B. 1903. A.M. 1908. M.B., B.C.
—	Geoffrey	Pem.	M 1909 [1910. M.D. 1912
—	Geoffrey Hare	Pem.	M 1903 A.B. 1906. *Pet. 1908. A.M. 1910
—	Harold	Pem.	M 1893 A.B. 1896. A.M. 1906
—	Hor. Sam.	Down.	M 1905 A.B. 1908. A.M. 1912
—	Ja.	Cla.	M 1905 A.B. 1908
—	Lancelot Ja.	Pem.	M 1898 A.B. 1901
—	Lewis	Em.	M 1856 A.B. 1860. A.M. 1863. D.D. 1903
—	Will. Dixon	N. C.	M 1903
Cleary,	Will. Castle	Trin.	M 1905 A.B. 1908. LL.B. 1909. A.M. 1912
Cleeve,	Cha. Edw.	Chr.	M 1909 A.B. 1912
—	Fre. Cuthbert Aylmer	Chr.	M 1908 A.B. 1911
Clegg,	Hugh Vincent	H. Sel.	M 1902
—	Ja. Art.	Trin.	M 1905 A.B. 1908
—	John	Trin. H.	M 1898 A.B., LL.B. 1902
—	Marcus Tho.	Jes.	M 1907 M. T. de Gonzalez, A.B. 1910
Cleland,	John Rob.	Joh.	M 1908 A.B. 1911
Clement,	Leon.	Sid.	M 1903 A.B. 1906. A.M. 1911
Clements,	Will. Tho.	Joh.	M 1894 A.B. 1897. A.M. 1908
Clemetson,	Dav. Louis	Trin.	M 1912
Cleminson,	Frederic John	Cai.	M 1897 A.B. 1901. A.M. 1904. B.C. 1909
Clemmow,	Cha. Art.	Pet.	M 1907 A.B. 1910
—	Ern. Phil.	Pet.	M 1908 A.B. 1911
Clemo,	Fre. Alf.	H. Sel.	M 1910
Cleworth,	Tho. Hartley	Qu.	M 1906 A.B. 1909
Cliff,	Arnold Pearse	Joh.	M 1910
Cliff-McCulloch,	Adam Edw.	Cla.	M 1910
Clifford,	Anth. Clifford	Em.	M 1906 A.B. 1909
—	Eric Cha.	Cla.	M 1908
—	Fra. Awdry	King's	M 1903 A.B. 1906. A.M. 1910
—	Maur. Will.	Cai.	E 1906
Clifton,	Art. Benj.	Cla.	M 1895 A.B. 1898. A.M.† 1903
—	Edw. Noël	Trin.	M 1909 A.B. 1912
—	(*Lord*) Esme Ivo ...	King's	M 1905
—	Geo. Fre.	Down.	M 1908 A.B. 1911
—	Hub. Everard	Trin.	M 1910
Clissold,	Will.	Joh.	M 1903 A.B. 1906
Clogg,	Frank Bertram	Em.	M 1903 A.B. 1906. A.M. 1910
Close,	Archib. Victor	H. Sel.	M 1911
—	Herb. Skillicorn	Sid.	M 1894 A.B. 1897. A.M. 1902

Close,	Rob. Will. Mills	H. Sel.	M 1907 A.B. 1910
Close-Brooks,	Art. Brooks	Trin.	M 1903 A.B. 1906
Cloudsley,	Hugh	Cai.	M 1902 A.B. 1905. LL.B. 1907. A.M.1911.
Clough,	John	Chr.	M 1912 [post Cloudesley, H.
—	Tho.	Joh.	M 1906 A.B. 1909
—	Vernon	Chr.	M 1908 A.B. 1911
Clouts,	Phil.	Joh.	M 1911
Clow,	And. Gourlay	Joh.	M 1909 A.B. 1912
Clutton,	Brian	Trin.	M 1902
Coad,	Claude Norman	Joh.	M 1902 A.B. 1905. M.B., B.C. 1910. A.M.
Coad-Pryor,	Eric Augustus	Trin.	M 1910 [1911
Coaks,	Herb. Cyril	Jes.	M 1909 A.B. 1912
Coast,	Ja. Percy Chatterton	Qu.	M 1901 A.B. 1904
Coates,	Alan Dav.	Cai.	M 1912
—	Alwyn Scrivener ...	Mag.	M 1909 A.B. 1912
—	Basil Montgomery ...	Qu.	E 1912
—	Dav. Wilson	Joh.	M 1904 A.B., LL.B. 1907. A.M. 1911
—	Ern. Will.	Cath.	M 1893 A.B. 1896. A.M. 1904
—	Hamish Hustler Howard	Trin.	M 1909 A.B. 1912
—	Hen. John	Chr.	M 1899 A.B. 1902
—	Norman Hen.	Cai.	M 1910
—	Vincent Middleton ...	Cai.	M 1907 A.B. 1911
—	Will.	Pet.	M 1909 A.B. 1912
—	Will. Jos.	Cath.	M 1904 A.B. 1907
Cobb,	Hen. Venn	Trin.	M 1883 LL.B. 1886. A.B. 1894. A.M. 1903
—	Herb. Stanley	C. C.	M 1901
Cobbold,	Cha. Townsend	Cai.	M 1912
—	Clem. John Fromanteel	Trin.	M 1900 A.B. 1903. A.M. 1909
—	Fra. Alf. Worship ...	Pem.	M 1901 A.B. 1904. LL.B. 1905
—	Geoffrey Wyndham Nevill	Pem.	M 1911
—	Guy Fromanteel	Trin.	M 1903 A.B. 1906
—	Rob. Hen. Wanklyn	Joh.	M 1912
Cobham,	Elijah	Em.	M 1900 A.B. 1903. A.M. 1907
Cochrane,	Aubrey Kenneth Ormesby	Trin.	M 1909
—	Gerald Douglas	Trin.	M 1904
—	Keith Dav.	Trin.	M 1908 A.B. 1911
—	Kenneth Alex. Basil	Cai.	M 1910
—	Roy Dundonald	Pem.	M 1911
Cock,	John Lucius Astley	Trin.	M 1894 A.B. 1898. A.M. 1902
Cockayne,	Alan Andreas	Cai.	M 1909 A.B. 1912
Cockburn,	Archib. Fre.	Trin.	M 1909 A.B. 1912
Cockell,	Fre. Harold	Qu.	M 1902 A.B. 1905
Cockerell,	[1] Syd. Carlyle		A.M. 1908. *Jes.
Cockerton,	Jos. Stewart	Jes.	L 1889 A.B. 1891. A.M. 1901
Cockin,	Geo. Sam.	C. C.	M 1895 A.B. 1898. A.M. 1902
—	Maur. Stanley	Cai.	M 1900 A.B. 1904. A.M. 1907
—	Reg. Percy	Cai.	M 1898 A.B. 1901. M.B., B.C., A.M. 1906
Cocks,	Hor. Sionnach	Cla.	M 1910
—	Will.	Cath.	M 1907
—	Wyllard Fleetwood ..	Trin.	M 1911
Cocksedge,	Tho. Abr. Bryan ...	Cai.	M 1902
Cockshott,	Fra. Geoffrey	Trin.	M 1899 A.B. 1902
—	Frank Will.	Trin.	M 1902 A.B. 1905. A.M. 1910
Cockton,	Jos. Curwen	Chr.	M 1910
Coddington,	Eustace	Down.	M 1896 A.B. 1899. A.M. 1903
Code,	Geo. Brereton	Pem.	M 1906 A.B. 1909
Coggan,	Frank Richmond ...	Chr.	M 1904 A.B. 1907
Coggin,	Hen. Fre. Fitzmaurice	Trin.	M 1902 A.B. 1905
—	Maur. Edw. Hen. ...	Joh.	M 1910

[1] Director of the Fitzwilliam Museum, 1908.

Coghlan,	Hen. Granville	......	Cla.	M 1887 H. Sel. A.B. 1890. A.M. 1902
Coham-Fleming, Blyth Bickford		...	Trin. H.	M 1903
Cohen,	Abr.	....	Em.	M 1906 A.B. 1909
—	Art. Merton	....	King's	M 1895 A.B. 1898. A.M. 1905
—	Aubrey Mendelssohn		Jes.	M 1909
—	Dav. Hor.	....	Trin.	M 1898 A.B. 1901. A.M. 1906
—	Dav. Lennard	....	Chr.	M 1900 A.B. 1903. A.M.† 1907
—	Dudley Sam.		Trin. H.	M 1903 A.B. 1906. LL.B. 1907
—	Ern. Merton	....	Trin.	M 1895 A.B. 1899. A.M. 1903
—	Geo. Hub.	....	Chr.	M 1897 A.B. 1900. LL.B. 1901
—	Ja. Cecil	....	Em.	M 1903 A.B. 1906. A.M. 1910
—	John Icely	....	Qu.	M 1911
—	Jos. Lewis	....	N. C.	M 1910
—	Rob. Waley	....	Em.	M 1896 A.B. 1900. A.M. 1906
—	Sam. Burnett	....	Jes.	M 1886 A.B., LL.B. 1890. LL.M. 1894.
Cohn,	Paul Victor	....	Trin.	M 1903 A.B. 1906 [A.M., LL.D. 1902
Coit,	Rich. Wetzlar	....	King's	M 1905 A.B. 1908
Coke,	Rich. Art. Sacheverell		Pem.	M 1909
Coker,	Ern. Geo.	....	Pet.	M 1893 A.B. 1896. A.M.† 1901
Colam,	Harold Nugent	......	Pem.	M 1900 A.B. 1903
Colbeck,	Leon. Geo.	....	King's	M 1903 A.B. 1906
Colchester,	Geoffrey Vivian	......	N. C.	M 1904 Qu. A.B. 1911
Colclough,	Will. Frank	....	Cai.	L 1883 A.B. 1885. M.B., B.C. 1894. A.M.,
Cole,	Alex. Caxton	....	C. C.	M 1905 A.B. 1908 [M.D. 1902
—	Art. Frederic And.	..	King's	M 1901 A.B. 1904
—	Bern. Hedley	....	H. Sel.	M 1908 A.B. 1911
—	Cha. Humphry	......	Sid.	M 1906 A.B. 1909
—	Cha. Leslie	....	Pem.	M 1904 A.B. 1907
—	Fra. Edw.	....	Joh.	M 1898 A.B. 1901. A.M. 1911
—	Fre. Geo.	....	Joh.	M 1884 A.B. 1887. A.M. 1902
—	Fre. Geo.	....	Joh.	M 1892 A.B. 1895. A.M. 1902
—	Geo. Lamont	....	Pem.	M 1906 A.B. 1910
—	Hugh Basil	....	King's	M 1894 A.B. 1897. A.M. 1901
—	Ja. Humphrey	....	Joh.	M 1909 A.B. 1912
—	John Will. Edw.	...	C. C.	M 1891 A.B. 1894. B.C. 1902. A.M. 1904.
—	Leslie Stewart	....	Cla.	M 1909 [M.B. 1906
—	Ralph Turney	....	Joh.	M 1903 A.B. 1906
—	Skelton	....	Trin. H.	E 1876 A.B. 1884 (2). A.M. 1909
—	Syd. Will.	....	Trin.	M 1896 A.B. 1900. A.M. 1904
—	Tho. Ern.	....	Joh.	M 1890 A.B. 1893. A.M. 1906
—	Will. Douglas	....	Qu.	M 1911
—	Will. Hor. de Vere	..	Trin.	M 1902
Coleman,	Cha. John	....	Trin.	M 1893 A.B. 1896. M.B., A.M. 1901. M.D.
—	Edw. Cha.	....	Pem.	M 1910 [1908
—	Edw. Hayling	....	Joh.	M 1891 A.B. 1894. M.B., B.C. 1901. A.M.,
—	Hen. Norreys	....	Chr.	M 1901 A.B. 1904. B.C. 1908 [M.D. 1910
—	Herb. Napier	....	Jes.	M 1903
—	Leon. Worsley	......	Qu.	M 1904 A.B. 1907
—	Noel Dolben	....	Joh.	M 1910
Colenso,	Nigel John Frankland		Trin.	M 1907 A.B. 1910
Colenutt,	Fabian Art.	....	Qu.	M 1906 A.B. 1909
—	Rich.	....	Qu.	M 1904 A.B. 1907
Coleridge,	Gerard Hartley Buchanan		H. Sel.	M 1901 A.B. 1904
Coles,	Cha. St Arnaud	......	Trin.	M 1899 A.B. 1903
—	Crewe	....	Jes.	M 1907 A.B. 1910
—	Edgar Ralph	....	Mag.	M 1907 A.B. 1910
—	Ern. Ja.	....	Trin.	M 1906 A.B. 1909
—	Geoffrey Will.	....	Trin. H.	M 1906 A.B. 1909
—	Rich. John	....	Down.	L 1906
—	Victor John Hulbert		Joh.	M 1909 A.B. 1912
Coley,	Colin	....	Chr.	M 1909 A.B., LL.B. 1912

Colgate,	Rob.	Trin.	M 1901
Colledge,	Lionel	Cai.	M 1901 A.B. 1904. M.B., B.C., A.M. 1910
Collet,	Gilb. Golding	Trin.	M 1901 A.B. 1904. M.B., B.C. 1908 (2).
—	John Stratfold	Em.	M 1902 A.B. 1905 [A.M. 1909
—	Jos. Penn	Em.	M 1912
Collett,	Gilb. Faraday	Pem.	M 1898 A.B. 1901. A.M. 1905
—	Ronald Leslie	Trin.	M 1905 A.B. 1908
—	Seymour	Pem.	M 1902 A.B. 1905. A.M. 1911
Colley,	Will. Harold	Em.	M 1907 A.B. 1910
Collie,	Arnold Edgar	Em.	M 1906 A.B. 1910
Collier,	Alan Egerton	Mag.	M 1910
—	Austin Grey	Jes.	M 1903 A.B. 1906
—	Cecil Massy	Trin.	M 1895 A.B. 1901
—	Donald Will	Trin. H.	M 1911
—	Geo. Hen.	H. Sel.	M 1907 A.B. 1910
—	Herb. Mayo Stanley	H. Sel.	M 1904 A.B. 1907. A.M. 1911
—	Herman Fra. Stanley	Pem.	M 1901 N. C., A.B. 1905
Collier-Johnston,	Norman Sykes ..	Trin.	M 1910
Collin,	Art. Compton	Pem.	M 1902 A.B. 1905
—	Edw. Phil. Compton	King's	M 1909
Collinge,	Rob. Maur.	Cai.	M 1901 A.B. 1904
Collingham,	Dav. Hor.	King's	M 1897 A.B. 1900. A.M. 1908
Collings-Wells,	Leon. Collings ...	Trin. H.	M 1907 A.B. 1910
Collingwood,	Bertram Ja.	Cai.	M 1890 A.B. 1893. M.B., B.C. 1900. M.D.
—	Cha. Art.	Down.	M 1909 A.B., LL.B. 1912 [1906
Collins,	Art. Jefferies	Mag.	M 1912
—	Barry Keyte Tenison	Trin.	M 1906 A.B. 1910
—	Dav. Cha.	Trin.	M 1907 A.B. 1910
—	Edw. Duppa	Pem.	M 1912
—	Edw. Laurence	Joh.	M 1904
—	Ern. Edwin	Trin. H.	E 1901
—	Fre. Hen.	Qu.	M 1906 A.B. 1909
—	Geoffrey Abdy	Chr.	M 1907 A.B., LL.B. 1910
—	Harry Rawle	Cath.	M 1892 A.B. 1895. A.M. 1902
—	Hen. Edwards	Cath.	M 1894 A.B. 1897. A.M. 1901
—	Ja. Tho.	Qu.	E 1897 A.B. 1899. A.M. 1906
—	John Basset Baron ..	Pet.	M 1894 A.B. 1897. A.M. 1901
—	John Stratford	Joh.	M 1901 A.B. 1904
—	Keith Earle	Qu.	M 1909
—	Reg. Frank	Trin.	M 1909 A.B. 1912
—	Reg. Lakeman	Em.	M 1900 A.B. 1903. A.M. 1908
—	Rich. Henn ....*Down.		M 1863 A.B. 1865. A.M. 1868. *LL.D.* 1902
—	Valentine St Barbe ..	Pem.	M 1912
—	Will. Edw.	H. Sel.	M 1884 A.B. 1887. A.M. 1891. B.D. 1902.
—	Will. Hen. Perry ...	Qu.	M 1904 [D.D. 1904
Collinson,	Ja. West	Trin.	M 1903 A.B. 1906 [1894. M.D. 1901
Collis,	Art. John	H. Sel.	M 1887 A.B. 1890. A.M. 1894. M.B., B.C.
—	Geo. Jennings	Cla.	M 1889 A.B. 1892. A.M. 1902
Collis-Browne,	Will. Hen. Montague	C. C.	M 1908
Collister,	Harold Ja.	Sid.	M 1903 A.B. 1906
Collot,	Tho. Alex.	Cai.	M 1912
Collyer,	Dan.	Cla.	M 1866 A.B. 1870. A.M.† 1903
Colman,	Claude John	Pet.	M 1911
—	Dudley Maple	Pem.	M 1904 A.B. 1907. A.M. 1911
—	Jerem.	Trin.	M 1905 A.B. 1908
—	Leon. Maple	Pem.	M 1904 A.B. 1907. A.M. 1911
Colonna,	(*Don*) Mario	Mag.	M 1908 A.B. 1912
Colquhoun,	Gideon Rob. Ern. ...	Trin.	M 1907
Colson,	Anth. Fra. Douglas	Pet.	M 1911
—	Cha. Gordon Tulloch	Joh.	M 1910
—	Frank Shettle	Em.	M 1908 A.B. 1911

Colston,	Edw. John	C. C.	M 1893 A.B. 1896. A.M. 1902
Colt,	Geo. Herb.	Sid.	M 1897 A.B. 1900. M.B., B.C. 1904. A.M.
Colthurst,	Geo. Oliver	Trin.	M 1901 [1906
—	Jos. Riversdale	Chr.	M 1893 A.B. 1896. A.M. 1901
	Rich. St John Jefferyes	Trin.	M 1906
Colton-Fox,	Barnard Broomhead	Trin.	M 1898 B. Fleming Hartley, B., A.B. 1901.
			[Broomhead-Colton-Fox, B. F. H.
Colville,	Dav.	Pem.	M 1909 A.B. 1912 [A.M. 1906
—	Dav. John	Trin.	M 1912
	(*Hon.*) John Gilb. ...	Trin.	M 1910
—	Rob. Neil Ker	Pet.	M 1901
—	Tho. Rich.	Trin.	M 1901
Colwell,	Clive Kear	Down.	M 1912
Combe,	Edm. Percy	Cai.	M 1909
—	Harvey Alex. Brabazon	Trin. H.	M 1903
	Rob. Geo. Nicholson	Cla.	M 1897 A.B. 1900. A.M. 1904. LL.M. 1908
Comeau,	Ern. Alex.	King's	M 1912
Comely,	John	Chr.	M 1910
Comline,	Rob.	Trin.	M 1901 A.B. 1904
Common,	Tho. And.	Trin.	M 1894 A.B. 1897. A.M. 1905
Compston,	Geo. Dean	Trin. H.	M 1906
—	Gerald Edmonds ...	Trin. H.	M 1904 A.B., LL.B. 1907
Compton,	Alb. Geo. Will.	Cai.	M 1903 A.B. 1906
—	Art. Will. Hen.	Em.	M 1887 A.B. 1890. A.M. 1903
—	Rob. Harold ....*Cai.		M 1905 A.B. 1908. A.M. 1912
Compton-Burnett,	Guy	King's	M 1904
—	Noël	King's	M 1907 A.B. 1910
Comyn,	Art. Fitzwilliam	Pem.	M 1899 A.B. 1902. M.B., B.C. 1910
—	Harold Fitzwilliam ..	King's	M 1903 A.B. 1906
—	Kenneth	H. Sel.	M 1902 A.B. 1906. B.C. 1909. M.B. 1910
Conacher,	Hamilton	Em.	M 1900 A.B., LL.B. 1903
Conan-Davies,	Brynmor Iwan	N. C.	M 1910
Conder,	Art. Clarence	Qu.	M 1911
	John Marmaduke ...	Joh.	M 1908 A.B. 1911
Coningham,	Will. Fra. Meyrick ..	C. C.	M 1909
Connett,	Tho. Oliphant	Chr.	M 1912
Connolly,	Rich. Hugh	N. C.	M 1896 Chr. A.B. 1899. A.M. 1904
Conolly,	Clifford Gover	Trin.	M 1896 A.B. 1899. LL.B. 1900. A.M. 1903
Considine,	Hugh Herb.	Cla.	M 1905 A.B. 1908
Constable,	Lionel Golding	Pem.	M 1908 A.B. 1911
—	Will. Geo.	Joh.	M 1906 A.B. 1909
Constantine,	Herb. Norman	Cla.	M 1910
—	Will. Whitesmith ...	Cla.	M 1905
Consterdine,	Ja. Harold	Em.	M 1904 A.B. 1907
—	Reg. Hen.	Trin.	M 1882 A.B. 1885. A.M. 1902
Conway,	Frank Gilb.	Trin.	M 1898 A.B. 1901
—	St Vincent	Cla.	M 1903 A.B. 1906. A.M. 1910
Conybeare,	Alf. Edw.	King's	M 1894 A.B. 1897. A.M. 1901
Cook,	Art. Lionel FitzRoy	Jes.	M 1902
—	Barry	Trin. H.	M 1903
—	Benj. Mason	Joh.	M 1895 A.B. 1898. LL.B. 1899. A.M. 1903
—	Edw. Bern.	Cai.	M 1898 A.B. 1901
—	Edw. Mitchener	Cla.	M 1899 A.B. 1902
—	Edw. Penketh	Jes.	M 1894 A.B. 1897. A.M. 1901
—	Edwin Art.	Qu.	M 1907 A.B. 1910
—	Hen. Arnold	Cai.	M 1893 A.B. 1896. A.M. 1902
—	Leon. Will.	Em.	M 1911
—	Victor Chandler	Chr.	M 1904 A.B. 1907
Cooke,	Alan Welldon Hands	King's	M 1906 A.B. 1909
—	Art. Ingram	Cai.	M 1899 A.B. 1902. B.C. 1907. M.B., A.M.
—	Art. Tulk	Qu.	M 1903 A.B. 1906. A.M. 1910 [1909

Cooke,	Cecil Pybus	Trin. H.	M 1907
—	Cyril Hands	King's	M 1902 A.B. 1905. A.M. 1909
—	Edw. Rob. Cecil	Em.	M 1905 A.B. 1909
—	Fre. Fra.	Pem.	M 1909 A.B. 1912
—	Fre. Hen.	Qu.	M 1899 A.B. 1902. A.M. 1906
—	Hen. Rob.	Qu.	M 1904 A.B. 1907
—	Hereward Lester ...	Em.	M 1903
—.	John Geo.	Sid.	M 1891 A.B. 1894. M.B., B.C., A.M. 1902
—	Norman Victor	Trin.	M 1906 A.B. 1909
—	Sid. Russell	King's	M 1911
—	Will. Cha. Cyril	Qu.	M 1900 A.B. 1903. A.M. 1907
—	Will. Ingram	Cai.	M 1906 A.B. 1909
—	Will. Seymour	Cai.	L 1904
Cookson,	Bryan	Trin.	E 1898 A.B. 1900. A.M. 1905
—	Herb. Hen. Osmond	Jes.	M 1892 A.B. 1896. A.M. 1902
—	Kenneth	Trin.	M 1900 A.B. 1903
—	Reg. Tho. Chorley ...	Qu.	M 1894 A.B. 1897. A.M. 1902
Coole,	Cha. Will.	C. C.	M 1898 A.B., LL.B. 1901
Coombs,	Art. Geo.	Joh.	M 1903 A.B. 1906. A.M. 1910
—	Harold Martin McCulloch	Em.	M 1901 A.B. 1904. M.B., B.C. 1912
—	Philip Gurney	Pem.	M 1910
Cooney,	Alex. Basil	Cath.	M 1910
—	Tho. Babington	Cath.	M 1909
Coop,	Frank Dickinson ...	King's	M 1912
—	Wilfrid	Joh.	M 1902 A.B. 1905. A.M. 1909
Cooper,	Alf. Cecil	Chr.	M 1901 A.B. 1904. A.M. 1908
—	Alf. Leslie	Em.	M 1906 A.B. 1909
—	Allan	Sid.	M 1904 A.B. 1907
—	Cha. Rob. Plant	Cai.	M 1901 A.B. 1904
—	Clive Forster	Trin.	M 1897 A.B. 1901. A.M. 1904
—	Edw. Geo.	Em.	M 1901
—	Fre. Tho.	N. C.	M 1907 Cath. A.B. 1910
—	Geo. Will.	C. C.	M 1908 A.B. 1911
—	Harold	Joh.	M 1908 A.B. 1911
—	Harold Octavius	C. C.	M 1907 A.B. 1910
—	Hen. Weatherly Frank	C. C.	M 1899 A.B. 1902
—	Herb. Edw.	N. C.	M 1900 Pet. A.B. 1903
—	Hor. Rowsell	H. Sel.	M 1890 A.B. 1893. A.M. 1904
—	John Gerald	Trin.	M 1893 B.C. 1903. M.B. 1904
—	John Russell	Trin. H.	M 1910
—	John Sephton	Jes.	M 1896 A.B. 1899. A.M. 1903. M.B., B.C.
—	John Smith	N. C.	E 1898 A.B. 1902. A.M. 1907 [1904
—	Maur. Cha.	Joh.	M 1898 A.B. 1901
—	Pat. Ashley	Trin. H.	M 1906 A.B. 1909
—	Phil. Howard	Trin.	M 1897 A.B. 1900. A.M. 1904
—	Rob. Granville	Trin.	M 1893 A.B. 1896. A.M. 1902
—	Tho.	Joh.	M 1904 A.B. 1907
—	Wilbraham Villiers ..	King's	M 1895 A.B. 1898. A.M. 1904
—	Will. Art.	King's	M 1905 A.B. 1908
Cooper-Hunt,	Cecil Lyon	Em.	M 1903 A.B. 1906
—	Dudley Lyon	Em.	M 1908
Coopland-Julian,	Tho. Ennor	Qu.	M 1901 A.B. 1905
Coore,	Cyril	Joh.	M 1899 A.B. 1902. A.M. 1907
Coote,	Art.	Em.	M 1895 A.B. 1898. A.M. 1905
—	Art. Phil.	Trin.	M 1909
—	Cha. Chenevix	Trin.	M 1902
Cope,	John Lachlan	Chr.	M 1911
—	Tho.	Chr.	M 1907 A.B. 1910
—	Tho. Geo.	Trin.	M 1902 A.B. 1905
Copeland,	Will. Brian	Trin.	M 1909 A.B. 1912
Copeman,	Cha. Edw. Fraser ...	H. Sel.	M 1886 A.B. 1889. King's A.M. 1907

Copeman,	Ern. Hugh	Chr.	M 1906 A.B. 1909
Copland,	Randolph	Trin. H.	M 1900 A.B., LL.B. 1903
Copland-Griffiths,	Felix Alex. ⎱ Vincent ⎰	Trin.	M 1912
Copleston,	Reg. Steph.		*LL.D.* 1908
Coplestone,	Will. Drake	Jes.	E 1898 A.B. 1901. A.M. 1907. B.C. 1912
Copplestone,	Wilfred Rob. John ..	N. C.	M 1912
Corban,	Laurence Herb. ⎱ Leslie Barrow ⎰	Cla.	M 1899 A.B. 1902. A.M. 1906
—	Will. Hen. Birch ...	Cla.	M 1897 A.B. 1900. A.M. 1904
Corbett,	Art. Edw.	Joh.	M 1900 A.B. 1903
—	Geo. Holmes Uvedale	King's	M 1898 A.B. 1901. M.B., B.C. 1906
—	Herb. Vincent	Cath.	M 1912
—	John Rooke	Joh.	M 1895 A.B. 1898. A.M. 1902
—	Kenneth Edw. Cyril	Down.	M 1907
—	Lionel Edw.	H. Sel.	M 1892 A.B. 1895. A.M. 1905
—	Reg. Harvey	Jes.	M 1911
—	Rupert Shelton	Cai.	M 1912
—	Sam. Sterndale	Chr.	M 1898 A.B. 1901
Corbin,	Ja. Lee	Trin.	M 1901 A.B. 1904
—	Rich. Beverley	Trin.	M 1900 A.B. 1903
Corbyn,	Ern. Nugent	Trin.	M 1900 A.B. 1903
Corder,	Phil.	Joh.	M 1912
Cordua,	Rudolf	Chr.	M 1910
Corfield,	Bern. Conyngham ...	Jes.	M 1909 A.B. 1912
—	Conrad Laurence ...	Cath.	M 1912
—	Will. Gordon	H. Sel.	M 1906 A.B. 1909
Corke,	Guy Harold	Down.	M 1909 A.B. 1912
Corless,	Rich.	Sid.	M 1903 A.B. 1906. A.M. 1910
Cornaby,	Edgar Edw.	N. C.	M 1887 A.B. 1891. A.M. 1901. B.C. 1903
Cornehls,	Eduard Friedrich Julius	N. C.	M 1910
Cornelius,	Norman Stanley	Cla.	M 1905
Corner,	Edred Moss	Sid.	M 1891 A.B. 1894. M.B., B.C., A.M. 1898.
Corney,	Leon. Geo.	Joh.	M 1905 A.B. 1908 [M.C. 1907
Cornish,	Art.	Sid.	M 1893 A.B. 1896. A.M. 1901
—	Cha. Lawson	Trin.	M 1905 A.B. 1908
—	John Rundle ....*Sid.		M 1855 A.B. 1859. A.M. 1862. D.D. 1906
Cornwell,	Leon. Cyril	N. C.	M 1911
Corrie,	Donald Welldon	King's	M 1905 A.B. 1909
—	Guy Temple	King's	M 1907 A.B. 1910
—	Owen Cecil Kirkpatrick	Trin.	M 1901 A.B. 1904
Corry,	Fre. Hen. Lowry ...	Trin.	M 1908 A.B. 1911
—	Harry Barrett	Cai.	M 1899 A.B. 1902
—	Ja. Perowne Ivo Myles	Trin.	M 1911
—	Will. Myles Fenton	Trin.	M 1912
Cort,	John Leon. Patchett	Joh.	M 1903 A.B. 1907
Cortazzi,	Fre. Edw. Mervyn ...	Qu.	M 1909 A.B. 1912
Cory,	Cha. Woolnough	Cai.	M 1906 A.B. 1909
—	John Fre. Towerson	N. C.	M 1905 Chr. A.B. 1910
—	Rob. Fra. Preston ...	Cai.	M 1904 A.B. 1907
——	Rob. Wilberforce ...	Cla.	E 1896 A.B. 1899. A.M. 1903
Coryton,	Augustus Fre.	Mag.	M 1911
—	Edm. Geo.	King's	M 1909 A.B. 1912
—	Hen. Haworth	Chr.	M 1900 A.B. 1903. A.M. 1907
Cosens,	Will. Reyner Hyde	H. Sel.	M 1903 A.B. 1907
Cossar,	Hor. Ja.	Qu.	M 1895 A.B. 1898. A.M. 1904
—	John Mackenzie	Pem.	M 1907 A.B. 1910. LL.B. 1911
Costalas,	Anth. John	N. C.	M 1905 A.B. 1908
Costello,	Leon. Wilfred Ja. ...	N. C.	M 1899 Pet. A.B., LL.B. 1902. A.M. 1906
Costigan,	Rob. Hampton	Cai.	M 1909
Costobadie,	Lionel Palliser	Cai.	M 1908 A.B. 1911

Coteman,	Ern.	Chr.	M 1907 A.B. 1910
Cotes,	John Cha. Cecil	Mag.	M 1909
Cotes-Preedy,	Digby Hen. Wor-⎱ thington ⎰	Em.	M 1895 ⎰A.B. 1899. Cotes-Preedy, Digby. ⎱ A.M. 1902. LL.M. 1910
Cott,	Alf. Will.	Cla.	M 1906
—	Art. Mackenzie	Cla.	M 1906
Cottam,	Hor. Cha. Bowman	Cai.	M 1909 A.B. 1912
Cotterill,	Hugh Edw.	Trin.	M 1886 A.B. 1910
Cottingham,	John Will.	Em.	M 1912
Cotton,	Brian Gorden Hamilton	Trin. H.	M 1908
—	Cha. Kenneth	Down.	M 1906 A.B. 1909
—	Fre. Art. Stapleton	H. Sel.	M 1902 A.B. 1905. A.M. 1910
—	Geo. Vincente	Qu.	M 1906 A.B. 1909
—	Rob. Hugh Alban ...	Joh.	M 1908 A.B. 1911
—	Vere Egerton	Mag.	M 1907 A.B. 1910
Couch,	Archib. Will.	Mag.	M 1904 A.B. 1907
—	Claud Ja.	Qu.	M 1912
—	Wilfrid Cha.	Qu.	M 1912
Couchman,	Hugh John	Cai.	M 1904 A.B. 1907
—	Maur. Lionel	Qu.	M 1910
Coulby,	Geo. Art.	Trin.	M 1884 A.B. 1887. M.B., B.C. 1892. A.M.,
Coulcher,	Goodricke Bohun ...	C. C.	M 1901 A.B. 1904 [M.D. 1908
Couldrey,	Alf. Edm.	H. Sel.	M 1901 A.B. 1904
Couldridge,	Will. Hen. French ...	N. C.	M 1908 Chr. A.B. 1911
Coulson,	Geo.	Qu.	M 1906 A.B. 1909
—	Norman	Pem.	M 1910
—	Rich. Niven	Cai.	M 1898 A.B. 1901. A.M. 1907
Coultas,	Tho. Bestwick	Qu.	M 1912
—	Will. Whitham	Sid.	M 1909 A.B. 1912
Coupe,	Geo. Alb.	N. C.	E 1906 A.B. 1909
—	Tom Openshaw	H. Sel.	M 1905 A.B. 1908, Tho. O. A.M. 1912
Couper,	John Duncan Campbell	Trin.	M 1894 A.B. 1897. A.M. 1901
Courtauld,	John Sewell	King's	M 1899 A.B. 1902
—	Louis	Trin.	M 1895 A.B. 1898. B.C., A.M. 1905. M.B.
—	Maitland Savill	Trin.	M 1896 A.B. 1901. A.M. 1905 [1906
—	Rich. Minton	Pem.	M 1897 A.B. 1900. A.M. 1904. M.B., B.C.
—	Steph. Lewis	King's	M 1901 A.B. 1904. A.M. 1910 [1907
Courtenay,	Ashley Reg.	Em.	M 1907 A.B. 1910
—	Reg. Herb.	Em.	M 1904 A.B. 1907
Courthope,	Rob.	Mag.	M 1911
Courthope-Munroe,	Caryl Hen. ...	Trin. H.	M 1908 A.B. 1911
—	John Wilfrid	Trin. H.	M 1911
Courtis,	Alan Osborne	Pem.	M 1909 A.B. 1912
Cousins,	Noel Art. Cavendish	Trin. H.	M 1910
Coutts,	Hub. Allan Tucker	Trin.	M 1912
Coventon,	Alb. Will. Duncan ...	Trin.	M 1897 A.B. 1900. B.C., A.M. 1904. M.D.
Cow,	Cha. Stuart	Cla.	M 1898 A.B. 1901. A.M. 1905 [1910
—	Douglas Vernon	Trin.	M 1899 A.B. 1902. M.B., B.C. 1905. A.M.,
Cowan,	Cha. John Alex.	Pem.	M 1912 [M.D. 1911
—	Dav. Tho.		*A.M.* 1907
—	Geoffrey	King's	M 1897 A.B. 1900. M.B., B.C. 1905. M.D.
—	Geo. Herb.	C. C.	M 1898 A.B. 1901 [1910
—	Hugh Montgomerie	Chr.	M 1903
—	John Marshall	King's	M 1888 A.B. 1891. M.B., B.C. 1895. M.D.
—	Noël Pat.	Pem.	E 1906 [1903
Coward,	Cecil John Griffith	Cla.	M 1906
—	Cha. Ern.	Cai.	M 1900 A.B. 1903
—	Hen.	King's	M 1906 A.B. 1909
—	John Cha. Lewis ...	C. C.	M 1870 A.B. 1875. A.M. 1903
Cowe,	Alex. Ewing	N. C.	M 1907 A.B. 1910
Cowell,	John	Down.	M 1912

Cowell,	John Brassey	Em.	M 1909 A.B. 1912
—	Stuart Jasper	Qu.	M 1909 A.B. 1912
Cowen,	Claude Herb. Grant	Chr.	M 1907 A.B. 1910
Cowie,	Alex. Gordon	Cai.	M 1909
—	Dav. Hen.	Em.	M 1910
—	Hugh Cameron	Trin.	M 1905 A.B. 1909
Cowley,	Bern. Paul	Chr.	M 1901 A.B., LL.B. 1904. A.M. 1908
—	John Norman	Trin.	M 1904 A.B. 1907
—	Rob. Baynes	Pem.	M 1907
Cowlin,	Frank Ern.	Trin.	M 1909 A.B. 1912
Cowper,	Geoffrey Moore	Trin.	M 1908 A.B. 1911
Cox,	Art. Hen.	C. C.	M 1907 A.B. 1910
—	Aubrey Paul	Trin.H.	M 1909 A.B. 1911
—	Clem. Harlow	Jes.	M 1902 A.B. 1905
—	Douglas Howard	Cai.	M 1900 A.B. 1903
—	Euan Hillhouse Methven	Trin. H.	M 1912
—	Frank Buchanan Hen.	Jes.	M 1906
—	Frederic	Trin.	M 1894 A.B. 1897. A.M. 1906
—	Geo. Lissant	Chr.	M 1898 A.B. 1901. B.C., A.M. 1906. M.B. [1908. M.D. 1911
—	Harold	Jes.	M 1878 A.B. 1882. A.M. 1911
—	Harold Aldwyn Machell	Cath.	M 1898 A.B. 1901
—	Hor. Beresford	Joh.	M 1901
—	Isaac Spencer	Down.	M 1879 A.B. 1883. A.M., LL.M. 1887.
—	John Ward	Trin. H.	M 1910 [LL.D. 1902
—	Methven Geo. Crerar	Qu.	M 1901
—	Ralph	Cai.	M 1902 A.B. 1905. M.B., B.C. 1909
—	Reg. Cha.	Cai.	M 1899 A.B. 1902. A.M.† 1906
—	Ronald Bentley	Cla.	M 1912
—	Stanley John	Joh.	M 1896 A.B. 1899. A.M. 1903
—	Tho. Hunter Cecil ...	Jes.	M 1904
—	Tho. Percy	N. C.	M 1903
Coxe,	Knightley Holled ...	Em.	M 1909
Coxon,	Art. Cedric Mears ...	Mag.	M 1907 A.B. 1910
—	Hen. Ern. Ja.	N. C.	L 1904 Down. A.B. 1906. A.M. 1910
Coxwell,	Cha. Blake	Chr.	M 1908 A.B. 1911
Coy,	John Chris.	Jes.	M 1909 A.B. 1912
Coyajee,	Jehangirshah Cooverjee	Cai.	M 1907 A.B. 1910
Coyte,	Stanley Edw.	Sid.	M 1912
Cozens,	Fre. Cyril	Em.	M 1911
Crabb,	Will. Johnston	Em.	M 1908 A.B. 1911
Crabbe,	Reg. Percy	C. C.	M 1902 A.B. 1905. A.M. 1910
Crabtree,	Harold	Pem.	M 1893 A.B. 1896. A.M. 1905
—	Harold Gathorne ...	Chr.	M 1898 A.B. 1901. A.M. 1905
—	Will. Art.	Cath.	M 1886 A.B. 1889. A.M. 1907
Crace,	Herb. Stanley	Cla.	M 1904 A.B. 1907. A.M. 1911
—	John Foster	King's	M 1897 A.B. 1901. A.M. 1905
Cracknell,	Ern. Walt.	Em.	M 1897 A.B. 1900. A.M. 1904
Cradock,	Norman	Trin.	M 1900 A.B. 1903. A.M. 1907
Crafer,	Tho. Wilfrid	Chr.	E 1889 A.B. 1892, Jes. A.M. 1896. B.D. [1907
Craft,	Herb. Baynes	C. C.	M 1904
Craggs,	Geo. Craggs	Joh.	M 1902 A.B. 1905
—	Percy Beaumont	Em.	M 1902
Craig,	Archib. Dav. Edmonstone	Trin. H.	M 1904
—	Geo. Will.	Em.	M 1898 A.B. 1901
—	Rich. Dudley	Pem.	M 1903 A.B. 1906. LL.B. 1909
—	Stewart Graham	Joh.	M 1877 A.B. 1881. A.M. 1901
Craigs,	Will. Nixon	Qu.	M 1910
Crake,	Ralph Vandeleur ...	Trin.	M 1903
Cramphorn,	Fre. Tho.	Em.	M 1896 A.B. 1899. A.M. 1905
Crampton,	Ern. Bryant	Cla.	M 1899 A.B. 1903

Crampton,	Gerald Phil.	Down.	M 1912 [1907. M.D. 1911
—	Harold Percy	Cla.	M 1897 A.B. 1900. A.M. 1904. M.B., B.C.
Crane,	Cha. Edw. Dav.	Sid.	M 1891 A.B. 1895. A.M. 1902
—	Hen. Ern.	Chr.	M 1903 A.B. 1906. A.M. 1910
—	Hen. Vincent	Qu.	M 1885 A.B. 1888. A.M. 1902
—	Lucius Fairchild Newton	Trin.	M 1898 L. F. LL.B. 1901
Cranston,	Hen. Norman	Pet.	M 1905
Crathorne,	Josiah Tho.	N. C.	M 1910
Crauford,	Leon. Geo.	Joh.	M 1904 A.B., LL.B. 1907. A.M. 1912
—	Will. Harold Lane ...	Pet.	M 1909
Craven,	Alf. Eric Lawrence	Jes.	M 1912
—	Edw. Musgrave	Cla.	M 1898 A.B. 1901. A.M. 1905
—	Hiram	King's	M 1909 A.B. 1912
—	Will. Lancelot	Jes.	M 1906 A.B. 1909
Crawford,	Colin Grant	Trin. H.	M 1909 A.B. 1912
—	Dav.	Trin.	M 1909 A.B. 1912
—	Geo. Reg.	Pem.	M 1892 A.B. 1895. A.M. 1903
—	Gerald Baynes	Chr.	M 1910
—	Rob.	Jes.	M 1901 A.B. 1904. M.B., B.C. 1910
—	Walt. Coulton	Pem.	M 1901 A.B. 1905
Crawhall,	Tho. Lionel	Cai.	M 1912
Crawley,	John Lloyd	H. Sel.	M 1910
—	Will. Hen. Terence Edw.	Trin. H.	E 1910
Crawshaw,	Aubrey Aitken	Em.	M 1910
—	Cedric Basil Hartley	Chr.	M 1912
—	Cha. Harold	Chr.	M 1906 A.B. 1909
Creasy,	Rob. Leon.	King's	M 1911
Credner,	Hermann		*Sc.D.* 1907
Creed,	John Martin	Cai.	M 1908 A.B. 1911
Crees,	Ja. Harold Edw. ...	Joh.	M 1901 A.B. 1904. A.M. 1908
Creighton,	Cuthbert	Em.	M 1895 A.B. 1898. A.M. 1902
Crellin,	Douglas	Joh.	M 1908 A.B. 1911
Cresswell,	Cyril Eystein	Pem.	M 1907
Creswell,	Harry Edm.	Cai.	M 1907 A.B. 1910
Crew,	Fre. Denys	Em.	M 1897 A.B. 1900. M.B., B.C. 1906
Crewdson,	Bern. Fra.	King's	M 1905 A.B., LL.B. 1908
—	Harold Escott	Pem.	M 1908 A.B. 1911
—	John Wright	Trin.	M 1888 A.B. 1891. A.M.† 1911
—	Roger Bevan	King's	M 1912
—	Will. Dillworth	Trin.	M 1898 A.B. 1901. LL.B. 1902. A.M. 1906
Crewe,	(*Earl of*)		*See* Milnes, R. O. A.
Creyke,	Edm. Ralph	Jes.	M 1905 A.B. 1909
Crick,	Hen.	Qu.	M 1908 A.B. 1911
—	Leslie Cha.	Mag.	M 1910
—	Louis Graham Minden	Joh.	M 1910
—	Phil. Cha. Thurlow	Pem.	M 1901 A.B. 1904. *Cla. A.M. 1908
Crimp,	Geo. Lidstone	Cai.	M 1894 A.B. 1897, G. Lydston. B.C. 1902.
Cripps,	Rich. Seymour	Joh.	M 1904 A.B. 1907. A.M. 1912 [M.B. 1905
—	Will. Lawrence	Trin.	M 1896 A.B. 1899. B.C. 1904. M.B. 1908
Crisford,	Geo. Northcote	Em.	M 1899 A.B. 1904
—	Kenneth Northcote	Em.	M 1906 A.B. 1909
Crisp,	Hope	Cath.	M 1909
Crispin,	Ern. Hen.	Joh.	E 1894 A.B. 1898. A.M. 1901
Critchett,	Geo. Montague	Cla.	M 1903
Croasdale,	Harold Jos.	Em.	M 1908 A.B. 1911
Crocker,	Gordon Geo.	Cla.	M 1912
—	Ja. Codrington	Joh.	M 1898 A.B. 1901. A.M. 1905
—	Reg. Tho.	Trin.	M 1907 A.B. 1911
—	Reg. Will.	Trin. H.	M 1906 A.B. 1909
Crockford,	Leslie Cha.	Pem.	M 1906 A.B., LL.B. 1909
Crocombe,	Frederic Rich.	H. Sel.	M 1911

Croft,	Chris. Barham	Em.	M 1898 A.B. 1901
—	John Art. Chris. ...	Trin.	M 1907 A.B. 1911
—	John Rob.	Qu.	M 1897 A.B. 1900. A.M. 1905
Crofton,	Hugh Denis	Trin.	M 1897 A.B. 1901
—	John Hutchinson ...	Pem.	M 1902 A.B. 1905. M.B., B.C. 1911
—	Rich. Hayes	Joh.	M 1898 A.B. 1901
Crofton-Atkins,	Will. Art.	Cla.	M 1896 A.B. 1899. A.M. 1903
Crofts,	Tho. Rob. Norman	Cai.	M 1893 A.B. 1896. A.M. 1901
Croggon,	Josiah Fenwick Sibree	Joh.	M 1899 A.B. 1902. A.M. 1906
Croghan,	Edw. Hen.	Pem.	M 1911
Crole-Rees,	Herb. Stanley	Joh.	M 1903 A.B. 1906. A.M. 1912
Cromer,	(*Earl of*)		*LL.D.* 1905
Cromie,	Will. Pat.	N. C.	E 1895 C. C. A.B. 1899. A.M. 1902
Crommelin-Brown,	John Louis ...	Trin.	M 1907 A.B. 1910
Crompton,	Claud	Trin.	M 1894 A.B. 1897. A.M. 1902
—	Ja.	Cai.	M 1905 A.B. 1908
—	Kenneth Edw.	Cai.	M 1894 A.B. 1897. M.B., B.C. 1901
—	Nigel Geo.	King's	M 1907 A.B. 1910
--	Reg.	Cai.	M 1908 A.B. 1911
Cronbach,	Abr.	Cath.	M 1911
Cronk,	Herb. Leslie	Jes.	M 1908 A.B. 1911
Crook,	Art. Hen.	Chr.	M 1902 A.B. 1905. A.M. 1909. M.B. 1912
Crookall,	Egerton	N. C.	M 1906 A.B. 1909
Crooke,	Roland Howard	Em.	M 1907 A.B. 1910
Crookes,	Will.		*Sc.D.* 1908
Crookham,	Hugh Anth. Rupert	Jes.	M 1912
Cropper,	Ja.	Trin.	M 1881 A.B. 1884 (2). A.M. 1907
—	Ja. Winstanley	Trin.	M 1898 A.B. 1901
—	John	Trin.	M 1883 A.B. 1886. B.C., A.M. 1892. M.B.
Crosbie,	Rob. Edw. Harold ..	Pem.	M 1905 A.B. 1908 [1893. M.D. 1902
Crosbie Oates,	Edw. Cecil	Mag.	M 1912
Crosby,	Josiah	Cai.	M 1899 A.B. 1902
Crosfield,	Bertram Fothergil ...	Trin.	M 1901 A.B. 1904. A.M. 1909
—	Hugh Theodore	King's	M 1902 A.B. 1905. A.M. 1910
Croshaw,	Fra. Peabody	Cla.	M 1900 A.B. 1903
Cross,	Alf. Will. Stephens	Cai.	M 1892 A.B. 1895. A.M. 1903
—	Kenneth Mervyn Baskerville	Cai.	M 1909 A.B. 1912
—	Martin Edw.	Qu.	M 1899 A.B. 1902
—	Percy Montague	N. C.	M 1907 A.B. 1910
—	Reg. Carlton	Cla.	L 1911
—	Walt. Ern.	Cai.	M 1892 A.B. 1895. A.M. 1909
Crosse,	Spencer Stawell	Pem.	M 1906 A.B. 1909
—	Tho. Latymer	Cai.	M 1908 A.B. 1911
Crossland,	Cyril	Cla.	M 1897 A.B. 1900. A.M. 1904
Crossley,	Alan Hastings	Cla.	M 1897 A.B. 1900. A.M. 1908
—	Brian	Trin.	M 1904
—	Erskine Alick	Cla.	M 1899 A.B. 1902
—	Fra. Marshall	Cla.	M 1904
—	Guy Hastings Irwin	C. C.	M 1909
Crosthwaite,	Will. Hen.	H. Sel.	M 1902 A.B. 1905
Crots,	Fre. Petrus	Chr.	M 1896 A.B., LL.B. 1898. A.M.† 1902
Crouch,	Harold Armstrong ...	Down.	M 1909 A.B. 1912
—	Will. Ja. Bryan	H. Sel.	M 1903 A.B. 1906. A.M. 1910
Crow,	Percy	Pem.	M 1909 A.B. 1912
Crowder,	Geo. Cyril Gordon ...	Chr.	M 1910
—	Will. Irwin Rob. ...	Trin.	M 1904 A.B. 1907
Crowe,	Dennis Marston	Cla.	M 1911
—	Hugh Barby	Trin.	M 1912
—	Tho. Mervyn	Jes.	M 1905 A.B. 1909
Crowfoot,	Alf. Henchman	Em.	M 1899 A.B. 1902. A.M. 1908 [1904
—	Will. Bayly	Em.	M 1896 A.B. 1899. B.C., A.M. 1903. M.B.

Crowley,	Fre.	Trin. H.	M 1902 A.B. 1906
Crowther,	Cha. Rowland	Joh.	M 1896 A.B. 1899. B.C. 1905. M.B. 1907
—	Harold Nayler	Em.	M 1902 A.B. 1906
—	Harold Oakes	Cla.	M 1907 A.B. 1910
—	Ja. Arnold ....*Joh.		M 1902 A.B. 1905. A.M. 1909
—	Wilfred Cooksey	C. C.	M 1904 A.B. 1907
Croyden-Burton,	Cyril Noel Brad-⎱ shaw ⎰	Pet.	M 1909 A.B. 1912
Croysdale,	John Hawkshaw ...	Cai.	M 1897 A.B. 1901. A.M. 1905
—	Rob. Beacock	Jes.	M 1892 A.B. 1898. A.M. 1901
Cruickshank,	Donald Edw.	Joh.	M 1906 A.B. 1909
—	Geo. Malcolm	Joh.	M 1905 A.B. 1908. A.M. 1912
—	Rob. Scott	Pet.	M 1898 A.B. 1901
Cruikshank,	Guy Lindsay	Em.	M 1908
Crump,	Geoffrey Herb.	Qu.	M 1909 A.B. 1912
Cubbon,	Hen. Tho.	Joh.	M 1912
Cubitt,	Victor Murray	Em.	M 1906
Cuffe,	Geo. Eustace	Jes.	M 1911
Cullen,	Alf. Edgar	Joh.	M 1902 A.B. 1905. M.B., B.C. 1910
—	Archib. Howard	Qu.	M 1912
—	Augustus Pountney	Joh.	M 1908 A.B. 1911
—	Cecil Donald	Trin.	M 1892 A.B. 1895. A.M. 1902
—	Harold Rigby	Cai.	M 1895 A.B. 1898. A.M. 1903
—	Rob. Art.	Cla.	M 1897 A.B. 1901
Culley,	Geo. Cha. Hen.	C. C.	M 1911
Cullimore,	Cha.	Cai.	M 1909 A.B. 1912
—	Ja.	Cai.	M 1904 A.B. 1907. A.M. 1911
—	John	Cai.	M 1912
—	Will.	Cai.	M 1906 A.B. 1909
Cullinan,	Maxwell Will. Frederic	Mag.	M 1912
Cullingworth,	Harry Edw.	H. Sel.	M 1892 A.B. 1895. A.M. 1909
Cullis,	Leon.	Joh.	M 1902 A.B. 1905. A.M. 1911
Culverwell,	Jos. Stanley	Cath.	M 1908 A.B. 1911
Cumberland,	Rich. Bentley Lorne	Pem.	M 1903
Cumberlege,	Barry Stephenson ...	Em.	M 1910
Cumberlidge,	Will. Isaac	Chr.	L 1899 A.B. 1901. M.B. 1908
Cumming,	Geo. Elder	Cath.	M 1911
—	John Hamilton	Pem.	M 1903
Cummins,	Cresswell Art.	Joh.	M 1902 A.B. 1905. A.M.† 1909
Cunard,	Edw.	Trin.	M 1909 A.B. 1912
Cuningham,	Martin Walpole Martin	Pem.	M 1901 A.B. 1904
Cunliffe,	Ja. Hen. Grave	Chr.	L 1912
—	Norman	Trin.	M 1908 A.B. 1911
Cunningham,	Art. John Wellington	Trin.	M 1901 A.B. 1904. M.B., B.C. 1910. A.M.
—	Ebenezer ....*Joh.		M 1899 A.B. 1902. A.M. 1906 [1911
—	Gilb. Matth.	Down.	M 1910
—	Ja. Michael	Trin.	M 1897 A.B. 1901. A.M. 1906
—	Ja. Sandeman	Trin.	M 1904 A.B. 1907
—	John Art.	Joh.	M 1900 A.B. 1902. A.M. 1908
—	Leslie	Down.	M 1911
—	Norman Rowsell	Cai.	M 1898 A.B. 1901
—	Norman Usher	Jes.	M 1907
—	Tom Eric	Trin.	M 1905 A.B. 1908
—	Will. And.	Trin.	M 1901 A.B. 1905
Cunnington,	Cecil Willett	N. C.	M 1896 A.B. 1899. M.B., B.C. 1905
—	Edw. Cha.	C. C.	M 1908 A.B. 1911
—	Will. Alf.	Chr.	M 1902 A.B. 1906. A.M. 1909
Curl,	Syd. Walt.	Down.	M 1893 A.B. 1896. M.B., B.C., A.M. 1900.
Curnock,	Geo. Ashwin	Pem.	M 1912 [M.D. 1905
Currey,	Lawrence Eustace ...	Trin.	M 1901
Currie,	J. D. L.		*See* Legge-Currie, J. D.

Currie,	Ja. Henderson	Jes.	M 1907
—	Will. Crawford	Trin.	M 1902 A.B. 1905
Curry,	Phil. Art.	Trin.	M 1902 A.B. 1905
Cursetjee,	Heerajee Jehangir } Manockjee }	Cai.	M 1908
Cursham,	Curzon	King's	M 1906
Curtis,	Art. Cecil	King's	M 1893 A.B. 1896. A.M. 1901
—	Art. Randolph Wormeley	Trin.	M 1908 A.B. 1911
—	Lewis	N. C.	M 1897 Cai. A.B. 1900. A.M. 1904
—	Sam. Waller	Cath.	M 1911
—	Tho. Lancelot Constable	Trin.	M 1907 A.B. 1910
—	Timothy Herb. Will.	Trin.	M 1901
—	Walt. Sept.	Trin. H.	M 1897 A.B. 1901. A.M. 1905
Curtois,	Peregrine Art.	Qu.	M 1911
Curwen,	Brian Murray	Cai.	M 1909 A.B. 1912
—	Cecil Niel	Cai.	M 1908 A.B. 1911
Curzon,	(*Baron*) of Kedleston		*LL.D.* 1907
—	Cecil Tho. Billage ...	Down.	M 1909 A.B. 1912
—	Cha. Edw.	Chr.	M 1897 A.B. 1900. A.M. 1904
—	Harry Edw. Ja.	N. C.	M 1900 A.B. 1903. Down. A.M. 1907
Cushing,	Will. Ewart Wittrick	Joh.	M 1909 A.B. 1912
Cushion,	Ern. John	King's	M 1905 A.B. 1908
Cuthbert,	Claude Art.	Trin.	M 1910
—	Will. Wilfred Larder	Chr.	M 1906 A.B. 1909
Cuthbertson,	Edw. Hedley	Cla.	M 1907
—	Hugh	Trin.	M 1909 A.B. 1912
—	Ja. Hen.	Em.	M 1900 A.B. 1903
—	Monro	Pem.	L 1912
Cutlack,	Will. Phil.	Pem.	M 1900 A.B. 1903. A.M. 1907
Cutler,	Cha. Edw.	H. Sel.	M 1900 A.B. 1903. A.M. 1909
—·	Donald Ward	Qu.	M 1910
—	Edw. Trevor	Cla.	M 1905
—	Hor. Art.	Cla.	M 1893 A.B. 1896. A.M. 1902. M.B., B.C.
Cutter,	Roy Carnegie	Jes.	M 1905 A.B. 1908 [1904
Cutting,	Ern. Melville	Joh.	M 1901 A.B. 1904. A.M. 1908
Cutts,	Fre. Ja.	Em.	M 1906 A.B. 1909

D

Daffarn,	Maur.	Trin.	M 1906 A.B. 1909
Daiches,	Herb. Salom	Down.	M 1909
Dain,	Geo. Rutherford	Cla.	M 1903
Daing,	Maung Sein	Down.	M 1909
Daintree,	Claud Neville	Jes.	M 1911
Daish,	Tho.	Mag.	M 1911
Daisley,	Geoffrey Will.	Trin.	M 1895 A.B. 1898. A.M. 1902
Dakin,	Alb.	Jes.	M 1900 A.B. 1903. A.M. 1907
Dalál,	Ardeshir Rustomji ...	Joh.	E 1905 A.B. 1907
Dalal,	Kaikhuaro Kharsedji	Chr.	E 1901
—	Rustomjee Dadiba ...	Jes.	E 1910
d'Albuquerque,	Nino Pedroso	Cla.	M 1912
Dalby,	Phil.	Pem.	M 1896 A.B. 1899. A.M. 1903
Dale,	Alwyne Percy	Cla.	M 1898 A.B. 1903
—	Fra. Rich.	Trin.	M 1902 A.B. 1905

Dale,	Frank	Joh.	M 1907 A.B. 1910
—	Hen. Hallett	Trin.	M 1894 A.B. 1897. B.C., A.M. 1903. M.D.
—	Hugh Frederic	Cai.	M 1905 A.B. 1910 [1909
—	Leon.	Jes.	M 1888 A.B. 1891. A.M. 1903
Dalgleish,	Ja. Pat.	Pem.	M 1912
Dalley,	John Pomeroy	Qu.	M 1911
—	Rich. Pomeroy	Pem.	M 1908 A.B. 1911 [M.D. 1908
Dally,	John Fre. Halls	Joh.	M 1895 A.B. 1898. M.B., B.C., A.M. 1903.
Dalrymple,	Cochrane Maxton ...	King's	M 1895 A.B. 1898. A.M. 1902
Dalton,	Cha. Reg.	Trin.	M 1894 A.B. 1897. A.M. 1901
—	Edw. Hugh John Neale	King's	M 1906 A.B. 1909
—	Llewelyn Chisholm ..	Trin.	M 1897 A.B. 1900. A.M. 1905
—	Tho. Edmonstone ...	Trin.	M 1892 A.B. 1895. A.M. 1901
Daltroff,	Edm. Mayer	Qu.	M 1909 A.B. 1912
Daltry,	Lionel Offley	Trin.	M 1908 A.B. 1912
Dalvi,	Vishvanath Ganpat ..	Joh.	M 1906 A.B. 1909. LL.B. 1911
Dalwigk,	Rabodo Elgar Rich.	Cla.	M 1908
Daly,	Ivan de Burgh	Cai.	M 1911
—	Ulick de Burgh	Cai.	M 1911
Dalzell,	(*Lord*) Rob. Hippisley	Trin.	E 1897 A.B. 1901
Dammers,	Eric. Hen. Falk	Pem.	M 1910
Damras,	Mom Chow	Trin.	M 1906 A.B. 1909
Dams,	Percy John	Cath.	M 1907 A.B. 1910
—	Victor	Cath.	M 1910
—	Will. Bell	Jes.	M 1899 A.B. 1902. A.M. 1906
Danckwerts,	Will. Otto Adolph } Julius }	Pet.	M 1873 Wilhelm O. A. J. A.B. 1877, Will. [O. A. J. A.M.† 1911
Dandridge,	Will. Leslie	Em.	M 1912
Dani,	Vishwanath Ganesh	Sid.	M 1912
Daniel,	Alf. Wilson	Em.	M 1891 A.B. 1894. M.B., B.C. 1899. M.D.
—	Jos. Abr.	Chr.	M 1903 A.B. 1906 [1903
Daniell,	Percy John	Trin.	M 1907 A.B. 1910
—	Phil. Foster	Pet.	M 1899 A.B. 1902
Daniels,	Alec Percy	Cla.	M 1908 A.B. 1911
—	Harold Geo.	King's	E 1901
—	Mark	Sid.	M 1910
—	Will. Ewart	N. C.	M 1910
Dannatt,	Will. Ja.	Qu.	M 1901 A.B. 1904. A.M. 1908
Dannhorn,	Theodore John	Cai.	M 1909 A.B. 1912
Danvers,	Geo. Cecil ....:	H. Sel.	M 1900 A.B. 1903
Daphtary,	Chandra Kisan	Mag.	M 1912
Darbishire,	Harold Dukinfield ...	Cla.	M 1900 A.B., LL.B. 1903
Darby,	Art. John Lovett ...	Cla.	M 1895 A.B. 1898. A.M. 1910
—	Cecil Alb.	N. C.	M 1899 Qu. A.B. 1902. A.M. 1907
—	Edw. Hen. d'Esterre	Cla.	M 1899 A.B. 1902
Darbyshire,	John Russell	Em.	M 1899 A.B. 1902. A.M. 1906
Darch,	Oswald Wallwyn ...	Jes.	M 1908 A.B., LL.B. 1911
Dare,	Alb. Geo.	C. C.	M 1902 A.B. 1905. A.M. 1909
—	Alf. Julius	Down.	M 1905 A.B. 1908
Darley,	Cecil Barrington	Cai.	M 1906
Darling,	Malcolm Lyall	King's	M 1899 A.B. 1902
Darlington,	Will. Aubrey Cecil	Joh.	M 1909 A.B. 1912
—	Willoughby Scott ...	Pem.	M 1902 A.B. 1905. A.M. 1909
Darlow,	Hen.	Down.	M 1904 A.B., LL.B. 1907
Darroch,	Alasdair Ronald	Trin.	M 1899 A.B. 1902. A.M. 1910
Dart,	Hugh	Trin.	M 1900 A.B. 1903. A.M. 1907
Darwin,	Bern. Rich. Meirion	Trin.	M 1894 A.B., LL.B. 1897. A.M. 1901
—	Cha. Galton	Trin.	M 1906 A.B. 1909
—.	Erasmus	Trin.	M 1901 A.B. 1904. A.M. 1910
—	Fra.	Trin.	M 1866 A.B. 1870. M.B., A.M. 1875. *Chr.
—	John Hen.	Joh.	M 1904 A.B. 1907 [*Sc.D.* 1909

Darwin,	Leon.		Sc.D. 1912
Das,	Dwarka	Jes.	M 1910
Dás,	Narám	Down.	M 1910
da Silva,	Claude Hen.	Chr.	M 1907 A.B., LL.B. 1910
Dassenaike,	Edw. Senerat	Chr.	M 1904 A.B., LL.B. 1907
Datta,	Rabindranath	Chr.	M 1904 A.B. 1906. A.M.† 1910
Daubeney,	And. Rob. Vaughan	Cla.	M 1893 A.B. 1903
Daughtry,	Edm. Osmond	Chr.	L 1903 A.B. 1905. Mus.B. 1907. A.M. 1909
Daukes,	Archib. Herb.	Trin.	M 1908 A.B. 1911
—	Sid. Herb.	Cai.	M 1897 A.B. 1900. M.B., B.C. 1906
Daun,	Edw.	Trin.	M 1904
Dauncey,	Arnold Falconer	C. C.	M 1908 A.B. 1911
—	Kingsley Erskine Dunlop	C. C.	M 1911
Davenport,	Art. Hen.	Sid.	M 1907 A.B. 1910
—	Cha.	N. C.	E 1902 Cath. A.B. 1905. A.M. 1912
—	Harold	Chr.	E 1909 A.B. 1912
—	Stanley	Chr.	M 1907 A.B. 1910
Davey,	Alf. Augustus	N. C.	M 1892 Joh. A.B. 1895. A.M. 1907
—	Archib. Paterson ...	Jes.	M 1905
—	Art. Hammond	N. C.	M 1901 Down. A.B. 1905
—	Hen. Norman	Cla.	M 1907 A.B. 1910
—	Ja. Ern.	King's	M 1909 A.B. 1912
—	John Kingsley	Jes.	M 1907
—	Roscoe Ellis Boyle ...	Cla.	M 1909 A.B. 1912
—	Syd.	Chr.	M 1894 A.B. 1897. LL.B. 1898. A.M. 1911
—	Syd. Guy	Cla.	M 1912
David,	Martin Sinclair	Pem.	M 1881 A.B. 1884 (2). A.M. 1910
—	Pet. Julius Paul		Mus.M. 1908
—	Will. Tho.	Trin.	M 1908 A.B. 1910
Davidge,	Hen. Tho.	Joh.	M 1902
Davidson,	Alex.	Chr.	M 1894 A.B. 1897. A.M. 1901
—	Alister Ja.	Mag.	M 1908
—	Eric Harry Lucas ...	Trin.	M 1906
—	Fra. Reg. Clear	Qu.	M 1911
—	Geo. Edw.	Cai.	M 1896 A.B. 1899. B.C., A.M. 1904. M.B.
—	Geo. Fre.	Cai.	M 1910 A.B. 1912 [1905
—	Geo. Stainforth	Qu.	M 1901 A.B. 1904. A.M. 1908
—	Gerard Markby	Cla.	M 1894 A.B. 1897. A.M. 1901
—	John Clarke Forbes	Mag.	M 1911
—	John Colin Campbell	Pem.	M 1907 A.B. 1910
—	Malcolm Gordon	Trin.	M 1912
--	Randall Geo.	Cla.	M 1894 A.B. 1897. A.M. 1902
—	Randall Tho.		LL.D. 1903
—	Walker Wheatley ...	Em.	M 1903 A.B. 1906
—	Walt. Eardley Freeling	Jes.	M 1911
Davie,	Hugh Symington ...	N. C.	E 1904
Davies,	Algernon Lionel	Cath.	M 1912
—	Art. Rob.	Trin.	M 1908 A.B. 1911
—	Art. Tho.	Joh.	M 1912
—	Art. Vaughan	Qu.	M 1887 A.B. 1890. A.M. 1901
—	Aubrey Hugh	Cai.	M 1893 A.B. 1896. M.B., B.C. 1901
—	Clem. Edw.	Trin. H.	M 1904 A.B., LL.B. 1907
—	Conway	H. Sel.	M 1908 A.B. 1911
—	Cyril Edw. Hughes	Jes.	M 1909 A.B. 1912
—	Dan.	N. C.	M 1882 Joh. A.B. 1886. A.M. 1908
—	Dan. Gordon	Down.	M 1910
—	Dav.	King's	M 1899 A.B. 1903. A.M. 1910
—	Dav. Ephraim	C. C.	M 1895 A.B. 1898. A.M. 1902
—	Dav. Ja.	N. C.	M 1892 Cath. A.B. 1895. A.M. 1903
—	Dav. John	Trin.	M 1901 A.B. 1904. A.M. 1908
—	Dav. John	Sid.	M 1904 A.B. 1906. A.M. 1911

Davies,	Dav. Rich.	Joh.	M 1900 A.B. 1903. A.M. 1907
—	Dav. Tho.	Chr.	M 1898 A.B., LL.B. 1902
—	Dewi Llewellyn Erasmus	Cath.	M 1912
—	Edw. Ja. Llewellyn	Mag.	M 1896 A.B. 1899. A.M. 1907
—	Eric	Joh.	M 1908 A.B., LL.B. 1911
—	Eric Dav. Despard	Chr.	M 1907
—	Fre. Cha.	Down.	M 1903 A.B. 1906. M.B., B.C. 1911
—	Fre. Middlecott	Em.	M 1903
—	Geoffrey Boisselier ...	H. Sel.	M 1912
—	Geo. Bevan	Down.	M 1902 A.B. 1905
—	Geo. Fre.	King's	M 1894 A.B. 1897. A.M.† 1902
—	Geo. Knoyle	N. C.	M 1907 A.B. 1910
—	Geo. Llewelyn	Trin.	M 1912
—	Herb.	Em.	E 1895 A.B. 1897. A.M. 1901
—	Herb. Barrs	Pem.	M 1910
—	Herb. Howel	Joh.	M 1891 A.B. 1894. A.M. 1903
—	Hugh Morriston	Trin.	M 1897 A.B. 1900. B.C., A.M. 1904. M.C.
—	Ivor Glyndwr	Joh.	M 1912 [1907. M.D. 1908
—	Ja. Cathcart	Em.	L 1904 A.B. 1906. A.M. 1910
—	Ja. Gordon	Em.	M 1910
—	Ja. Ramsbotham ...	N. C.	M 1910
—	Jenner Conway	Trin.	M 1911
—	John Bernard	Jes.	M 1897 A.B. 1900. A.M. 1906
—	John Bowen	Down.	E 1894 A.B., LL.B. 1897. A.M. 1902
—	John Ja.	N. C.	M 1897 Joh. A.B. 1901. A.M. 1904
—	John Llewellyn	Em.	M 1909 A.B. 1912
—	John Llewelyn	Chr.	M 1889 A.B. 1892. A.M. 1903
—	John Llewelyn	Em.	M 1901 A.B. 1904. A.M. 1908
—	John Phillips Hen.	Jes.	M 1902 A.B. 1905. B.C. 1911
—	John Rhys	Cai.	M 1899 A.B. 1902
—	Kenneth Cuthbert Johnson	Cath.	M 1912
—	Langford Geo.	Trin.	M 1898 A.B. 1901. M.B., B.C., A.M. 1906
—	Latimer Dan.	Qu.	M 1903 A.B. 1905
—	Leslie Frederic St John	Em.	M 1911
—	Lewis Cyril	Chr.	M 1906 A.B. 1909
—	Morgan Owen	Cath.	M 1907 A.B. 1910
—	Percy Marr	C. C.	M 1908 A.B. 1911
—	Reg.	Cath.	M 1906 A.B. 1909
—	Reg. Geo. Middlecott	Pem.	M 1906 A.B. 1909
—	Reg. Geo. Reynolds	King's	M 1909 A.B. 1912
—	Rich. Morgan	Joh.	M 1911
—	Rich. Rees	Trin.	M 1910
—	Rob.	N. C.	M 1905 A.B. 1908
—	Rob. Evan	N. C.	M 1898 Chr. A.B. 1902. A.M. 1906
—	Ronald Leslie	Down.	E 1909
—	Sam. Morris	Sid.	M 1898 A.B. 1901. A.M. 1905
—	Sid. Rich. Eccles ...	Qu.	M 1911
—	Steph. Harris	Em.	M 1902 A.B. 1905
—	Theoph. Maxwell ...	King's	M 1899 A.B. 1902. A.M. 1906
—	Tho. Edw.	N. C.	M 1903
—	Tho. Edw. Meurig ...	Trin.	M 1910
—	Tho. Hosegood	Pem.	M 1901 A.B. 1904. A.M. 1908
—	Trevor Art. Manning	C. C.	M 1912
—	Wilfred Eric	Jes.	M 1912
—	Will. Ja.	Trin.	M 1896 A.B. 1899. A.M. 1903
—	Will. Vivian	Jes.	M 1904 A.B. 1906
Davies-Colley,	Hugh	Trin.	M 1894 A.B. 1897. B.C., A.M. 1903 [1909
—	Rob.	Em.	M 1899 A.B. 1902. B.C., A.M. 1908. M.C.
d'Avigdor,	Osmond Elim	Trin. H.	M 1895 d'Avigdor-Goldsmid, O. E., A.B.,
Davis,	Bergen	N. C.	M 1902 [LL.B. 1898. A.M. 1903
—	Edw. Maximillian ...	Jes.	M 1911

Davis,	Frank Prosser	Cai.	M 1905 A.B. 1908	
—	Fre.	C. C.	M 1899 A.B. 1902. A.M. 1907	
—	Fre. Basil	H. Sel.	M 1907 A.B. 1911	
—	Fre. Mowbray	Cai.	M 1908 A.B. 1911	
—	Geo. Brocklesby	C. C.	M 1892 A.B. 1895. A.M. 1899. M.D. 1905	
—	Geo. Edgar Shuter ...	King's	M 1894 A.B. 1897. A.M. 1901	
—	Gilb. Fra. Shuter ...	King's	M 1905 A.B. 1908	
—	Harold Ja.	Joh.	M 1908 A.B. 1911	
—	Herb.	Joh.	M 1909 A.B. 1912	
—	Herb. Nath.	Em.	M 1909 A.B. 1912	
—	Hugh Cradock	Cla.	M 1904	
—	John Ogilvie	Mag.	M 1908	
—	Jos. Irving	Sid.	M 1908 A.B. 1911	
—	Kenneth Ja. Acton ...	King's	M 1902 A.B. 1905	
—	Lewis Fre.	Trin.	M 1910	
—	Mervyn	Sid.	M 1900 A.B. 1903	
—	Percy Fre.	N. C.	M 1901	
—	Phil. Brocklesby	C. C.	M 1893 A.B. 1896. A.M. 1901	
—	Rob. Gwynne	Trin.	M 1911	
—	Wilfrid Jervis	Cla.	M 1909	
—	Will.	Qu.	M 1898 A.B. 1901	
—	Will. Hen.	Joh.	M 1884 A.B. 1887. A.M. 1902	
Davison,	Alb. Edw.	Chr.	M 1910	
—	Alf.	N. C.	M 1894 A.B. 1897. A.M. 1901	
—	Gilderoy	Cath.	M 1912	
—	Ja. Fre.	Trin.	M 1901	
Davy,	Gaius	Jes.	M 1908 A.B. 1911	
—	Gerald Hen.	Cai.	M 1901 A.B. 1904. M.B. 1909	
—	John Ern. de Chatelain	Qu.	M 1908	
—	Paul Leigh	Trin. H.	M 1901	
—	Will. Ja.	Trin. H.	M 1907	
Daw,	Will. Fabyan Bennett	Pem.	M 1908 A.B. 1911	
Dawbarn,	Graham Richards ...	C. C.	M 1912	
Dawe,	Art. Purchas	Sid.	M 1894 A.B. 1897. A.M. 1901	
—	Leon. Sid.	Em.	M 1909 A.B. 1912	
Dawes,	Edyn Sandys	Mag.	M 1912	
—	Harold Ja.	N. C.	L 1907 Chr. A.B. 1909	
—	Hen. Franklin	Cai.	M 1906	
—	Herb. Edwin Tonge	Joh.	M 1900 A.B. 1903. M.B., B.C. 1910	
—	Mich. Cha. Burdett	Sid.	M 1900 A.B. 1903	
—	Mich. Stileman	Pem.	M 1908 A.B. 1911	
Dawkins,	Cha. John Randle ...	Pet.	M 1910	
—	Frederic Vincent ...	H. Sel.	M 1905 A.B. 1908. A.M. 1912	
—	John McGillivray ...	Em.	M 1906 A.B. 1909	
—	Rich. McGillivray ...*Em.		M 1898 A.B. 1901. A.M.† 1905	
Dawnay,	Cuthbert Hen.	Trin.	M 1910	
Dawson,	Ambrose Middleton	Joh.	M 1905 A.B. 1908	
—	Bartram Kendle	Pem.	M 1901	
—	Basil Hulse	H. Sel.	M 1909 A.B. 1912	
—	Chris. Wilford	Trin. H.	M 1903 A.B. 1909	
—	Edw. Courtenay	Pem.	M 1908 A.B. 1911	
—	Edw. Victor	N. C.	M 1910	
—	Ern. Edw.	Cai.	M 1905 A.B. 1908	
—	Fra. Gilmer Tempest	Pem.	L 1912	
—	Fre. Rowland	C. C.	M 1891 A.B. 1898. A.M. 1901	
—	Geo. Gordon	Cath.	M 1909 A.B. 1912	
—	Geo. Herb. Wrigley	Trin.	M 1896 A.B. 1899. A.M. 1903	
—	Harry	Em.	M 1907 A.B. 1911	
—	Hugh Pudsey	Trin.	M 1907 A.B. 1910	
—	Ja. Hamilton Tho. ...	Pem.	M 1905 A.B. 1908	
—	John	Trin.	M 1904 A.B. 1907. A.M. 1911	

Dawson,	Percy	Pet.	M 1912
—	Reg. Tho.	Joh.	M 1904 A.B. 1907. A.M. 1911
—	Will. Rob.	N. C.	M 1896 A.B. 1899. A.M. 1903
Dawswell,	Geo. Alec	King's	M 1912
Day,	Bern.	Cai.	M 1899 A.B. 1902. M.B., B.C. 1909
—	Cyril Douglas	Down.	M 1908 A.B. 1911
—	Dennis Ivor	Joh.	M 1911
—	Eric Cornwallis	Jes.	M 1909 A.B. 1912
—	Fra. Hen. Coryton ...	Trin. H.	M 1898 A.B., LL.B. 1901
—	Fra. Morland	Cai.	M 1909 A.B. 1912
—	Geoffrey Reynolds ...	Pet.	M 1907 A.B. 1910. *Em.
—	Geo. Lewis	Joh.	M 1910
—	Geo. Stanley	Qu.	M 1902 A.B. 1905. A.M. 1909
—	Gilb.	Cai.	M 1907 A.B. 1910
—	Gordon Phil. Jodrell	Cath.	M 1907 A.B. 1910
—	John Godfrey FitzMaurice	Pem.	M 1893 A.B. 1896. A.M. 1903
—	Maur. Cha.	Trin.	M 1910
—	Sam. Hulme	Qu.	M 1898 A.B. 1902. A.M. 1905
—	Will. Frank Lydston	Cai.	M 1895 A.B. 1898. M.B., B.C. 1904
Dé,	Birendranath	Joh.	M 1903 A.B. 1906
—	Prabodh Chandra ...	Down.	M 1904 A.B. 1906
Deacon,	Cha. Edw. Bourne ...	H. Sel.	M 1894 A.B. 1897. A.M. 1906
—	Phil. Leslie	Jes.	M 1901 A.B. 1904
Deakin,	Howard Vipond	Trin.	M 1907 A.B. 1910
de Ambrózy,	Geo. Victor	Trin. H.	M 1903
Dean,	Fre.	N. C.	M 1897 C. C. A.B. 1900. A.M. 1904
—	Lawrence Thompson	Sid.	M 1901 A.B. 1904. M.B., B.C. 1909
—	Percy Cecil	Down.	M 1894 A.B. 1897. A.M. 1901
Deane,	Art. Percival Williams	Trin.	M 1907 A.B. 1910
—	Art. Vernon	Em.	M 1906 A.B. 1909
—	Colin Hermann	Trin.	M 1902 A.B. 1905
—	Everard Duncan	Trin.	M 1909 A.B. 1912
—	Ja. Killen	Joh.	M 1905 A.B. 1910
Deans,	Harold	Sid.	E 1885 A.B. 1888. A.M. 1910
Dearbergh,	Jack	Cla.	M 1903
Dearden,	Harold	Cai.	M 1901 A.B. 1904
Debailleul,	Alexandre	Cai.	M 1904
de Baráthy,	Hen. Cha.	C. C.	M 1895 A.B. 1898. A.M. 1902
de Behr,	(*Baron*) Geo. Johann	Pem.	M 1907 A.B. 1911
de Brockdorff,	Georges Frederic } Schack {	Trin. H.	M 1908
de Bunsen,	Eric Hen.	King's	M 1908 A.B. 1911
de Burgh,	Lionel Nooth	Sid.	M 1899 A.B. 1902. A.M. 1906
de Castro,	Jean Paul François Lopez	Joh.	M 1892 A.B. 1898. A.M. 1901. post John
de Cerjat,	René Gaston	King's	L 1908 [Paul de Castro
de Chaumont,	Tho. Sandford } Blakiston François{	H. Sel.	M 1903 A.B. 1906. A.M. 1912
Deck,	Sam. Fre.	Cai.	M 1902 A.B. 1906
de Clermont,	Eric Fehrman	King's	M 1899 A.B. 1902
de Cordes,	Aubrey Lucas	Trin.	M 1906 A.B. 1909
de Czarkowski-Golejewski,	Wiktor	Pet.	L 1910
de Déchy,	Iwan Elemèr	Pem.	M 1907
de Dirsztay,	Gedeon	Joh.	M 1908
Dedman,	Art. Ja.	Chr.	M 1902 A.B. 1905
Deed,	Neville Gard	Em.	M 1907 A.B. 1910
—	Syd. Geo.	Trin.	M 1893 A.B. 1896. A.M. 1907
—	Will. Rob. Wheeler	Joh.	M 1893 A.B. 1896. A.M. 1901
Deedes,	John	Jes.	M 1912
Deeping,	Geo. Warwick	Trin.	M 1895 A.B. 1898. M.B., A.M. 1902
de Érdös,	Cha.	C. C.	M 1911
Deerr,	Geo. Hen.	H. Sel.	M 1887 A.B. 1890. A.M. 1911

de Fayal,	Anth.	Mag.	M 1911
Defoe,	Luther Marion	N. C.	M 1902
De Freitas,	Julian Mignon	Cla.	E 1909 A.B. 1912
de Geijer,	Erik Neville	Trin.	M 1912
—	Will.	Trin.	M 1907 W. Adam Valdemar Gustäf, A.B.
de Gex,	Ralph Octavus	Pem.	M 1895 A.B. 1898. A.M. 1902 [1910
de Grużewski, Geo. Marian Ivano-⎱ witsh ⎰		Down.	M 1911
de Hahn,	Constantin Pet.	Pet.	M 1912
de Hamel,	Herb. Gustave	King's	M 1899 A.B., LL.B. 1903
de Hatvany, (*Baron*) And. Ignatius		Trin.	M 1909
de Havilland, Walt. Augustus ...		H. Aye.	M 1890 A.B. 1893. N. C., A.M. 1902
Dehn,	Kurt Otto	Chr.	M 1909
Deighton,	Fra. John	N. C.	M 1903 A.B. 1907
—	Fre. Montague	Trin.	M 1905 A.B. 1908
—	Gerald Will.	King's	M 1911
—	John	Trin.	M 1906 A.B. 1909
de Jager,	Sam. Jacobus	Trin. H.	M 1899 A.B., LL.B. 1902
de Janasz,	Geo. Kazimir Art. ...	Trin.	M 1909 LL.B. 1912
de Jersey,	Eustace Bertram Rivers	H. Sel.	M 1893 A.B. 1897. A.M. 1903
De la Bere,	Fre. Bayard de Prickley	Cath.	M 1902
—	Ivan	Sid.	M 1911
Delahunt,	Cha. Geo.	N. C.	M 1904 Down. A.B. 1907
De la Mothe, Claude Douglas Fenelon		Pem.	M 1907 A.B. 1910
de la Motte,	Vital	N. C.	M 1897 Chr. A.B. 1900. A.M. 1904
Delap,	Louis Bredin	Pem.	M 1888 A.B. 1891. A.M. 1902
De Lapparent, Alb. Auguste			*Sc.D.* 1907
de la Rue,	Reg. Warren	Trin. H.	M 1904
Delius,	Steph. St Martin ...	Cla.	M 1908 A.B. 1911
Dellschaft,	Max Eberhard	Jes.	M 1904 A.B. 1907. M.B., B.C. 1910
Delph,	Leon. Will.	Cath.	M 1910
de Mazaraki, Aleksander Kazimir		Mag.	L 1911
De Mel,	Vidanalagé Fre. Jos.	Joh.	M 1897 A.B., LL.B. 1900. A.M.†1905
de Mello,	Aloysius	Pet.	M 1901
—	Roque	Down.	E 1911
de Menasce,	Rene Alf.	Trin. H.	M 1901
de Mesa,	Tirso Lucian	Mag.	M 1904
de Montigny, Baudouin de Marotte		Trin.	M 1912
de Montmorency, Ja. Edw. Geoffrey		Pet.	M 1886 A.B. 1889. LL.B. 1890. A.M. 1907
de Morpurgo, Frederick Gustave ⎱ Adolphe Bela ⎰		King's	M 1903 A.B. 1906
—	Jean Gabriel Cha. Etienne	King's	M 1910
—	Lionel Maur. Joachim	King's	M 1908 A.B. 1911
de Motta Maia, José		Pet.	M 1911
Dempsey,	Geo. Barlow	Cath.	M 1912
Denby,	Art. Peel	Jes.	M 1902 A.B. 1905. LL.B. 1906
Dendy,	Edw. Herb.	Cai.	M 1910
—	Rob. Will. Miller ...	N. C.	M 1912
Denham,	Harold Art.	Joh.	M 1898 A.B. 1901
—	Jos. Percival	Joh.	M 1908 A.B. 1911
—	Ronald Kynaston ...	C. C.	M 1907 A.B. 1910
Denham-Cookes, Art. Brownlow ...		Trin. H.	M 1910
Denne,	Alured John de Den	H. Sel.	M 1899 A.B. 1905
Dennehy,	Harold Geo.	Em.	M 1909 A.B. 1912
Dennes,	Wilfrid	Chr.	M 1908 A.B. 1911. LL.B. 1912
Dennett,	Fre. Sid.	Pet.	M 1894 A.B. 1897. A.M. 1902
Denning,	Howard	Cai.	M 1904 A.B. 1907
—	Will. Frederic	Trin.	M 1899 A.B. 1903
Dennis,	Alf. Will.	Joh.	M 1887 A.B. 1890. A.M. 1901
—	John Neville	Mag.	M 1912
—	Trevor	Cla.	M 1901 A.B. 1904. A.M. 1908

Dewar,	Alex.	Cla.	M 1904 A.B. 1907
—	Dav.	Down.	M 1912
—	Hub. Steph. Lowry	Jes.	M 1911
—	Mich. Bruce Urquhart	Trin.	M 1905 A.B. 1908. A.M. 1912
Dewé,	Cha. Douglas Eyre	Qu.	M 1898 A.B. 1901. A.M. 1905
Dewhurst,	Cyril	Trin.	M 1907 A.B. 1910
—	Geo. Charnley Littleton	Trin.	M 1910
—	Hen.	N. C.	L 1895 Cath. A.B. 1897. A.M. 1903
Dewick,	Edw. Chisholm	Joh.	M 1903 A.B. 1906. A.M. 1910
de Witt,	Lothar Cornelius ...	Mag.	M 1906
Dewrance,	John Lowthian	Trin.	M 1902
Dexter,	Edw. Norman	Jes.	M 1911
—	John Eric	Jes.	M 1909 A.B. 1912
—	Ralph Marshall	Jes.	M 1910
Dey,	Navendra Krishna ...	Down.	L 1908
de Yarburgh-Bateson, (*Hon.*)Eustace		Trin.	M 1903 A.B. 1906
de Yrarrázaval, Gabriel	....	N. C.	M 1912
—	Sergio	Trin.	M 1906
Dhar,	Will.	Chr.	M 1908
Dhavle,	Shankar Balaji	Joh.	M 1901 S'ankara B., A.B. 1904
Dhawan,	Piara Lal	Chr.	M 1902 A.B. 1905
Dias,	Edgar Osmund	Cath.	M 1912
—	Reg. Felix	Trin. H.	M 1909 A.B. 1912
Dibb,	Chris. Ern.	C. C.	M 1895 A.B. 1898. A.M. 1902
Dibben,	Ern. Sheppard	C. C.	M 1887 A.B. 1890. A.M. 1905
—	Harold Herb.	C. C.	M 1910
—	Norman Cecil	C. C.	M 1904 A.B. 1907
Dibble,	Tho. Edwin	Mag.	M 1911
Dice,	Alb. Edw.	N. C.	M 1892 King's A.B. 1895. A.M. 1905
Dick,	Hen. Pfeil	Trin.	M 1910
—	Ja. Reid	Down.	M 1903 A.B. 1906. M.B., B.C. 1912
—	John Bern. Goodrich	Cai.	M 1900 A.B. 1903. A.M. 1911
—	Norman Brabazon ...	Sid.	M 1901 A.B. 1904
Dicken,	Cha. Vernon	Pem.	M 1900 A.B. 1903. A.M.† 1907
Dickens,	Cedric Cha.	Trin. H.	M 1907 A.B. 1910
—	Phil. Cha.	Trin. H.	M 1906 A.B. 1909
Dickenson,	Laurence Aubrey } Fiennes Wingfield }	H. Sel.	M 1912
—	Lenthall Greville ...	H. Sel.	M 1888 A.B. 1891. A.M. 1904
Dickey,	Edw. Montgomery O'Rorke	Trin.	M 1911
Dickin,	Hen. Bern.	Sid.	M 1889 A.B. 1892. A.M. 1904
Dickins,	Bruce	Mag.	M 1909
Dickinson,	Alan Peile	Pem.	M 1910
—	Geo. Fryer	Pem.	M 1904 A.B., LL.B. 1908. A.M. 1911
—	Gerald Will.	Trin.	M 1888 A.B. 1891. A.M. 1905
—	Godfrey Nix	Trin.	M 1892 A.B. 1895. A.M. 1904
—	Ja.	Trin.	M 1903
—	Percy Parkin	King's	M 1902 A.B.1905. Mus.B.1907. A.M. 1909
—	Raymond Scott	Trin.	M 1912
—	Will. Tyson	N. C.	E 1889 Chr. A.B. 1892. A.M. 1903
Dickson,	Alan	Pet.	M 1901 A.B. 1904
—	Art. Fra.	Cai.	M 1909 A.B. 1912
—	Art. Norman	N. C.	M 1898 Down. M.B. 1907
—	Cha. Cecil	Jes.	M 1903 A.B. 1906
—	Cyril Garlies	Sid.	M 1909 A.B. 1912
—	Eric Dav.	Em.	M 1906 A.B. 1909
—	Ern. Cha. Scott	Trin.	M 1906 A.B. 1909
—	Fra. Cyprian	Jes.	M 1905 A.B. 1908
—	Fra. Pat.	Pem.	M 1907 A.B. 1910
—	Fredrick Ja. Catling	Em.	M 1908
—	Geo. Yarker	Em.	M 1903 A.B. 1907

Dickson,	Harold Stewart	Chr.	M 1898 A.B. 1901
—	Jos. Will. Edm.	Trin.	M 1908 A.B. 1911
—	Kenneth Bruce	Trin.	M 1906 A.B. 1909
—	Rob. St John	Joh.	M 1899 A.B. 1902
Diels,	Hermann		*LL.D.* 1909
Dier,	Claude Vernon	Cath.	M 1908 A.B. 1911
Dietrichsen,	Fre. Christian	Cai.	M 1901 A.B., LL.B. 1904
Digby,	Kenelm Geo.	Trin.	M 1909 A.B. 1912
—	Tho. Hankinson	Trin. H.	M 1910
Dill,	John Martin Gordon	Trin.	M 1908 A.B. 1911
Dillon,	Harold Geo. Sid. ...	Chr.	M 1907 H. G. Syd. A.B. 1910
Dimock,	Hor.	Sid.	M 1899 A.B. 1903. M.B., B.C. 1907
Dimond,	Fre. Martyn	Mag.	M 1908
Din,	Geo. Kyan	Down.	M 1903 A.B. 1906. LL.B. 1907
Dines,	John Somers	Em.	M 1903 A.B. 1906. A.M. 1910
—	Lewen Hen. Geo. ...	Em.	M 1903 A.B. 1906. A.M. 1910
Dingwall,	Cha. Fre.	Trin.	M 1911
—	Eric John	Pem.	M 1911
Dinn,	Hugh Kennett	Cla.	M 1903 A.B., LL.B. 1906
Dippie,	Herb.	N. C.	M 1905 Chr. A.B. 1908
Disney,	Hen. Anth. Pat.	Cai.	M 1912
Divatia,	Virmitra Bhimrao ...	Sid.	M 1907 A.B. 1909
Dive,	Hen. Aston	Jes.	M 1905 A.B. 1908
Diver,	Oswald Fra.	Joh.	M 1894 A.B. 1897. A.M. 1901
Dix,	Archib. Will.	Sid.	M 1895 A.B. 1898. A.M. 1902
Dixit,	Moreshwar Rajaram	Chr.	E 1900 A.B. 1903
Dixon,	Art. Frederic Will.	Chr.	M 1911
—	Art. Harold	Chr.	M 1911
—	Art. Lewis	Sid.	M 1899 A.B. 1902
—	Cuthbert	Joh.	M 1906
—	Douglas Gilb.	Joh.	M 1908
—	Fra. Netherwood ...	Cai.	M 1898 A.B. 1901
—	Geo. Percival Allsop	Qu.	M 1910
—	Hamlet Gill	C. C.	M 1898 A.B. 1901. A.M. 1905
—	Harry Livesey	H. Cav.	M 1883 A.B. 1886. M.B., B.C., A.M. 1890.
—	Herb. Hen.	Pem.	M 1906 A.B. 1909 [N. C. M.D. 1910
—	Hor. Alb.	C. C.	M 1908 A.B. 1911
—	Hor. Hen.	N. C.	L 1890 A.B. 1892. A.M.† 1909
—	John Howard	N. C.	M 1899 Qu. A.B. 1902
—	Oscar	Trin.	M 1901 A.B. 1905 [ney-Dixon, S.
—	Sam.	Trin.	M 1897 A.B. 1901. A.M. 1904. post Gur-
—	Tho. Harold	N. C.	M 1892 A.B. 1895. A.M.† 1908
—	Walt. Ern.	Down.	A.M. 1902
—	Will. Scarth	Cai.	M 1901 A.B. 1904. Mus.B., A.M. 1911
Dixson,	Hugh Fitzmaurice ...	Trin.	M 1910
Doak,	Ja. Kidd Robertson	Cai.	M 1909 A.B. 1912
Dobb,	Geo. Conway	Pem.	M 1911
—	Harry Raymond	Pem.	M 1909
—	Rob. Alan	Pem.	M 1912
Dobbin,	Alf. Will.	Chr.	M 1906 A.B. 1909
Dobbs,	Archib. Edw. ....*King's		M 1901 A.B. 1904. A.M. 1908
—	Fra. Wellesley	Trin.	M 1895 A.B. 1898. A.M. 1902
—	Will. Evelyn Jos. ...	Trin.	M 1899 A.B., LL.B. 1902
Dobell,	Cecil Clifford ....*Trin.		M 1903 A.B. 1906. A.M. 1910
—	Hub.	Chr.	M 1901 A.B. 1904. A.M. 1911
Dobson,	Alban Tabor Austin	Em.	M 1904 A.B. 1907
—	Bern. Hen.	Em.	M 1900 A.B. 1903
—	Cyril Comyn	H. Sel.	M 1898 A.B. 1901. A.M. 1905
—	Darrell Rich.	Cai.	M 1898 A.B. 1902. A.M. 1908
—	Eric Leon.	King's	M 1906 A.B. 1909
—	Gordon Miller Bourne	Cai.	M 1907 A.B. 1910

Dobson,	Harry Desborough	... Cai.	M 1909
—	Hen. Montagu	...... Trin.	M 1905 A.B. 1908
—	John Frederic	.... Trin.	M 1894 A.B. 1898. A.M. 1904
—	Rich. Rhimes	.... Chr.	M 1907 A.B. 1910
—	Will. Steele	.... Qu.	M 1910
Dockerill,	Will Harry Atkin	... N. C.	M 1897 A.B. 1900. Down. A.M. 1906
Dockray,	Kenneth Titus Smalley	Trin.	M 1895 A.B. 1898. A.M. 1902
Dodd,	Alf. Herb.	.... Chr.	M 1910
—	Edw. Norman	.... H. Cav.	M 1888 A.B. 1891. Down. A.M. 1902
—	John Maur.	.... Cath.	M 1906 A.B. 1910
—	Mich.	.... Pet.	M 1912
—	Rowland Pocock	...... Joh.	M 1905 A.B. 1908
—	Stanley	.... Cai.	M 1896 A.B. 1899. M.B., B.C., A.M. 1905
—	Walt. Edw. Fagan	... Cai.	M 1903 A.B. 1906
—	Walt. Prichard	...... Joh.	M 1908 A.B. 1911
—	Will. Geo.	.... N. C.	L 1899 Qu. A.B. 1901. A.M. 1906
Doddrell,	Curling Finzel	...... Chr.	M 1893 A.B. 1899. A.M. 1903
Dodds,	Maitland Theoph.	... Em.	M 1902 A.B. 1905. A.M. 1912
—	Steph. Roxby	.... Trin.H.	M 1899 A.B. 1902. LL.B. 1903. A.M. 1906
Dodgshun,	Ern. Ja.	.... Joh.	M 1899 A.B. 1902
Dodgson,	Fra.	.... Trin.	M 1908 A.B. 1911
—	Phil. Henley	.... Trin.	M 1910
Dodson,	Cha. Sherborne	...... Qu.	M 1908 A.B. 1911
—	Fre. Kite	.... Down.	M 1909 A.B. 1912
—	Gerald	.... Down.	M 1902 A.B., LL.B. 1905
Dodwell,	Geo. Melville	.... Chr.	M 1902 A.B., LL.B. 1905. A.M. 1910
—	Howard Branson	... Em.	M 1911
Doggart,	Hugh	.... Em.	M 1904 A.B. 1907
—	Will. Edw.	.... Joh.	M 1907 A.B. 1910
Doherty,	Rich. Edw. Ern. Biggs	Trin.	L 1906 A.B. 1907 (Dubl. incorp.)
—	Will. Dav.	.... King's	M 1912
Dolbey,	Roger Clarke	.... Trin.H.	L 1907 A.B. 1911
Dole,	Harold Will. Jackson } Roeckel }	Jes.	M 1910
Doll,	Christian Cha. Tyler	Trin.	M 1898 A.B. 1901. A.M. 1906
—	Mordaunt Hen. Caspers	Trin.	M 1907 A.B. 1910
—	Will. Alf. Millner	... Trin.H.	M 1904 A.B. 1907. A.M. 1911
Dollman,	Hereward Chune	... Joh.	M 1907
—	John Guy	.... Joh.	M 1905 A.B. 1908
Dollo,	Louis Antoine Marie Jos.		*Sc.D.* 1907
Don,	Archib. Will. Robertson	Trin.	M 1909 A.B. 1912
—	Fra. Percival	.... Trin.	M 1904 A.B. 1907. A.M. 1912
Donagan,	Alf. Edw.	.... N. C.	E 1883 A.B. 1886. A.M. 1901
Donald,	Alex. Gostling	.... Sid.	M 1911
—	Jonat.	.... C. C.	M 1908
—	Kenneth John Lenny	Qu.	L 1907 A.B. 1909
Donaldson,	Alastair	.... Jes.	M 1905 A.B. 1908
—	Alex. Hen.	.... Cai.	M 1888 A.B. 1892. A.M. 1902
—	Chris. Herb.	.... C. C.	M 1903 A.B. 1908
—	Eric	.... Trin.	E 1907 A.B. 1910
—	Euan Aidan Lewis	Sid.	M 1912
—	Geoffrey Boles	.... Cai.	M 1912
—	Harold	.... Sid.	M 1907 A.B. 1910
—	Harold Tho.	.... N. C.	M 1909 A.B. 1912
—	John Thomlinson	... Em.	M 1912
—	Malcolm	.... Trin.	E 1902 A.B. 1905. M.B., B.C. 1912
—	St Clair Geo. Alf.	... Trin.	M 1882 A.B. 1885. A.M. 1890. D.D. 1904
—	[1] Stuart Alex.	.... Trin.	M 1873 A.B. 1877. A.M. 1880. B.D. 1905.
—	Stuart Hay Marcus	Trin.	M 1905 [D.D. 1910

[1] Master of Magdalene, 1904.

Doncaster,	Basil Wilson	King's	M 1903 A.B. 1907
—	Leon. ....*King's		M 1896 A.B. 1900. A.M. 1903
Donington,	Geo. Caulton	Cai.	M 1893 A.B. 1896. A.M. 1902
Donne,	Cha. Edw.	Cai.	M 1888 A.B. 1891. A.M. 1908
—	Reg. Felix	Joh.	M 1907 A.B. 1911
Donnell,	Jos. Hollins	Cai.	M 1896 A.B. 1899. M.B., B.C. 1904
Donner,	Julius Dunlop	Trin.	M 1906
Donnithorne,	Stuart	Pet.	M 1900 Clarence Edw. Stuart Comyn
—	Vyvyan Hen.	Cla.	M 1911 [A.B. 1903
Donovan,	Edm. Lawrence	Joh.	M 1907 A.B. 1910
Doongaji,	Sheriarji Nusserwanji	N. C.	M 1907 A.B. 1910
Doorly,	Cha. Stokely	H. Sel.	M 1900 A.B. 1903
—	Martin Edw.	H. Sel.	M 1899 A.B. 1902
Dore,	Alan Syd. Whitehorn	Jes.	M 1901 A.B. 1904. A.M. 1908
—	Sam. Ern.	Joh.	M 1891 A.B. 1894. M.B., B.C., A.M. 1900.
Doria Pamphilj,	Filippo Andrea ...	Mag.	M 1909 [M.D. 1907
Dorman,	Art. Cha.	Trin.	M 1892 A.B. 1895. A.M.† 1903
—	Art. John	Trin.	M 1900 A.B. 1903. A.M.† 1908
Dornhorst,	Frederic Schultsze ...	Joh.	M 1898 A.B. 1903
Dorrell,	Benj. Cha.	N. C.	M 1895 H. Sel. A.B. 1898. A.M. 1902
—	Harold Geo.	Em.	M 1910
Dorward,	Alan Ja.	Trin.	M 1910
Dottridge,	Cecil Alf.	Cla.	M 1903 A.B. 1906. M.B., B.C., A.M. 1912
Doudney,	Ern. Edw.	Chr.	M 1896 A.B. 1899. A.M. 1904
—	Harold	N. C.	L 1898 Em. A.B. 1900. A.M. 1904
—	Herb. Will.	C. C.	M 1892 A.B. 1895. A.M.† 1905
Dougall,	Eric Stuart	Pem.	M 1905 A.B. 1908
Doughty,	Edgar Penrice	Pem.	M 1899 A.B. 1902. A.M. 1906
—	Hugh	H. Sel.	M 1910
—	Wilfrid Vere	Trin.	M 1899 A.B. 1902
—	Will. Harford	Cla.	M 1905 A.B. 1908
Douglas,	And. Halliday	Joh.	L 1894 A.B. 1898. A.M. 1901
—	And. Wilmot	Mag.	M 1906 A.B. 1909
—	Cecil Howard	Cai.	M 1901
—	Cha. Kenneth Mackinnon	King's	M 1912
—	Clifford Hugh	Pem.	L 1910
—	Eric Campbell	Qu.	M 1904 A.B. 1907. A.M. 1911
—	Fra. Will. Gresley ...	Cla.	M 1905 A.B. 1908. A.M. 1912
—	Geo. Hamilton	Qu.	M 1909
—	Gerald Wybergh ...	King's	M 1894 A.B. 1897. A.M. 1901
—	Harold Archib.	H. Sel.	M 1905 A.B. 1908
—	Hen. Kenneth	Pem.	M 1904 LL.B. 1907
—	John Fre.	C. C.	L 1898 A.B. 1900. A.M. 1908
—	Justyn Langton	Mag.	M 1907 A.B. 1910
—	Kenneth Justyn	Qu.	M 1899 A.B. 1903
—	Mellis Stuart	Qu.	M 1898 A.B. 1901. A.M. 1905
—	Rob. Hen.	Pem.	M 1900 A.B. 1903. A.M. 1907
—	Stuart Monro	Joh.	M 1898 A.B. 1901
—	Will. Ewart	Joh.	M 1909
Douglas-Hamilton,	Claud Archib. ⎰ Aubrey ⎱	Trin.	M 1907 A.B. 1910
Douglass James,	Will.	Pem.	M 1911
Doune,	(*Lord*) Fra. Douglas Stuart	Trin.	M 1911
Douthwaite,	Alf. Will. Stanley ...	Cla.	M 1907 A.B. 1910
—	John Bullough	Pem.	M 1898 A.B. 1901
Douty,	Edw. Hen.	N. C.	M 1881 King's A.B. 1884 (2). A.M. 1888. [M.B., B.C. 1890. M.D. 1898.
Dove,	Cha. Kingsley	Mag.	M 1905 A.B. 1908 [M.C. 1908
—	Fre. John	Trin.	M 1910
Dow,	Stewart	King's	M 1908
Dowdall,	Launcelot Fra. Raymond	Cath.	M 1898 A.B. 1903. A.M. 1906

Dowell Lee,	Reg. Will.	H. Sel.	M 1910
Dowling,	Geoffrey Cha. Walt.	Trin.	M 1910
Downey,	Ja.	N. C.	M 1909 A.B. 1912
—	Will. Percy	Trin.	M 1897 A.B. 1901
Downie,	Ja. Maitland	Chr.	M 1911
Downing,	Art. Bern.	Sid.	M 1899 A.B. 1902. A.M. 1907
—	Lionel Edw. Lowder	King's	M 1906 A.B. 1909
Downman,	Leon. Cha.	Jes.	M 1905 A.B. 1909
Downs,	Brian Westerdale ...	Chr.	M 1912
Downton,	Art. Murray	Cla.	M 1906
—	Basil Murray	Em.	M 1897 A.B. 1900. A.M. 1907
—	Edm. Murray	Em.	M 1903 A.B. 1907
Dowsett,	Art. Arnold	N. C.	M 1910
Dowson,	Edw. Maur.	Trin.	M 1899 A.B. 1903
—	Humphrey	King's	M 1908 A.B. 1911
—	Walt. John	Chr.	M 1906 A.B. 1909
Doyle,	Ralph Will.	N. C.	E 1898 Qu. A.B. 1901
Dracup,	Athelstane Hamleigh	Cai.	M 1907 Cath. A.B. 1910
Drake,	Art. Will. Courtney	Pem.	M 1900 A.B. 1903. M.B., B.C. 1908
—	Bern. Audley Mervyn	King's	M 1910
—	Gerald Edw.	Trin. H.	M 1900 A.B. 1903
—	Humphrey Rich. Owen	Trin.	M 1912
Dransfield,	Gordon Burdett	C. C.	M 1905 A.B. 1910
Draper,	Fre. Will. Marsden	Qu.	M 1901 A.B. 1904
—	John Rob.	Joh.	M 1900 A.B. 1903. M.B., B.C. 1906
—	Jos. Ja.	N. C.	L 1908 Cath. A.B. 1910
—	Julian Mawby	Qu.	M 1901
Drapes,	Tho. Lambert	Sid.	M 1897 A.B. 1900. M.B., B.C. 1906
Drawbridge,	Cyprian Leycester ...	H. Aye.	M 1888 Pet. A.B. 1891. A.M. 1904
—	Will. Hamilton	C. C.	M 1889 A.B. 1892. A.M. 1905
Dredge,	Edm. John Ingle ...	Pet.	M 1906 A.B. 1909
Drennan,	Cha. Maxwell	Em.	M 1906 A.B. 1909
Dressler,	Phil. d'Hue	Cla.	M 1911
Drew,	Alf. Edw.	C. C.	M 1894 A.B. 1897. A.M. 1902
—	Alf. Lionel	Trin.	M 1905 A.B. 1908. LL.B. 1911
—	Cha. Leon.	Trin.	M 1891 A.B. 1894. A.M. 1901
—	Geo. Harold	Chr.	M 1900 A.B. 1903
—	John Alex.	Pet.	M 1899 A.B. 1902
—	Rob. Stanbanks	Pem.	M 1895 A.B. 1898. B.C. 1903. M.B. 1904
—	Vincent	Em.	M 1910
Drewe,	Adrian	Trin.	M 1910
Drewry,	Geo. Hayward	Cai.	M 1907 A.B. 1910
Drey,	Nich.	King's	M 1912
—	Oscar Raymond	Chr.	M 1903 A.B. 1906
Dreyfus,	Bertram Edw.	Qu.	L 1911
Driffield,	Herb. Geo.	Cath.	M 1901 A.B. 1904
—	Lancelot Townshend	Cath.	M 1899 A.B. 1902
Drinkwater,	John Roddam	King's	M 1906 A.B., LL.B. 1909
—	Roddam Collingwood	Trin.	M 1912
Driver,	Darab Cursetji	Em.	M 1908 A.B. 1911
—	Sam. Rolles		*Litt.D.* 1905
Droop,	Art. Hen.	Trin.	M 1899 A.B. 1902. LL.B. 1903
—	Cha. Edw.	Trin.	M 1896 A.B. 1899. B.C., A.M. 1905. M.B. [1907
—	John Percival	Trin.	M 1901 A.B. 1904
Druce,	Cyril		*A.M.* 1906
—	Cyril Lemuel	Joh.	M 1904 A.B. 1907
—	Phil. Milton	Em.	M 1897 A.B. 1900. A.M.† 1906
—	Rob. Mervyn Powys	Cla.	M 1899 A.B. 1902
Dru Drury,	Clem.	Trin.	M 1901 A.B. 1904. A.M. 1908
Druitt,	Cecil Hen.	C. C.	M 1894 A.B. 1897. A.M. 1901. D.D. 1911
—	Cha. Edw. Hobart ...	Sid.	M 1911

Drummond,	Geo. Hen.	Trin.	M 1901
—	Harold John	Trin.	M 1900 A.B. 1903. A.M. 1907
—	Ja. Montagu Frank	Cai.	M 1900 J. F. M. A.B. 1904
—	John Graham	Chr.	M 1903 A.B. 1906
Drury,	Alan Nigel	Cai.	M 1909 A.B. 1912
—	Alf. Dru	Mag.	M 1890 A.B. 1893. A.M. 1902
—	Tho. Wortley	Chr.	M 1866 A.B. 1870. A.M. 1873. B.D. 1900.
—	Will.	C. C.	M 1895 A.B. 1898. A.M. 1906 [D.D. 1907
Dry,	Ern. Fre. Kenneth ...	Pet.	M 1901
Dryland,	Gilb. Winter	Cai.	M 1900 A.B. 1903
Drysdale,	And. Howard	Trin. H.	M 1898 A.B. 1901
—	Art.	Trin.	M 1910
—	Eric Gordon	Cla.	M 1904
—	Ern. Jos.	Cla.	M 1901
—	Geo. Frederic	Joh.	M 1902 A.B. 1905
—	John Ebenezer	Jes.	M 1906 A.B. 1909
—	John Mortimer	Pet.	M 1905 A.B. 1908
—	Kenneth Gordon	Trin. H.	L 1907
—	Malcolm Blair	Trin. H.	M 1911
—	Percy Douglas	Cla.	M 1901
—	Reg. Keith	Trin.	M 1909
—	Roger Gillespie	Pet.	M 1908 A.B. 1911
—	Theodore	Jes.	M 1898 A.B. 1901. M.B., B.C. 1906
D'Souza,	Fra. Xavier	Joh.	M 1889 A.B., LL.B. 1893. de Souza, A.M.,
Duberly,	Evelyn Hugh Ja. ...	Trin. H.	M 1905 [LL.M. 1899. LL.D.+ 1905
Dubois,	Harold Anth.	N. C.	M 1910
Dubs,	Clarence Ivor Alistair	Trin.	M 1909
—	Ralph Rae Art.	Trin.	M 1904 A.B. 1909. A.M. 1912
Ducat,	Reg.	Trin.	M 1904 A.B. 1907. A.M. 1911
Duchemin,	Cha. Leslie Hawksford	Trin.	M 1911
Duchesne,	Alf.	Jes.	M 1899 A.B. 1902. A.M. 1906
Ducket,	Alex. Armstone	Em.	M 1909 A.B. 1912
Duckham,	Tho. Hen.	Cla.	M 1906 A.B. 1909
Duckworth,	Leslie	Cai.	M 1910
—	Walt. Clarence	H. Sel.	M 1909 C. C. A.B. 1912
—	Wynfrid Laurence Hen.*Jes.		E 1889 A.B. 1892. A.M. 1896. M.D. 1905.
Duddell,	Alb. Graham	Cai.	M 1912 [Sc.D. 1906
Duff,	Alex. Gordon	Trin.	M 1902 A.B. 1905. A.M. 1909
—	Beauchamp Pat.	Trin.	M 1911
—	Douglas Garden	Trin.	M 1906 A.B. 1910
—	Kenneth Dunscombe Johnston	Trin. H.	E 1908
—	Ludovic Ja. Colquhoun	Trin.	M 1908
—	Walt. Norwich	Trin.	M 1902 A.B. 1905
Duffield,	Cha. Alban Will. ...	Qu.	M 1906
—	Hen. Cha.	Cla.	M 1899 A.B. 1902
—	Kenneth Launcelot	Trin.	M 1903 A.B. 1906
—	Walt. Geoffrey	Trin.	M 1901 A.B. 1903
Duffin,	Cha. Grimshaw	Trin.	M 1908 A.B. 1911
Dufton,	John Thornton	Trin.	M 1911
Duggan,	Ern. Fre.	Qu.	M 1910
Duigan,	Will.	Chr.	M 1883 A.B. 1886. M.B., B.C. 1890. A.M.
Duisberg,	Carl Ludwig	Cai.	E 1908 [1905
Duke,	Art. Rob. Aubrey Hare	Cath.	M 1905 A.B. 1908
—	Herb. Lyndhurst ...	Cai.	M 1902 A.B. 1905. M.B., B.C. 1910
—	Mervyn Olliver Molesworth	C. C.	L 1906 A.B. 1908
—	Mich.	Mag.	M 1909
—	Will. Holden ....*Jes.		M 1905 A.B. 1908. A.M. 1912
Duke-Baker,	Cecil Ayshford	Qu.	M 1911
Dukes,	Eric Harford	Trin.	M 1911
—	Lawrence	Trin.	M 1898 A.B. 1901. B.C., A.M. 1905

Duly,	Sid. John	C. C.	M 1910
Dumaresq,	Onfrey Will.	Sid.	M 1900 A.B. 1903. A.M. 1909
Dunbar,	Archib. Edw.	Pem.	M 1907 A.B. 1910
Duncan,	Clarence Will.	Mag.	M 1912
—	Geo. Bruce	Pem.	M 1901 A.B. 1904
—	Geo. Simpson	Trin.	M 1906 A.B. 1909
—	Ja. Grant	Pem.	M 1899 A.B. 1902
—	Jos. Hugh	Cai.	M 1905 A.B. 1908
—	Oliver Cha. Edgar ...	Trin.	M 1909
Duncan-Hughes, John Grant		Trin.	M 1902 A.B. 1905. LL.B. 1906. A.M.† 1910
Duncan-Jones			*See* Jones, A. S. D.
Duncanson,	Edw. Ford	Em.	M 1898 A.B. 1903. A.M. 1907
Dundas,	Alan Charlesworth ...	Joh.	M 1899 A.B. 1902
Dunderdale,	Roland John	Sid.	M 1903 A.B. 1906
Dunham,	Phil.	Cla.	M 1903
Dunkels,	Ern.	Trin.	M 1898 A.B., LL.B. 1901. A.M., LL.M.
—	Walt.	Trin.	M 1904 A.B. 1908　　　　　　　 [1905
Dünkelsbühler, Reg. John		Chr.	M 1909
Dunkerley,	Cecil Lawrence	Joh.	M 1911
—	Harold	Down.	M 1907 A.B. 1910
—	John Victor	Cai.	M 1911
—	Roylance	Trin. H.	M 1901
Dunkley,	Geo. Will.	Pem.	M 1911
—	Herb. Fra.	Joh.	M 1905 A.B. 1908
Dunlop,	Colin John	King's	L 1889 A.B. 1892. A.M. 1903
—	John Beattie	Sid.	M 1894 A.B. 1897. A.M. 1903. M.B., B.C.
—	John Gunning Moore	Cai.	M 1905 A.B. 1909. A.M. 1912　　 [1904
—	John Kinninmont ...	Joh.	M 1910
—	Walt. Nigel Usher ...	Cai.	M 1912
—	Will. Craufurd Carstares	C. C.	E 1907
Dunn,	Cha. Marshman	King's	M 1901 A.B. 1904
—	Geo. Hunter	Pem.	M 1899 A.B. 1902. A.M. 1906. B.C. 1911
—	Harold Curling	Sid.	M 1905 A.B. 1908
—	Hen. Edw.	N. C.	M 1909
—	Hen. Gordon	Cla.	M 1903 A.B. 1906
—	John Drysdale	Cla.	M 1906 A.B. 1909
—	Jos. Harrison	Cla.	M 1898 A.B. 1901. A.M.† 1908
—	Phil. Morgan	Cla.	M 1908 A.B. 1911
—	Tho. Will. Newton	Cai.	M 1898 A.B. 1902. M.B., B.C., A.M. 1906
—	Walt. Geo.	Cath.	M 1898 A.B. 1901
—	Will. Alex.	Pem.	M 1895 A.B. 1898. A.M. 1902
Dunne,	Art. Briggs	Qu.	M 1888 A.B. 1891. M.B., B.C. 1902
Dunnett,	Will. Herb.	Qu.	M 1906
Dünnhaupt,	Paul	N. C.	E 1910
Dunnicliff,	Hor. Barratt	Down.	M 1904 A.B. 1908. A.M. 1911
Dunning,	Geo. Cameron	N. C.	M 1909 A.B. 1912
Dunphy,	Victor	H. Sel.	M 1906 A.B. 1909
Dunscombe,	Geo. Will.	Em.	M 1898 A.B. 1901
Dunsheath,	Percy	N. C.	M 1910 A.B. 1912
Dunwell,	Fre. Leslie	H. Sel.	M 1907 A.B. 1910
Du Pontet,	Raymond Jules Eugéne	Qu.	M 1906
Du Puy,	Harry Wilfred	Trin.	M 1903
Durack,	Jerem. Jos. Ern. ...	Trin.	M 1900 A.B. 1903. A.M.† 1907
Durand,	Percy Fisher	Em.	M 1907 A.B. 1910
Durant,	Will. Maitland	Joh.	M 1908 A.B. 1911
Duranty,	Walt.	Em.	M 1903 A.B. 1906
Durell,	Clem. Vavasor	Cla.	M 1900 A.B. 1903. A.M. 1907
—	John Carlyon Vavasor*Cla.		M 1889 A.B. 1892. A.M. 1896. B.D. 1906
Durham,	Alex. Cha.	C. C.	M 1903 A.B. 1906. A.M. 1910
—	Herb. Edw.	King's	M 1884 A.B. 1887. A.M. 1891. M.B., B.C.
Durie,	Ja. Alf.	Em.	M 1907 A.B. 1910　　 [1892. Sc.D. 1909

Durnford,	Fra. Hen.	C. C.	M 1901 A.B. 1904. A.M. 1908
—	Hugh Geo. Edm. ...	King's	M 1905 A.B. 1908
—	Rich. Selby	King's	M 1904 A.B. 1907
Durrad,	Walt. John	Jes.	M 1897 A.B. 1900. A.M.† 1909
Durrant,	Cha. Edw.	Qu.	M 1907 A.B. 1912
—	Hub. Art.	Qu.	M 1908
—	Ja. Falconer	N. C.	M 1904 A.B. 1907
—	Reg. Bickersteth	Pem.	M 1898 A.B. 1901. A.M. 1911
Durst,	Austin	Cai.	M 1894 A.B. 1897. A.M. 1901
—	Cha. Sumner	Pem.	M 1907 A.B. 1910
Dutfield,	Dudley	Jes.	M 1911
Duthie,	Will. Leon.	Trin.	M 1911
Dutt,	Aaron Chunder	C. C.	M 1880 A.B. 1884. M.B. 1887. Aroon C.
—	Asoka Chunder	N. C.	M 1908 [M.D. 1906
—	Clemens Palme	Qu.	M 1912
—	Guru Saday	Em.	M 1904
—	Praphulla Kumàr ...	N. C.	M 1899 A.B. 1902. A.M.† 1906
—	Prithwi Chandra ...	Down.	M 1910
—	Promothonath	Chr.	E 1905 A.B. 1907
Dutta,	Indu Bhushan	Joh.	M 1901
Dutton,	Harold	Joh.	M 1907 A.B. 1910
Duval,	Herb. Phil.	Cai.	M 1891 A.B. 1894. LL.B. 1895. A.M.†
Duvall,	John Rich.	H. Sel.	E 1908 A.B. 1911 [1899. LL.M. 1906
Dvorkovitz,	Victor	Em.	M 1911
Dwai,	Saw Pha		*See* Yin Saw Ba
Dwelly,	Fre. Will.	Qu.	M 1903 A.B. 1906. A.M. 1911
Dworzak,	Alf. Edgar	Trin. H.	M 1907 A.B. 1910
Dyas,	Geo. Eldridge	Cai.	M 1905 A.B. 1908
Dyer,	Art. Cyril	Em.	M 1907 A.B. 1910
—	Basil Saunders	H. Sel.	M 1898 A.B. 1901
—	Cecil Macmillan	Chr.	M 1912
—	Cha. Hen.	Joh.	M 1903 A.B. 1905. A.M. 1910
—	Fra. Gilb.	C. C.	L 1897 A.B. 1899. Mus.B. 1902. A.M. 1907
—	Fra. Norman Victor	Cla.	M 1912
—	Harry Frank	C. C.	M 1904 A.B. 1907
Dykes,	Fre. Ja. ....*Trin.		M 1899 A.B. 1902. A.M. 1906
Dymes,	Frank Rawling	Joh.	M 1868 A.B. 1875. A.M.† 1910
Dyne,	Hugh Edw. Lubbock	King's	M 1904 A.B. 1907
—	John Bradley	King's	M 1894 A.B. 1897. A.M. 1901
Dyson,	Cha. Bertram	Trin.	M 1908 A.B. 1911
—	Ern.	N. C.	M 1912
—	Ern. Andrews	Jes.	M 1903 A.B. 1906. M.B., B.C. 1912
—	Hub. Archib.	Cla.	M 1912
—	Ja. Will.	Joh.	M 1894 A.B. 1897. A.M. 1902
—	Will. Hub.	King's	M 1910
—	Will. Lionel	Qu.	M 1911

E

Eade,	Art. Neville	Trin.	M 1901 A.B. 1905
—	Aylmer	Trin.	M 1910
—	Cha.	Pem.	M 1909 A.B. 1912
Eaden,	John	Trin.	M 1900 A.B. 1903
Eadie,	Rob. Allan	Qu.	M 1912
Eady,	Crawfurd Wilfrid Griffin	Jes.	M 1909 A.B. 1912
Eagles,	Cha. Edw.	Chr.	L 1884 A.B. 1890. A.M. 1901
Eales,	Will. Harold Fulford	Em.	M 1901 A.B. 1904. B.C. 1910. M.B., A.M.
Eames,	Arnold John	Chr.	M 1911 [1912
—	Ewart Ja. Hyatt ...	Trin.	M 1907 A.B. 1909
—	John	N. C.	M 1894 Chr. A.B. 1897. A.M. 1901
—	John Wallace	Trin.	M 1900 A.B. 1904
Eardley-Wilmot,	Cha. Revell	Cla.	M 1899 A.B. 1902. A.M. 1906
Earle,	Geo. Foster	Joh.	M 1908
—	Herb. Gastineau	Down.	M 1901 A.B. 1905
—	Lawrence Mathew ...	Trin.	M 1900 A.B. 1903. A.M. 1908
Earles,	Fra. John	Chr.	M 1912
Earp,	Freeling Oswald Millns	Joh.	M 1912
—	John Rosslyn	Joh.	M 1910
Eason,	Alec Birks	Jes.	M 1905 A.B. 1908. A.M. 1912
—	Edw. Keith	Jes.	M 1903 A.B. 1906
East,	Gordon Doulton	Em.	M 1907 A.B. 1910
Easter,	Art. John Talbot ...	Cath.	M 1912
—	Fre. Ern. Clow	N. C.	M 1880 H. Sel. A.B. 1884. A.M. 1904
Easterling,	Claude	H. Sel.	M 1911
—	Hen. Garnett	Trin.	M 1906 A.B. 1909
Eastgate,	Art. Bern.	Mag.	M 1898 A.B. 1901. A.M. 1905
Eastick,	Fre. Cha.	Joh.	M 1908 A.B. 1911
Easton,	Frank Reg. Ja.	Joh.	M 1902 A.B. 1905. A.M. 1909
—	Gervaise Lennard Edw.	Trin.	M 1912
—	Ja. Will.	Joh.	M 1906 A.B. 1909
Eastwell,	Maur. Mansfield	Cath.	M 1908 A.B. 1911
Eastwood,	Art. Will.	Joh.	E 1894 A.B. 1898. A.M. 1906
—	Harold Edm.	Trin.	M 1907 A.B. 1910
—	John Fra.	Trin.	M 1906 A.B. 1909
—	Noel Walt.	Trin.	M 1909 A.B. 1912
Eatherley,	Will.	Qu.	M 1900 A.B. 1910
Eaton,	John Edw. Caldwell	King's	E 1892 A.B. 1895. A.M.† 1903
Ebden,	Ja. Wylde	Cai.	M 1901 A.B. 1904
—	Will. Sydenham	Cai.	M 1906 A.B. 1909
Eber,	Reynold Lionel	Chr.	M 1905 A.B. 1908
Eberli,	Will. Felix	Joh.	M 1910
Eccles,	Alex. Gerald	Mag.	M 1910
—	Gregory Will.		*A.M.* 1911
—	Ja. Ronald	King's	M 1893 A.B. 1897. A.M. 1901
Eckenstein,	Tho. Cyril	Chr.	M 1904 A.B. 1907
Eckersley,	Tho. Lydwell	Trin.	L 1910 A.B. 1912
—	Walt. Herb.	Trin.	M 1893 A.B. 1896. A.M. 1903
Eckhard,	Oscar Philip	King's	M 1907 A.B. 1911
Eddington,	Art. Stanley ....*	Trin.	M 1902 A.B. 1905. A.M. 1909
Eddison,	Fre. Will.	Trin.	M 1894 A.B. 1897. A.M. 1901
—	Herb. Wilfred	Chr.	M 1911
—	John Radley	Pem.	M 1908 A.B. 1911
Eddleston,	Reg. Saumarez	Cath.	M 1909 A.B. 1912
Eddowes,	Art.	Qu.	E 1902 A.B. 1905

Eddowes,	Edm. Edw.	Jes.	M 1890 A.B. 1898. A.M. 1905
—	Hen. Cyril	C. C.	M 1899 A.B. 1902. A.M. 1906
Eddy,	Jerome Orrell	Mag.	M 1912
Ede,	Cuthbert	King's	M 1905 A.B. 1908. M.B., B.C. 1911
—	Ern. Elton	Cath.	M 1911
—	Ja. Chuter	Chr.	M 1903
—	Max Crutchley	King's	M 1912 [M.D. 1907
—	Will. Edw. Moore ...	King's	M 1894 A.B. 1897. B.C. 1901. M.B. 1903.
—	Will. Moore	Joh.	M 1868 A.B. 1872. A.M. 1875. D.D. 1908
Eden,	John Rodney	Pem.	M 1911
Edgar,	Walt. Herb.	Trin. H.	M 1906
Edge,	Art. Ern.	Em.	M 1894 A.B. 1897. A.M. 1901
—	Art. Stanley	Jes.	M 1911
—	Cha. Noel	Cai.	M 1900 A.B. 1903
—	Steph. Rathbone Holden	Cai.	M 1911
Edge-Partington,	Ellis Foster	Trin.	M 1904 A.B. 1907. A.M. 1911
Edgeworth,	Fra. Hen.	Cai.	M 1883 A.B. 1887. M.B., B.C. 1889. M.D.
Edghill,	Ern. Art.	King's	M 1898 A.B. 1901. A.M. 1906 [1908
Edkins,	John Syd.	Cai.	M 1882 A.B. 1886. M.B. 1890. A.M. 1892.
Edleston,	Rob.	Trin.	M 1898 A.B. 1901. A.M. 1905 [Sc.D. 1911
Edmond,	Fra. John	Trin.	M 1900 A.B. 1903. A.M. 1907
Edmonds,	Cecil John	Pem.	L 1911
—	Cha. Douglas	Em.	M 1894 A.B. 1897. A.M. 1901
—	Ern. Fritz	Em.	M 1908 A.B. 1911
—	Harold	Joh.	M 1902 A.B. 1905. A.M. 1909
—	Hen. Fénélon	Em.	M 1909 A.B. 1912
—	John	N. C.	M 1900 Em. A.B. 1903
—	John Maxwell	Jes.	M 1894 A.B. 1898. A.M. 1902
—	Sam. Frank	Sid.	M 1898 A.B. 1901. A.M. 1910
—	Syd. Art.	Joh.	M 1903
—	Tho. Acland	Qu.	M 1901 A.B. 1904. A.M. 1910
—	Will.	Trin.	M 1889 A.B. 1892. A.M. 1910
—	Will. Stanley	King's	M 1901 A.B. 1904
Edmondson,	Herb.	Cla.	M 1889 A.B. 1892. M.B., B.C. 1901
Edmunds,	Cecil Harry	Down.	M 1908 A.B. 1911
—	Cha. Vincent	H. Sel.	M 1902 A.B. 1905. A.M. 1909
—	Claud Hen.	Trin.	M 1899 A.B. 1902. A.M. 1906
—	Herb. Weston	Sid.	M 1899 A.B. 1902
—	Horace Vaughan ...	Jes.	M 1905 A.B. 1908. A.M. 1912
—	Norman Gunnery ...	Cla.	M 1903 A.B. 1907. A.M. 1910
—	Percy Michael Lewis	King's	M 1912
Edridge-Green,	Fre. Will.	Joh.	M 1904
Edwardes-Evans,	Dav.	Joh.	M 1896 A.B. 1903
Edwards,	Art. Ern.	N. C.	L 1898 Qu. A.B. 1900. A.M. 1904
—	Art. Lionel	Mag.	M 1899 A.B. 1902
—	Art. Tudor	Joh.	M 1908 A.B. 1911
—	Cha. Derwent	Joh.	M 1889 A.B. 1892. M.B., B.C. 1896. M.D.
—	Cha. Greig	Cai.	M 1911 [1910
—	Cha. Jos.	King's	M 1905 A.B. 1908. A.M. 1912
—	Donald Will.	N. C.	L 1909
—	Douglas Leonel Payne	N. C.	M 1902
—	Edw.	Joh.	M 1889 A.B. 1892. A.M. 1902
—	Edw.	Chr.	M 1900 A.B. 1903
—	Evan Percy	Cla.	M 1901
—	Fra. Millward	Qu.	M 1904 A.B.† 1911
—	Frank Payne	Down.	M 1893 M.B., B.C. 1904
—	Fre. Wallace	Chr.	M 1906 A.B. 1909
—	Geoffrey Lloyd	Trin.	M 1899 A.B. 1902
—	Geoffrey Rich.	Joh.	M 1910
—	Gerald Bracton	Trin.	M 1910
—	Guy Threlkeld	King's	M 1909 A.B. 1912

Edwards,	Harold Walt.	N. C.	M 1906 Chr. A.B. 1909
—	Harrison Stewart ...	Cla.	M 1911
—	Hub. Edwin	Em.	M 1904 A.B. 1907. A.M. 1911
—	John Bryn	Trin. H.	L 1910
—	John Llewellyn Art.	Qu.	M 1908 A.B. 1911
—	John Nassau	N. C.	M 1906
—	John Stanley	Pem.	M 1899 A.B. 1902
—	Langdon Percival Lorimer	Trin.	M 1912
—	Lionel L'Estrange Waller	Jes.	M 1910
—	Maur. Hen.	Qu.	M 1907 A.B. 1911
—	Morgan Hen.	N. C.	M 1902 A.B. 1905. Down. A.M. 1912
—	Reg. Guy	Qu.	M 1910
—	Reg. Herb.	Cla.	M 1905
—	Sid. Ja.	Sid.	M 1906 A.B. 1909
—	Tho.	Sid.	M 1908 A.B. 1911
—	Tho. Groves	Em.	M 1906 A.B. 1909
—	Vincent	Mag.	M 1907 A.B. 1910
—	Walt. Hen.	Cath.	M 1892 A.B. 1895. A.M. 1901
—	Wilfred Norman	Chr.	M 1908 A.B. 1911
—	Will.	Pem.	M 1893 A.B. 1896. A.M. 1901
—	Will. Armine	Trin. H.	M 1909
—	Will. Griffith	Joh.	M 1911
—	Will. Lionel Godfrey	Cla.	M 1901 A.B. 1904. A.M. 1908
Edwards-Moss,	John	Trin.	M 1901
Edyvean,	Rob. Geo. Alb.	Sid.	M 1909
Efflatoun,	Hassan	Trin. H.	M 1900 A.B. 1904
—	Hassan	Trin. H.	M 1912
Egerton,	Leon. Rhodes	Qu.	M 1912
Eggar,	Ja.	Trin.	M 1899 A.B. 1904
Ehlvers,	Fre. Will. Victor ...	H. Sel.	M 1909
Ehrenborg,	Göstaf Bramwell ...	Chr.	M 1902 A.B. 1905. A.M.† 1909
Ehrhardt,	Will. Hereward	Down.	M 1911
Ehrle,	Fra.		*Litt.D.* 1905
Ehrlich,	Cha. Worsley	Trin.	M 1902 A.B. 1905
Eiloart,	Horace Anson	Trin.	M 1908 A.B. 1911. LL.B. 1912
Eisdell,	Hub. Mortimer	Cai.	M 1901 A.B. 1904
Ekanayake,	Geo. Benj.	H. Sel.	M 1899 A.B. 1902. A.M. 1907
El Alaily,	Ibraheem Abd El Salam	Trin.	L 1907
El Arab,	Mohamed Tewfik ...	Trin.	M 1904 Mohammed T. A.B. 1907
Elborne,	John	Trin.	M 1912
—	Syd. Lipscomb	Trin.	M 1909
—	Will.	Cai.	M 1911
Elder,	Alex. Lang	Pem.	M 1909 A.B. 1912
Elderton,	Merrick Beaufoy ...	Cla.	M 1903 A.B. 1906
—	Tho. Howard	Cla.	M 1905 A.B. 1908
Eldridge,	Basil Edgar	Qu.	M 1911
Eley,	Hen. Gerard	Cai.	M 1906
Elger,	Tho. Gwyn	Cai.	M 1901 A.B. 1904
Elgin and Kincardine,	(*Earl of*)		*LL.D.* 1907
Elias,	Rhys	N. C.	E 1901 Down. A.B. 1904. A.M. 1908
Eliott,	Ralph	Trin.	M 1898 A.B. 1901
Eliott-Lockhart,	Allan	N. C.	L 1906
Elischer,	Max Hans	Pem.	M 1904 A.B. 1907. A.M. 1911
Elkington,	Tho. Garrett	Pet.	M 1912
Ellett,	Geo. Grigson	Cath.	M 1895 A.B. 1898. M.B., B.C. 1904. M.D.
Ellice-Clark,	Stuart Tulk	Trin.	M 1905 A.B. 1909 [1908
Ellicott,	Fre. Art. John	Trin.	M 1911
Ellington,	Noel Bayzand	King's	M 1899 A.B. 1902
Elliot,	Edw. Ja.	Trin.	M 1902 A.B. 1905
—	Hub. Will. Art.	Trin.	M 1909 A.B. 1912
—	Wilfrid Edm.	Trin.	M 1912

Elliot,	Wilfrid Thompson ...	Em.	M 1901 A.B. 1905
Elliott,	Art. Dormand	Chr.	M 1902 A.B. 1905
—	Art. Forbes	Em.	M 1896 A.B. 1899. B.C. 1902. M.B. 1903
—	Art. Godfrey	Mag.	M 1898 A.B. 1901
—	Claude Aurelius	Trin.	M 1906 A.B. 1909 *Jes. 1910
—	Claude Temple	Trin. H.	M 1906
—	Edw. Chris. Bowes ...	Trin.	M 1912
—	Edw. Crewdson	Em.	M 1907 A.B., LL.B. 1910
—	Ern. Geo.	Qu.	M 1905 A.B. 1908
—	Gilb. Lewes Lloyd ...	Trin.	M 1912
—	Hen. Venn	Trin.	M 1888 A.B. 1891. A.M. 1904
—	Herb. Denis Edleston	Sid.	M 1905 A.B. 1908
—	John Stanley	H. Sel.	M 1901 A.B. 1904. A.M. 1908
—	Myles Layman Farr	Cla.	M 1909 A.B. 1912
—	Norman	N. C.	M 1911
—	Tho. Reg. Hatchard	Chr.	M 1912
—	Tho. Renton	Trin.	M 1896 A.B. 1900. A.M. 1904. M.D. 1908.
—	Walt. Will.	N. C.	M 1906 A.B. 1909 [*Cla. 1908
—	Will. Hen. Hatchard	Chr.	M 1901 A.B. 1904. A.M. 1908
Elliott-Cooper,	Malcolm	King's	M 1900 A.B. 1903. A.M. 1907
Elliott-Smith			*See* Smith, G. E.
Ellis,	Archib. Gwynne	Trin.	M 1906 A.B. 1908
—	Art. Isaac	Joh.	M 1903 A.B. 1906. A.M. 1910
—	Basil Aird Whittaker	Cla.	M 1901
—	Bern. Jos.	N. C.	L 1899 Chr. A.B. 1903
—	Donald Wilson	Cla.	M 1910
—	Edw. White	Pet.	M 1911
—	Ern. Alf.	Down.	M 1897 A.B. 1900. B.C. 1903. M.B., A.M.
—	Fre.	N. C.	M 1900 A.B. 1903. A.M. 1910 [1904
—	Gordon Stuart Marcon	C. C.	M 1909 A.B. 1912
—	Harold Thornton ...	Trin.	M 1894 A.B. 1898. A.M. 1906
—	Ja. Will. Condell ...	Sid.	M 1904 A.B. 1907
—	Joe	H. Sel.	M 1909 A.B. 1912
—	John Hen.	Cai.	M 1902 A.B. 1905. A.M. 1911
—	John Stanley	Trin.	M 1910
—	Martin Fra.	Chr.	M 1889 A.B. 1892. A.M. 1904
—	Phil. Davenport	Em.	M 1899 A.B. 1902. A.M. 1906
—	Rob.	Cath.	M 1903 A.B. 1906. M.B., B.C. 1912
—	Tho. Pat.	Pem.	M 1910
—	Wilfrid Frank Proffitt	Trin.	M 1907 A.B. 1910
—	Will. Geo. Pharoe ...	N. C.	M 1884 Cath. A.B. 1887. A.M. 1891. B.C.
Ellison,	Art. Dav.	Qu.	M 1912 [1905. M.D. 1906
—	Edm. Geo.	Pem.	M 1911
—	Harold Blades	Cai.	M 1900 A.B. 1903. M.B., B.C., A.M. 1910
—	John	Down.	M 1904 A.B. 1907. B.C. 1912
—	Will. Julius	Em.	M 1910
Ellis Roberts,	Rob.	Jes.	M 1907 A.B. 1912
Ellson,	Syd. Edw.	Trin.	M 1899 A.B. 1902
Ellwood,	Gerald Rob. Maur. ...	H. Sel.	M 1897 A.B. 1901
—	Rupert	Chr.	M 1900 A.B. 1903
El Masry,	Ibrahim	Pem.	M 1912
Elmer,	Tho.	N. C.	L 1907 A.B. 1909
Elmhirst,	Leon. Knight	Trin.	M 1912
Elmslie,	Gordon Forbes	Jes.	M 1908
—	Kenward Wallace ...	King's	M 1906 A.B. 1909. LL.B. 1911
—	Will. Alex. Leslie ...	*Chr.	M 1904 A.B. 1907. A.M. 1911
—	Will. Gray	Pem.	M 1905 A.B., LL.B. 1908
Eloff,	Johan Sarel	Trin. H.	M 1910
Elphick,	Hugh Clifford	Trin.	M 1912
Elphinston,	Tho. Geo.	Em.	M 1901 A.B. 1904
Elphinstone,	Kenneth Vaughan ...	Trin.	M 1897 A.B. 1902. A.M.† 1905

Elphinstone,	Lancelot Hen.	Trin.	M 1898 A.B. 1902. A.M. 1905
Elrington	Bisset, Walt. Favère ...	Pem.	M 1907 A.B. 1910
Elsee,	Cha.	Joh.	M 1895 A.B. 1898. A.M. 1903
Eltham,	Ern. Will.	Qu.	M 1907 A.B. 1910
Elton,	Geoffrey York	Chr.	M 1912
—	Hen. Brown	Cai.	M 1901 A.B. 1905. M.B., B.C. 1909
Eltringham,	Hugh Cyril	Cai.	M 1911
Elverson,	Ronald Whidborne ...	Jes.	M 1909 A.B. 1912
Elvin,	Cha. Fre. Cory	H. Sel.	M 1903 A.B. 1906
Elwell,	Clarence	C. C.	M 1906 A.B. 1909
—	Geo. Hen. Willmott	N. C.	M 1898 A.B. 1901. A.M. 1905
—	Rob. Graham	Trin.	M 1895 A.B. 1898. B.C. 1904. M.B. 1908
Elwin,	Ern. And.	Cla.	M 1896 A.B. 1899. A.M. 1906
—	Walt. Douglas	C. C.	M 1899 A.B. 1906
Elwood,	Augustus Geo. Fredrick	Cath.	L 1908
Elworthy,	Tho.	Cai.	M 1911
Embleton,	Dennis	Chr.	M 1900 A.B. 1903. M.B. 1912
Emerson,	Ambrose	Cai.	M 1894 A.B. 1897. M.B., B.C., A.M. 1901.
—	Herb. Will.	Mag.	M 1900 A.B. 1903 [M.D. 1904
Eminson,	Rob. Astley Franklin	Down.	M 1909 A.B. 1912
Emmett,	Roger Hen.	Trin.	M 1912
—	Will. Gidley	Cai.	M 1905 A.B. 1909. A.M. 1912
Emrys-Evans,	Paul Vychan	King's	M 1912
Emrys-Jones,	Mansel Franklin ...	Cai.	M 1900 Franklin A.B. 1903
Emson,	Percy Algernon Embleton	Jes.	M 1876 A.B. 1882. A.M. 1910
Emtage,	Will. Lashley	Qu.	M 1911
Ende,	Friedrich Wilhelm ...	N. C.	L 1912
Engelhorn,	Curt Maria	Mag.	M 1910
Engineer,	Akhrur Ardeshir ...	Trin.	M 1904 A.B. 1907. LL.B. 1908. A.M. 1911
England,	Edwin Thirlwall	Trin.	M 1896 A.B. 1899. A.M. 1903
—	Frank	Cla.	M 1902 A.B. 1905. LL.B. 1908
—	Frank de Fontayne	Trin.	M 1907 A.B. 1910
—	John Ayres	Mag.	M 1912
—	Walt. Brassington ...	Chr.	M 1911
Engledow,	Frank Leon.	Joh.	M 1910
Englefield,	Fre. Ronald Hastings	Joh.	M 1910
Engler,	Heinrich Gustav Adolf		*Sc.D.* 1904
English,	Burleigh Art.	King's	M 1904 A.B. 1907
—	Fre. Hubert	Joh.	M 1911
—	Hen. Bazely Chris.	C. C.	M 1896 A.B. 1902. A.M. 1908
—	Marcus Claude	Pem.	M 1905 A.B. 1908
Ennos,	Fre. Raine	Joh.	M 1909 A.B. 1912
Ensor,	Geo. Herb.	C. C.	M 1894 A.B. 1897. A.M. 1902
—	Rupert Cha. Handly	Cla.	M 1899 R. C. Handley A.B. 1902
Epping,	Johann Dietrich Wilhelm	N. C.	L 1910
Epps,	Claude Hen. Boudeville	Chr.	M 1899 A.B. 1902. A.M. 1906
—	Geo. Selby Washington	Em.	M 1904 A.B. 1907
Erikson,	Hen. Anton	N. C.	M 1908
Erith,	Lionel Edw. Pat. ...	N. C.	M 1903 A.B. 1906. Jes. A.M. 1910
Ermen,	Walt. Fra. Anth. ...	Em.	M 1894 A.B. 1898. A.M. 1904
Ern,	Otto	Cai.	E 1909
Errazuriz,	Max	Trin. H.	M 1906
Errera,	Alf. Jacques Jos. Harald	King's	M 1904
Erulkar,	Dav. Solomon	Down.	E 1909 A.B. 1912
Eschwege,	Fritz Salo	Chr.	M 1901 A.B. 1904
Escolme,	John Burton	Cai.	M 1898 A.B. 1906
Esdaile,	Arundell Ja. Kennedy	Mag.	M 1899 A.B. 1902
—	Everard Geo. Kennedy	Cai.	M 1901 A.B. 1904
Espin,	Cyril Espinell	Chr.	M 1900 A.B. 1903
Esskildsen,	Erik Yelverton	Chr.	M 1907 A.B. 1910
Estcourt.	Art. Cha.	Mag.	M 1912

Estcourt,	Walt. Bucknall	Mag.	M 1909 A.B. 1912
Etches,	Walt. Parker	N. C.	M 1882 C. C. A.B. 1885. A.M. 1902
Etherington	Smith, Raymond ⎱ Broadley ⎰	Trin.	M 1895 A.B. 1899. B.C., A.M. 1903. M.B. [1904
Eustace,	Alex. Anderson	Trin.	M 1899 A.B., LL.B. 1904
—	Eustace Mallabone ...	Sid.	M 1899 A.B. 1902. A.M. 1910
—	Will. Rowland Geo.	Mag.	M 1910
Evans,	Aidan Oswald	Cath.	M 1906 A.B. 1909
—	Alan Fre. Reg.	Pem.	M 1910
—	Alb. Ern.	Joh.	M 1904
—	Art. Geoffrey	Trin.	M 1905 A.B. 1908
—	Art. Llewelyn	Qu.	M 1910
—	Bern.	Trin.	M 1906 A.B., LL.B. 1909
—	Cha. Alf. Markham	Joh.	M 1893 A.B. 1897. A.M. 1904
—	Cha. Heyland	Pem.	M 1910
—	Cha. Lewis	King's	M 1900 A.B. 1903. A.M. 1907
—	Clifford Calow	C. C.	M 1903
—	Cyril Ern.	N. C.	M 1900 A.B. 1903
—	Dan. Davies	King's	M 1908
—	Edgar Dav.	Joh.	M 1901 A.B. 1904
—	Edw. Griffith	Cla.	M 1888 A.B. 1891. A.M. 1906
—	Emrys	Trin. H.	M 1911
—	Ern.	Trin. H.	M 1905 A.B., LL.B. 1908
—	Evan Laming	Trin.	M 1889 A.B. 1892. M.B., B.C., A.M. 1896. [M.D. 1902
—	Evelyn Ward	Trin.	M 1902 A.B. 1905
—	Frank Dav.	Trin.	M 1896 A.B. 1901. A.M. 1904
—	Frank Noël	Trin.	M 1904 A.B. 1907
—	Fre. Reg.	Qu.	M 1889 A.B. 1892. A.M. 1902
—	Geoffrey	Down.	M 1901 A.B. 1904. A.M.† 1912
—	Geoffrey Farrington ⎱ Farrington ⎰	King's	M 1907 A.B. 1911
—	Geo. Herb.	Down.	M 1903 A.B. 1906
—	Godfrey Theodore Major	Joh.	M 1894 A.B. 1897. A.M. 1904
—	Harold Gaspar	Pem.	M 1908 A.B. 1911
—	Hen. Rich.	Trin. H.	M 1908 A.B. 1910
—	Herb. Clyde	N. C.	M 1908 Joh. A.B. 1911. LL.B. 1912
—	Herb. Godfrey	Qu.	M 1912
—	Howell Tho.	Joh.	M 1902 A.B. 1904. A.M. 1908
—	Hugh Pickering	Chr.	M 1898 A.B. 1901. A.M. 1910
—	Humphrey Silvester	Trin.	M 1909 A.B. 1912
—	Illtyd Buller Pole ...	H. Sel.	M 1903 A.B. 1905. A.M.† 1910
—	Ivor	Cath.	M 1912
—	Ivor Hugh Norman	Cla.	M 1906 A.B. 1909
—	Ja. Will. Douglas ...	Trin.	M 1903 A.B. 1906
—	Jenkin	N. C.	M 1899 Joh. A.B. 1902
—	Jocelyn Herle	Trin.	M 1899 A.B. 1902
—	John Maur. Llewellyn	Cla.	M 1889 A.B. 1899. A.M. 1903
—	John Rich.	Trin. H.	M 1909 A.B. 1911
—	Leon. Hen. Brittan	King's	M 1908 A.B. 1912
—	Leon. Scholes	Cla.	M 1898 A.B. 1901
—	Llewellyn Rankin ...	C. C.	M 1908 A.B. 1911
—	Percy	Trin.	M 1911
—	Percy Dan.	Pem.	M 1900 A.B. 1903. A.M. 1907
—	Percy Edwin	Joh.	M 1907 A.B. 1910
—	Ralph Du Boulay ...	Pem.	M 1910
—	Reg. Wilfrid	Trin.	M 1911
—	Rhys Dav.	Joh.	M 1912
—	Rich. Landreth	Cai.	M 1894 A.B., LL.B. 1897. A.M. 1906
—	Rob. Jocelyn	H. Sel.	M 1911
—	Rupert Ancrum	Trin.	M 1910
—	Tho. Jos.	H. Sel.	M 1905 A.B. 1907

Evans,	Trevor Morse	Pet.	M 1898 A.B. 1901. A.M. 1905
—	Ulick Richardson ...	King's	M 1907 A.B. 1910
—	Vernon Lavington ...	Trin.	M 1905 A.B. 1908
—	Vivian Wentworth Eyre	Trin. H.	M 1907 A.B., LL.B. 1910
—	Will.	Cla.	L 1891 A.B. 1895 Swete-Evans, W. Benj.
			[A.M. 1903. B.C. 1904. M.B. 1905.
—	Will. Cha.	Em.	M 1908 A.B. 1910 [M.D. 1910
—	Will. Dav.	King's	M 1905 A.B. 1908. A.M. 1912
—	Will. Emrys	Joh.	M 1911
—	Will. Marsh Lee	Trin.	M 1893 A.B. 1898
Evatt,	Ja. Millar	Cai.	M 1908 A.B. 1911
Eve,	Frank Cecil ....i...	Em.	M 1890 A.B. 1893. M.B., B.C. 1900. M.D.
—	Herb. Frederic Harwood	Cai.	M 1911 [1903
Evelegh,	John Hen. Carter ...	Cath.	M 1894 A.B. 1897. A.M. 1905
Evelyn-White,	Bern.	Mag.	M 1901 A.B. 1904
—	Cha. Augustin	C. C.	M 1908 C. Augustine A.B. 1911
—	Kenneth Victor	Qu.	M 1905 A.B. 1908
Everard,	Bern.	Trin.	M 1898 A.B. 1901. A.M. 1906
—	Cha. Miskin	Cla.	M 1898 A.B. 1902
—	Hugo Erskine	Trin. H.	M 1906
—	Will. Lindsay	Trin.	M 1909 A.B. 1912
Everatt,	Reg. Will.	Joh.	M 1907
Everett,	Bern. Cha. Spencer	Cai.	M 1894 A.B. 1897. A.M. 1902
—	Will. Wallis	Down.	M 1910
Everington,	Geo. Fre.	Cath.	M 1910
Everitt,	Humphrey Leggatt	Cai.	M 1910
Evers,	Bertram Saxelbye ...	Jes.	M 1910
—	Mervyn Saxelbye ...	Cla.	M 1906 A.B. 1909
Every,	Austin Rimmington	Joh.	M 1912
—	Edw. Fra.	Trin.	M 1881 A.B. 1884 (2). A.M. 1888. D.D.
—	Edw. Oswald	Trin.	M 1905 A.B. 1908 [1906
—	John Morris	Joh.	M 1906 A.B. 1909
Eves,	Ralph Shakspeare ...	Trin. H.	M 1906 A.B., LL.B. 1909
Evington,	Hen. Bedford	Mag.	M 1902 A.B. 1905
Evison,	Reg. Rob.	Chr.	M 1904 A.B. 1909
Evitt,	Edw. Upham	Em.	M 1904 A.B. 1907. A.M. 1912
—	Ern.	H. Sel.	M 1911
—	John Edw. Tho.	Qu.	M 1899 A.B. 1902
Ewald,	Pet. Paul ....:...	Cai.	M 1905
Ewart,	Cha. Gordon	King's	M 1903
—	Geo. Art.	Chr.	M 1906 A.B. 1909
—	Hen. John	King's	M 1910
Ewbank,	Art. Leslie John	Qu.	M 1910.
Ewen,	Guy Cuthbert	Sid.	M 1908 A.B. 1912
—	John Fre. Brodrick	Cla.	M 1912
Ewens,	Bern. Creasy	Cai.	M 1907 A.B. 1910
Ewer,	Will. Norman	Trin.	M 1904 A.B. 1907
Ewing,	Alf. Washington	Chr.	M 1900 A.B. 1903
—	Art. Geo.	Qu.	M 1912
—	Will. Turner	Cai.	M 1906 A.B. 1910
Exham,	Lionel Art.	H. Sel.	M 1902 A.B. 1905
Exmouth,	(*Viscount*) Edw.)	Trin.	M 1909
	Addington Hargreaves Pellew)		
Exshaw,	Tho. Sandford Noel	Cla.	M 1912
Exton,	Geo. Fra.	Jes.	M 1895 A.B. 1898. A.M. 1902
Eyre,	Cha. Howard	Pem.	M 1902 A.B. 1905. A.M. 1911
—	Edw. John	Em.	M 1872 A.B. 1876. A.M. 1905
—	John	Em.	M 1898 A.B. 1901. A.M. 1907
—	Leon. Bucknall	Cai.	M 1909 A.B. 1912
Eyton-Jones,	Hugh Art.	Jes.	M 1910
Ezard,	Edw. Hen.	N. C.	M 1910

Ezechiel,	Victor Gerald	Cai.	M 1902 A.B. 1905
Ezra,	Dav.	Trin.	M 1902 A.B. 1905
—	Ellis	Pet.	L 1907

F

Fabricius,	Leslie	Qu.	M 1906 A.B. 1909
Fagan,	Tho. Wallace	N. C.	M 1895 A.B. 1898. A.M. 1902
Fahmy,	Hassanein	Down.	M 1910
Failes,	Bern. Ja.	Qu.	M 1906 A.B. 1909
—	Frank Chris.	Qu.	M 1904 A.B. 1907
Fair,	Cha. Herb.	Pem.	M 1904 A.B. 1907. A.M. 1911
—	Ja. Conroy	Chr.	M 1912
Fairbairn,	Cha. Osborne	Jes.	M 1912
—	Clive Prell	Jes.	M 1905
—	Geo. Eric	Jes.	M 1906
—	Gordon Armytage ...	Jes.	M 1911
Fairbourn,	Art. Norman	Mag.	M 1908 A.B. 1911
Fairbrother,	Ja.	Cai.	M 1908 A.B. 1911
Fairchild,	Geo. Cranston	Sid.	L 1906 A.B. 1908
Fairfax,	Bradford Lindsay ...	Mag.	M 1912
Fairgrieve,	Mungo McCallum ...	Pet.	M 1895 A.B. 1898. A.M. 1902
Fairhurst,	Chris. Sedgwick	Qu.	M 1906
—	Mark	N. C.	M 1900 Trin. H. A.B. 1903. A.M. 1908
Fairley,	Will.	Mag.	M 1910
Fairrie,	Ja. Leslie	Cai.	M 1910
Falcon,	Jos. Hen.	Pem.	M 1911
—	Michael	Pem.	M 1907 A.B., LL.B. 1910
—	Will.	Joh.	M 1892 A.B. 1895. A.M.† 1902
Falconer,	John Ja. McLennan	Mag.	M 1893 A.B. 1904
Falk,	Geo. Adolph	King's	M 1895 A.B. 1898. A.M. 1907
—	Herman	King's	M 1897 A.B. 1900. B.C. 1904. M.B. 1905
Falkner,	Art. Hen.	Pet.	M 1894 A.B. 1897. B.C. 1908
—	Cha. Gaskell	Trin.	M 1887 A.B. 1890. A.M. 1903
Falloon,	Will. Marcus	Qu.	M 1891 A.B. 1894. A.M.† 1907
Fallowes,	John Tyrell Champion	Cla.	M 1910
Fallowfield,	Hugh Jos. Fre. Alger-non Gordon	Cath.	M 1903 A.B. 1906
Fallows,	Leon.	Qu.	M 1911
Famintsyn,	Andrej Sevgejevich		*Sc.D.* 1904
Fan,	Lien Shao	Pem.	M 1906
Fancourt,	Will.	Cai.	M 1900 A.B. 1903. A.M. 1907
Fanshawe,	Rich. Evelyn	Trin. H.	M 1896 A.B. 1899. A.M. 1903
Fantham,	Harold Benj.	Chr.	M 1908 A.B. 1910 [M.D. 1908
Fardon,	Alb. Hen.	Chr.	M 1897 A.B. 1901. A.M. 1904. B.C. 1907.
—	Harold Jos.	Chr.	M 1897 A.B. 1900. A.M. 1904. B.C. 1907.
Fargus,	Archib. Hugh Conway	Pem.	M 1898 A.B. 1902. A.M. 1905 [M.D. 1909
Farie,	Allan Ja. Crawford	Cla.	M 1901
Farkas,	Tibor	N. C.	M 1910
Farley,	Cha. Finch	Trin.	M 1911
—	Reuben Llewellyn ...	Trin.	M 1909 A.B. 1912
Farmer,	Allix Fra. Gamul ...	Trin.	M 1909 A.B. 1912
—	Eric	Trin.	M 1911
—	Eric Onslow	Pem.	M 1901
—	Fre. Rich.	Qu.	M 1901 A.B. 1904

Farmer,	Hen. Cha. Maclean	Trin.	M 1911
—	Herb. Hen.	Pet.	M 1911
—	Will. Gray	C. C.	M 1902 A.B. 1905. A.M. 1909
Farmiloe,	Geo. Fre.	Trin. H.	L 1905
—	Tho. Howard	Trin. H.	M 1908
Farnell,	Edw. Nigel	Jes.	E 1907 A.B. 1910
—	Hen. Leigh	King's	M 1907 A.B. 1911
Farnfield,	Algernon Sam.	Qu.	M 1893 A.B. 1904. A.M. 1907
—	Archib. John	Qu.	M 1900 A.B. 1903. A.M. 1907
—	Bern. Stanley	Qu.	M 1909
—	Gilb. Sydney	Qu.	M 1903 A.B. 1906
—	Herb. Vernon	Qu.	L 1904 A.B. 1908
—	Percy Hamilton	Qu.	L 1908
Farnham,	Frank Jefferson	Chr.	M 1912
Farnsworth,	Cha. Roy	C. C.	M 1910
Farquhar,	Ja. Taylor Floyd ...	Pem.	M 1877 A.B. 1881. A.M. 1892. B.D. 1904
—	Will. Muir	Pem.	M 1882 A.B. 1885. A.M. 1907
Farquharson,	Fre. Ja.	Trin. H.	M 1901
Farr,	Herb. Foulkes	Cath.	M 1904 A.B. 1907. A.M. 1911
—	Laurence Ern. Augustus ⎱ Bolton ⎰	Cai.	M 1908
Farrant,	Melvil	Trin.	M 1903
Farrar,	Ern.	Trin.	M 1908 A.B. 1911
—	Frederic Percival ...	Pem.	M 1894 A.B. 1897. A.M. 1901
—	Herb. Ronald	Qu.	M 1906 A.B. 1910
Farrell,	Hugh	Jes.	M 1907 A.B. 1910. LL.B. 1911
—	Wilfrid Jerome ......*Jes.		M 1901 A.B. 1904. A.M. 1909
Farren,	Will. Scott	Trin.	M 1911
Farrer,	Edw. Rich. Blackburne	C. C.	M 1910
Farrie,	Hugh	Qu.	M 1907 A.B. 1910
Farrokh Khan,	Mirza	Pem.	M 1907
Farrow,	Ern. Pickworth	Trin.	M 1911
—	Will. Pickworth	Cath.	M 1911
Fathallah,	Mohamed	Trin. H.	M 1910
Faulconbridge,	Frank Tho.	Chr.	M 1912
Faulder,	Tho. Jefferson	Cla.	M 1889 A.B. 1892. M.B., B.C., A.M. 1905
Faulkner,	Alex. Keith	King's	M 1906 A.B. 1909
—	Alf. Mortland	Cai.	M 1904
—	Bertram	King's	M 1900 A.B. 1903. A.M. 1909
—	Odin Tom	Cai.	M 1909 A.B. 1912
—	Roy	Trin.	M 1911
Faulks,	Major Ja.	Joh.	M 1895 A.B. 1898. A.M. 1902
Fauquet-Lemaitre,	Pierre Alf.	Cla.	L 1906
Favell,	Norman Bainbridge	Pem.	M 1905 A.B. 1908
Fawcett,	Rich.	N. C.	M 1911
—	Rich. Wilfrid	Cai.	M 1910
—	Rob. Heath	Em.	M 1912
Fawcus,	Louis Reg.	Trin.	M 1906 A.B. 1909
Fawdry,	Reg. Cha.	C. C.	M 1894 A.B. 1897. A.M. 1901
Fawell,	Cha. Leon.	Pem.	M 1901 A.B. 1904. A.M. 1908
—	Stafford Hen.	Pem.	M 1904 A.B. 1907
Fawkes,	Herb. Beattie	H. Sel.	M 1909 A.B. 1912
Fawsitt,	Tho. Rubie	Chr.	M 1905
Fay,	Cha. Ryle	King's	M 1902 A.B. 1905. *Chr. A.M. 1909
—.	Percy Ja.	Chr.	M 1906 A.B. 1909
—	Stanley John	Chr.	M 1901 A.B. 1905
Fayerman,	Alec Geo. Percy	Joh.	M 1904
Fayle,	Barcroft Jos. Leech	Em.	M 1908 A.B. 1911
Fazl-i-Husain	....	Chr.	M 1899 A.B. 1901. A.M.† 1909
Fearfield,	Cecil John	Cai.	M 1910
—	Jos.	Cai.	M 1901 A.B. 1904

Ferris,	Sam. Bern. Clutton	Joh.	M 1908 A.B. 1911
—	Will. Edw.	Joh.	M 1907 A.B. 1910
Ferry,	Geo. Edm. Hen.	H. Sel.	M 1907 Pet. A.B. 1910
Fetherstonhaugh,	Godfrey Cha. ...	Pem.	M 1900 A.B. 1903. A.M. 1907
—	Rob. Geoffrey	Trin. H.	M 1908
Few,	John Edw.	King's	E 1896 A.B. 1899. A.M. 1903. LL.B. 1908
Fewings,	John Alb.	Joh.	M 1906 A.B. 1909
—	Percy Ja.	Joh.	M 1901 A.B. 1904
Ffrench,	Will. Kyrle Percy ...	Pem.	M 1898 A.B. 1901
Fiddian,	Cedric Moulton	King's	M 1909 A.B. 1912
—	Eric Alf.	Em.	M 1911
—	Guy Vasey	Down.	M 1906 A.B. 1909. M.B., B.C. 1912
—	Ja. Victor	Em.	M 1907 A.B. 1910
—	Will. Moulton	King's	M 1908 A.B. 1911
Field,	Alb. Thurlow	Em.	M 1898 A.B. 1902
—	Allan Bertram	Joh.	M 1896 A.B. 1899. A.M.† 1904
—	Hen. Trevor Cromwell	Qu.	M 1909 A.B. 1912
—	Ja. Hermann	Joh.	M 1898 A.B. 1903. A.M.† 1907
—	John Valentine	C. C.	M 1912
—	Lawrence Percy	Em.	M 1891 A.B. 1894. A.M. 1910
—	Marshall	Trin.	M 1912
Fielden,	Cecil Middleton	Trin.	M 1905
—	Fre. Joshua	Cai.	M 1912
Fieldhouse,	Edwin Ewart	Down.	M 1908 A.B., LL.B. 1911
Fielding,	Edw. Fleming	Cai.	M 1898 A.B. 1901. LL.B. 1909
Figgis,	John Neville	Cath.	M 1885 A.B. 1888. A.M. 1892. Litt.D. 1908
Figueiredo,	José Borges	Joh.	M 1901
Filandi,	Rodolfo	Cai.	M 1910
Fildes,	Geoffrey Phil. Agnew	Trin.	M 1906 A.B. 1909
—	Paul Gordon	Trin.	M 1900 A.B. 1904. B.C. 1909. M.B., A.M. [1910
Filon,	Louis Napoleon Geo.	King's	M 1898 A.B. 1901
Finch,	Cha. Edw. Oscar ...	Jes.	M 1908 A.B. 1911
—	Edwin Gorringe	N. C.	M 1901 Chr. A.B. 1904
—	Geo.	Em.	M 1912
—	Geo. Adolphus Andr.	N. C.	M 1903 A.B. 1906. Qu. A.M. 1911
—	Hen. Kingsley	Joh.	M 1902 A.B. 1905. A.M. 1910
—	John Douglas	Trin.	M 1898 A.B. 1901
—	John Ja.	C. C.	M 1908 A.B. 1911
Findlay,	Archib.	Cai.	E 1898 A.B. 1901. LL.B.† 1903
—	Hen. Alex.	Cai.	M 1900 A.B. 1903
—	Ja. Alex.	Mag.	M 1899 A.B. 1902. A.M. 1907
—	John Galloway	C. C.	M 1902
Finlay,	Eric Lionel	King's	M 1910
—	Rich. Vary Kirkman	Cai.	M 1902
—	Rob. Bannatyne		*LL.D.* 1905
Finlayson,	John Geo.	Chr.	M 1904 A.B. 1907. A.M. 1912
Finlow,	Leon. Will.	Jes.	M 1911
Finn,	Geo. Newport	Jes.	M 1899 A.B. 1902. A.M. 1909
Finter,	Fra. Boyne	Em.	M 1912
Firbank,	Art. Annesley Ronald	Trin. H.	M 1906
Firkins,	Harold Ludlow	Cath.	M 1898 A.B. 1901. A.M. 1905
Firth,	Alec Mark Bernard	Trin.	M 1908 A.B. 1912
—	Arnold	Trin.	M 1901 A.B. 1904
—	Art. Cha. Douglas ...	Trin.	M 1898 A.B. 1901. A.M. 1905. B.C. 1909.
—	Cha. Harding		*Litt.D.* 1910 [M.B. 1911
—	Edw. Loxley	Trin. H.	M 1905
—	Fred Garland	H. Sel.	M 1898 A.B. 1901. A.M. 1907
—	Harold Josiah Rose	Pem.	M 1895 A.B. 1898. A.M. 1902
—	John Cha.	King's	M 1908 A.B. 1911
—	Lewis Gerald	Trin.	M 1906 A.B. 1909
—	Rob. Browning	King's	M 1906 A.B. 1909

Firth,	Tho. Hubert	Trin.	M 1903 A.B., LL.B. 1906. A.M. 1910
Fischer,	Carl Edw.	H. Sel.	M 1912
—	Emil		*Sc.D.* 1907
—	Fre. Stanley	Cla.	M 1891 A.B. 1894. A.M. 1907
—	Hermann Otto Laurenz	Trin.	E 1907
Fischl,	Leopold	Chr.	L 1904
Fisher,	Art. Reg. Colborne	Pet.	M 1910
—	Basil Owen Fra.	N. C.	L 1912
—	Bern. Horatio Parry	Pem.	M 1894 A.B. 1897. A.M. 1901
—	Charley	Joh.	M 1902 Charlie A.B. 1907
—	Edw. Garlick	Em.	M 1902 A.B. 1905
—	Edw. Humbert	Em.	M 1902 A.B. 1905
—	Frank	Cla.	M 1905 A.B., LL.B. 1908
—	Frederic Browell	Joh.	M 1907 A.B. 1910
—	Geoffrey Herb.	Cla.	M 1906 A.B. 1909
—	Geo. Annesley	Jes.	M 1910
—	Geo. Will.	Jes.	M 1910
—	Hen. Frederic	Chr.	M 1896 A.B. 1899. A.M. 1908
—	Hen. Richmond	Em.	M 1895 A.B. 1898. M.B., B.C. 1904
—	Herb. Douglas	Sid.	M 1898 A.B. 1901
—	John Arbuthnot		*LL.D.* 1908
—	John Desmond	Down.	M 1910
—	John Lionel	Sid.	M 1905 A.B. 1908
—	John Wilfred	Trin.	M 1910
—	Kenneth	Trin.	M 1901 A.B. 1904. A.M. 1908
—	Legh Atherton	Sid.	M 1894 A.B. 1897. A.M. 1907
—	Leon. Noel	Sid.	M 1900 A.B. 1903. A.M. 1909
—	Oakden	Trin. H.	M 1904 A.B. 1907
—	Reg.	Sid.	M 1903 A.B. 1906
—	Rob.	Pem.	M 1906 A.B. 1909
—	Rob. Hankinson Williams	Em.	M 1903 A.B. 1906. A.M. 1911
—	Ronald Aylmer	Cai.	M 1909 A.B. 1912
—	Tho. Cathrew	Trin.	M 1889 A.B. 1892. A.M. 1896. D.D. 1911
—	Walt. Harington	Em.	M 1895 A.B. 1898. B.C. 1903. M.B. 1904.
—	Will. Rogers	Joh.	M 1863 A.B. 1867. A.M. 1906 [M.D. 1911
Fishwick,	Cha.	Em.	M 1902 A.B. 1905
—	John Frankland	King's	M 1894 A.B. 1897. A.M. 1901
Fisk,	Anth. Alan	Pem.	M 1902 A.B. 1905
Fison,	Alex. Key	Joh.	M 1910
—	Fre. Jonat.	Pet.	M 1908 A.B. 1911
—	Will. Ja.	Sid.	M 1902 A.B. 1905. A.M. 1909. B.C. 1912
Fitch,	Cha. Harold	Jes.	M 1903 A.B. 1906
Fitchett,	Will. Alf. Robertson	H. Sel.	M 1895 A.B. 1898. A.M. 1902
Fitton,	Rich.	Cai.	M 1909 A.B. 1912
FitzAucher,	R. A.		*See* Rappoport, R. A.
FitzGerald,	Dermot	Trin.	M 1910
—	Gerald Hartas	Qu.	M 1910
—	Gerald Milnes	Trin.	M 1902 A.B. 1905. A.M. 1909
—	Gerald Tho.	King's	M 1902 LL.B. 1905
Fitzgerald,	Harold Snowdon	Cai.	M 1902 A.B. 1907
FitzGerald,	Ja. Ferrier	Trin.	M 1891 A.B. 1904
—	Maur. Pembroke	Trin.	M 1906 A.B. 1909
—	Will. Jos.	Pet.	M 1905 A.B. 1908
FitzHerbert,	Hen. Edw.	Trin. H.	L 1910 A.B. 1912
—	Nicholas Hepburn	Pem.	M 1907 A.B. 1910
FitzMaurice,	Will. Herb.	H. Sel.	M 1905
Fitzpatrick, [1]	Tho. Cecil	*Chr.	M 1881 A.B. 1885. A.M. 1889
Fitzroy,	Hen. Somerset	Trin. H.	M 1889 A.B., LL.B. 1892. LL.M.† 1904
FitzRoy,	Will. Hen. Alf.	Trin.	M 1903

[1] President of Queens' College, 1906.

Fixsen,	Bern. Augustine	Mag.	M 1912	
—	Fra. Alban	Trin.	M 1907	
—	John Fre. Chris.	Pem.	M 1898 A.B. 1902. A.M. 1905	
Flanagan,	Maur. Jos.	N. C.	M 1909 A.B. 1912	
Flannery,	Brian Antony	Chr.	M 1908 A.B. 1912	
—	Harold Fortescue ...	Trin. H.	L 1907 A.B. 1910	
Flawn,	Neville Geo.	Trin. H.	M 1899 A.B., LL.B. 1902	
Flaxman,	Walt. Ja.	N. C.	M 1908 Cath. A.B. 1911	
Flecker,	Herman Elroy	Cai.	E 1908	
Fleet,	Cha. Stanley	Joh.	M 1906 A.B. 1909	
—	Will. Walt. Strong ...	Joh.	M 1903 A.B. 1906. A.M. 1910	
Fleming,	Art. Leslie	Pem.	M 1910	
—	Geoffrey Balmanno ...	King's	M 1900 A.B. 1903. B.C.† 1908. M.B. 1910	
—	John	Mag.	M 1909	
—	Noël	Pet.	E 1907	
—	Will. Dav. Harold ...	Jes.	M 1897 A.B. 1901	
Fleming-Brown,	Gerald Fra.	Cla.	M 1912	
Flemming,	Maximilian Geo.	Cai.	M 1911	
Fletcher,	Alex.	Trin.	M 1898 A.B. 1901	
—	Ambrose John Art.	Cla.	M 1910	
—	Art. Barry	Cai.	M 1912	
—	Art. Will.	Em.	M 1912	
—	Edw.	Jes.	M 1897 A.B. 1901	
—	Ern. Tertius Decimus	Mag.	M 1908 A.B. 1911	
—	Frank Castle	Trin.	M 1908 A.B. 1911	
—	Frederic	Joh.	M 1897 A.B. 1900. A.M.† 1904	
—	Hugh Greenwell	Pem.	M 1898 A.B. 1901	
—	John Holland Ballett	Joh.	M 1899 A.B., LL.B. 1902. A.M. 1906	
—	Matth. Hen. Rawcliffe	Jes.	M 1898 A.B. 1901	
—	Maur. ....,......	H. Sel.	M 1904 A.B. 1907	
—	Nigel Corbet	Qu.	M 1896 A.B. 1900. B.C. 1905. M.B. 1906	
—	Reg. Ja.	Pet.	M 1885 A.B. 1888. A.M. 1892. B.D. 1907.	
—	Rob. Ronald Rawcliffe	Sid.	M 1905	[D.D. 1911
—	Sam. Sigmund Fechheimer	King's	A.M. 1901	
—	Tho. Cha.	Joh.	M 1911	
—	Walt. Morley ....*	Trin.	M 1891 A.B. 1894. A.M. 1898. M.B. 1900.	
—	Wilfrid Taylor	Cla.	M 1902	[M.D. 1908
—	Will.	Cai.	M 1890 A.B. 1893. M.B., B.C. 1896. M.D.	
—	Will. Giffard	Pem.	M 1908 A.B. 1911	[1910
—	Will. Wolfe	Jes.	M 1909 A.B. 1912	
Fleuret,	Frank Stuart	Trin.	M 1904 A.B. 1907. LL.B. 1908	
Flinn,	Oswald Sterndale ...	Pem.	M 1902 A.B. 1905. LL.B. 1906	
Flint,	Algernon Hor.	Trin.	M 1901 LL.B. 1904	
—	Cha. Nigel	Cai.	M 1902	
—	John Walt.	Mag.	M 1904 A.B. 1907	
—	Will. Fielder	Cla.	M 1903	
Flintoff,	Kit Herb.	King's	M 1905 A.B. 1908	
Flitch,	John Ern. Crawford	King's	M 1900 A.B. 1903. A.M. 1907	
Float,	Wilfrid Laurence Palk	Cla.	M 1904 A.B., LL.B. 1907. A.M. 1911	
Flood,	Cha. Bertram	Jes.	M 1900 A.B. 1904	
—	John Cyril	Jes.	M 1896 A.B. 1899. A.M. 1903	
—	John Garnar	Qu.	M 1890 A.B. 1896. A.M. 1906	
—	Sam.	Qu.	M 1906 A.B. 1909	
Flook,	Hub. Syd.	Trin.	M 1894 A.B. 1897. A.M. 1902	
Florence,	Tom Hen.	Chr.	M 1901 A.B. 1904. A.M. 1908	
Flower,	Neville Alf. Cyril ...	Trin.	M 1902	
—	Will. John	N. C.	M 1903 A.B. 1906	
Flude,	Harry	Trin.	M 1894 A.B. 1897. A.M. 1911	
Flynn,	Alb. Ja.	Trin.	M 1911	
—	Tho. Edw.	N. C.	M 1908 Down. A.B. 1911	
Foad,	Ahmed	Trin. H.	M 1912	

Foakes-Jackson,	Fre. John	Trin.	M 1875 A.B. 1879. A.M. 1882. *Jes. B.D.
Foden,	Will. Bertram	Joh.	M 1911 [1903. D.D. 1906
Foister,	Jack	Cath.	M 1912
Foley,	Mich.	Em.	M 1900 A.B. 1903
Follett,	Cecil Walt.	Trin. H.	M 1903 A.B. 1906. A.M. 1911
Follit,	Harold Harry Baily	Cla.	M 1900 A.B. 1904. A.M. 1909
Fonseca,	Victor	Pem.	M 1912
Fontaine de Mazinghen, Achille ...		Down.	M 1912
Foord,	Geo. Howard	Pem.	M 1903 A.B. 1906. A.M. 1910
Foot,	Steph. Hen.	Em.	M 1906 A.B. 1909
Foote,	Fre. Cha.	N. C.	M 1901 A.B. 1904
Footner,	Geo. Rammell	Pem.	M 1897 A.B. 1900. M.B., B.C. 1906
Forbes,	Barré Cassels	King's	E 1900 A.B. 1903
—	Ja. Graham	Chr.	M 1891 A.B. 1894. M.B., B.C. 1898. A.M.,
—	John Foster	Cla.	M 1908 [M.D. 1902
—	Mansfield Duval ......*Cla.		M 1908 A.B. 1911
Forbes Adam,	Colin Gurdon	King's	M 1908 A.B. 1911
—	Eric Graham	King's	L 1908 A.B. 1911
Forchheimer,	Philip Josef	Trin.	M 1912
Ford,	Cha. Whitmore	Joh.	L 1884 A.B. 1890. A.M.† 1901
—	Edw. Baunton	Jes.	M 1895 A.B. 1898. A.M. 1902
—	Fra. Will.	H. Sel.	M 1912
—	Frank Tho.	H. Sel.	M 1906 A.B. 1909
—	Rawlinson Cha.	Cla.	M 1899 A.B. 1902
—	Ronald Mylne	Trin. H.	M 1902 A.B. 1905
Forde,	Cecil Ledward	Cla.	M 1900 A.B. 1903. B.C. 1909. M.B. 1910
Forder,	Frank Geo.	Chr.	M 1902 A.B. 1905. A.M. 1909
—	Hen. Geo.	Em.	M 1907 A.B. 1910
—	Herb. Ja.	H. Sel.	M 1909
Fordham,	Edw. King	Trin.	M 1899 A.B. 1902
—	Edw. Wilfrid	Trin.	M 1893 A.B., LL.B. 1896. A.M. 1903
—	Hugh Alex.	Trin.	M 1911
—	Oswald	Trin.	M 1907 A.B. 1910
—	Will. Herb.	Down.	M 1902 A.B. 1906
Foreman,	Fre. Will.	Cai.	E 1908 A.B. 1910
Forester,	Orlando St Maur ...	Trin.	M 1896 A.B. 1899. O. St M. Weld A.M.
Forgas,	Fra. Jos. Salvador ...	Em.	M 1912 [1903
Forman,	Adam	Pem.	M 1903 A.B. 1906. A.M. 1910
—	Art.	Pem.	M 1889 A.B. 1892. A.M. 1907
—	Dudley Perry	Cai.	M 1906 A.B. 1909
—	Edw. Hugh	Em.	M 1901
—	Geo. Edw. Gibson ...	Jes.	M 1911
—	Humphrey	Pem.	M 1907
—	Tho. Pears Gordon	Pem.	M 1904 A.B. 1907
Formby,	Tho. Hope	Pet.	M 1909
Formoy,	Ronald Ralph	Cai.	M 1905 A.B., LL.B. 1910
Forrer,	Hen. Augustus	Mag.	M 1905 A.B. 1908
Forrest,	Alb. Edw.	Down.	M 1905 A.B. 1908
—	John Will.	Trin.	M 1912
Forrester-Paton,	Ern.	King's	M 1910
Forse,	Edw. John Geo.	Trin.	M 1895 A.B. 1898. A.M. 1902
—	Leslie Napier	C. C.	M 1903 A.B. 1906. A.M. 1910
Forster,	Cha. Michael	Cai.	M 1905 A.B. 1908
—	Edw. Morgan	King's	M 1897 A.B. 1900. A.M. 1911
—	Geo. Wells	Jes.	M 1910
—	Tho.	Trin.	M 1910
—	Will.	Trin.	M 1910
Forster Brown,	Ja. Cameron	Cai.	M 1911
Forsyth,	Archer Baxter	Down.	M 1912
—	Gerald	Cai.	M 1899 A.B. 1903. A.M. 1908
—	Ja. Peters	Cai.	M 1902 A.B. 1905

Forsyth,	Lennard Will.	Cai.	M 1893 A.B. 1898. A.M. 1903
Fortescue,	Cecil Lewis	Chr.	M 1900 A.B. 1903. A.M. 1910
Forwood,	Phil. Lockton	Trin.	M 1909 A.B. 1912
Fosbrooke,	Hen. Leon.	Cla.	M 1902 A.B. 1905. A.M. 1912
Foss,	Will.	Em.	M 1908
Foster,	Art. Webster	Down.	M 1912
—	Basil Le Neve	Cai.	M 1898 A.B. 1902. A.M. 1906
—	Bern. La Trobe	Trin.	M 1912
—	Cuthbert Wellesley	Trin. H.	M 1905
—	Denis Beauchamp Lisle	H. Sel.	M 1908 A.B. 1911
—	Hen. Evans	Trin.	M 1907 A.B. 1910
—	Hugh Perceval Ross	King's	M 1905 A.B. 1908. LL.B. 1909
—	Ja. Rich.	Joh.	M 1894 A.B. 1897. A.M. 1902
—	Joe Hen.	Jes.	M 1900 A.B. 1903. A.M. 1912
—	John	Cla.	M 1896 A.B. 1901
—	John Birkhead	Cai.	M 1912
—	Leon. Charlie	Jes.	M 1905 A.B. 1908
—	Michael Reg.	Trin.	M 1911
—	Pelham La Trobe ...	Trin.	M 1910
—	Raymond Leslie Vachell	King's	M 1893 A.B. 1896. M.B., B.C., A.M. 1904
—	Reg.	N. C.	M 1912
—	Reg. Le Neve	Mag.	M 1895 A.B. 1898. A.M. 1902
—	Rob. Douglas	Joh.	M 1910
—	Vivian Le Neve	King's	M 1894 A.B. 1897. A.M. 1901 [1901
—	Will.	N. C.	M 1873 Joh. A.B. 1877. M.B. 1885. A.M.
—	Will. Hen.	N. C.	L 1901 Joh. A.B. 1903. A.M. 1907
—	Will. Martin	Trin. H.	M 1905
Fothergill,	Claud Fra.	Em.	M 1898 A.B. 1901. B.C. 1906. M.B. 1907
—	Leslie Adolphe	Em.	M 1899 A.B. 1902
Foulds,	Ja. Green	Sid.	M 1909 A.B. 1912
Foulger,	Harry Cecil	Pem.	M 1910
Foulston,	Sam. Vernon	C. C.	M 1912
—	Will. Fre.	C. C.	M 1907 A.B. 1910
Fowke,	Laurence Archdale ...	Mag.	M 1906
Fowle,	Tho. Ernlé	Trin.	M 1881 A.B. 1893. A.M. 1905
Fowler,	Art. Humphries	Sid.	M 1901 A.B. 1904. A.M. 1908
—	Bern. Will.	Pem.	M 1909
—	Cha. Hen.	Trin.	M 1905 A.B. 1908
—	Geo. Starr	H. Sel.	M 1886 A.B. 1889. A.M. 1904
—	Hen. Candler Neilly	Chr.	M 1909
—	John Dudley	Trin.	M 1910
—	Ralph Howard	Trin.	M 1908 A.B. 1911
—	Tho. Geo. Will.	Trin.	M 1899 A.B. 1902
—	Tracy Grant	Cai.	M 1910
—	Wilfrid Ralph Merrick	Cla.	M 1909
Fox,	Alb. Geo.	Cath.	M 1896 A.B. 1899. A.M. 1905
—	Alex. Douglas	Em.	M 1893 A.B. 1897. A.M. 1901
—	And. Stewart	Pem.	M 1912
—	Cha.	N. C.	M 1897 Chr. A.B. 1900. A.M. 1908
—	Cha. Beresford	Trin.	M 1894 A.B. 1897. A.M. 1902
—	Christian Eric	Trin.	M 1907 A.B. 1910
—	Cuthbert Lloyd	King's	M 1903 A.B. 1906
—	Edwin Aubrey Storrs	Em.	M 1907 A.B. 1910
—	Geo. Townshend	Trin.	M 1899 A.B. 1902. A.M. 1906
—	John Crofton	Trin.	M 1900 A.B. 1903
—	Jos. Tylor	Sid.	M 1903 A.B. 1907. M.B., B.C. 1911
—	Lewis Cha.	Trin. H.	M 1909 A.B. 1912
—	Seaton Hen. Elliott	Cai.	M 1911
—	Theodore Harold ...	Cla.	M 1905
—	Tho. Sid. Waterlow	Joh.	M 1897 A.B. 1900. A.M. 1904 [1905
—	Wilfrid Steph.	Trin.	M 1893 A.B. 1896. A.M. 1901. B.C., M.D.

Fox-Andrews, Norman Roy ...... Trin. H. M 1912
Fox-Strangways, Walt. Angelo ... Pem. M 1906 A.B. 1911
Foxton, John .... Em. M 1907
Foyster, Harold Tillard ...... Trin. M 1902 A.B. 1905
— Lionel Algernon ...... Pem. M 1897 A.B. 1900. A.M. 1907
— Phil. Tillard .... Trin. M 1906 A.B. 1909
Fraenkel, Adolph .... Trin. H. M 1910
Fraenkl, Edwin Geo. .... Trin. H. M 1899 A.B. 1902. A.M. 1906
France, Walt. Fre. .... Cai. M 1905 A.B. 1908
Francillon, Fra. Edw. .... Chr. M 1907 A.B. 1911
— Fra. Ja. .... Chr. M 1899 A.B. 1902
Francis, Edw. Cubitt .... H. Sel. M 1905 A.B. 1908
— Edw. Geoffrey .... Trin. M 1903 A.B. 1906
— Guy Lancelot Brereton Cai. M 1904 A.B. 1907
— Ja. Aylmer .... Chr. M 1894 A.B. 1898. A.M. 1902
— Ja. Burleigh .... Sid. M 1896 A.B. 1899. A.M. 1903
— John Clem. Wolstan Pem. M 1907 A.B. 1910
— John Philip .... Cla. L 1904
— Kenneth .... Pem. M 1903 A.B. 1906. A.M. 1910
— Ronald .... Pem. M 1912
— Will. .... N. C. M 1904 Cath. A.B. 1907. A.M. 1912
Franken, Johan Lambertus Machiel Trin. H. M 1901
Frankland, Cha. Art. .... Cla. M 1905
— Edw. .... N. C. M 1900 Em. A.B. 1903. A.M. 1907
— Edw. Percy .... Trin. M 1902 A.B. 1906
— Fra. Will. Barrett ...*Cla. M 1894 A.B. 1897. A.M. 1901
— John Naylor .... Cla. M 1899 A.B. 1901. A.M. 1907
Franklen-Evans *See* Evans, F. P.
Franklin, Cecil Douglas Gilbey Cai. M 1903
— Cha. Reed .... Pem. M 1907 A.B. 1910
— Geo. Denne .... King's M 1895 A.B. 1898. M.B., B.C. 1903
— Hugh Art. .... Cai. M 1907
— Jos. Hen. .... Joh. M 1898 A.B. 1901
— Rich. Penrose .... Pem. M 1904 A.B. 1907. A.M.† 1912
— Rob. .... Chr. M 1907 A.B. 1910
— Tho. Bedford .... Joh. M 1901 A.B. 1904
— Walt. Bell .... Trin. M 1910
Franklin-Smith, Noel Cunliffe ... Trin. M 1903
Franklyn, Alwyne Hollond ...... Trin. M 1905
Franks, Guy Lovell Temple Cla. M 1908
Franquet, Amable Charles (Comte de Franqueville) *Litt.D.* 1904
Fraser, Alex. Tho. .... Cai. M 1892 A.B. 1895. B.C. 1900. M.B. 1902
— Art. Leslie .... Pem. M 1907
— Clive Stuart .... Trin. M 1907 A.B. 1910
— Dav. Hammand ...... Cai. M 1896 A.B. 1900. B.C. 1904. M.B., A.M.
— Donald Stuart .... Joh. M 1906 A.B. 1909 [1905
— Fra. Rich. .... Chr. M 1904 A.B. 1907
— Gordon Travers ...... Trin. M 1900 A.B. 1903
— Ja. .... Joh. M 1902 A.B. 1906. A.M. 1909
— John .... Trin. M 1903 A.B. 1907
— John Hen. Pearson Jes. M 1891 A.B. 1894. M.B., B.C. 1902
— John Horatio .... Cla. M 1897 A.B. 1901
— Mackenzie Hamilton Trin. H. M 1908 A.B. 1911
— Pet. .... Qu. M 1902 A.B. 1905. A.M. 1910
— Rob. Leslie .... Trin. M 1902 A.B. 1906
— Rowland .... Pem. M 1908 A.B. 1911
— Tho. Rich. .... *Sc.D.* 1907
— Will. Arnold .... Chr. M 1911
Fraser-Mackenzie, Evelyn Rob. } Trin. M 1911
  Leopold
— John Ord Alistair ... Trin. M 1909

Frazer,	Norman Lewis	C. C.	M 1892 A.B. 1895. A.M. 1910
—	Rob. Alex.	Pem.	M 1909 A.B. 1912
Fream,	Will.	Trin. H.	M 1911
Frean,	Hen. Geo.	Joh.	M 1901 A.B. 1904. B.C., A.M. 1908. M.B.
—	Herb. Peek	Pem.	M 1888 A.B. 1891. A.M. 1907 [1908 (2)
Frearson,	Alf.	N. C.	M 1901 A.B. 1904. A.M. 1909
Frecheville,	Geo.	Pem.	M 1908
Frederick,	Tho.	Joh.	M 1912
Freeborn,	John Howard Rich.	Cla.	M 1911
Freeman,	And. Ja.	N. C.	M 1893 A.B. 1896. Mus.B. 1903
—	Art. Ja.	King's	M 1896 A.B. 1899. LL.B. 1900. A.M. 1903
—	Cecil Rayner	Pem.	M 1912
—	Cha. Tho.	Cath.	M 1905 A.B. 1908. A.M. 1912
—	Geo. Cyril	Cai.	M 1910
—	Harold	Em.	M 1898 A.B. 1902
—	Harold John Jourdan	Jes.	M 1900 A.B. 1903. A.M. 1912
—	Harry	Chr.	M 1906 A.B. 1909
—	Hen.	Pem.	M 1912
—	John Art.	Pem.	M 1892 A.B. 1895. A.M. 1903
—	John Edw.	Cla.	M 1900 A.B., LL.B. 1903
—	Kenneth John	Trin.	M 1901 A.B. 1904
—	Percy	Down.	M 1905 A.B. 1908
—	Percy Broke	Trin.	M 1906 A.B. 1909
—	Phil. Hor.	Trin.	M 1897 A.B. 1901. A.M. 1905
—	Reg. De Wyckersley	H. Sel.	M 1901
—	Rob. Hen.	N. C.	M 1899 Cath. A.B. 1902
—	Walt. Hanson	Pem.	M 1910
Freer,	Geoffrey Hub.	Trin.	M 1905
Freeth,	Rob. Evelyn	H. Sel.	M 1905 A.B. 1908. A.M. 1912
Freke,	Cecil Geo.	Joh.	M 1906 A.B. 1909
French,	Douglas Gordon	Em.	M 1903 A.B. 1906
—	Fra. Cha.	Trin.	M 1902
—	John Denton Pinkstone		*LL.D.* 1903
—	Reg. Tho. Geo.	Joh.	M 1900 A.B. 1903
—	Rob.	Down.	M 1912 [1906. M.D. 1909
—	Ronald Edgar	King's	M 1899 A.B. 1902. B.C. 1905. M.B., A.M.
—	Will. Douglas	Em.	M 1896 A.B. 1899. A.M. 1905
Frere,	John Edw.	Pem.	M 1895 A.B. 1898. B.C. 1903. A.M. 1907
—	Walt. Howard	Trin.	M 1882 A.B. 1885. A.M. 1889. B.D. 1909.
Freshfield,	Ja. Will.	Trin.	M 1895 A.B. 1898. A.M. 1902 [D.D. 1910
Freshwater,	John Douglas Hope	Trin.	M 1895 A.B. 1899. A.M. 1902. M.B., B.C.
Fretz,	Wilmot Theodore Stuart	Chr.	M 1910 [1903. M.D. 1912
Frewen,	Hugh Moreton	Trin.	M 1904
Frewer,	Cyril Charsley	H. Sel.	E 1897 A.B. 1900. A.M. 1905
—	John	H. Sel.	M 1902
Freyer,	Dermot Johnston ...	Trin.	M 1901 A.B. 1905
Friedlaender,	Kurt Theodor	Trin.	M 1910
Friedman,	Myer	Pet.	M 1908 A.B. 1912
Frift,	Walt.	C. C.	M 1906 A.B. 1910
Frith,	Cha. Alb.	H. Sel.	M 1905 Chr. A.B. 1908. A.M. 1912
—	John Brien	Pem.	M 1902 A.B. 1905. A.M. 1909
—	Will. Rob.	Pem.	M 1904 A.B. 1907
Fritsch,	Georg Friedrich	Chr.	E 1910
Frost,	Edm. Lionel	Trin.	M 1909 A.B. 1912
—	Edw. Granville Gordon	Pem.	M 1905
—	Edwin Brant		*Sc.D.* 1912
—	Hugh Kelsall	Cla.	M 1904
—	Maur.	C. C.	M 1907 A.B. 1910
—	Norman Percival ...	Pem.	M 1898 A.B. 1901. A.M. 1905
—	Percival Ryder	Cla.	M 1909 A.B. 1912
—	Tho. Lawrence	Cla.	M 1907 A.B. 1910

Fruhe-Sutcliffe, Reg. .... Cai. M 1909 A.B. 1912
Fry, Alf. Harold .... King's M 1904 A.B. 1907. A.M. 1911
— Cecil Roderick ...... Trin. M 1907
— Douglas Gaskoin ... Qu. M 1898 A.B. 1901
— Edw. .... *LL.D.* 1907
— Fra. McGregor .... Trin. M 1912
— Geoffrey Storrs ...... King's M 1905 A.B. 1908
— Kenneth Rob. Burgess Cla. M 1901 A.B. 1907. A.M. 1910
— Leslie Harrington ... Cla. M 1910
— Lewis Salisbury ...... King's M 1908 A.B. 1911
— Lucius Geo. Pownall Cai. M 1900 A.B. 1903
— Theodore Penrose ... King's M 1910
— Tho. .... Trin. M 1908 A.B. 1911
Fryar, John Rob. .... N. C. L 1902
Fryer, John Claud Fortescue *Cai. M 1904 J. Claude F. A.B. 1907
— Syd. Ern. .... Joh. M 1900 A.B. 1903
Fryers, John Lawrence ...... Joh. M 1908 A.B. 1911
Fuchs, Harold Munro .... Cai. M 1908 A.B. 1911
Fulford, Fra. Woodbury ...... Jes. M 1898 A.B. 1901. A.M. 1905. B.D. 1912
— Reg. Hardwick ...... Em. M 1905 A.B. 1908
Fullagar, Hugh Fra. .... Joh. M 1894 A.B. 1897. A.M. 1907
— Leo Alf. .... Cai. M 1904 A.B. 1907
Fullalove, Alan Lindsey .... Pem. M 1909 A.B. 1912
Fuller, Ashbury Jos. Stuart Em. M 1891 A.B. 1894. M.B., B.C., A.M. 1912
— Frank Jos. .... N. C. M 1894 Cath. A.B. 1897. A.M. 1901
— Ja. Fra. .... Down. M 1906 A.B. 1909
— Walt. Pearson .... Em. M 1903 A.B. 1905. A.M. 1910
— Will. .... N. C. M 1894 A.B. 1897. A.M. 1909
Fulton, Eustace Cecil .... Chr. M 1897 A.B. 1900. A.M. 1904
— John Hen. Westropp Pem. M 1899 A.B. 1902
Funduklian, Arto Artavasd ...... King's M 1911
Furmston, Edw. Bentley .... Chr. M 1903 A.B. 1909
Furness, Everard Haslam ...... King's M 1892 A.B. 1895. A.M. 1906
— John Monteith ...... King's M 1888 A.B. 1891. A.M. 1903
— Rob. Allason .... King's M 1902 A.B. 1905. A.M. 1912
— Will. .... Mag. M 1906 A.B. 1909
Fursdon, Geo. Ellsworth Sydenham Trin. M 1912
Furse, Will. King .... Chr. M 1902 A.B. 1905
Furze, Alf. .... H. Sel. M 1911
— Claude .... Jes. M 1910
Fushimi, (*Prince*) Sadanare ... *LL.D.* 1907
Fyson, Geoffrey .... Sid. M 1904 A.B. 1907
— Hugh .... Jes. M 1899 A.B. 1902
— Phil. Kemball .... Chr. M 1866 A.B. 1870. A.M. 1873. D.D. 1903

G

Gabain,	Will. Geo.	Pem.	M 1909 A.B. 1912
Gabb,	Harry Secretan	Down.	M 1895 A.B. 1898. M.B., B.C. 1901
—	Ja. Desmond	Cai.	M 1910
Gabbatt,	John Percy	Pet.	M 1900 A.B. 1903. A.M. 1907
Gabriel,	Bern.	N. C.	M 1901
—	Dav. Tho.	N. C.	E 1899 A.B. 1902
—	Gwilym Phillips	N. C.	L 1892 Cath. A.B. 1894. A.M. 1901
—	John Beresford Stuart	Em.	M 1907 A.B. 1910
—	Osman Broad	Em.	M 1909 A.B. 1912
—	Tho. Godfrey	N. C.	E 1905 Cath. A.B. 1909
Gaddum,	Walt. Fre.	Trin.	M 1907
Gaekwad,	Chandra Sinha	Sid.	M 1911
Gaekwar,	(*Prince*) Fatehsinh ...	Down.	L 1905
Gaffikin,	Geo. Horner	Cla.	M 1905 A.B. 1908
Gage,	Edw. Tregurtha	C. C.	M 1907 A.B. 1910
Gaikwad,	Sitaram Sampatrao	Cai.	M 1912
Gaitskell,	Herb. Ashley	Cla.	M 1891 A.B. 1894. A.M. 1898. M.B., B.C.
Galbraith,	Harold Graham	Cai.	M 1911 [1899. M.D. 1902
Gale,	Cuthbert Courtenay	Joh.	M 1908 A.B. 1911
Galer,	Ralph Fry	C. C.	M 1903
—	Reg. Vincent	C. C.	M 1898 A.B. 1902. A.M. 1908
Gall,	Alban	H. Sel.	M 1909
Gallimore,	Hen. Burrows	King's	M 1904 A.B. 1907
Galloway,	Syd. John	Jes.	M 1905 A.B. 1908. A.M. 1912
—	Will.	Qu.	M 1904 A.B. 1907
—	Will. Dawson	Cla.	M 1907 A.B. 1910
Gallwey,	Frank Payne	Trin.	M 1879 Fra. Hen. P., A.B. 1883. Frank
Galstaun,	Shanazar Galstaun ...	Trin.	M 1910 [H. P., A.M. 1910
Gamble,	Hen. John	N. C.	M 1908 A.B. 1911
Game,	Art. Kingsley	Cai.	M 1908 A.B., LL.B. 1911
Gamlen,	Rob. Long	Cai.	M 1899 A.B. 1903. M.B., B.C. 1908 (2).
Gamlin,	Gerald	Pem.	M 1902 [A.M. 1909. M.D. 1912
—	Raymond	King's	M 1903 A.B. 1906. A.M. 1910
Gammell,	Ja. And. Harcourt ...	Pem.	M 1911
Gandhi,	Nadirshaw Hormazshaw	Cai.	M 1899 Nadir H. A.B. 1902
Gandy,	Edgar Stansby	Chr.	M 1905 A.B. 1908. A.M. 1912
—	Eric Worsley	Em.	M 1898 A.B. 1903
—	Hen.	Joh.	M 1904 A.B. 1907. A.M. 1911
Gantillon,	Fre. Nepean	Qu.	M 1895 A.B. 1898. A.M. 1904
Garabedian,	Dikran Garabed	Joh.	M 1908 A.B. 1911
Garbett,	Colin Campbell	Jes.	M 1900 A.B. 1903. LL.B. 1904
Gard,	Herb. Garrard	Em.	M 1901 A.B. 1904. A.M. 1908
Gardener,	Edw. Geo. Augustine	Chr.	M 1908 A.B. 1911
Gardiner,	Allan Fre.	C. C.	M 1900 A.B. 1903. A.M. 1907
—	Art. Ja.	Chr.	M 1906 A.B. 1909
—	Art. Leslie	Cai.	M 1912
—	Felix John Sterndale	H. Sel.	M 1895 A.B. 1898. A.M. 1902
—	Hen. Hamilton	Cai.	M 1910
—	Herb. Alf. Phelps ...	Joh.	M 1889 A.B. 1895. A.M. 1902
—	Ja.	Trin.	M 1905 A.B. 1908
—	Ja. Ern.	Qu.	M 1898 A.B. 1901. A.M. 1905
—	[1]John Stanley	*Cai.	M 1891 A.B. 1895. A.M. 1898
—	Jos. Napier	Trin. H.	M 1890 A.B. 1893. M.B., B.C. 1898. M.D.
—	Kenneth John Rattray	Joh.	M 1909 [1902
—	Oliver Cordery	Chr.	M 1903 A.B. 1906

[1] Professor of Zoology and Comparative Anatomy, 1909.

Gardiner,	Tho. Watson	Em.	M 1904 A.B. 1907. A.M. 1911
—	Walt. ....*Cla.		M 1878 A.B. 1882. A.M. 1885. Sc.D. 1905
—	Will. Chetwynd	H. Sel.	M 1895 A.B. 1898. A.M. 1909
—	Winthrop	C. C.	M 1906
Gardiner-Hill,	Clive	Pem.	M 1910
Gardiner Hill,	Harold	Pem.	M 1909 A.B. 1912
Gardner,	Art.	King's	M 1897 A.B. 1901. A.M. 1904
—	Cha.	King's	M 1899 A.B. 1902. A.M. 1906
—	Cha. Gladstone	Down.	M 1908
—	Eric	Cai.	M 1896 A.B. 1899. M.B., B.C. 1904
--	Fra. Will.	Qu.	M 1909 A.B. 1912
—	Geo. Herb.	Em.	M 1901 A.B.•1904
—	Harold Will.	Qu.	M 1912
—	Hugh	King's	M 1911
—	Humphrey Douglas	Trin.	M 1911
—	Ja. Hen.	Pem.	M 1907 A.B. 1910
—	John Campbell	Trin.	M 1901 A.B. 1904. A.M. 1909
—	John Lawrence	H. Sel.	M 1899 A.B. 1902. A.M. 1909
—	Jos.	C. C.	M 1899 A.B. 1904
—	Kenneth Austen	Cath.	M 1901 A.B. 1907
—	Rob.	Em.	M 1908 A.B. 1911
—	Rob. Cotton Bruce ...	Cai.	M 1908 A.B. 1911
—	Rob. Geoffrey	Trin.	M 1904 A.B. 1907
---	Ronald Leslie	Qu.	M 1904 A.B. 1907
—	Theodore Alb.	Trin. H.	M 1901 A.B., LL.B. 1905
Gardner-Brown,	Fra. Sid. Gardner	Pem.	M 1900 A.B. 1903. A.M. 1907
—	John Gerald Gardner	Pem.	M 1895 A.B. 1898. A.M. 1903
Gardner-Smith,	Percival	Jes.	M 1906 A.B. 1909
Gardnor-Beard,	Will. Edw.	Trin.	M 1909 A.B. 1912
Garfit,	Tho. Noel Cheney ...	Trin.	M 1910
Garland,	Harry Will. Fox ...	King's	M 1903..
Garle-Browne,	John Babington ...	Joh.	M 1900 A.B. 1903
Garne,	Tho.	Jes.	M 1902
Garner, ·	Harry Mason	Joh.	M 1911
Garner-Richards,	Dan. Boghurst	Joh.	M 1894 A.B. 1907. A.M. 1910
Garnett,	Ivan Will.	Mag.	M 1912
—	Ja. Clerk Maxwell ...*Trin.		M 1899 A.B. 1902. A.M. 1906
—	Ja. Newstead	Pem.	M 1909 A.B. 1912
—	Kenneth Gordon	Trin.	M 1911
—	Rich. Tolson	Em.	M 1907 A.B. 1910
—	Will. Hub. Stuart ...	Trin.	M 1900 A.B. 1903
Garnett-Botfield,	Alf. Clulow Fitz-} Gerald {	Trin.	M 1912
—	Will. McLean	Trin.	M 1901 A.B. 1906
Garnsey,	Ern.	Cai.	M 1898 A.B. 1901. LL.B. 1910
Garrad,	Cha. Edw. ....*Cla.		M 1894 A.B. 1897. A.M. 1901
—	Will. Rolfe	Cla.	M 1903 A.B. 1906. A.M. 1910
Garrard,	Geo. Gilb. Crowther	Cla.	M 1909 A.B. 1912
—	Norman	Pem.	M 1906 A.B. 1909
Garratt,	Geo. Campbell	Trin.	M 1887 A.B. 1890. M.B., B.C. 1893. M.D.
Garrett,	Cha. Alf. Blythe	Em.	M 1905 [1903
—	Douglas Thornbury	Em.	M 1902 A.B. 1905
—	Geoffrey Dunnell ...	Pem.	M 1909
—	Geo. Galloway	Em.	M 1899 A.B. 1902. A.M. 1906
—	Gerald Will. Blackman	Cai.	M 1904 A.B. 1907
—	Hen. Fawcett	Pem.	M 1904 A.B. 1907
—	Herb. Leon.	Joh.	M 1899 A.B. 1902. A.M. 1912
—	Howard Geo.	Trin.	M 1909 A.B. 1912
—	Jos. Hugh	Cai.	M 1899 A.B. 1902
—	Leslie Cha.	Trin.	M 1906 A.B. 1909. LL.B. 1910
—	Reg. Will. Burnham	Cath.	M 1904 King's A.B. 1907. A.M. 1911

Garrett,	Steph.	N. C.	M 1903 A.B. 1906. A.M. 1910
—	Tho. Rich. Hen.	Jes.	M 1899 A.B. 1902. A.M. 1909
—	Victor Rich.	Pem.	M 1906 A.B. 1909
—	Will.	Cla.	M 1908 A.B., LL.B. 1911
Garrison,	Rob. Harold	Cath.	M 1911
Garrod,	Alf. Noël	Em.	M 1906 A.B. 1909
—	Ralph Eddowes	Cla.	M 1908 A.B. 1911
—	Wilfrid Edwin Evan	Qu.	M 1912
Garrood,	Jesse Rob.	Joh.	M 1892 A.B. 1895. M.B., B.C. 1899. M.D.
Garry,	Art. Nicholas Melville	King's	M 1909 A.B. 1912　　　　　[1904
Garsden,	John Ja.	Qu.	M 1901 A.B. 1904
Garson,	Herb. Leslie	Cla.	M 1909 A.B. 1912
Garstin,	Denys Norman	Sid.	M 1909
—	Edw. John Langford	Sid.	M 1911
Gartside-Tippinge,	Geoffrey	Pem.	M 1908 A.B. 1911
Gascoigne,	Tho.	Cla.	M 1900 A.B. 1903. A.M. 1910
Gaselee,	Alec Mansel	King's	M 1912
—	Steph.	King's	M 1901 A.B. 1904. A.M. 1908. *Mag. 1909
Gaskell,	Clive Hunter	Pem.	M 1905 A.B. 1908
—	Evelyn Milnes	Trin.	M 1896 A.B. 1899. A.M. 1910
—	John Foster	Cai.	M 1897 A.B. 1900. A.M. 1904. M.B., B.C.
—	Jos. Gerald	Cla.	M 1903　　　　　　　[1907. M.D. 1912
—	Leon. Sadgrove	Chr.	M 1889 A.B. 1892. A.M. 1898. M.B., B.C.
—	Will.	Joh.	M 1892 A.B. 1895. A.M. 1910　　[1901
Gaskoin,	Cha. Jacinth Bellairs	N. C.	M 1895 A.B. 1898. Jes. A.M. 1902
Gaster,	Hugh Frederic	C. C.	M 1892 A.B. 1895. A.M. 1901
Gates,	Cha. Edw.	Sid.	M 1907 A.B. 1910
—	Sid. Barrington	C. C.	M 1911
Gathergood,	Leslie Somerville ...	Sid.	M 1911
Gathorne,	Chris.	Joh.	M 1902 A.B. 1905. A.M. 1909
Gauld,	Alex. Geo.	Em.	M 1912
Gaunt,	Tho.	Mag.	M 1894 A.B. 1897. A.M. 1908
Gaussen,	John MacCulloch ...	Joh.	M 1912
Gauvain,	Hen. John	Joh.	M 1899 A.B.1902. A.M.1906. B.C.1908(2)
Gavin,	Alex. Gordon Douglas	Pet.	M 1911
—	Will.	Trin.	M 1907 A.B. 1910
Gawler,	Alec Edw. Ja.	Cla.	M 1912
Gawne,	Herb. Douglas	H. Sel.	M 1910
Gay,	John Jos.	Chr.	E 1890 A.B. 1894. A.M. 1910
—	Will. Hayne	Chr.	M 1895 A.B. 1898. A.M. 1902
Gaye,	Alan Willis	Cai.	M 1904 A.B. 1907. M.B., B.C. 1912
—	Art. Stretton	Trin.	M 1900 A.B. 1903. A.M. 1907
—	Russell Kerr	*Trin.	M 1896 A.B. 1900. A.M. 1903
Gayne,	Art. Agathos Alenson	Cla.	M 1909 A.B. 1912
Gayner,	Fra.	King's	M 1895 A.B. 1898. A.M. 1905. M.B., B.C.
Gaze,	Alf. Malcolm Brockway	N. C.	M 1907 A.B. 1910　　　　　　[1907
—	Edwin Howard	Joh.	M 1900 A.B. 1903
Gazieh,	Fathalla Mohamed ...	Trin. H.	M 1908 A.B. 1912
—	Mahmoud Hassan ...	Trin. H.	M 1910
Geach,	Geo. Hender	Trin.	M 1908 A.B. 1911
Geake,	Anth.	Joh.	M 1904 A.B. 1907. A.M. 1911
Geard,	Douglas Art. Ayrton	Trin.	M 1912
Geare,	John Wilding Arundel	Pem.	M 1908 A.B. 1911
—	Will. Duncan	Qu.	M 1909 A.B. 1912
Geary,	Alf.	Joh.	M 1912
Geddes,	Rex Wilshire	Jes.	M 1904
Gedge,	Basil Johnson	H. Sel.	M 1901 A.B. 1904
—	Pet.	H. Sel.	M 1909 A.B. 1912
Gee,	Edw. Maitland	Trin.	M 1898 post Maitland, E. M. A.B. 1906
—	Ern.	Cla.	M 1898 A.B. 1901. A.M. 1905
—	Ern. Cresswell	C. C.	M 1895 A.B. 1898. A.M. 1902

Gee,	Hub. Cecil	N. C.	M 1903 Down. A.B. 1906. A.M. 1910
Geider,	Egon Lothar Alb. ...	Trin. H.	M 1909
Geldard,	Nicholas	Trin.	M 1908 A.B. 1911
—	Stuart	Trin.	M 1908 A.B. 1911
Gelderd-Somervell,	Roger Fre. } Churchill	Trin.	M 1904
Gell,	Edw. Anth. Syd. ...	C. C.	M 1894 A.B. 1897. A.M. 1902
—	Will. Cha. Coleman	Cai.	M 1907 A.B., LL.B. 1910
Gelling,	Lawrence Douglas ...	Cla.	M 1902
Gemmell,	Alan Cecil	Trin.	M 1900 A.B., LL.B. 1904. A.M. 1907.
—	Art. Alex.	King's	M 1911 [M.B., B.C. 1912
—	Geo.	Qu.	M 1907
—	Kenneth Tho.	Pem.	M 1902 A.B. 1905. A.M. 1910
Gent,	Frank Ern.	King's	M 1912
Gentle,	Fre. Will.	Qu.	M 1912
George,	Athelstan Key Durancé	Cai.	M 1905
—	Chris. Owen	H. Sel.	M 1910
—	Eric John	Trin.	M 1898 A.B. 1901. A.M. 1905
—	Frank Hen.	Jes.	M 1890 A.B. 1893. A.M. 1909
—	Herb. Horace	Trin.	M 1909 A.B. 1912
—	Howard Trevelyan ...	Cai.	M 1894 A.B. 1897. A.M. 1905
Gerard,	(*Baron*) Fre. John ...	Trin.	M 1902
Gerliczy,	(*Baron*) Felix Geza } Vincenz Gustav Franz Maria	Trin. H.	M 1903
German,	Ralph Lionel	Em.	M 1911
Gerrish,	Frank Wilfred	Cath.	M 1898 A.B. 1901
Gething,	Hugh Bagnall	Trin.	M 1902 A.B. 1906
—	John Eric	Pem.	M 1903 A.B. 1906
Getty,	Ja. Houghton	Cai.	M 1907 A.B. 1910
Ghadge,	Vishwasrao Bajirao ...	Down.	M 1903
Ghani,	Syed Abdul	Down.	M 1908 A.B., LL.B. 1911
Gharpurey,	Hari Ganpat Rao ...	Joh.	M 1898 A.B. 1901
Ghatala,	Mahomed Ziaullah ...	Down.	M 1907
Ghose,	Hem Chandra	N. C.	M 1898 A.B. 1901
—	Sarat Kumar	Trin.	M 1899 A.B. 1903
Ghosh,	Bimal Chandra	Joh.	M 1896 A.B. 1898. A.M. 1902. M.B., B.C.
—	Mahim Chandra	Joh.	M 1900 A.B. 1903. A.M. 1911 [1908 (2)
Gibb,	Cha. Courtenay	Pem.	M 1894 A.B. 1897. A.M. 1901
—	Dav. Eric Wilson ...	Trin.	M 1901 A.B. 1904
—	Edw. Austin	Em.	M 1908 A.B. 1911
—	Harold Pace	Sid.	M 1897 A.B. 1900. M.B., B.C. 1907
—	Ja.	Cath.	M 1905 A.B. 1908. A.M. 1912
—	John		*A.M.* 1906
—	John Harold Onslow	Pet.	M 1905 A.B. 1908
—	Paul	Em.	M 1906 A.B., LL.B. 1909
Gibbings,	Will. Tho.	Joh.	M 1897 A.B. 1900. A.M. 1904
Gibbins,	Hen. Chorley	King's	M 1907 A.B. 1910
—	Norman Martin	Pem.	M 1900 A.B. 1903. A.M. 1909
—	Roland Bevington ...	King's	M 1904 A.B. 1907
—	Tho. Will. Horn	Joh.	M 1903 A.B. 1906
Gibbon,	Edw. Llewellyn Lloyd	Trin.	M 1898 A.B. 1901. A.M. 1905
—	John Houghton	Trin.	M 1897 A.B. 1912
—	Owen Llewelyn	N. C.	M 1903 Down. A.B. 1906. A.M. 1910
Gibbons,	Edwyn Ingram	Trin.	M 1911
—	Geo. Fre.	Pem.	M 1891 A.B. 1894. A.M. 1904
—	Rumney	King's	M 1907
—	Stanley Alex.	Trin. H.	M 1909 A.B. 1912
Gibbs,	Art. Rob.	Mag.	M 1904 A.B. 1907
—	Bern.	Pem.	M 1912
—	Cecil Armstrong	Trin.	M 1908 A.B. 1911
—	Ja. Walt.	Cla.	M 1901

Gibbs,	Reg. Will. Malyon ...	Qu.	M 1903 A.B. 1906
—	Walt. Durant	Trin.	M 1907 A.B. 1910
—	Will. John Rich. ...	N. C.	M 1903 Qu. A.B. 1906. Mus.B. 1909
Giberne,	Harold Buller	Pem.	M 1903 A.B. 1906
Gibson,	Cha. Stanley	Sid.	M 1909 A.M. Incorp. Oxf. 1909
—	Daryl Keith	Cla.	M 1908 A.B. 1911
—	Frank Arnould Sumner	Mag.	M 1912
—	Fre. Harris	C. C.	M 1892 A.B. 1895. A.M. 1909
—	Geo. Middleton	Cla.	M 1899 A.B. 1903
—	Hamilton Hen.	Cath.	M 1897 A.B. 1900. A.M. 1907
—	Harold	N. C.	M 1903 A.B. 1906. A.M. 1910
—	Herb.	Qu.	M 1898 A.B. 1901
—	Herb. Bright	Qu.	M 1900 A.B. 1903
—	Ivor Frederic	Chr.	M 1909
—	Ja. Guthrie	Pem.	M 1911
—	Ja. Lambert	N. C.	M 1902
—	John Paul Stewart Riddell	Sid.	L 1902 A.B. 1906. A.M.† 1909
—	Jos.		*See* Hollins
—	Norman	Down.	M 1910
—	Paul O'Bryen	Em.	M 1909 A.B. 1912
—	Rob. Milner	Chr.	M 1908 A.B. 1911
—	Rob. Will. Beor	Jes.	M 1903 A.B. 1906
—	Rowland Ja. Theodore	Pem.	M 1902 A.B., LL.B. 1905
—	Stanley Rutherford	Qu.	M 1909 A.B. 1912
—	Tho. Alex.	Qu.	M 1899 A.B. 1903
—	Tho. Bainbridge	H. Sel.	M 1907 A.B. 1910
—	Tho. Geo.	Pem.	M 1905 A.B. 1908
—	Tho. Sid.	Em.	M 1901 A.B. 1904
Gibson-Craig,	Archib. Cha.	Trin.	M 1902 A.B. 1905
Gidlow Jackson,	Cha. Will.	Pem.	M 1908 A.B. 1911
—	Geoffrey Herb.	Trin.	M 1911
Gidney,	Fra.	H. Sel.	L 1912
Gidwani,	Sahijram Hassasing	N. C.	M 1909 A.B. 1911
Gielgud,	Hen. Lex Fra. Adam	Pem.	M 1900 A.B. 1903
Giesecke,	Ernst Franz Rudolf Hans	Joh.	M 1910
Giffard,	Edw. Cha.	Trin.	M 1903
—	Hardinge Stanley (*Earl* of Halsbury)		*LL.D.* 1908
—	John Steph.	Jes.	M 1908 A.B. 1911
Gifford,	Ralph Eric	Cla.	M 1903 A.B. 1906
Gilbart-Smith,	Claud Denham ...	Trin.	M 1899 A.B. 1902
—	Mervyn	Trin.	M 1889 A.B., LL.B. 1892. LL.M. 1897. [LL.D. 1911
Gilbert,	Bern. Will.	Joh.	M 1910
—	Ern. Denby	Qu.	M 1902 A.B. 1907. A.M. 1910
—	Frank Mottram	Chr.	M 1890 A.B. 1893. A.M. 1901
—	Geoffrey Gilb. Tho.	H. Sel.	M 1899 A.B. 1902
—	Geo. Saunders	Em.	M 1898 A.B. 1901. A.M. 1905
—	Harry	Em.	M 1912
—	Herb. Edw.	Cai.	M 1886 A.B. 1889. A.M. 1906
—	Leon. Armitage	Cath.	M 1903 A.B. 1906. A.M. 1910
—	Tho.	Trin. H.	M 1907 A.B. 1910
Gilbey,	Walt. Ewart	Trin.	M 1904
—	Wilfrid Holland	Trin.	M 1905
Gildersleeve,	Basil Lanneau		*Litt.D.* 1905
Giles,	Allen Fra.	Em.	M 1911
—	Bertram	Chr.	E 1901
—	Claude Harold	Cla.	M 1900 A.B. 1903
—	Eric	Pem.	M 1912
—	Granville Cha. Trelawny	King's	M 1910
—	Hew O'Halloran	Trin. H.	M 1908 A.B. 1911 [Litt.D. 1910
—	[1] Pet. ....*Cai.		M 1882 A.B. 1885. A.M. 1889. *Em.

[1] Master of Emmanuel College, 1911.

Gilham,	Cecil Walt.	Pet.	M 1910
Gill,	Cha. Hope	Qu.	M 1880 A.B. 1884. A.M.† 1887. D.D. 1905
—	Cyril Illingworth Carswell	King's	M 1912
—	Dav.		Sc.D. 1904
—	Hen. Vincent	Down.	M 1907 A.B. 1909
—	Hub. Alex.	Qu.	M 1906 A.B. 1909
—	Kenneth Carlyle	Cath.	M 1912
—	Reg. Geo.	Joh.	M 1903 A.B. 1908
—	Will.	N. C.	L 1907 Cath. A.B. 1909
—	Will. Conrad	King's	M 1908 A.B. 1910
Gillan,	Geo. van Baerle	Pem.	M 1909 A.B. 1912
Gillespie,	Alex. Marshall	King's	M 1896 A.B. 1899. A.M.† 1903
—	Tho.	Joh.	M 1894 A.B. 1897. M.B., B.C., A.M. 1902
Gillett,	Art. Bevington	King's	M 1898 A.B. 1901. A.M. 1906
Gilliat-Smith,	Bern. Jos.	Cai.	L 1907
Gillibrand,	Art.	C. C.	M 1904 A.B. 1907
Gillies,	Cha. Percivale	Pem.	M 1911
—	Harold Delf	Cai.	M 1901 A.B. 1904
Gilliland,	Geo. Fra.	Trin.	M 1902 A.B. 1905. A.M. 1912
—	Valentine Knox	Trin.	M 1907 A.B. 1910
Gillison,	Wilfred	Pet.	M 1903 A.B. 1906
Gillson,	Alb. Hen. Steward	Joh.	M 1908 A.B. 1911
Gillum,	Sid. Julius	King's	M 1895 A.B. 1898. A.M. 1904
Gilmour,	Alastair Stuart	Trin.	M 1906 A.B. 1909
Gilroy,	Paul Knighton	H. Sel.	M 1903 A.B. 1906. M.B., B.C. 1910
Gilson,	Rob. Quilter	Trin.	M 1912
Gimblett,	Cha. Alf.	Trin.	M 1905 A.B. 1908. A.M. 1912
—	Cha. Leon.	Cai.	M 1908 A.B. 1911
Ginnlette,	Cha. Hart Medlicott	Cai.	M 1908 A.B. 1911
Gimson,	Basil Lovibond	Em.	M 1909
—	Chris.	Em.	M 1906 A.B. 1909
Gingell,	Walt. Craven	Cai.	M 1908 A.B., LL.B. 1911
Ginistelli,	Edouard Plançon ...		See Plançon, E.
Ginn,	Dennis Barton	Trin. H.	M 1898 A.B. 1902. A.M. 1906
Ginsburg,	Hyam Hirsch	Down.	M 1912
Girard,	Dan. Lucien Marie	Down.	L 1908
Girdlestone,	Frederic Stanley ⎱ Pears Lynn ⎰	N. C.	M 1900 A.B. 1904. A.M. 1908
Girling,	Edw. Art.	H. Sel.	M 1907 A.B. 1910
—	Fra. Black	Em.	M 1900 A.B. 1903. A.M. 1908
Girtin,	Tho.	Pem.	M 1893 A.B. 1896. A.M. 1903
Gjers,	Lawrence	Trin.	M 1912
Gladstone,	Art. Lawrence	Cla.	M 1908 A.B. 1911
—	Hugh Steuart	Trin. H.	M 1896 A.B. 1899. A.M. 1904
—	Rob. Theodore	Trin.	M 1904 A.B. 1907. A.M. 1912
Gladwell,	Reg. John	C. C.	M 1897 A.B. 1900. A.M. 1905
Glaister,	Geo. Fre.	N. C.	M 1908 A.B. 1911
Glaisyer,	Hen. Ern.	Cai.	M 1902 LL.B. 1905
Glanville,	Walt. Josolyne	Cai.	M 1901 A.B. 1904
Glare,	Tho. Will.	Sid.	M 1906 A.B. 1909
Glaser,	Herb.	Chr.	M 1904 A.B. 1907. A.M. 1911
—	Will. Hen.	Chr.	M 1900 A.B. 1903. A.M. 1907
Glasson,	Alf. Kirby	C. C.	M 1907 A.B. 1910
—	Jos. Leslie	Cai.	M 1909 A.B. 1911
—	Lancelot	King's	M 1908 A.B. 1911
Glasspool,	Reg. Tho. Booth ...	Mag.	M 1899 A.B. 1902
Glauert,	Hermann	Trin.	M 1910
—	Otto	Cla.	M 1899 A.B. 1902
Glazebrook,	Art. Rimington	Trin.	M 1910
Glazounow,	Alex.		Mus.D. 1907
Gleave,	John Wallace	Joh.	M 1909 A.B. 1912

Gledhill,	Art.	H. Sel.	M 1895 A.B. 1898. A.M. 1908
—	Walt. Geo.	Joh.	M 1899 A.B. 1902. A.M. 1906
Gledstone,	Fre. Farrar	Joh.	M 1904 A.B. 1907. A.M. 1911
Gleed,	Rich. Wilson Arnall	Trin.	M 1908 A.B. 1911
Glen,	Alex.	Chr.	M 1868 A.B. 1872. LL.B. 1873. A.M. 1875.
—	Bruce Cunningham	Trin.	M 1905 [LL.M. 1906
—	Randolph Alex.	Chr.	M 1894 A.B., LL.B. 1897. A.M. 1905
—	Rob. Rodger	Trin.	M 1911
Glen-Bott,	Carl Lotherington	Em.	M 1902 A.B. 1905
Glencross,	Ja. Reg. Morshead	Trin.	M 1896 A.B. 1899. A.M. 1903. LL.B. 1904
Glenday,	Roy Gonçalves	Em.	M 1908 A.B. 1911
Glendenning,	John Will.	C. C.	M 1899 A.B. 1902. A.M. 1906
Glenister,	Douglas Ja.	Chr.	M 1906 A.B. 1909
Glenn,	Cecil Hayward	Pem.	M 1893 A.B. 1896. B.C. 1901. M.B. 1902
Glerawly,	(*Viscount*) Fra.	Trin. H.	M 1904
Glover,	Alb. Edw.	Jes.	M 1907 A.B. 1911
—	Hulbert Edw. Toone	Cla.	M 1879 A.B. 1883. A.M. 1907
—	Ja. Alison	Joh.	M 1894 A.B. 1897. B.C. 1901. M.B., A.M.
—	Ja. Irving	N. C.	E 1897 Mus.B. 1901 [1902. M.D. 1905
—	Ja. Rodolph Heber	Down.	M 1909 A.B. 1912
—	John Gibson	Qu.	M 1911
—	John Hen.	Trin.	M 1889 A.B. 1892. A.M. 1906
Gloyne,	Will. Ja. Maynard	Trin.	M 1909
Gluckstein,	Isidore Montagu	Sid.	M 1909
Glyn,	John Paul	Cai.	M 1905 A.B. 1908
Glynn,	Dashper Hen.	Cla.	M 1901 A.B. 1904
—	Eric Hardy	Cla.	M 1912 [M.D. 1909
—	Ern. Edw.	Cla.	M 1892 A.B. 1895. M.B., B.C., A.M. 1901.
—	Tho. Rawdon	Cla.	M 1898 A.B. 1901. M.B., B.C., A.M. 1910
Glynne,	Arvon	Cla.	M 1910
Goatcher,	Fred	H. Sel.	M 1908 A.B. 1911
Godber,	Hen. Trevor	Trin.	M 1909 A.B. 1912
Godbole,	Yeshwant Anant	N. C.	M 1910
Godby,	Trevor Austin	Mag.	M 1906 A.B. 1909
Goddard,	Archib. Spencer	Trin.	M 1905 A.B. 1909
—	Fre. Walt.	Chr.	M 1912
—	Harry	Joh.	M 1899 A.B. 1902. A.M. 1906
—	John	Chr.	M 1899 A.B. 1903. A.M. 1906
—	Rob. Edw.	Trin.	M 1877 A.B. 1881. A.M. 1907
Godfrey,	Alf. Rob.	N. C.	M 1895 A.B. 1898. A.M. 1903
—	John Bates Dashwood	Pet.	E 1898 A.B. 1903. A.M. 1908
Godlee,	Steph.	Pem.	M 1902 A.B. 1906
Godsal,	Hugh	Trin.	M 1912
Godsell,	Rich. Tho.	Trin.	M 1899 A.B. 1903
Godson,	Art. Talbot	Pet.	M 1903 A.B. 1906. A.M. 1911
—	Fre. Phil.	Pem.	M 1906 A.B. 1909
Goffin,	Syd. Fre. Herb.	Jes.	M 1897 A.B. 1900. LL.B. 1901
Goh,	Lai Hee	Em.	M 1899 A.B. 1902. A.M. 1906
Goho,	Saroda Churn	Pet.	M 1901
—	Srish Chander	Pet.	M 1910
Going,	Claude Art. Hedley	Pem.	M 1892 A.B. 1895. A.M. 1908
—	John	Cla.	M 1893 A.B. 1896. A.M. 1907
Gold,	Cha. Millen	King's	E 1908
—	Ern.	*Joh.	M 1900 A.B. 1903. A.M. 1907
Goldberg,	Stuart Victor	Cath.	M 1910
Goldie,	Archib. Hayman Robertson	} Joh.	M 1910
—	Noël Barré	Trin.	M 1901 LL.B. 1904. A.B. 1905
Golding,	Hen. Cha.	Pem.	M 1911
Goldney,	Hen. Hastings	Trin.	M 1905 A.B. 1908
Goldschmidt,	Ernst Philipp	Trin.	M 1905 A.B. 1908

Goldschmidt,	Ja. Parlane	Trin.	M 1912
—	Julius Hen.	N. C.	L 1903
--	Louis Moritz	Trin. H.	M 1903
—	Will. Noel	Pem.	M 1912
Goldsmid-Stern-Salomons, Dav. ⎫ Reg. Herman Phil.⎬		Cai.	M 1904 A.B. 1907. A.M. 1911
Goldsmith,	Edm. Onslow	Pem.	M 1910
—	Geo. Harvey	Cai.	M 1886 A.B. 1889. M.B. 1893. M.D. 1902
—	Hen. Mills	Jes.	M 1904 A.B. 1908
—	John Hen.	Jes.	M 1909
Goldstein,	Wolfe	Em.	M 1911
Goldziher,	Ignatius		*Litt.D.* 1904
Gollancz,	Israel	Chr.	M 1883 A.B. 1887. A.M. 1891. Litt.D. 1906
Gomes,	Edwin Herb.	Joh.	M 1882 A.B. 1896. A.M.† 1901
Gomme,	Arnold Wycombe ...	Trin.	M 1905 A.B. 1908
—	Edw. Elfred Coote ...	Trin. H.	M 1904 A.B. 1907
—	Geoffrey Ja. Lyon ...	Trin.	M 1910
—	Ralph Eliot	Trin. H.	M 1907 A.B., LL.B. 1910
Gomperz,	Theodor		*Litt.D.* 1904
Gonehalli,	Venkanna Hosabnaik	Joh.	M 1906 A.B. 1908. A.M.† 1912
Gonin,	Hugh Ern. Geo.	Em.	M 1900 A.B. 1906
Gonne,	Fra.	N. C.	M 1904 A.B. 1907. A.M. 1911
Gooch,	Cha. Trevor	Pem.	M 1907 A.B. 1910
—	Geo. Will.	Sid.	M 1911
—	Hen. Wyard	Sid.	M 1904 A.B. 1907. A.M. 1911
—	Kenneth Thackeray	Pem.	M 1912
Good,	Claude Wilfrid	Qu.	M 1911
Goodacre,	John	Jes.	M 1894 A.B. 1897. A.M. 1901
Goodall,	Armitage	Qu.	M 1894 A.B. 1897. A.M. 1902
—	Cha. Cunliffe	Cai.	M 1909
—	Cha. Hen.	King's	E 1901 A.B. 1905
—	Edw. Basil Herb. ...	Jes.	M 1904 A.B. 1907
—	John Fre.	Em.	M 1910
—	Jos. Brittain	Em.	M 1909 A.B. 1912
Goodbody,	Art. Brand	Cai.	M 1910
—	Jonat.	Cla.	M 1900 A.B. 1903
Goodchild,	Edw. Lionel	Cai.	M 1910
—	Ern. John	N. C.	M 1909 A.B. 1912
—	Geo. Fre.	Sid.	M 1895 A.B. 1898. A.M. 1906
—	Harold Hicks	Down.	M 1903
—	Hugh Napier	Jes.	M 1908 A.B., LL.B. 1911
—	John	Cla.	M 1898 A.B. 1901
Goodden,	Cecil Phelips	King's	M 1899 A.B. 1902
Gooddy,	Cha. Brian Walton	Cla.	M 1904
Goode,	Alf. Geo.	Cath.	M 1902 A.B. 1905
--	Geo.	N. C.	M 1881 A.B. 1886. A.M. 1901
—	Reg. Hen.	Joh.	M 1908 A.B. 1911
—	Sam. Walt.	Cai.	E 1899 A.B. 1901
Gooderham,	Ern. John Robinson ⎫ Briggs ⎬	Cai.	M 1908 A.B. 1911
Goodhart,	Alf. Warner	C. C.	M 1899 A.B. 1902. A.M. 1909
—	Art. Lehman	Trin.	M 1912 [1908
—	Gordon Wilkinson ...	Trin.	M 1899 A.B. 1902. B.C., A.M. 1907. M.B.
Goodhart-Rendel,	Harry Stuart ...	Trin.	M 1905 Mus.B. 1909 [1906. M.D. 1909
Gooding,	Simonds	Joh.	M 1898 A.B. 1901. A.M. 1905. M.B., B.C.
Goodland,	Joshua	Trin. H.	M 1900 A.B., LL.B. 1904. A.M. 1907
Goodliffe,	Arnold	King's	M 1897 A.B. 1900. A.M. 1905
Goodman,	Benj. Mark	Pem.	M 1911
—	Edw. Leonce	Jes.	M 1905 A.B. 1908
Goodrich,	Alex. Thorpe	C. C.	M 1892 A.B. 1895. A.M. 1909
—	Harold Spencer	Joh.	M 1912

Goodwin,	Alb. Desborough	Trin.	M 1904 A.B. 1907
—	Ern.	Em.	M 1896 A.B. 1899. A.M. 1903
—	Ern. St George Sagar	Cai.	M 1904 A.B. 1907. M.B., B.C., A.M. 1911
—	Harold Desborough	Trin.	M 1908 A.B. 1912
—	Harold Ja.	Jes.	M 1905 A.B. 1908
—	Hen. Art. Chris.	Jes.	M 1907 A.B. 1910
Goodwyn,	Phil. Will.	Qu.	M 1911
Goolden,	Alex. Wood	Trin.	M 1908 LL.B. 1911
—	Cha. Denis	N. C.	M 1901 Chr. A.B. 1904. A.M. 1908
—	Cha. Edw.	Em.	M 1911
—	Geo. Anth.	Cai.	M 1910
—	Hugh Jos.	Joh.	M 1912
—	Percy Pugh Goolden	Trin.	M 1879 A.B. 1883. A.M. 1908
Gordon,	Alan Fra. Lindsay ...	Trin. H.	M 1911
—	Alan Sam.	Pem.	M 1907 A.B. 1910
—	Art. Granville	Trin. H.	M 1901 A.B. 1904
—	Art. Reynault	Trin.	M 1912
—.	Art. Wiener	Trin.	M 1897 A.B. 1901
—	Cosmo Alexander ...	King's	M 1904 A.B. 1907. A.M. 1911
—	Edw. Basil	Mag.	M 1912
—.	Edw. Fra. Strathearn	Joh.	M 1912
—	Eldred Pottinger	Cla.	M 1909 A.B. 1912
—	Fra. Jervis	Chr.	M 1900 A.B. 1903
—	Geoffrey	Cai.	M 1904
—	Geo. Art.	Em.	M 1907
—	Geo. Fra. Carter	Trin.	M 1895 A.B. 1898. A.M. 1903
—	Hamilton	Trin.	M 1905
—	Ja. Geoffrey	Trin.	M 1900 A.B. 1903. A.M. 1907
—	John Edm.	N. C.	M 1904
—	Keith Roy	Trin.	M 1906
—	Rich. Edw. Clifton ...	Pem.	M 1908 A.B. 1911. LL.B. 1912
—	Rob. Abercromby ...	Pet.	M 1893 A.B. 1897. A.M. 1901. LL.M. 1907
—	Roland Graham	H. Sel.	M 1899 A.B. 1902
—.	Steph.	Pem.	M 1903 A.B. 1906. B.C. 1911
—	Walt. Maxwell	Chr.	M 1896 A.B. 1899. A.M. 1904
—	Will. Bonnalie	Cla.	M 1908 A.B. 1911
—	Will. Hyde Eagleson	Sid.	M 1912
—	Will. Tho.	Em.	M 1908 A.B. 1910
Gordon-Cumming,	Alex. Penrose	Trin.	M 1912
Gordon-Smith,	Harry	Trin.	M 1894 A.B. 1897. B.C., A.M. 1901. M.B.
Gordon Walker,	Robin Ern.	King's	M 1906 [1902
Gore,	Cha.		*LL.D.* 1909
Gore Browne,	Harold Tho. Thirlwall	Trin.	M 1904
Gornall,	Harold Kenyon	Cath.	M 1893 A.B. 1896. A.M. 1903
Gorrell,	John Gregory	H. Sel.	M 1903 A.B. 1905
Gorringe,	Allan Lindsay	Joh.	M 1903 A.B. 1907
Gorst,	John Eldon	Trin.	M 1879 A.B. 1883. A.M.† 1903
Gosling,	Will. Rich.	H. Sel.	M 1910
Gosnell,	Ralph Percy	Trin.	M 1899 A.B. 1902. A.M. 1906
Goss,	John	Jes.	M 1896 A.B. 1900. B.C. 1904. M.B. 1905
Gossage,	Art. Fre. Winwood	Trin.	M 1909 A.B. 1912
—	Ern. Leslie	Trin.	M 1909 A.B. 1912
Gosse,	Alf. Hope	Cai.	M 1903 A.B. 1906. A.M. 1910. M.B., B.C.
—	Reg. Wilkes	Cai.	M 1910 [1912
Gossling,	Brian Stephen	Trin.	M 1909 A.B. 1912
—	Frank Newbery	Em.	M 1908 A.B. 1911
Gosvámí,	Satya dás	Chr.	M 1906
Gotch,	Duncan Hepburn ...	Cai.	M 1910
—	Mervyn Spencer	Trin.	M 1910
Gott,	John Addison	Mag.	M 1896 A.B. 1899. A.M. 1903
Gotto,	Edw. Thornton	Qu.	M 1902 A.B. 1905

Gotto,	Hen. Stanley	Trin. H.	M 1902
Gottstein,	Kurd Felix Waldemar	Joh.	M 1911
Goudy,	Alexander Porter ...		A.M. 1902
Gough,	Harold Art.	Em.	M 1907 A.B. 1910
—	Harry Percy Bright	Sid.	M 1899 A.B. 1902
—	Hen. Jos.	Joh.	M 1902
Gough Calthorpe, Fre. Somerset		Jes.	M 1911
Gould,	Cha. Ja. Baines	N. C.	M 1899 A.B. 1902
—	Edwin	Cla.	M 1898 A.B. 1901. A.M. 1907
—	Harold Utterton	Trin.	M 1894 A.B. 1898. M.B., B.C., A.M. 1903
—	Hen. Chris.	Cla.	M 1911
—	Hen. Hilton Monk ...	Cla.	M '1908 A.B. 1911
—	Herb. Fre.	Pem.	M 1906 A.B. 1909
—	Ja. Douglas	Trin. H.	M 1893 A.B. 1897. A.M. 1903
—	Kenneth Luke	Pem.	M 1896 A.B. 1900. A.M. 1903
—	Phil. Oliver	Em.	M 1903 A.B. 1906. A.M. 1910
—	Roger	Jes.	M 1911
Gould-Butson, Hen. Strange		Pem.	M 1902 [Down. M.C. 1906
Goulden,	Cha. Bern.	N. C.	E 1896 A.B. 1899. M.B., B.C., A.M. 1904.
Goulston,	Art.	Cla.	M 1872 A.B. 1883. A.M. 1886. M.B., B.C. [1911. M.D. 1912
Goult,	Ja. Ern.	Em.	M 1895 A.B. 1898. A.M. 1902
Gour,	Harpasad Sing	Down.	M 1889 Harprasad S. N. C. A.B. 1892. [A.M.† 1896. LL.M. 1902. Down.
Gourlay,	Will. Balfour	Trin.	M 1899 A.B. 1902 [LL.D.† 1908
Gover,	Clem. Edw. John ...	Pem.	M 1909 A.B. 1912
Gow,	Alex.	Cai.	M 1900 A.B. 1903. A.M. 1907
—	And. Sydenham Farrar	*Trin.	M 1905 A.B. 1908. A.M. 1912
—	Cha. Humphry	Em.	M 1909 A.B. 1912
—	Leon. Harper	Pem.	M 1910
—	Pet. Graham	Cath.	M 1903 A.B. 1906. A.M. 1910
Gowdy,	Rob. Clyde	Trin.	M 1909
Gower,	Joshua Reg.	Trin. H.	M 1909 A.B. 1912
—	Lawford Cha.	Down.	M 1909
—	Rob. Pat. Malcolm ...	Em.	M 1906 A.B. 1909
Gowers,	Ern. Art.	Cla.	M 1899 A.B. 1902
Goyder,	Fra. Willoughby	Joh.	M 1896 A.B. 1899. B.C. 1903. M.B. 1906
Grabham,	Geo. Walt.	Joh.	M 1899 A.B. 1902. A.M. 1906
Graburn,	Godfrey Newall	C. C.	M 1903 A.B. 1906
Grace,	Cha. Lindesay Playfair	Trin.	M 1910
—	Cleveland Raphael ...	Cla.	M 1905 A.B. 1910
—	Edgar Mervyn	Chr.	M 1905 A.B. 1908
—	Handley Carleton ...	Qu.	M 1910
—	Harold Myers	Qu.	M 1907 A.B. 1910
—	Will. Gilb.	Pem.	M 1893 A.B. 1896. A.M. 1903
Gracey,	Horace Cha.	Trin.	M 1911
—	Rob. Lloyd	Trin.	M 1910
Graham,	Chris.	N. C.	M 1897 Cai. A.B. 1901. A.M. 1905
—	Constantine		*See* Michaelides, C. C.
—	Geo.	Trin.	M 1901 A.B. 1904. B.C., A.M. 1908. M.B.
—	Geo. Walford	Cla.	M 1892 A.B. 1901 [1910
—	Harold Ern.	Jes.	M 1896 A.B. 1899. M.B., B.C., A.M. 1906
—	Harold Ja.	Em.	M 1895 A.B. 1898. A.M. 1902
—	Hen. Archib. Roger	Trin.	M 1911
—	John Cha. Will.	Trin.	M 1890 A.B. 1893. A.M. 1901. B.C., M.D.
—	John Reg. Noble ...	Trin.	M 1911 [1909
—	Jos. Ivon	Em.	M 1910 A.B. 1912
—	Lionel Augustine ...	Cai.	M 1906
—	Oswald	Trin.	M 1902 A. 1905
—	Rob. Fra.	Trin.	M 1894 A.B. 1897. A.M. 1902
—	Sam. Irvine	Trin.	M 1884 A.B. 1887. A.M. 1912

Graham,	Will. Ja. .... Pem.	M 1909
—	Will. Sharpe .... Cla.	M 1891 A.B. 1894. A.M. 1902
Graham Brown, Geo. Fra. .... Cath.		M 1910
Graham-Hodgson, Harold Kingston Cla.		M 1910
Graham-Jones, John Lawrence ... Em.		M 1899 A.B. 1902. M.B., B.C. 1910
Graham Montgomery, Graham John Early } Jes.		M 1912
Graham-Smith, Geo. Stuart .... Pem.		M 1894 A.B. 1897. M.B., B.C., A.M. 1902.
Grail,	Clifford Geo. .... N. C.	M 1908 Joh. A.B. 1911 [M.D. 1905
Grandage,	Will. Briggs .... Cla.	M 1899 A.B. 1902. B.C., A.M. 1908
Granger,	Edw. Harold Hertslet Cla.	M 1909 A.B. 1912
Grant,	Alan Fra. Montagu Trin.	M 1911
—	Alex. Phil. Fullerton Trin. H.	M 1906
—	Alister Campbell ...... King's	M 1900 N. C. A.B. 1906
—	Bramwell Dundas ... Trin.	M 1910
—	Ern. Boase .... Qu.	M 1906 A.B. 1909
—	Fra. Hen. Symons ... Joh.	M 1902 A.B. 1905
—	Frank .... Qu.	M 1897 A.B. 1900. A.M. 1904
—	Fre. Geo. .... Chr.	M 1902 A.B. 1905. LL.B. 1906. A.M. 1910
—	Geo. Leon. .... Qu.	M 1908 A.B. 1912
—	Gregor Hugh .... Trin.	M 1898 A.B. 1902. A.M. 1907
—	Harry Alex. Gwatkin Trin.	M 1901
—	Hen. Stirling .... Trin.	M 1895 A.B. 1899. A.M. 1902
—	John .... King's	M 1902 A.B. 1905
—	John Cha. .... King's	M 1908 A.B. 1911
—	Montagu Fre. .... Trin.	M 1896 A.B. 1899. B.C.†, A.M. 1905
—	Norman Maling ...... Trin.	M 1907 A.B. 1910
—	Rob. Melville .... Pem.	M 1908 A.B. 1911
Grantham,	Ja. .... Down.	M 1909 A.B. 1912
—	Stanley Geo. .... Trin.	M 1901 A.B. 1904
Grantham-Hill, Clermont .... Cai.		M 1909 A.B. 1912
Grasemann, Cuthbert .... Trin.		M 1908 A.B. 1911
Grasett,	Elliot Blair .... N. C.	L 1908 Jes. A.B. 1911
Graves,	Basil .... Chr.	L 1907 A.B. 1910
—	Rich. Massie .... King's	M 1903
Graveson,	Art. Will. .... King's	M 1911
Gray,	Anth. Fre. .... Mag.	M 1911
—	¹ Art. ....*Jes.	M 1870 A.B. 1874. A.M. 1877
—	Art. Phil. .... Em.	M 1904 A.B. 1907
—	Austin Keyingham ... Jes.	M 1907 A.B. 1911
—	Basil .... Trin.	M 1907 A.B. 1910
—	Douglas Leslie .... Cai.	M 1903 A.B. 1906
—	Ern. Godfrey .... Sid.	M 1898 A.B. 1901
—	Frederic Harold Arbuthnot H. Sel.	M 1896 A.B. 1899. A.M. 1903
—	Fre. Laurence .... Trin.	M 1905 A.B. 1908
—	Fre. Steele .... Em.	M 1896 A.B. 1899. A.M. 1903
—	Gabriel .... Qu.	M 1901 A.B. 1904. A.M. 1908
—	Geo. Harold Magrath King's	M 1899 A.B. 1903. A.M. 1906
—	Hamish .... Jes.	M 1900 A.B. 1903. A.M. 1907
—	Harry Tyrrell .... Trin.	M 1899 A.B. 1902. B.C., A.M. 1906. M.C.
—	Hen. Malcolm Franklin Cai.	M 1902 A.B. 1905 [1908
—	Ja. .... King's	M 1909 A.B. 1912
—	John .... Trin.	M 1905
—	John Milner .... King's	M 1908 A.B. 1911
—	Maur. .... Trin.	M 1908
—	Norman .... Em.	M 1907 A.B. 1910
—	Phil. .... Mag.	M 1907 A.B. 1910
—	Ronald Evelyn Gordon Pem.	M 1897 A.B. 1900. A.M. 1904. M.B., B.C.
—	Syd. Tho. .... Jes.	M 1909 [1905. M.D. 1911

¹ Master of Jesus, 1912.

Gray,	Walt. Stuart Wingate	Pem.	M 1909 A.B. 1912
—	Will.	N. C.	M 1896 King's A.B. 1899. A.M. 1903
—	Will. Athelstan	Cai.	M 1904 A.B. 1907
—	Will. Hornigold	Chr.	M 1911
—	Will. Stanger	Pem.	M 1910
Grayrigge,	Rob. Stockdale	Trin.	M 1903
Grayson,	Denys Hen. Harrington	Pem.	M 1912
—	Geo. Hastwell	Em.	M 1889 A.B. 1892. A.M. 1902
Grazebrook,	Owen Fra.	Cai.	M 1904 A.B. 1907
Grear,	Art. Tho. Lantsbury	Mag.	M 1906 A.B. 1909
—	Edw. Lantsbery	N. C.	M 1902 A.B. 1905
—	Ern. John Lantsbery	Joh.	M 1910
Greathead,	Art. Merriman	Cla.	M 1904 A.B. 1907
—	Ja. Hen.	Cai.	M 1905 A.B. 1908
—	Ja. Merriman	Chr.	M 1904 A.B. 1907
Greatorex,	Walt.	Joh.	M 1895 A.B. 1898. A.M. 1904
Greatrex,	Ferdinand Cecil	Cai.	M 1903 A.B. 1906
Greaves,	Alan	Chr.	M 1904 A.B. 1907
—	Fra. Neville	Qu.	M 1899 A.B. 1902
—	Geo. Methuen	Trin.	M 1907
—	Hen. Gordon	Em.	M 1903 A.B. 1906. M.B., B.C. 1911
—	Maxwell John	Sid.	M 1905 A.B. 1908
—	Ralph Cha. Johnstone	Trin.	M 1908
—	Wilfrid Golden	Down.	M 1906 A.B. 1909
Green,	Alan Baldrey	Down.	E 1890 A.B. 1893. A.M. 1897. M.B., B.C.
—	Archib. Geo. Noble	Chr.	M 1908 A.B. 1911 [1898. M.D. 1901
—	Bern.	Trin.	M 1907 A.B. 1910
—	Cha. Fre.	Sid.	M 1894 A.B. 1897. A.M. 1901
—	Dan. Stanley	Down.	M 1907
—	Dav.	Trin.	M 1912
—	Edw. Cowper	Qu.	M 1903 A.B. 1906
—	Edwin Augustus	Em.	M 1910
—	Ern. Will.	Joh.	M 1902 A.B. 1906. A.M. 1910
—	Eustace Hub.	Em.	M 1894 A.B. 1897. A.M. 1901
—	Fra. Gilb.	Trin.	M 1901 A.B. 1904. A.M. 1908
—	Fre. Will.	Jes.	M 1887 A.B. 1898. A.M. 1901
—	Gabriel	N. C.	M 1904 Chr. A.B. 1907
—	Geo.	Chr.	M 1894 A.B. 1897. A.M. 1901
—	Harold	Trin.	M 1903 A.B. 1906. A.M. 1910
—	Hen. Frank	Sid.	M 1912
—	Hen. Gwynedd	Cai.	M 1912
—	Hen. Tyrrell	Qu.	M 1905 A.B. 1908
—	Hor. Salkeld	Trin.	M 1902 A.B. 1905
—	Ja.	Qu.	M 1907 A.B. 1910
—	John Eric Sid.	Pet.	M 1905 A.B. 1908. A.M. 1912. *Trin. H.
—	John Hanson	C. C.	M 1886 A.B. 1889. A.M. 1907 [1912
—	John Leslie	Down.	E 1907 A.B. 1910
—	John Rich. Eling ...	King's	M 1903 A.B. 1908
—	Leon. Newman	Cla.	M 1899 A.B. 1904
—	Norman	Joh.	M 1906 A.B. 1909
—	Pet.	Joh.	M 1890 A.B. 1893. A.M. 1902
—	Robin Fre.	Qu.	M 1907
—	Ronald John	Qu.	M 1910
—	Sam. Arnold Collier	Cai.	M 1910
—	Stanley Jos.	Down.	M 1908 A.B. 1911
—	Stanley Willoughby	Cla.	M 1904
—	Stuart Montagu	Joh.	M 1907 A.B. 1910. LL.B. 1911
—	Tho. Reg.	C. C.	M 1910
—	Will. Harold	Qu.	M 1912
Green-Armytage,	Geoffrey	Qu.	M 1906 A.B. 1909
Greenberg,	Art. Will.	Cai.	M 1911

Greenberg,	Bern. Morris	Em.	M 1911
Greene,	Alf. Ern.	King's	M 1896 A.B. 1899. A.M. 1903
—	Cha. Will.	Em.	M 1900 A.B. 1903. M.B., B.C. 1907. M.C.
—	Fra. Carleton	Pem.	M 1900 A.B. 1903 [1910
—	Geo. Watters	Down.	M 1895 A.B. 1899. M.B., B.C., A.M. 1903.
—	Gerald Edw.	Cai.	M 1899 A.B. 1903 [M.D. 1906
—	Lovell	Chr.	M 1901 A.B.† 1907
—	Will. Hen. Clayton	C. C.	M 1893 A.B. 1896. M.B., B.C. 1901
—	Will. Pomeroy Crawford	Trin.	M 1903 A.B. 1906
Greenfield,	Will. Montague	Jes.	M 1903
Greenhalgh,	Will. Rawson	Pem.	M 1902 A.B. 1905. A.M. 1909
Greenham,	Raymond Geo. Harvey	Jes.	M 1905 A.B., LL.B. 1909
Greenhill,	Ja. Kenneth	Pem.	M 1907 A.B. 1910
—	Tho. Watson	Pem.	M 1911
Greenhough,	Harold	Cath.	M 1910
Greenidge,	Cha. Wilton Wood ...	Down.	M 1907 A.B. 1910. LL.B. 1911
Greening,	Will.	Chr.	M 1899 A.B. 1904. A.M. 1907
Greenish,	Fre. Harold Sellick	Cai.	M 1908 A.B. 1911
Greenlees,	Ja. Robertson Campbell	Joh.	M 1898 A.B. 1901. B.C. 1905. M.B. 1907
Greenop,	Herb. Barton	Em.	M 1903 A.B. 1906. A.M. 1910
Greenough,	Tho. Rigby	Cai.	M 1904 A.B. 1907
Greensill,	Art. Will.	Cath.	M 1904 A.B. 1908. A.M. 1912
—	Bern. Heynes	Trin. H.	E 1906
Greenstreet,	Norman Bern. de Medina	Joh.	M 1912
Greenwood,	Art. Will.	Qu.	M 1898 A.B. 1901
—	Ern. Talbot	Sid.	M 1912
—	Frank Braithwaite ...	Mag.	M 1903 A.B. 1906
—	Geo. Frederick	Sid.	M 1899 A.B. 1902. B.C. 1907. M.B. 1909
—	Harry Bordley	Trin.	M 1898 A.B., LL.B. 1901. A.M. 1908
—	Hub. Fra.	H. Sel.	M 1902 C. C. A.B. 1910
—	John	Pet.	M 1905 A.B. 1909
—	John	N. C.	M 1905 A.B. 1908
—	John Eric	King's	M 1910
—	Leon. Hugh Graham *King's		M 1899 A.B. 1902. A.M. 1906. *Em. 1909
—	Oliver	Cla.	M 1908
—	Wilfrid Edm. Carwithen	H. Sel.	M 1902 A.B. 1906
Greer,	Hugh	Pem.	M 1901 A.B. 1904
—	Syd. Herb. Armstrong	Trin.	M 1899 A.B. 1902
—	Will.	Pem.	M 1899 A.B. 1902
Greg,	Art. Hyde	Trin.	M 1891 A.B. 1894. M.B., B.C., A.M. 1902
—	Walt. Wilson	Trin.	M 1894 A.B. 1897. A.M. 1901. Litt.D. 1909
Gregg,	Hamlet Pilkington Huband	Cla.	M 1907
—	Ivo Fra. Hen. Carr	Chr.	M 1902 A.B. 1905. A.M. 1910
—	John Allen FitzGerald	Chr.	M 1891 A.B. 1894. A.M. 1898. B.D. 1909
—	Rob. Gordon Cromwell Carr	Chr.	M 1902 A.B. 1905. A.M. 1910
Gregory,	Art. Reg.	Joh.	M 1909 A.B. 1912
—	Cha. Hebden	Em.	M 1896 A.B. 1899. M.B., B.C., A.M. 1903.
—	Edm. Douglas	Em.	M 1903 [M.D. 1911
—	Galiston Marcar	Trin.	M 1908 A.B. 1911
—	Geo. Monro Allan ...	Trin. H.	M 1896 A.B. 1900. A.M.† 1903
—	Herries Smith	Em.	M 1896 A.B. 1899. A.M. 1903
—	John Sheridan	Trin.	M 1908 A.B., LL.B. 1911
—	Reg. Phil. ....*Joh.		M 1898 A.B. 1901. A.M. 1905
—	Tho. Leslie Clarke ...	Trin.	M 1901 A.B. 1906
Gregory Jones,	Cecil	Cai.	M 1909 A.B. 1912
Gregson,	Hen. Geo.	Trin.	M 1912
—	Hen. Wilson	Chr.	M 1900 A.B. 1903. A.M. 1910
—	Phil.	Pem.	M 1910
Greig,	Alex. Will.	Jes.	M 1893 A.B. 1896. B.C. 1901
—	Algernon Frank Macgregor	Pet.	M 1908

Greig,	Cha. Alexis	King's	M 1903
Grell,	Jesse Mitchinson Potter	H. Sel.	M 1899 A.B. 1902. M.B., B.C. 1907
Grellier,	Ern. Franz Waldemar	Down.	M 1905 B.C. 1912
Grenfell,	Eric Blake	Jes.	M 1911
—	(*Lord*) Francis Wallace		*LL.D.* 1903
Grenside,	Chris. Fre.	Pem.	M 1903 A.B. 1906
Grepe,	Hector Will.	Pem.	M 1884 A.B. 1887. A.M. 1909
Gresley,	Geo. Nigel	H. Sel.	M 1883 A.B. 1886. A.M. 1904
Greville,	Perceval Eden	H. Sel.	M 1907 A.B. 1910
Greville-Smith,	Stanley Howard	Trin.	M 1907 A.B. 1912
Grew,	Edwin Sharpe	Chr.	M 1885 A.B. 1888. A.M. 1904
Grey,	Alb. Hen. Geo.	Trin.	M 1870 A.B.1874. LL.M. 1879 (*Earl* Grey)
Grey-Wilson,	Rob. And.	Trin.	M 1910 [*LL.D.* 1911
Gribble,	Cha. Herb.	Trin.	M 1907 A.B. 1910
—	Harry Wagstaff Graham	Em.	M 1910
Grice,	John Eric	Down.	M 1912
—	John Will.	King's	M 1900 A.B. 1903
—	Norman	Joh.	M 1912
Grice-Hutchinson,	Rowan Ernest	Trin.	M 1904 A.B. 1907
Grierson,	Hen.	Pem.	M 1910
Grieve,	Alex. Barrie	Cla.	M 1908 A.B. 1911
Griffin,	Art. Wilfrid Michael } Stewart	Trin.	M 1906 A.B. 1910
—	Everard Jervis Fullagar	Qu.	M 1905 A.B. 1908
—	Frederic Will. Waudby	King's	M 1900 A.B. 1903. M.B., B.C., A.M. 1908
—	Herb. John Stewart	Trin.	M 1903 A.B. 1906
—	John	Trin. H.	M 1904 A.B. 1907. A.M. 1912
—	Tho. Noel Rathbone	Pem.	M 1894 A.B. 1897. A.M. 1902
Griffith,	Anth. Wykeham	Sid.	M 1912
—	Art. Lefroy Pritchard	Cla.	M 1905 A.B. 1908
—	Geoffrey Foster	Trin.	M 1910
—	Harold Kinder	Trin.	M 1904 A.B. 1907. M.B., B.C. 1912
—	Hen. Hall	Chr.	M 1909 A.B. 1912
—	Herb. Cecil	King's	M 1895 A.B. 1898. A.M. 1907
—	Hugh Gethin Hanmer	Jes.	M 1906 A.B. 1909
—	Hugh Lyons Waldie	Trin.	M 1909 A.B. 1912
—	John Rich.	Chr.	M 1905 A.B. 1908
—	Jos.	Trin.	M 1899 A.B. 1902. LL.B. 1905. A.M. 1906
—	Lewis Evan Holliday	Pet.	E 1892 A.B. 1895. A.M. 1906
—	Malcolm Lloyd	Trin.	M 1905 A.B. 1908
—	Rob. Gladstone	Em.	M 1904 A.B. 1907
—	Tho. Syd. Phillips ...	Pet.	E 1894 A.B. 1897. A.M. 1906
—	Will. St Bodfan	Trin.	M 1902 A.B. 1905
Griffiths,	Art. Rees	N. C.	M 1908
—	Cha. Hen. Will.	Jes.	M 1902
—	Cuthbert Cyril	Trin.	M 1910
—	Ern. Howard ....*Sid.		M 1870 A.B. 1874. A.M. 1877. Sc.D. 1902
—	Geo. And. Montagu	Cath.	M 1907 A.B. 1910
—	Geo. Art. Mence ...	Joh.	M 1908 A.B. 1911
—	Hen. Stokes Douglas	Cath.	M 1899 A.B. 1902. A.M. 1906
—	Hugh Peregrine	Joh.	M 1909 A.B. 1912
—	John	N. C.	M 1912
—	John Herb.	N. C.	E 1897 Qu. A.B. 1900. A.M. 1909
—	Jos.		A.M. 1890. post King's M.C. 1905
—	Melville Cha.	Em.	M 1900 A.B. 1903. A.M. 1907
—	Rich.	C. C.	M 1893 A.B. 1896. A.M.† 1902
—	Rich. Evelyn	Trin.	M 1907
—	Sam. Victor Floyd ...	Qu.	M 1906 A.B. 1909
—	Will. Herb. Selwyn	Cath.	M 1904 A.B. 1907
—	Will. Mawe	H. Sel.	M 1905 A.B. 1908

Griffith-Williams, Art.	....	Trin.	M 1905
Grigg,	Percy Ja.	Joh.	M 1909 A.B. 1912
Grigson,	Pawlet St John Baseley	Joh.	M 1901 A.B. 1904
Grille,	Fre. Louis	Jes.	M 1908 A.B. 1911
Grimble,	Art. Fra.	Mag.	M 1906 A.B. 1909
Grimes,	Cha. Hugh Duffy ...	Jes.	M 1893 A.B. 1896. A.M. 1904
—	Gerald Hub.	Joh.	M 1902 A.B. 1905
—	Hen. Syd. King	Jes.	M 1901 A.B. 1910
—	John Bryan	Jes.	M 1894 A.B. 1897. J. B. Madden, A.M.
Grimké-Drayton, Chris. de Vere ⎱ Drayton ⎰		Trin.	M 1900 A.B. 1903 [1907
—.	Norman Drayton ...	King's	M 1907 A.B. 1910
Grimshaw,	Phil. Stott	Em.	M 1909 A.B. 1912
Grimston, Hugh Dorrington Kendal		Cai.	M 1890 A.B. 1902
Grimwade,	Edw. Ern.	Cai.	M 1906 A.B. 1909
Grindon,	Art. Will. Harvey ...	N. C.	M 1892 Cath. A.B. 1895. Mus.B. 1897.
Grinsell,	Art. Lorenzo	H. Sel.	M 1901 A.B. 1905 [A.M. 1906
Grissell,	Tho. De la Garde ...	Trin.	M 1897 A.B. 1900. A.M. 1904
Grist,	Will.	N. C.	M 1909 Chr. A.B. 1912
Grocock,	Stanley	Qu.	M 1907 A.B. 1910
Grogan,	John Douglas	Sid.	M 1908 A.B. 1911
Groner,	Reg. Edw. Ern.	Trin.	M 1903 A.B. 1906
Gronow,	Wilfrid Hen. Lettsom	Cla.	L 1909
Groom,	Art. Holdsworth	Pem.	M 1899 A.B. 1902
—	Reg. Walt.	Mag.	M 1911
—	Syd. Herb.	Sid.	M 1906 A.B. 1909
Groos,	Adolph Wilhelm Jacob	Joh.	M 1896 A.B. 1899. LL.B. 1901
Grose,	Syd. Will.	Chr.	M 1905 A.B. 1908. A.M. 1912
—	Tho. Alex.	Cla.	M 1902 A.B. 1905. A.M. 1909
Grose Hodge, Humphrey		Pem.	M 1910
Grosjean,	John Cecil Frederic	Joh.	M 1894 A.B. 1897. A.M. 1901
Gross,	Will. Stovell	Jes.	M 1911
Ground,	Edw. Geo.	Sid.	M 1904 A.B. 1907
Grove,	Alf. John	Em.	M 1910
—	Oswald Harry	Chr.	M 1909 A.B. 1912
—	Will. Reg.	Sid.	M 1887 A.B. 1890. M.B., B.C. 1894. M.D.
Groves,	Cecil Tom	Chr.	M 1906 A.B. 1909 [1906
—	Hen. Leigh	Trin.	M 1899 A.B. 1902
—	John Percival Knight	Qu.	M 1908
—	Keith Grimble	Trin.	M 1906 A.B. 1909. LL.B. 1910
—	Will. Peer	Chr.	M 1897 A.B. 1901
Growse,	Rob. Hen.	Cai.	M 1905 A.B. 1910
Grubb,	Harold Crichton Stuart	Jes.	M 1912
Gruggen,	Geo. Will.	H. Sel.	M 1889 A.B. 1892. A.M. 1902
Grünbaum,	Otto Fritz Frankau	Trin.	M 1892 A.B. 1895. A.M. 1899. B.C. 1900. [M.B. 1902. M.D. 1904
Grundy,	Morris	Joh.	M 1899 A.B. 1902. M.B., B.C., A.M. 1906
—	Wilfred Walker	King's	M 1904 A.B. 1907
Grylls,	Edw. Anth. Hawke	Cai.	M 1911
Gubbay,	Ezekiel Abraham ...	Trin.	M 1904
Gubbins,	Cha. Frederic Ross	Mag.	M 1898 A.B. 1901
—	Edw. Ern.	H. Sel.	M 1894 A.B. 1897. A.M. 1902
Gudgeon,	Clifford John	Cath.	M 1905 A.B. 1908
Gudgin,	Syd. Harry	Down.	M 1907 A.B. 1910
Guest,	Ern. Bryan	Chr.	M 1895 A.B. 1898. LL.B. 1899. A.M. 1902
—	Oscar Montague	Trin.	M 1906 A.B. 1910
Guest-Williams, Alyn Art.		Joh.	M 1907 A.B. 1910
—	Warren Kirkham ...	Joh.	M 1906 A.B. 1909
Guggenheim, Harry Frank		Pem.	L 1911
Guilford,	Edw. Montmorency	Qu.	M 1907 A.B. 1910

Guilford,	Everard Leaver	...... Cla.	M 1903 A.B. 1906. A.M. 1910
Guillebaud,	Claude Will.	.... Joh.	M 1909 A.B. 1912
—	Eric Cyril	.... Pem.	M 1912
—	Harold Ern.	.... Pem.	M 1907 A.B. 1910
—	Walt. Hen.	.... Joh.	M 1909 A.B. 1912
Guinness,	Art. Ern.	.... Trin.	M 1898 A.B. 1901. A.M. 1905
—	Hugh Spencer	.... King's	M 1909
—	John Frith Grattan	Cai.	M 1908 A.B., LL.B. 1911
—	Kenelm Edw. Lee	... Trin. H.	M 1906
—	Rich. Smythe	... . Trin.	M 1907 A.B. 1910
Gull,	Edw. Manico	.... Trin.	M 1902 A.B. 1905
Gullick,	Art. Louis	.... Cath.	M 1904 A.B. 1908
—	Cha. Donald	.... Jes.	M 1911
—	Leon. Bowery	.... Cath.	L 1906
Gulliland,	John Hutchison	...... Cai.	M 1911
Gunasekara,	Edwin Ivers	.... Down.	M 1909 ....
—	Victor Roland	.... Cath.	M 1912
Gunn,	John Donald	.... Pem.	M 1902 A.B. 1906
—	John Will.	.... Pet.	M 1899 A.B. 1902. A.M. 1910
—	Leslie Lionel	.... C. C.	M 1907 A.B., LL.B. 1910
Gunner,	Walt. Robin	.... Trin.	M 1904 A.B. 1907
Gunning,	Cardwell Sinclair	... Pem.	M 1908 A.B. 1911
Gunston,	Derrick Wellesley	... Trin.	M 1910
Gunter,	Will. Hector	.... Cai.	M 1903 A.B. 1906. A.M. 1912
Gunther,	Cha. Emil	.... Trin. H.	M 1910
Gupta,	Shoilendra Chandra	Trin.	M 1910...
Gurney,	Art. Gerard	.... Trin. H.	M 1899 A.B. 1903
—	Chris. Rich.	.... Trin.	M 1903 A.B. 1906
—	John Cedric	.... Pet.	M 1912
—	Quintin Edw.	.... Trin.	M 1901 A.B. 1904
Gurnhill,	Chris. Ja.	.... Em.	M 1908 A.B. 1911
—	Geoffrey Delamere	... H. Sel.	M 1910
Guruswami,	Krishnaswamireddiar	Joh.	M 1912
Gutch,	Alf. Pitt	.... N. C.	M 1895 A.B. 1898. A.M. 1902
—	Clem.	.... King's	M 1894 A.B. 1897. A.M. 1901
—	John	.... Chr.	M 1889 A.B. 1892. A.M. 1896. B.C. 1900.
Güterbock,	Paul Gottlieb Julius	Trin.	M 1905 A.B. 1908. A.M. 1912 [M.D. 1901
Guthrie,	Alex. Gordon	.... Cla.	M 1904 A.B. 1907
—	Cha. Clem.	.... Cla.	M 1909
—	Fra. Clint	.... Cla.	M 1907 A.B. 1910
—	Rob. Forman	.... King's	M 1910
—	Tho.	.... N. C.	M 1896 King's A.B. 1899. B.C., A.M. 1903.
Gutmann,	(*Baron*) Géza	.... Trin.	M 1909 . [M.B. 1904
—	(*Baron*) Hen. Alex.	Trin.	M 1908
Gutteridge,	Harold Cook	.... King's	M 1895 A.B. 1898. A.M. 1902
Güttler,	Gerhard	Em.	M 1909
Guy,	Allan Whiston Ferrers	Trin.	M 1891 A.B. 1894. A.M. 1908
—	Henwood	.... Qu.	M 1906 A.B. 1909
—	Oswald Vernon	...... Jes.	M 1910
Guyomar,	Alf. Honoré	.... N. C.	M 1910
Gwalior,	Maharaja of	....	*See* Scindia, Madharao
Gwatkin,	Edw. Art.	.... Joh.	M 1897 Gwatkin-Graves, E. A. A.B. 1901
—	Fra. Ley	.... Joh.	M 1895 A.B. 1899. A.M. 1902
Gwatkin-Graves			*See* Gwatkin, Edw. Art.
Gwillim,	Geoffry Sheward	...... Qu.	M 1908 A.B. 1911
Gwinn,	Frank Baker	.... C. C.	M 1897 A.B. 1900. A.M. 1904
Gwinner,	Johannes Philipp Wilhelm Alex. }	King's	M 1906
Gwyer,	Herb. Linford	.... Mag.	M 1902 A.B. 1905
Gwyn,	Cyril Postle	.... Em.	M 1910
—	Rich. Fryer	.... Em.	M 1906 A.B. 1908

Gwynne,	Hub. Llewelyn	Joh.	M 1911
—	Roderick Thynne } Sackville }	Trin.	M 1912
Gwyther,	Cyril Edryk	Sid.	M 1901 A.B. 1904
Gyles,	Walt. Hen. Keane ...	Cla.	M 1903 A.B. 1906

H

Habershon,	Edw. Fra.	Cla.	M 1904 A.B. 1907. A.M. 1911
—	Leon. Osbourn	Trin.	M 1912
—	Phil. Hen.	Cla.	M 1912
—	Sid. Heathcote	Cla.	M 1908 A.B. 1911
Habgood,	Art. Hen.	Jes.	M 1900 A.B. 1903. M.B., B.C. 1909
—	Geo.	Cla.	M 1909 A.B. 1912
Habich,	Leopold Sylvester Morrice	Joh.	M 1904 A.B. 1907
Hack,	Cha. Edwin	Cath.	M 1900 A.B. 1903
—	Ja. Hen.	N. C.	M 1896 A.B. 1899. A.M. 1911
Hacker,	Hugh Will. Lawton	Jes.	M 1906 A.B. 1910
Hackforth,	Edgar	Trin.	M 1897 A.B. 1900. A.M. 1906
—	Reg.	Trin.	M 1905 A.B. 1908. A.M. 1912. *Sid. 1912
Hacking,	Egbert Melville	Pem.	M 1901 A.B. 1904. A.M. 1912
—	Hen.	N. C.	M 1900 Cath. A.B. 1903
Hackworth,	Alan	Jes.	M 1909 A.B. 1912
Haddon,	Ern. Balfour ....'	Chr.	M 1901 A.B. 1904. A.M. 1911
Hadfield,	Cha. Fre.	Trin.	M 1894 A.B. 1897. A.M. 1901. M.D. 1906
—	Ern. Harry Loverseed	Joh.	M 1898 A.B. 1903. A.M. 1912
Hadley,	¹Will. Sheldon ....*Pem.		M 1878 A.B. 1882. A.M. 1885
Hadrill,	Eric Walt.	Trin.	M 1910
—	Herb. Murton	Trin.	M 1906 A.B. 1910
Hafez,	Aly	N. C.	M 1901
Haggard,	Amyand Ja. Rider ...	King's	M 1908 A.B. 1911
Hagger,	Norman Watson	Joh.	M 1912
Haggie,	Frank Reg.	Trin. H.	L 1912
Haggis,	Alf. Josiah	N. C.	M 1903 A.B. 1906
Hagon,	Alb. Cha.	Trin. H.	M 1910
Hague,	Tho. Hen.	Sid.	L 1910
Hahn,	Fre. Meinerts	Em.	M 1911
Haidar,	Mohomad	Mag.	M 1911
—	Sayad Agha	Chr.	M 1901 A.B., LL.B. 1904. A.M.† 1908
Haider,	Kazi Ali	Down.	M 1910
Haigh,	Art. Gordon	Chr.	M 1903 A.B. 1906
—	Bern.	Cai.	M 1897 A.B. 1902. B.C. 1912
—	Percy Barnes	Joh.	M 1897 A.B. 1900. A.M. 1910
—	Will.	H. Sel.	M 1909 A.B. 1912
Hailstone,	Edm.	H. Sel.	M 1908 A.B. 1911
—	Geo. Rupert	H. Sel.	M 1912
—	John Edw.	H. Sel.	M 1895 A.B. 1898. A.M. 1902
Haines,	Frank Percy	Cla.	M 1907 A.B., Mus.B. 1910
—	Fre. Edw. Church ...	Cai.	M 1910
—	Hub. Yelverton	Em.	M 1911
—	Rob. Tho. Moline ...	Cai.	M 1910
—	Will. Ribton	Trin. H.	M 1903

¹ Master of Pembroke College, 1912.

Hains,	Art. Phil. Frederic ...	C. C.	M 1889 A.B. 1898. A.M. 1903
Hake,	Hen. Mendelssohn ...	Trin.	M 1910
Hakim,	Meherban Hormusjee	Joh.	M 1904
Haldane,	Ja. Oswald	Jes.	M 1898 A.B. 1902
—	Ric. Burdon		*LL.D.* 1907
Hale,	Geo. Alex.	Sid.	M 1894 A.B. 1897. A.M. 1904
—	Geo. Ellery		*Sc.D.* 1911
—	Herb. Edw.	Cai.	M 1901 A.B. 1904. A.M. 1911
—	John	Cai.	M 1911
—	Rob. Eugene Vaughan	Cai.	M 1897 A.B. 1900. M.B., B.C. 1910
Hales,	Geoffrey Trafford ...	Chr.	M 1905 A.B. 1908. A.M. 1912
—	Hen. Ward	Pem.	M 1909 A.B. 1912
—	John Baseley	Trin.	M 1907 A.B. 1910
Haley,	Leon.	N. C.	M 1910
Halford,	Reg. Hosier	Cath.	M 1911
Halid,	Halil		A.M. 1902
Hall,	Alb. Clifford	Chr.	M 1906 A.B. 1909
—	Alex. Furneaux	C. C.	M 1911
—	Alf. Fra.	Joh.	M 1906 A.B. 1909
—	Art. John	Cai.	M 1884 A.B. 1887. M.B., B.C. 1889. A.M.
—	Art. Kenrick Dickinson	Cla.	M 1904 A.B. 1907 [1900. M.D. 1905
—	Art. Leon.	C. C.	M 1908 A.B. 1911
—	Cecil Sept.	N. C.	M 1892 Em. A.B. 1895. A.M. 1910
—	Cecil Symes	H. Sel.	M 1904 A.B. 1907. A.M. 1911
—	Charlton Rob. Fre.	Trin.	M 1896 A.B. 1899. B.C., A.M. 1906
—	Dav. Alston	Cath.	M 1896 A.B. 1899. A.M. 1903
—	Donald Geo.	Em.	M 1894 A.B. 1897. M.B., B.C. 1900. A.M.,
—	Edw. Basil	Cath.	M 1909 [M.D. 1903
—	Eric Watson	Cai.	M 1912
—	Frank Gardner	King's	M 1907 A.B. 1910
—	Frederic Grainger ...	Trin.	M 1909 A.B. 1912
—	Geoffrey Bertram ...	Trin. H.	M 1902
—	Geo. Elsmie	Pem.	M 1908 A.B. 1911
—	Geo. Gordon	C. C.	M 1905 A.B. 1908
—	Geo. Lewtas	Em.	M 1906 A.B. 1909
—	Geo. Noel Lankester	Joh.	M 1910
—	Geo. Rob.	N. C.	L 1884 Pet. A.B. 1899. A.M. 1906
—	Geo. Sadler	C. C.	M 1884 A.B. 1887. A.M. 1905
—	Harry Spencer	Pem.	M 1899 A.B. 1902. A.M. 1911
—	Hen.	Cla.	M 1911
—	Ja.	Sid.	M 1911
—	Ja. Griffith	Joh.	M 1912
—	John	Em.	M 1900 A.B. 1903. A.M. 1907
—	John Ashley	Cla.	M 1905 A.B., LL.B. 1908
—	John Fre.	Cla.	M 1901 A.B. 1904
—	John Herschel	N. C.	L 1910 Pet. A.B. 1912
—	John Maxwell	Mag.	M 1903
—	John Percy	Cai.	M 1901 A.B. 1904. A.M. 1909
—	John Smith	Sid.	M 1904 A.B. 1907
—	John Thornton	C. C.	M 1912
—	Leslie Mackinder ...	Cai.	M 1907 A.B. 1910
—	Phil. Ashley	Cla.	M 1910
—	Rob.	Down.	M 1911
—	Rob. Sinclair	Trin.	M 1904 A.B. 1907
—	Robin Hen. Edw. ...	Trin. H.	M 1901
—	Vincent Claud	Mag.	M 1900 A.B. 1903
Hallack,	Will. Collin	Joh.	M 1904 A.B. 1907
Hallam,	Jos. Hen.	Pet.	M 1902 A.B. 1905. A.M. 1910
—	Stuart Griffith	Sid.	M 1894 A.B. 1897. A.M. 1902
Halland,	John Tho.	C. C.	M 1877 A.B. 1881. A.M. 1912
Haller,	Bertram Conrad	Trin.	M 1901 A.B. 1905. A.M. 1908

Hallett,	Hen. Gerard	Trin.	M 1895 A.B. 1899. A.M. 1906
—	Herb. Jodrell	Qu.	M 1911
Hall Hall,	Art.	Jes.	M 1901
—	Herb.	Jes.	M 1898 A.B. 1901
Halliday,	Cha. Walt. Alex. ...	King's	M 1904 A.B. 1907
—	Dav. Rupert Johnstone	Trin.	M 1907 LL.B. 1911
—	Matth. Alf. Corrie ...	Trin.	M 1905
Hallimond,	Art. Fra.	Pem.	M 1908 A.B. 1911
Halliwell,	Wilfrid Newbold	Joh.	M 1909
Hallowes,	Basil John Knight ...	Cai.	M 1902 A.B. 1905
—	Kenneth Alex. Knight	Cai.	M 1898 A.B. 1901. A.M.† 1912
Hallows,	Ralph Watson	Mag.	M 1904 A.B. 1907
Hall-Smith			*See* Smith, P. H.
Halnan,	Edw. Tho.	Trin.	M 1908 A.B. 1911
Halsall,	John Rich.	N. C.	M 1896 A.B. 1899. A.M. 1903
Halsbury,	(*Earl of*)		*See* Giffard
Halse,	Lionel Will.	Qu.	M 1912
Halsey,	Reg. Tom	Joh.	M 1907 A.B. 1910
Ham,	Gordon Lupton	Chr.	M 1904 A.B. 1907
—	Paul Sison	Down.	M 1910
Hamaguchi,	Rokunosuke	Pem.	M 1904
—	Tan		*See* Tajima, Tan
Hamblin,	Edw. Cha. Clifford ...	Cai.	M 1910
Hambro,	Ronald Olaf	Trin.	M 1905
Hamer,	Herb. Barningham ...	Joh.	M 1894 A.B. 1897. A.M. 1901
Hamid,	Abdul	N. C.	M 1910 [M.D. 1908
Hamill,	John Molyneux	Trin.	M 1898 A.B. 1901. M.B., B.C., A.M. 1905.
—	Phil.	Trin.	M 1902 A.B. 1905. A.M. 1909
Hamilton,	Archib.	Chr.	M 1902 A.B. 1905. A.M. 1909. M.B., B.C.
—	Archib. Hen. de Burgh	C. C.	M 1905 A.B. 1908 [1910
—	Art. Ja. Stanley	Joh.	M 1901 A.B., LL.B. 1905. A.M. 1912
—	Cha. Jos.	Cai.	M 1898 A.B. 1901. A.M. 1908
—	Clarence Haselwood	Chr.	M 1895 A.B. 1898. A.M. 1902
—	Cuthbert Art.	Trin.	M 1899 A.B. 1902. A.M. 1908
—	Cyril Julien	Sid.	M 1910
—	Edw.	C. C.	M 1897 A.B. 1900. A.M. 1904
—	Edw. Will.	Trin.	M 1912
—	Eric Will.	Sid.	M 1906 A.B. 1909
—	Geoffrey Hubert	Sid.	M 1908 A.B. 1911
—	Geo. Hall	Trin.	M 1904 A.B. 1907. A.M.† 1912
—	Gerald	Trin.	M 1911
—	Herb. Otho	Trin.	M 1911
—	Ja.	C. C.	M 1898 A.B. 1901
—	John Livingston	Down.	M 1908
—	John Will.	Cath.	M 1909
—	Kenneth	Trin.	M 1905 A.B. 1908
—	Kismet Leland Brewer	Joh.	M 1902 A.B. 1905. A.M.† 1909
—	Noel Crawford	Jes.	M 1912
—	Tho.	N. C.	M 1900 King's A.B. 1903. A.M.† 1912
Hammack,	Rupert Godwin	Trin. H.	M 1901
Hammersley,	Sam. Schofield	King's	M 1912
Hammick,	Hen. Alex.	Pem.	M 1909 A.B. 1912
Hammond,	Cyril Elmore	Trin.	M 1908 A.B. 1911 ..
—.	Fre. Will.	Mag.	M 1912
—	Hue Mason FitzHammond	Em.	M 1892 A.B. 1895. A.M. 1905
—	John	Down.	M 1907 A.B. 1910
—	Nich. Will.	Sid.	M 1897 A.B. 1900. A.M. 1911
—	Phil. Warrener	Cai.	M 1895 A.B. 1901. A.M. 1905
—.	Rob. Woodward	Pet.	M 1895 A.B. 1902. A.M. 1911
Hammond-Chambers, Hen. Borgnis Barêt		King's	M 1905 A.B. 1909

Hamond,	Ern. Will.	Qu.	M 1902 A.B. 1906
—	John Hen. Bell	Trin.	M 1895 A.B. 1898. A.M. 1902
Hampson,	Rob. Hamer	Trin. H.	M 1891 A.B., LL.B. 1894. A.M., LL.M.
—	Stuart Hirst	Qu.	M 1912 [1898. LL.D. 1904
Hanbury,	Hor.	Trin.	M 1898 A.B. 1902
Hance,	Ja. Bennett	Chr.	M 1905 A.B. 1908
Hancock,	Fre.	Cla.	M 1902 A.B. 1905
—	Herb. Art.	N. C.	M 1900 A.B. 1903
—	Walt. Ralegh	Cai.	M 1906
—	Will. Hugh Mundy	Chr.	M 1894 A.B. 1897. A.M. 1902
Hand,	Harry Sheerman ...	Joh.	M 1912
Handcock,	Will. Art. Stanley ...	N. C.	E 1903 Chr. A.B. 1907. A.M. 1910
Handford,	Hen. Basil Strutt ...	Trin.	M 1912
—	John Rich.	Qu.	M 1911
Hands,	Harry	Down.	M 1909 A.B., LL.B. 1912
—	Hen. Ja.	N. C.	M 1903 Pet. A.B. 1906. A.M. 1911
—	Will. Jos. Geo.	Jes.	M 1911
Hanford,	Hugh Duncan	Cath.	M 1898 A.B. 1901. A.M. 1905
Hanhart,	Art. Anderson	Pem.	M 1898 A.B., LL.B. 1901
Hanitsch,	Karl Vernon	Sid.	M 1911
Hankey,	Cyril Patrick	Pem.	M 1905 A.B. 1908
Hankin,	Ern. Hanbury ....*Joh.		M 1886 A.B. 1889. A.M.† 1893. Sc.D. 1905
Hanna,	Cha. Bushra	Trin.	M 1912
—	Ern.	C. C.	M 1901 A.B. 1904
—	Godfrey FitzGerald	Trin.	M 1910
—	John Hen.	C. C.	M 1901 A.B. 1904. A.M. 1908
—	Will. Bushra	Trin.	M 1911
Hannam,	Frederic And.	Joh.	M 1898 A.B. 1901. A.M. 1905
Hannay,	Tho.	Qu.	M 1907 A.B. 1910
Hannington,	Gilb. Jos.	Chr.	M 1903
—	Ja. Edw. Meopham	Pem.	M 1896 A.B. 1899. A.M. 1903
Hansell,	Geo. Fra.	Chr.	M 1912
Hans-Hamilton,	Geo. Cecil	King's	M 1906 A.B., LL.B. 1910
Hanson,	Edw.	Qu.	M 1900 A.B. 1903
—	Edw. Kenneth	Trin.	M 1897 A.B. 1900. A.M. 1904
—	Edw. Taylor	Chr.	M 1901 A.B. 1904
—	Edwin Cha.	H. Sel.	M 1912
—	Herb. Ja.	Trin.	M 1893 A.B. 1896. A.M. 1903
—	Ja.	Joh.	M 1909 A.B. 1912
—	Oswald Hesketh	Trin.	M 1891 A.B. 1894. A.M. 1903
—	Reg. John Edw.	Trin.	M 1888 M.B., B.C. 1896. A.B. 1899. A.M.
—	Rich. Harold	Joh.	M 1911 [1902
—	Wilfrid Julius	Trin.	M 1882 A.B. 1885. A.M. 1903
Hanumanta	Rao, Chintakindi ⎱ Venkata ⎰	Trin.	M 1912
Hanworth,	Will. Cha.	Sid.	M 1904 A.B. 1907
Happell,	Art. Comyn	King's	M 1911
Happold,	Fre. Crossfield	Pet.	M 1912
Harari,	Ralph And.	Pem.	M 1910
Harber,	Ern. Will.	Trin. H.	M 1905 A.B. 1908
Harbord,	Harry Collett	Trin.	M 1902 LL.B. 1905
—	John	Cla.	M 1911
Harcourt,	Guy Hanmer	Jes.	M 1903 A.B. 1906
Hardcastle,	Hen. Rob.	Trin.	M 1892 A.B. 1900. A.M. 1903
—	Steph. Brindley	Chr.	M 1902 A.B. 1905
—	Walt. Edwin	Jes.	M 1907 A.B. 1910
Hardie,	Alec Dav.	Pet.	M 1902 A.B. 1905. A.M. 1909
—	Alf.	Trin. H.	M 1885 A.B., LL.B. 1888. A.M. 1892. [LL.M. 1902. LL.D. 1911
—	Cha. Fre.	Qu.	M 1895 A.B. 1899. A.M. 1902. B.C. 1904.
—	Edw. Eccles	Cai.	M 1912 [M.B. 1906

Hardie,	Vivian	Em.	L 1903
—	Will. Geo.	Em.	M 1897 A.B. 1900. A.M. 1904
Harding,	Alb. Fra. Sid.	Qu.	M 1903 A.B. 1906. A.M. 1910
—	Aubrey Milward	Mag.	M 1908
—	Edm. Wilfrid	Cai.	M 1902 A.B. 1905
—	Edw.	Trin.	M 1910
—	Egerton Steph. Somers	King's	M 1905 A.B. 1908. A.M. 1912
—	Fre. Howard	Chr.	M 1888 A.B. 1891. A.M. 1904
—	Geo. Will. Hen.	Joh.	M 1895 A.B. 1897. A.M. 1901
—	Norman Sydney	Em.	M 1906 A.B. 1910
—	Walt. Ambrose Heath	Pet.	M 1889 A.B. 1906. A.M. 1909
—	Walt. Harry	Joh.	M 1906 A.B. 1909
—	Wilfrid John	Chr.	M 1904 A.B. 1907. A.M. 1912
—	Will. Iliff	Joh.	M 1900 A.B. 1903. A.M. 1907
Hardinge,	(*Hon.*) Alex. Hen. Louis	Trin.	L 1912
Hardingham,	Cha. Hen.	Chr.	M 1896 A.B. 1899. A.M. 1903
—	John	Joh.	M 1900 A.B. 1903
Hardisty,	Cha. Will.	Joh.	M 1911
Hardman,	Fre. McMahon	King's	M 1909 A.B. 1912
—	John Rob.	Em.	M 1910
—	Will. Howard	Down.	M 1907 A.B., LL.B. 1910
Hardwich,	John Manisty	Joh.	M 1892 A.B. 1895. A.M. 1902
Hardwick,	Frank	Jes.	M 1910
Hardwicke,	Edwin Cecil	C. C.	M 1898 A.B. 1901
Hardwick-Smith,	Hen.	Joh.	M 1896 A.B. 1899. M.B., B.C. 1907
Hardy,	Clive	Trin.	M 1906 A.B. 1909
—	Eric Howieson	Chr.	M 1902 A.B. 1905
—	Fred	Pet.	M 1908 A.B. 1911
—	Frederic Wynne	Jes.	M 1883 A.B. 1886. M.B., B.C. 1902
—	Gateshill	Em.	M 1911
—	Geo. Bern.	N. C.	E 1898 A.B. 1901. A.M. 1904
—	Godfrey Harold ......*Trin.		M 1896 A.B. 1899. A.M. 1903
—	Gordon Sidey	Joh.	M 1902 A.B. 1905
—	Jack	Cai.	M 1908
—	Maur. Victor	Sid.	M 1906 A.B. 1909
—	Percy	Trin. H.	M 1896 A.B. 1899. M.B., B.C. 1904
—	Tho. John	Qu.	M 1888 A.B. 1891. A.M. 1911
—	Tho. Lionel	H. Sel.	M 1905 A.B. 1908
Hare,	Adrian Church	Cai.	M 1910
—	Fred	Trin.	M 1912
—	Sam. Hen.	Cai.	M 1904 A.B. 1908
—	Syd. Geo. Steels	Cath.	M 1906 A.B. 1909
—	Will. Theodore	Chr.	M 1907 A.B. 1910
Harford,	Hen. Dundas Battersby	Jes.	M 1908 A.B. 1911
Hargrave,	Aud. Bracken	Cai.	M 1885 A.B. 1889. A.M. 1901
Hargrave-Carroll,	Featherstone ...	Jes.	M 1907
Hargreaves,	Alf. Ridley	Trin.	M 1903 A.B. 1906
—	Art. Gerard	Cai.	M 1902
—	Cyril Alf.	N. C.	M 1911
—	Harman	Trin. H.	M 1899 A.B. 1906
—·	Hen. Cecil	Pem.	M 1899 A.B. 1911
—	Herb. Lyde	H. Sel.	M 1907 A.B., Mus.B. 1910
—	Herb. Price	Pem.	M 1909 A.B. 1912
—	John Art.	Trin.	M 1898 A.B. 1901. A.M. 1905
—	Rich.	Cath.	M 1894 C. C. A.B. 1897. A.M. 1902
—	Rich.	Chr.	M 1910
—	Rob.	Cla.	M 1899 A.B. 1902. LL.B. 1906
—	Rob.	Cai.	M 1908 A.B. 1911
—	Will. Fra. Carlile ...	Pem.	M 1902 A.B. 1905. A.M. 1912
Hargrove,	Cha. Rodolph	Pet.	M 1900 A.B. 1903
Harke,	Syd. Lawrence	Pem.	M 1895 A.B. 1898. M.B., B.C., A.M. 1907

Harker,	Alf. Ja. Shuttleworth	H. Sel.	M 1893 A.B. 1896. A.M. 1911
—	Geo. Cuthbert Warburton	Pem.	M 1910
—	Rob. Grange	Pem.	M 1904 A.B. 1907
Har Kishan Singh			*See* Singh, H. K.
Harkness,	Ariel Law	Pem.	M 1904 A.B. 1907. A.M. 1911
Harland,	Horace Claude	Em.	M 1907 A.B. 1910
—	Rob. Ern. Compton	Em.	M 1910
Harman,	John Eustace	King's	M 1880 A.B. 1884. A.M. 1903 [A.M. 1901
—	Nath. Bishop	N. C.	E 1894 Joh. A.B. 1897. M.B., B.C. 1898.
Harmens,	Wyger	Trin.	M 1901 A.B. 1904. B.C. 1909. M.B. 1910
Harmer,	Will. Douglas	King's	M 1892 A.B. 1895. M.B., B.C., A.M. 1899.
Harmstone,	Rich.	N. C.	M 1908 A.B. 1911 [M.C. 1901
Harnett,	Walt. Lidwell	Joh.	M 1896 A.B. 1899. M.B., B.C., A.M. 1904
Harper,	Cecil Humphries ...	Chr.	M 1906 A.B. 1909
—	Edw. Russell	Cai.	M 1904
—	Frederic Art.	King's	M 1907 A.B. 1910
—	Ja. Erskine	Em.	M 1907 A.B. 1912
—	Kenneth John	Pem.	M 1900 A.B. 1903
—	Leon. Vyse	Chr.	M 1900 A.B. 1903
—	Walt. Edw.	H. Sel.	M 1907 A.B. 1910
Harper-Smith,	Geo. Hastie	Cai.	M 1896 A.B. 1899. B.C. 1906. A.M. 1909
Harraton,	John Reg.	Trin.	M 1909
Harries,	Gerald Hollidge	Joh.	M 1890 A.B. 1893. A.M. 1901
—	Hen. Martyn	N. C.	M 1907 A.B. 1910
—	Owen Will.	Jes.	M 1895 A.B. 1901
Harries-Jones,	Jos. Standring } Dronsfield }	Cla.	M 1910
Harris,	Alan Dale	Em.	M 1905
—	Alf. Morgan	Jes.	M 1903 A.B. 1906
—	Arnold Frank Stapleton	Cla.	M 1908 A.B. 1911
—	Art. John	Cla.	M 1904 A.B. 1907
—	Boris Gordon	Pem.	M 1903 A.B. 1907
—	Cyril Raymond	Pem.	M 1911
—	Dav. Rob.	Joh.	M 1896 A.B. 1898. A.M. 1903
—	Edw. Temple	Chr.	M 1896 A.B. 1899. B.C. 1903. M.B. 1904
—	Fre. Knox	Mag.	M 1908
—	Geo. Herb.	N. C.	M 1910
—	Geo. Woodrouffe	Cai.	M 1899 A.B. 1905
—	Hen.	Joh.	M 1899 A.B. 1905
—	Hen. Lyn	Joh.	M 1911
—	Hen. Wilson	Joh.	M 1902 A.B. 1905. A.M. 1909
—	Herb.	Cath.	M 1903 A.B. 1906. A.M. 1912
—	Herb. Sextus	Trin. H.	M 1902 A.B., LL.B. 1906. A.M.† 1910
—	Heywood	Em.	M 1896 A.B. 1899. A.M. 1903
—	Hub. Alf.	Em.	M 1899 A.B. 1902
—	John Cha. Neville ...	Pem.	M 1910
—	John Fre.	Joh.	M 1910
—	John Rich.	Qu.	M 1910
—	Jos. Bastable	H. Sel.	M 1910
—	Murray Geo.	Pem.	M 1909
—	Raymond John	Cla.	M 1901
—	Reg. Fra.	H. Sel.	M 1907 A.B. 1910
—	Rob. Graham	N. C.	M 1912
—	Rob. Vernon	C. C.	M 1904 A.B. 1909
—	Sid. John	Qu.	M 1894 A.B. 1897. A.M. 1901
—	Stanley Shute	Pem.	M 1900 A.B. 1903. A.M. 1909
—	Tom	Em.	M 1909 A.B. 1911
—	Walt. Bruce	Pem.	M 1908 A.B. 1911
—	Will. Eastwood	Pem.	M 1909 A.B. 1912
—	Will. Stuart Twelves	Jes.	M 1909 A.B. 1912
Harrison,	Aelfric Milton	Sid.	M 1908

Harrison,	Cecil Cantilupe	...... Cai.	M 1903 A.B. 1907
—	Cha. Fancourt	.... Cai.	M 1911
—	Cholmondeley	.... Jes.	M 1888 A.B. 1891. A.M. 1895. LL.B. 1912
—	Donald Howard	...... Em.	M 1912
—	Edw. Phil.	.... King's	M 1903
—	Eric Fairweather	... Trin.	M 1898 A.B. 1901
—	Eric Marshall	.... Chr.	M 1912
—	Ern.	.....................*Trin.	M 1896 A.B. 1899. A.M. 1903
—	Ern. Cha.	.... Cla.	M 1895 A.B. 1899. A.M. 1903
—	Ern. Reed	.... N. C.	L 1906 A.B. 1908. A.M.† 1912
—	Ern. Wivelsfield	...... N. C.	M 1895 A.B. 1898. A.M. 1905
—	Everard	.... Trin.	M 1897 A.B. 1900. B.C. 1904. M.B. 1905
—	Frank	.... Down.	M 1912
—	Frank Eric	.... C. C.	M 1911
—	Fred	.... King's	M 1903 A.B. 1906. A.M. 1910
—	Frederic	....	*Litt.D.* 1905
—	Geo.	.... Pet.	M 1901 A.B. 1904
—	Geo. Lee	.... Qu.	M 1903 A.B. 1906
—	Hen. Edw.	.... King's	M 1901 A.B. 1905
—	Hen. Geo.	.... Sid.	M 1898 A.B. 1901. A.M. 1905
—	Hub. English	.... Trin.	M 1898 A.B. 1902. A.M. 1906
—	John	.... Chr.	M 1902 A.B. 1905
—	John Pittman	.... Qu.	M 1904 A.B. 1907. A.M. 1911
—	John Raymond	...... Qu.	M 1912
—	John Will.	.... Chr.	M 1894 A.B. 1897. A.M. 1903
—	Lionel Gordon	.... Sid.	M 1904 A.B. 1908
—	Mark Wilks	.... Em.	M 1896 A.B. 1899. A.M. 1903
—	Percy	.... Chr.	M 1893 A.B. 1897. A.M. 1901
—	Will. John	............*Cla.	M 1903 A.B. 1906. A.M. 1910
—	Will. Phillip	.... Jes.	E 1904
Harrisson,	Ern. Hen.	.... Cla.	M 1896 A.B. 1899. B.C. 1902. M.B. 1903.
Harrowing,	John Stanley	.... Trin.	M 1907 A.B. 1911 [A.M., M.D. 1907
Harry,	Norman Geo.	.... Jes.	M 1896 A.B. 1899. M.B., B.C. 1905
Harse,	Tho. Harwood	.... Em.	M 1911
Harston,	Frank Northey	...... C. C.	M 1909 A.B. 1912
Hart,	Alex. Hutton	.... Pem.	M 1904
—	Ern. Parsons	.... Joh.	E 1898 A.B. 1901. .A.M. 1905
—	Geo. Fre. Will.	...... Qu.	M 1906 A.B. 1909
—	Harold Eaton	.... Cai.	M 1911
—	Howard Percy	.... C. C.	M 1909 A.B. 1912
—	John Hen. Art.	......*Joh.	M 1895 A.B. 1898. A.M. 1902
—	Norman Basset	...... Down.	M 1909 A.B., LL.B. 1912
—	Phil. Hannington	... N. C.	L 1908
—	Rich. Gilbert Keppel	Trin.	M 1898 A.B. 1901. A.M. 1912
—	Rich. Neville	.... Sid.	M 1897 A.B. 1900. M.B., B.C., A.M. 1906.
—	Rob. Edw.	.... Pem.	M 1896 A.B. 1899. A.M. 1903 [M.D. 1909
—	Seymour	.... Cla.	M 1907 A.B. 1910
—	Tho. Clifford	.... Pem.	M 1902 A.B. 1905
Hartcup,	Geoffrey Hamilton Will.	Cla.	M 1904 A.B. 1907
—	John Archib.	.... Pem.	M 1908
—	Roderick Edw.	...... Cla.	M 1907 A.B. 1911
Hart-Davis,	Hugh Vaughan	...... Trin.	M 1902
Harter,	Ja. Collier Foster	... Mag.	L 1908
Hartley,	Bern. Cha.	.... Jes.	M 1897 A.B. 1904
—	Cecil Rich.	.... Trin.	M 1905 A.B. 1910
—	Cecil Stewart	.... Trin.	M 1894 A.B. 1897. A.M. 1903
—	Dav. Harvey Johann	Cla.	M 1898 A.B. 1901. A.M. 1909
—	Joshua Edw. Thompson	Mag.	M 1909 A.B. 1912
—	Leslie Briggs	.... King's	M 1912
—	Rich. Jos. Middelton	Trin. H.	M 1909
—	Walt. John	.... Pet.	M 1907 A.B. 1910

Hartley,	Will. Ern.	Trin.	M 1896 A.B. 1899. A.M. 1904
Hartmann,	Raymond Theobald	Em.	M 1912
Hartog,	Gustave	Trin. H.	M 1898 LL.B. 1901
Hartree,	Kenneth	Cai.	M 1908 A.B. 1911
—	Raymond	Cai.	M 1904 A.B. 1907
Hartridge,	Hamilton	*King's	M 1905 A.B. 1908. A.M. 1912
Harverson,	Percy Ambrose	Pet.	M 1902 A.B. 1905. A.M. 1911
Harvey,	Art. Geo.	Joh.	M 1894 A.B. 1897. M.B., B.C. 1905. M.D.
—	Art. Gordon	Cath.	M 1912 [1909
—	Bern. Will.	Trin.	M 1894 A.B. 1897. A.M. 1901
—	Clyde	Trin.	M 1903 A.B. 1906. A.M. 1911
—	Cyril Herb.	Chr.	M 1898 A.B. 1901. A.M. 1905
—	Douglas Lennox	Trin.	M 1911
—	Edwin Josiah Will.	Trin.	L 1908 A.B. 1910
—	Frank Lennox	Trin.	M 1909 A.B. 1912
—	Fre. Ern. Edwin	N. C.	M 1896 A.B. 1905. A.M. 1908
—	Geo. Macdonald	Trin. H.	M 1904
—	Godfrey Tho. Benedict	C. C.	M 1910
—	Hector Raymond ...	C. C.	M 1911
—	Hildebrand Wolfe ...	Down.	M 1906 A.B. 1909
—	John Edm.	Trin.	M 1912
—	Oliver Cha.	Trin.	M 1912
—	Phil.	Trin.	M 1905 A.B. 1908. A.M. 1912
—	Rob. Cha. Percy Gerald	Em.	M 1901 A.B. 1904
—	Walt.	N. C.	M 1907 A.B. 1910
—	Will.	Chr.	L 1911
—	Will. Morton	Chr.	M 1877 A.B. 1881. A.M. 1902
—	Willoughby Henwood	Chr.	E 1906 A.B. 1908
Harvie,	John Keith	Chr.	M 1912
Harwood,	Alf. Hen. Fairfax ...	Cai.	M 1911
—	Sam. Davenport Fairfax	Joh.	M 1898 A.B. 1901. A.M. 1906
Hasan,	Mohamed Haider ...	Em.	M 1901 A.B. 1905
—	Naziruddin	N. C.	M 1904 Down. A.B. 1907. LL.B. 1909.
—	Syed Agha	Pet.	L 1902 [A.M.† 1911
—	Syed Mahmoodul ...	Down.	M 1909
Haseler,	Donald	Chr.	M 1906 A.B. 1909
—	Hub. Leslie	Cath.	M 1909 A.B. 1912
Haskins,	Fra. Winstanley	Trin.	M 1908 A.B. 1911
Haslam,	Ralph Alex. McEwen	Trin. H.	M 1906
—	Reg. Kingdon	Joh.	M 1909 A.B. 1912
—	Victor Kingdon	Joh.	M 1906 A.B. 1909
—	Will. Aitken	Pem.	M 1899 A.B. 1902. A.M. 1907
—	Will. Heywood	King's	M 1908 A.B. 1911
—	Will. Kenneth Seale	Trin.	M 1911 [A.M. 1911
Haslehurst,	Rich.	Trin.	M 1904 A.B. 1907, R. Stafford Tyndale.
Hasluck,	Fre. Will.	*King's	M 1897 A.B. 1901. A.M. 1904
—	Reg. ffolliott	Pem.	M 1910
Hassall,	Art.	Qu.	M 1894 A.B. 1897. A.M. 1901
Hassé,	Hen. Ronald	*Joh.	M 1903 A.B. 1906. A.M. 1910
Hastings,	Harry Coghill	Trin. H.	M 1905
—	Will.	Chr.	M 1898 A.B. 1901. M.B., B.C. 1904
—	Will. Howitt	Trin.	M 1897 A.B. 1901. M.B., B.C., A.M. 1906
Haswell,	John Vincent	Sid.	M 1902 A.B., LL.B. 1905. A.M. 1909
—	Phil.	Sid.	M 1907 A.B. 1910
—	Tho. Geo.	N. C.	E 1909 A.B. 1912
Hatch,	Laurence Collier	Pem.	M 1912
—	Phil. Randall	Chr.	M 1911
—	Sid. Cuthbert Lawson	Trin.	M 1910
Hatchell,	Chris. Frederic Wellesley	Chr.	M 1888 A.B. 1891. A.M. 1908
Hathorn,	Alex. Anth. Roy ...	Cai.	M 1900 A.B. 1903
—	Geo. Rutherford	Trin.	M 1900 A.B. 1903

Hathorn,	Walt. Blaikie	Cai.	M 1912	
Hatley,	Alf. John	Sid.	M 1912	
Hatt-Cook,	Geo.	Pem.	M 1901 A.B. 1904	
Hatten,	Art. Will.	Joh.	M 1900 A.B. 1903	
—	Geoffrey	Cai.	M 1902 A.B., Mus.B. 1905	
—	John Cha. Le Pelley	H. Sel.	M 1896 A.B. 1899. A.M. 1905	
—	Wilfrid Hayley Spark	Catb.	M 1907	
Hattersley,	Alan Fre.	Down.	M 1912	
—	Sid. Martin	Em.	M 1906 A.B. 1909	
—	Will. Hanchett	Joh.	M 1908	
Hatton,	Geo. Art. Lyon	Cai.	M 1907 A.B. 1910	
Hatton-Hall,	Hub. Chris.	Trin. H.	M 1911	
Haughton,	Alf. John	Qu.	M 1900 A.B. 1903	
—	Sid. Hen.	Trin. H.	M 1906 A.B. 1909	
—	Will. Theodore Hoghton	Trin.	M 1903 A.B. 1906	
Haultain,	Will. Fra. Theodore	Cai.	M 1911	
Hauner,	Vilém Julius	N. C.	M 1902	
Havard			*See* Jones, Alban Jenkins	
—	Godfrey Tho.	Trin.	L 1907	
Havelock,	Tho. Hen.	*Joh.	E 1897 A.B. 1900. A.M. 1904	
Haverfield,	Hen Wyld	H. Sel.	M 1898 A.B. 1903	
Havers,	Cecil Rob.	C. C.	M 1908 A.B. 1911. LL.B. 1912	
—	Geoffrey Gordon	Down.	M 1912	
Haviland,	Edm. Art.	King's	E 1893 A.B. 1896. A.M. 1901	
—	John	Trin. H.	M 1901 LL.B. 1904	
—	Wilfred Pollen	King's	M 1899 A.B. 1903	
Havinden,	Eric	Em.	M 1912	
Haward,	Lawrence Warrington	King's	M 1897 A.B. 1900. A.M. 1904	
—	Tristram Warrington	King's	M 1903 A.B. 1906	
Hawcridge,	Rob. Stuart	Joh.	M 1905 A.B. 1909	
Hawdon,	Hugh Will.	Jes.	M 1909 A.B. 1912	
—	Noel Elliot	Jes.	M 1905 A.B. 1908. A.M. 1912	
Hawes,	Bertram Lowth	Cai.	M 1905 A.B. 1908	
—	Cha. Hen.	Trin.	M 1896 A.B. 1899. A.M. 1903	
Hawk,	John Clemence	Trin. H.	M 1910	
Hawke,	Eric Ludlow	Trin.	M 1911	
Hawken,	Will. Dallinger	N. C.	M 1897 Chr. A.B. 1900. A.M. 1904	
Hawker,	Geo. Poole Dav.	Cai.	M 1894 A.B. 1897. B.C. 1902. M.B. 1904	
Hawkes,	Cha. Pascoe	Trin.	M 1894 A.B. 1897. A.M. 1901	
—	Will. John	Joh.	M 1900 A.B. 1903. A.M. 1907	
Hawkins,	Alan Geo.	Em.	M 1898 A.B. 1901	
—	Alban Goring Bailey	Trin. H.	M 1907 A.B. 1911	
—	Alb. Gordon Jones	Chr.	M 1906 A.B. 1909	
—	Caesar Hugh Geo. Wills	Cai.	M 1908	
—	Herb. Hervey Baines	Trin.	M 1895 A.B. 1898. A.M. 1903	
—	Hugh Douglas	Trin.	M 1901	
—	Oliver Luther	Jes.	M 1912	
—	Osmond Crutchley	Jes.	M 1908 A.B. 1911	
—	Rich. Ja.	Chr.	M 1911	
Haworth,	Cha. Wilfrid Buckenham	Sid.	M 1911	
—	Harold Wilfred	Trin. H.	M 1896 A.B. 1899. LL.B. 1900. A.M. 1904	
—	John Ja.	N. C.	M 1899 A.B. 1902	
—	Will.	Em.	M 1899 A.B. 1902. A.M. 1912	
Hawthorne,	Cha. Barnard	Cla.	M 1901	
Hawtrey,	Michael Chequers	Trin.	M 1904 A.B. 1907	
—	Ralph Geo.	Trin.	M 1898 A.B. 1901	
Hay,	Alex. Cyril	Jes.	M 1907	
—	Harry Algernon	Trin. H.	M 1900 A.B. 1904	
—	Kenneth Rob.	Cai.	M 1892 A.B. 1895. M.B., A.M. 1902	
—	Mortimer Cecil	Cath.	M 1909 A.B. 1912	
—	Will. King	Joh.	M 1904 A.B. 1907. A.M. 1912	

Hayashi,	Tadasu		*LL.D.* 1902
Haydon,	Art. Dodsworth	Cai.	M 1907 A.B. 1910
—	John Frederic	N. C.	M 1894 Em. A.B. 1897. A.M. 1903
—	Rob. Alex.	Em.	M 1902 A.B., LL.B. 1905
Hayes,	Cecil	Down.	M 1905
—	Ja. Gordon	C. C.	M 1906 A.B. 1909
—	Ja. Hurst	Joh.	M 1894 A.B. 1897. A.M. 1901
—	Robin Arden	Qu.	M 1905 A.B. 1908. A.M. 1912
Hayllar,	Montagu Hayllar ...	H. Sel.	M 1895 A.B. 1898. A.M. 1903
Hayman,	Cha. Hen. Telford ...	Joh.	M 1899 A.B. 1905
—	Eric	Cai.	M 1912
—	Victor Alex. Palmer	Qu.	M 1912
Haynes,	Art. John	Down.	M 1908 A.B. 1912
—	Geo. Secretan	King's	L 1899 M.B., B.C. 1904. M.D. 1907
—	Hugh Lankester	H. Sel.	M 1899 A.B. 1902. A.M. 1912
Hay-Robertson, John Will.		Cla.	M 1908 A.B. 1911
Hayter,	Geo. Keith Homfray	Em.	M 1906 A.B. 1909
—	Kenneth Sid. Randall	Joh.	M 1895 A.B. 1898. A.M. 1903
Haythornthwaite, Ja.		Em.	M 1899 A.B. 1902. A.M. 1908
Hayton,	Ja. Dawson Wray ...	Chr.	L 1911
Hayward,	Archib. Dav.	Qu.	M 1910
—	Art. Will.	Joh.	M 1899 A.B. 1902
—	Cha. Oswald	Pem.	M 1912
—	Edw.	Sid.	M 1903 A.B. 1906. A.M. 1910
—	Frank Herb.	N. C.	M 1899 Cai. A.B. 1901
—	Gerald	N. C.	M 1910
—	Leon. Cha.	Pet.	M 1902 A.B. 1905
—	Milward Cecil	Cai.	M 1889 A.B. 1892. A.M. 1900. M.B., B.C.
—	Ronald Livingston ...	C. C.	M 1912 [1903
—	Will. Edw.	Sid.	M 1910
Hazel,	Hub. Hen.	Sid.	M 1910
Hazeldine,	Donald	Cai.	M 1910
—	Syd.	C. C.	M 1909 A.B. 1912
Hazeltine,	Harold Dexter ......*Em.		*A.M.* 1906. A.M. 1907
Hazlehurst,	Cha. Art. Cheshyre	Trin.	M 1906 A.B. 1909
Hazlerigg,	Art. Grey	Trin.	M 1898 A.B. 1901
––	Grey	Joh.	M 1897 A.B. 1900. LL.B. 1906
Head,	Benj. Wrightson	Em.	M 1896 A.B. 1899. A.M. 1903
—	Geo. Herb.	Pem.	M 1888 A.B. 1891. A.M. 1905
—	Harold Geo.	Jes.	M 1907 A.B. 1910
Heading,	Bertie	Qu.	M 1909 A.B. 1912
Headlam,	Walt. Geo. ....*King's		M 1884 A.B. 1887. A.M. 1891. Litt.D. 1903
Headley,	Hor. Harper	N. C.	L 1906
Heads,	John Ern. Blacklock	Sid.	M 1907 A.B. 1910
Heald,	Cha. Brehmer	Cai.	M 1902 A.B. 1905. M.B., B.C., A.M. 1910
—	Walt. Marsden	Cai.	M 1904 A.B. 1908. A.M. 1911
—	Will. Hen. Art.	Trin.	M 1912
Healey,	Frank Gray	King's	M 1911
—	Randolph Eddowes	Trin.	M 1866 A.B. 1870. A.M. 1907
—	Rich. Elkanah Hownam	H. Sel.	M 1904 A.B. 1907
Healy,	Fra. Dolores	N. C.	M 1902 A.B. 1905
Heany,	Wilfrid Percival	Em.	M 1912
Heap,	Frank Gustav	King's	M 1911
—	Jos. Milne	Trin.	M 1907 A.B. 1910
—	Steph.	Trin.	M 1894 A.B. 1897. LL.B. 1898. A.M. 1901
Heape,	Brian Ruston	Trin.	M 1911
Heard,	Alex. St John	Cai.	M 1904 A.B. 1907. A.M. 1911
—	Hen. FitzGerald	Cai.	M 1908 A.B. 1911
—	Ja.	Trin.	M 1899 A.B. 1902
—	Nigel	Pem.	M 1903 A.B. 1906
—	Will. Nevill	Down.	M 1891 A.B. 1894. M.B. 1901

Hearn,	John Stanley	Em.	M 1908 A.B. 1911
—	John Whitcombe ...	Sid.	M 1903 A.B., LL.B. 1906
—	Reg. John	Jes.	M 1908 A.B. 1911
—	Rob. Cecil	Joh.	M 1911
Hearsey,	Geo. Art. Canning ...	Jes.	M 1905
Hearson,	Hen. Fra. Pengelly	King's	M 1904 A.B. 1907
Heath,	Archie Edw.	Trin.	M 1907 A.B. 1910
—	Art. Fra.	Pem.	M 1912
—	Cha. Noel	Em.	M 1906 A.B. 1909
—	Fra. Clifford	Joh.	M 1894 A.B. 1897. A.M. 1901
—	Geo. Hen.	Qu.	M 1890 A.B. 1893. A.M. 1904
—	Ja. Shafto	Pet.	M 1894 A.B. 1897. A.M. 1901
—	John Rippiner	Trin.	M 1905 A.B. 1908
—	Leopold Cuthbert ...	Trin.	M 1912
—	Oliver	Trin.	M 1896 A.B. 1902. B.C., A.M. 1908. M.B
—	Rob. Will.	Trin.H.	M 1895 A.B. 1899. A.M. 1902 [1910
—	Roland John	Pem.	M 1911
—	Sid. Phippen	N. C.	M 1911
—	Walt. Ern.	Qu.	M 1912
Heathcock,	Tho.	Pem.	M 1912
Heathcote,	Edgar Hor.	Trin.	M 1900 A.B. 1904. A.M. 1907
—	Gilb. Stanley	Jes.	M 1902 A.B. 1905
—	Leon. Vyvyan	Cla.	M 1905 A.B. 1908
Heathcote-Smith, Clifford Edw. ...		Pem.	M 1903
Heather,	Cha. Herb.	H. Sel.	M 1895 A.B. 1898. A.M. 1903
Heatley,	Leon.	Pet.	M 1911
Heaton,	Dav. Rinnington	Trin.	M 1912
—	Frank	Em.	M 1898 A.B. 1902. A.M. 1905
—	Fre. Alphonse Art. Will.	Joh.	M 1906 A.B. 1909
—	Rainald	Chr.	M 1904 A.B. 1907
Heaton-Armstrong, John Dunamace		Trin.H.	L 1907 A.B. 1910
—	Will. Duncan Fra. ...	Trin.	M 1904
Heaton-Ellis, Cha. Edw. Rob.		H. Sel.	M 1912
Heaver,	Herb.	H. Aye.	M 1893 Chr. A.B. 1896. A.M. 1903
Heblethwaite, Chris. John		Trin.	M 1903
Hebron,	Will. Reg.	H. Sel.	M 1911
Hedderwick,	Art. Stuart	Cla.	M 1904 A.B. 1907
—	Gerald	Cla.	M 1912
Hedding,	Cecil Geo.	Down.	M 1909
Hedgecock,	Art. Tho.	Joh.	M 1909 A.B. 1912
Hedges,	Killingworth Michael Fentham	Trin.	M 1908 A.B. 1911
Hedin,	Sven Anders		Sc.D. 1909 [1900. M.D. 1905
Hedley,	Edw. Williams	King's	M 1892 A.B. 1895. A.M. 1899. M.B., B.C.
—	Illtyd	King's	M 1901 A.B. 1904. A.M. 1911
—	Ivor Mathews	King's	M 1910
—	John Prescott	King's	M 1895 A.B. 1898. B.C., A.M. 1902. M.B.
—	Oswald Will. Edw. ...	Trin.	M 1902 [1903. M.C. 1910
—	Walt.	King's	M 1898 A.B. 1902. A.M. 1906
Heelas,	Raymond John	King's	M 1902 A.B. 1905
Heigelin,	Hermann	Trin.H.	M 1911
Heimann,	Herman Paul	Joh.	M 1910
Heineken,	Georg August	N. C.	E 1906
Heinichen,	Friedrich Wilhelm Eberhard	Chr.	M 1911
Hele,	Tho. Shirley ....*Em.		M 1900 A.B. 1903. M.B., B.C., A.M. 1907.
Hellings,	Geoffrey Stuart	Joh.	M 1907 A.B. 1910 [M.D. 1911
Hellins,	Edgar Will. Ja.	Cath.	M 1894 A.B. 1897. LL.B. 1898. A.M. 1901
Hellyer,	Fra. Edgcombe	Trin.	M 1907 A.B. 1910
Helm,	Cyril	King's	M 1907 A.B. 1910
—	Hen. Paul Dundas ...	Trin.	M 1912

Helm,	Ja. Howard	Trin. H.	M 1899 A.B. 1902
Helme,	Ja.	Trin.	M 1902 A.B. 1905. A.M. 1909
—	Ja. Milner	Trin.	M 1907 A.B., LL.B. 1910
—	Rob. Egerton	Trin.	M 1910
—	Tho. Wilson	Trin.	M 1899 A.B. 1902. A.M. 1907
Helps,	Edm. Art. Plucknett	Cla.	M 1907 A.B. 1910
Hemmant,	Edw. Vincent	Pem.	M 1903 A.B. 1906
—	Geo.	Pem.	M 1899 A.B. 1902
—	Maur.	Pem.	M 1906 A.B. 1909
Henderson,	Alec Stewart	Trin.	M 1905
—	Alex. Iselin	Trin.	M 1912
—	Donald	Cla.	M 1912
—	Hub. Douglas	Em.	M 1909 A.B. 1912
—	John Allardice	Chr.	M 1900 A.B. 1903. A.M. 1907
—	John Kenneth	Trin.	M 1902 A.B. 1905
—	Mervyn	Joh.	M 1901 A.B. 1906. A.M. 1910
—	Percival	Joh.	M 1901 A.B. 1904. A.M. 1908
—	Rolf Keith	Cla.	M 1903 A.B. 1906
—	Will. Ashwin	Cla.	M 1903 A.B. 1906
—	Will. Lewis	Pet.	M 1902 A.B. 1905
Hendrie,	Hugh Alb.	H. Sel.	M 1910
Hendriks,	Cecil Augustus Cha. } John	Cla.	M 1902 A.B. 1905
Heneage,	Tho. Rob.	Trin. H.	M 1898 A.B. 1902
Henkel,	Fre. Will.	Jes.	M 1903
—	Wilfred Edw. Gustav	Pem.	M 1910
Henman,	Will. Whitefield	Pet.	M 1898 A.B. 1901
Henn,	Hen. ....*Trin. H.	M 1877 A.B. 1881. A.M. 1884. D.D. 1909
—	Will. Fra.	Mag.	M 1911
Hennessy,	Theodore Harber ...	Joh.	M 1895 A.B. 1898. Jes. A.M. 1902
Henri,	Frank	Trin.	M 1912
Henry,	Augustine	Cai.	A.M. 1908
—	Claud Dawson	Joh.	M 1886 A.B. 1889. A.M. 1893. M.B., B.C.
—	Douglas Cecil	Trin.	M 1912 [1894. M.D. 1906
—	Ja. Griffiths	Trin.	M 1902 Down. A.B. 1906. A.M. 1909
—	Syd. Alex.	Trin.	M 1898 A.B. 1901. A.M. 1905. M.B., B.C.
—	Will. Dav. Murray ...	Joh.	M 1909 A.B. 1912 [1906. M.D. 1910
Henryson Caird, Alister Ja.		Mag.	M 1902
Hensley,	Egerton Hen. Valpy	King's	M 1910
Henslow,	Cyril John Wall	Joh.	M 1906 A.B. 1910
—	Tho. Geoffrey Wall	H. Sel.	M 1897 A.B. 1901. A.M. 1904
Hensman,	Will. Alwin	Chr.	M 1899 A.B. 1901
Henstock,	Art. John	H. Sel.	M 1898 A.B. 1901. A.M. 1907
Henty,	Edwin Claude	Jes.	M 1906 A.B. 1909
Henwood,	Alf. Norman	Jes.	M 1908 A.B. 1911
—	Art. Dimble	Cath.	M 1908 A.B. 1911
Hepburn,	Fre. Cha.	Pem.	M 1896 A.B. 1902
—	Malcolm Arnold	Mag.	M 1910
—	Roger Paul	Mag.	M 1911
Hepburne-Scott, Walt. Tho.		Trin.	M 1909 post Scott, W. T. H.
Hepworth,	Bern. Gilpin	Em.	M 1905 A.B. 1908
—	Frank Art.	Joh.	M 1897 A.B. 1900. M.B., B.C., A.M. 1904
Herald,	Will.	N. C.	M 1896 Qu. A.B. 1899. A.M. 1905
Herapath,	Cyril Alex.	Qu.	M 1909 A.B. 1912
Herbert,	Alf. Bern.	Cath.	M 1898 A.B. 1901. A.M. 1905
—	Art. Grenville	Trin.	M 1897 A.B. 1900. LL.B.1901. A.M. 1904.
—	Basil	N. C.	M 1912 [LL.M. 1906
—	Elidyr John Bernard	King's	M 1899 A.B. 1902
—	Fra. Falkner	Em.	M 1898 A.B. 1901. A.M. 1911
—	Geo. Cha.	Joh.	M 1880 A.B. 1885. A.M. 1905
—	Percy Mark	Trin.	M 1904 A.B. 1907. A.M. 1911

Herbert,	Phil. Lee Will.	Cai.	M 1901
Herbert-Smith,	Gwenffrwd Mostyn	Trin.	M 1910
Herd,	John Geo. Manners McKaig	Cath.	M 1896 A.B. 1902. A.M. 1912
Herder,	Art. John	Sid.	M 1902 A.B. 1905
Herdman-Newton,	Cha.	Pem.	M 1909
Hereford,	Ja. Cecil	Cai.	M 1905 A.B. 1908
Heriz-Smith,	Eustace Edw. Art.	Pem.	M 1907 A.B. 1910
Herklots,	Bern.	C. C.	M 1891 A.B. 1894. A.M. 1901
Herman,	Ashley Ern.	King's	M 1905 A.B. 1908
—	Geo. Alf.	Trin.	M 1911
—	Geo. Lawrence	King's	M 1905 A.B. 1908. A.M. 1912
—	Walt. Sebastian	Sid.	M 1906 A.B. 1909
Hermon,	Horace Vincent	Trin. H.	M 1910
Heron,	Rich. Cobden	Joh.	M 1890 A.B. 1893. A.M. 1901
Herries,	Alex. Dobrèe Young	Trin.	M 1911
Herring,	Armine Will. Hen.	Pem.	M 1901 A.B. 1904
—	John Leigh	Trin.	M 1909
—	Justin Howard	Chr.	M 1908
Herriot,	Dav. Robertson	Cai.	M 1912
—	Ja. Allan	Cla.	M 1904
Herrmann,	Paul Millington	Joh.	E 1911
Hertslet,	Edw. Lewis Augustine	Jes.	M 1897 A.B. 1900. A.M. 1904
Hertwig,	Ric.		*Sc.D.* 1909
Hertz,	Oskar Heinrich	Chr.	M 1906
Hervey,	Art. Cha. Constantine	King's	M 1905 A.B. 1909
—	Eric Sedgwick	Trin.	M 1898 A.B. 1902
—	Gerald Art.	Pem.	M 1900 A.B. 1903
Herzl,	Hans	Joh.	M 1910
Herzog,	Ewald Alb. Ludwig	Joh.	E 1911
—	Fre. Jos.	Trin.	M 1908 A.B. 1911
Heseltine,	Norfor Evelyn	Trin.	M 1904
Hesford,	Isaac	N. C.	M 1911
Heshmat,	Hassan	Pem.	M 1906
Hesketh,	Geo. Evan	Pem.	M 1900 A.B. 1903. A.M. 1907
—	Gerald Manley	Cla.	M 1906
Heslop,	Gerald Gwydyr	Cla.	M 1897 A.B. 1901
Hesmondhalgh,	Will.	N. C.	E 1898 Cath. A.B. 1901. A.M. 1904
Hesse,	Harold Will.	Trin. H.	M 1900 A.B. 1903
Hetherington,	Art. Lonsdale	Trin.	M 1900 A.B. 1903. A.M.† 1907
—	Hen. Anstruther	Trin.	M 1903 A.B. 1907
—	John Railton	Pem.	M 1902 A.B. 1905
—	Roger Gaskell	Trin.	M 1894 A.B. 1897. A.M. 1901
—	Tho. Will.	Trin.	M 1911
Hett,	Arnold Innes	Chr.	M 1912
—	Hen. Alex.	Trin.	M 1901
Heurtley,	Walt. Abel	Cai.	M 1902 A.B. 1905
Hewett,	Cecil Douglas	Cai.	M 1903
—	Fre. Stanley	Cai.	M 1898 A.B. 1901. M.B., B.C. 1907. M.D. [1911
Hewgill,	Rupert Percy Alex.	Pem.	M 1894 A.B. 1897. A.M. 1901
Hewitt,	Fre. Whitmore	C. C.	M 1898 A.B. 1901. A.M. 1908
—	Geo. Herb.	N. C.	M 1910
—	Halford Wotton	Cla.	M 1889 A.B. 1893. A.M. 1907
—	John	Jes.	M 1899 A.B. 1902
—	Lelean McNeill	Qu.	M 1909
—	Norman Sinclair	Sid.	M 1911
—	Rupert Conrad	Cai.	M 1909 A.B. 1912
Heycock,	Morris Sadler	Pem.	M 1903 A.B. 1906. A.M. 1910
Heydon,	Geo. Aloysius Makinson	Chr.	M 1900 A.B. 1903
Heyes,	Will.	N. C.	M 1901 A.B. 1905. A.M. 1911
Heyland,	Hector Miles	Pem.	M 1909
Heyn,	Rich. Gustavus	Pem.	M 1907 A.B. 1910

Heywood,	Art. Geo. Percival ...	Trin.	M 1904 A.B. 1908. A.M. 1911
—	Cyril Garnett	Pem.	M 1907 A.B. 1910
—	Graham Percival	Trin.	M 1897 A.B. 1900. A.M. 1907
—	Leon. John	Pem.	M 1906 A.B. 1909. LL.B. 1910
—	Will. Benj.	Em.	M 1889 A.B. 1892. M.B., B.C. 1897. A.M.,
Heyworth,	Edw. Lawrence	King's	M 1910 [M.D. 1907
—	Geo. Alex. Fredrick	Trin.	M 1900 A.B. 1903. B.C. 1909
Hibberd,	And. Stuart	Joh.	M 1912
—	Hen.	C. C.	M 1897 A.B. 1900. A.M. 1912
Hibbert,	John Percy Maghull	King's	M 1903 A.B. 1906. A.M. 1910
Hibbins,	Fre. Art.	Joh.	M 1897 A.B. 1900. A.M. 1904
Hick,	Reg. Heber Prowde	Chr.	M 1903 A.B. 1906. B.C. 1911
Hickie,	Eric Wynne	Qu.	M 1912
Hicklin,	Jos. Herb.	N. C.	M 1903 Pet. A.B. 1906. A.M. 1910
Hickling,	Art. Raymond	Trin. H.	M 1906
Hickman,	Cha. Edw.	Trin.	M 1909 A.B. 1912
—	Terence	King's	M 1907 A.B. 1910. LL.B. 1911
—	Will. Christie	Cai.	M 1906 A.B. 1909
Hicks,	Basil Perrin	Trin.	M 1911
—	Edw. Jeffery	Cla.	M 1910
—	Eric Perrin	Trin.	M 1910
—	Fra. Edw.	Cath.	M 1890 A.B. 1893. A.M. 1902
—	Fra. Will.	Joh.	M 1905 A.B. 1908
—	Geo. Bruno	N. C.	M 1900 Pet. A.B. 1903. A.M. 1907
—	Geo. Dawes	Trin.	M 1903 A.B. 1909. A.M. 1912
—	Hen. Geo. Fra.	C. C.	M 1903 A.B. 1906. A.M. 1910
—	Rivers Keith	Em.	M 1898 A.B. 1901
Higgin,	Rob. Fra.	Cai.	M 1902 A.B. 1905. M.B., B.C. 1911
Higgins,	Alex. Pearce	Down.	M 1888 A.B., LL.B. 1891. A.M. 1895.
			[LL.M. 1898. LL.D. 1904
—	Cha. Alleyne	Pem.	M 1905 A.B. 1908. LL.B. 1909
—	Frank Edm.	Joh.	M 1909 A.B. 1912
—	Fre. Alf. Raymond	Joh.	M 1903 A.B. 1906
—	Hub.	King's	E 1890 A.B. 1893. A.M. 1901
—	Lionel Geo.	Cla.	M 1912
—	Syd. Ja.	Cai.	M 1903 A.B. 1906
.—	Tho. Hutchinson ...	Cai.	M 1894 A.B. 1897. A.M. 1901
—	Walt. Norman	Em.	M 1898 A.B. 1901. A.M. 1905
—	Will. Rob.	Cai.	M 1896 A.B. 1899. B.C. 1905. M.B., A.M.
Higginton,	John Martin	Joh.	M 1912 [1906. M.D. 1911
Higgs,	Hen. Jos.	Mag.	M 1905 A.B. 1908
—	Syd. Limbrey	Joh.	M 1912
Higham,	Cha. Strachan Sanders	Trin.	M 1909 A.B. 1912
Highfield,	Hen.	N. C.	L 1892 A.B. 1894. A.M. 1902
Highfield-Jones, Phil.		Joh.	M 1912
Hight,	Harold Edw.	King's	M 1908 A.B. 1911
Highton,	Douglas Clifford	King's	M 1899 A.B. 1902. A.M. 1908
Hignell,	Harold	Jes.	M 1903
Higson,	Ern.	Mag.	M 1897 A.B. 1900. M.B., B.C. 1904
—	Leslie Art.	Joh.	M 1912
Hilary,	Rob. Jephson	Joh.	M 1912
Hildyard,	Ern.	Qu.	M 1910
Hiles,	Morton	Pem.	M 1902 A.B. 1905
Hill,	Alb. Edw.	N. C.	M 1906 A.B. 1909
—	Alex. Galloway Erskine	Trin.	M 1912
—	Alex Woodward	Em.	M 1903 A.B. 1906. A.M. 1910
—	Alf. John Bostock ...	Trin.	M 1905 A.B. 1908
—	Archib. Vivian ......*Trin.		M 1905 A.B. 1908. A.M. 1912
—	Art.	Em.	M 1897 A.B., LL.B. 1900. A.M. 1904
—	Art. Croft	Trin.	M 1892 A.B. 1895. A.M. 1899. M.B., B.C.
—	Art. Theodore	Em.	M 1906 A.B. 1909 [1901. M.D. 1903

Hill,	Art. Will.	*King's	M 1894 A.B. 1897. A.M. 1901
—	Beresford Winnington	Mag.	M 1911
—	Cha. Alex.	Trin.	M 1886 A.B. 1889. M.B., B.C. 1894. A.M.
—	Cha. Loraine	Trin.	M 1909 [1907
—	Ern. Edw.	H. Sel.	M 1892 A.B. 1895. A.M. 1907
—	Geoffrey	Pem.	M 1909 A.B. 1912
—	Geo. Ja.	Pet.	M 1906 A.B. 1909
--	Guy Marshall	Cla.	M 1911
—	Harold Percivale	Jes.	M 1907 A.B. 1910
—	Hen. Lancelot Hingston	Pem.	M 1901 A.B. 1904. A.M. 1911
—	Hen. Oliver	Trin.	M 1906 A.B. 1909
—	Herb. Will.	N. C.	M 1910
—	Hub. Luff	Em.	M 1911
—	John Clarence	Jes.	M 1909 A.B. 1912
—	John Robertshaw ...	Joh.	M 1902 A.B. 1906
—	Jos. Ja. Sterling	Down.	M 1908 A.B. 1912
—	Jos. Lawrence	Em.	M 1901 A.B. 1903
—	Phil. Aubrey	Cai.	M 1891 A.B. 1895. A.M. 1901
—	Rich. Athelstane Parker	Cai.	M 1899 A.B. 1902. M.E. 1909
—	Ronald Guy	Trin.	M 1910
—	Russell Ja.	Pem.	M 1901 A.B. 1904. A.M. 1908
—	Stanley Paris	H. Sel.	M 1886 A.B. 1889. A.M. 1903
—	Tho. Archib. Montgomerie	Trin.	M 1908 A.B. 1911
—	Walt. Noel	Joh.	E 1898 A.B. 1902. A.M. 1907
—	Will.	Em.	M 1894 A.B. 1897. M.B., B.C., A.M. 1904
—	Will.	Cla.	M 1903 A.B. 1906
—	Will.	Trin.	M 1905 A.B. 1908
—	Will. Douglas Penneck	King's	M 1903 A.B. 1906. A.M. 1910
—	Will. Edw.	Joh.	M 1906 A.B. 1909
—	Will. Fre.	H. Sel.	M 1902 A.B. 1905
Hillbrook,	Wallace	Em.	M 1910
Hilleary,	Edw. Langdale	Trin.	M 1890 A.B. 1893. A.M. 1902
—	Leicester Mount	Trin.	M 1885 A.B. 1888. A.M., LL.M. 1892.
—	Roland	Trin.	M 1892 A.B. 1895. A.M. 1902 [LL.D. 1902
Hiller,	Hub. Geo.	King's	M 1909 A.B. 1912
Hilliard,	Gerald Will.	N. C.	M 1906
Hills,	Alf.	King's	M 1893 A.B. 1896. A.M. 1901
—	Art. Hyde	Cai.	M 1902 A.B. 1905
—	Cecil Hyde	C. C.	M 1909 A.B. 1912
—	Geo. Fredric Sowden	Trin.	M 1900 A.B. 1903
—	Herb. John	N. C.	E 1902 A.B. 1905
—	Tho. Will. Selwyn ...	Down.	M 1897 A.B. 1900. B.C. 1911. A.M. 1912
—	Walt. Hyde	Pem.	M 1896 A.B. 1899. M.B., B.C. 1904
—	Will. Fre. Waller ...	Trin.	M 1912
Hill-Thomson,	Ern. Will.	Pem.	M 1899 A.B. 1902
Hilpern,	Wilfred Tho. Hen. ...	Cai.	M 1909 A.B. 1912
Hilton,	Hen. Denne	Trin.	M 1902 A.B. 1905. A.M. 1909
—	Sam	C. C.	M 1898 A.B. 1901. A.M. 1905
Hime,	Alb. Hen.		*LL.D.* 1902
Hin,	Lim Kar	Pet.	M 1911
Hinchcliffe,	Harry Watson	Jes.	L 1908 A.B. 1910
—	John Will.	Cai.	M 1912
Hincks,	Edw. Harrison	Mag.	M 1902 A.B. 1906
Hind,	Alf. Ern.	Trin. H.	M 1897 A.B. 1901
—	Art. Mayger	Em.	M 1899 A.B. 1902
—	Cha. Raymond	Pem.	M 1912
—	Harold Ashover	King's	M 1898 A.B. 1901
—	Lawrence Art.	Trin. H.	M 1896 LL.B. 1899. A.B. 1903
Hinde,	Bertram Fountain ...	Em.	M 1905 A.B. 1908
—	Ern. Bertram	Em.	M 1900 A.B. 1903. M.B., B.C. 1908
—	Herb. Will.	Pem.	M 1896 A.B. 1899. A.M. 1903

Hinde,	Percy Montague	Em.	M 1903 A.B. 1907. A.M. 1910
—	Sid. Downton	Pem.	M 1899 A.B. 1902. A.M. 1906
Hinderlich,	Alb.	C. C.	M 1912
Hindle,	Alf.	C. C.	M 1894 A.B. 1897. A.M. 1901
—	Edw.	Mag.	M 1910 A.B. 1912
Hindley,	Eric Paton	Pet.	M 1911
—	Oliver Walt.	King's	E 1898 A.B. 1901
—	Will. Talbot	Chr.	M 1899 A.B. 1902. A.M. 1906
Hindley-Smith,	Ja. Dury	Mag.	M 1912
Hindmarsh,	Heriot	Sid.	M 1902
Hine,	Tho. Guy Macaulay	King's	M 1892 A.B. 1896. A.M. 1900. B.C. 1904.
Hinnell,	Tho. Squier	Pem.	M 1912 [M.D. 1907
Hippisley,	Edw. Townsend	Trin.	M 1912
Hird,	Bern. Hollis	Cath.	M 1902 A.B. 1905
Hirjee,	Rustom	Joh.	M 1908
Hiron,	John Bennett	N. C.	M 1900 Joh. A.B. 1903. A.M. 1907
Hirsch,	John Gauntlett	Cla.	M 1902
Hirst,	Gerald Scott	Trin.	M 1906
—	John	Trin.	M 1903 A.B. 1906
—	Reg. John	Pem.	M 1899 N. C., A.B. 1912
—	Wilfrid Bertram	N. C.	M 1911
Hiscott,	Leslie Stephenson ...	Pem.	M 1912
Hislam,	Percival Art.	C. C.	L 1906
Hislop,	Tho. Cha. Atkinson	Cai.	M 1907
Hissey,	John Bouch	Trin.	L 1904 A.B. 1906
Hitchcock,	Aldous Edw. North	Qu.	M 1906 A.B. 1909
—	Ja. Vincent	Cath.	M 1908 A.B. 1911
—	Rob. Jack	Qu.	M 1907 A.B. 1910
—	Roger Knight	Cai.	M 1906
—	Will. Hume Lane ...	Pem.	M 1904 A.B. 1907
Ho,	Shai Chuen	Joh.	M 1911
—	Shai Leung	Joh.	M 1907
Hoare,	Alan Brodie	Pem.	M 1901
—	Benj. Sumner	Trin.	M 1910
—	Chris. Gurney	King's	M 1901 A.B. 1904
—	Dav. Gurney	Trin.	M 1900 A.B. 1903
—	Edw. Godfrey	Trin.	M 1898 A.B. 1901
—	Edw. Ralphe Douro	Trin.	M 1912
—	Fre. Russell	Trin.	M 1906 A.B. 1909
—	Geoffrey de Monteney / Gerard	Trin.	M 1890 G. de Mounteney G. A.B. 1893.
—	Hen. Colt Art.	Trin.	M 1907 A.B. 1910 [A.M. 1910
—	Louis Gurney	King's	M 1898 A.B. 1901
Hobbs,	Cha. Richardson	Jes.	M 1910
—	Edw. Neville Bailey	Pem.	M 1903
—	Fre. Dudley	King's	M 1911
—	Victor Will. John ...	Joh.	M 1905 A.B. 1908. LL.B. 1909
Hobday,	Rich. Hen.	Sid.	M 1898 A.B. 1901. A.M. 1906
Hobhouse,	Art. Lawrence	Trin.	M 1904 A.B. 1907
Hobson,	Alan Faber	Cai.	M 1911
—	Cha. Kenneth	Trin.	M 1905 A.B. 1908. A.M. 1912
—	Cha. Mortimer	Qu.	M 1912
—	[1] Ern. Will.	*Chr.	M 1874 A.B. 1878. A.M. 1881. Sc.D. 1892
—	Fra. Will. Eland ...	Jes.	M 1902 LL.B. 1905
—	Frank	H. Aye.	M 1894 Cath. A.B. 1897. A.M. 1902
—	Oscar Rudolf	King's	M 1905 A.B. 1908. A.M. 1912
Hockey,	Harold Hub. Hibbert	Joh.	M 1900 A.B. 1903. A.M. 1910
Hodder,	And. Edw.	King's	M 1895 A.B. 1898. B.C. 1901. M.B. 1903
—	Fra. Edwin	·C. C.	M 1902 A.B. 1905

[1] Sadlerian Professor of Pure Mathematics, 1910.

Hodder,	Geo. Will.	Cath.	M 1899 A.B. 1902. A.M. 1907
—	Harold Geo.	Cath.	M 1911
—	Will.	N. C.	M 1898 Cla. A.B. 1901. A.M. 1905
Hodge,	Alex. Dingwall	Trin.	M 1907 A.B. 1910
—	Dorrien Edw. Grose	Pem.	M 1911
—	Edw. Humfrey Vere	Cla.	M 1902 A.B. 1905. M.B., B.C. 1910
—	Hugh Sydenham Vere	Trin.	M 1900 A.B. 1903. A.M. 1908
—	John Douglass Vere	Pem.	M 1906 A.B. 1909
—	Reg. Felix Vere	Em.	M 1899 A.B. 1902. M.B., B.C. 1906. M.D.
Hodges,	Alban Goderic Art.	King's	M 1912 [1912
—	Art. Noel	Qu.	M 1902 A.B. 1906
—	Cha. Frederic	Joh.	M 1903 A.B. 1907
—	Cyril Evelyn	N. C.	M 1902 Chr. A.B. 1905. A.M. 1910
—	Edw. Cha.	Trin.	M 1903 A.B. 1906. A.M. 1910
—	Geo. Edm. Ja.	Pet.	M 1912
—	Leslie Noel	Em.	M 1905 A.B. 1908
—	Reg. Alb.	H. Sel.	M 1911
—	Will.	N. C.	L 1901 Jes. A.B. 1903. A.M. 1907
—·—	Will. Cliff	Trin. H.	M 1902 A.B. 1905
—	Will. Geo.	H. Sel.	L 1898 A.B. 1901
Hodgkin,	Geo. Lloyd	Trin.	M 1898 A.B. 1903
—	Hen. Theodore	King's	M 1895 A.B. 1898. M.B., B.C., A.M. 1902
—	Ronald	Trin.	M 1899 A.B. 1902. A.M. 1907
Hodgson,	Alb. Ern.	Chr.	M 1903
—·—	Art. Claude Waterhouse	Qu.	M 1903 A.B. 1906
—	Art. Douglas	H. Sel.	M 1908 A.B. 1911
·—	Art. Hammond Fra.	Trin.	M 1901
—	Art. John	Cla.	M 1906 A.B. 1909
—	Cyril Art. Godwin ...	Trin.	M 1902 A.B. 1905
—	Geo. Will. Houghton	Trin.	M 1907 A.B. 1912
—	Gerald Augustus Tylston	Trin.	M 1891 A.B. 1894. A.M. 1908
—	Harold Edw. Austen	Trin.	M 1904
—	Herb. Hen.	Trin.	M 1901 A.B. 1904. A.M. 1908
—	Lionel Chris.	Chr.	M 1887 A.B. 1890. A.M.† 1901
—	Nigel Linnhe Tylston	Trin.	M 1901 A.B. 1904. A.M. 1908
—	Randolph Llewelyn	Qu.	M 1890 A.B. 1905
—	Tho. Reg.	Chr.	M 1901 A.B. 1904. A.M. 1908
—	Will.	N. C.	L 1904 A.B. 1907
—	Will. Hammond	Chr.	M 1899 A.B. 1902. M.B., B.C., A.M. 1911
—	Will. Harry	Chr.	M 1904 A.B. 1907
Hodsdon,	Cha. Walt.	Cla.	M 1912
Hodson,	Edmond Adair	Trin.	M 1912
—	John	Trin. H.	M 1911
—	Ronald	Pem.	M 1905 A.B. 1908
—	Vernon	C. C.	M 1901
Hoerber,	Florian Milward	Pet.	M 1911
Hoexter,	Oscar Hendrik	Em.	M 1912
Hoff,	Hen. Gilson	Cai.	M 1908 A.B. 1911
Höffding,	Harald		*Sc.D.* 1909
Hoffman,	Cha. Isaiah	N. C.	L 1902
—	Geo. Spencer	Trin.	M 1894 A.B. 1897. A.M. 1901
—	Harry Drummond ...	Trin.	M 1895 A.B. 1898. B.C. 1904. M.B., A.M.
Hoffmann,	Art. Rupert	Trin.	M 1907 A.B. 1910 [1905
—	Cecil Duncan	Sid.	M 1900 A.B. 1903
—	Geoffrey	Cai.	M 1901 A.B. 1904. B.C. 1911
—	Will. Arnold	Chr.	M 1897 A.B. 1900. A.M. 1905
Hoffmeister,	Cha. Edw.	Cath.	M 1905 A.B. 1908
—	Cyril John Roby ...	Cai.	M 1899 A.B. 1902
Hofmeyr,	Will. Hendrik	Em.	M 1899 A.B. 1902. A.M.† 1907
Hogan,	Claud Douglas Devereux	Joh.	M 1905 A.B. 1908. LL.B. 1909
—	Fra. Pat.	N. C.	M 1903 A.B. 1906

Hogan,	Reg. Victor John } Somerville	Joh.	M 1904 A.B. 1907
Hogarth,	Tho. John	Chr.	M 1902 A.B. 1905
Hogben,	Eric O'Neill	H. Sel.	M 1912
Hogg,	Will. Lindsay	Trin. H.	M 1901
Hoisington,	Hen. Martyn Howland	N. C.	M 1902 Down. A.B. 1905
Holbech,	Laurence	Qu.	M 1907
Holberton,	Tho. Edm.	Pem.	M 1901 A.B. 1904
Holborn,	Rob. Will.	Em.	M 1903
Holden,	Art.	Qu.	M 1900 A.B. 1903. A.M. 1907
—	Bern. Tomlyn	Sid.	M 1907 A.B. 1910
—	Edwin Greener	Cath.	M 1903 A.B. 1906. A.M. 1912
—	Frank	Joh.	M 1911
—	John Railton	Joh.	M 1911
—	John Stuart	N. C.	M 1894 C. C. A.B. 1899. A.M. 1902
—	Norman Edw.	Trin. H.	M 1897 A.B., LL.B. 1902
—	Norman Victor	Joh.	M 1909 A.B. 1912
—	Will.	Joh.	M 1880 A.B. 1884. A.M. 1909
Holder,	Norman Fra.	Pem.	M 1903 A.B. 1907
Holdich,	Tho. Hungerford ...		*Sc.D.* 1907
Hole,	Edwyn Cecil	Pem.	M 1911
—	Herb. Wray	Em.	M 1911
—	Hub. Northcote	Trin.	M 1899 A.B. 1903
Holland,	Cha. Benj.	C. C.	M 1906
—	Ern. Steph.	Cla.	M 1901 A.B. 1904
—	Franklin	King's	M 1900 A.B., LL.B. 1904
—	John Dixon Cuyler	Trin. H.	M 1911
—	John Gibson	Pet.	M 1908
—	Phil. Fielder	Jes.	M 1905 A.B. 1908
—	Vyvyan Beresford ...	Trin. H.	M 1905 A.B. 1910
—	Wallace Derry Ayre	Cai.	M 1911
—	Walt. Glen Cuyler ...	Trin. H.	M 1909
Holland-Hibbert, Thurstan		Trin.	M 1907 A.B. 1910
Hollender,	Alb. Harold Solomon	Trin.	M 1901
Hollings,	John Herb. Butler ...	Mag.	M 1906
Hollingworth, Edw. Will.		Pem.	M 1892 A.B. 1895. A.M. 1902
—	John	Pet.	M 1904 A.B. 1907. A.M. 1911
Hollins,	Edw. Ralph Lambert	Em.	M 1903 A.B. 1906
—	Esmond Mawdesley	King's	M 1901 A.B., LL.B. 1904
—	Jos.	Pem.	M 1896 post Gibson, J. A.B., LL.B. 1899
—	Noël Clinton	Em.	M 1905 A.B. 1908 [A.M. 1903
—	Percy Ryder	Trin.	M 1910
—	Rich. Roger	Cla.	M 1904
Hollis,	Augustus Theodore	Qu.	M 1891 A.B. 1894. A.M. 1906
—	Walt.	Cai.	M 1902 A.B. 1906
—	Will. Pushee Bertram	N. C.	M 1912
Hollond,	Hen. Art. ....*Trin.		M 1903 A.B., LL.B. 1906. A.M. 1910.
—	Raymond Claude ...	King's	M 1910 [LL.M. 1912
Holloway	Bern. Hen.	Jes.	M 1907 A.B. 1911
—	Norman Ja.	Jes.	L 1909 A.B. 1912
Hollyer,	Leslie Theodore	N. C.	M 1894 Cath. A.B. 1902
Holman,	Alb. Basset	Cath.	M 1890 A.B. 1893. A.M. 1903
—	Alex. McArthur	Trin.	M 1908 A.B. 1911
—	Alwyn Haswell	Jes.	M 1908 A.B. 1911
—	Cha. Colgate	Cai.	M 1903 A.B. 1906. M.B., B.C. 1909
—	Frank Macdonald Holman	Sid.	M 1908 A.B. 1911
—	Paul	Jes.	M 1910
—			*See* Taylor, J. H.
Holme,	Bertram Lester	Qu.	M 1906 A.B. 1909
—	Hen. Redmayne	Jes.	M 1908 A.B. 1911
—	Maur. Ingram	Jes.	M 1899 A.B. 1902. A.M. 1907

Holmes,	Alf. Kenward	....	Cla.	M 1900 A.B., LL.B. 1903
—	Art. Beresford	....	Joh.	M 1884 A.B. 1887. A.M. 1908
—	Basil Scott	....	Sid.	M 1903 A.B. 1906
—	Ern. Percy Worthington		Em.	M 1910
—	Geoffrey	....	Cai.	M 1903 B.C. 1910. M.B. 1911
—	Herb. Tho.	....	Joh.	M 1893 A.B. 1896. A.M. 1902
—	Jasper Cyril	....	Jes.	M 1910
—	John Backhouse	......	Qu.	M 1889 A.B. 1892. A.M. 1909
—	Reg. Yarborough	...	Em.	M 1906 A.B. 1909
—	Steph.	....	King's	M 1905 [M.B. 1902. M.D. 1905
—	Tho. Edw.	....	Cai.	M 1894 A.B. 1897. B.C. 1900. A.M. 1901.
—	Tho. Scott	....	Sid.	M 1871 A.B. 1875. A.M. 1878. B.D. 1910.
—	Tho. Symonds	....	King's	M 1912 [D.D. 1911
—	Tho. Victor	....	Trin. H.	M 1911
Holmwood,	Lionel Snowdon	......	Chr.	M 1908 A.B. 1912
Holmyard,	Eric John	....	Sid.	M 1908 A.B. 1911
Holroyd,	Gilb.	....	Chr.	M 1898 A.B. 1901. M.B., B.C. 1906
Holroyde,	Douglas	....	Trin.	M 1895 A.B. 1898. A.M. 1902. B.C. 1903
Holt,	Alf.	....	Pem.	M 1897 A.B. 1900. A.M. 1905 [M.B. 1908
—	Fra. Neville	....	C. C.	M 1912
—	Frederic Appleby	...	King's	M 1906 A.B., LL.B. 1909
—	Herb. Wilfred	....	King's	M 1907 A.B. 1910
—	Jos.	....	Cath.	M 1909 A.B. 1912
—	Reg.	....	Chr.	M 1910
Holthouse,	Cuthbert Lempriere		Joh.	M 1906 A.B. 1909
Holthusen,	Walt. Ernst	....	N. C.	M 1903
Holtzapffel,	John Geo. Holtzapffel		Joh.	M 1907 A.B. 1910
Holtzmann,	Wilfred Watkinson	...	Chr.	M 1896 A.B. 1899. B.C. 1903. M.B., A.M.
Home,	Alwyn Douglas	......	Chr.	M 1903 A.B. 1906 [1905
—	Cecil Fredrick Morton		Pem.	M 1910
—	John Norval	....	Cla.	M 1902 A.B. 1907
Homer,	Lionel Victor Cyril		Pet.	M 1901 A.B. 1905. LL.B. 1909
Homfray,	Sam. Geo.	....	King's	M 1906 A.B. 1909
Homolle,	Jean Théophile	......		*Litt.D.* 1903
Hone,	Jos. Maunsell	....	Jes.	L 1901 A.B. 1903
Honeyball,	Frederic Ralph	......	H. Sel.	M 1910
Honeybourne,	Harry Cecil	....	Joh.	M 1903 A.B. 1906. A.M. 1910
—	Victor Cyril	....	Joh.	M 1899 A.B. 1902
Honeyburne,	Will. Rob.	....	Pet.	M 1896 A.B. 1899. B.C. 1905. M.B. 1906
Honter,	Rich. Fre.	....	Em.	M 1897 A.B. 1900. A.M. 1905
Hony,	Geo. Bathurst	....	Chr.	M 1912
—	Hen. Cha.	....	Trin.	L 1907
Hood,	Alban	....	Chr.	M 1898 A.B. 1901
—	Hugh Meggison	......	Jes.	M 1903 A.B. 1906
—	John Alex.	....	Chr.	M 1907
—	John Cha. Fulton	...	Chr.	M 1902 A.B. 1905. A.M. 1909
—	John Will.		H. Sel.	M 1909 A.B. 1912
Hook,	Cha. Wilfrid Theodore		Joh.	M 1911
Hooker,	Cha. Will. Ross	......	Cla.	M 1904 A.B. 1908
—	Rich. Symonds	......	Em.	M 1905 A.B. 1908
Hoole,	Brian	....	Qu.	M 1911
—	Douglas	....	Qu.	M 1908 A.B. 1911
—	Norman	....	Em.	M 1912
Hooley,	Leon. Jos.	....	C. C.	M 1912
—	Terah Franklin	......	Trin.	M 1901
Hoon,	Pran Nath	....	N. C.	L 1908
Hooper,	Alb. Cha.	....	Qu.	M 1896 A.B. 1899. A.M. 1910
—	Art. Norman	....	Em.	M 1907 A.B. 1910
—	Aubrey Will.	....	Em.	M 1908 A.B. 1911
—	Edwyn Buchanan	...	Qu.	M 1893 A.B. 1896. A.M. 1910
—	Frank Hen.	....	Cla.	M 1905 A.B. 1908

Hooper,	Geo. Graham	.... Em.	M 1905 A.B. 1908
—	Handley Douglas	... Qu.	M 1909 A.B. 1912
—	Harold Geo.	.... Em.	M 1907 A.B. 1910
––	John	.... Pem.	M 1898 A.B. 1901. A.M. 1906
—	Kenneth Anderson	... Qu.	M 1907 A.B. 1910
—	Percival Ridley	...... Em.	M 1898 A.B. 1901
—	Percy John	.... H. Sel.	M 1907
—	Sam. Gordon	.... Em.	M 1909 A.B. 1912
Hopcraft,	Ern. Geo. de Lathom	Jes.	M 1906 A.B. 1909
Hope,	Art. Hen. Monger	... Cla.	M 1898 A.B. 1902. A.M. 1905
—	Bertram Liddell	...... Em.	M 1899 A.B. 1902. A.M. 1907
—	Geo. Leon. Nelson	... Pem.	M 1902 A.B. 1905
—	Geo. Meredyth	...... Cai.	M 1901 A.B. 1905
—	Hen. Norman	.... Cla.	M 1902
—	John Humphrey	...... Trin.	M 1910
—	Laurence Nugent	... Trin. H.	M 1909 A.B. 1912
—	Selwyn Pet.	.... Cla.	M 1909
—	Will. Hen. St John	Pet.	M 1877 A.B. 1881. A.M. 1884. Litt.D.
Hope Johnstone,	Cha. John	...... King's	M 1903 [1912
Hope-Jones,	Will. Hope	.... King's	M 1903 A.B. 1906
Hopewell,	Alan Fra. John	...... Qu.	M 1911
—	Donald Gardner	...... Trin. H.	M 1909
––	Ern. Roland	.... Mag.	M 1908 A.B. 1911
Hopkin,	Dan.	.... Cath.	M 1910
Hopkins,	Edw. Augustus	...... H. Sel.	M 1903 A.B. 1906
—	Geoffrey Art.	.... N. C.	E 1898 Joh. A.B. 1902. A.M. 1908
—	Noël Tho.	..............; Cla.	M 1910
—	Oliver Scatcherd	...... Trin.	M 1911
—	Rich. Valentine Nind	Em.	M 1899 A.B. 1902
—	Walt. Donald	.... Trin. H.	M 1901 A.B. 1904
—	Will. Hen.	.... N. C.	L 1904 Down. A.B. 1907
––	Will. Jos.	.... H. Sel.	M 1908 A.B. 1911
Hopkinson,	[1] Bertram	.... Trin.	M 1892 A.B. 1895. A.M. 1903
—	Harry Cunliffe	...... Em.	M 1911
––	Rudolf Cecil	.... Trin.	M 1909 A.B. 1912
Hopkirk,	Kenneth Rob.	.... Em.	M 1912
Hopley,	Fre. John Vander Byl	Pem.	M 1902
—	Geoffrey Will. Vander Byl	Trin.	M 1910
Hopton,	Mich.	.... Trin.	M 1858 A.B. 1862. A.M. 1901
Horan,	Art. Kevin	.... Sid.	M 1906 A.B. 1909
—	Will. Horace Stuckey	C. C.	M 1904
Hordern,	Lebbeus	.... Trin. H.	L 1910
Hore,	Cha. Will. Conybeare	Mag.	M 1908
Hori,	Timothy Keishi	...... Joh.	M 1901 N. C. A.B. 1906
Horikiri,	Zembe	.... N. C.	M 1906
Horn,	Allen	.... Trin. H.	M 1900 A.B. 1903
—	D'Arcy	.... Trin. H.	M 1900 A.B. 1903
Horne,	Cha. Wynn Ellis	... H. Sel.	E 1896 A.B. 1899. A.M. 1903
—	Gerald Cassan	.... Em.	M 1899 A.B. 1902. A.M. 1906
—	Harold Forster	...... King's	M 1897 A.B. 1900. M.B., B.C., A.M. 1904.
—	Ja. Anth.	.... Chr.	M 1910 [M.D. 1909
—	John Willoughby	... Pem.	M 1899 A.B. 1902
—	Maynard	.... Trin.	M 1889 A.B. 1892. M.B., B.C., A.M. 1901
—	Walt. Jobson	.... Cla.	M 1884 A.B. 1887. M.B., B.C., A.M. 1892.
			[M.D. 1901
Horner,	Norman Gerald	...... Cai.	M 1899 A.B. 1902. M.B., B.C. 1910
Hornibrook,	Murray	.... Joh.	L 1895 A.B. 1898. A.M. 1902
Hornidge,	Edw. Stewart	.... Trin. H.	M 1906 A.B. 1910
Horniman,	John Eric	.... Chr.	M 1909

[1] Professor of Mechanism and Applied Mechanics, 1903.

Hornsby,	Ja. Art.	Mag.	M 1909
—	Rich. Lionel Will. ...	Trin.	M 1911
Hornung,	Geo.	Trin.	M 1908 A.B. 1912
Horowitz,	Solomon	Joh.	M 1900 A.B. 1903
Horrocks,	John Art.	H. Sel.	M 1902 A.B. 1905
—	John Wesley	Chr.	L 1903
Horrox,	Harold Thompson ...	Cath.	M 1909 A.B. 1912
Horsefield,	Cha. Stanley Ward	Pem.	M 1910
Horsfall,	Cedric Fawcett	King's	M 1908 A.B. 1911
—	John	Cai.	M 1902 A.B. 1906
—	Rob. Elcum	King's	M 1912
Horsfield,	Ralph Beecroft	Trin.	M 1905 A.B. 1908
Horsley,	Sid. Gilb.	King's	M 1900 A.B. 1903
—	Stanley	Cla.	M 1901 A.B. 1904
—	Will. Edw.	H. Sel.	M 1907 A.B. 1910
Hort,	Fre. Aylmer	Em.	M 1890 A.B. 1902. A.M.† 1906
Horton,	Cuthbert Theodore ...	Joh.	M 1899 A.B. 1902. A.M. 1906
—	Ern. Fra.	Em.	M 1903 A.B. 1906. A.M. 1910
—	Frank ....*Joh.		M 1901 A.B. 1903. A.M. 1908
--	Harry	N. C.	M 1906 King's A.B. 1909
—	Le Gendre Geo.	Trin.	M 1878 A.B. 1882. A.M. 1903
—	Le Gendre Geo. Will.	Trin.	M 1912
—	Will. Rob.	Trin. H.	M 1908
Horwood,	Oswald Ryle	C. C.	M 1902 A.B. 1905. A.M. 1910
—	Tho.	N. C.	M 1904 A.B. 1907
Hosain,	Sheikh Shahid	Chr.	M 1900 A.B., LL.B. 1903
—	Syed Ahmad	Pet.	L 1912
Hosbons,	Percy	N. C.	M 1901
Hose,	Eustace	Jes.	M 1899 Reg. E. A.B. 1902
—	Hen. Christian Thorn	Em.	M 1902 A.B. 1905. A.M. 1910
Hosken,	Hub.	Chr.	M 1905 A.B., LL.B. 1908
Hoskin,	Alan Simson	Trin.	M 1905 A.B. 1908
—	Theophilus Jenner Hooper	Trin.	M 1907 A.B. 1910
Hosking,	Rich.	N. C.	M 1902 A.B. 1904
Hoskins,	Leander Miller	N. C.	M 1901
Hoskyns,	Edwyn	Jes.	M 1870 A.B. 1874. A.M. 1880. D.D. 1901
—	Edwyn Clement	Jes.	M 1903 A.B. 1906. A.M. 1911
Hosny,	Mohammed	Pet.	M 1908
Hotblack,	Geo. Finch	Pem.	M 1901 A.B. 1904. LL.B. 1905. A.M. 1908
, —	Gerald Vernon	Cai.	M 1909 A.B. 1912
—	Herb. Seymour	Cla.	M 1908
Houchen,	Gerald Saye	H. Sel.	M 1883 A.B. 1887. A.M. 1906
Hough,	Ja. Fisher	Joh.	M 1899 A.B. 1902. A.M. 1906
—	John Will.	C. C.	M 1908 A.B. 1911
—	Will.	Pem.	M 1904
Houghton,	John Christian	H. Sel.	M 1898 A.B. 1901
—	Ralph Lawrence	Trin.	M 1911
Hoult,	Jos. Murray	Trin.	M 1908 A.B. 1911
Houlton,	John Wardle	Chr.	M 1911
Housden,	Edwin Ja. Tilleard ...	Pet.	M 1907 A.B. 1910
—	Ern. Fre.	Pet.	M 1911
—	Rich. Ja.	Sid.	M 1908 A.B. 1911
Houseman,	Cecil Rob.	H. Sel.	M 1912
—	Fre. Oliver	Qu.	M 1895 A.B. 1898. A.M. 1903
Housman,	¹ Alf. Edw. ....*Trin.		A.M. 1911
Houstoun,	Rob. Alex.	Em.	M 1905
How,	John Cha. Halland	Joh.	M 1900 A.B. 1903. A.M. 1907
—	Syd.	Mag.	M 1888 A.B. 1891. A.M. 1901
Howard,	Addison Ja.	King's	M 1911

---

¹ Kennedy Professor of Latin, 1911.

Howard,	Alb.	Joh.	M 1896 A.B. 1899. A.M. 1903
—	(*Hon.*) Bern. Edw. ...	Trin.	M 1903
—	Cha. Gordon	Em.	M 1911
—	Cha. Reg.	Pem.	M 1893 A.B. 1896. M.B., B.C. 1904. M.D.
—	Claude Felce	Trin.	M 1910 [1907
—	Dav.	Cla.	M 1907 A.B. 1910
—	Donald Sterling Palmer	Trin.	M 1910
—	Geoffrey Will. Algernon	Trin.	M 1895 A.B. 1898. A.M. 1905
—	Geo. Will. Allen	Cath.	M 1909
—	Geo. Wren	Trin.	M 1911
—	Gilb.	Trin.	M 1894 A.B. 1897. LL.B. 1898. A.M. 1902
—	Hen. Southey	Trin.	M 1899 A.B. 1902. A.M. 1907
—	Hor. Reg.	H. Sel.	M 1911
—	Ja.	Jes.	M 1912
—	John Curtois	Cla.	M 1906 A.B. 1909
—	John Philip	Trin.	M 1907 A.B. 1910
—	John Reg.	Jes.	M 1902 A.B. 1905
—	Neville Martin Cha.	Trin.	M 1908
—	Percival	Cath.	M 1894 A.B. 1897. A.M. 1901
—	Rich. Tho.	Jes.	M 1903 A.B. 1906. A.M. 1910
—	Rob. Wilmot	Trin.	M 1906 A.B. 1909
—	Stanley Wathen	Trin.	M 1901
—	Tho. Hen.	Em.	M 1902 A.B. 1905
—	Walt. Stewart	Trin.	M 1906 A.B. 1909
—	Will. Evelyn Wykeham	H. Sel.	M 1906 A.B. 1909
—	Will. Harry	Cath.	M 1900 A.B. 1903. A.M. 1909
Howard-Flanders,	Rich. Leon. ...	Em.	M 1901
Howarth,	Walt. Goldie	King's	M 1897 A.B. 1900. B.C., A.M. 1905. M.B.
Howden,	Amaral	Down.	M 1904 [1906
—	Harold Ja.	Cla.	M 1895 A.B. 1898. A.M. 1906
—	Pat. Fraser	Trin.	M 1906
Howe,	Geo. Art.	Joh.	M 1911
—	Hen.	Mag.	M 1902 A.B. 1905
—	John Chris.	Pem.	M 1912
—	Rob. Geo.	Cath.	M 1912
Howell,	Eric Earnshaw	King's	M 1905 A.B. 1908. A.M. 1912
—	Evelyn Berkeley	Em.	M 1895 A.B. 1898. A.M. 1907
—	Geo. Fre.	King's	M 1908 A.B. 1911
—	Rapelje Hunting	Trin. H.	M 1897 A.B. 1902
—	Rob. Geo. Dunett ...	Em.	M 1896 A.B. 1899, R. G. Dunnett. A.M.
—	Roland Aneurin	Em.	M 1908 A.B. 1911 [1903
Howells,	Geo.	Chr.	L 1906 A.B. 1906. A.M.† 1911
Howell-Smith,	Art. Denner	C. C.	M 1899 A.B. 1902
Howett,	Frank	Trin. H.	M 1903 A.B. 1907. A.M. 1911
Howick,	(*Viscount*) Cha. Rob. Grey	Trin.	M 1898 A.B. 1901
Howitt,	Alf. Bakewell	Cla.	M 1898 A.B. 1901. M.B., B.C., A.M. 1906
—	Alf. Will.		Sc.D. 1904
Howland,	Tho. Walt.	Em.	M 1893 A.B., LL.B. 1896. A.M., LL.M.
Howlden,	Rich. Cyril	Cai.	M 1902 [1901
Howlett,	Cha. Edgar	H. Sel.	M 1907 A.B. 1910
—	Edwin John	Trin.	M 1896 A.B. 1899, E. J. Evans. A.M. 1903
—	John Montagu	Down.	M 1907 A.B. 1910
Howse,	Cha. Aubrey	Cla.	M 1903 A.B. 1906
Howson,	Hugh Edm. Elliot ...	King's	M 1907 A.B. 1910
—	John Lamb	King's	M 1910
—	Roger Saul	Trin.	M 1901 A.B. 1904
Hoyland,	Geoffrey	Joh.	M 1912
—	John Somervell	Chr.	M 1907 A.B. 1910
Hoyle,	John Baldwin	Pem.	M 1911
Htoon,	Moung Kyaw	Cath.	M 1907
Hubback,	Fra. Will.	Trin.	M 1903 A.B. 1907

Hubbard,	Gilb. Ern.	Trin.	M 1903 A.B. 1906
—	Harry Lovett	H. Sel.	M 1911
—	John Alf.	H. Sel.	M 1902 A.B. 1905. A.M. 1911
—	Phil. Waddington ...	Trin.	M 1911
Hubble,	Harry Ronald	H. Sel.	M 1911
Hubbuck,	Geoffrey Martin	Trin.	M 1909
—	Rupert Edw.	Pem.	M 1906 A.B., LL.B. 1909
Hubrecht,	Jan Bastiaan	Chr.	L 1906 A.B. 1907. A.M. 1912
Huck,	John	H. Sel.	M 1901 A.B. 1904. A.M. 1908
Huckle,	Hen. Will.	Down.	M 1907 A.B. 1912 [LL.M. 1901
Huda,	Sayyid Nurul	N. C.	L 1878 Joh. A.B., LL.B. 1881. A.M.,
Huddart,	Lindow Hereward Leofric }	Em.	M 1898 A.B. 1901. A.M. 1905
Huddleston,	Art. Ja. Croft	King's	M 1899 A.B. 1902. A.M. 1907 [M.D. 1906
Hudson,	Art. Cyril	Trin.	M 1895 A.B. 1898. M.B., B.C., A.M. 1902.
—	Bern.	Cla.	M 1896 A.B. 1899. A.M. 1903. M.B., B.C. [1904. M.D. 1907
—	Cha. Bamford	King's	M 1896 A.B. 1899. LL.B. 1901
—	Cha. Edw.	Joh.	M 1892 A.B. 1895. A.M. 1901
—	Edm. Foster	Joh.	M 1895 A.B. 1898. A.M. 1902
—	Egbert Claud	Trin.	M 1902 A.B. 1905. A.M. 1911
—	Eric Phillippo Ern.	Cla.	M 1905
—	Fra. Gerald	Jes.	M 1904 A.B. 1908
—	Fre. Audley	Trin.	M 1908 A.B. 1911
—	Geo. Harrington	Cath.	M 1910
—	Godfrey	Trin. H.	M 1912
—	Hen. Cecil Harland	Jes.	M 1906 A.B. 1910
—	Lynton Cha. Alf. ...	Pem.	M 1905
—	Noel Baring	Chr.	M 1912
—	Norman	Cla.	M 1911
—	Ralph Palliser Milbanke	Trin.	M 1910
—	Rob. Ja.	Cai.	M 1905 A.B., LL.B. 1908
—	Roland Burton	Trin. H.	M 1910
—	Ronald Will. Hen. Turnbull }	*Joh.	M 1895 A.B. 1898. A.M. 1902
—	Tho. Edgley	N. C.	M 1910
—	Tho. Heylyn	H. Sel.	M 1908 A.B. 1911
—	Will. Fre. Art.	Mag.	M 1894 A.B. 1898. A.M. 1904
Hue,	Art. Corbet	Mag.	M 1885 A.B. 1888. A.M. 1907
Huelin,	Edw. Scotton	Cai.	M 1907 A.B. 1910
Huggins,	Hen. Will.	Trin.	M 1910
Huggonson,	Rich. Pritchard	Chr.	M 1908 A.B. 1911
Hughes,	Alec Manston	H. Sel.	M 1912
—	Arnold	Joh.	M 1906 A.B. 1909
—	Art. Edgar	C. C.	M 1885 A.B. 1888. A.M. 1901
—	Art. Llewelyn	Em.	M 1908 A.B. 1910
—	Basil	H. Sel.	L 1898 A.B. 1903. A.M. 1908. B.C. 1909.
—	D'Arcy Wynne Aylward	Pet.	M 1908 A.B. 1910 [M.B. 1910
—	Dav.	Trin. H.	M 1906
—	Dav.	Cath.	L 1910 A.B. 1912
—	Edw. Art.	Trin.	M 1906 A.B. 1909
—	Edwin Watkin	Cla.	M 1895 A.B. 1898. A.M. 1902
—	Ern. Cranmer	Cla.	M 1898 A.B. 1901. B.C., A.M. 1906. M.C.
—	Evan	N. C.	M 1905 Cai. A.B. 1907 [1907
—	Frank Art.	Sid.	M 1906 A.B. 1909
—	Geo. Edw.	Trin.	M 1903
—	Geo. Hill	Cla.	M 1893 A.B. 1896. A.M. 1909
—	Geo. Ravensworth ...	Trin.	M 1906 A.B. 1909
—	Harold Cha.	Mag.	M 1911
—	Harry Halcomb	Qu.	M 1906
—	Hen. Castree	Pet.	M 1911

Hughes,	John Evans	Joh.	M 1905 A.B. 1908
—	John Lawrence	Joh.	M 1910
—	John Whitehouse Ward	Em.	M 1902 A.B. 1905
—	Jos. Edw.	Qu.	M 1897 A.B. 1900. A.M. 1905
—	Lancelot Hall	Pem.	M 1895 A.B. 1898. A.M. 1903
—	Lewis Art.	Qu.	L 1900 A.B. 1906. A.M. 1909
—	Lionel Worsley	Em.	M 1911
—	Maur. Blackburn	Pem.	M 1904 A.B. 1907. A.M. 1911
—	Noel Wilfrid	Pem.	M 1912
—	Norman Alf.	Trin.	M 1907 A.B. 1910
—	Owen	Cla.	M 1908
—	Percy Gladstone	N. C.	M 1907
—	Reg. Johnasson	Trin.	M 1901
—	Rich.	Joh.	M 1882 A.B. 1885. A.M. 1902
—	Sam. John	H. Sel.	M 1903 A.B. 1906
—	Tho. Geoffrey	Trin.	M 1905 A.B. 1908
—	Tho. McKenny	Trin.	M 1902 A.B. 1905. A.M. 1909
—	Tho. Will. Gillilan Johnson	Pem.	M 1908 A.B. 1911
—	Tom	Qu.	M 1898 A.B. 1901. A.M. 1905
—	Vivian de Courcy	Jes.	M 1903
—	Will. Owen	H. Sel.	M 1894 A.B. 1897. A.M. 1906
—	Will. Ravenscroft	*Jes.	M 1899 A.B. 1902. A.M. 1906
Hughes-Games,	Cyril Tomlinson Wynn	C. C.	M 1886 A.B. 1889. A.M. 1906
—	Joshua Bower	Qu.	M 1907 A.B. 1910
Hughes Gibb,	Aubrey Patrick	Trin.	M 1903 A.B. 1906
—	Harold Fra.	Trin.	M 1910
Hughes Jones,	Oswald	Joh.	M 1907 A.B., LL.B. 1910
Hugill,	Will. Lawson	Chr.	M 1881 A.B. 1884 (2). A.M. 1902
Hugo,	Louis du Buisson	King's	L 1903 A.B. 1904. A.M.† 1908
Hulbert,	Cha. Geoffrey Keith	Pem.	M 1906 A.B. 1909
—	Fra. Seymour	Trin.	M 1902 A.B. 1905
—	Hen. Bourchier	Cai.	M 1911
—	Hen. Louis Powell	Trin.	M 1891 A.B. 1894. A.M. 1900. M.B., B.C. [1903. M.D. 1910
—	John Norman	Cai.	M 1910
—	Maur. Leon.	Cla.	M 1905 A.B. 1909
Hulk,	Frederic Martines	N. C.	M 1902
Hull,	Hen. Cha.	Em.	M 1905
Hulme,	Tho. Ern.	Joh.	M 1902
Hulton,	Will. Penton	Trin.	M 1905 A.B. 1908
Hulton-Sams,	Fre. Edw. Barwick	Trin.	M 1900 A.B. 1904
—	Kenneth Assheton	Jes.	M 1903 A.B. 1906
Humby,	Spencer Rob.	Qu.	M 1910
Hume,	Dudley Basil Mackenzie	N. C.	E 1912
—	Martin And. Sharp		*A.M.* 1908
—	Percy John	Joh.	M 1904 A.B. 1907
—	Will. Errington	Pem.	M 1897 A.B. 1900. M.B., B.C., A.M. 1904
Hume-Williams,	Roy Ellis	Trin. H.	M 1907
Humfrey,	John Cha. Willis	Joh.	M 1900 A.B. 1902
Humm,	Harry	N. C.	M 1896 A.B. 1899. A.M. 1903
Humphreys,	Dudley Fra.	Pem.	M 1909
—	Geo. Will.	Qu.	M 1891 A.B. 1894. A.M. 1901
—	Gordon Noël	Cath.	M 1901 A.B. 1905. A.M.† 1909
—	Guy Howard	Trin.	M 1912
—	Iorwerth Hen. Maur.	Em.	M 1912
—	Will. Averill	Trin.	M 1905
—	Will. Herb.	Chr.	L 1906 A.B. 1908. LL.B. 1909
Humphries,	Rob. Percival	Trin. H.	M 1912
Humphry,	Alex. Murchison	Trin.	M 1907
—	Stewart	H. Sel.	M 1897 A.B. 1900. A.M. 1904
Humphrys,	Cha. Geo.	Pem.	M 1904 A.B. 1907

Humphrys,	Herb. Edw.	Cai.	M 1901 A.B. 1904. B.C. 1910. M.B. 1911
—	Reg. Percy	Cla.	M 1909 A.B. 1912
Hungerford,	Rich. Stanley	N. C.	M 1884 A.B. 1899. A.M.+ 1906
Hunkin,	Jos. Wellington	Cai.	M 1906 A.B. 1909
Hunt,	Alf. Edw.	Pet.	M 1899 A.B. 1902
—	Alf. Garrod Leedes	Joh.	M 1902 A.B. 1905. A.M. 1909
—	Dav. Ja.	N. C.	L 1888 Cath. A.B. 1890. A.M. 1912
—	Edw. Geoffrey	Cla.	M 1898 A.B. 1901 [M.D. 1903
—	Ern. Rivaz	Trin.	M 1891 A.B. 1894. M.B., B.C., A M. 1899.
—	Frank Geo.	N. C.	M 1896 Chr. A.B. 1899. A.M. 1904
---	Fre. Rich. Will.	Qu.	M 1910
--	Geo. Hen.	Cla.	M 1887 A.B. 1892. A.M. 1900. M.B., B.C.
—	Hen. Leslie	Cla.	M 1908 A.B. 1911 [1901
—	Holdsworth	Trin.	M 1902
—	John Brian	Em.	M 1909 A.B. 1912
—	Tho. Will.	N. C.	M 1898 Joh. A.B. 1901. A.M. 1905
—	Walt. Wingyett	H. Sel.	M 1894 A.B. 1897. A.M. 1901
—	Will. Edgar	H. Sel.	M 1902 A.B. 1905
Huntbach,	Gerald Will	Em.	M 1907 A.B. 1910
Hunter,	Archib.		*LL.D.* 1903
—	Campbell Murray ...	Trin.	M 1899 A.B. 1902. A.M. 1906
—	Cha. Michael	Pem.	M 1906
—	Cyril Ja.	C. C.	M 1907 A.B. 1910
—	Eric John	Cla.	M 1909
—	Geo. Ja.	Mag.	M 1907
—	Godfrey Jackson	Trin. H.	M 1907 A.B. 1910. LL.B. 1911
--	Herb. Kenneth	Qu.	M 1900 A.B. 1903. A.M. 1908
—	Hugh Connop	Trin. H.	M 1903 A.B., LL.B. 1906
—	Ja. de Graaff	Pem.	M 1900 A.B. 1903. A.M. 1907
—	John Adams	Joh.	M 1910
—	John Bowman	Joh.	M 1909 A.B. 1912
—	John Hubert	Cai.	M 1908 A.B. 1911
—	Mark Oliver	Trin.	M 1892 A.B. 1895. A.M. 1907
—	Michael John	Cla.	M 1909 A.B. 1912
—.	Wilfrid Clare	Cla.	M 1894 A.B. 1897. A.M. 1904
—	Will. Turner	Em.	M 1903 A.B. 1906. A.M. 1910
Huntington,	Cha. Philip	King's	M 1907
—	Lionel Welby	Trin.	M 1903 A.B. 1906
Huntley,	Douglas Evelyn Kingsby	Trin.	M 1903
Hunton,	Claude Wensley	Cath.	M 1899 A.B. 1904. A.M. 1912
Huntriss,	Edw. Mitchell	Trin. H.	M 1899 A.B. 1902. A.M. 1906
Hurrell,	John Norman	Trin.	M 1902 A.B., LL.B. 1905
—	John Will.	N. C.	M 1911
—	Stuart Cavendish ...	C. C.	M 1909
Hurry,	Art. Gordon	Joh.	M 1912
—	Cecil Baldwin	N. C.	M 1907
Hurst,	Alf. Will.	Em.	M 1902 A.B. 1905
—	Archib. Jos.	H. Sel.	M 1900 A.B. 1904
—	Cha. Benj.	Chr.	M 1900 A.B. 1904. A.M. 1912
--	Edw. Eumeralla	Pet.	M 1908
—	Fre. Geo.	Cath.	M 1908
—	Leon. Hen.	Pem.	E 1908
—	Ronald Fra.	N. C.	L 1906 Joh. A.B. 1908
—	Will. Hutchinson ...	Chr.	M 1909 A.B. 1912
Husain,	Syed Ishrat	Chr.	M 1900 A.B. 1904
—	Syed Jamil	Down.	L 1908
Husbands,	John Edwin	C. C.	M 1898 A.B. 1901
Hussey,	Rich. Lionel	N. C.	M 1907 A.B. 1910
Hussey-Macpherson, Lachlan Fowke			*See* Macpherson
Hutchence,	Byron Levick	Cai.	M 1907 A.B. 1910
—	Will. Gordon	Cai.	M 1903 A.B., LL.B. 1906. A.M. 1910

Hutchings,	Cyril Eustace	Em.	M 1908 A.B. 1911
—	Hugh Will.	Em.	M 1906 A.B. 1909
Hutchinson,	Anth. Chris. Campbell	Trin. H.	M 1902 A.B. 1905
—	Archib. Campbell ...	C. C.	M 1902 A.B. 1905
—	Cha. Hilton	Cai.	M 1901 A.B. 1904
—	Edw. Walt.	Pet.	M 1900 A.B. 1903
—	Ern. Gordon	C. C.	M 1908 A.B. 1911
—	Fra. Downes	Joh.	M 1905
—	Fra. Ern.	King's	E 1904 A.M. 1904 (Oxf. Incorp.)
—	Fre. Arundel Stewart	Trin.	M 1888 A.B. 1891. B.C., A.M. 1896. M.B.
—	Geoffrey Clegg	Cla.	M 1912 [1897. M.D. 1905
—	Geo.	Jes.	M 1908 A.B. 1911
—	Godfrey Cresswell ...	Trin. H.	M 1903 A.B. 1906. LL.B. 1907
—	Ja. Hely	C. C.	M 1912
—	Leslie Gwynne	Cla.	M 1912
—	Leslie Thomason Rose	Trin.	M 1889 A.B. 1892. M.B., B.C., A.M. 1897.
—	Noel Wilfrid	Cla.	M 1907 A.B. 1910 [M.D. 1902
—	Rob. Hilton	Cla.	M 1901 A.B. 1904
—	Tho. Will.	Joh.	M 1869 A.B. 1873. A.M. 1902
Hutchison,	John Colville	Cai.	M 1909 A.B. 1912
Hutt,	Cecil Will.	Trin.	M 1899 A.B. 1902. B.C., A.M. 1908
Hutton,	Art. Rob. Russell ...	Joh.	M 1890 A.B. 1893. A.M. 1911
—	Fra. Hen.	Trin.	M 1894 A.B. 1897. A.M. 1901
—	Martin Burnup	Cai.	M 1895 A.B. 1898. A.M. 1903
—	Rob. Jermyn	Joh.	M 1908 A.B. 1911
Huxley,	Geo. Art.	Trin.	M 1906 A.B. 1909
Hyams,	Alex.	Joh.	M 1902 A.B. 1905. A.M. 1911
Hybart,	Art. Ja. Fre.	H. Sel.	M 1905 A.B. 1908
Hyde,	Edwin	C. C.	M 1894 A.B. 1897. A.M. 1904
—	Harold Augustus ...	Down.	M 1910
—	Laurence Bentley ...	N. C.	M 1903 Down. A.B. 1906
—	Norman Bentley	Down.	M 1908
—	Ronald Will.	Joh.	M 1907
Hyde Parker,	Will. Steph.	Mag.	M 1910
Hyder,	Lodhi Karim	N. C.	M 1909 King's A.B. 1912
Hyder Beg,	Mirza Mohamed	Chr.	M 1900 A.B. 1903
Hylton Stewart,	Art. Cha. Lestoc	Pet.	M 1903 A.B. 1906. Mus.B. 1907. A.M. 1910
—	Bruce Delacour	Pet.	M 1910
Hyne,	Warwick Melville ...	Cath.	M 1908 A.B. 1911

I

Ibbetson,	Ern. Fre. Ilford	Mag.	M 1907 A.B. 1910
Ibbotson,	Archie Will.	Pem.	M 1905 A.B. 1908
Igglesden,	Reg. Swatman	Pem.	M 1908
Ilangakoon,	John Will. Ronald ...	Trin. H.	M 1903 A.B. 1906
Ilbert,	Courtenay Adrian ...	King's	M 1906 A.B. 1910
Iles,	Fra. Geo. Vernon ...	C. C.	M 1892 A.B. 1900. A.M. 1903
—	Geo. Ehret	Joh.	M 1894 A.B. 1898. A.M. 1902
—	John Hyde	Cai.	M 1896 A.B. 1899. B.C., A.M. 1907
—	John Owen	Cai.	M 1912
Iliffe,	Cecil Art. Mountford	Em.	M 1911
Illing,	Vincent Cha.	Sid.	M 1909 A.B. 1912
Illingworth,	Leon.	Trin.	M 1905 A.B. 1908

Illingworth,	Norman Holden	Cla.	M 1892 A.B. 1899. A.M. 1902
—	Oswald	C. C.	M 1906. A.B. 1909
—	Walt.	N. C.	M 1902 Chr. A.B. 1905. A.M. 1909
Ilott,	Cha. Hor.	Cai.	M 1890 A.B. 1893. A.M. 1902
—	Cyril Herb. Tho. ...	Cai.	M 1898 A.B. 1901. M.B., B.C. 1908 (2).
Imamura,	Schigezo	Trin.	M 1899 Shigezo, A.B. 1902 [A.M. 1909
Imbert-Terry,	Fre. Bouhier	Cla.	M 1906
Imison,	Chris. Savage	Trin.	M 1905 A.B. 1908
Imlay,	Alan Durant	Em.	M 1904 A.B. 1907. A.M. 1911
Imms,	Augustus Daniel ...	Chr.	M 1905 A.B. 1907
Inayat Ullah	....	Chr.	M 1907 A.B. 1909
Ince,	Rich. Basil	Pet.	M 1903 A.B. 1906. A.M. 1910
—	Stanley Robertson ...	Chr.	M 1904 A.B. 1907. A.M. 1911
Inchbald,	Chris. Chantrey Elliot	Cla.	M 1909
Inchley,	Orlando	Joh.	M 1892 A.B. 1895. A.M. 1899. B.C. 1900.
Inder,	Rob. Wilfred	Down.	M 1904 A.B. 1907 [M.B. 1902. M.D. 1905
Infeld,	Harry	King's	M 1912
—	Louis	Qu.	M 1907 A.B. 1910
Inge,	[1] Will. Ralph ....*King's		M 1879 A.B. 1883. A.M. 1886 *Jes. B.D.
Inger,	Hen. Edw.	Cath.	M 1901 A.B. 1904 [1909. D.D. 1910
Ingham,	Harold	Cath.	M 1907
—	Wilfrid	H. Sel.	M 1908 A.B. 1911
Ingle,	Laurence Mansfield	King's	M 1909 A.B. 1912
—	Norman Lee ....*Chr.		M 1904 A.B. 1907. A.M. 1911
—	Roland Geo.	Qu.	M 1905. A.B. 1908
Ingleby,	Bertram Edw.	Cai.	M 1901 A.B. 1904
—	Rich. Art. Oaks	Trin.	M 1897 R. A. Oakes, A.B. 1900. A.M. 1904
Ingles,	Fra. Hamilton	Jes.	M 1898 A.B. 1902
—	Phil. Hen. Bligh ...	Sid.	M 1896 A.B. 1899. A.M. 1906
Ingleson,	Phil.	Qu.	M 1911
Inglis	Alex. Evan Johnston	King's	M 1906 A.B. 1909
—	Alex. Raymond	Trin.	M 1908 A.B., LL.B. 1911
—	Art. Loveday	King's	M 1900 A.B. 1903
—	Cha. Edw. ....*King's		M 1894 A.B. 1897. A.M. 1901
—	Will. Morley	Qu.	M 1912
Ingoldby,	Roger Hugh	Em.	M 1905 A.B. 1908
Ingpen,	Donald Lane	Trin. H.	M 1903 A.B. 1906
Ingram,	Art. Cha.	Joh.	M 1895 A.B. 1898. M.B., B.C. 1902. M.D.†
—	Art. Foley Winnington		*LL.D.* 1908 [1905
—	Art. Geo.	Trin. H.	M 1889 A.B. 1892. A.M. 1901
—	Art. Ralph	Joh.	M 1895 A.B. 1899. A.M. 1905
—	Beresford	Joh.	M 1897 A.B. 1900. A.M. 1911
—	Edw. Maur. Berkeley	King's	M 1909
—	Geo. Skinner	Trin.	M 1900 A.B. 1905. A.M. 1909
—	John Ja.	Down.	M 1909 A.B. 1912
—	Ralph Edw. Alston	Down.	M 1904
—	Tom Lewis	Trin.	M 1894 Tho. L., A.B. 1898. A.M. 1906
Inman,	Ern. Cha.	Cai.	M 1906 A.B. 1909
—	Roy Talfourd	Trin.	M 1902
Innes,	Pet. Dav.	Trin.	M 1905 A.B. 1907
—	Will. Kedie	Pem.	M 1912
Innes-Cross,	Art. Cha. Wolseley	Trin.	M 1906 LL.B. 1909
Innocent,	Art.	Chr.	M 1906
Inskip,	John Hampden	King's	M 1898 A.B. 1902
Insole,	Eric Raymond	Trin.	M 1908
—	Geo. Claud Lathom	Trin.	M 1907 A.B. 1910
Iqbal.	Ali Khan	N. C.	M 1912
—	Muhammad	Trin.	M 1905 Sheikh, M., A.B. 1907
Iredale,	Hen. Cecil	Chr.	M 1909 A.B. 1912

[1] Lady Margaret's Professor of Divinity, 1907.

Ireland,	Geo. Harvey	Trin.	M 1904 A.B. 1907
—	John Fre.	Trin.	M 1907
—	Roy FitzGerald	Jes.	M 1909 A.B. 1912
—	Tho. Wilson	N. C.	M 1890 Sid. A.B. 1893. A.M. 1905
—	Will. Fra.	Joh.	M 1906 A.B. 1909
Iremonger,	Edw. Victor	Joh.	M 1905 A.B. 1908
—	Rich.	Pem.	M 1900 A.B. 1903. A.M. 1911
Ironside,	Reg. Will.	Pem.	M 1898 A.B. 1901
Irvine,	Leon. Cockburn Dundas	Em.	M 1905 A.B. 1908
Irving,	Aubrey Gordon	King's	M 1908 A.B. 1910
—	Dav. Whiteley	Qu.	M 1910
—	John Chris.	Joh.	M 1907 A.B. 1910
—	Percy Alex.	Joh.	M 1906 A.B. 1909
—	Will.	Cai.	M 1887 A.B. 1890. M.B., B.C. 1897. M.D.†
—	Will. Ross	H. Sel.	M 1911 [1911
Irwin,	Alf. Percy Bulteel ...	Cai.	M 1906 A.B. 1910
—	Cuthbert	Trin.	M 1907 A.B. 1910
—	Dav.	Sid.	M 1900 A.B. 1903
—	Hen. Mark	H. Sel.	M 1904 A.B. 1908
—	Will. Livingstone ...	Joh.	M 1903
Isaac,	Alb. Tudor	Jes.	E 1898 A.B., LL.B. 1902
—	Cha. Leon.	Joh.	E 1896 A.B. 1899. M.B., B.C. 1909
—	Dudley Cha.	Pem.	M 1912
Isaacs,	Marcel Godfrey	Down.	M 1911
Isitt,	Geoffrey Holt	Pem.	M 1904 A.B. 1907. A.M. 1912
Ismail,	Mohamed Cassim ...	Sid.	M 1908
Ison,	Art. Jesse	C. C.	L 1911
—	Leon. Ja.	N. C.	M 1911
Israel,	Judah	Qu.	M 1888 A.B. 1891. J. Dav., LL.M. 1897.
Isserlis,	Leon	Chr.	M 1900 A.B. 1903 [LL.D. 1902
Ives,	Geo. Cecil	Mag.	M 1885 A.B. 1892. A.M. 1901
—	Louis	Qu.	M 1898 A.B. 1901. A.M. 1905
Iwasaki,	Koyata	Pem.	M 1902 A.B. 1905
Izard,	Arnold Woodford ...	Trin.	M 1893 A.B. 1896. M.B., B.C., A.M. 1903.
—	Keith Halsted	Pem.	M 1906 [M.D. 1909

J

Jack,	Alex. Fingland	Trin.	M 1910 A.B. 1912
Jacklin,	Ja. Valentine	Joh.	M 1911
Jackson,	Amiend Cecil Desmond	Chr.	M 1901 A.B. 1904. LL.B. 1905
—	And. Eric	Pem.	M 1901 A.B., LL.B. 1904. A.M. 1908
—	Art. Ern.	N. C.	L 1893 A.B. 1897. A.M. 1906
—	Art. Frame	Pet.	M 1902 A.B. 1905. B.C. 1908. M.B. 1909
—	Bern. Cecil	Chr.	M 1898 A.B. 1901. A.M. 1905
—	Bertram Rolfe	Trin.	M 1906 LL.B. 1910
—	Cha. Alb.	Joh.	M 1903 A.B. 1906. A.M. 1910
—	Cyril Rob.	Mag.	M 1912
—	Donald Fisher	Jes.	M 1906 A.B. 1909
—	Edw. Phillips	Trin.	M 1912
—	Evelyn Willan	Trin. H.	M 1899 A.B., LL.B. 1902
—	Fra. Bern.	King's	M 1895 A.B. 1898. A.M. 1905
—	Fre. Keith	Chr.	E 1912
—	Geo. Clive	Trin.	M 1912

Jackson,	Geo. Stiebel	Trin. H.	M 1899 A.B. 1904
—	Gilb. Edw.	Joh.	M 1908 A.B. 1911
—	Gordon Balmbra	Trin.	M 1905 A.B. 1908
—	Griffith Art. Jones ...	Qu.	M 1912
—	Guy Howland	King's	M 1905 A.B. 1908
—	Harley Douglas	Joh.	M 1907 A.B. 1910
—	¹ Hen. ....*Trin.		M 1858 A.B. 1862. A.M. 1865. Litt.D.
—	Hen. ....*Down.		M 1894 A.B. 1898. A.M. 1901 [1884
—	Hen. Beecher	Cla.	M 1898 A.B. 1901. A.M. 1905
—	Hen. Latimer	Chr.	M 1878 A.B. 1882. A.M.† 1885. B.D. 1906
—	Hor. Art.	Trin.	M 1904 A.B. 1907. A.M. 1911
—	Ivor	Pem.	M 1904 A.B., LL.B. 1907. A.M., LL.M.
—	John	Trin.	M 1909 A.B. 1912 [1912
—	John Broadhurst ...	Sid.	M 1908 A.B. 1911
—	John Edw. Norman	Joh.	M 1905 A.B. 1908. A.M. 1912
—	John Gildart	Cla.	M 1896 A.B. 1902
—	Langford Pridden ...	Qu.	M 1904 A.B. 1907. A.M. 1911
—	Leon. Ja.	Chr.	M 1903 A.B. 1906. A.M. 1911
—	Reg. Will.	Sid.	M 1912
—	Rupert Will. Percival	Cla.	M 1909 A.B. 1912
—	Tho. Graham		*LL.D.* 1910
—	Tho. Hartley	H. Sel.	M 1897 A.B. 1902. A.M. 1909
—	Tho. Will.	Pem.	M 1896 A.B. 1899. A.M. 1905
—	Wesley Pickard	Trin. H.	M 1908 A.B. 1911
—	Will. Edm.	Trin.	M 1900 A.B. 1903
—	Will. Hartas	Cla.	M 1898 A.B. 1901. A.M. 1905
Jacob,	Anstey Ross	Joh.	M 1912
—	Art. Cecil	Cai.	M 1909 A.B., LL.B. 1912
—	Clyde Will.	Sid.	M 1901 A.B. 1904
—	Fre.	Cai.	E 1894 A.B. 1897. A.M. 1901
—	Geo. Archib. Forlong	King's	M 1907 A.B. 1910
—	Hugh Fra.	Trin.	M 1901 A.B. 1904
—	Lancelot Geo.	Chr.	M 1909 A.B. 1912
Jacoby,	Alf. Hen. Maur.	Jes.	M 1903
Jacomb,	Will. Hor.	Pem.	L 1901 A.B. 1903
Jacot,	Edouard	Em.	M 1910 A.B. 1912
Jacquest,	Sam. Percy	Joh.	M 1907 A.B. 1910
Jaffé,	Alf. Cecil	Em.	M 1902
—	Art. Dan.	King's	M 1899 A.B. 1902. A.M. 1906
—	Geo. Cecil	Trin.	M 1903
—	Will. Edw. Berthold	Em.	M 1902 A.B. 1905. A.M. 1912
Jaffee,	Mark	Trin.	M 1908 A.B. 1911
Jagg,	Herb. Vernon Ralph	H. Sel.	M 1912
—	Victor Tho. South ...	H. Sel.	M 1906 A.B. 1910
Jagger,	Art.	Pem.	M 1887 A.B. 1890. A.M. 1903
Jago,	Edwin Osborne	Em.	M 1905 A.B. 1908
Jaini,	Mansumrat Das	Down.	M 1905 A.B. 1908
Jalland,	Ern. Hen.	Cla.	M 1902 A.B. 1905
James,	Adrian Ingram	Trin.	M 1909
—	Archib. Will. Hen. ...	Trin.	M 1912
—	Art. Edw. Geo.	N. C.	M 1911
—	Art. Lloyd	Trin.	M 1908 A.B. 1910
—	Cha. Clem. Hancock	Mag.	M 1909 A.B. 1912
—	Cha. Edw. Noel	King's	M 1893 A.B. 1896. A.M. 1905
—	Cha. Kenneth	Cai.	M 1910
—	Dan Ivor	Sid.	M 1905 A.B. 1907. A.M. 1911
—	Dav.	Down.	M 1907
—	Dav. Basil	Pet.	M 1909
—	Dav. Watkin	Cla.	M 1895 A.B. 1898. LL.B. 1901

¹ Regius Professor of Greek, 1906.

James,	Edw. Bankes	Cai.	M 1889 A.B. 1892. A.M. 1902
—	Edw. Haughton	Cai.	M 1909
—	Eric Sam. Pennant Kingsbury	C. C.	M 1906 A.B. 1909
—	Fra. Art.	Joh.	M 1905 A.B. 1908
—	Gwilym	Joh.	M 1901 A.B. 1905
—	Harold Morton	Jes.	M 1903
—	John Allen	Cai.	M 1912
—	John Dan.	Mag.	M 1881 A.B. 1884 (2). A.M. 1889. B.D.
—	John Harold	Qu.	M 1902 A.B. 1905 [1906
—	John Neville Abraham	Pem.	M 1910
—	John Paton	Em.	M 1906 A.B. 1910
--	Kenneth Pascoe	Chr.	M 1910
—	Lewis Hen.	Em.	M 1909 A.B. 1912
—.	¹ Montague Rhodes ...*King's		M 1882 A.B. 1885. A.M. 1889. Litt.D. 1895
—	Reg. Hetling Lancelot	Cla.	M 1890 A.B. 1893. A.M. 1902
—	Reg. Will.	Joh.	M 1909 A.B. 1912
—	Tho. Campbell	Trin.	M 1899 A.B. 1902. A.M. 1906
—	Tho. Jos.	Chr.	M 1895 A.B. 1898. A.M. 1904
--	Tho. Maur.	Em.	M 1910
—	Tudor Stanley	Trin. H.	M 1909
—	Will. Browne	N. C.	M 1902 Down. A.B. 1907
Jameson,	Algernon Ja. Durand	Trin.	M 1906 A.B. 1909
—	Cecil Will.	C. C.	M 1909 A.B. 1912
—	Frank Rob. Wordsworth	Em.	M 1912
—.	Geoffrey Ja.	Trin.	M 1907 A.B. 1910
—	Geo. Dearden	Pem.	M 1907 A.B. 1910
—	Laurence Watson ...	Trin. H.	M 1902
—	Will. Luxmoore	Em.	M 1905 A.B. 1908. A.M. 1912
Jamieson,	Ern. Art. Oliphant Auldjo	Trin.	M 1899 A.B. 1903
—	Pet. Edwin	King's	M 1899 A.B. 1902
Jansz,	Paul Lucien	Em.	M 1908 A.B. 1911
Janvrin,	Claud Will.	N. C.	M 1907 A.B. 1910
—	Reg. Beavis Le Breton	Joh.	M 1899 A.B. 1902. A.M. 1906
Jaques,	Art.	Pem.	M 1907 A.B. 1910
Jaquet,	Douglas Austin	Em.	M 1906 A.B. 1909
—	Ern. Godfrey	Jes.	M 1908 A.B. 1911
Jarchow,	Chris. John Fre. ...	Joh.	M 1898 A.B. 1901. A.M. 1905
Jardine,	Douglas Ja.	Trin.	M 1907 A.B. 1910
—	Ja. Willoughby	King's	E 1899 A.B. 1902. LL.B. 1903. A.M. 1907
Jareja,	Bhoputsingjee Bhug-vatsingjee	Trin.	M 1907
Jármay,	Istvan Basil	Trin.	M 1903 A.B. 1908
Jarratt,	Geo. Lansdell	Joh.	M 1900 A.B. 1903
Jarvie,	Ja. Milne	Em.	M 1903 A.B. 1906. B.C. 1912
Jarvis,	Cha. Hooper	N. C.	M 1903 Joh. A.B., LL.B. 1906. A.M. 1910
—	Frederic	Cai.	M 1906 A.B. 1910
—	Fre. John	N. C.	M 1903 Chr. A.B. 1907
—	Hor. Eustace Geo. ...	Down.	M 1909 A.B., LL.B. 1912
Jary,	Rob. Ja. Alb.	N. C.	E 1899 A.B. 1902. A.M. 1911
—	Will. Fre.	Qu.	M 1912
Jasper,	Reg. Frederic Tudor	Cai.	M 1909 A.B. 1912
Jassawalla,	Cawasjee Burjorjee ...	N. C.	M 1907
Jathar,	Ganesh Bhaskar	N. C.	M 1907 A.B. 1910
Jay,	Cha. Douglas	Trin.	M 1908
—	Drue Drury Butler	H. Sel.	M 1905 A.B. 1908
—	Edw. Aubrey Hastings	Trin.	M 1888 A.B., LL.B. 1892. A.M. 1901
Jayaratnam,	Tho. Cooke Sam. ...	Cla.	M 1912

¹ Provost of King's College, 1905.

Jeakes,	John Will.	Trin.	M 1899 A.B. 1902
Jeans,	Frank Alex. Gallon	Joh.	M 1896 A.B. 1899. A.M. 1903. M.B., B.C.
—	Ja. Hopwood ....*Trin.		M 1896 A.B. 1899. A.M.† 1903 [1906
Jeayes,	Wilfrid Art.	Qu.	M 1907 A.B. 1910
Jebb,	Reg. Douglas	King's	M 1903 A.B. 1906. A.M. 1910
Jeejeebhoy,	Jeejeebhoy Piroshaw } Bomanjee {	Trin.	M 1909
Jeeves,	Frederic Will.	N. C.	M 1910
—	Leon. Lambart Garnet	N. C.	M 1907 L. Lambert G., C. C. A.B. 1910
Jeff,	Alf. Hen.	N. C.	M 1908 A.B. 1911
Jeffcock,	Harold Cha. Firth ...	Jes.	L 1904
—	Phil. Eric	Jes.	M 1906
—	Tho. Roy	Mag.	M 1910
—	Will. Hen. Claude ...	Jes.	M 1907
—	Will. Phil.	Trin. H.	M 1911
Jefferson,	Will. Brundrit	C. C.	M 1907 A.B. 1910
Jeffery,	Edw. John Bennetto	H. Sel.	M 1911
—	Frank Herb.	Trin.	M 1896 A.B. 1899. A.M. 1903
Jefferys,	Ern. Walt.	Em.	M 1893 A.B. 1896. A.M. 1907
Jeffreys,	Harold	Joh.	M 1910
—	Howel Gabriel Gwyn	Trin.	M 1904 A.B. 1908
—	John Gwyn	Trin.	M 1901 A.B. 1904. A.M. 1908
—	Rob. Syd.	Joh.	M 1906 A.B., LL.B. 1909
—	Walt. Marmaduke ...	Trin.	M 1897 A.B. 1900. M.B., B.C. 1909
Jeffries,	Fra. Jos.	Cai.	M 1892 A.B., LL.B. 1896. A.M. 1907.
—	Will. Fra. Carey	Trin.	M 1909 A.B. 1912 [LL.M.† 1909
Jeffs,	Will. Conyngham ...	Cath.	E 1902
Jehanghier,	Cowasjee	Joh.	M 1897 A.B. 1901. A.M.† 1906
Jehu,	Tho. John	Joh.	M 1895 A.B. 1898. A.M. 1902
Jelf,	John Ja.	King's	M 1901 A.B. 1904
Jemmett,	Cha. Will.	Cla.	M 1905
—	Frank Rupert	Trin.	M 1904 A.B. 1907. A.M. 1912
Jenkin,	Cha. Oswald Frewen	King's	M 1909 A.B. 1912
—	Hen. Archib.	Jes.	M 1903 A.B. 1906
—	Nelson West	Chr.	M 1901 A.B. 1904
—	Reg. Trevor	Jes.	M 1906 A.B. 1909
Jenkins,	Alb. Ern.	Joh.	M 1901 A.B. 1904
—	Cha. Edw.	N. C.	M 1895 Jes. A.B. 1900. A.M. 1908
—	Dav. Jones Capenhurst	Down.	M 1912
—	Edgar Ern.	King's	M 1906 A.B. 1909
—	Edw.	Sid.	M 1892 A.B. 1895. A.M.† 1902
—	Evan John	N. C.	M 1903
—	Fre.	Joh.	M 1904 A.B. 1907
—	Hammond Beaconsfield	Joh.	M 1900 A.B. 1903. A.M. 1908
—	Harry Lionel	N. C.	M 1910
—	Ja. Heald	Em.	M 1894 A.B. 1897. A.M. 1901
—	John	Chr.	M 1909 A.B. 1911
—	John Edwardes	N. C.	M 1894 Em. A.B. 1897. A.M. 1901
—	Reg. Edw.	Jes.	M 1909
—	Rich. Syd.	Joh.	M 1899 A.B. 1902
—	Rob. Tho.	Trin.	M 1901 A.B. 1904. A.M. 1909
—	Walt. Allen	Em.	M 1912
—	Will. Canning	Qu.	L 1901
Jenkinson,	Cha. Hilary	Pem.	M 1901 A.B. 1904
—	Stanley Noël	Cai.	M 1905
Jenner Fust,	Denton	Trin. H.	M 1898 A.B. 1901. A.M. 1906
Jennings,	Art. Rich.	Jes.	M 1904 A.B. 1907. A.M. 1911
—	Cha.	Pem.	M 1900 A.B. 1903
—	Eric Parry	Qu.	M 1911
—	John Herb.	Down.	M 1907 A.B. 1910
—	Leon. Art.	N. C.	M 1904

Jennings,	Rich. Will.	Jes.	M 1907 A.B., LL.B. 1910
—	Rob. Ingilby	Pem.	M 1900 A.B. 1903. A.M. 1907
—	Sutcliffe Hales	Qu.	M 1895 A.B. 1898. A.M. 1902
Jephcott,	Alex.	Qu.	M 1909 A.B. 1912
—	Ern. Woodward	Cai.	M 1907 A.B. 1910
Jephson,	Phil. Hen. Reiss	Pem.	M 1906 A.B. 1909
Jeppe,	Otto Rich.	Trin. H.	M 1905
—	Theodor Julius Juta	Cai.	M 1905
Jepson,	Alf. Cha.	Pem.	M 1904 A.B. 1907. B.C. 1912
—	Frank Price	Pem.	M 1903 A.B. 1909
—	Rowland Walt.	Mag.	M 1907 A.B. 1910
Jerusalem,	Geo.	Joh.	M 1908 A.B. 1910
Jervis,	Art. Cyril	H. Sel.	M 1906
—	Bern. Aubrey	Qu.	M 1904 A.B. 1907
—	Ern. Oswald	H. Sel.	L 1892 A.B. 1894. A.M. 1901
—	Tho. Haworth	H. Aye.	M 1889 A.B. 1892. A.M. 1911
Jerwood,	Bern. Ellery	Sid.	M 1911
—	Fre. Harold	Jes.	M 1905 A.B. 1908
—	Hen. Art.	Sid.	M 1897 A.B. 1902. A.M. 1905
—	John Hugh	Jes.	M 1909 A.B. 1912
Jesse,	Walt. John	Trin. H.	M 1902
—	Will.	H. Sel.	M 1888 A.B. 1891. A.M. 1902
Jeudwine,	Wilfrid Wynne	H. Sel.	M 1895 A.B. 1898. B.C. 1902. M.B. 1903.
Jevons,	Herb. Stanley	Trin.	M 1894 A.B. 1897. A.M. 1901 [M.D. 1912
—	Tho. Seton	Cla.	M 1893 A.B. 1901
Jewell,	Bertram Sam.	Trin.	M 1899 A.B. 1902
—	Cha. John Sam.	Trin.	M 1910
Jewitt,	Dermod Pat.	Chr.	M 1912
Jewson,	John Chris.	Pem.	M 1909 A.B. 1912
—	Norman	Cai.	M 1901 A.B. 1906
Joannides,	Geo. Spyro	King's	M 1904 G. Spyros, A.B. 1907
Job,	Cyril Dyon	Qu.	M 1905 A.B. 1908. A.M. 1912
Jobson,	Ja. Stanley	Sid.	M 1903 A.B. 1906. M.B., B.C. 1910
—	John Oswald	Pem.	M 1894 A.B., LL.B. 1897. A.M. 1901
—	Rich. Fitton	Cai.	M 1900 A.B. 1903
Joce,	John Burden Dunn	Joh.	M 1901 A.B. 1904
Joel,	Woolf Solomon	Trin. H.	M 1911
Johannes,	Mark	N. C.	M 1910
John,	Dav. Will.	Cla.	M 1906 A.B. 1909
—	Jordan Constantine	King's	M 1905 A.B. 1908. M.B. 1912
Johns,	Bradley Cooper	Mag.	M 1899 A.B. 1902 [1909, *Jes.
—	[1] Claude Hermann Walt.	Qu.	M 1875 A.B. 1880. A.M. 1885. Litt.D.
—	Nich. Allen	Em.	M 1908 A.B. 1911. LL.B. 1912
—	Owen Llewelyn	Em.	M 1911
—	Sam. Hen. Mannings	Cla.	M 1909 A.B. 1912
Johnson,	Alan Douglas	Trin.	M 1903 A.B. 1906. A.M. 1911
—	Alb. Victor	Chr.	M 1912
—	Alf. Spencer	Pet.	M 1898 A.B. 1901. A.M. 1905
—	Art. Carveth	Down.	M 1905 A.B. 1908. B.C. 1911
—	Art. Laurence	Trin.	M 1905 A.B. 1909. A.M. 1912
—	Augustine Hen.	N. C.	E 1884 Em. A.B. 1887. A.M. 1905
—	Cuthbert	King's	M 1911
—	Cuthbert Rowland Ingram	Mag.	M 1901 A.B. 1904
--	Donald Frederic Goold	Em.	M 1911
—	Edw. Will. Peach ...	Em.	M 1900 A.B. 1905. A.M. 1908
—	Eric Blake Herb. ...	Trin. H.	M 1910
—	Eric Townsend	Trin. H.	M 1899 A.B., LL.B. 1902
—	Ern. Alf.	C. C.	M 1895 A.B. 1898. A.M. 1904
—	Ern. Hugh	King's	M 1911

[1] Master of St Catharine's College, 1909.

Johnson,	Ern. Stapley Heming	Cla.	M 1899 A.B. 1902
—	Ern. Will.	Joh.	M 1901 A.B. 1904
—	Ern. Wright	Down.	M 1905 A.M. 1905 (Oxf. incorp.)
—	Frank Garnet	Trin.	M 1901 A.B. 1904
—	Frederic Cha.	Sid.	M 1909 A.B. 1912
—	Fre. Victor	Trin.	M 1905 A.B. 1908
—	Geoffrey Barham ...	Jes.	M 1912
—	Geo. Bern. Brimley	Trin. H.	M 1906 A.B. 1909
—	Geo. Geoffrey Floyd	King's	M 1909 A.B. 1912
—	Geo. Peach	Trin.	M 1903 A.B. 1906. A.M. 1910
—	Gordon Saffery	Pem.	M 1910
—	Harold Cecil John ...	Cai.	M 1902 A.B. 1906
—	Hen. Grindley	Trin.	M 1901 A.B. 1906
—	Ja. Gerald Thewlis ...	Trin. H.	M 1904 A.B. 1907
—	John Barham	H. Sel.	M 1909 A.B. 1912
—	Jos. Hen. Fyffe	Qu.	M 1906
—	Leslie	Joh.	M 1911
—	Maur. Rich. Wheatley	Pem.	M 1907 A.B. 1910
—	Noel Digby	Jes.	M 1905
—	Owen Bennett Goold	Sid.	M 1912
—	Pet. Randall	Trin.	M 1898 A.B. 1901
—	Phil. Bulmer	Trin.	M 1906 A.B. 1909
—	Rich. Garrett	Qu.	M 1881 A.B. 1889. A.M. 1910
—	Rob. Harrington	H. Sel.	M 1905 Cai. A.B. 1908
—	Ronald Lindsay	King's	L 1909 A.B. 1911
—	Rowland Theodore ...	H. Sel.	M 1896 A.B. 1899. A.M. 1907
—	Roy Frank	Cla.	E 1910
—	Stanley Currie	N. C.	M 1900 A.B. 1903 Down. A.M. 1907
—	Tho. Edgar	Em.	M 1896 A.B. 1899. A.M. 1903
—	Trevor Griffith	Jes.	E 1897 A.B. 1901
—	Vernon Yate	Joh.	M 1910
—	Walt. Harrison	N. C.	M 1899 A.B. 1902
—	Wilfrid Harry Cowper	Trin.	M 1898 A.B. 1901. A.M. 1909
—	Will. Hardy	Cath.	M 1901 A.B. 1904. A.M. 1909
—	Will. Lawrence	Pem.	M 1905 A.B. 1908. M.B., B.C. 1912
—	Will. Morton	Trin.	M 1900 A.B. 1903. A.M. 1909
—	Will. Rob.	Qu.	M 1896 A.B. 1901
Johnston,	Alec Bowman	Joh.	M 1903 A.B. 1906. A.M. 1910
—	Alf. And.	Pem.	M 1902 A.B., LL.B. 1905. A.M. 1909
—	Basil	Pem.	M 1898 A.B. 1901
—	Donald Vaughan	Joh.	M 1901 A.B. 1904. A.M. 1910
—	Douglas Hope	Trin. H.	M 1894 A.B. 1898. A.M.† 1903
—	Edm. Tho. Rob.	Qu.	M 1895 A.B. 1898. A.M. 1903
—	Ern.	Joh.	M 1898 A.B. 1901
—	Fra. Benj.	King's	M 1912
—	Frank	Joh.	M 1904 A.B., LL.B. 1907
—	Hen.	Trin.	M 1893 H. Lindsay, A.B. 1897. A.M. 1904
—	Hen. Bennett	Cai.	M 1911
—	Hen. Gordon Lawson	Trin. H.	M 1905
—	Hen. Hamilton		*Sc.D.* 1902
—	Ja. Farquharson	Chr.	M 1902
—	John Alex.	King's	M 1891 A.B. 1894. A.M. 1901
—	John Alex.	Pem.	M 1894 J. A. Hope, A.B. 1897. A.M. 1909
—	Rob. Matteson	Pem.	M 1885 A.B. 1889. A.M. 1901
—	Rob. Will.	Pem.	M 1902 A.B., LL.B. 1905. A.M. 1909
—	Syd.	Joh.	M 1900 A.B. 1903
Johnstone,	Cha. Art.	Mag.	M 1905 A.B. 1908
—	Cha. Campbell	Jes.	M 1908 A.B. 1911
—	Donald	King's	M 1903 A.B. 1906
—	Geo. Alex.	Pem.	M 1887 A.B. 1890. A.M. 1907
—	Geo. Gordon	King's	M 1905 A.B. 1908. M.B., B.C., A.M. 1912

Johnstone,	Geo. Hor.	Trin.	M 1900 A.B. 1904
—	John Jeffry	Trin.	M 1908
—	Will.	Jes.	L 1907 A.B. 1909
Joicey,	Clive Montague	Trin. H.	L 1911
—	Drever	Trin.	M 1905
—	Edw. Raylton	Trin. H.	M 1910
—	Syd. Ja. Drever	Trin.	M 1903 A.B. 1906. A.M. 1911
Jolley,	Leon. Benj. Will. ...	Trin.	M 1904 A.B. 1907
Jolliffe,	Tom And.	Trin. H.	M 1902
Jolly,	Cha. Neville	Pet.	M 1912
—	Evelyn Hugh Parker	Joh.	M 1904 A.B. 1907
—	Harold Lee Parker	Trin.	M 1906 A.B. 1909
—	John Catterall	King's	M 1906 A.B. 1909
—	Leon. John Parker ...	Joh.	M 1901 A.B. 1904
—	Newman Harold Harding	Qu.	M 1901 A.B. 1904. A.M. 1912
—	Reg. Bradley	Em.	M 1905 A.B. 1908. A.M. 1912
Jolowicz,	Herb. Felix	Trin.	M 1909 A.B. 1912
Jomaron,	Adolphe Cha.	C. C.	M 1912
Jonas,	Gerald John	Sid.	M 1912
Jones,	Abel John	Cla.	M 1906 A.B. 1908. A.M. 1912
—	Alban Jenkins	N. C.	M 1890 A.B. 1893. post Havard, A. J.
—	Alb. Victor	King's	M 1906 A.B., LL.B. 1909 [A.M. 1903
—	Alcwyn Elkington ...	N. C.	L 1907
—	Arnold	King's	M 1902 A.B. 1905. A.M. 1909
—	Art. Hawkins	Chr.	M 1904 A.B. 1907. A.M. 1911
—	Art. Probyn	King's	M 1910
—	Art. Stuart Duncan *Cai.		M 1898 A.B. 1901. A.M. 1905. post Dun-
—	Bennett Melvill	Em.	M 1906 A.B. 1909 [can-Jones, A. S.
—	Bern. Collier	C. C.	E 1911
—	Bern. Tho. White ...	Joh.	M 1895 A.B. 1899. A.M. 1905
—	Bertram	Trin.	M 1901 A.B. 1904. A.M. 1908
—	Cecil Hugh	Trin.	M 1906 A.B. 1909
—	Ceri McColm	Down.	M 1911
—	Cha. Edw. Mellersh	King's	M 1900 A.B. 1903. B.C. 1908. M.B. 1909
—	Cha. Lloyd	N. C.	M 1901 Pet. A.B. 1904 [A.M. 1903
—	Cha. Martin	Trin.	M 1895 Martin-Jones, C. M., A.B. 1898.
—	Cha. Stafford	Cai.	M 1896 A.B. 1899. A.M. 1905
—	Chris. John	Em.	M 1910 A.B. 1912
—	Clem. Harold	Qu.	M 1905 A.B. 1908
—	Clem. Wakefield	Trin.	M 1899 A.B. 1902. A.M. 1907
—	Cynfelyn Madoc	Qu.	M 1895 A.B. 1898. A.M. 1903
—	Cyril Challenor Lloyd	Em.	M 1893 A.B. 1896. A.M. 1901
—	Cyril Edgar	Jes.	M 1910
—	Dan.	King's	M 1900 A.B. 1903. A.M. 1907
—	Dav.	N. C.	M 1909
—	Dav.	Cath.	M 1910
—	Dav. Caradog	Pem.	M 1902 A.B. 1905. A.M. 1909
—	Dav. Ja.	Em.	M 1912
—	Dav. Lloyd	Sid.	M 1905 A.B. 1908
—	Dav. Owen	N. C.	M 1898 Joh. A.B. 1901
—	Dav. Treborth	Joh.	M 1901 A.B. 1904
—	Douglas Doyle	Pem.	M 1905 A.B., LL.B. 1908
—	Edw. Alf.	Cla.	M 1912
—	Edw. Evan Whittingham	Qu.	M 1896 A.B. 1901. A.M. 1912
—	Edw. Hub. Gunter ...	Cai.	M 1903 A.B., LL.B. 1906
—	Edwyn Llewellin ...	Pet.	M 1902 A.B. 1905
—	Eric Gregory	Em.	M 1907 A.B. 1910
—	Ern.	Chr.	M 1911
—	Evan	N. C.	M 1892 Chr. A.B. 1895. A.M. 1909
—	Evan Davies	N. C.	L 1901
—	Evan Davies	Trin.	M 1911

Jones,	Fra. Hor.	Em.	M 1897 A.B. 1900. A.M. 1904
—	Fra. Jos.	Cai.	M 1897 A.B. 1903. A.M. 1906
—	Fra. Stacey	Trin.	M 1906 A.B. 1909
—	Frank Butler	Joh.	M 1911
—	Fre. Rob.	Chr.	M 1902 A.B. 1905. A.M. 1910
—	Geo. Ellis	C. C.	M 1893 A.B. 1896. A.M. 1903
—	Geo. Milton	Trin.	M 1910
—	Guy Maclean	C. C.	M 1910
—	Harold Ivor	N. C.	M 1903 Sid. A.B. 1908
—	Harold Spencer	Jes.	M 1908 A.B. 1911
—	Harold Syd.	Chr.	M 1885 A.B. 1888. A.M. 1903
—	Harry Bithel	Sid.	M 1900 A.B. 1903
—	Harry Llewellyn	Cla.	M 1905 A.B. 1908
—	Hen. Geo. Tetley ...	Joh.	M 1888 A.B. 1891. post Taylor-Jones,
—	Hen. Kirkpatrick ...	Pem.	M 1902 [H. G. T. A.M. 1901
—	Herb. Chris. Basil ...	Em.	M 1905 A.B., LL.B. 1908
—	Humphrey Owen ...*Cla.		M 1897 A.B. 1899. A.M. 1903
—	Ivan FitzRoy Hippisley	Em.	M 1906
—	Ivone Kirkpatrick ...	Trin.	M 1909 A.B. 1912
—	Ja. Dennistoun	H. Sel.	M 1906 A.B. 1909
—	Ja. Harries	N. C.	M 1894 Cath. A.B. 1897. A.M. 1907
—	Ja. Sid.	Pem.	M 1907
—	Jenkin	N. C.	M 1898 Qu. A.B. 1901. A.M. 1905
—	John Art.	Em.	M 1902 [A.B. 1906
—	John Edw. Sheppard	Mag.	M 1902 post Sheppard-Jones, J. E. S.
—	John Llewellyn Sylovanus	Cath.	M 1894 A.B. 1897. A.M. 1901
—	John Rich.	N. C.	M 1904 Down. A.B. 1908
—	John Steph. Langton	Jes.	L 1908
—	John Will.	N. C.	M 1898 Joh. A.B. 1901. A.M. 1905
—	Leslie Art. Steph. ...	Qu.	M 1905 A.B. 1908. A.M. 1912
—	Leslie Will.	Em.	M 1910
—	Maur. Herb.	Trin.	M 1908 M. H. Lawrence, A.B. 1911
—	Owen Tho.	Trin.	M 1900 A.B. 1902. A.M. 1906
—	Pendrill Cha. Varrier	Joh.	M 1902 A.B. 1905. A.M. 1909
—	Reg. Tho. Pryce	Chr.	M 1897 A.B. 1901
—	Rhys Rich. Percy ...	C. C.	M 1905 A.B. 1908
—	Rich. Archib.	King's	M 1901 A.B. 1904
—	Rich. Evan	Cla.	M 1899 A.B. 1902. A.M. 1907
—	Rich. McNair	Joh.	M 1905 A.B. 1908
—	Rob. Fra.	Joh.	M 1904 A.B. 1907
—	Rob. Leetham	King's	M 1896 A.B. 1899. A.M. 1906
—	Rob. Thornely	N. C.	M 1892 A.B. 1896. A.M.† 1901
—	Sam.	Cai.	E 1905
—	Tho. Aneurin	N. C.	E 1905
—	Tho. Art.	Cai.	M 1899 A.B. 1902
—	Tho. Edgar	Cla.	M 1910
—	Tho. Hen.	Trin. H.	M 1900 A.B. 1902. A.M. 1908
—	Tho. Lewis	Qu.	M 1870 A.B. 1874. A.M. 1901
—	Tom	Sid.	M 1907 A.B. 1910
—	Tom Barry	Trin.	M 1907 A.B. 1910
—	Trevor Hywel	Qu.	M 1897 A.B. 1900. A.M. 1904
—	Vernon Stanley	King's	M 1894 A.B. 1897. *Mag. A.M. 1901. post
—	Walt. Benton	Trin.	M 1899 A.B. 1902 [Vernon-Jones, V. S.
—	Walt. Foulkes	King's	M 1901 A.B. 1904
—	Walt. Hewitt	Chr.	M 1900 A.B. 1903
—	Walt. Pateshall	Trin.	M 1876 A.B. 1880. A.M.† 1912
—	Will. Art.	Cai.	E 1899 A.B. 1901
—	Will. Emlyn Dav. ...	Em.	M 1912
—	Will. Havercroft	Joh.	M 1902
—	Will. Hen.	Down.	M 1912
—	Will. Hen. Sam.	H. Sel.	M 1894 A.B. 1897. A.M. 1902. *Cath.

Jones,	Will. Neilson	Em.	M 1903 A.B. 1906. A.M. 1910
—	Will. Piers Montagu	Trin.	M 1901
—	Will. Woodgate	C. C.	M 1894 A.B. 1901. A.M. 1904
Joppen,	Cha.	Pet.	M 1912
Jopson,	Norman Brooke	Joh.	M 1909 A.B. 1912 [1902
Jordan,	Alf. Cha.	Sid.	M 1891 A.B. 1894. M.B., B.C. 1899. M.D.
—	Anson Robertson ...	Cla.	M 1901 A.B. 1904. M.B., B.C. 1907. M.D.
—	Geo. Paul	C. C.	M 1908 [1911
—	Humfrey Robertson	Pem.	M 1902 A.B. 1905
—	John Herb.	Em.	M 1908 A.B. 1911
—	Will. Hen.	Pem.	M 1901 A.B. 1904. A.M. 1908
Joscelyne,	Cyril Hedley	H. Sel.	M 1910
Jose,	Chris. Hen.	Joh.	M 1898 A.B. 1901
—	Steph. Walt.	Chr.	M 1892 A.B. 1895. A.M. 1908
Joseph,	Cha. Gordon	N. C.	E 1912
—	Ern. Llewellyn	Em.	M 1907 A.B. 1910
—	Hen.	King's	M 1903 A.B. 1906
—	Hen. Mich.	Trin.	M 1897 A.B. 1900. M.B., B.C., A.M. 1904
—	Maitland Raymond	Trin. H.	M 1904 A.B. 1907. A.M. 1911
—	Tho. Morgan	Cai.	M 1874 A.B. 1879. post Joseph-Watkin, [T. M. A.M. 1907
—	Will. Franklin Geo.	Chr.	M 1901 A.B. 1904. A.M. 1911
Jourdain,	Phil. Edw. Bertrand	Trin.	M 1898 A.B. 1902. A.M.† 1906
Jowett,	Art. Craven	Trin.	M 1911
Joy,	Neville Holt	Trin.	M 1908 A.B. 1911
Joyce,	Geo. Edgar	N. C.	M 1906 Qu. A.B. 1909
—	Ja. Leon.	King's	M 1901 A.B. 1904. M.B., B.C., A.M. 1909
—	Ja. Will.	Pet.	M 1905
—	John Will. Hen.	N. C.	M 1905 Chr. A.B. 1908. A.M. 1912
Joyner,	Cerdric Batson	Em.	M 1901 A.B. 1904. A.M. 1908
Joynson,	Ralph	Mag.	M 1906
Joynt,	Ivor Will.	Em.	M 1905 A.B. 1908
Jubb,	Edwin Cha.	Pem.	M 1903 A.B. 1906
Juckes,	Ralph	Pem.	M 1912
Judd,	Fra. Art.	H. Sel.	M 1901 A.B. 1904. A.M. 1908
Judge,	Jos. Terence	N. C.	M 1903
Judson,	John Fre.	H. Sel.	M 1907 A.B. 1910
Jukes,	John Edwin Clapham	Pem.	M 1898 A.B. 1902
Juler,	Frank Anderson	Trin.	M 1898 A.B. 1901. M.B., B.C., A.M. 1909
Jump,	Hen.	Trin.	M 1901 A.B. 1904
—	Ralph Lyon	Trin.	M 1907 A.B. 1911
Jung,	Alf. Edgar	Pem.	E 1908
—			*See* Zoolcadur, M. M.
Jupe,	Fra. Isaiah Maggs ...	N. C.	E 1891 Down. A.B. 1894. A.M. 1904
—	Montagu Hor.	Cai.	M 1912
Just,	Theodore Hartmann	Trin.	M 1905 A.B. 1908. M.B., B.C. 1912

K

Kabbadias,	Panagiotis		*Litt.D.* 1904
Kachorn,	Mom Chow	Trin.	M 1906 A.B., LL.B. 1909
Kadir,	Mohamed	Trin.	M 1908
Kafka,	Emil Julius	Qu.	E 1901 A.B. 1904
Kahn,	Cha. Jos.	Cath.	M 1894 A.B. 1897. A.M. 1901
—	Fra. John	Cath.	M 1899 A.B. 1902. A.M. 1909
—	Percy St Goar	Qu.	M 1905 post Kelton, P. St G.
Kak,	Dharam Narain	Down.	M 1906 A.B. 1909
Kalé,	Vithal Dhondo	Joh.	M 1911
Kamodia,	Matilal Chhotalal ...	Pet.	E 1898 A.B. 1901
Kane,	Wilfrid Bern.	N. C.	M 1902 A.B. 1905
Kanjilal,	Manindra Nath	Down.	M 1908 A.B. 1910. LL.B. 1911
Kann,	Ern. Alex.	Em.	M 1908
Kantawala,	Mohan Hargovinddas	Qu.	M 1911
Kaplan,	Isaac	Trin. H.	E 1907 A.B. 1910
Kapp,	Edm.	Chr.	M 1910
Kapur,	Badri Nath	N. C.	M 1910
—	Kundan Lal	N. C.	M 1910
Kariappa,	Apparandra Bopana	Chr.	M 1898 A. Bopanna, A.B. 1901. A.M.†
Karn,	Ja. Chavasse	Down.	M 1908 A.B. 1911 [1906
Karney,	Art. Baillie Lumsdaine	Trin.	M 1893 A.B. 1896. A.M.† 1901
Karran,	Tho. Will.	Sid.	M 1908
Karsondas,	Mansen	Cath.	M 1908
Kashyap,	Shiv Ram	N. C.	M 1910 A.B. 1912
Kastner,	Léon Emile	Qu.	M 1895 Cla. A.B. 1898. A.M. 1902
Katchkaryov,	Vasilij Callinikovich	Pet.	M 1910
Kato,	Yasumichi	Pet.	M 1904
Kauffmann,	Allan Louis	Cai.	M 1912
Kaufmann,	Hilary Pilkington ...	Pet.	M 1911
Kay,	Arnold Innes	Mag.	M 1907 A.B. 1910
—	Rich. Percy	Sid.	M 1907 A.B. 1910
—	Syd. Entwisle	Em.	M 1906 A.B. 1909
Kaye,	Abr. Edw.	Em.	M 1899 A.B. 1902
—	Everard Astley	Pem.	M 1911
—	Geo. Will. Clarkson	Trin.	M 1905 A.B. 1908
Keable,	Rob.	Mag.	M 1905 A.B. 1908
Keane,	Fra. Stanley	Trin.	M 1898 A.B. 1901
Kearney,	Ja. John	Down.	M 1902
Kearns,	Hen. Ward Lionel ...	Chr.	M 1909 A.B. 1912
—	Jos. Rich. Carden ...	Chr.	M 1898 A.B. 1901
Keat,	Quah Sin	Joh.	M 1898 A.B. 1902
Keating,	Geo. Hen.	C. C.	M 1911
—	John FitzStephen ...	C. C.	L 1873 A.B. 1876. A.M. 1879. B.D. 1898.
—	John Hervey	Cai.	M 1912 [D.D. 1901
—	Leslie Charlton	N. C.	M 1895 A.B. 1898. A.M. 1905
Keats,	Fre. Thorold	Pem.	M 1911
—	John Rochfort	Jes.	M 1912
Keay,	Ern. Douglas	Cla.	M 1908 A.B., LL.B. 1911
Keddie,	Cha. Mackay	King's	M 1909
Keeble,	Cyril Fra. Allan	Joh.	M 1903 A.B. 1906
—	Fre. Will.	Cai.	M 1889 A.B. 1893. A.M. 1898. Sc.D. 1906
Keelan,	Vivian Leathem	N. C.	M 1890 A.B. 1893. A.M. 1902
Keeling,	Bertram Fra. Eardley	Trin.	M 1898 A.B. 1901. A.M. 1908
—	Frederic Hillersdon	Trin.	M 1904 A.B. 1907. A.M. 1911
—	Geo. Syd.	Cai.	M 1891 A.B. 1895. M.B., B.C. 1900. M.D.
—	Guy Will.	King's	M 1908 A.B. 1911 [1907

Keeling,	Owen Hugh	Trin.	M 1904 A.B. 1907
Keely,	Alf. Will. Johnson ...	Joh.	M 1874 A.B. 1878. A.M. 1903
Keen,	Austin		*A.M.* 1907
—	Geoffrey Percy	Cla.	M 1908 A.B. 1911
Keesey,	Geo. Ern. Howard ...	Down.	M 1905 A.B. 1908. A.M. 1912
Keeton,	Geo. Haydn	Em.	M 1897 A.B. 1900. A.M. 1910
Keeves,	Jos. Allan Coningsby	Cla.	M 1909 A.B. 1912
Keey,	Edgar Cha.	N. C.	M 1893 A.B. 1896. A.M. 1906
Kefford,	Will. Kingsley	Joh.	M 1894 A.B. 1897. A.M. 1901
Keighley,	Will. Geo. Macgregor	Cai.	M 1898 Trin. H. A.B. 1901
Keightley,	Frederic Richardson	C. C.	M 1887 A.B. 1890. A.M. 1905
Keigwin,	Art. Lawrence	Pet.	L 1908
—	Cha. Hen. Skarratt	Trin. H.	M 1909
—	Hen. Dav.	Pet.	M 1900 A.B. 1903. Mus.B. 1905. A.M.
—	Herb. Stanley	Pet.	M 1897 A.B. 1900. A.M.† 1904 [1907
—	Rich. Prescott	Pet.	M 1902 A.B. 1905. A.M. 1912
—	Walt. Skarratt	Cla.	M 1907
Keir,	Ja. Laurence Young	Cai.	M 1903 A.B., LL.B. 1906. A.M. 1910
Keith,	Alex. Ja.	Down.	M 1912
Kekulawala,	Alb.	Sid.	M 1907 A.B. 1910
Kelavkar,	Shamrao Krishnarao	N. C.	M 1912
Kelham,	Marmaduke Hen. Cogan	C. C.	M 1907 A.B. 1910
Kelk,	Art. Fre. Hastings ...	Mag.	M 1910
—	Art. Hastings	Mag.	M 1882 A.B. 1885. A.M. 1909
Kelkar,	Ganesh Hari	N. C.	M 1912
Kelland,	Walt. Harold Casimir	Em.	M 1912
Kelleher,	Hen.	Chr.	M 1910
Kellgren,	Jonas Henrik	Trin.	M 1895 A.B. 1898. A.M. 1910 [1905
Kellie,	Kenneth Harrison } Alloa {	Cai.	M 1893 A.B. 1898. B.C., A.M. 1904. M.B.
Kellock,	Tho. Herb.	Em.	M 1880 A.B. 1884. M.B., B.C., A.M. 1891.
Kellow,	Will.	Cai.	M 1911 [M.D. 1894. M.C. 1909
Kelly,	Denis Pat. Jos.	Down.	M 1906 A.B. 1909
—	Edw. Harding	N. C.	M 1879 King's A.B. 1883. A.M. 1903
—	Fra. Geo. Minchin ...	Em.	M 1900 A.B. 1904. A.M. 1910
—	Hen. Percy	Pet.	M 1899 A.B. 1902
—	Ignatius Geo.	Qu.	M 1904 A.B. 1907. LL.B. 1908
—	Norman Edw.	Pem.	M 1899 A.B. 1902
—	Phil. Ja.	Qu.	M 1900 A.B. 1903
Kelsey,	Art. Edw.	Trin.	M 1883 A.B. 1886. M.B., B.C. 1890. A.M.
—	Art. Ray	Mag.	M 1909 A.B. 1912 [1910
—	Herb. Slade	Em.	M 1895 A.B. 1898. A.M. 1902
Kelton,	Gerald St Goar	Qu.	M 1908 A.B. 1912
—			*See* Kahn, P. St G.
Kelway,	Kenneth Stevenson	Cai.	M 1912
Kelynack,	Will. Syd.	Joh.	M 1898 A.B. 1901. A.M. 1906
Kemp,	Ern. Wentworth Guy	Qu.	M 1904 A.B. 1908
—	Hen. Cha. Edw.	Cla.	M 1888 A.B. 1891. A.M. 1912
—	Kenneth McIntyre ...	C. C.	M 1903 A.B. 1906. A.M.† 1910
—	Percy Vickerman ...	Joh.	M 1910
—	Phil. Geo.	Mag.	M 1912
Kempe,	Edw. Challis	Trin.	M 1899 A.B. 1902. A.M. 1906
—	Wilfrid Noël	C. C.	M 1907 A.B. 1910
—	Will. Alf.	Trin.	M 1901 A.B. 1904. A.M. 1908
Kempsey,	Frank	King's	M 1910
Kempson,	Eric Will. Edw.	Trin.	M 1899 A.B. 1902
—	Fre. Claude	Cai.	M 1886 A.B. 1889. M.B. 1893. A.M. 1911
Kempthorne,	John Augustine	Trin.	M 1882 A.B. 1886. A.M. 1890. D.D. 1910
Kemp-Welch,	Hub. Annesley	Trin.	M 1906 LL.B. 1909
—	Maur.	King's	M 1899 A.B. 1902
Kendall,	Eric Angerstein	King's	M 1906

Kendall,	Fre. Ralph Norman	Trin.	M 1910
—	Guy Melville	Joh.	M 1911
—	Hen. Ewing	Pem.	L 1908 A.B. 1910
—	Hugh Berenger	Pem.	M 1904 A.B. 1907
—	John Michael Angerstein	C. C.	M 1911
—	Locke Fra. Will. ...	Cai.	M 1911
—	Will. Atkinson	Cath.	M 1911
Kennaway,	Rich. Harold	Pem.	M 1906
Kennedy,	Alex. Kenelm Clark	Trin.	M 1902 A.B. 1905
—	Alf. Ravenscroft	King's	M 1897 A.B. 1903
—	Anth.	Cai.	M 1905 A.B. 1908
—	Donald Ja.	Jes.	M 1900 A.B. 1904. A.M. 1908
—	Hen. Cha. Donald } Cleveland Mackenzie }	Cla.	M 1908 A.B. 1911
—	Hor.	Pem.	M 1899 A.B. 1902. A.M. 1908
—	Horas Tristram	Trin.	M 1908 A.B. 1912
—	John de Navarre ...	Trin.	M 1906
—	John Murray Stewart	Trin.	M 1912
—	John Oswald	Em.	M 1909 A.B. 1912
—	John Scott	King's	M 1906 A.B. 1910
—	Myles Storr Nigel ...	Trin.	M 1908 A.B. 1911
—	Rob. John	Trin.	M 1898 A.B. 1900. A.M.† 1905
—	Ronald Sinclaire	Chr.	M 1906 A.B. 1909
—	Sam. Dav.	Trin.	M 1900 A.B. 1903
—	Will. Ja. Rann	H. Sel.	M 1900 A.B. 1903
—	Will. Theodore	Trin.	M 1902 A.B. 1905
Kennett,	Bern. Lawrence } Augustine }	Qu.	M 1910
—	Edw. John Benedict } Manners }	Qu.	M 1909 A.B. 1912
—	[1] Rob. Hatch	*Qu.	M 1882 A.B. 1886. A.M. 1890. B.D. 1906.
—	Walt. Holman	Joh.	M 1899 A.B. 1902 [D.D. 1911
Kennett-Barrington, Guy Nevill } Eaglestone }		Mag.	M 1906 A.B. 1910
Kennington, Syd.		Cla.	M 1891 A.B. 1894. A.M. 1903
—	Will. Davy	Cai.	L 1909
Kenny,	[2] Courtney Stanhope	*Down.	M 1871 LL.B. 1875. LL.M. 1878. LL.D.
Kensington,	Hugh Le Geyt	Pem.	M 1905 A.B. 1908 [1887
Kent,	Art. Rob.	Qu.	M 1902
—	Cecil	Trin.	M 1902 A.B. 1905
—	John Ja. Percy	N. C.	M 1894 Joh. A.B. 1897. A.M. 1901
—	Leighton Udall	Pem.	M 1905 Leigh U., A.B. 1908
—	Norman Braund	Chr.	M 1905 A.B. 1908
—	Tho. Percival Platt	Em.	M 1910
—	Will. Andrews	Joh.	M 1889 A.B. 1892. A.M. 1910
Kenwood,	Syd. Harris	Em.	M 1910 A.B. 1912
Kenworthy,	Cha. Houldsworth ...	Cla.	M 1911
—	Cuthbert Reg. Leatham	Em.	M 1912
Kenworthy Browne, Bern. Evelyn		Jes.	M 1908 A.B. 1911
Kenyon,	Harold Godfrey	Pem.	M 1899 A.B., LL.B. 1902
—	Myles Noel	Trin.	M 1905 A.B. 1908. A.M. 1912
Keogh,	Cha. Geo. Peterson	Pem.	M 1901 A.B. 1904
Keown,	Rob. White	Pem.	M 1912
Ker,	Reg. Art.	H. Sel.	M 1900 A.B. 1903. A.M. 1907
Kerby,	Caleb	Cath.	M 1904
—	Clem. Carlyon	Trin.	M 1904 A.B. 1907
—	Edwin Tho.	Cla.	M 1896 A.B. 1899. A.M. 1903
—	Will. Moseley	N. C.	M 1904 Down. A.B. 1906. A.M. 1911

[1] Regius Professor of Hebrew, 1903.
[2] Downing Professor of the Laws of England, 1907.

Kernick,	John Wilson	.... Sid.	M 1910
Kerr,	Art. Edgar	.... Chr.	M 1897 A.B. 1900. M.B., B.C. 1907
—	Colin Causton	.... Em.	M 1909 A.B. 1912
—	Dugald Lawrenson	... Qu.	M 1905 A.B. 1908. A.M. 1912
—	John Bruce	.... Trin. H.	L 1900 A.B. 1904
—	Kenelm	.... Trin.	M 1900 A.B. 1903
—	Melville Ja. Douglas	Cla.	M 1903 A.B. 1906. A.M. 1910
—	Phil. Walt.	.... Pem.	M 1904 A.B. 1907
Kerridge,	Harold Ja.	.... N. C.	M 1906 A.B. 1909
—	Will. And. Leo	...... N. C.	M 1911
—	Will. Hen.	.... C. C.	M 1903 A.B. 1906. Mus.B. 1907
Kerry,	Will.	.... Joh.	M 1896 A.B. 1899. A.M. 1903
Kerschbaum,	Friedrich Paul	...... Cai.	M 1911
Kersey,	Rob. Hogarth	.... Trin.	M 1909 A.B. 1912
Kershaw,	Art.	.... Joh.	M 1900 A.B. 1903. A.M. 1907
—	Hor.	.... Qu.	M 1890 A.B. 1893. A.M. 1901
—	Jack Reginalde	...... Trin.	M 1912
—	Jos.	.... Trin.	M 1912
—	Kersley	.... Pet.	M 1895 A.B. 1898. A.M. 1902
—	Milton	.... Pet.	M 1905 A.B. 1908
Kesteven Balshaw,	Newton	.... H. Sel.	M 1911
Keswick,	Harry Gordon	.... Trin.	M 1905
Kettlewell,	Harold Herb.	.... H. Sel.	M 1907 A.B. 1910
—	Lancelot	.... H. Sel.	M 1912
Keuneman,	Art. Eric	.... Pem.	M 1905 A.B. 1908. LL.B. 1909
Kewley,	Ja.	.... King's	M 1898 A.B. 1901. A.M. 1905
—	Will. Chris.	.... H. Sel.	M 1910
Key,	Fre. John	.... Pet.	M 1893 A.B. 1895. A.M. 1901
—	Sam. Whittell	.... Joh.	M 1892 Cath. A.B. 1898. A.M. 1901
Keyes,	Harold Edw.	.... N. C.	M 1893 A.B. 1896. A.M. 1906
Keymer,	Bern. Will.	.... Pem.	M 1894 A.B. 1897. A.M. 1912
—	Edw. Hen.	.... Joh.	M 1894 A.B. 1897. A.M. 1901
Keynes,	Geoffrey Langdon	... Pem.	M 1906 A.B. 1909
—	John Maynard	......*King's	M 1902 A.B. 1905. A.M. 1909
—	[1] John Neville	.........*Pem.	M 1872 A.B. 1876. A.M. 1879. Sc.D. 1891
Keyworth,	Fre. Munday	.... Joh.	M 1901 A.B. 1904
—	Will. Dav.	.... H. Sel.	M 1899 A.B. 1902. B.C. 1906. M.B. 1909
Khalifa,	Mahmoud Ibrahim	... Chr.	M 1911
Khan,	Abdul Rahim	.... Trin. H.	M 1899 A.B. 1903
—	Aga Jafar Ali	.... Cath.	M 1910
—	Ahmad Ali	.... Pem.	M 1903 A.B. 1906
—	Fazl Muhammad	... Joh.	M 1902 A.B. 1905
—	Framjee Pestonjee	... Cai.	M 1902 A.B. 1905. A.M. 1909
—	Imtiaz Ali	.... Cath.	M 1910
—	Mohamed Islam-ullah	Joh.	M 1907
—	Mohammed Ibrahim	Cla.	M 1905
—	Mohommed Ismail	... Joh.	L 1901 A.B. 1905
—	Muhammad Noor-ul-Hussain	Down.	M 1909
—	Shafaat Ahmad	...... Sid.	M 1910
—	Shujaat Ali	.... N. C.	M 1910
Khannah,	Lok Nath	.... N. C.	M 1910
Kharé,	Laxman Ganesh	...... N. C.	M 1906 Chr. A.B. 1910
Khare,	Prabhakar Daji	...... Down.	M 1909 A.B. 1912
Kharegat,	Pheroze Merwan	...... Cla.	M 1908 A.B. 1911
Khayatt,	Ameen Bastawros	... Jes.	M 1912
Khayru'd Din,	Ahmed Abdu	...... N. C.	E 1912
Khong,	Kam Tak	.... Joh.	M 1904 A.B. 1907. M.B., B.C. 1910
Khoo,	Bong Kee	.... Cath.	E 1908
Khosla,	Lal Chand	.... Pet.	L 1907

---

[1] Registrary of the University, 1910.

Khwaja,	Abdul Majid	Chr.	M 1906 A.B. 1909
—	Mohomed Yahya	N. C.	L 1907
Kidd,	Cha. Bern.	Trin.	M 1898 A.B. 1905
—·	Eric Leslie	Pem.	M 1909 A.B. 1912
—	Ern. Starkey	Cai.	M 1897 A.B. 1900. A.M. 1905
—	Fra. Seymour	Trin.	M 1896 A.B. 1899. B.C. 1903. M.B. 1905
—	Franklin	Joh.	M 1909 A.B. 1912
—	Gerald Christobel	Chr.	L 1904 A.B. 1906
—	Hugh Lionel	Trin.	M 1898 A.B. 1901
—	Lewis Selkirk	Pem.	M 1912
—	Will. Alex. Trotter	Jes.	M 1907 A.B. 1910
Kidner,	Art. Rich.	Joh.	M 1898 A.B. 1901
Kidston,	Rob. Alex. Pat. Rich.	Pem.	M 1912
Kilburn,	Drysdale	Cath.	E 1911
—	Paul	Trin.	M 1908 A.B. 1911. Mus.B. 1912
Killick,	Cha.	Trin.	M 1893 A.B. 1896. M.B., B.C., A.M. 1901.
Kilner,	Strangman Davis	Em.	M 1908 A.B. 1911 [M.D. 1907
Kim,	Lim Ew	Pem.	M 1909
Kinder,	Tho. Harry	Cai.	M 1912
Kindersley,	Cha. Edw.	Mag.	M 1909 A.B. 1912
—	Rich. Frampton	Mag.	M 1906 A.B. 1909
King,	Art. Steele	Qu.	M 1899 A.B. 1902. A.M. 1908
—	Bullard Nowell	Trin.	M 1904 A.B. 1908. A.M. 1911
—	Cecil Bishop Redman	Sid.	M 1911
—	Colin	Trin.	M 1897 A.B. 1900. B.C., A.M. 1906. M.B.
—	Edm. Harold	Qu.	M 1910 [1908
—	Eric Frank Hulme	Cai.	M 1911
—	Fra. Lambourne	C. C.	M 1899 A.B. 1902. A.M. 1908
—	Geo. Cha.	Cai.	M 1905 A.B. 1910
—	Geo. Kemp	Joh.	M 1899 A.B. 1902
—	Geo. Lanchester	Cla.	M 1879 A.B. 1883. A.M. 1889. D.D. 1904
—	Harold Cha.	N. C.	M 1895 Qu. A.B. 1898. A.M. 1902
—	Harold Wardley	H. Sel.	M 1898 A.B. 1901. A.M. 1908
—	Hen. Medwin	Em.	M 1891 A.B. 1894. A.M. 1901
—	Herb. Ryder	Trin. H.	M 1907
—	Hor. Herb.	King's	M 1908 A.B. 1911
—	Hugh	Em.	M 1906 A.B. 1909
—	Hugh Basil	Sid.	M 1911
—	Humphrey Hastings	Pem.	M 1898 A.B. 1901. LL.B. 1902
—	Ja. Kirkman	Pet.	M 1901 A.B. 1904. A.M. 1912
—	John Fra. Oliver	Trin.	M 1912
—	Kenneth	Cla.	M 1911
—	Leon. Augustus Lucas	Joh.	M 1898 A.B. 1901. A.M. 1906
—	Leslie Reg.	Pem.	M 1901 A.B. 1904
—	Louis Vessot	Chr.	M 1905 A.B. 1908
—	Norman	Sid.	M 1900 A.B. 1903
—	Paul Edm.	H. Sel.	M 1909 A.B. 1912
—	Phil. Banks	Trin. H.	M 1911
--	Reg. Herb.	Pem.	M 1911
—	Reg. Ratcliffe	N. C.	M 1912
—·	Stanley	Cla.	M 1902 A.B. 1905. A.M. 1912
—	Walt. Hen. Robinson	Jes.	M 1905
—	Will. Bern. Robinson	Jes.	M 1908 A.B. 1911
—	Will. Oliver Redman	Sid.	M 1906 A.B. 1909
Kingdom,	Fra. Windsor Pelham	N. C.	M 1909
—	Tho.	King's	M 1901 A.B. 1904. A.M. 1909
—	Will. Alex.	Joh.	M 1911
Kingdon,	Campbell	Joh.	M 1897 A.B. 1900. A.M. 1910
—	Donald	Joh.	M 1902 A.B., LL.B. 1905
—	Frank Maynard	Sid.	M 1896 A.B. 1899. A.M. 1903
—	Geo. Herb.	Qu.	M 1912

Kingdon,	John	Qu.	M 1907 A.B. 1910
—	John Phillipps	Jes.	M 1900 A.B. 1903
—	Rob. Geo.	Jes.	M 1905 A.B. 1908
Kingham,	Bern. Vickers	Em.	M 1908 A.B. 1911
—	Will. Randolph	Trin.	M 1906 A.B. 1909
Kinghorn,	Ern. Carr	King's	M 1910
Kingsford,	Algernon Beechey ...	Qu.	M 1895 A.B. 1898. A.M. 1909
—	Cecil Edw. Beechey	Qu.	M 1907 A.B. 1910
—	Guy Thornhill	Cai.	M 1900 A.B. 1903. LL.B. 1904
Kingsland,	Art. Ambrose	Trin.	M 1910
—	Harold Lovett	Trin.	M 1908
Kingston,	Geo. Malcolm	Joh.	M 1877 A.B. 1881. A.M.† 1903
Kinloch,	Geo.	Trin.	M 1898 A.B. 1901
Kinnaird,	Douglas Art.	Trin.	M 1898 A.B. 1901. A.M. 1905
—	Kenneth Fitzgerald	Trin.	M 1899 A.B. 1902
Kipling,	Rudyard		*Litt.D.* 1908
Kipping,	Cyril Hen. Stanley	Trin. H.	M 1910
Kirby,	Hen. Rich.	Pem.	M 1908 A.B. 1912
—	Walt. Ern.	Em.	M 1902 A.B. 1905. A.M. 1910
Kirbyshire,	Art. Scarr	Down.	M 1910
Kirk,	Alf. Eric Kenny	Joh.	M 1896 A.B. 1900. A.M. 1908
—	Art.	Cai.	M 1906 A.B. 1910
—	Geo. Lascelles	Trin.	M 1906
—	John Haydn	Joh.	M 1909 A.B. 1912
—	Will. Temperley	N. C.	M 1899 Pet. A.B. 1902
Kirkby,	Art. Tuke	King's	M 1906
—	Cha. Will.	Trin.	M 1871 A.B. 1888. A.M.† 1911
—	Noel Walt.	Pem.	M 1908 A.B. 1911
Kirke,	Geo. Grieve	Cla.	M 1907
—	Percy St Geo.	Trin.	M 1900 A.B. 1903. A.M. 1909
Kirke Smith,	Art.	Trin.	M 1896 A.B. 1899. A.M. 1903
Kirkland,	Alf. Ern.	Em.	M 1908 A.B. 1911
—	Walt. Newman	Qu.	M 1912
Kirkman,	Reg. Will.	Down.	M 1909
Kirkness,	Lewis Hawker	Joh.	M 1901 A.B. 1904. A.M. 1908
Kirkpatrick,	[1] Alex. Fra.	*Trin.	M 1867 A.B. 1871. A.M. 1874. B.D. 1889.
—	Alex. Pemberton	Trin.	M 1904 A.B. 1907. A.M. 1911 [D.D. 1892
—	Herb. Fra.	Jes.	M 1907 A.B. 1910
—	John Bartlett	Jes.	M 1912
—	Leslie Gordon	Trin.	M 1904
—	Roger Maning	C. C.	M 1909 A.B. 1912
Kirkus,	Cuthbert Hayward ...	Cath.	M 1899 A.B. 1902
Kirkwood,	Ja. Millar	Pem.	M 1908 A.B. 1911
Kirloskar,	Vinayak Ganesh	Joh.	M 1906 A.B. 1909
Kirtland,	Jos.	H. Sel.	M 1907 A.B. 1910
Kisch,	Ern. Royalton	Cla.	M 1905 A.B. 1908. LL.B. 1909
Kissack,	Bern. Keble	Em.	M 1900 A.B. 1903. A.M. 1908
Kissan,	Bern. Will.	Jes.	M 1898 A.B. 1901
Kitchin,	Ern. Hugh	Down.	M 1895 A.B. 1898. M.B., B.C., A.M. 1903
—	Shepherd **Braithwaite**	Trin. H.	M 1898 LL.B. 1901
—	Vernon **Parry**	Pem.	M 1895 A.B. 1898. A.M. 1908
Kitching,	Alf. Everley	Jes.	M 1909
—	Art. Leon.	Em.	M 1894 A.B. 1897. A.M. 1901
—	Cecil Ross	Cai.	M 1902 A.B. 1905. A.M. 1909
—	Geoffrey Cha.	Jes.	M 1911
—	Harold **Edw.**	Trin. H.	M 1904
—	Tho.	Pet.	M 1909 A.B. 1912
Kitchlew,	Saifud **Din**	Pet.	M 1907 A.B. 1911
Kitson,	Art. John	Pem.	M 1895 A.B. 1898. A.M. 1902

[1] Lady Margaret's Professor of Divinity, 1903.

Kitson,	Bern. Meredyth	Pet.	M 1905 A.B. 1908
—	Cha. Herb.	H. Sel.	M 1893 A.B. 1896. A.M. 1904
—	Edw. Christian	Trin.	M 1892 A.B. 1895. A.M. 1902
—	Rob. Hawthorn	Trin.	M 1892 A.B. 1895. A.M. 1901
—	Roland Dudley	Trin.	M 1901 A.B. 1904
Kittermaster,	Digby Bliss	Cla.	M 1896 A.B. 1899. A.M. 1903
Kitto,	John Lemon	Joh.	M 1901 A.B. 1904
Kjellberg,	Edvard	N. C.	M 1904
Kleeman,	Rich. Dan.	Em.	M 1905 A.B. 1907
Klinger,	(*Baron*) Erich	Trin. H.	M 1911
Knapman,	Herb.	*Em.	M 1898 A.B. 1901. A.M. 1905
Knapp,	Bertie Edwin	Cath.	M 1904
Knappett,	Percival Geo.	Mag.	M 1907 A.B. 1910
Knaster,	Roland Marcus Igna- tius Julius }	Sid.	M 1908 A.B. 1911
Kneen,	Clem. Wallace	Cath.	M 1912
—	Edwyn Corlett	Pem.	M 1905 A.B. 1908
Kneese,	Rupert Heinrich Wilhelm	Trin.	M 1907 A.B. 1910
Knight,	Alf. Gordon	Qu.	M 1906 A.B. 1909
—	Art. Cecil	Pem.	M 1894 A.B. 1897. A.M. 1901
—	Art. Mesac	Pem.	M 1883 A.B. 1886. A.M. 1891. *Cai. D.D.
—	Cha.	Joh.	M 1902 A.B. 1905 [1903
—	Clifford Edw.	Jes.	M 1908
—	Edw. Foley	Cai.	M 1907 A.B. 1910
—	Ern. Alex.	C. C.	M 1905 A.B. 1908. A.M. 1912
—	Fra. Howard	Qu.	M 1900 A.B. 1903. A.M. 1907
—	Gilb. Tho.	C. C.	M 1908 A.B. 1911
—	Harry	C. C.	M 1905
—	Hen. Foley	Cai.	M 1905 A.B. 1908
—	Hen. Jos. Corbett ...	Cath.	M 1878 A.B. 1882. A.M. 1885. *C. C. B.D.
—	Hugh Fre. Parker ...	Joh.	M 1903 [1906. D.D. 1907
—	John Edw. Horton ...	Cath.	M 1907
—	Phil. Clifford	Trin.	M 1911
—	Rich.	Chr.	M 1911
—	Tho. Harold	Cla.	M 1893 A.B. 1896. A.M. 1902
—	Walt. Forster	Em.	M 1908 A.B. 1911
—	Will. Lowry Craig ...	Pem.	M 1909
Knight Bruce,	Rob. Evelyn Cleave	Trin.	M 1909
Knighton,	Gerald Godfrey	Pem.	M 1906 A.B. 1909
Knights,	Harold Ja. West ...	Em.	M 1899 A.B. 1902. A.M. 1908
—	Kenneth Merriman West	Em.	M 1904 A.B. 1907
Knipe,	Randolph Cha.	Sid.	M 1909 A.B. 1912
Knobel,	Will. Bern.	Trin.	M 1893 A.B. 1896. A.M. 1900. M.D. 1905
Knollys,	Edw. Erskine	H. Sel.	M 1894 A.B. 1897. A.M. 1903
Knowles,	Claude Kingsley	Cla.	M 1911
—	Felix	Pem.	M 1910
—	Guy John Fenton ...	Trin.	M 1898 A.B. 1901
—	Maur. Hinton	H. Sel.	M 1907 A.B. 1910
—	Rob.	Down.	M 1902 A.B. 1905
—	Rob. King	Trin.	M 1908 A.B. 1911
—	Stanley	Pem.	M 1900 A.B. 1903. A.M. 1907
Knox,	Alf. Dillwyn	*King's	M 1903 A.B. 1906. A.M. 1910
—	Bryce	Cla.	M 1910
—	Geoffrey Geo.	Trin.	E 1906
—	Hen. Tho.	Trin. H.	M 1906
---	Ja.	Trin.	M 1902
—	Rob. Uchtred Eyre	Joh.	M 1908 A.B. 1911
—	Will.	Cai.	M 1906 A.B. 1909
---	Will. Barr	Trin.	M 1905
Knubley,	Cha.	Mag.	M 1907 A.B. 1910
—	Edw. Miles	Mag.	M 1897 A.B. 1900. A.M.† 1905

Knubley,	Rob. Leavitt	Mag.	M 1906 A.B. 1909
Koenig,	Karl Rob. Ludwig ...	Chr.	M 1911
Koga,	Manjiro	Pet.	M 1908
Koh,	Kheng Seng	Joh.	M 1902 A.B. 1905
Kohan,	Cha. Mendell	Trin.	M 1903 C. Mendel, A.B. 1906
—	Rob. Mendell	Cai.	M 1901 A.B. 1904
Kohn,	Wilfrid Art.	Cai.	M 1912
Koko,	....	Chr.	M 1908 A.B. 1911
Kölber de Páka, Josef		Sid.	M 1910
Kolhapur,	*Maharaja of*		*See* Chhatrapati, Shahu
Kolwey,	Emil Alb.	N. C.	M 1906
Komarovsky, Boris Markoff		Trin.	M 1908 A.B., LL.B. 1911
Kon,	Geo. Armand Rob. ...	Cai.	M 1909 A.B. 1912
Koop,	Gerhard Gottfried ...	Cai.	M 1903 Gerard Godfrey, A.B. 1906
Kossel,	Albrecht Carl Ludwig} Martin Leonhard }		*Sc.D.* 1904
Koudela,	Jan	N. C.	L 1904
Kraemer,	Adolf Ernst	Joh.	M 1901
—	Edm.	Chr.	M 1912
Krajewski-Landau, Casimir		Trin.	E 1908
Kraus,	Martin	Joh.	M 1905 A.B. 1908
Krause,	Ern. Howard Frc. Brown	Jes.	M 1911
Krige,	Leo Jacobus	Cai.	M 1907 A.B. 1911
Krishnamma, John Ratnam		Em.	M 1903 A.B. 1907
—	Noble Ratnam	Qu.	M 1906 A.B. 1909
Krishnamurti, Tanjore Sadasiva ...		Chr.	M 1909
Krishnan,	Cheruvari	Chr.	M 1887 A.B. 1890. A.M. 1902
Kroenig,	Hugh Sept. Nathanael	C. C.	M 1895 A.B. 1900. Kroenig-Ryan, H. S.
Kroenig-Ryan, Alex. Cha. Tho. ...		Cath.	M 1912 [A.M. 1904
Krönig,	Hermann	Em.	M 1902
Kruckenberg, Ja.		Qu.	M 1904 A.B. 1909
Krumbacher, Karl			*Litt.D.* 1904
Kuhn,	Rob.	N. C.	E 1901
Kujo,	Yoshimune	Cla.	M 1910
Kumamoto, Saichi		N. C.	M 1909
Kung,	Anching	Chr.	M 1910
Kuntay,	Yashvant Krishna ...	N. C.	L 1910 A.B. 1911
Kuroda,	(*Baron*) Nagatoshi ...	King's	M 1907
Kurwa,	Shujavoddeem Esmailjee	Down.	M 1904
Kutnow,	Hen. Sigismund	Jes.	M 1907 A.B. 1912
Kutsuzawa, Genichiro		Cai.	M 1909 A.B. 1912
Kuypers,	Art. Benedict	King's	M 1896 A.B. 1898. A.M. 1903
Kyle,	John Latimer	Cath.	M 1884 A.B. 1888. A.M. 1903
Kynaston,	Phil. Edmond	King's	M 1890 A.B. 1893. A.M. 1910

L

Labey,	Tho. Hen.	H. Sel.	M 1912	
Laby,	Tho. Howell	N. C.	M 1905 Em. A.B. 1907	
Lacey,	Alf. Travers	King's	M 1911	
—	Fre. Art.	Trin.	M 1906 A.B. 1909	
Lacson,	Domingo	Joh.	M 1911	
Lacy,	Fre. Hugh	Pem.	M 1893 A.B. 1896. A.M. 1901	
Ladd,	Leslie Scrivener	Chr.	M 1911	
Laddu,	Tukaram Krishna ...	N. C.	M 1909 A.B. 1911	
Ladenburg,	Rudolf Walt.	Trin.	M 1906	
La Fontaine,	Ja. Syd.	Cai.	M 1912	
—	Syd. Hub.	Cai.	M 1905 A.B. 1908	
Lagden,	Reg. Bousfield	Pem.	M 1911	
Lahusen,	Diedrich Duncan ...	Chr.	M 1908	
—	Johann Heinrich Gustav	Jes.	E 1910	
—	Johannes Christian ...	Chr.	E 1910	
Laidlaw,	Cha. Glass Playfair	Joh.	M 1907 A.B. 1910	
—	Douglas Hunter	N. C.	M 1898 Em. A.B. 1901	
—	Frank Fortescue	Trin.	M 1895 A.B. 1898. A.M. 1905	
—	Geo. Muir	Joh.	M 1897 A.B. 1900. A.M.† 1904	
—	Hugh Alex. Lyon ...	Joh.	M 1904 A.B. 1907	
—	Pat. Playfair	Joh.	M 1900 A.B. 1903. B.C. 1907. A.M. 1909	
—	Walt. Sibbald	Joh.	M 1909 A.B. 1912	
Laidlay,	John Chris.	Trin. H.	M 1908	
Laidman,	Will. Ern.	Chr.	M 1895 A.B. 1898. A.M. 1902	
Laing,	Alex. Torrance	C. C.	M 1907 A.B. 1910	
—	Colin Moncrieff	Trin.	M 1904 A.B. 1907	
Laird,	And. John	Joh.	M 1910	
—	Geo. Ern.	Pem.	M 1908 A.B. 1911	
—	John	Trin.	M 1908 A.B. 1911	
—	Pat. Ramsay	Pem.	M 1906 A.B. 1909	
Laird Clowes,	Geoffrey Swinford	Sid.	M 1902 A.B. 1905	
Laistner,	Max Ludwig Wolfram	Jes.	M 1909 A.B. 1912	
Lake,	Lionel Hen.	H. Sel.	M 1896 A.B. 1899. A.M. 1908	
—	Walt. Ivan	Cai.	M 1907 A.B. 1910	
Lal,	Dewan Manohar	N. C.	M 1909 A.B. 1912	
—	Manohar	Chr.	M 1907 A.B. 1910	
Láll,	Panna	Joh.	M 1904 A.B. 1906. LL.B. 1907	
Lamb,	Cecil Mortimer	Cai.	M 1909 A.B. 1912	
—	Chris. Hen.	Trin.	M 1906 A.B. 1909	
—	Geo. Johnstone	Trin.	M 1909 A.B. 1912	
—	Gerald Gore Elmsley	Pem.	M 1906 A.B., LL.B. 1909 (G. G. Elmslie)	
—	Hor.	*Trin.	M 1868 A.B. 1872. A.M. 1875. Sc.D. 1908	
—	Percy Cecil Chalmers	Down.	M 1907 A.B. 1911	
—	Reg. Phipps	Trin.	M 1900 A.B. 1903	
—	Rich. Edgar	Trin.	M 1898 A.B. 1901. A.M. 1906	
—	Walt. Rangeley Maitland	*Trin.	M 1901 A.B. 1905. A.M. 1908	
Lambart,	Julian Harold Legge	King's	M 1912	
Lambert,	Cyril Claude	Sid.	M 1906 A.B. 1909	
—	Frank	Chr.	M 1902 A.B. 1905. A.M. 1909	
—	Gordon Ormsby	Joh.	M 1895 A.B. 1898. M.B., B.C. 1901. M.D.	
—	Harold Ern.	Qu.	M 1912	[1906
—	Hen.	Trin.	M 1899 A.B. 1902. A.M. 1908	
—	Hen. Holmes	Pem.	M 1901 A.B. 1905. LL.B. 1907	
—	John	Down.	M 1898 A.B. 1901. B.C. 1904. M.B. 1905.	
—	Jos. Edgar Hugo ...	Pem.	M 1909 A.B. 1912 [M.D. 1908. A.M. 1909	
—	Reg. Everitt	Trin.	M 1901 A.B. 1904. A.M. 1908	

Lambert,	St John Murray	Trin.	M 1903
—	Syd. Herb. Art.	Joh.	M 1884 A.B. 1887. M.B., B.C. 1893. M.D.
—	Will.	C. C.	M 1909 A.B. 1912 [1904
Lambrinudi,	Constantine	Chr.	M 1907 A.B. 1910
Lambton,	John Fre.	Mag.	M 1905
Laming,	Walt. Cecil	Joh.	M 1888 A.B. 1891. A.M. 1905
Lamm,	Martin	N. C.	L 1903
La Mothe,	Hugo Dominique ...	C. C.	M 1909 A.B. 1912
Lamplough,	Fra. Edw. Everard ...	*Trin.	M 1900 A.B. 1903. A.M. 1907
Lamplugh,	Alf. Amoz Fletcher	Joh.	M 1901 A.B. 1904
—	Lancelot John	Joh.	M 1904 A.B. 1907
Lamprey,	Art. Syd.	C. C.	M 1887 A.B. 1890. A.M. 1910
Lancaster,	Egbert Townsend ...	Qu.	M 1906 A.B. 1909
—	Hen.	Pem.	M 1898 A.B. 1901. A.M. 1905
—	Steph.	Trin.	M 1911
Lanchester,	Cha. Compton	H. Sel.	M 1895 A.B. 1898. A.M. 1903
—	Hen. Craven Ord ...	*Pem.	M 1896 A.B. 1899. A.M. 1903
Landale,	Dav. Gordon	Trin. H.	M 1903
—	Douglas Blackwood	Trin.	M 1909 A.B. 1912
Landau,	Hen.	Cai.	M 1910
Lander,	Gerard Heath	Trin.	M 1881 A.B. 1884 (2). A.M. 1888. D.D.
—	Harold Drew	Cai.	M 1902 A.B. 1906 [1907
—	John Vernon	Cla.	M 1902 A.B., LL.B. 1905. A.M. 1909
—	Percy Edw.	Down.	M 1907 A.B. 1910
Landon,	Jos. Whittington ...	Sid.	M 1898 A.B. 1901. A.M. 1905
Landsberg,	Alb. Clinton	Trin. H.	M 1908
Lane,	Frank Dav.	Qu.	M 1904
—	Gilb. Roberts	Chr.	M 1909 A.B. 1912
—	Hen. Clarence Horsburgh	Joh.	M 1906 A.B. 1909
—	Hen. John	Cai.	M 1905
—	John Art. Cha.	Em.	M 1895 A.B. 1898. A.M. 1903
—	Phil.	Chr.	M 1912
—	Sam. Fra. Beeke	Pem.	M 1902 A.B. 1905
—	Tho. Willington	Cla.	M 1912
—	Will. Woodhouse ...	Em.	M 1902 A.B. 1905
Lang,	Art.	Em.	M 1902 A.B. 1905. A.M. 1910
—	Art. Hor.	Trin.	M 1909 A.B. 1912
—	Basil Thorn	Trin.	M 1899 A.B. 1902. B.C., A.M. 1908
—	Frank Hope	Em.	M 1896 A.B. 1902. A.M. 1910
—	Harold Montgomery	Pem.	M 1896 A.B. 1899. A.M. 1903
—	Hor.	Cai.	M 1910
—	Leslie Hamilton	Trin.	M 1909 A.B. 1912
—	Rob. Cha. Vaughan	Pem.	M 1890 A.B. 1893. A.M. 1903
—	Rob. Stanley	Trin.	M 1903
—	Will. Dickson	Pem.	M 1898 A.B. 1901. A.M. 1905
Langdale,	Art. Hugh	Cai.	M 1909 A.B. 1912
—	Clifford Marmaduke	Cla.	M 1906 A.B. 1909
—	Harold Carthew	Cai.	M 1912
—	Kenneth Marmaduke	Cla.	M 1903 A.B. 1906
Langdon,	Alf. Geo.	King's	M 1887 A.B. 1890. A.M. 1911
—	Cecil	H. Sel.	M 1901 A.B. 1904. A.M. 1909
—	Cha. Godfrey	H. Sel.	M 1895 A.B. 1898. A.M. 1909
Langdon-Davies,	Bern. Noël	Pem.	M 1896 A.B. 1899. A.M. 1903
Lange,	Moses Reuben	Trin.	M 1901
Langerman,	Austen Hill-Rennie	Chr.	M 1903
—	Ern. Struben	Chr.	M 1907
Langham,	Basil Jomini	H. Sel.	M 1907 A.B. 1910
—	Cecil Rich.	Trin. H.	M 1910
—	Cyril Norman	Em.	M 1908 A.B. 1911
Langhorne,	Herb. Edw.	Qu.	M 1893 A.B. 1896. A.M. 1905
Langlands,	Norman Mann Smart	Trin.	M 1912

Langley,	Art. Syd.	N. C.	M 1902 Down. A.B. 1905
—	Edw. Ralph	Cai.	M 1908
—	Fre. Oswald	Cai.	M 1902 A.B., LL.B. 1905
—	¹ John Newport	Joh.	M 1871 A.B.1875. *Trin. A.M.1878. Sc. D.
Langley-Smith,	Nelson Humphries	Qu.	M 1911 [1896
Langmead,	Lydstone Geo. Norman	Em.	M 1911
Langridge,	Walt. Osborn	Pet.	M 1907 A.B. 1910
Langton,	Algernon Cha. } Mainwaring	Pem.	M 1897 A.B. 1901
—	Geo. Bernard	Sid.	M 1911
—	Harold McKee	Joh.	M 1912
—	Hugh Banastre	Pem.	M 1895 A.B. 1898. A.M. 1902
Lankester,	Ronald Farrer	Em.	M 1907 A.B. 1910
Lansberry,	Harold Geo.	Down.	M 1910
Lapage,	Fra. Claud	King's	M 1907 A.B. 1911
—	Reg. Hen.	H. Sel.	M 1909
Lapsley,	Gaillard Tho. ....*Trin.		A.M. 1904
Laredo,	Mordecai Abr.	Down.	M 1904
Large,	Rupert Jerome	N. C.	M 1906 Chr. A.B. 1909
Larke,	Ern. Edw.	N. C.	L 1904
Larking,	Ronald Guy	King's	M 1910
Larmor,	² Jos. ....*Joh.		M 1876 A.B. 1880. A.M. 1883
Larmour,	Alwin Corden	Trin.	M 1905 A.B. 1909
Larpent,	John Planta Geo. } De Hochepied	Pem.	M 1900 A.B. 1903
Larymore,	Hen. Douglas	Chr.	E 1903
Lasbrey,	Bertram	Cath.	M 1900 A.B. 1903. A.M. 1908
—	Ern. Will.	Em.	M 1903 A.B. 1906
—	Percy Urwick	Joh.	L 1900 A.B. 1902. A.M. 1907
Lascelles,	Percy Lindsay	H. Sel.	M 1900 A.B. 1905. A.M. 1908
—	Rich.	Trin.	M 1901
Last,	Fre. Will.	C. C.	M 1910
Latham,	Edw.	Chr.	M 1882 A.B. 1885. A.M. 1905
—	Jos. Art. Victor	Cath.	M 1911
Lathbury,	Rob. Ja.	Em.	M 1912
Latif,	Abdullatif Camrudin } Amirudin Abdul	Joh.	M 1898 A.B. 1901. LL.B. 1902. LL.M.† [1905. post Latifi, Alma. A.M.
—	Sarhan Camrudin ...	Joh.	M 1912 [1907
Latifur-Rahman,	Abu Sharf } Muhammad	Pem.	M 1909 A.B. 1912
La Touche,	Geo. Godfrey Digges	Trin.	M 1907 A.B. 1910
—	Hugh Norman Digues	Joh.	L 1910
—	Tho. Hen. Digues ...	Joh.	M 1876 A.B.1880, T. H. Digges, A.M. 1912
La Trobe,	Will. Sanderson	Joh.	M 1894 A.B. 1896. A.M. 1901
Lattey,	Hen. Pat. Tabor	Pem.	M 1902 A.B. 1905
—	Will. Tabor	C. C.	M 1904 A.B. 1907
Lattimer,	Will.	Cla.	M 1888 A.B. 1891. A.M. 1906
Lauder,	John Currie	Jes.	M 1910
Lauderdale,	Edw. Maitland	Cai.	M 1902 A.B. 1905
Laurance,	John Bidwell	Pem.	M 1908 A.B. 1911
Laurence,	Claud	Trin.	M 1900 A.B. 1903. A.M. 1907
—	Reg. Vere ....*Trin.		M 1895 A.B. 1898. A.M. 1902
Laurie,	Fre. Grieve	Cai.	M 1912
—	Fre. Will.	N. C.	M 1904
Laver,	Laurence Saville	Joh.	M 1899 A.B. 1902. A.M. 1909
Laville,	Louis Victor	C. C.	M 1907 A.B. 1910
Lavington,	Fre.	Em.	M 1908 A.B. 1911
Lavy,	Ern. Edw.	Pem.	M 1899 A.B. 1902. A.M.† 1906

¹ Professor of Physiology, 1903.
² Lucasian Professor of Mathematics, 1903; Representative in Parliament, 1911.

Law,	Alan Rokeby	....	Trin.	M 1899 A.B. 1902. A.M. 1906
—	Art. Tho. Will.	......	H. Sel.	M 1894 A.B. 1897. A.M. 1901
—	Cha.	....	Pem.	M 1909 A.B. 1912
—	Cha. Ewan	....	Pem.	M 1907
—	Harry	....	Pem.	M 1911
—	Hen. Duncan Graves		Trin.	M 1905
—	Nigel Walt.	....	Trin.	M 1909 A.B. 1912
—	Percival John Knight		Chr.	M 1902
—	Ralph Arnold	....	Trin.	M 1911
—	Shau Pang	....	Trin. H.	M 1910
—	Yan Pak	....	Jes.	M 1909 A.B. 1912
Lawn,	John Gunson	....	Sid.	M 1912
Lawrance,	Baldeo Will.	....	Down.	E 1901 A.B. 1904
—	Walt. John	....	Trin.	M 1858 A.B. 1862. A.M. 1865. D.D. 1906
Lawrence,	Alex. Carson Clarke		Trin.	M 1901
—	Art. Lyndon	....	Trin.	M 1902 A.B. 1905. A.M. 1910
—	Basil Ranger	....	Pem.	M 1911
—	Brian Lyndon	....	Trin.	M 1909 A.B. 1912
—	Cha. Hen.	....	Trin.	M 1899 A.B. 1903
—	Fra. Hen.	....	Qu.	M 1901 A.B. 1904
—	Hen. Rundle	....	Pem.	M 1897 A.B. 1909
—	Ja. Taylor	....	Trin.	M 1908
—	John Sothoron Gower		Cai.	M 1911
—	Oliver John	....	Trin.	M 1912
—	Tho.	....	Pem.	M 1903
—	Will.	....		*LL.D.* 1908
—	Will. Hen. Art.	......	Trin.	M 1912
Laws,	Sam. Cha.	....	Joh.	M 1901 A.B. 1904. A.M. 1908
Lawson,	Chris. Geo.	....	Pem.	M 1904 A.B. 1907
—	Digby	....	Trin. H.	M 1898 A.B. 1902
—	Godfrey	....	Trin.	M 1899 A.B. 1902
—	Harry Sackville	......	Pet.	M 1895 A.B. 1898. A.M. 1910
—	Reg. Hugh	....	Sid.	M 1912
—	Rob. Chris.	....	Trin.	M 1893 A.B. 1896. A.M. 1901
—	Tho. Dav.	....	Down.	M 1908 A.B. 1911
—	Will. Rogers	....	H. Sel.	M 1902 A.B. 1905. A.M. 1909
Lawson Johnston,	Art. McWilliam		Trin.	M 1904 A.B. 1907
Lawton,	Art.	....	N. C.	M 1896 Pet. A.B. 1899. A.M. 1912
Lawton Roberts,	John Chambers		Cla.	M 1898 A.B. 1901. M.B., B.C., A.M. 1906.
Laxon,	Herb.	....	Pem.	M 1901 A.B. 1904 [M.D. 1909
Layard,	John Willoughby	...	King's	M 1910
Laycock,	Alb. Penard	....	Joh.	M 1895 A.B. 1898. M.B., B.C. 1902. A.M.
Laye,	Pet. Art. Webb	......	Trin. H.	L 1908 [1903
Layton,	Douglas Harrison	...	Down.	M 1907
—	Harold Noel	....	H. Sel.	M 1906 A.B. 1909
—	Walt. Tho.	....	Trin.	M 1904 A.B. 1907. *Cai. A.M. 1911
Lazarus,	Eric Lewis	....	Chr.	M 1910
—	Geo. Maitland	....	King's	M 1900 A.B. 1903. LL.B. 1904. A.M. 1907
Lea,	Donald Hen.	....	Jes.	M 1900 A.B. 1903
—	Harold Art. Holt	...	Em.	M 1896 A.B. 1899. A.M. 1903
—	John	....	Cai.	M 1889 A.B. 1892. A.M. 1907
—	Max	....	Cai.	M 1903
—	Ronald Syd. Harris		Trin.	M 1910
Leach,	Gerald Kemball	......	Mag.	M 1902
—	Norman Kershaw	...	Chr.	M 1900 A.B. 1903. A.M. 1907
—	Rob.	....	Mag.	M 1900 A.B. 1904
—	Rob. Wild	....	Chr.	M 1903 A.B. 1906. LL.B. 1907
—	Roger Chadwick	......	Cla.	M 1908 A.B. 1911
—	Wilfrid John	....	Trin.	M 1905 A.B. 1908
Leach Lewis,	Allan Fra.	....	Pem.	M 1901 A.B. 1904. A.M. 1908
—	Will.	....	Cai.	M 1902

Lee,	Hor. Will.	Qu.	M 1908 A.B. 1911
—	John Mitchell	Trin. H.	M 1908 A.B. 1911
--	John Romanis	Trin.	M 1895 A.B. 1898. A.M. 1904
—	Norman	Sid.	M 1912
—	Rich. Hen. Lovelock	Pet.	M 1898 A.B. 1901. A.M.† 1908
—	Rob. Dalway	Chr.	M 1907 A.B., LL.B. 1910
—	Rob. Steph. Norris	Jes.	M 1905 A.B. 1908
—	Rocliffe Stanley Osborne	Em.	M 1902 A.B. 1905. A.M. 1912
—	Ronald Outram	Em.	M 1895 A.B. 1898. B.C. 1904. M.B. 1906
—	Walt. Evelyn	Chr.	M 1909 A.B. 1912
—	Will. Emerson	Trin.	M 1894 A.B. 1898. A.M. 1906. B.C. 1907.
Lee Booker,	Roland	Trin. H.	L 1909 [M.D. 1910
Leech,	Benj.	Cla.	M 1896 A.B. 1899. A.M. 1903 [M.D. 1907
—	Ern. Bosdin	Chr.	M 1894 A.B. 1897. M.B., B.C., A.M. 1903.
Leeds,	Frank	N. C.	L 1906 Cath. A.B. 1908. A.M. 1912
Leeke,	Cha.	Trin.	M 1906
—	Cha. Harold	Trin.	M 1906 A.B. 1909
—	Chris.	Trin.	M 1901 A.B. 1904. A.M. 1908
—	Edw. John	Trin.	M 1903 A.B. 1906. A.M. 1911
—	John Alan	Trin.	M 1904 A.B. 1910
—	John Cox	Trin.	M 1862 A.B. 1866. A.M. 1869. D.D. 1906
—	Will. Meynell	Trin.	M 1898 A.B. 1901. A.M. 1906
—	Will. Wordsworth ...	Cla.	M 1901 A.B. 1904. A.M. 1908
Leeming,	Alf. Johnson	C. C.	M 1908 A.B. 1911
Lee-Norman,	Fra. Tho.	Pem.	M 1905 A.B. 1908
Lees,	Alan Hen.	King's	M 1902 A.B. 1906. A.M. 1910
—	Alec Antony	Em.	M 1908 A.B. 1911
—	Denzil Clark	Qu.	M 1906
—	Edm. Hartley	Trin. H.	M 1906
—	Kenneth Art.	King's	M 1900 A.B. 1903. M.B., B.C. 1909. A.M.
—	Sam.	*Joh.	M 1906 A.B. 1909 [1910
—	Tho. Prior	Cla.	M 1893 A.B. 1896. A.M. 1901
—	Will. Donald	Pet.	M 1898 A.B. 1901. A.M. 1909
—	Will. Edw.	H. Sel.	M 1911
Leeser,	Herb.	Joh.	E 1907
Leete,	Will. John Hurstwaite	Cai.	M 1905 A.B. 1908
Lee Warner,	Roland Paul	Joh.	E 1911
—	Will.	Joh.	M 1865 A.B. 1869. A.M.† 1872. *LL.D.*
Lee-Williams,	Owen Llewellyn ...	Mag.	M 1910 [1911
Le Fleming,	John	Cla.	M 1884 A.B. 1887. A.M. 1902
Lefroy,	Cha. Edwin	Trin.	M 1901 A.B. 1904
—	Edw. Jeffry	Trin.	M 1911
—	Harold		*See* Maxwell Lefroy, Harold
Legg,	Geo. Turner	King's	M 1899 A.B. 1902
—	Hor. Gordon	King's	M 1900 A.B. 1903
—	Will. Hen.	N. C.	M 1909 A.B. 1912
Leggatt,	Reg. Remington	H. Cav.	M 1890 Chr. A.B. 1898. A.M. 1902
Legge,	Percy Anlagnier	N. C.	E 1911
—	Reg. Ja.	Down.	M 1906 A.B. 1911
Legge-Currie,	John Duncan	Cla.	M 1904
Leggett,	Geo. Malcolm Kent	King's	M 1900 A.B. 1904
Le Goc,	Maur.	N. C.	M 1908 M. Jacques, A.B. 1911
Le Gros,	Fre. Gervaise	Jes.	M 1912
Lehmann,	John Rob.	Cla.	M 1909 A.B. 1912
Le Huray,	Cyril Pet.	N. C.	M 1912
Leicester,	Will. Sam.	Em.	M 1900 A.B. 1903
Leigh,	Bern. Hen.	Pet.	M 1908
—	Edw. Hen.	Pem.	M 1907 A.B. 1911
—	Frank	Down.	E 1911
—	Ja.	Chr.	M 1895 A.B. 1898. A.M. 1902
—	John Franklen Will.	Cla.	M 1901 A.B. 1904. A.M. 1908

Leigh,	Rob.	Trin. H.	M 1909
Leigh-Clare,	Harry Ja. Leigh	Qu.	M 1910
Leigh-Smith,	Benj. Valentine	Trin.	M 1907
Leighton,	Art. Fra.	Cai.	M 1907 A.B. 1910
—	Fre. Fra.	Joh.	M 1896 A.B. 1899. B.C. 1906. M.B. 1907
—	John Wright	Down.	M 1907 A.B. 1910
—	Rob. Leighton	Down.	M 1906 A.M. 1906 (Oxf. incorp.)
Leite,	Hub. Marie Jos. François-{ de-Paul Pinto	Cai.	M 1899 A.B. 1902
Le Jeune,	Yves	N. C.	M 1901 A.B. 1904. A.M.† 1908
Le Lacheur,	Edw. Tom	King's	M 1901 A.B. 1904
—	Will. John	Trin.	M 1895 A.B. 1898. A.M. 1903
Lely,	Will. Gerald	Em.	M 1905 A.B. 1908
le Maistre,	Stanley Girault	Cla.	M 1906 A.B. 1910
Leman,	Herb. Mayo	Mag.	M 1889 A.B.1892. LL.B.1893. LL.M.1902.
Lembcke,	Gustave Mich.	Pem.	M 1905 A.B. 1908 [A.M.† 1911
Lemon,	Guy Talbot	Cla.	M 1904 A.B. 1908
Lempfert,	Rudolf Gustav Karl	Em.	M 1894 A.B. 1898. A.M. 1901
Le Neve Foster,	Bern. Antoine } Jeffrey Chevalier {	Jes.	M 1912
Leney,	Ronald John Barcham	Cai.	M 1902 A.B. 1905. B.C., A.M. 1912
Lenfestey,	Stanley de Jersey ...	Pet.	M 1895 A.B. 1898. A.M. 1903
Lennox,	Norman Gordon	Trin.	M 1907 A.B. 1910
Lenon,	John Walt.	Jes.	M 1899 A.B. 1903
Lenox-Conyngham,	Geo. Hugh ...	Cai.	M 1878 A.B. 1882. A.M. 1903
Leonard,	Douglas	Sid.	M 1902 A.B. 1905
—	Hen. Verdon	Cla.	M 1912
—	Percy Ja.	Joh.	M 1905 A.B. 1908
Leong,	Tek Khean	Chr.	M 1911
—	Yin Khean	Chr.	M 1911
Lepper,	Rob. Stewart	King's	M 1889 A.B. 1892. LL.B. 1893. A.M.†
Leroy-Beaulieu,	Pierre Paul		*Litt.D.* 1904 [1896. LL.M. 1903
Leschallas,	Gilb. Pigé	Trin.	M 1897 A.B. 1901
Lescher,	Frank Graham	Cai.	M 1907 A.B. 1910
Lesley,	Ja. Wyvill	Em.	M 1907 A.B. 1910
Leslie,	Alan	H. Sel.	M 1898 A.B. 1901. A.M. 1905
—	Alan	Trin.	M 1908 A.B. 1911. LL.B. 1912
—	John Randolph	King's	M 1904 A.B. 1907. A.M. 1911
—	Jos. Derek	Chr.	M 1899 A.B. 1903
—	Roger	Trin.	M 1911
Lesser,	Reg. Wolff	Trin.	M 1903 A.B. 1907
Lester,	Cha. Valentine	N. C.	M 1899 Cai. A.B. 1902
—	Fra. Harold	Pem.	M 1901 A.B. 1904. B.C. 1909
—	Ronald Kingsley	Cai.	M 1906 A.B. 1909
L'Estrange,	Gilb. Rich.	C. C.	M 1904
Le Sueur,	Walt. Rondel	Joh.	M 1889 A.B. 1892. A.M. 1908
Letchworth,	Geo. Howard Strettell	Pem.	M 1904 A.B. 1907
Lethbridge,	Edwin Herb.	Joh.	M 1898 A.B. 1901
Letts,	Christian Fra. Campbell	Jes.	M 1907 A.B. 1910
—	Egerton Michael	Trin. H.	M 1910
—	Reg.	Jes.	M 1876 A.B. 1880. A.M. 1912
Lever,	Darcy	Trin.	M 1906 A.B. 1909
—	Percy Fogg	Chr.	M 1897 A.B. 1900. LL.B. 1901
—	Will. Hulme	Trin.	M 1906 A.B. 1909
Levett,	Ern. Chris.	Trin.	M 1907 A.B. 1910
—	Laurence Rawdon ...	Trin.	M 1902 A.B. 1906. A.M. 1910
Levett-Prinsep,	Tho. Art.	Cla.	M 1898 A.B. 1902
Levi,	Anth. Angelo	Trin.	M 1898 A.B. 1902
Levien,	Edwin Goldsmid	Em.	M 1898 A.B. 1901. A.M.† 1910
Levine,	Ephraim	Jes.	M 1906 A.B. 1909
Levinstein,	Gerald Edw.	Pem.	M 1905 A.B. 1908. A.M. 1912

Levy,	Hen.	Chr.	M 1910
—	Isaac	Cath.	M 1911
—	Leon. Angelo	Cla.	M 1904 A.B. 1907. A.M. 1911
—	Leslie Cha.	Joh.	M 1906 LL.B. 1909
—	Lewis	Pem.	M 1899 A.B. 1902
—	Stanley Isaac	Joh.	M 1909 A.B. 1912
—	Wilfred Rhodes	Trin.	M 1900 Wilfrid R. A.B. 1903. post [Rhodes, W. R., A.M. 1907
Lewin,	Herb. Will.	Cla.	M 1901 A.B. 1905. A.M. 1908
—	Kenneth Rob.	Trin.	M 1906 A.B. 1909
—	Will. Geo.	Cai.	M 1902
Lewis,	Alf. Dale	King's	L 1902 A.B. 1904. A.M.† 1909
—	Brinley Rich.	Trin. H.	M 1909 A.B., LL.B. 1912
—	Cha. Bertram	Em.	M 1900 A.B. 1903
—	Chris. Sothern	Cla.	M 1892 A.B. 1895. LL.B. 1896. A.M. 1905
—	Clifford Mich.	King's	M 1903 A.B., LL.B. 1907
—	Dav. John Watts ...	N. C.	M 1898 A.B. 1912
—	Edm. Oliver	N. C.	L 1906 Joh. A.B. 1907. A.M. 1911
—	Edw. Phil.	Em.	M 1904 A.B. 1907
—	Edwin Hugh	Trin.	M 1901 A.B. 1904. A.M. 1908
—	Emrys Llewellyn ...	Qu.	M 1907 A.B. 1910
—	Ern. Isaac	Cai.	M 1899 A.B. 1902. A.M. 1912
—	Fra. Herb.	Chr.	M 1908 A.B. 1911
—	Frank Tom	N. C.	M 1896 A.B. 1899. F. Tho. A.M. 1903
—	Frank Warburton ...	Trin.	L 1908 A.B. 1910
—	Gerald Vyvyan	Trin.	M 1903
—	Hen.	Trin. H.	M 1905 A.B. 1908. A.M. 1912
—	Hen. Godfrey	Joh.	M 1900 A.B., LL.B. 1903
—	Hen. Howard	Cai.	M 1907
—	Hugh Ja.	Chr.	M 1908 A.B. 1911
—	John Biddulph Strafford	Down.	M 1912
—	Jos.	Trin. H.	M 1894 A.B. 1897. A.M.† 1902
—	Julius Heinrich	Cath.	M 1908
—	Lewis Fra. Gurslave	Chr.	M 1900 A.B. 1903
—	Lewis Hewitt	Cla.	M 1912
—	Lionel Will. Pelling	Pet.	M 1891 A.B. 1894. A.M. 1904
—	Malcolm Meredith ...	Down.	M 1910
—	Martin Bonnell	Qu.	M 1910
—	Michael Art.	Trin.	M 1909 A.B. 1912
—	Oliver Geo.	N. C.	M 1911
—	Owen Rhydderch ...	Joh.	M 1893 A.B. 1904
—	Percy Ja.	Joh.	M 1903 A.B. 1906. A.M. 1910
—	Reg. Cameron	Chr.	M 1911
—	Rich. Morgan	N. C.	M 1906 Chr. A.B. 1910
—	Rob. John Bailey ...	Qu.	M 1897 A.B. 1902. A.M. 1905
—	Rupert Edw.	H. Sel.	M 1889 A.B. 1893. A.M. 1902
—	Trevor Edw.	Cai.	M 1906 A.B. 1909
—	Trevor Gwyn Elliot	Trin.	M 1890 A.B. 1894. A.M. 1903
—	Will. Augustus Howe	Down.	M 1909 A.B. 1912
—	Will. Basil Aylmer ...	Chr.	M 1911
—	Will. Hawthorne	Cai.	M 1907 A.B. 1910
Lewtas,	Fre. Geo.	Cai.	M 1910
Lewthwaite,	Cha. Gilfrid	Trin.	M 1903 A.B. 1906
—	Will.	Trin.	M 1901 A.B. 1905
Ley,	Chris. Fra. Aden ...	Pem.	M 1912
—	Rich. Leon.	Pem.	M 1901 A.B. 1904. M.B. 1909
Leyland,	Geoffrey Rich.	Pem.	M 1908
Leytham,	Cha. Edgar	H. Sel.	M 1885 A.B. 1888. A.M. 1912
Li,	Gaston	Chr.	M 1908 A.B. 1911
Liang,	Pow Kan	Cai.	M 1909 A.B. 1912
Lias,	Art. Godfrey	King's	M 1907 A.B. 1910

Lias,	Edm. Tho. Mortlock	Pet.	M 1911
—	Ronald John Mortlock	Trin.	M 1909 A.B. 1912
Lichtenberg,	Will. Adolf	Trin.	M 1911
Lidbetter,	Ja. Staples	Em.	M 1910
Liddell,	Cecil Fre. Jos.	Trin.	M 1908
—	Hen. Gordon Trevor	C. C.	M 1912
Lidderdale,	Fra. John	Trin.	M 1886 M.B., B.C. 1899. M.D. 1905
Liddiard,	Tho. Herne	C. C.	M 1910
Liddle,	Geo. Ern.	Pet.	M 1904 A.B. 1907. A.M. 1911
—	Hen. Weddell	N. C.	M 1906 Down. A.B. 1909
Lidgett,	John Cuthbert	Em.	M 1904 A.B. 1907. LL.B. 1911
Light,	Donald Owen	Pem.	M 1908 A.B. 1911
—	Edwin Mellor	Cla.	M 1880 A.B. 1884. A.M. 1887. M.B., B.C.
—	Percy	Jes.	M 1901 A.B. 1904 [1888. M.D. 1904.
Lightbody,	Wilfrid Petre	Trin.	M 1911
Lightburne,	Harcourt Rob. Hen.	H. Sel.	M 1904 A.B. 1907. A.M. 1911
Lightfoot,	Ben	Pet.	M 1906 A.B. 1909
—	Gerald	Pem.	M 1895 A.B. 1898. A.M.† 1912
Liley,	Hen. Deakin	Chr.	M 1907 A.B. 1910
Lilley,	Eric Gordon	Mag.	M 1906 A.B. 1909
Lillie,	Cecil Firmin	Joh.	M 1891 A.B. 1894. M.B., B.C. 1897. A.M.
—	Denis Gascoigne	Joh.	M 1906 A.B. 1909 [1898. M.D. 1901
Lillingston,	Claude	Pem.	M 1899 A.B. 1902. B.C. 1906. M.B. 1911
Lilly,	Cha. Otto	Jes.	M 1908 A.B. 1911
—	Geo. Austen	Cai.	M 1907 A.B. 1910
Lim,	Cheng Ean	Cla.	M 1911
—	Guan Cheng	Joh.	M 1904 A.B. 1907. B.C. 1910. M.B. 1911
Limantour,	Guillermo Manuel ...	Trin. H.	M 1912
Lincoln,	Norman	Joh.	M 1904 A.B. 1907
Lindemere,	Victor	Trin.	M 1900 A.B. 1903
Lindenbaum,	John Benj.	Cai.	M 1903 A.B., LL.B. 1906. A.M., LL.M.
Lindesay,	Ja. Hen. Coddington	Sid.	M 1912 [1910
Lindley,	Edw. Searles	Trin.	M 1900 A.B. 1903
—	Tinsley	Cai.	M 1884 A.B. 1888. LL.M. 1898. LL.D.
—	Will. Maximilian ...	Trin.	M 1910 [1903
Lindsay,	Geo. Reg.	N. C.	M 1912
—	Will. Jos.	Sid.	M 1890 A.B. 1893. M.B., B.C. 1898. A.M.,
Lindsell,	Art. Ja. Gurney	Chr.	M 1899 A.B. 1902 [M.D. 1902
—	John	Joh.	M 1911
—	Roger Edw.	King's	M 1905 A.B. 1908
Line,	Ja.	Em.	M 1911
Linford,	Will. Alan Milroy ...	Cla.	L 1911
Ling,	Gerard Alston	King's	M 1898 A.B. 1901
—	Herb. Westwood	Pem.	M 1908
Lingard,	John Reg.	Trin.	M 1903 A.B. 1906. A.M. 1910. LL.B. 1912
Lingwood,	Bertie Alb.	N. C.	M 1908
Linnell,	Cha. Darby	Joh.	L 1902 A.B. 1903
—	Harry Leofwin	Down.	M 1908
—	John Wycliffe	Joh.	M 1899 A.B. 1902. M.B., B.C. 1907
—	Rob. McCheyne	Joh.	M 1900 A.B. 1904
Linney,	Duncan	Joh.	M 1896 A.B. 1899. A.M. 1910
Linthorne,	Edw. Lester Roope	Mag.	M 1912
Linton,	Edw. Cox	Trin.	M 1892 A.B. 1895. A.M. 1909
—	Fra. Ja.	Pem.	M 1904 A.B. 1907. LL.B. 1908. A.M. 1911
Lipkind,	Goodman	Joh.	M 1901
Lippmann,	Gabriel		*Sc.D.* 1908
Lipschitz,	Julius	Cla.	M 1912
Lipshytz,	Gordon Tho.	Em.	M 1912
Lipson,	Dan. Leopold	C. C.	M 1905 A.B. 1908. A.M. 1912
—	Ephraim	Trin.	M 1907 A.B. 1910
Liptrot,	Roger Norman	Chr.	M 1908 A.B. 1911

List,	John Napier	King's	M 1902 A.B. 1906. A.M.† 1910
Lister,	Art. Venning	Pem.	M 1910
—	Art. Will.	Chr.	M 1899 A.B. 1902. A.M. 1906
—	John	Joh.	M 1897 A.B. 1904
—	John Geo.	Cath.	M 1904 A.B. 1907. A.M. 1911
—	John Venning	Pem.	M 1898 A.B. 1901. A.M. 1909
—	Tom	Joh.	M 1906 A.B. 1909
—	Wilfred Mackay	H. Sel.	M 1909 A.B. 1912
Litchfield,	Geo.	N. C.	M 1911
Little,	And. Hunter	C. C.	M 1909 A.B. 1912
—	Art. Wentworth Roberts	Trin. H.	M 1899 A.B. 1902. A.M. 1906
—	Cha. Scott	H. Sel.	M 1908 A.B. 1912
—	Harold Lowthian	Sid.	M 1911
—	Harold Norman	Cai.	M 1901 A.B. 1904. B.C. 1908. A.M. 1909
—	Ja. Armstrong	Cai.	M 1904 A.B. 1907. A.M. 1912
—	John Caruthers	Cai.	M 1905
—	Tho. Gurney	Pet.	M 1864 A.B. 1868. A.M. 1902
Littledale,	Aubyn	Qu.	M 1910
Littlejohn,	Hugh Ascot	Pem.	M 1912
—	Ja. Crombie	C. C.	M 1898 A.B. 1902
Littler,	Cha. Guy Matheson	H. Sel.	M 1907 A.B. 1910
Littlewood,	Art.	Down.	M 1908 A.B. 1911
—	John Edensor	*Trin.	M 1903 A.B. 1906. A.M. 1910
Litton,	Edw. Leslie	Qu.	M 1906
—	Will. Roy Upton	Trin. H.	M 1905 A.B. 1908
Liu,	Liang-hsun	Chr.	M 1910
Liveing,	Geo. Downing	*Joh.	M 1846 A.B. 1850. A.M. 1853. *Sc.D.* 1908
Livens,	Geo. Hen.	*Jes.	M 1906 A.B. 1909
—	Will. Howard	Chr.	M 1908 A.B. 1911
Livesey,	Alan Geo. Hilton	Pem.	M 1908 A.B. 1911
—	Algernon Montague	Trin.	M 1893 A.B. 1899. A.M. 1905
—	Frank	Pem.	M 1901 A.B. 1904
—	Rich. Edmondson	Cath.	M 1912
—	Tho. Reg. Montagu	King's	M 1910
Livingston,	Clive Percy	Trin. H.	M 1911
—	Phil. Clermont	Jes.	M 1912
Livingstone,	Frank Darley	Pet.	M 1904 A.B. 1908
Llewellyn,	Evan Edwards	Chr.	M 1912
Llewelyn,	Dav. Edw. Kershaw	Down.	M 1910
—	Will. Hen.	Down.	L 1912
Llewelyn Davies,	Roland Art.	Trin.	M 1911
Lloyd,	Alan Cha. Gore	Qu.	M 1898 A.B. 1901
—	Alan Hub.	Cai.	M 1902 A.B. 1905
—	Alan Scrivener	Trin.	M 1907 A.B. 1910
—	Art. Cresswell	Cai.	M 1906
—	Cha. Geoffrey	Sid.	M 1902
—	Cyril Gascoigne	Trin.	M 1905
—	Edm.	Em.	M 1898 A.B. 1901. B.C. 1905. M.B. 1907
—	Edw. Aubrey	Trin.	M 1904 A.B. 1907. A.M. 1911
—	Eric Ivan	Trin.	M 1911
—	Ern. Llewelyn	Joh.	M 1912
—	Geo. Tho.	Cla.	M 1902 A.B. 1905. A.M. 1912
—	Gerald Braithwaite	Trin.	M 1904 A.B. 1907
—	Harold Rhys	Cai.	M 1899 A.B. 1902. A.M. 1912
—	Hen. Clifford	Trin.	M 1909 A.B. 1912
—	Hen. Greame	Trin.	M 1912
—	Herb. Marsden	Joh.	M 1909 A.B., LL.B. 1912
—	Humphrey Willis Chetwode	Jes.	M 1910
—	Ja. Davidson	Trin.	M 1900 A.B. 1903. A.M. 1907
—	John Dan.	Sid.	M 1903 A.B. 1906
—	John Fra. Selby	Trin.	M 1900 A.B. 1903

Lloyd,	John Pemberton	Trin.	M 1902 A.B. 1906. A.M. 1909
—	John Pryse	King's	M 1912
—	John Wheller	Cla.	M 1900 A.B. 1903
—	Lancelot Walt.	Cla.	M 1912
—	Leslie Steeds	Trin.	M 1908 A.B. 1912
—	Llewelyn Southworth	Chr.	M 1895 A.B. 1898. A.M. 1902
—	Montague Aubrey ...	Pem.	M 1906 A.B. 1909
—	Murray Tenison	Joh.	M 1908 A.B. 1911
—	Reg. Broughton	Em.	M 1900 A.B. 1903. B.C. 1907. M.B. 1908
—	Tho. Glyn	Cla.	M 1910
—	Will. Hutchinson ...	Trin.	M 1903
—	Will. Reg.	Joh.	M 1906 Pet. A.B. 1909
Lloyd-Barrow,	Reg. Awbrey	Jes.	L 1909
Lloyd George,	Rich.	Chr.	M 1907 A.B. 1910
Lloyd-Jones,	Edw. Wynne	Em.	M 1907 A.B. 1910
—	Ivor Gordon	Trin.	M 1888 A.B. 1891. A.M. 1901
—	John	Em.	M 1910
—	Percy	Cai.	M 1903 A.B. 1906
—	Percy Arnold	Joh.	M 1895 A.B. 1898. M.B., B.C. 1907
Lloyd-Williams,	Aldborough Rupert Caulfield	Trin.	M 1899 A.B. 1902
Lluellyn,	Raymond Chester ...	Cai.	M 1904
Lo,	Tsing Hien	Cath.	M 1904
—	Tsung Yee	Jes.	M 1906 A.B. 1909
Lob,	Hyman	King's	M 1905 A.B. 1908
Lobo,	Paschal Constantine	Trin. H.	L 1899 A.B. 1901
Loch,	Dav. Hen.	King's	M 1902 A.B. 1905
Lock,	John Lewis	Cai.	M 1893 A.B. 1896. M.B., B.C., A.M. 1901
—	Lyonel John	N. C.	M 1905 A.B. 1909
—	Norman Fra.	Cai.	M 1904 A.B. 1908. M.B., B.C., A.M. 1912
—	Percy Gonville	Cai.	M 1893 A.B. 1897. A.M. 1904
—	Rob. Heath ....*Cai.		M 1898 A.B. 1902. A.M. 1905. Sc.D. 1910
Locke,	Cha. Edw. Leatham	Qu.	M 1903 A.B. 1908
—	Geo. Tho.	Joh.	M 1894 A.B. 1897. A.M. 1901
Locker-Lampson,	Oliver Stillingfleet	Trin.	L 1900 A.B. 1903
Lockett,	John	Trin.	M 1900 A.B. 1903
Lockhart,	John Harold Bruce	Jes.	M 1908 A.B. 1911
—	Laurence	Pem.	M 1910
—	Rob. Bruce	C. C.	M 1881 A.B. 1884 (2). A.M. 1906
Lockspeiser,	Benny	Sid.	M 1910
Lockton,	Will.	Joh.	M 1897 A.B. 1900. Jes. A.M. 1904
Lockwood,	Edw. Marston	Trin. H.	M 1909
—	Phil. Kendall	Mag.	M 1910
Lockyer,	Jos. Norman		Sc.D. 1904
Loder,	Norman Wilfrid	Trin.	M 1905
—	Rob. Egerton	Trin.	M 1906 A.B. 1909
Lodge,	Oliver Jos.		Sc.D. 1910
—	Ronald Fra.	King's	M 1908 A.B. 1911
—	Tho.	Trin.	M 1901 A.B. 1904
Loeb,	Jacques		Sc.D. 1909
Loeffler,	Carl Ludwig Henrik	Trin.	M 1895 A.B. 1898. A.M. 1902
Loewe,	Herb. Martin Ja. ...	Qu.	M 1901 A.B. 1904. A.M. 1908
—	Lionel Louis	Jes.	M 1911
Loewenthal,	Fre. Kimberley	Trin. H.	M 1896 A.B. 1901
Logan,	Fre. Lafferty	N. C.	M 1898 A.B. 1902
—	Hugh	Trin. H.	M 1903
—.	John Montagu	Trin. H.	M 1902
Logeman,	Willem Hendrik	Trin.	M 1904
Logothetes,	Porphyrios		LL.D. 1904
Loly,	Gerard Masterman ...	Trin. H.	M 1907 A.B. 1910
Lomas,	Ern. Gabriel	Trin.	L 1902

Loseby,	Percy John	Em.	M 1894 A.B. 1897. A.M. 1901
Lound,	Hugh Alf.	H. Sel.	M 1904
—	Reg. Stanley	H. Sel.	M 1901 A.B. 1904
—	Vivian Stanley	H. Sel.	M 1909 A.B. 1912
Love,	Art. Harold	Chr.	M 1894 A.B. 1897. A.M.† 1904
—	Fra. Stanley	Joh.	M 1908
Loveband,	Fra. Yerburgh	Cai.	M 1907 A.B. 1910
—	Guy Yerburgh	Jes.	M 1911
Loveday,	Alex.	Pet.	M 1907 A.B. 1911
—	Geo. Edw.	Cai.	M 1895 A.B. 1898. B.C. 1902. A.M. 1903.
Loveless,	Maynard Lambert ...	Pem.	M 1908 A.B. 1911 [M.B. 1904
—	Will. Bird	Pem.	M 1907 A.B. 1911
Lovell,	Edw. Norman	Jes.	M 1907 A.B. 1910
Lovelock,	Art. Reg.	Cai.	M 1908
—	Cha. Prior	Down.	M 1908 A.B. 1912
Lovett,	Fre. Ja.	Trin.	M 1897 A.B. 1901. A.M. 1904
Lovett Henn,	Edw. Hen.	Trin.	M 1910
Low,	Alban	Jes.	M 1912
—	Alex. Halley	Sid.	M 1910
—	Alf. Moore	Pem.	M 1890 A.B. 1893. A.M. 1910
—	Archib. Reith	Cla.	M 1900 A.B. 1903
—	Ja. Mitchell	Em.	M 1898 A.B. 1901. A.M. 1905
—	Rob. Allan	H. Sel.	M 1892 A.B. 1895. A.M.† 1910
—	Walt. Percival	Chr.	M 1895 A.B. 1898. A.M. 1909
Lowcock,	Douglas Raymond ...	Cla.	M 1903
Lowe,	Cha. Augustus Herb.	Chr.	M 1909 A.B. 1912
—	Cyril Nelson	Pem.	M 1911
—	Fra. Gordon	Cla.	M 1902 A.B. 1907
—	Fre. Ern.	Jes.	M 1885 A.B. 1888. A.M. 1910
—	Geoffrey Burman ...	Cla.	M 1911
—	Hen. St Alban	Trin.	M 1894 A.B. 1897. A.M. 1901
—	Will.	Cai.	M 1896 A.B. 1900. B.C. 1905. W. Picker-
[ing, M.B. 1906
—	Will. Douglas	Pem.	M 1898 A.B. 1901. A.M. 1905
Lowndes,	Ashley Gordon	Cath.	M 1910
—	John	H. Sel.	M 1908 A.B. 1911
—	Rich. Grant	Cla.	M 1901 A.B. 1904
—	Will. Parker	Pem.	M 1910
Lowry,	Sid. Hen.	Pem.	M 1907 A.B. 1910
—	Will. Augustine Harper	Cai.	M 1908
Lowson,	Kenneth John	Cai.	M 1904 A.B. 1907. LL.B. 1909
Lowther,	Chris. Will.	Trin.	M 1905
—	Ja. Will.	Trin.	M 1874 LL.B. 1879. LL.M. 1882. *LL.D.*
Löwy,	Alb. Ern.	Pet.	M 1907 A.B. 1910 [1910
Loxdale,	Ronald Geo. Maclean	Trin.	M 1905 A.B. 1908
Loyd,	Edw. Noel Farnham	Trin.	M 1899 A.B. 1904. A.M. 1907
—	Phil. Hen.	King's	M 1903 A.B. 1906. A.M. 1912
—	Reg. Art.	Trin.	M 1904 A.B. 1908
—	Rob. John Hen.	Trin.	M 1902
—	Will. Lewis Brownlow	Trin.	M 1908
Luard,	Edwin Percy	H. Sel.	M 1888 A.B. 1891. A.M. 1905
—	Harold	Trin. H.	M 1894 A.B. 1897. A.M. 1904
—	Syd. d'Albiac	Cla.	L 1912
Luard-Selby,	Reg. Bertram	H. Sel.	M 1904 A.B. 1907. A.M. 1911
Lubbock,	Harold Fox Pitt ...	Trin.	M 1906 A.B. 1909
—	Percy	King's	M 1898 A.B. 1902. A.M. 1907
—	Roy	King's	M 1911
—	Sam. Gurney	King's	M 1892 A.B. 1895. A.M. 1902
Lucas,	Alan Reg. Farrar ...	Trin.	M 1912
—	Alf. Eyre Owen	H. Sel.	M 1905 A.B. 1908
—	Algernon	H. Sel.	M 1899 A.B. 1903

Lucas,	Cha. Eric	Trin.	M 1904 A.B. 1908	
—	Dallyn	Trin.	M 1906 A.B. 1909	
—	Ern.	Em.	M 1906 A.B. 1909	
—	Ern. Cha.	Joh.	M 1904 A.B. 1907. A.M. 1911	
—	Fra. Herman	Trin.	M 1897 A.B. 1900. A.M. 1905	
—	Geoffrey Morton Ern.	Trin.	M 1906 A.B. 1909	
—	Harold Will.	Pem.	M 1898 A.B. 1901	
—	Harry Audley	Trin.	M 1904 A.B. 1907	
—	John Cuthbert	H. Sel.	M 1909 A.B. 1912	
—	Keith .... *Trin.		M 1898 A.B. 1901. A.M. 1905. Sc.D. 1911	
—	Stainforth John Chadwick	Pet.	M 1897 A.B. 1903	
—	Travis Clay	Cla.	M 1895 A.B. 1898. M.B.† 1905. B.C. 1908	
—	Vernon Ruskin	Trin. H.	M 1905	
—	Walt. Randolph	Mag.	M 1903 A.B. 1906	
—	Will. Haslam	Cla.	M 1903 A.B. 1908. A.M. 1912	
—	Will. Thornton	Trin. H.	M 1908 A.B. 1911	
—	Will. Wrathal	Trin. H.	M 1897 A.B. 1911	
Luce,	Gordon Hannington	Em.	M 1908 A.B. 1911	
Lucey,	Will. Harding	Cla.	M 1901	
Luckock,	Art. Mortimer	Trin.	M 1899 A.B. 1902. A.M. 1907	
Lucy,	Rich. Spencer	Cla.	M 1912	
Ludinszky,	Lewis Zoltan	Down.	L 1910	
Ludlow,	Frank	Sid.	M 1905 A.B. 1908	
Luker,	Stanley Gordon	Pem.	M 1900 A.B. 1903. A.M. 1907. B.C. 1908.	
Lukis,	Syd.	Cai.	M 1907 A.B. 1910 [M.D. 1911	
Lukyn-Williams, Art. Oswald ...			*See* Williams, A. O.	
Lumb,	Herb.	Cla.	M 1905 A.B. 1908. A.M. 1912	
—	Will.	Joh.	M 1907 A.B. 1910	
Lumby,	Art. Friedrich Rawson	Chr.	M 1909 A.B. 1912	
—	Chris. Dittmar Rawson	Mag.	M 1907 A.B. 1910	
Lumley,	Cha. Hugh	Trin.	M 1898 A.B. 1904	
Lummis,	Edw. Will.	King's	M 1912 A.M. (incorp.) 1912	
Lumsden,	Alex. Louis Courtenay	Trin.	M 1910	
—	Harry Basil	Pem.	M 1903 A.B. 1906	
—	John Art.	Trin.	M 1897 A.B. 1900. A.M. 1909	
—	Rob.	Pem.	M 1912	
Lund,	John	Cath.	L 1904 A.B. 1907. A.M. 1911	
Lundie,	Rob. Cha.	Chr.	M 1904 A.B. 1907	
Lunn,	Harold Fernie	Qu.	M 1894 A.B. 1897. A.M. 1901	
—	Herb. Cha.	Jes.	M 1908	
Lunniss,	Syd. Fre.	Cai.	M 1904	
Lunt,	Art. Temple	Chr.	M 1890 A.B. 1893. A.M. 1904	
Lupton,	Art. Sinclair	Joh.	M 1895 A.B. 1898. A.M. 1906	
—	Fra. Ashford	Trin.	M 1904 A.B. 1907	
—	Geoffrey Art.	King's	M 1912	
—	Hugh Ralph	Trin.	M 1912	
—	Jos. MacDougal	King's	M 1886 A.B. 1889. A.M. 1893. B.D. 1908	
—	Lionel Martineau ...	Trin.	M 1910	
—	Maur.	Trin.	M 1906 A.B. 1909	
—	Reg. Ellison	Em.	M 1904 A.B. 1907. A.M. 1911	
—	Reg. Hamilton	Cla.	M 1903	
—	Will. Mawhood	Cla.	M 1907 A.B. 1910	
Lurion,	Raoul Ollivier	Pem.	M 1905 Down. A.B. 1909	
Lusby,	Syd. Gordon	Em.	M 1909 A.B. 1911	
Luscombe,	Bern. Porter	Cath.	M 1912	
—	Popham Street	N. C.	M 1898 Qu. A.B. 1901. A.M.† 1905	
Lush,	Ern. Jos.	H. Sel.	M 1907 A.B. 1910	
—	John Art.	H. Sel.	M 1900 A.B. 1903	
Lusk,	Ja.	Joh.	M 1902 A.B. 1905	
Luttman,	Willie Lewis	Pet.	M 1894 A.B. 1897. A.M. 1901. Mus.B. 1903	
Lycett,	Cyril Vernon Lechmere	Trin.	M 1912	

Lydekker,	Cuthbert John	H. Sel.	M 1909 A.B. 1912	
—	Lionel Edw.	H. Sel.	M 1905 A.B. 1908. A.M. 1912	
—	Neville Wolfe	H. Sel.	M 1906 A.B. 1909	
Lyell,	Geo. Drummond	Trin.	M 1905 A.B. 1908	
—	Tho. Reg. Guire	King's	M 1905	
Lyle,	Cha. Ern. Leon.	Trin. H.	M 1901	
—	Rob. Cha.	C. C.	M 1906 A.B. 1909	
Lyman,	Theodore	Trin.	M 1901	
Lynch,	Percy Algernon	Trin. H.	M 1899 A.B. 1903. LL.B., A.M. 1910	
—	Rich. Irwin		*A.M.* 1906	
Lyne,	Cha. Wadham	H. Sel.	E 1894 A.B. 1897. A.M. 1901	
Lyon,	Cha. Geo.	Trin. H.	M 1900 A.B. 1904	
—	Harry Limnell	Trin.	M 1898 A.B. 1903	
—	Ralph Cuthbert Grant	Mag.	M 1909	
—	Will. Alf.	Trin. H.	M 1910	
—	Will. John	Em.	M 1906 A.B. 1909	
—	Will. Towers	King's	M 1905 A.B. 1908. A.M. 1912	
Lyons,	Rich. Jenkins	Joh.	M 1908 A.B. 1911	
Lyon Smith,	Geo.	Em.	M 1912	
Lyster,	Anth. St George	Pem.	M 1906 A.B. 1909	
—	Lumley FitzGerald ...	Trin.	M 1909 A.B. 1912	
Lyttelton,	Archer Geoffrey	Trin.	M 1903 A.B. 1906	
—	Cha. Fre.	Trin.	M 1905 A.B. 1909	
—	Edw.	Trin.	M 1874 A.B. 1878. A.M. 1881. B.D. 1907.	
—	Geo. Will.	Trin.	M 1902 A.B. 1905 [D.D. 1912	
—	Oliver	Trin.	M 1912	

M

Maasdorp,	Eric John	Chr.	M 1911	
—	Vivian Hayton	Chr.	M 1906	
McAfee,	Lewis Alex.	Pem.	M 1907 A.B. 1910	
McAlister,	Art.	N. C.	M 1899 A.B. 1902	
Macalister,	Geo. Hugh Kidd ...	Joh.	M 1898 A.B. 1901. M.B., B.C., A.M. 1906.	
McAllister,	Hugh Cecil	C. C.	M 1900 A.B. 1903 [M.D. 1910	
Macalpine,	John Leon.	Jes.	M 1904	
McAlpine,	Rob. Geo.	N. C.	E 1909 A.B. 1912	
MacAndrew,	Cha. Glen	Trin.	M 1906	
McArthur,	Alex. Gordon Finley	King's	M 1912	
—	Cha.	N. C.	M 1911	
—	Gordon Kelf	Sid.	M 1910	
—	Ronald	Cath.	M 1912	
Macartney,	Maxwell Hen. Hayes	Pem.	M 1899 A.B. 1902	
—	Mervyn Edw.	Cla.	M 1902 A.B. 1905	
Macaulay,	Aulay	Mag.	M 1870 A.B. 1874. A.M. 1912	
—	Colin Campbell	H. Sel.	M 1899 A.B. 1902	
—	Donald	Joh.	M 1903 A.B. 1906	
McAulay,	Fra. Willmer	Joh.	M 1909 A.B. 1912	
McAuliffe,	Rob. Paton	Cath.	M 1900 A.B. 1903. A.M. 1907	
McBain,	Geo. Brown Sievewright	Trin.	M 1910	
—	Will. Rob. Brown ...	Jes.	M 1910	
Macbeth,	Athole Harold	Trin.	M 1903 A.B. 1907	
MacBrayne,	Laurence	Pem.	M 1885 A.B. 1888. A.M. 1910	
McBride,	Lancelot Geo.	Cai.	M 1911	
MacBryan,	Edw. Crozier	Jes.	M 1912	

McBryde,	Ja.	King's	M 1893 A.B. 1896. M.B., B.C., A.M. 1903
McCall,	Harold Will. Lockhart	Trin.	M 1900 A.B. 1904
—	Hen. Dundas	Chr.	M 1907 A.B. 1910
—	Rob. Home	Chr.	M 1902 A.B. 1905
—	Tho. Hardy	H. Sel.	M 1912
McCance,	Dav.	Trin. H.	M 1896 A.B. 1904
McCarthy,	Ja. Desmond	Pet.	M 1894 A.B. 1897. A.M. 1901
—	Pelling Hotham	Qu.	M 1909 [1909
McCaskie,	Harry Bertram	Cai.	M 1896 A.B. 1899. M.B., A.M. 1904. M.D.
—	Norman Ja.	Cai.	M 1893 A.B. 1896. M.B., A.M. 1900. M.D.
McCaughey,	Sam.	Jes.	M 1912 [1904
McCaw,	Osmond Calbraith ...	Cai.	M 1908
MacCaw,	Vivian Hardy	Trin.	M 1901 A.B. 1904
McCleary,	Geo. Fre.	Trin. H.	L 1890 A.B. 1892. M.B. 1898. M.D. 1902
McCleland,	Nial Pat. Kenneth } Ja. O'Neill }	Pem.	M 1906 A.B. 1909
McClelland,	John Alex.	Trin.	L 1896 A.B. 1898. A.M. 1903
McClement,	Fre. Jos. Carr	Trin.	M 1904 A.B. 1907. A.M. 1912
McCliment,	Rob. Ja.	N. C.	M 1912
McClintock,	Edw. Louis Longfield	Trin.	M 1905 A.B. 1908. A.M. 1912
McClintock-Bunbury,	Tho. Leopold	Trin.	M 1898 A.B. 1901. A.M. 1906
McClung,	Rob. Kenning	Trin.	M 1901 A.B. 1903
McClure,	Ivor Herb.	Cla.	M 1910
—	Keith Alister Johnstone	Trin.	M 1911
Maccoby,	Ephraim Myer	Joh.	M 1910
MacColl,	Hugh Herb.	Chr.	M 1912
—	Will. Lawrence	H. Sel.	M 1912
McComas,	Herb. Will.	Chr.	E 1901
MacCombie,	Will. John	Cai.	M 1910
McConnel,	Ern. Whigham Jardine	Cai.	M 1886 A.B. 1889. A.M.† 1904
McConnell,	Alf. Edw.	Jes.	M 1899 A.B. 1903
—	Will. Edw.	Mag.	M 1907 A.B. 1911
McCorkell,	Dudley Evelyn Bruce	Pem.	M 1902
McCormick,	Alister Hamilton ...	Trin.	M 1910
—	Edw. Hamilton	Trin.	M 1908 A.B. 1911
—	Fra.	Mag.	L 1908 A.B. 1911
—	Jos. Gough	Joh.	M 1893 A.B. 1896. A.M. 1901
—.	Leander Ja.	Trin.	M 1907 A.B. 1910
—	Will. Pat. Glyn	Joh.	M 1896 A.B. 1899. A.M. 1907
McCorquodale,	Edm. Geo.	Trin.	M 1900 A.B. 1903
McCosh,	And. Kirkwood	Trin.	M 1899 A.B. 1902
—	Edw.	Cla.	M 1910
—	Rob.	Trin.	M 1904 A.B. 1907
—	Will. Waddell	Trin.	M 1902
McCowan,	Hugh Wallace	Joh.	M 1905 A.B. 1908. A.M.† 1912
McCraith,	Douglas	Trin.	M 1896 A.B. 1899. A.M. 1903
—	Kenneth Yorke	Trin.	M 1909
McCririck,	Douglas Howard Gwyn	Cla.	M 1912
McCrossan,	Hugh Mansure	C. C.	M 1910
McCubbin,	John Harold	Trin.	M 1906 A.B. 1909
McCulloch,	Will.	Joh.	M 1911
—	Will. Reed	Pem.	M 1902
MacDaniel,	Ja. Rich. Lane	Cla.	M 1904
Macdona,	Cuthbert Laud	Trin.	M 1906 A.B. 1909
McDonald,	Alex.	Em.	M 1903 A.B. 1906
—	Art.		*See* Brown, A. M.
Macdonald,	Allan John Smith ...	Trin.	M 1906 A.B. 1909
—	Art. Kennan	Joh.	M 1897 A.B. 1900. A.M. 1904
—	Cha. Leslie	Em.	M 1900 A.B. 1903
—	Geo. Mackay	Chr.	M 1886 A.B. 1890. M.B., B.C. 1897. A.M.,
—	Guyon Kenneth	Pem.	M 1908 [M.D. 1905

Macdonald,	John	Em.	M 1910
MacDonald,	John Norman	Cai.	M 1906 A.B. 1909
McDonald,	Ranald Geo.	Qu.	M 1900 A.B., LL.B. 1903
Macdonald,	Stuart Hugh	Pem.	M 1911
MacDonald,	Syd. Gray	Joh.	M 1899 A.B. 1902. M.B., B.C., A.M. 1907
McDonell,	Harold Clark	C. C.	M 1901 A.B. 1904. A.M. 1908
McDonnell,	John	King's	M 1897 A.B. 1901
MacDonnell,	John Carlyle	Pem.	M 1889 A.B. 1892. J. Carlile, A.M. 1901
McDonnell,	Mich. Fra. Jos.	Joh.	M 1901 A.B. 1904
McDougal,	Ern. Trevor Murray	Trin.	M 1912
McDougall,	Art.	Chr.	M 1904 A.B. 1907
—	Ronald	Pem.	M 1908 A.B. 1911
McDowall,	Stewart And.	Trin.	M 1901 A.B. 1904. A.M. 1908
Mace,	Cecil Alec	Qu.	M 1912
McEwen,	John Helias Finnie	Trin.	M 1912
Macfadyen,	Will. Archib.	Joh.	M 1912
McFarland,	John Beattie	Sid.	M 1908 A.B. 1911
Macfarlane,	Cha. Bate	Cai.	M 1905 A.B. 1908
McFarlane,	Geo.	Sid.	M 1894 A.B. 1897. A.M. 1901
—	John	King's	M 1898 A.B. 1902
McFayden,	Donald	N. C.	M 1905
Macfie,	John Will. Scott ...	Cai.	M 1898 A.B. 1901. A.M.† 1912
McGeagh,	Geo. Rob. Denison ...	Cai.	M 1906 A.B. 1909
—	Ja. Paul	Cla.	M 1912
Macgillivray,	Geo. John	Trin.	M 1896 A.B. 1899. A.M. 1903
McGowan,	Hen.	Cath.	M 1910
—	Ivor Alex. Whitworth	Jes.	M 1904 A.B., LL.B. 1907
—	Norman Stanley	Chr.	M 1909
—	Oswald	Cath.	M 1899 A.B. 1902. A.M. 1906
McGrady,	Sam. Hugh	Joh.	M 1904 A.B. 1907. A.M. 1911
Macgregor,	Alex. Miers	Qu.	M 1907 A.B. 1910
—	And. Hamilton	Cai.	M 1909 A.B. 1912
—	Dav. Hutchison ......*Trin.		M 1898 A.B. 1901. A.M. 1905
—	Geo. Hogarth Carnaby	Cai.	M 1911
McGregor,	John Scott Ivan	Jes.	M 1906 A.B. 1909
MacGregor,	Malcolm	Cai.	M 1907 A.B. 1910. LL.B. 1911
—	Malcolm Evan	Trin.	M 1910
McGrigor,	Alex. Muir	Pem.	M 1906 A.B. 1909
Machell,	Humphrey Gilb.	King's	M 1906 A.B. 1909
Machin,	Arnall Edw.	Down.	M 1908 A.B. 1911
—	Will.	King's	M 1904 A.B. 1907. A.M.† 1911
Mächtig,	Eric Gustav Siegfried	Trin.	M 1908 A.B. 1911
McIlroy,	Howard Douglas	Jes.	M 1910
Macintosh,	Hen. Maitland	C. C.	M 1911
Macintyre,	Donald Livingstone	Cla.	M 1912
McIntyre,	Edgar	Trin.	M 1904
—	Harold	Trin.	M 1900 Macintyre, H. A.B. 1904
—	John	King's	M 1899 A.B. 1902. B.C. 1906. M.B., A.M.
—	Norman	Trin.	M 1902 A.B. 1906 [1908
MacIver,	Cha. Ronald	Trin.	M 1910
Mack,	Isaac Alex.	Jes.	M 1911
Mackarness,	Ronald Geo. Campbell	Trin.	M 1903 A.B. 1906
Mackay,	Alex. Morrice	Trin.	M 1895 A.B. 1898. A.M. 1902
—	Alex. Sutherland ...	Jes.	M 1909 A.B. 1912
—	Eric Reay	Trin.	M 1903 A.B. 1906. A.M. 1910
—	Geo. Roger	Trin.	M 1911
—	Kenneth	Trin.	M 1906 A.B. 1910
—	Rob. Donald	Trin.	M 1908 A.B., LL.B. 1912
—	Rob. Ferrier Burns	King's	M 1910
McKenna,	Jos. Pat. Llewellyn	Em.	M 1909 A.B. 1912
Mackennal,	Will. Leavers	Trin.	M 1903 A.B. 1906. A.M. 1910

Mackenzie,	Boyce Mackay Scobie	Cla.	M 1908 A.B. 1911
—	Colin	Em.	M 1901 A.B. 1904. A.M. 1908
—	Colin Roy	Trin.	M 1910
—	Geo. Annand	N. C.	M 1907 A.B. 1910
—	Gilb. Marshall	Pem.	M 1908 A.B. 1911
MacKenzie,	Ja. Wesley	Down.	M 1912
McKenzie,	John Cormack	Pem.	M 1905
Mackenzie,	John Mitchell Douglas	Trin.	M 1906 A.B. 1909 [Litt.D. 1901
—	John Stuart	N. C.	M 1886 *Trin. A.B. 1889. A.M. 1893.
—	Kenneth Ja. Jos. ...	Chr.	*A.M.* 1908. A.M. 1911
—	Louis Hope Lovat ...	Trin.	M 1899 A.B. 1902. B.C., A.M. 1907. M.B.
—	Rob. Theodore Hope	Pem.	M 1906 A.B. 1909 [1908
—.	Roderick Simcox ...	Pem.	M 1906
—	Steph. Morton	Trin.	M 1898 A.B. 1901. M.B., B.C., A.M. 1905
Mackern,	Geo. Theodore Gibson	Pem.	M 1911
McKerrell Brown,	John	Trin.	M 1907 A.B. 1910
McKerrow,	Cha. Kenneth	Cla.	M 1902 A.B. 1905. M.B., B.C., A.M. 1911
—	Geo.	Cai.	M 1910
—	Ronald Brunlees	Trin.	M 1894 A.B. 1897. A.M. 1901. Litt.D. 1911
Mackeson,	Geo. Peyton	King's	M 1911
Mackeurtan,	Harold Graham	Trin.	M 1902 LL.B. 1905
McKibbin,	Alex. Geo.	Cla.	M 1906
Mackie,	Alf. Will. White	C. C.	M 1898 A.B. 1901
—	Augustine Clark	C. C.	M 1898 A.B. 1901. A.M. 1905
—	Leon. Shirras	Jes.	M 1912
—	Osbert Gadesden ...	Cla.	M 1895 A.B. 1898. A.M. 1902
McKiever,	Victor Comley	H. Sel.	M 1908
McKinlay,	Alan Burdon	Trin.	M 1911
Mackinlay,	Dav. Murray	Joh.	M 1912
McKinney,	John Cha.	N. C.	M 1894 Cath. A.B. 1905
MacKinnon,	Kenneth	Jes.	M 1901 A.B. 1905. A.M. 1912
Mackintosh,	Cha.	Trin.	M 1890 LL.B. 1893. LL.M. 1897. LL.D.
—	Geo. Will.	Trin.	M 1909 A.B. 1912 [1903
—	Hugh	Cai.	M 1898 A.B. 1901
—	Leslie Parkin Fraser	Cai.	M 1905
Macklem,	Tho. Clark Street ...	Joh.	M 1882 A.B. 1885. A.M. 1901
Macklin,	Ern. Fra.	Pet.	M 1904 A.B. 1907. A.M. 1911
McKnight,	Ja. Rob.	Qu.	M 1910
Mackrill,	Oscar Whittick	Cla.	M 1902 A.B. 1905. A.M. 1909
Mackworth-Praed,	Cyril Winthrop	Trin.	M 1911
Maclagan-Wedderburn,	Jos. Hen.	N. C.	E 1906
MacLaren,	Alisdair Iain	Cla.	M 1907 A.B. 1910
McLaren,	Art. Duncan	N. C.	M 1908
—	Cha. Walt. de Bois	Pem.	M 1908
Maclaren,	Malcolm	Trin.	M 1902 A.B. 1905
—	Norman	Trin.	M 1894 A.B. 1897. B.C. 1901. M.B. 1909
McLaren,	Sam. Bruce	Trin.	M 1897 A.B. 1900. A.M. 1905
Maclaurin,	Rich. Cockburn ......*Joh.		M 1892 A.B. 1895. LL.M. 1899. LL.D.†
Maclay,	Ebenezer	Joh.	M 1909 A.B. 1912 [1905. Sc.D. 1908
Maclean,	Adrian John	H. Sel.	M 1892 A.B. 1895. A.M. 1901
McLean,	Alan	Trin.	M 1895 A.B. 1898. A.M. 1905
Maclean,	Art. John	King's	M 1876 A.B. 1880. A.M. 1883. D.D. 1904
McLean,	Colin	Trin.	M 1900 A.B. 1906
—	Donald	Cai.	M 1898 A.B. 1901
Maclean,	Eric Wanklyn	Em.	M 1904 A.B. 1907
—	Fra. Sid.	Jes.	M 1911
McLean,	Hugh	Cai.	M 1898 A.B. 1901
Maclean,	Kenneth Edw.	Jes.	M 1907 A.B. 1910
McLean,	Rob. Colquhoun	Joh.	L 1912
—	Wilfrid	N. C.	M 1912
Macleod,	Douglas Noël	Cai.	M 1905 A.B. 1910. B.C. 1911

Macleod,	Kenneth Grant	Pem.	M 1905 A.B. 1908
—	Lewis Macdonald ...	Pem.	M 1903 A.B. 1906
—	Will. Art.	H. Sel.	M 1888 A.B. 1891. A.M. 1908
McLintock,	Leslie	Chr.	M 1908
Maclure,	Frederic Cavendish	Pem.	M 1882 A.B. 1886. A.M. 1901
MacMahon,	Percy Alex.		Sc.D. 1904
McMeekin,	Herb. Will. Porter ...	Cath.	M 1910
MacMichael,	Art. Will.	Trin.	M 1904 A.B. 1907. A.M. 1911
McMichael,	Douglas Will.	Cla.	M 1912
MacMichael,	Geo. Woodham	Cath.	M 1910
—	Harold Alf.	Mag.	M 1901 A.B. 1904
—	Humphrey Curzon ...	Mag.	M 1909 A.B. 1912
McMichael,	John Fisher	H. Sel.	M 1905 A.B. 1908
Macmillan,	Duncan	Trin.	M 1909
McMillan,	John Furse	Trin. H.	M 1908 A.B., LL.B. 1911
Macmillan,	Will. Edw. Frank ...	King's	M 1899 A.B. 1903. A.M. 1908
Macmorran,	Kenneth Mead	King's	M 1902 A.B. 1905. LL.B. 1907. A.M. 1909
MacMullan,	Cha. Walden Kirk- }patrick }	Pem.	M 1908 A.B. 1911
—	Harold Wilfred	Jes.	M 1912
MacMullen,	Alf. Robinson	Cai.	M 1907 A.B. 1910
—	Edm. Ronalds	Trin.	M 1903 A.B. 1907
—	Will. Alb.	Joh.	M 1909
MacMunn,	Howard Fletcher ...	Em.	M 1897 A.B. 1900. A.M. 1905
MacMurtrie,	Stanley Gibson	Cath.	M 1896 A.B. 1899. A.M. 1910
Macnab,	John Theodore	Chr.	M 1898 A.B. 1901. M.B., B.C., A.M. 1908
MacNaghten,	Angus Cha. Rowley }Steuart }	Trin.	M 1906
Macnaghten,	Cha. Melville	Trin.	M 1898 A.B. 1901
—	Hen. Pelham Wentworth	King's	M 1899 A.B. 1902
—	Norman Donnelly ...	King's	M 1900 A.B. 1903
McNair,	Arnold Duncan ......*Cai.		M 1906 A.B., LL.B. 1909
—	Art. Ja.	Em.	M 1905 A.B. 1908
—	Lindsay John	N. C.	M 1886 A.B. 1890. A.M. 1905
—	Will. Lennox	Cai.	M 1911 [1903. M.D. 1908
Macnamara,	Eric Danvers	Pet.	M 1887 A.B. 1890. A.M. 1899. M.B., B.C.
McNaught-Davis,	Ja. Walden }Fortune }	Cath.	M 1912
Macnaughton,	Donald Allan	Chr.	M 1895 A.B. 1898. A.M. 1905
McNaughton,	Hen. Leck	Pem.	M 1906 A.B. 1909
Macnee,	Eustace Alberic	Cla.	M 1904 A.B. 1907. A.M. 1911
McNeil,	Cha.	Jes.	M 1907 A.B. 1910
—	John	Jes.	M 1907 A.B. 1910
—	Will. Arnott	Trin. H.	M 1907 [1904. D.D. 1909
McNeile,	Alan Hugh	Pem.	M 1889 A.B. 1893. A.M. 1897. *Sid. B.D.
—	Ja. Duncan	Sid.	M 1898 A.B. 1901. A.M. 1905
—	John Hen.	Trin.	M 1911
McNeill,	Alex. Hen.	Cla.	M 1902
—	Neil Ian	Trin.	M 1904 A.B. 1907
—	Tennent	Trin.	M 1905 A.B. 1908. A.M. 1912
McNulty,	John Fra.	N. C.	M 1906 A.B. 1909
Macnutt,	Art. Cha.	Jes.	L 1898 A.B. 1900. A.M. 1904
—	Fre. Brodie	Trin.	M 1894 A.B. 1897. A.M. 1901
Macpherson,	Cha. Edw. Hen. Cardew	H. Sel.	M 1909
—	Donald Geo.	Cla.	M 1912
—	Duncan Gordon	Cai.	M 1898 A.B. 1901. A.M. 1906
—	Lachlan Fowke	Cla.	M 1908 post Hussey-Macpherson, L. F.
McQuade,	Will. Frederic	Pem.	M 1903 [A.B. 1912
Macquarrie,	Edm. Jeffrey	Cai.	M 1902 A.B., LL.B. 1905
MacQuarrie,	Hector	Cai.	M 1911
Macqueen,	Harry Quilter	N. C.	M 1909 A.B. 1912

Macqueen,	Percy	H. Sel.	M 1902
McQuistan,	Dougald Black	Cai.	M 1904
Macrae,	Lachlan	Em.	M 1911
—	Russell Duncan	Sid.	M 1907 A.B. 1910
MacRobert,	Tho. Murray	Trin.	M 1906 A.B. 1909
MacRury,	Evan	Cai.	L 1907 A.B. 1909
McTaggart,	Geo. Hen. Somerset } Gardner	N. C.	E 1907
—	Hen. Allen	N. C.	E 1912
—	Herb. Theodore Gardner	N. C.	E 1907
—	John McTaggart Ellis *Trin.		M 1885 A.B. 1888. A.M.† 1892. Litt.D. [1902
McWatters,	Hector Morgan	H. Sel.	M 1910
—	Will. Montgomerie ...	H. Sel.	M 1903 A.B. 1906
McWilliam,	Ja.	Mag.	M 1911
Madan,	Art. Gresley	Trin.	M 1912
—	Janardan Atmaram	Trin.	M 1908
Madden,	John Clements } Waterhouse	Trin. H.	L 1889 A.B. 1892. A.M. 1903
—	John Grevile	Pem.	M 1909 A.B. 1912
—	Owen	Cla.	M 1890 A.B. 1893. A.M. 1905
Maddison,	Geoffrey	Trin. H.	M 1905
—	Tho. Rowland Story	Jes.	M 1895 A.B. 1901
Maddocks,	Reg. Heber	H. Sel.	M 1902 A.B. 1905
Madge,	Hen. Ashley	Pet.	M 1898 A.B. 1901
—	Quintus	Em.	M 1906 A.B. 1909
—	Raymond	Em.	M 1899 A.B. 1902
—	Reg. Ellice	H. Sel.	M 1911
Mager,	Leon.	Chr.	M 1902 A.B., LL.B. 1905
Magnay,	Chris. Boyd Will. ...	Pem.	M 1903
Mahadeva,	Arunachalam	Chr.	M 1904 A.B. 1907
Mahli,	Sna Ullah	N. C.	E 1896 Chr. A.B. 1908
Maile,	Will. Cha. Drayson	Pem.	M 1906 A.B. 1909
Maine,	Hen. Cecil Sumner	Trin. H.	M 1903
Mainprice,	Humphrey	Jes.	M 1902 A.B. 1906
Mainwaring,	Alex. Gordon Max ...	Trin.	M 1901 A.B. 1905
—	Cyril Lyttelton	C. C.	M 1906 A.B. 1909
Mainwaring-Ellerker-Onslow, Art. } Guildford		Trin.	M 1908 A.B. 1911
Mair,	Alex. Will. ....*Cai.		M 1893 A.B. 1898. A.M. 1901
—	Edw. Millett	Sid.	M 1905 A.B. 1908
—	Gilb. Robertson	Cai.	M 1901 A.B. 1904
—	Rob. Pascoe	Trin.	M 1904
Maish,	Edw. Hen.	Qu.	M 1905 A.B. 1908. A.M. 1912
Maitland,	Eardley Tho.	Trin.	M 1906 A.B. 1909
—	Edw. Maitland		*See* Gee, E. M.
—	Graham Macdowall	Trin.	M 1897 A.B. 1901
—	Hen. Comyn	Mag.	M 1903 A.B. 1906
—	Hen. Maitland	H. Sel.	M 1907
—	John	Trin.	M 1898 A.B., LL.B. 1901
—	John Dalrymple	Jes.	M 1910
—	Peregrine Neave	Trin. H.	M 1903 A.B. 1906
—	Rob. Lindley	Pem.	M 1887 A.B. 1890. A.M. 1909
—	Rob. Prescott Fuller	Trin.	M 1906
—	Rowland Will.	Cla.	M 1897 A.B. 1901. A.M. 1905
Maitra,	Surendra Nath	N. C.	M 1911
Majid,	Abdul	N. C.	L 1903 Chr. A.B., LL.B. 1905
Majumdar,	Hem Chandra	Joh.	M 1903
—	Khagendra Nath ...	Joh.	M 1903 A.B. 1907. A.M.† 1912
Makant,	Angus Virtue	Cla.	M 1908 A.B. 1911
—	John Will.	Cla.	M 1904 A.B. 1908. A.M. 1911
Makepeace,	Fra. Lucas	Em.	M 1901 A.B. 1904. A.M. 1908

Makins,	Fre. Kirkwood	Trin.	M 1908 A.B. 1911
Makinson,	Jos. Crowther	Joh.	M 1910
Makovski,	Eric Waterlow	Trin.	M 1896 A.B. 1900. A.M. 1904
Makower,	Alf. Jacques	Trin.	M 1895 A.B. 1898. A.M. 1908
—	Walt.	Trin.	M 1902 A.B. 1904. A.M. 1909
Malaher,	Hen. Tho.	Em.	M 1906 A.B. 1909
Malcolm,	Alan Sam. Lack	Cai.	M 1906 A.B. 1910
—	Hugh Wilmott	Cla.	M 1906 A.B. 1909
Malcolm-Dickinson,	Will.	Trin.	M 1911
Malcomson,	Hub.	Pem.	M 1909 A.B. 1912
—	Llewellyn	Em.	M 1910
—	Will. Douglas	Pem.	M 1910
—	Will. Theodore	Em.	M 1908 A.B. 1911
Malden,	Edm. Claud	Cai.	M 1909 A.B. 1912
—	Edw. Elliot	Trin. H.	M 1898 A.B. 1905
—	Eustace Walt.	Em.	M 1911
—	Hen. Russell	Qu.	M 1903 A.B. 1906
—	Hen. Will.	N. C.	M 1904
—	Phil. Humfrey	Trin. H.	M 1910
—	Rich. Hen.	King's	M 1898 A.B. 1901. A.M. 1906
—	Walt.	Trin.	M 1877 A.B. 1881. A.M. 1885. M.B. 1887.
—	Will. Ern. Pelham	Trin.	M 1887 A.B. 1891. A.M. 1905 [M.D. 1905
Male,	Harold Will.	Joh.	M 1893 A.B. 1896. A.M. 1901
Malet,	Hugh Art. Grenville	Cai.	M 1910
Malik,	Jaswant Singh	Down.	M 1908
—	Mukhbain Singh	Down.	M 1907 A.B., LL.B. 1910
Malkin,	Herb. Will.	Trin.	M 1902 A.B. 1905
Mallalieu,	Will.	Trin.	M 1912
Malleson,	Will. Miles	Em.	M 1908 A.B. 1911
Mallet,	Eugène Hugo	King's	M 1884 LL.B. 1887. LL.M. 1907
Mallett,	Fre. John	Down.	M 1909 A.B. 1912
—	Howard Rothwell	N. C.	M 1907 A.B. 1911
—	Laurence Cecil	Em.	M 1899 A.B. 1903
Mallinson,	Edw. Cyril	Cla.	M 1906 A.B. 1909
Mallman,	Carl	Trin. H.	M 1903
Mallock,	Rawlyn Rich. Maconchy	Trin.	M 1904 A.B. 1908
—	Roger Champernowne	Trin.	M 1899 A.B. 1902
Mallory,	Geo. Herb. Leigh	Mag.	M 1905 A.B. 1908
—	Trafford Leigh	Mag.	M 1911
Malpas,	Cecil Culme	Cla.	M 1909
Maltby,	Fra. Edw.	Cath.	M 1906
Malthus,	Rob.	Trin.	M 1900 A.B. 1903. A.M. 1907
Mamlock,	Phil.	Pem.	M 1905 A.B. 1908
Man,	Morrice Lionel	Em.	M 1896 A.B. 1899. A.M. 1906
Manasse,	Max Maur.	Trin.	M 1911
Mandall,	John Alb.	Mag.	M 1902 A.B. 1905. A.M. 1909
—	Will. Alf.	Mag.	M 1900 A.B. 1904. A.M. 1907
Mander,	Cha. Art.	Trin.	M 1903 A.B. 1906
—	Fre. Will.	Trin.	M 1891 A.B. 1894. A.M. 1903
—	Geoffrey Le Mesurier	Trin.	M 1900 A.B. 1903. A.M. 1907
—	Gerald Poynton	Trin.	M 1904 A.B. 1907
Mandleberg,	Jos. Harold	Trin.	M 1904 A.B. 1907. A.M. 1911
—	Lennard Cha.	Trin.	M 1911
Manduell,	Matthewman Donald	Jes.	M 1896 A.B. 1899. A.M. 1910
Manekjee,	Sorabjee	Chr.	M 1907
Manfield,	Neville Phil.	Pem.	M 1912
Manford,	Ronald Fre.	N. C.	M 1911
Manger,	Alf. Stuart	Trin.	M 1908 A.B. 1911
Mangham,	Syd.	Em.	M 1905 A.B. 1908. A.M. 1912
Mango,	Alex. Anth.	Trin.	M 1902 A.B., LL.B. 1906. A.M. 1910
Manifold,	Edw. Walford	Jes.	M 1911

Manifold,	John	Jes.	M 1907 A.B. 1910
Manley,	Harry Fleming	Joh.	M 1898 A.B. 1902
—	John Dundas	Em.	M 1910
—	John Herb. Hawkins	Em.	M 1875 A.B. 1879. A.M. 1882. M.B., B.C.
—	Roger Shawe	Trin.	M 1911 [1884. M.D. 1903
Mann,	Art. Hen.	King's	*A.M.* 1910
—	Cha. Julian	Pem.	M 1911
—	Edw. John	Pem.	M 1901 A.B. 1904
—	Eric Will.	Trin.	M 1901 A.B. 1905. A.M. 1908
—	Fra. Tho.	Pem.	M 1907
—	John Will.	Cath.	M 1907 A.B. 1910
—	Rich.	Em.	M 1900 A.B. 1905
—	Rob. Lamplough	Jes.	M 1910
—	Tho. Clifford	Em.	M 1907 A.B. 1910
—	Tho. Eagling	Joh.	M 1906
Mannering,	Leslie Geo.	Sid.	M 1902 A.B. 1905. A.M. 1909
—	Reg.	Jes.	M 1910
Manners,	Geo. Rob.	N. C.	M 1904
—	Will. Fra.	Pem.	M 1877 A.B. 1881. A.M. 1908
Manning,	Bern. Lord	Jes.	M 1912
—	Cha. Rosedale Upwood	Sid.	M 1909 A.B. 1912
—	John Carlton	Cai.	M 1908 A.B., LL.B. 1911
—	Kenrick John Abbott Owen	Em.	M 1910
—	Rich.	Jes.	M 1908 A.B. 1911
—	Tho. Edgar	Jes.	M 1902 A.B. 1905
—	Warner	Cath.	M 1904 A.B. 1907
Mannington,	Ewart Gladstone ...	Chr.	M 1910
Mannooch,	John Kingscote	Qu.	M 1907 LL.B. 1910
Manohar Lál	....	Joh.	M 1900 A.B. 1902
Mansel,	Rob. Trevor Llewellin	Trin.	M 1901 A.B. 1904. A.M. 1909
—	Will. Cha. Grenville	Qu.	L 1903
Mansell,	Ralph	Qu.	M 1912
—	Reg. Anson	Em.	M 1909 A.B. 1912
Mansell-Moullin,	Oswald	King's	M 1906 A.B. 1909
Mansel-Pleydell,	John Morton ...	Trin.	M 1903 A.B. 1906
Manser,	Frank Hosmer	Cath.	M 1910
—	Fre. Bailey	Pet.	E 1894 A.B. 1897. M.B., B.C. 1903
Mansfield,	Harold Young	Em.	M 1907 A.B. 1910
—	Ja.	C. C.	M 1894 A.B. 1898. A.M. 1901
—	Phil. Theodore	Pem.	M 1910
—	Ralph Sheldon	Trin.	M 1910
—	Tho. Cha.	Pem.	M 1899 A.B. 1902
—	Wilfrid Steph.	Em.	M 1912
Mappin,	Frank Crossley	Cai.	M 1903
Marais,	Abr. Johannes	Trin. H.	M 1902 A.B. 1906
—	Wilfred Ford	Trin. H.	E 1904 A.B., LL.B. 1906
Marburg,	Cha. Lewis Hermann	Pem.	M 1909
Marc,	Geo. Ja. Alex.	Trin.	M 1908
March,	Walt. Will.	Cath.	M 1910
Marchand,	Geoffrey Isidore Cha.	Joh.	M 1907 A.B. 1910
Marchbank,	Fre. Furnivall	Sid.	M 1907 A.B. 1910
Mardon,	Heber Austin	Trin.	M 1911
Marett Tims,	Ronald Douglas ...	Cai.	M 1909
Margesson,	Hen. Dav. Reg.	Mag.	M 1908
Mariette,	Edgar Hen.	Pem.	M 1885 A.B. 1888. A.M. 1905
Marigold,	Ja. Evelyn	Trin.	M 1912
Maritz,	Gerald John	Trin. H.	L 1907
Markham,	Cha. Fre.	Jes.	M 1904 A.B. 1907
—	Clements Rob.		*Sc.D.* 1907
—	Edwin Bennett	Chr.	M 1912
—	Frank Reynolds	Cai.	M 1903

Markham,	Rich. Geo. .... Cai.	M 1901 A.B. 1904. M.B., B.C. 1907
—	Will. Art. .... N. C.	M 1903 A.B. 1906. A.M. 1910
Marklove,	John Carrington ...... Cai.	M 1901 A.B. 1904. B.C. 1912
Marks,	Alf. Dav. Tho. ...... Cai.	M 1888 A.B. 1891. A.M. 1911
—	Julian Dav. .... Trin.	M 1907 A.B. 1910
Marley,	Fra. Lindsay .... Qu.	M 1903 A.B. 1907
—	Harold .... Em.	M 1907 A.B. 1910
Marlowe,	John Morrison ...... Pem.	M 1911
Marnham,	Art. Ewart .... Jes.	M 1909 A.B. 1912
Marples,	Percy Morris .... Jes.	M 1897 A.B. 1900. A.M. 1905
Marpole,	Dav. Williams .... Joh.	M 1901
Marr,	Cecil Bruce Shand ... Cla.	M 1911
—	John Edw. ....*Joh.	M 1875 A.B. 1879. A.M. 1882. Sc.D. 1904
Marrack,	John Richardson ... Joh.	M 1905 A.B. 1908. M.B., B.C. 1912
—	Phil. Edw. .... Trin.	M 1900 A.B. 1903. A.M. 1910
Marriage,	Edw. Cha. Dacre ... Cla.	M 1900 A.B. 1903
Marriott,	Cecil Edw. .... Cla.	M 1888 A.B. 1891. M.B., B.C. 1900. M.C.
—	Cha. Geo. Lee .... Cla.	M 1912 [1904
—	Edw. Augustin ...... C. C.	M 1892 A.B. 1895. A.M. 1905
—	Fre. Claud .... H. Sel.	M 1894 A.B. 1897. A.M.† 1901
—	Fre. Geo. .... Chr.	M 1912
—	Geo. Armstrong ...... Cai.	M 1911
—	Geo. Edw. Jos. ...... Pet.	M 1907 A.B. 1910
—	John Fra. Laycock ... C. C.	M 1907 A.B. 1910
—	Steph. Jack .... H. Sel.	M 1904 Chr. A.B. 1907
Marris,	Eric Denyer .... Em.	M 1910
—	Hen. Fairley .... Cai.	M 1897 A.B. 1900. A.M. 1904
Marrs,	Fra. Will. .... Joh.	M 1899 A.B. 1902. A.M. 1906
Marsden,	Tho. Pickles .... Sid.	M 1895 A.B. 1898. A.M. 1902
—	Tom .... Cai.	M 1903 A.B. 1906
—	Walt. Gibson .... Em.	M 1905 A.B. 1908
Marsdin,	Fre. Bladworth ...... Pem.	M 1896 A.B. 1899. A.M. 1903
Marsh,	Alf. Stanley .... Trin.	M 1909 A.B. 1912
—	Bertie Cecil .... Pem.	M 1908 A.B. 1911. LL.B. 1912
—	Cecil John .... H. Cav.	M 1886 Down. A.B. 1912
—	Frank Douglas ...... Trin.	M 1907 A.B. 1910
—	¹ Fre. Howard ....*King's	A.M. 1903. M.C. 1904. Sc.D. 1912
—	Fred Shipley .... H. Sel.	M 1903 A.B. 1906. A.M. 1910
—	Harry Evelyn .... Pem.	M 1899 A.B. 1903
—	Herb. Geo. .... Cath.	M 1908 A.B. 1911
—	Ja. Will. .... Jes.	M 1900 A.B. 1903
—	John Fre. .... Jes.	M 1901 A.B. 1904. A.M. 1909
—	Lewis .... Em.	M 1899 A.B. 1902. A.M. 1906
—	Octavius de Burgh ... Pem.	M 1904 A.B. 1907. B.C. 1911
—	Rich. Jos. .... Joh.	M 1912
—	Rob. Alban .... Qu.	M 1909 A.B. 1912
—	Theodore Hen. ...... Pem.	M 1882 A.B. 1885. A.M. 1905
—	Will. .... Pem.	M 1905 A.B., LL.B. 1908. A.M. 1912
Marshall,	Alf. ....*Joh.	M 1861 A.B. 1865. A.M. 1868. *Sc.D.* 1908
—	Alf. Russel .... Em.	M 1905 A.B. 1908
—	Alf. Turner .... C. C.	M 1899 A.B. 1902. A.M. 1907
—	Art. Raymond ...... Cai.	M 1909
—	Douglas .... Cai.	M 1910
—	Edw. Norman .... Joh.	M 1884 A.B. 1887. A.M. 1905
—	Edwin Ern. .... N. C.	M 1889 Trin. H. A.B. 1892. A.M. 1897.
—	Eustace Art. .... Cla.	M 1911 [LL.M. 1901
—	Fra. Hugh Adam ...*Chr.	M 1896 A.B. 1899. A.M. 1905. Sc.D. 1912
—	Fre. Hen. ....*Em.	M 1897 A.B. 1900. A.M. 1904
—	Frederic Will. Dyson Pet.	M 1908 A.B. 1910

¹ Professor of Surgery, 1903; Master of Downing College, 1907.

Marshall,	Hannath Arnold	...... Jes.	M 1902 A.B. 1905. A.M. 1911
—	Hen.	.... Sid.	M 1903 A.B. 1905. A.M. 1910
—	Hen. Geo.	.... King's	M 1902 A.B. 1908
—	Herb. Edw. Champion	Chr.	L 1885 A.B. 1888. A.M. 1902
—	Hor. Cecil	.... Trin.	M 1906 A.B. 1909
—	Howard Gabb	.... Em.	M 1901 A.B. 1904. A.M. 1911
—	Ja.	.... Trin.	M 1904 A.B. 1907
—	Ja. Stevenson Denny	Jes.	M 1900 A.B. 1903. A.M. 1907
—	John Hub.	.... King's	M 1895 A.B. 1898. A.M.† 1902
—	Norman Edwyn	...... Em.	M 1908 A.B. 1911
—	Phil. Twells	.... Pet.	M 1898 A.B. 1901. A.M. 1905
—	Reg. Egbert	.... Down.	M 1910
—	Roger Cha.	.... Pem.	M 1907
—	Tho. Humphrey	...... Trin.	M 1912
—	Wilfrid	.... Joh.	M 1912
—	Will.	.... Pet.	M 1893 A.B. 1899. A.M. 1905
—	Will.	.... Pem.	M 1907 A.B., LL.B. 1910
—	Will. Burton	.... Joh.	M 1899 A.B. 1902. B.C. 1908 (2). M.B.
—	Will. Hen.	.... Pem.	M 1907 A.B. 1910 [1912
Marsham,	Art. Frederic	.... Trin.	M 1904 A.B. 1907. A.M. 1911
Marsland,	Syd. Hammond	...... Cla.	M 1910
Marson,	Art. Aylmer	.... Trin.	M 1909
Marston,	Cecil Gifford	.... Trin.	M 1908
—	Stewart Jasper	...... Pem.	M 1900 A.B. 1903. A.M. 1909
Martell,	Edw. Alf.	.... Joh.	M 1899 A.B. 1903. A.M. 1907
Marten,	Alf. Amberson Barrington	Trin.	M 1889 A.B. 1892. LL.B. 1893. A.M.,
			[LL.M. 1897. LL.D. 1903
—	Geo. Hen.	.... King's	M 1894 A.B. 1898. A.M. 1901
—	Hen. Humphrey	...... Cai.	M 1912
—	Rob. Humphrey	...... Cai.	L 1885 M.B., B.C. 1888. M.D. 1905
—	Rob. Humphrey	...... Cai.	M 1909 A.B. 1912
Martin,	Alf. Eugène	.... Down.	M 1893 A.B. 1896. M.B., B.C., A.M. 1900.
—	Baynard Steven	...... Jes.	M 1910 [M.D. 1909
—	Cha.	.... Chr.	M 1899 A.B. 1902
—	Cyril Fre.	.... Pem.	M 1905 A.B. 1908
—	Edw. Graeme	.... Trin. H.	M 1903 A.B. 1906
—	Edw. Walter	.... Pem.	M 1908
—	Edwin McGrath	...... Pem.	M 1896 A.B. 1899. A.M. 1903
—	Ern. Will. Lunn	...... Cla.	M 1908 A.B. 1911
—	Eustace Meredyth	... C. C.	M 1893 A.B. 1897. LL.M. 1903
—	Fra.	.... N. C.	M 1911
—	Fra. Hen.	.... Pem.	M 1907 A.B. 1910
—	Fredrick John	.... H. Sel.	M 1910
—	Geo. Alb.	.... Joh.	M 1898 A.B. 1901
—	Geo. Westcott	.... N. C.	M 1903 Down. A.B. 1906. A.M. 1910
—	Herb. Craven	.... Cla.	M 1896 A.B. 1901. A.M. 1904
—	Hor. Edm.	.... N. C.	M 1910
—	John	.... N. C.	M 1901 A.B. 1904. A.M. 1908
—	John Aston	.... Pem.	M 1906 A.B. 1909
—	John Baptist	.... N. C.	M 1908 A.B. 1911
—	John Bosworth	.... Trin.	M 1905 A.B. 1908
—	John Harding Baynes	Em.	M 1900 A.B. 1903. B.C. 1907. M.B. 1908
—	John Middleton	...... Pet.	M 1889 A.B. 1892. M.B., B.C. 1897. M.D.
—	Maur. Bonamy	..... King's	M 1909 [1904
—	Oscar Harry	.... Trin. H.	M 1901
—	Oswald Lunn	.... King's	M 1911
—	Percy Tho.	.... N. C.	M 1905 A.B. 1908
—	Rich. Clare	.... Cla.	M 1905 A.B., LL.B. 1908
—	Rob. Edm.	.... King's	M 1893 A.B. 1896. A.M. 1901
—	Rolfe Geo.	.... Chr.	M 1909 A.B. 1912
—	Sid. Todd	.... Sid.	M 1909 A.B. 1912

Martin,	Steph. Staffurth	King's	M 1912
—	Tho. Leslie	Trin.	M 1903 A.B. 1906
—	Tho. Lyttle	Em.	M 1912
—	Trice	Pet.	M 1904 A.B. 1907
—	Walt. Baird	Cai.	M 1902 A.B. 1905. LL.B. 1906
—	Will.	C. C.	M 1883 A.B. 1886. A.M. 1912
—	Will.	Down.	M 1889 A.B. 1892. LL.B. 1893. A.M., [LL.M. 1896. LL.D. 1902
—	Will. Art.	Chr.	M 1905 A.B. 1908
—	Will. Herb.	C. C.	M 1908
—	Will. Muir	Trin.	M 1904 A.B. 1907
—	Will. Neville	Qu.	M 1900 A.B. 1903
Martindale,	Rob. Gunson	C. C.	M 1907 A.B. 1910
Martineau,	Wilfrid	Trin. H.	M 1908 A.B. 1911
Martinet,	Marcel Henri	Trin.	M 1911
Martin-Jones, Cha. Martin			*See* Jones, C. M.
Martin Smith, Julian Hor.		Trin.	M 1906
Martin-Tomson, Will. John		Trin.	M 1907 A.B. 1910
Martius,	Hans Konrad Götz	N. C.	E 1910
Martyn,	Rendel Vivian	Pem.	M 1912
—	Ronald Flower	Pet.	M 1912
Martyn-Linnington, Adolphus } Littell		Pem.	M 1911
Marwitz,	Georg Eduard	Trin.	E 1910
Maryon Wilson, Augustus Geo. ...		Trin.	M 1900 A.B. 1904
—	Tho. Spencer	Trin. H.	M 1907
Marzetti,	Claude	Pem.	M 1908 A.B. 1911
—	Leon.	Pem.	M 1910
Marzials,	François Maur.	Pem.	M 1887 A.B. 1890. A.M. 1906
Masefield,	Will. Beech	Jes.	M 1904 A.B. 1908
Masham,	John	Sid.	M 1887 A.B. 1890. A.M. 1906
Masom,	Will. Fre.	N. C.	M 1888 Joh. A.B. 1891. A.M. 1902
Mason,	Art. Denis Clarkson	Trin. H.	M 1908 A.B. 1911
—	[1] Art. Ja. ....*Trin.		M 1868 A.B. 1872. A.M. 1875. B.D. 1887. [D.D. 1890. *Jes. 1896
—	Cecil Cha.	Trin. H.	M 1899 A.B. 1902. A.M. 1906
—	Edm. Will.	Joh.	M 1909 A.B. 1912
—	Frank Louis Lionel	King's	M 1907 A.B. 1910
—	Geo. Haworth	Em.	M 1903 A.B. 1906
—	Geo. Hen.	Trin. H.	M 1897 A.B. 1902
—	Ja. Herb.	Cai.	M 1906 A.B. 1910
—	John Wharton	Cai.	M 1910
—	Kenneth Ralph	Jes.	M 1909
—	Louis	Pem.	M 1895 A.B. 1898. A.M. 1904
—	Mark Theakston	Em.	M 1898 A.B. 1901
—	Mich. Geo.	N. C.	M 1892 A.B. 1895. A.M. 1907
—	Noel	Sid.	M 1908 A.B. 1911
—	Randall Stewart	Jes.	M 1912 [Mason, R. S., A.M. 1903
—	Swann	N. C.	L 1894 Cath. Rich. S., A.B. 1897. Swan-
Masser,	Bern. Rich.	Cla.	M 1901 A.B., LL.B. 1904
—	Cha. Sylvester	Cla.	M 1910
Massey,	Bern. Wilfrid Arbuthnot	King's	M 1903 A.B. 1906
—	Edwyn Leslie	Pet.	M 1900 A.B. 1903
—	John Hamon	Jes.	M 1912
Masson,	Keith	King's	M 1909 A.B. 1912
Master,	Dudley Cyril	Cai.	M 1899 A.B. 1902
—	Legh Chichele Hoskins	Trin.	M 1909 A.B. 1912
Masters,	Percival Geo.	H. Sel.	M 1904 A.B. 1908
Masterton,	Hen. Will.	Trin.	M 1907 A.B. 1910

[1] **Master of Pembroke College, 1903.**

Masud,	Sheikh Zaman	Down.	M 1910
Mather,	Alf. Lushington	Trin.	M 1904 A.B. 1907
—	Aubrey	Trin.	M 1904
—	Basil	Pem.	M 1895 A.B. 1898. A.M. 1902
—	Edm. Lawrence	Pem.	M 1909
—	Ern. Gerald	Trin.	M 1901
—	Geo. Rupert	Pem.	M 1908
—	Herb.	Trin.	M 1893 A.B. 1896. A.M. 1902
—	Loris Emerson	Trin.	M 1905
—	Tho. Ja. Elton	Cla.	M 1905 A.B. 1908
Matheson,	Cha. Fre.	Cai.	M 1910
—	Ian Mackenzie	Trin. H.	M 1912
—	John Lee	Trin.	M 1904 A.B., LL.B. 1907
—	Norman Macdonald	Trin.	M 1908 A.B. 1911
—	Sam. Pritchard		*LL.D.* 1908
Mathew,	Felton Art. Hamilton	Trin.	M 1911
Mathews,	Art. Guest	Pem.	M 1892 A.B. 1895. A.M. 1905
—	Cha. Myles	King's	M 1897 A.B. 1900. LL.B. 1903
—	John Kenneth	Cla.	M 1903
—	Paul	King's	M 1910
Mathias,	Cha. Dav.	Trin.	M 1895 A.B. 1898. M.B., B.C., A.M. 1905
—	Hen. Hugh	King's	M 1906 A.B. 1909
Mathieson,	Will.	Sid.	M 1901 A.B. 1905
Matsumoto,	Genichiro	Jes.	M 1908
Matterson,	Rob. Henderson	Sid.	M 1906 A.B. 1909
Matthaei,	Ernst Roger	Trin. H.	M 1902 A.B. 1905
Matthai,	Geo.	Em.	M 1911
Matthew,	Austin Frederic	Em.	M 1901 A.B. 1904. A.M. 1908
Matthews,	Art.	Jes.	M 1905 A.B. 1908. A.M. 1912
—	Art. Silvester	Mag.	M 1906 A.B. 1909
—	Bern.	Pem.	M 1904 A.B. 1907. A.M. 1911
—	Cecil	Pem.	M 1904 A.B. 1907
—	Cha. Hen. Selfe	King's	M 1893 A.B. 1896. A.M. 1902
—	Douglas Gilb.	N. C.	M 1908 A.B. 1911
—	Edgar Cha.	Trin.	M 1911
—	Eric Walt.	King's	M 1909 A.B. 1912
—	John Burnett	Cla.	M 1908 A.B. 1911
—	John Cha.	Joh.	M 1894 A.B. 1897. B.C. 1900. M.B. 1909
—	John Cuthbert	Down.	M 1896 A.B. 1899. M.B., B.C. 1904
—	Jos. Keith	Down.	M 1905 A.B. 1908
—	Marmaduke Humphrey	Pem.	M 1909
—	Noël Anwyl	H. Sel.	M 1911
—	Tho. Humphrey	Em.	M 1899 A.B. 1902. A.M. 1906
—	Trevor Jocelyn	Cla.	M 1901 A.B. 1904. A.M. 1908
—	Will. Dav. Woodside	Pem.	M 1904
Matthey,	Geo. Augustus	Pem.	M 1906
Mattiesen,	Emil	N. C.	M 1904
Mattingly,	Harold	*Cai.	M 1903 A.B. 1906. A.M. 1910
Mattock,	Fra. Clifford	N. C.	M 1912
Mattoon,	Art. Martyn	N. C.	M 1903
Maude,	Gerald Will. Urquhart	H. Sel.	M 1902 A.B. 1905
Maude-Roxby,	Ja. Howard Trevelyan Maude		*See* Roxby, J. H. T. M.
Maufe,	Herb. Brantwood ...		*See* Muff, H. B.
Maule,	Geoffrey Lamb	Chr.	M 1910
—	Rob.	Chr.	M 1904 A.B. 1907. A.M. 1911
—	Will. Harry Fowke	Mag.	M 1908 A.B. 1911
Maulik,	Samarendra	N. C.	L 1912
Maundrell,	Ern. Barton	Jes.	M 1899 A.B. 1902
—	Will. Herb.	C. C.	M 1895 A.B. 1898. A.M. 1904
Maung,	Maung Thein	Down.	M 1910 A.B., LL.B. 1912
—	Nyun	Cath.	M 1911

Maunsell,	Art. Edm. Lloyd ...	Trin.	M 1899 A.B. 1902. LL.B. 1903
—	Fre. Wyndham	Cai.	M 1908 A.B. 1911
—	Syd. Augustus Wray	Trin.	M 1909
Mavor,	Ivan	Sid.	M 1906 A.B. 1909
—	Ja. Watt	Trin.	M 1902 A.B. 1905
Maw,	Fra. Reg.	Pem.	M 1894 A.B. 1897. A.M. 1901
—	Geo. Oliver	Pem.	M 1906 A.B. 1909
Mawdesley,	John Leyland	C. C.	M 1911
Mawe,	Eric Spanton	King's	M 1908 A.B. 1911
—	Montague Denoon ...	King's	M 1905 A.B. 1908
Mawer,	Allen ....*Cai.		M 1901 A.B. 1904. A.M. 1908
Mawhood,	Reg. Hawksworth ...	Trin.	M 1902 A.B. 1905. M.B., B.C. 1911
Maxwell,	Cha. Herb.	Chr.	M 1904 A.B. 1907. A.M. 1911
—	Ian Constable	Trin.	M 1910
—	Malcolm Laurie	Pem.	M 1906 A.B. 1909
—	Malcolm Theodore ...	Trin.	M 1907 A.B. 1910
—	Noël	Cai.	M 1909 A.B. 1912
—	Ronald Constable ...	Trin.	M 1910
—	Stanley	Joh.	M 1894 A.B. 1897. LL.B. 1898. A.M. 1901
—	Will. Fra. John	Trin.	M 1905 A.B. 1908
Maxwell-Lefroy,	Harold	King's	M 1895 A.B. 1898. A.M. 1902
May,	Alb. John	Sid.	M 1902 A.B. 1905. B.C. 1908. M.B. 1911
—	Cedric Armyn Cecil	H. Sel.	M 1911
—	Clarence Ja.	Pet.	M 1906 A.B. 1909
—	Cyril Phil.	Chr.	M 1909
—	Edw. Geoffrey	Cai.	M 1889 A.B. 1892. A.M. 1912
—	Fra. Hawtrey Morgan	Trin.	M 1898 A.B. 1901. A.M. 1905
—	Gerald Henderson ...	Trin.	M 1907 A.B. 1911
—	Herb. Rich. Dudfield	Joh.	M 1897 A.B. 1900. LL.B. 1901. A.M. 1904
—	Otto	Joh.	M 1897 A.B. 1900. A.M. 1904. M.B., B.C.
—	Percy Rob.	Pem.	M 1902 A.B. 1905 [1907. M.D. 1910
—	Reg. Carr	Qu.	M 1901 A.B. 1906
—	Valentine Delabère ...	Trin.	M 1902 A.B. 1905
Mayall,	Cha. Augustine	C. C.	M 1893 A.B. 1896. A.M. 1906
—	John Bardsley	Sid.	M 1910
—	Reg.	C. C.	M 1891 A.B. 1894. A.M. 1905
—	Rob. Cecil	Sid.	M 1912
—	Rob. Percival Walkden	Sid.	M 1895 A.B. 1900. A.M. 1908
Maybrey,	Herb. John	Chr.	M 1912
Maybury,	Cha. Garde	Trin.	M 1912
Mayer,	Frank Chazal	Chr.	M 1911
—	Gerald Max	Pem.	M 1911
—	Norman Edw.	Chr.	E 1908 A.B., LL.B. 1911
—	Percy Geo.	Trin.	M 1912
Mayes,	Reg. Metcalf	Sid.	M 1905 A.B. 1908. A.M. 1912
Mayhew,	Art. Farr	Cai.	M 1902 A.B. 1906. A.M. 1909
—	Evelyn Hill	Em.	M 1898 A.B. 1901. M.B., B.C., A.M. 1906
Mayhewe,	Keith Guy	Trin.	M 1903 A.B. 1906. A.M. 1910
Maynard,	Alf. Clarkson Martin	N. C.	M 1903 Qu. A.B. 1906. A.M. 1910
—	Alf. Fre.	Em.	M 1912
—	Cha. Bowman	Pet.	M 1910
—	Herb. Art. Vernon ...	Cai.	M 1911
—	Herb. Athelstan	Em.	M 1911
Mayne,	Cyril Fre.	Cai.	M 1907 A.B. 1910
—	Walt. Nath.	Jes.	M 1885 A.B. 1889. A.M. 1911
—	Will. Cyril	Trin.	M 1896 A.B. 1899. A.M. 1904
Mayo,	Herb. Reg.	Cai.	M 1893 A.B. 1897. M.B., B.C. 1902
—	Herb. Theodore	Trin.	M 1908 A.B. 1911
—	Hub. Giles	Qu.	M 1899 A.B. 1902
—	John Fre.	Qu.	M 1898 A.B. 1901. A.M. 1905
—	Rob. Hobart	Mag.	M 1909 A.B. 1912

Mayo	Will. Cha.	Cath.	M 1905 A.B. 1908
Mayor,	Fred	Em.	M 1908 A.B. 1911
—	Hamlet Hor.	Joh.	M 1888 A.B. 1893. A.M. 1903
May-Oung		N. C.	M 1904 Down. A.B., LL.B. 1906. A.M.†
Mead,	Art. Will.	Trin.	M 1912 [1910
—	Edgar Walt.	Pem.	M 1906 A.B. 1909
—	Godfrey Cha. Fre. ...	Pem.	M 1910
Meade,	Lionel Grant	H. Sel.	M 1902 A.B. 1908
—	Syd.	H. Sel.	M 1895 A.B. 1898. A.M. 1902
Meadowcroft,	Lancelot Vernon ...	Trin.	M 1904 A.B. 1907
Meakin,	Bern.	Trin.	M 1903 A.B. 1906
—	Cyril Hugh	Trin.	M 1901
—	Fre. Guy	Jes.	M 1903 A.B. 1907
—	Gerald	Trin.	M 1896 A.B. 1899. A.M. 1905
—	Leslie	Trin.	M 1901 A.B. 1904. B.C., A.M. 1910
—	Walt.	Trin.	M 1895 A.B., LL.B. 1898. A.M., LL.M.
Mears,	Rob. Peel	Trin.	M 1903 A.B. 1906 [1907
Medcalf,	Dav. Hen.	Pem.	M 1887 A.B. 1890. A.M. 1901
—	Herb.	Trin.	M 1905 A.B. 1908
Medley,	Rob. Percival	Cai.	M 1900 A.B. 1903. A.M. 1907
Medrington,	Art. Cha. Percy	Qu.	M 1909 A.B. 1912
Medwin,	Herb.	Pem.	M 1906 A.B., LL.B. 1909
Mee,	John Theodore Martin	Chr.	M 1908 A.B. 1911
Meek,	Jos.	Trin.	M 1906 A.B. 1909
Meeres,	Hen. Will. Hugh ...	Jes.	M 1899 A.B. 1902
Meers,	Rupert Hart	Pem.	M 1898 A.B. 1901. A.M. 1905
Mees,	Gustavus Eric	Cath.	M 1903 A.B. 1906. A.M.† 1910
Megarry,	Rob. Lindsay	Trin. H.	M 1898 A.B., LL.B. 1902
Meggeson,	Rich. Ronald Hornsey	Cai.	M 1906 A.B. 1909
Megson,	Manfred	Sid.	M 1901 A.B. 1904 [A.M.† 1904
Mehra,	Lal Chand	N. C.	M 1897 Down. A.B. 1900. LL.B. 1901.
--	Nehal Chand	Down.	L 1902 A.B. 1904. LL.B. 1905
Mehta,	Bhala Nath	Down.	M 1902
—	Gaupatlal Dayashankar	N. C.	M 1906 Down. A.B. 1909
--	Jagan Nath	Chr.	L 1909 A.B. 1910
—	Nanalal Chamanlal	N. C.	M 1909 A.B. 1912
—	Vasudeo Batukram ...	N. C.	M 1899 Pet. A.B. 1902
Mehtá,	Vinayak Nandshankar	King's	M 1904
Meier,	Fre. Alf.	Trin.	M 1907 A.B. 1910
Meimarachi,	Anth.	Chr.	M 1902 A.B. 1905
Meister,	Gerald Carl Quintus	King's	M 1895 A.B. 1898. A.M. 1902
—	Heinrich Georg Hans Alb.	N. C.	M 1911
Meixner,	Fre.	N. C.	M 1910
Meldrum,	Roy	Joh.	M 1903 A.B. 1906
Melhuish,	Frank	H. Sel.	M 1908 A.B. 1911
—	Tho. Walt.	Pem.	M 1907 A.B. 1910
Mellanby,	Edw. ..:..................	Em.	M 1902 A.B. 1905. M.B., A.M. 1910
—	John	Em.	M 1896 A.B. 1899. A.M. 1903. M.D. 1907
Meller,	Rob. Will.	Trin.	M 1905 A.B. 1908
—	Sherard Alf.	Trin.	M 1904 A.B. 1907
Mellersh,	Eric Leslie	H. Sel.	M 1909 A.B. 1912
Melles,	Gordon Frank	Trin. H.	M 1903
Mellin,	Eric Lawrence	Cla.	L 1907
—	Gustave Lassen	Cla.	M 1902
Melling,	John Geo.	H. Sel.	M 1898 A.B. 1901. A.M. 1905
—	John Stanley	Chr.	M 1909
—	Will. Hill	Chr.	M 1906 A.B. 1910
Mellis,	Geo. Duncan	Cla.	M 1907 A.B. 1910
Melliss,	Hugh John	Trin.	M 1898 A.B. 1901
Mellor,	Alf. Shaw	King's	M 1894 A.B. 1897. M.B., B.C., A.M. 1901
—	Arnold	Trin. H.	M 1908 A.B. 1911. LL.B. 1912

Mellor,	Arnold Kilver	Trin.	M 1898 A.B. 1901
—	Geoffrey	Trin.	M 1910
—	Hen.	Qu.	M 1898 A.B. 1901. A.M. 1905
—	Ja. Edgar	Jes.	M 1903 A.B. 1906. A.M. 1910
—	John Sam.	C. C.	M 1897 A.B. 1902
—	Phil. Hor. Leyland	Pem.	M 1906 A.B. 1909
—	Phil. Seddon	Pem.	M 1901 A.B. 1904
—	Walt. Sam.	Qu.	M 1906 A.B. 1909
Mellows,	Frank	N. C.	M 1899 Chr. A.B. 1902. A.M. 1906
Melvill,	Ivo Eedes	Trin. H.	M 1903 A.B., LL.B. 1907. A.M.† 1910
—	Lionel Vintcent	Cai.	M 1906 A.B. 1909
Melville,	Hugh Colquhoun ...	Trin.	M 1905 A.B. 1909
Melville-Smith,	Hen. MacLane ...	Trin.	M 1912
Mencke,	Hans Wilhelm Bern-	N. C.	E 1907
	hard August		
Menneer,	Rich. Wellington ...	Down.	M 1909
Mennell,	Ja. Beaver	Pem.	M 1899 A.B. 1902. A.M. 1906. B.C. 1908.
Menon,	Idichanadath Ramen	N. C.	M 1911 [M.B. 1908 (2). M.D. 1910
—	Konkoth Ramunni ...	Chr.	M 1893 A.B. 1896. A.M.† 1912
—	Konkoth Sankara ...	Chr.	M 1912
Menzies,	Rob. Cha.	Cla.	M 1905
—	Victor Malcolm Graham	Trin. H.	M 1912
Mercer,	Donald	Pem.	M 1889 A.B. 1892. A.M. 1910
—	Geoffrey Hamish ...	H. Sel.	M 1910
—	Ja. ....*Trin.		M 1903 A.B. 1907. A.M. 1910
—	John Launcelot Capel	King's	M 1909 A.B. 1912
—	John Will.	Cai.	M 1889 A.B. 1892. A.M. 1903
—	Will.	N. C.	L 1904 Chr. A.B. 1906. A.M. 1910
Merchant,	John Alb. Edw.	H. Sel.	M 1902 A.B. 1908
Mere,	Colin Leigh	Chr.	M 1907 A.B. 1910
Meredith,	Art. Radclyffe	Qu.	M 1900 A.B. 1903
—	Hugh Owen ....*King's		M 1897 A.B. 1901. A.M. 1904
Merivale,	Bern.	Joh.	M 1900 A.B., LL.B. 1903
Merrick,	Frank Geo.	N. C.	M 1898 Trin. H. A.B. 1901. A.M. 1906
Merriman,	Art. Douglas	Down.	M 1912
—	Ern. Steward	C. C.	M 1905 A.B. 1908. A.M. 1912
—	Gordon	Trin. H.	M 1903
—	Mark Marshall	Trin. H.	M 1895 A.B. 1898. A.M. 1903
—	Rich. Will.	Trin.	M 1902 A.B. 1905. A.M. 1911
Merrin,	John	Chr.	M 1900 A.B. 1903. A.M. 1907
Merritt,	Edm. Douglas	Em.	M 1898 A.B. 1901. A.M. 1905
Merryweather,	Cha. Walt.	Trin.	M 1900 A.B. 1903. A.M. 1907
Merson,	Ronald Kelburne ...	Em.	M 1906 A.B. 1910
Merton,	Gerald		*See* Schmiechen, Gerald
—	Wilfred		*See* Schmiechen, Wilfred
Meryon,	Lewis Kennard	Pem.	M 1899 A.B. 1902
Merz,	Ern. Leisler	King's	M 1900 A.B., LL.B. 1904
Messer,	Cha. McIlvaine	Em.	M 1893 A.B. 1896. A.M. 1906
Messiter,	Cyril Cassan	Cai.	M 1902 A.B. 1906
Metcalf,	Fra. Will. Rucker ...	Em.	M 1894 A.B. 1897. A.M. 1901
Metcalfe,	Chris. Hen. Frank ...	Pem.	M 1906 A.B. 1909
—	Edw. Parr	Em.	M 1907
—	Frederic Will.	Sid.	M 1905 A.B. 1908
—	Geo. Chris.	Cai.	M 1906 A.B. 1911
—	Percy Kynaston	Pem.	M 1899 A.B. 1902. A.M. 1906
—	Sid.	N. C.	M 1904 A.B. 1907. A.M. 1911
—	Theoph. Ja.	Jes.	M 1909
Metcalfe-Gibson,	Anth.	Pem.	M 1907 A.B. 1910
—	Art. Edw.	Cai.	M 1906 A.B. 1909
—	Rupert Anth.	Em.	M 1905 A.B. 1909
Metcalfe-Walton,	John Brian	H. Sel.	M 1911

Methuen,	Art. Pemberton	......	Trin.	M 1903 A.B. 1907
Methven,	Colin Malcolm	......	Mag.	M 1908
—	Ja. Norman	....	Mag.	M 1905 A.B. 1908
—	Malcolm Dav.	....	Cai.	M 1909 A.B. 1912
Meyendorff,	Geo.	....	Chr.	L 1907
Meyer,	Geo. Meyer	....	Em.	M 1904 A.B. 1907
—	Harold Gustave	......	Trin.	M 1902 A.B. 1905. LL.B. 1906. A.M. 1909
—	Rich.	....	Joh.	L 1904
Meyrick,	Evan Eckhard	......	Trin.	M 1912
Meyricke,	Art. Llewelyn	....	Pem.	M 1898 A.B. 1901. A.M. 1905
Meysey-Thompson,	Algar de Clifford Cha.	}	Trin.	M 1905 A.B. 1908
Meysey Thompson,	Hub. Cha.	...	Trin.	M 1902 A.B. 1905
Michaelides,	Constantine Cleanthes		King's	M 1901 A.B. 1905. post Graham, Constantine
Michaelson,	Sam. Morris Percy	...	King's	M 1901 [stantine
Micheli,	Gaston Hor. Louis	...	Cla.	M 1912
Michell,	Alf. Hen.	....	Sid.	M 1901 A.B. 1904
—	Art. Matth. Lee	......	C. C.	M 1909
—	Geo. Eric	....	Em.	M 1904
—	Noel Burgess	....	Trin.	M 1905 A.B. 1908
Michie,	John Lundie	....	Trin.	M 1904 A.B. 1907. A.M.† 1911
Micklethwait,	Geo. Whitley	......	Trin.	M 1891 A.B. 1896. A.M. 1900. B.C. 1903.
Middlebrook,	Syd.	....	Cath.	M 1911 [M.D. 1907
Middleditch,	Bern.	....	Jes.	M 1891 A.B. 1894. A.M. 1909
Middlemas,	Percy	....	Pem.	M 1912
Middleton,	Chris. Basil	....	Joh.	M 1903 A.B. 1906
—	Leon.	....	Pem.	M 1903 A.B. 1906
—	Leon. Eadon	....	Qu.	M 1905 A.B. 1908
—	Rob. Harris	....	Qu.	M 1909
—	Rupert Cha. Godfrey		Trin.	M 1909 LL.B. 1912
—	¹ Tho. Hudson	....		A.M. 1902
Midgley,	Edwin Craven	....	Trin.	M 1900 A.B. 1903
—	Harold Edw.	....	Qu.	M 1899 A.B. 1902. A.M. 1906
—	Will. Alex. Lewis	...	Chr.	M 1905 A.B. 1909
Milburn,	Anth.	....	Trin.	L 1911
—	Archib. Will.	....	Trin.	M 1905 A.B. 1910
—	Booker	....	Jes.	M 1907
—	Cha. Stamp	....	Chr.	M 1897 A.B. 1900. A.M. 1904
—	John Davison	....	Trin.	M 1904 A.B. 1908. A.M. 1911
—	Leon. John	....	Trin.	M 1902
—	Rich. Gerald	....	Trin.	M 1912
—	Rob.	....	Cla.	M 1903 A.B. 1906
—	Will. Hewlins	....	Jes.	M 1902
—	Will. Hudson	....	Em.	M 1910
Miles,	Amos Bertram	......	Qu.	M 1901 A.B. 1904
—	Archie Rich. Will.	...	Mag.	M 1907 A.B. 1911
—	Bevis Lipscomb	......	Pem.	M 1903 A.B. 1906
—	Cyril Vernor	....	Pem.	M 1911
—	Harley	....	N. C.	M 1909
—	Stanley Howard	......	Cla.	M 1908 A.B. 1911
—	Will. Hen.	....	Pem.	M 1906 A.B. 1909
Miley,	Miles	....	Trin.	M 1908 A.B. 1911
Millar,	Art. Liberty	....	Cla.	M 1906 A.B. 1910
—	Gilb. Hen.	....	Pem.	M 1903 A.B. 1906
Millard,	Alan Carthew	....	H. Sel.	M 1904 A.B. 1907
—	Cha. Stuart	....	Em.	M 1911
Miller,	Alex. Grant Schaw		Pet.	M 1909
—	Art. Congreve	....	H. Sel.	M 1895 A.B. 1898. A.M. 1903
—	Art. Hallowes	....	Trin.	M 1898 A.B. 1901. B.C., A.M. 1906. M.B.
—	Austin Timæus	......	Cai.	M 1906 A.B. 1910 [1907. M.D. 1910

¹ Professor of Agriculture, 1902.

Miller,	Cecil John Whitworth	Trin.	M 1909 A.B. 1912
—	Cha Alex. Morell ...	Cai.	M 1912
—	Cha. Hewitt	Trin.	M 1894 A.B. 1897. B.C., A.M. 1901. M.D.
—	Cha. Phil.	Jes.	M 1909 A.B. 1912 [1906
—	Donald Campbell ...	Down.	M 1912
—	Douglas Owen d'Elboux	Trin. H.	M 1910
—	Edw. John	N. C.	M 1895 A.B. 1898. A.M. 1910
—	Emanuel	Joh.	M 1911
—	Ern. Cyril	Trin.	M 1897 A.B. 1901
—	Geo. Handscomb ...	H. Sel.	M 1910
—	Hen. Hugh Lingwood	Pem.	M 1901 A.B. 1904
—	Hugh Fra. Ridley ...	Joh.	M 1909 A.B. 1912
—	Jack Humphry	Trin. H.	M 1902
—	Leon. Victor	N. C.	M 1912
—	Norman	Qu.	M 1910
—	Paul Tennant	Pem.	M 1903
—	Ralph Will. Richardson	Trin.	M 1910
—	Rob. Molineux	Cla.	M 1896 A.B. 1900, R. Molyneux. M.B.
—	Roland	Trin.	M 1903 [1912
—	Roland Brice	Trin.	M 1905 A.B. 1908
—	Will. Murdoch	Pem.	M 1912
Miller-Hallett, Geo.		Trin.	M 1902 A.B. 1905
Miller-Williams, Eustace Ja.		N. C.	M 1907 Down. A.B. 1910. LL.B. 1911
Milligan,	Derrick Warden	Cai.	M 1912
—	Rob. Alex.	Cai.	M 1906
—	Will.	Pem.	M 1910
Milligen,	Alb. McCracken	Trin.	M 1901 A.B. 1905. A.M. 1909
—	Edgar John	Trin.	M 1904
Milliken,	Herb. Ern.	Pem.	M 1907 A.B. 1910
Millington,	John Price	Chr.	M 1900 A.B. 1902. A.M. 1906
Million,	Alf. Baker	Em.	M 1909 A.B. 1912
Millner,	Hen. Lloyd	Chr.	M 1897 A.B. 1900. A.M. 1904
Mills,	Art. Edw.	Pem.	M 1908 A.B. 1911
—	Cha. Fre.	C. C.	M 1892 A.B. 1901
—	Cha. Gordon	Cla.	M 1912
—	Eric	C. C.	M 1910
—	Ern. Ja.	Joh.	M 1904 A.B. 1907. A.M. 1912
—	Fra. Rich.	Trin.	M 1898 A.B., LL.B. 1901. A.M. 1905
—	Frank Symons	C. C.	M 1902
—	Gerald Rusgrove	Cai.	M 1895 A.B. 1898. A.M. 1902
—	Hen. Forster	Trin. H.	M 1904
—	Herb.	Cath.	M 1911
—	Ja. Webb	Cla.	M 1908 A.B. 1911
—	Jos. Travis	N. C.	M 1898 A.B. 1902. A.M. 1908
—	Kenneth Laurence ...	Cai.	M 1903
—	Rich. Sawbridge	C. C.	M 1900 A.B. 1903. A.M. 1907
—	Tho. Gundry	Pem.	M 1904
—	Tom Rethman	Trin.	M 1906
—	Will. Eustace	King's	M 1900 A.B. 1903. A.M. 1907
Millward,	Geoffrey Duncan ...	Down.	M 1906 A.B. 1909
—	Geo. Alf.	Qu.	M 1902 A.B. 1905. A.M. 1910
Millyard,	Tho.	Joh.	M 1912
Miln,	Crichton Jordan	Pem.	M 1906
Milne,	Alan Alex.	Trin.	M 1900 A.B. 1903
—	Douglas Duart Williamson	Cla.	M 1906
—	Geo.	Joh.	M 1907 A.B. 1910
—	Herb. John Mansfield	Cai.	M 1909 A.B. 1912
—	Ja. Barclay	Trin. H.	M 1904
—	Ja. Sinclair	Trin.	M 1911
—	Rob. Moir	Jes.	M 1894 A.B. 1897. A.M. 1902
—	Will. Proctor	Cla.	M 1903 A.B. 1906. A.M. 1910

Milne Home,	Archib. Cha.	Pem.	M 1901 A.B. 1904
—	Cha. Alex.	King's	M 1909 A.B., LL.B. 1912
Milner,	Dermod Ross	Cath.	M 1909 A.B. 1912
—	Geoffrey	King's	M 1912
—	Geo. Rob.	Em.	M 1909 A.B. 1912
—	Hen. Brewer	Trin.	M 1912
—	Hugh Cantis	C. C.	M 1903 A.B. 1906
—	Paul Ross	Pet.	M 1911
—	(*Viscount*)		LL.D. 1907
—	Will. Alf.	Trin.	M 1906
Milner-White,	Eric	King's	M 1903 A.B. 1907. A.M. 1911
—	Rudolph	Pem.	M 1905 A.B. 1908
Milnes,	John Harrison	Joh.	M 1898 A.B. 1901
—	Rob. Offley Ashburton	Trin.	M 1875 A.B. 1880. A.M. 1885 (*Earl of*
Milne-Thomson,	Louis Melville ...	C. C.	M 1910 [*Crewe*). LL.D. 1911
Milroy,	Geo. Will. Winck- ⎱ worth Wallace ⎰	Em.	M 1906 A.B. 1909
Milsom,	Cecil Fra.	Trin.	M 1901
—	Edwin Theodore	C. C.	M 1898 A.B. 1901. A.M. 1905
—	Ern.	Cai.	M 1904 A.B. 1907
—	Harry Lincoln	Trin.	M 1907 A.B. 1911
—	Sid.	H. Sel.	M 1905
Milton,	Archib. Rob. Bewicke	Mag.	M 1902 A.B. 1905. A.M.† 1910
—	Harold Aubrey	Trin. H.	M 1900 A.B. 1903
Milward,	Fra. Norman	H. Sel.	M 1911
Minchin,	Geo. Rob. Neville ...	Chr.	M 1907 A.B. 1910
Mines,	Geo. Ralph ....*Sid.		M 1904 A.B. 1907. A.M. 1911
Minnitt,	Rob. Ja.	Trin.	M 1908
Minson,	Herb.	Chr.	M 1905 A.B. 1908
Minto,	(*Earl of*) Gilb. John ⎱ Murray Kynynmond Elliot⎰		LL.D. 1911
Minton,	Hor. Donald Leolin	Jes.	M 1911
Minton-Senhouse,	Bern. Darby ...	Sid.	M 1906 A.B. 1909
Mir,	Hasan Ali	Pet.	M 1901
—	Shaik Mohomed	Chr.	M 1908 A.B. 1911
Mirza,	Ali Akbar Husein Khan	Joh.	M 1901 A. A. Hussein K. A.B. 1903
Miskin,	Geoffrey	Cai.	M 1908
—	Stanley Croft	Em.	M 1909 A.B. 1912
Misquith,	Oscar Gerald	Chr.	M 1911
Misra,	Harkaran Nath	Cai.	M 1911
—	Jaikaran Nath	Trin.	M 1911
Mitchell,	Alan Alex. McCaskyll	Pet.	M 1901 A.B. 1904
—	Alec Lea	Cai.	M 1902 A.B. 1905
—	Alex. Cha. Oswald ...	Jes.	M 1905
—	Alf. Gordon	Sid.	M 1904 A.B. 1907
—	Alf. Will. Coutts ...	Cai.	M 1909 A.B. 1912
—	And.	Pem.	M 1905 A.B. 1908
—	Bertram Everett	Joh.	M 1899 A.B. 1902. A.M. 1906
—	Cha. Wand	Em.	M 1902 A.B. 1904. A.M. 1912
—	Fre. MacLellan	Cla.	M 1910
—	Geo. Douglas	Trin. H.	M 1906
—	Godfrey Will.	Cla.	M 1903 A.B. 1907
—	Hen.	N. C.	M 1891 Em. A.B. 1895. A.M. 1902
—	John Cory	H. Sel.	M 1911
—	John Roderick	Cla.	M 1912
—	John Stewart	Joh.	M 1902
—	Percy Rob.	Trin.	M 1895 A.B. 1898. A.M. 1902
—	Steph.	Jes.	M 1903
—	Walt.	Trin.	M 1895 A.B. 1907. A.M. 1910
—	Wilfred John	Trin.	M 1900 A.B. 1904
—	Will.	N. C.	M 1900 Cath. A.B. 1903. *Chr. A.M. 1907

Mitchell,	Will. Edm. White ...	Trin.	M 1901
Mitchell-Carruthers,	Alex. Douglas	Trin.	M 1901
Mitchelson,	Ja. Kendall	Jes.	M 1907 A.B. 1910
Mitchison,	Alan	Sid.	M 1910
Mitford,	Cuthbert Will.	Jes.	M 1904 A.B. 1907
Mitra,	Nagendra	N. C.	M 1894 A.B. 1897. A.M.† 1901
Mitsuchi,	Chuzo	N. C.	M 1902
Mittell,	Hen. Hastings	Mag.	M 1904 A.B. 1907
Mitton,	Launcelot Edgar Dury	Pem.	M 1899 A.B. 1902. A.M. 1906
Mittra,	Raj Narain	N. C.	M 1872 Cath. LL.B. 1876. LL.M.† 1905
Moberly,	Art. Hamilton	King's	M 1903 A.B. 1906. A.M. 1910
Mody,	Naoroz Hormusji Naoroji	Trin. H.	M 1895 A.B. 1898. A.M. 1902
Moeran,	Will. Graham	Em.	M 1908 A.B. 1911
Moffatt,	Cecil Harold	Trin. H.	L 1902
—	Chris. Will. Paget ...	Cla.	M 1897 A.B. 1900. M.B., B.C. 1905
Moffitt,	Ja. Prior	Jes.	M 1911
Mogg,	Alb. Oliver Dean ...	Cai.	M 1909
—	John Leslie Heaven	Trin.	M 1897 A.B. 1900. A.M. 1904
Mogridge,	Hen. Theodore	Joh.	M 1910
Mohan,	Rai Radha	N. C.	M 1905 Down. A.B. 1909
Mohiuddin,	Ghulam	Down.	M 1907 A.B., LL.B. 1910
Moir,	Reg.	Cai.	M 1911
Mojsisovics,	Edm. (Edler von Mojsvár)		*Sc.D.* 1904
Moline,	Rob. Will. Haines ...	Em.	M 1909 A.B. 1912
Moller,	Nils Hen.	Cai.	M 1911
Mollison,	Will. Mayhew	King's	M 1897 A.B. 1900. B.C. 1904. A.M. 1905.
Molony,	And. Chartres Brew	Sid.	M 1911 [M.C. 1906
—	Art. Williams	Pem.	M 1912
—	Brian Cha.	Trin.	M 1911
—	Herb. Ja.	Pem.	M 1884 A.B. 1887. A.M., D.D. 1908
—	Ja. Alex.	Sid.	M 1909 A.B. 1912
Molson,	Harold Elsdale	Pem.	M 1911
—	John Elsdale	Em.	M 1882 M.B., B.C. 1891. M.D. 1905
Molteno,	Hen. Anderson	Pem.	M 1898 A.B. 1901
Molyneux,	John Howard	Cath.	M 1897 A.B. 1900. LL.B. 1908
Momber,	Alb. Reg. Theodore	Mag.	M 1910
—	Rob. Mary Steph. Theodor	Trin.	M 1903 A.B. 1906. A.M. 1910
Monakhoff,	Dimitri	Pem.	M 1906 Monahov, D. A.B. 1909
Monck-Mason,	Geo. Evelyn Art. Cheyne	Joh.	E 1908
Monckton,	Edw. Phil.	Trin.	M 1859 A.B. 1864. A.M. 1905
—	Fre. Hardy	Down.	M 1911
—	Ja. Fre. Edw.	Cai.	M 1912
—	Oliver Paul	King's	M 1898 A.B. 1901. A.M.† 1909
—	Tho. Anth.	Trin.	M 1905 A.B. 1908. A.M. 1912
Moncrieff,	Alan	Chr.	M 1912
—	Duncan Campbell ...	Trin.	M 1909 A.B. 1912
Mond,	Fra. Leopold	King's	M 1912
Money,	Archib.	N. C.	M 1901 A.B. 1907
—	Dav. Washbourne ...	Qu.	M 1898 A.B. 1901. A.M. 1905
—	Roger Noel	Cla.	M 1910
Mongia,	Gurmukh Singh	N. C.	M 1911
Monks,	Fre. Remund	Pem.	M 1903
—	Gilb.	Jes.	M 1908
Monro,	Grosvenor Herb. Loftus	Qu.	M 1901
—	Harold Edw.	Cai.	M 1898 A.B. 1901
—	Kenneth Neal	King's	M 1897 A.B. 1900. A.M. 1910
—	Rob. Godfrey	Trin.	M 1895 A.B. 1898. A.M. 1904
Monson,	Claude Sach	Mag.	M 1902

Monson,	(*Sir*) Edm. John			*LL.D.* 1905
Montagnon,	Art.	Joh.	M 1912	
Montagu,	Alb. Hen.	Jes.	M 1903 A.B. 1906	
—	Edwin Sam.	Trin.	M 1898 A.B. 1902. A.M. 1905	
—	Geo. Hen. Simon ...	C. C.	M 1911	
—	Ja. Fountayne	Trin. H.	M 1906	
—	Ja. Gerard Edgar Drogo	Trin.	M 1911	
Montague,	Paul Denys	Cai.	M 1909	
Monteith,	Hugh Glencairn	Pem.	M 1902 A.B. 1905. B.C., A.M. 1910	
—	Will. Ambrose Ja. And.	Pem.	M 1902 post Monteith-Winstanley, W. A.	
Montennis,	Louis Emslie	Trin. H.	M 1901	[J. A. A.B. 1906
Montford,	Douglas Raymond ...	Pem.	M 1908 A.B. 1911	
Montgomerie, Will. Stirling		Joh.	M 1905 A.B. 1908	
Montgomery, Allen Fiennes		Cla.	M 1908	
—	Basil Russell	Trin. H.	M 1904	
—	Colin Fra.	Pem.	M 1887 A.B. 1890. A.M. 1904	
—	Donald Stanley	H. Sel.	M 1905 A.B. 1908	
—	Hen.	King's	M 1907	
—	Hugh Roger Greville .	Cla.	M 1909	
—	Neville	H. Sel.	M 1905 A.B. 1908	
—	Will.	Joh.	E 1906 A.B. 1909	
Moody,	Basil	Joh.	M 1908 A.B. 1911	
—	Reg. Fre.	Qu.	M 1892 A.B. 1895. A.M. 1901	
—	Rob. Hector	Em.	M 1905 A.B. 1908. A.M. 1912	
Mookerjie,	Jitendra Nath	Down.	M 1906	
Moon,	Leon. Ja.	Pem.	M 1896 A.B. 1900. A.M. 1912	
Moor,	Cha. Fre.	Chr.	E 1902	
—	Chris.	Pem.	M 1910	
—	Frewen	Trin.	M 1911	
Moore,	Alan Hilary	Trin.	M 1900 A.B. 1903. M.B., B.C. 1911	
—	Alex. Knight	Chr.	M 1894 A.B. 1899. A.M. 1902	
—	Alf. Will.	Em.	M 1899 A.B. 1903. M.B., B.C. 1907	
—	Art. Crompton	Cla.	M 1896 A.B. 1899. A.M. 1904	
—	Athol Raymond	Cai.	M 1896 A.B. 1899. M.B., B.C., A.M. 1905	
—	Barron	Cath.	M 1876 A.B. 1880. A.M.† 1903	
—	Cecil Arbuthnot St George	Pem.	M 1900 A.B. 1903. A.M.† 1909	
—	Cha. Gordon Holland	Cai.	M 1903 A.B. 1906	
—	Claude Douglas Hamilton	N. C.	M 1894 Trin. H. A.B. 1897. A.M.† 1901	
—	Cyril Ashton Glover	H. Sel.	M 1904 A.B. 1907. A.M. 1911	
—	Edw. Stapleton	Trin.	M 1901 A.B. 1906. A.M. 1909	
—	Frank Reg.	Cla.	L 1907 A.B. 1909	
—	Frederic Ja. Stevenson	Joh.	M 1892 A.B. 1895. A.M. 1901	
—	Geo. Guy	H. Sel.	M 1907 A.B. 1910	
—	Gerald Alex. Clifford	Trin.	M 1910	
—	Gilb.	Cla.	M 1904 A.B. 1907	
—	Gillachrist	Cath.	M 1912	
—	(*Viscount*) Hen. Cha. } Ponsonby }	Trin.	M 1902	
—	Hen. Monck-Mason	Jes.	M 1906 A.B. 1909	
—	John	Jes.	M 1910	
—.	John Roland	Joh.	M 1905	
—	John Walt. Barnwell	H. Sel.	M 1905 A.B. 1908. A.M. 1912	
—	Jos. Alex.	King's	M 1893 A.B. 1896. A.M. 1912	
—	Noël Christian	C. C.	M 1910	
—	Norman	Jes.	M 1907 A.B. 1910	
—	Reg. Mark	Joh.	M 1902 A.B. 1905. M.B., B.C. 1910. A.M.	
—	Rich. Temple	Chr.	M 1910	[1911
—	Rob. Foster	N. C.	E 1897 Chr. A.B. 1900. B.C., A.M. 1905	
—	Tho. Cumming Rainsford	Chr.	M 1903 A.B. 1906. A.M. 1911	
—	Will. Geoffrey	Cai.	M 1911	
—	Will. Leslie Wilton	Trin. H.	M 1902	

Moore-Brabazon,	John Theodore } Cuthbert	Trin.	M 1902
Moorhouse,	Will. Barnard Rhodes	Trin. H.	M 1908
Moorsom,	Alf. Edgar	Trin.	M 1912
—	Jermyn	King's	M 1899 A.B. 1902
—	Raisley Stewart	King's	M 1911
—	Rob. Pearson	N. C.	M 1897 Qu. A.B. 1900. A.M. 1912
Moos,	Sorab Nanabhoy	King's	M 1910
Morcom,	Alf. Farr	Cla.	M 1903 A.B. 1906. M.B., B.C. 1911. A.M.
—	Edgar Llewellyn	Cla.	M 1898 A.B. 1901. A.M. 1906 [1912
—	Reg. Keble	Trin.	M 1896 A.B. 1899. A.M. 1903
Mordell,	Louis Joel	Joh.	M 1907 A.B. 1910
More,	Tho.	Cai.	M 1904
Moreing,	Adrian Cha.	Trin.	M 1909 A.B. 1912
—	Algernon Hen.	Trin.	M 1907 A.B. 1910
Morgan,	Art.	C. C.	M 1900 A.B. 1903. A.M. 1908
—	Art. Conway Osborne	Trin.	M 1903 A.B. 1906
—	Chris. And.	N. C.	M 1890 Cath. A.B. 1893. A.M. 1902
—	Dav. Alban	Down.	M 1909
—	Dav. Fra.	Down.	M 1912
—	Dav. Ja.	Joh.	M 1893 A.B. 1896. M.B., B.C. 1902. A.M.,
—	Ern. Cha.	Cai.	M 1904 A.B. 1907 [M.D. 1906
—	Evan Dav.	King's	M 1910
—	Evan Hone	Em.	M 1898 A.B. 1905. A.M. 1911
—	Frederic Ja.	Cai.	M 1907
—	Fre. Cleveland	Trin.	M 1900 A.B. 1903
—	Geo. Will. Faulconer	Pem.	M 1900 A.B. 1903
—	Harold Riversdale ...	Mag.	M 1905 A.B. 1908
—	Hopkin Trevor	Cai.	M 1912
—	Ivor Bertie	Trin.	M 1901
—	Ja.	H. Sel.	M 1894 A.B. 1897. A.M. 1901
—	Ja.	Pem.	L 1905
—	Ja. Douglas	Trin.	M 1899 A.B. 1902
—	Ja. Hill Faulconer ...	Pem.	M 1905 A.B. 1908. A.M. 1912
—	John	N. C.	M 1884 A.B. 1887. A.M. 1904
—	Osborne	Down.	M 1905 A.B. 1909
—	Oswald Gayer	Cla.	M 1907 A.B. 1910
—	Percival Campbell ...	N. C.	M 1911
—	Rob. Trevor	Jes.	M 1897 A.B. 1900. A.M. 1904
—	Sid. Conrad	C. C.	M 1907 A.B. 1910
—	Syd. Cope	Trin.	M 1906 A.B. 1909
—	Telford Dav.	Jes.	M 1909 A.B. 1912
—	Tho.	Mag.	M 1894 A.B. 1897. A.M. 1902
—	Will. Edgar	Em.	M 1906 A.B. 1909
—	Will. Parry	Cla.	M 1895 A.B. 1898. A.M. 1902. B.C. 1906.
—	Will. Watkins	Trin. H.	M 1905 A.B., LL.B. 1908 [M.B. 1908
Morgan Jones,	John	N. C.	M 1895 Joh. A.B. 1898. A.M. 1903
Morgans,	Godfrey Ewart	Pet.	M 1901 A.B. 1905
Morgan-Smith,	Gerald Oscar	N. C.	M 1907 Cath. A.B. 1910
Moriarty,	Gerald Herb.	Cai.	M 1912
Morier,	Cha. Eliot	Em.	M 1908 A.B. 1911
Morison,	Douglas Rutherford	Cla.	M 1905 A.B. 1908
Moritz,	Manfred	Em.	M 1905 N. C. A.B. 1908
Morland,	Denys Max Thomson	Cla.	M 1911
—	Harold John	King's	M 1891 A.B. 1894. A.M. 1908
Morley,	Bern. Cha.	Pem.	L 1911
—	Cha.	Trin.	M 1903 A.B. 1906. A.M. 1912
—	Claude Hope	Trin.	M 1906
—	Denys Warwick	Pem.	M 1912
—	Geoffrey Hope	Trin.	M 1904
—	Geo. Stanley	Mag.	L 1897 A.B. 1898. A.M. 1909

Morley,	Gordon Harpur	Joh.	M 1912
—	Ja.	Trin.	M 1886 LL.B. 1889. LL.M. 1902. A.B.
—	John	Mag.	M 1907 [1905
—	Reg. Wragge	H. Sel.	M 1909 A.B. 1912
—	Vincent	Cath.	M 1906 A.B. 1909
Morrice,	Geoffrey Wilmot	Trin.	M 1902 A.B. 1907
—	Rich. John	Trin.	M 1898 A.B. 1901. A.M. 1910
—	Will.	Pem.	M 1912
—	Will. Walt.	Cla.	M 1900 A.B. 1903
Morris,	Art. Capel	Jes.	M 1912
—	Austin Rob.	Qu.	M 1904 A.B. 1907
—	Edw. Harry	Cath.	M 1900 A.B. 1904
—	Edw. Pat.		*LL.D.* 1911
—	Frank Basil	Pem.	M 1899 A.B. 1902
—	Frank Mosedale	Joh.	M 1910
—	Geoffrey Grant	Trin.	M 1907 A.B. 1910. *Jes.
—	Geo. Fre. Bingley ...	Qu.	M 1907 A.B. 1910
—	Geo. Phil.	Chr.	M 1911
—	Herb. Cha.	N. C.	M 1904 Down. A.B. 1908. A.M.† 1911
—	Herb. Norman	Jes.	M 1902 A.B. 1905
—	Ja. Outram	Em.	M 1905 A.B. 1910
—	John Child	Mag.	M 1911
—	John Fre.	Jes.	M 1899 A.B. 1902
—	Jos.	C. C.	M 1906 A.B. 1909
—	Rob. Straw	Qu.	M 1897 A.B. 1900. A.M. 1904
—	Stuart Denton	C. C.	M 1909 A.B. 1912
—	Tho. Norman	Joh.	M 1907 A.B. 1910
—	Walt. Edm. Harston	Trin.	M 1891 A.B. 1894. A.M. 1905
—	Walt. Fre.	Cath.	M 1911
—	Wilson Clark	N. C.	M 1908
Morrisey,	Hugh	N. C.	M 1906 A.B. 1909
Morris Eyton,	Rob. Edw.	Trin.	M 1911
Morrish,	John	N. C.	M 1911
Morrison,	Alf.	King's	M 1894 A.B. 1897. A.M. 1903
—	Douglas Cha. Adey	Joh.	M 1898 A.B., LL.B. 1901
—	Edw. Oliver	Cai.	M 1910
—	Gresham Wynter ...	C. C.	M 1893 A.B. 1896. A.M. 1902
—	Hans Hamilton	H. Sel.	M 1902 A.B. 1905. A.M. 1909. LL.B. 1912
—	Ja.	Em.	M 1912
—	John Harold	N. C.	M 1907 A.B. 1908
—	John Stanton Fleming	Trin.	M 1911
—	Jos. Alb. Colquhoun	Trin. H.	M 1901 A.B. 1904
—	Martin Ja.	Jes.	M 1912
—	Reg. John	Trin. H.	M 1909
—	Rob. Ja. Alex.	Trin. H.	E 1886 A.B., LL.B. 1889. LL.M. 1902.
—	Rob. Thackray	Chr.	M 1904 A.B. 1907 [LL.D. 1907
Morritt,	Hen. John Graveley	Trin. H.	M 1912
Morsbach,	Adolf Maria Aloysius	Trin.	M 1909
Morse,	Cha. Geo. Hugh	Em.	M 1904 A.B. 1907
—	Chris.	Pem.	M 1912
—	Eric Victor	Pem.	M 1910
—	Leopold Geo. Esmond	King's	M 1904 A.B. 1907
Morshead,	Reg. Sperling	Trin.	M 1905 A.B. 1908
Mortada,	Ismail	Trin. H.	M 1907 A.B. 1910
Mortimer,	Art.	Sid.	M 1899 A.B. 1903
—	Fre. Geo. Crofton ...	Trin. H.	L 1901
—	Herb. Clifford	Trin.	M 1901 A.B., LL.B. 1904
Mortimore,	Alf. John	Cath.	M 1905 A.B. 1908
—	Geo. Rae	Cath.	M 1910
Mortlock,	Cha. Bern.	N. C.	M 1910
—	John And. Tennant	Jes.	M 1912

Mortlock,	Will. Fre. Walt.	Trin.	M 1909
Morton,	Cha. Edw.	N. C.	L 1897 A.B. 1905
—	Clem. John	Pem.	M 1904 A.B. 1907. A.M. 1911
—	Cyril Evelyn	H. Sel.	M 1903 A.B. 1906. A.M. 1910
—	Cyril Shadforth	Pet.	M 1904 A.B. 1908
—	Ellys Art.	Cla.	M 1897 A.B. 1900. A.M. 1904
—	Fergus Dunlop	Joh.	M 1906 A.B. 1909. LL.B. 1910
—	Fred	Cath.	M 1909 A.B. 1912
—	Geo. Art.	Qu.	M 1904 A.B. 1908
—	Geo. Fletcher	Em.	M 1903 A.B. 1906. A.M. 1910
—	Harold Ja. Storrs ...	Pem.	M 1905 A.B. 1908
—	Harold Swithun	C. C.	M 1908 A.B. 1911
—	Hen. Thorne	Em.	M 1909 A.B., LL.B. 1912
—	Ja. Fairfax Amphlett	Cla.	M 1911
—	John Aylmer Fitz-Hardinge	King's	M 1912
—	John Geo.	N. C.	M 1900 A.B. 1903. A.M. 1909
—	Lawrence Knyvett ...	Em.	M 1894 A.B. 1897. A.M. 1905
—	Rowland Fra. Storrs	Trin.	M 1905 A.B. 1912
—	Victor Chalmers	Joh.	M 1906 A.B. 1909
Mosely,	Fre. Maur.	Joh.	M 1906
Moses,	Cha. Basil	Cath.	M 1908 A.B. 1911
Mosley,	Isaac Hen.	Chr.	M 1901 A.B. 1904. LL.B. 1905
Moss,	Cha. Edw.	Em.	E 1908 A.B. 1910
—	Fre. Wood Collins ...	Pem.	M 1897 A.B. 1901. A.M. 1906
—	Geo.	H. Sel.	M 1910
—	Fre. Blundell	Trin.	M 1891 post Moss-Blundell, F. B. A.B., [LL.B. 1894. A.M., LL.M. 1898. [LL.D. 1904
—	Hen. Seymour	Joh.	M 1890 post Moss-Blundell, H. S. A.B. [1893. LL.B. 1894. A.M., LL.M.
Mosse,	Cha. Herb.	Jes.	M 1908 A.B. 1911 [1898. LL.D. 1904
—	Cotton Grimley Tenison	Cai.	M 1909 A.B. 1912
Mosseri,	Felix Nezzim	Pem.	M 1912
—	Lionel Néssim	Pem.	M 1908 A.B. 1911
Mossop,	Allan Geo.	Pem.	M 1904 A.B., LL.B. 1908
—	Harold Evan	Cla.	M 1902 A.B. 1906
Mostyn Owen,	Guy Cha.	Trin. H.	M 1910
Mott,	Cha. Fra.	Trin.	M 1896 A.B. 1900. A.M. 1903
—	Raymond Culver ...	Trin.	M 1895 A.B. 1899. A.M. 1903. B.C. 1905.
Mottram,	Ja. Cecil	Joh.	M 1905 [M.B. 1906
—	Vernon Hen.	*Trin.	M 1901 A.B. 1904. A.M.† 1908
Mould,	Herb. Bertram Jos.	N. C.	M 1907 Pet. A.B. 1911
—	Sam Carter	Jes.	M 1899 A.B. 1902
Moulden,	John	N. C.	M 1911
Moule,	Hen. Cha. Cautley ...	Trin.	M 1912
—	Hor. Fre.	Cla.	M 1893 A.B. 1896. A.M. 1904
—	Walt. Steph.	C. C.	M 1883 A.B. 1886. A.M. 1908
Moullin,	Eric Balliol	Down.	M 1912
Moulton,	Wilfrid Johnson	Cla.	M 1889 A.B. 1892. A.M. 1902
—	Will. Ralph Osborn	King's	M 1910
Moung,	Moung	King's	M 1907
—	Moung Aye	Cla.	M 1910
Mounsey,	Geo. Fryer	King's	M 1899 A.B. 1902
—	Jasper Percy	C. C.	M 1906 A.B. 1909
—	John Edw.	King's	M 1898 A.B. 1901. A.M. 1906
—	Reg. Jos.	King's	M 1902 A.B. 1905
Mountain,	Bern.	Sid.	M 1902 A.B. 1905. A.M. 1910
—	Harold	Chr.	M 1898 A.B. 1902. LL.B. 1905. A.M. 1906
—	Stanford Walton	Pem.	M 1911
Mountfield,	Dav. D'Oyly	Pem.	M 1904 A.B. 1907
Mountford,	Art. Wilfrid	N. C.	M 1909 Cath. A.B. 1912

Mountfort,	Cha. Clayton	Em.	M 1902 A.B. 1905. A.M. 1909
Mountjoy,	Victor Ulric Allin ...	Joh.	M 1901 A.B. 1904. A.M. 1908
Mourilyan,	Cha. Archib.	Cla.	M 1901 A.B. 1904. A.M. 1908
Moursi,	Mahmoud Muhammad	Pem.	M 1909
Mousley,	Edw. Opotiki	Em.	M 1912
—	Tho. Harold	N. C.	M 1907 Cath. A.B. 1912
Moutray,	Basil	Pem.	M 1899 A.B. 1902. B. Moutray A.M. 1910
Mowatt,	Osmond	Cai.	M 1899 A.B. 1904. A.M. 1907
Mowforth,	Herb. Hen.	N. C.	M 1910
Mowlam,	Harold Jesse	Down.	M 1907 A.B. 1910
Mowll,	Basil Chris.	Em.	M 1909 A.B. 1912
—	Chris. Kilvinton	Cai.	M 1911
—	Edw. Worsfold	Jes.	M 1900 A.B. 1903. A.M. 1907
—	Herb. Ja.	Jes.	M 1898 A.B. 1901. A.M. 1905
—	Howard West Kilvinton	King's	M 1909 A.B. 1912
Mowton,	Walt. Edw.	Joh.	M 1911
Moxey,	Edgar Reg.	Pem.	M 1910
—	John Llewellyn	Pem.	M 1908 A.B. 1911
Moxley,	Chris. Hen.	Qu.	M 1900 A.B. 1903. A.M. 1907
—	Hen. Roberts	N. C.	M 1905 A.B. 1908
Moxon,	Herb. Ern.	Qu.	M 1907
—	Herb. Will.	Joh.	M 1899 A.B. 1902
—	Reg. Stewart	Cai.	M 1894 A.B. 1897. A.M. 1901. B.D. 1908
—	Tho. Allen	Joh.	M 1896 A.B. 1899. A.M. 1903
Moylan,	John Fitzgerald	Qu.	M 1901 A.B. 1904
Mozley,	Bern. Cha.	King's	M 1912
—	John Hen.	King's	M 1906 A.B. 1909
—	John Kenneth ....*Pem.		M 1902 A.B. 1905. A.M. 1909
Mudd,	Norman	Trin.	M 1907 A.B. 1910
Mudie,	Rob. Fra.	King's	M 1908 A.B. 1911
Muff,	Herb. Brantwood ...	Chr.	M 1898 A.B. 1901. post Maufe, H. B.
—	Statham Broadbent	Cla.	M 1906 A.B. 1909
Mugaseth,	Jal Jehangir	N. C.	M 1908 A.B. 1911
Muggeridge,	Gordon Denne	Pem.	M 1896 A.B. 1899. A.M. 1903
Mugliston,	Frank Hugh	Pem.	E 1905 Francis H. A.B. 1908
Muir,	Burleigh Leycester ...	Trin.	M 1909 A.B. 1912
—	Clive Robertson Pattison	Cai.	M 1893 A.B. 1896. A.M. 1901
—	Dav. Miller	Trin.	M 1907 A.B. 1910
—	Ja.	Trin.	M 1897 A.B. 1899. A.M. 1904
—	Jos. Corbett	Em.	M 1891 A.B. 1894. M.B., B.C. 1897. A.M. [1900. M.D. 1901
—	Romney Moncrieff Pattison	Cai.	M 1903 A.B. 1906. A.M. 1912
Muirhead,	Ja. Alex. Orrock ...	Cai.	M 1909 A.B. 1912
Muir Mackenzie,	Kenneth Ja. ...	Jes.	M 1901
—	Montague Ronald Alf.	Jes.	M 1900 A.B. 1903
—	Rob. Cecil	Jes.	M 1910
Mujtaba,	Husain	Pet.	M 1904 Chondhari H. A.B. 1908
Mukarji,	Satya Nand	Qu.	M 1909 Satia, N. A.B. 1911
Mukerjea,	Devabrata	Em.	L 1906 A.B. 1910
Mukhi,	Mangharam Gurudinamal	N. C.	M 1906
Mules,	Cha. Oliver	Trin.	M 1856 A.B. 1860. A.M. 1863. D.D. 1908
—	Fra. John	Trin.	M 1892 A.B. 1895. A.M. 1905
Mulholland,	Godfrey John Art. } Murray Lyle	Trin.	M 1911
—	Hen. Geo. Hill	Trin.	M 1909
—	Will.	Joh.	M 1910
Muller,	Hugh Christian } Andreas Sigvald	Em.	M 1896 A.B. 1900. A.M.† 1906
Müller,	John Stewart	Joh.	M 1892 A.B. 1895. A.M. 1904
Mullineux,	Matth.	Joh.	M 1893 A.B. 1896. A.M. 1903
Mullinger,	Ja. Bass	Joh.	M 1862 A.B. 1866. A.M. 1870. *Litt.D.* 1912

Mullings,	Will. Tho.	Chr.	M 1893 A.B. 1896. M.B., B.C., A.M. 1900.
Mullins,	Alban Ferris	Cath.	M 1909　　　　　　　[M.D. 1903
—	Cha. de Courcy Cochrane	Sid.	M 1910
Mulock,	Edw. Homan	Trin.	M 1904
Mumford,	Cecil Geo.	Cla.	M 1912
—	Gerald Blomfield ...	King's	M 1897 A.B. 1901
—	Noël Geo.	H. Sel.	M 1895 A.B. 1898. A.M. 1903
—	Phil. Stearn	Jes.	M 1912
—	Will. Hugh Nottage	N. C.	M 1910
Mummery,	John Percy Lockhart	Cai.	M 1893 A.B. 1897. M.B., B.C. 1902
Muncaster,	Eric	Trin.	M 1908 A.B. 1911
Muncey,	Edw. Howard Parker	Joh.	M 1905 A.B. 1908. A.M. 1912
—	Raymond Waterville Luke	Trin.H.	M 1911
Munday,	Edw.	Cla.	M 1909 A.B. 1912
Mundle,	Indu Bhusan	Pet.	M 1904
Mundy,	Cecil Trelawney	Pem.	M 1891 N. C. A.B. 1901
Munesinghe,	Menickpure Lenty ...	Qu.	M 1908 A.B. 1911
Munford,	Tho. Nettleship	Sid.	M 1900 A.B. 1903. A.M. 1908
Mungavin,	Will. Malcolm Wiseham	Em.	M 1909
Munns,	Rob. Douglas Gatty	Jes.	M 1907 A.B. 1910
Munro,	Donald	N. C.	M 1912
Munshi,	Rafieuddin Faziduddin	N. C.	M 1909
Munthe af Morgenstierne, Wilhelm⎰ Herman Ludvig ⎰		Joh.	L 1910
Murdoch,	Alan Ja.	Cla.	M 1912
—	Colin Belton	N. C.	M 1904 Down. A.B. 1910
Murfet,	Alec Tho. Morton ...	Pet.	M 1910
Murly-Gotto,	Ja.	Pem.	M 1908 A.B. 1911
Murota,	Koichiro	N. C.	M 1909
Murphy,	Art. Will. Gerald ...	H. Sel.	M 1906 A.B. 1909 [M.D. 1900. M.C. 1904
—	Ja. Keogh	Cai.	M 1888 A.B. 1891. M.B., B.C., A.M. 1896.
—	Will. Lombard	Joh.	M 1896 A.B. 1899. A.M. 1903. M.B., B.C.
Murray,	Alan Rob.	Pem.	M 1910　　　　　　　　　　[1907
—	Alex. Gordon Wynch	Trin.	M 1903 A.B. 1906. A.M. 1912
—	Alex. Will. Ramsay	Cath.	L 1903 A.B. 1905
—	Art. Hugh	H. Sel.	M 1902 A.B. 1905
—	Art. Richmond	Chr.	M 1906 A.B. 1909
—	Cha. Molteno	Pem.	M 1895 A.B. 1898. A.M. 1903. M.B., B.C.
—	Donald Cecil Laird	C. C.	M 1908 A.B. 1911　　　　　　[1904
—	Donald Wynch	Em.	M 1905 A.B. 1908. A.M. 1912
—	Eric	Pet.	M 1904 A.B. 1908
—	Everitt Geo. Dunne	Chr.	M 1909 A.B. 1912
—	Frank Everitt	Joh.	M 1894 A.B. 1897. M.B., B.C. 1901
—	Geo. Anth.	Trin.	M 1912
—	Geo. John Rob.	Trin.	M 1884 A.B., LL.B. 1887. LL.M. 1909
—	John	N. C.	E 1886 Chr. A.B. 1889. A.M. 1901
—	John	King's	M 1902 A.B. 1905
—	John Challenger	Trin.	M 1912
—	1 John Owen Farquhar	Trin.	M 1877 A.B. 1881. A.M. 1884. *Em. B.D.
—	John Stanley	Trin.	M 1905 A.B. 1908　　　[1903. D.D. 1904
—	Keith Rich.	Mag.	M 1907 A.B. 1911
—	Malcolm Geo. Douglas	Trin.	M 1907 A.B. 1910
—	Penry John	Trin.	M 1900 A.B. 1903
—	Rich. Brian	Trin.	M 1909
—	Rob. Leslie	Jes.	M 1912
—	Thorkill Howard Everitt	Trin.	M 1910
Murray-Aynsley, Alf. Evans			*See* Vinter, A. E.
Murray-Jardine, Gordon		Cla.	M 1906
Murray Johnson, Fra. Kinloch ...		Trin.	M 1902

1 Master of Selwyn College P. H., 1909.

Murray Smith,	Art. Geo.	Trin.	M 1905 A.B. 1909
—	John Edw.	Mag.	L 1909 A.B. 1911
Muscio,	Bern.	Cai.	M 1911
Musgrave,	Tom	Mag.	M 1908
Muslehudin,	Mohomed	Chr.	M 1886 Trin. H. A.B. 1889. A.M.† 1902
Muspratt,	Percy Knowles	Chr.	M 1895 A.B. 1898. B.C., A.M. 1903. M.B.
Musson,	Tho. Meadows Barrow	Jes.	M 1910 [1904
Mutch,	Nathan	Em.	M 1904 A.B. 1907. M.B., B.C., A.M. 1911
Mutzenbecher,	Franz Matthias ...	Chr.	M 1902
Myddelton,	Edw. Geoffrey	Jes.	M 1912
Myer,	Hor. Stuart	Trin.	M 1904 A.B., LL.B. 1907
Myers,	Cha. Sam.	Cai.	M 1891 A.B. 1895. M.B., B.C. 1898. A.M.
			[1901. M.D. 1902. Sc.D. 1910
—	Edw.	N. C.	M 1896 A.B. 1899. A.M. 1904
—	Harold Hawthorn ...	N. C.	E 1903
—	Will.	Sid.	M 1889 A.B. 1892. A.M. 1904
Myles,	Dav.	Em.	M 1912
—	Herb. Blythe	Cai.	M 1909 A.B. 1912

N

Nabeshima,	Nawomitsu	Cai.	M 1895 A.B. 1898. A.M.† 1903
Nadin,	Russell	Jes.	M 1899 A.B. 1902
Naesseth,	Alf. Lianna Treweeke	Trin.	M 1912
Naggiar,	Syd.	Trin.	M 1910
Naidoo,	Ramdas Crishna	Down.	M 1907
Nainby-Luxmoore,	Chave Cha. ...	Trin. H.	M 1910
Nair,	Kalipurayath Ramunni	Em.	M 1904 [1905. B.D. 1906
Nairn,	John Arbuthnot ......*Trin.		M 1892 A.B. 1896. A.M. 1899. Litt.D.
Nairne,	Bern. Domett	Jes.	M 1896 A.B. 1899. A.M. 1903
Naish,	Alb. Ern.	Trin.	M 1890 A.B. 1893. M.B., B.C., A.M. 1901
—	Christofer Garrison	Chr.	M 1904 A.B. 1907
—	Fra. Clem. Prideaux	Sid.	M 1900 A.B. 1903. A.M. 1908
—	Will. Vawdrey	Em.	M 1892 A.B. 1895. B.C., A.M. 1904. M.B.
Naldrett,	Harold Carter ....:	Jes.	M 1912 [1905. M.D. 1911
Nanavati,	Dhirajlal Dayabhai	Joh.	M 1905 A.B. 1907
Nánávutty,	Erachshah Maneckji	King's	M 1897 A.B. 1901
Nancarrow,	John Vivian ..ı......	King's	M 1903 A.B., LL.B. 1906. A.M. 1912
Nand Lal	....	N. C.	M 1905 Down. A.B., LL.B. 1908
Nandi,	Surendra Nath	N. C.	M 1909 Down. A.B. 1912
Nangle,	Edw. Jocelyn	Cai.	M 1906
Nankivell,	Art. Hay Aitken ...	Trin.	M 1887 A.B. 1890. A.M. 1905
Naoröji,	Jal Ardeshir Dadabhai	Chr.	M 1904 A.B. 1909
Naoroji,	Karesasp Ardeshir ⎱ Dadabhai ⎰	Chr.	M 1912
Napier,	Guy Greville	Pem.	M 1903 A.B. 1907
—	Lennox Pelham	King's	M 1909
—	Oswald Ja. Walt. ...	Chr.	M 1908 A.B. 1911
—	Phil. Hen.	Trin.	M 1902 A.B. 1905
Narayan,	Hitendra	Pem.	M 1908
—	Yegna	N. C.	M 1909
Nardone,	Carlo Maria Geltrude⎱ Errico Francesco Marco⎰	Chr.	L 1900 A.B. 1901
Nash,	Geo.	Mag.	M 1909 A.B. 1912
—	John Victor	Trin.	M 1911
—	Will. Wallace Hayward	H. Sel.	M 1903 A.B. 1906. A.M. 1912

Nash-Wortham,	Fra. Leslie Dalton	Pem.	M 1901
Nason,	John Will. Washington	Qu.	M 1908
—	Will. Fre. Cha.	Qu.	M 1905 A.B. 1908
Naters,	Cuthbert Cha. Trewhitt	Em.	M 1900 A.B. 1903. A.M. 1907
Nath,	Dewan Badri	Trin.	M 1904 A.B. 1907
—	Jagan	Trin.	M 1907
Nathan,	Alb. Alex.	Jes.	M 1905 A.B. 1908
—	Cha. Edw.	Cla.	M 1902
—	Edw.	Trin. H.	M 1904
—	Edw. Jonah	King's	M 1907 A.B. 1910
—	Julian	Cla.	M 1907 A.B. 1910
—	Rob. Frederic	Cai.	M 1911
—	Sid. Herb.	Trin.	M 1890 A.B. 1893. A.M. 1897. B.C., M.D.
Nathorst,	Alf. Gabriel		Sc.D. 1907 [1905
Naumann,	John Harold	King's	M 1912
Naunton,	Will. Johnson Smith	Joh.	M 1907 A.B. 1910
Navalkar,	Moreshwar Vinayak	Trin. H.	M 1897 A.B., LL.B. 1901
Nawaz,	Mian Haq	N. C.	M 1904 Down. A.B., LL.B. 1907
—	Mohammed Shah ...	N. C.	M 1897 Chr. A.B., LL.B. 1901
Nayler,	Jos. Lawrence	Pet.	M 1909 A.B. 1912
—	Will. Arnold	Trin.	M 1904 A.B. 1907
Naylor,	Alf. Tho. Art.	Em.	M 1908 A.B. 1911
—	Hen.	Qu.	M 1910
—	John Murray	Trin.	M 1907 A.B. 1911
—	Tho. Humphrey	Trin.	M 1909 A.B. 1912
Nazimuddin,	Khaja	Trin. H.	M 1912
Neal,	Art. Westall	King's	M 1912
—	John	King's	M 1907 A.B. 1910. LL.B. 1911
—	Rich.	N. C.	L 1908 A.B. 1910
—	Will. Hen.	N. C.	M 1910
Neale,	Algernon Kenneth Hastings	Trin.	M 1911
—	John Basil	Jes.	M 1909 A.B. 1912
Neales,	Art. Ern.	Down.	M 1910
Neame,	Tho.	Cai.	M 1904 A.B. 1907 [M.D. 1909
Neatby,	Tho. Miller	Joh.	M 1885 A.B. 1888. A.M. 1892. B.C. 1906.
Nedwill,	Courtney Llewellyn	Trin.	M 1894 A.B. 1898. M.B., B.C. 1904
Need,	Geo. Spofforth	Joh.	M 1912
Needham,	Eglin	Chr.	M 1907 A.B. 1910
—	Ja. Nall	H. Sel.	M 1911
Negroponte,	Jean Jacques	Trin.	M 1912
Nehru,	Jawaharlal	Trin.	M 1907 A.B. 1910
—	Shri Shridhara	Mag.	M 1905 A.B. 1907. A.M. 1912
Neighbour,	Phil. Morgan	Sid.	M 1912
Neild,	Will. Cecil	Cla.	M 1910
Neill,	Norman Clark	Joh.	M 1902 A.B. 1905
Neilson,	Drevor Fre. Acton ...	Trin.	M 1909
—	Geo. Edw.	Trin.	M 1905
—	Hen. John Tullis ...	Trin.	L 1912
—.	Hen. Vere	Cai.	M 1909 A.B. 1912
Nelder,	Gordon Cha. Aldridge	Chr.	M 1912
Nelson,	Edw. Will.	Chr.	M 1902
—	Ern. Bertram	C. C.	M 1909 A.B. 1912
—	Geo. Geoffrey	Chr.	M 1905 A.B. 1908
—	Lionel	Em.	M 1904 A.B. 1907
—	Rich. Albany	Pet.	M 1899 A.B. 1902. LL.B. 1903
—	Roland Hugh	Trin.	M 1900 A.B. 1903
—.	Ronald Duckworth ...	Chr.	M 1907 A.B. 1911
—	Tho. Basil	Chr.	M 1902 A.B. 1909
Nemes,	(*Count*) Bálint Tános		
	Dénes	Trin. H.	M 1903
Nesbit,	Ja. Widdowson	Qu.	M 1908 A.B. 1911

Nesbitt,	Will. Hen. Alex.	Jes.	M 1899 A.B. 1902
Ness,	Gordon Stewart	Cla.	M 1904
Nettlefold,	Edw. John	Trin.	M 1904 A.B. 1907
—	Jos. Hen.	Trin.	M 1909 A.B., LL.B. 1912
Neuburg,	Victor Benj.	Trin.	M 1906
Neumann,	Karl Otto	Trin.	E 1911
Neumark,	Otto	Trin.	M 1908 A.B. 1911
Nevett,	Rich. Brian	Em.	M 1909 A.B. 1912
Nevile,	Bern. Phil.	Trin.	M 1910
—	Gervas Clifton	Trin.	M 1903 A.B. 1906
—	Hugh Geo.	Trin.	M 1898 A.B. 1901
Nevill,	Warwick	Cla.	M 1911
Neville,	Alf. Geoffrey	Mag.	M 1909
—	Art. Will.	Jes.	M 1903 A.B., LL.B. 1906
—	Eric Harold ....*Trin.		M 1907 A.B. 1910
—	Geo. John Ern.	Jes.	M 1904 A.B. 1907
—	Hen. Allen Dugdale	Em.	L 1911 A.B. 1912
—	Jos. Tho. Donovan ...	C. C.	M 1907
Neville-Bagot,	Will. Hugh	Trin. H.	M 1897 A.B. 1901
Nevins,	Hugh Nevin	H. Sel.	M 1907 A.B. 1910
Nevinson,	Guy Roger Grisewood	C. C.	M 1907
New,	Frank Ossian Walt.	Em.	M 1907 A.B. 1910
—	Tho. Gladstone	Pem.	M 1900 A.B. 1903. LL.B. 1905. A.M. 1907
—	Will.	Down.	E 1907 A.B. 1910
Newall,	Geoffrey Stirling	Trin.	M 1901
—	¹ Hugh Frank ....*Trin.		M 1876 A.B. 1880. A.M. 1884
—	Lionel Beresford	Trin.	M 1904
Newberry,	Ern. Edgar	Trin. H.	M 1903 A.B. 1910
Newbery,	Herb. Edw. Lightfoot	Trin.	M 1893 A.B. 1896. A.M. 1901
—	Lionel Archib. McClintock	Chr.	M 1890 A.B. 1893. A.M. 1903
—	Rob. Edwin	Joh.	M 1903 A.B. 1907. A.M. 1912
Newbold,	Cha. Jos.	Cai.	M 1900 A.B. 1903
Newbould,	Herb. Simpson	Trin. H.	M 1898 A.B. 1902. A.M. 1909
Newcomb,	Wilfrid Davison	Trin.	M 1908 A.B. 1911
Newcombe,	Harry Wyndham ...	Trin.	M 1911
—	Will. Art.	Trin.	M 1892 A.B. 1895. A.M. 1902
Newell,	Herb. Will.	N. C.	M 1908 A.B. 1911
Newgass,	Edgar Isaac Augustus	Trin.	M 1906 A.B. 1911
Newham,	Art.	Joh.	M 1879 A.B. 1883. A.M. 1907
—	Cyril Ern.	Jes.	M 1912
Newman,	Art. Edwin Tweed ...	Trin. H.	M 1886 A.B. 1889. A.M. 1901
—	Cha. Herb. Alf.	Jes.	M 1906 A.B. 1909
—	Edw. Devon	Trin. H.	M 1906
—	Eric	Chr.	M 1901
—	Frank Chafen	Down.	M 1902 A.B. 1906. A.M. 1911
—	Fre. Hen. Cha.	Jes.	M 1899 A.B. 1902
—	Geo. Campin	Mag.	M 1901
—	John Burton	Trin.	M 1907 A.B. 1910
—	John Campin	Trin.	M 1891 A.B. 1894. M.B., B.C., A.M. 1905
—	Leslie Frank	Down.	M 1906 A.B. 1909
—	Rowland Allen Webbe	Trin.	M 1905 A.B. 1908
Newmarch,	John Hen.	Pem.	M 1904 A.B. 1907
Newnes,	Frank Hillyard	Cla.	M 1894 A.B., LL.B. 1897. A.M. 1901
Newnum,	Fra. Cecil	Pem.	M 1902 A.B. 1905
Newport,	Geo. Bern.	Sid.	M 1895 A.B. 1898. A.M. 1903
—	Harold	H. Sel.	M 1908 A.B. 1912
Newton,	Alan Fra.	Cath.	M 1904 A.B. 1907. A.M. 1912
—	Basil Cochrane	King's	M 1908
—	Fre. Hen. Jos.	Em.	M 1905 A.B. 1908

¹ Professor of Astrophysics, 1909.

Newton,	Geo. Douglas Cochrane	Trin.	M 1898 A.B. 1902. A.M. 1905
—	Gilb. Ford	N. C.	M 1900 Chr. A.B. 1903. A.M. 1910
—	Hor. Gerard Townsend	Joh.	M 1904
—	Hor. Will. Goodwin	King's	M 1902 A.B. 1905
—	John	Pem.	M 1908
—	John Raphael	Trin.	M 1900 A.B. 1907. A.M. 1910
—	Percy	Cla.	M 1901 A.B. 1906
—	Rob. Hen. Herdman	Pem.	M 1905 A.B. 1908
—	Tho. Hotham	Em.	M 1902 A.B. 1905
—	Will. Hen.	Em.	M 1897 A.B. 1900. M.B., B.C. 1907
Newton-Clare,	Edw. Tho.	Cla.	M 1901 A.B. 1904. A.M. 1909
—	Herb. John	Cla.	M 1906 A.B. 1909
—	Walt. Shackfield	Cla.	M 1906
Nibandhu,	(*Prince*) Praong Chow	Trin.	M 1903 (*Prince*) Nipandh Parnupaungse
Nichol,	Rob. Will.	Cai.	M 1911 [A.B. 1906
Nicholas,	Archib. John	N. C.	M 1906 Chr. A.B. 1910
—	Fre.	Em.	M 1910
—	Fre. Parry	Jes.	M 1909 A.B. 1912
—	Henric Clarence	Trin.	M 1900 A.B. 1904
—	Tressilian Cha.	*Trin.	M 1907 A.B. 1910
Nicholl,	Archib. Mich. Cyprian	Joh.	M 1899 A.B. 1902. A.M. 1907
—	Cha. Bowen	Qu.	M 1890 A.B. 1893. A.M. 1906
—	Cha. Carlyon	Em.	M 1898 A.B. 1901
—	Dav. Art.	Joh.	M 1887 A.B. 1890. A.M., LL.M. 1906
—	Esmond Mackillop	Qu.	M 1910
—	Jos. Warren McKillop	Qu.	M 1912
—	Vincent	Pem.	M 1911
Nicholls,	Alb. Cha.	Joh.	M 1907 A.B. 1910
—	Douglas Maine	Down.	M 1905 A.B., LL.B. 1908. A.M. 1912
—	Fra. John	Joh.	M 1889 M.B., B.C. 1901
—	Guy Syd.	Down.	M 1909
—	Herb. Lee	C. C.	M 1908 A.B. 1911
—	John Rich. Lee	Trin.	M 1897 A.B. 1900. A.M. 1904
—	Lucius	N. C.	M 1901 Down. A.B. 1904. M.B., B.C. 1907
—	Stanley Harold	Cai.	M 1899 A.B. 1902
Nichols,	Alb. Russell	Cla.	M 1878 A.B. 1882. A.M. 1902
—	Cecil Walt.	Em.	M 1909 A.B. 1912
—	Frank Howard	Trin.	M 1903 A.B. 1906. A.M. 1910
Nicholson,	Archib. Fre.	Trin.	M 1899 A.B. 1902
—	Brinsley Darracott	Trin.	M 1912
—	Clem. Octavius Edw.	Trin.	M 1893 A.B. 1896. A.M. 1901
—	Cuthbert John	Cai.	M 1902 A.B. 1905
—	Edgar Cyril	Joh.	M 1910
—	Fra.	Chr.	M 1895 A.B. 1898. A.M. 1904
—	Frank Carr	Chr.	M 1894 A.B. 1898. A.M. 1902
—	Fre. Dering	King's	M 1896 A.B. 1899. B.C. 1902. M.B. 1904.
—	Fre. Victor	Qu.	M 1906 A.B. 1909 [M.D. 1909
—	Geo. Crosfield Norris	Cla.	M 1904
—	Gilb. Will. de Poulton	Jes.	M 1896 A.B. 1899. A.M. 1903. B.C. 1906.
—	Harold	King's	M 1902 A.B. 1905 [M.D. 1907
—	Harry Helstrip	H. Sel.	M 1911
—	Humphrey John	Trin.	M 1912
—	John Gifford	Cla.	M 1907
—	John Will.	Trin.	M 1902 A.B. 1905. A.M. 1909
—	Malcolm	Trin. H.	M 1907 A.B. 1910
—	Otho Will.	Mag.	M 1910
—	Phil. Chris.	Trin.	M 1908
—	Reynold Alleyne	*Trin.	M 1887 A.B. 1890. A.M. 1894. Litt.D. 1909
—	Ronald Scholfield	Cla.	M 1889 A.B. 1892. A.M. 1903
—	Wilfrid Walmsley	Joh.	M 1885 A.B. 1888. A.M. 1902
Nickal,	Geo. Brockbank	Chr.	M 1909 A.B. 1912

Nickels,	Rob. Norman	Cai.	M 1908 A.B. 1911
Nicklin,	Geo. Norman	Joh.	M 1908 A.B. 1911
Nickse,	Hermann Georg	Chr.	M 1911
Nickson,	Geo.	C. C.	M 1884 A.B. 1887. A.M. 1891. D.D. 1906
Nicol,	Ja.	Trin.	M 1900 A.B. 1903
Nicoll,	Hen. Maur. Dunlop	Cai.	M 1903 A.B. 1906
Nicoll-Griffith,	Hub. Victor	H. Sel.	M 1908 A.B. 1911
Nicolson,	Leslie Gibson	Down.	M 1910
Nield,	Cha. Herb.	Trin. H.	M 1910
Nielsen,	Edgar Emil Manicus	Cla.	M 1911
Nightingale,	Cuthbert Leathley ...	Qu.	M 1910
—	Dudley Art.	Trin.	M 1899 A.B. 1902
—	Herb. Paul	Chr.	M 1907
Nihál-Singh,	Sirdar	Pet.	M 1904 A.B. 1908
Nihill,	John Harry Barclay	Em.	M 1911
Nimr,	Alb. Faris	Chr.	M 1908
Nishigori,	Sozaburo	N. C.	E 1904
Nishihara,	Hiroshi	N. C.	M 1906
Nishiwaki,	Seizaburo	N. C.	L 1906
Nissim,	Jos.	Joh.	M 1902 A.B.1904. LL.B.1906. A.M.†1908
—	Simon	Joh.	M 1912
Niven,	Ern. Ogilvie	Pem.	M 1909 A.B. 1912
—	Hugh	Joh.	M 1907 A.B. 1911
Nivin,	Ern. Fielden	N. C.	M 1894 Em. A.B. 1897. A.M. 1901
Nix,	Cha. Geo. Ashburner	Trin.	M 1892 A.B. 1898. A.M. 1904
Nixon,	Art. Lyndon	Em.	M 1904 A.B. 1907
—	Brinsley Hampton ...	Trin.	M 1903 A.B. 1906
—	Frank Horsfall	Pem.	M 1908 A.B. 1911
—	Sam. Hen.	N. C.	M 1898 Em. A.B. 1901
Nobbs,	Ja. Alf.	N. C.	M 1899 A.B. 1902 Down. A.M. 1906
Nobes,	Fortescue Jerman ...	Cla.	M 1906 A.B. 1909
Noble,	Ambrose Edw.	Cath.	M 1898 A.B. 1901
—	And.		*Sc.D.* 1908
—	Art. Hen.	Qu.	M 1905 A.B. 1908
—	Art. Heywood	Cla.	M 1906 A.B. 1910
—	Ern. Rich.	Sid.	M 1905 A.B. 1908. A.M. 1912
—	Humphrey Brunel ...	King's	M 1911
Nock,	Tho. Art.	Pem.	M 1900 A.B. 1903. A.M. 1907
Noel,	Evan Baillie	Trin.	M 1898 A.B. 1901
— (Hon.)	Rob. Edm. Tho. Moore	Trin.	M 1907
Nolan,	Edmond	Trin.	L 1897 A.B. 1899. A.M. 1903
Nolte,	Carl Hanns	Chr.	E 1911
Noon,	Leon.	Trin.	M 1896 A.B. 1899. B.C., A.M. 1903
—	Theodore Woods	Em.	M 1906
Nooruddin,	Muhmmad	Mag.	M 1909
Norbury,	Fra. Campbell	Joh.	M 1901 A.B. 1904. A.M. 1908
Norby,	Rob. Harold	Cath.	M 1912
Norman,	Cha. Archib. Kensit	Trin.	M 1902 A.B. 1905
—	Cha. Wake	Trin.	M 1910
—	Duncan Tho.	Em.	M 1908 A.B. 1911
—	Geo. Blake	Joh.	M 1894 A.B. 1897. B.C. 1903. M.B. 1904
—	John	Em.	M 1912
—	Newman Fre.	Em.	M 1902
—	Raymond Elder	Cla.	M 1908 A.B. 1911
—	Ronald Collet	Trin.	M 1891 A.B. 1894. A.M. 1902
—	Theodore Vassie	Jes.	M 1911
—	Tho. Stanley	Em.	M 1908 A.B. 1911
—	Will. Hen.	N. C.	M 1907 A.B. 1910
Norquoy,	Fre.	Em.	M 1901 A.B. 1904. A.M. 1908
Norrington,	Guy Pat. Terrell ...	Sid.	M 1905
Norris,	Cha. Gilb.	Cath.	M 1910

Norris,	Cha. Lloyd	Pem.	M 1887 A.B. 1890. A.M. 1901
—	Will. Forbes	Trin.	M 1912
—	Will. Hen. Hobbs ...	C. C.	M 1903 A.B. 1906
Norris-Elye,	Leon. Towne Sterndale	H. Sel.	M 1903 A.B. 1906
Norrish,	John Comins	Jes.	M 1906 A.B. 1909
Norsworthy,	Edwal	Cai.	M 1909
North,	Geo. Dudley	Jes.	M 1912
—	Walt. Grosvenor Bertie	Cai.	M 1901 A.B. 1904
Northam,	Percy Cuthbert	Em.	M 1894 A.B. 1901. A.M. 1904
Northcote,	Dudley Stafford	Trin.	M 1909
Northen,	Frank	Trin.	M 1894 A.B. 1897. A.M. 1902
—	Harold Abr.	Trin.	M 1899 A.B. 1903
Northorp,	Frederic	Joh.	M 1906 A.B. 1909
Northumberland (*Duke of*)			*See* Percy
Norton,	Dav. Geo.	Cai.	M 1905 A.B. 1908
—	Gilb. Paul	Cai.	M 1900 A.B. 1903. A.M. 1907
—	Hen. Tertius Ja. ...*Trin.		M 1905 A.B. 1908. A.M. 1912
—	John Grantley	Sid.	M 1894 A.B. 1897. A.M. 1906
—	Josiah Geo.	N. C.	M 1877 A.B. 1881. A.M. 1901
—	Leon. Martin	H. Sel.	M 1906
—	Rob. Holland	King's	M 1896 A.B. 1899. LL.B. 1900. A.M. 1905
—	Stanley Hen.	Qu.	M 1899 A.B. 1902. A.M. 1907
—	Victor Eustace Brampton	Em.	M 1906 A.B. 1909
—	Will. John	Cai.	M 1905 A.B. 1908
Norton-Fagge,	Frederic Walt. } Langford Grantley}	N. C.	L 1906 A.B. 1909
Norwood,	Gilb. ....*Joh.		M 1899 A.B. 1903. A.M. 1906
Nosworthy,	John Leon.	H. Sel.	M 1912
Nothwanger,	Rob. Geo.	Joh.	M 1895 A.B. 1898. A.M. 1902. M.B., B.C.
Nott, ·	Louis Cameron	Em.	M 1912 [1905
—	Percy Pleydell Neale	Pem.	M 1894 A.B. 1897. A.M. 1901
—	Tho. Walker	Em.	M 1907 A.B. 1910
Nowell,	Geo. Harold	N. C.	M 1885 Cath. A.B. 1888. M.B. 1893. B.C.
Nowers,	Will. Art.	Em.	M 1909 A.B. 1912 [1894. A.M. 1903
Noyes,	Harry Fra. Golding	Cai.	M 1899 A.B. 1902. M.B., B.C. 1907
—	John Curtis	Cla.	M 1912
Nugent,	Roland Tho.	Trin.	M 1904 A.B. 1909
Nunn,	Hen. Preston Vaughan	Joh.	M 1896 A.B. 1899. A.M. 1903
—	Tho. Hancock	Chr.	M 1880 A.B. 1884. A.M. 1904
Nunns,	Bern. Tho.	Joh.	M 1887 A.B. 1890. A.M. 1902
Nurse,	Sam. Dav.	Joh.	M 1908
Nutley,	Cha. Edw.	Joh.	M 1894 A.B. 1897. A.M. 1901
Nutman,	Basil Knox	Jes.	M 1900 A.B. 1903. B.C., A.M. 1907. M.D.
Nuttall,	Edw. Duncan	N. C.	M 1908 Chr. A.B. 1911 [1912
—	Enos		*LL.D.* 1908
—	[1] Geo. Hen. Falkiner		A.M. 1900 *Chr. Sc.D. 1906 *Mag.
Nutter,	Steph. Bern.	Em.	M 1904 A.B. 1907. A.M. 1912
Nutting,	Art. Ronald Stansmore	Trin. H.	M 1907 A.B. 1910
—	John Godfrey Stansmore	Trin.	M 1906

[1] Quick Professor of Biology, 1906, 1909, 1912.

O

Oakden,	John Gould	Cath.	M 1902 A.B. 1905
—	Will. Marshall	Pet.	M 1906 A.B. 1909
Oakeley,	Hen. Eckley Herb.	Joh.	M 1895 A.B. 1898. B.C. 1908
Oakes,	Montague Waddington	Em.	M 1909 A.B. 1912
Oakey,	Godfrey Ja.	Trin. H.	M 1895 A.B. 1898. A.M. 1902
—	John Martin	Trin.	M 1907 A.B. 1910
—	Phil. Herb.	Trin.	M 1902 A.B. 1905
Oakley,	Fre. Christian	Joh.	M 1908 A.B. 1911
—	Rob. Will.	H. Sel.	M 1903 A.B. 1907. A.M. 1912
Oaten,	Edw. Farley	Sid.	M 1903 A.B. 1906. LL.B. 1907. A.M.†
—	Walt. Sam.	Sid.	M 1911 [1910
Oates,	Bryan Will. Grace ...	Trin.	M 1901
Oatfield,	Will. John	King's	M 1910
Oats,	Giles	Trin.	M 1903 A.B., LL.B. 1906
—	Wilfrid	Cai.	M 1901 A.B. 1907
Obeyesèkere,	Donald	Trin.	M 1898 A.B. 1902. A.M.† 1908
—	Forester Augustus ...	Trin.	M 1899 A.B. 1903. A.M. 1908
—	Ja. Pet.	Trin.	M 1898 A.B. 1902. A.M.† 1905
—	Ja. Stanley	Trin.	M 1900 A.B. 1903
O'Brien,	Brian Fanning	Trin.	M 1911
—	John Crooke Power	Cai.	M 1903 A.B. 1906. A.M. 1910
—	Will. Frank	Em.	M 1903
O'Connell,	Jephson Byrne	N. C.	M 1912
O'Connor,	Art. Cathal	Trin.	M 1910
—	Ja.	N. C.	M 1907 Cath. A.B. 1911
Odam,	Cha. Leslie	Sid.	M 1911
Oddie,	Geo. Scudamore	Jes.	M 1901 A.B. 1904
Oddin Taylor,	John Frederic	C. C.	M 1902 A.B. 1905
Odgers,	Fra. Will.	Trin.	M 1898 A.B. 1901. A.M. 1905
—	Lindsey Noel Blake	Joh.	M 1911
—	Rob. Blake	Joh.	M 1908 A.B. 1911
Odling,	Egbert Fra.	Trin.	M 1900 A.B. 1903
—	Fra. Crawford	Cla.	M 1912
Oesterley,	Will. Oscar Emil ...	Jes.	M 1885 A.B. 1889. A.M. 1893. B.D. 1902.
O'Ferrall,	Cyril Lucian	Trin.	M 1910 [D.D. 1908
—	Ronald Stanhope More	Trin.	M 1909
Offer,	Clifford Jesse	C. C.	M 1907 A.B. 1910
Officer,	Harry Henley	H. Sel.	M 1911
Ogden,	Alf.	Chr.	M 1906 A.B. 1909
—	Alwyne Geo. Neville	C. C.	M 1908 A.B. 1911
—	Cha. Kay	Mag.	M 1908 A.B. 1911
—	John Basil	Chr.	M 1904 A.B., LL.B. 1907. A.M. 1911
Ogilvie,	Alex.	Trin.	M 1901 A.B. 1904
—	Gavin Lang	Trin.	M 1901 A.B. 1904
—	Geo. Norman	Trin.	M 1903
—	Hen.	King's	M 1900 A.B. 1903
—	Norman	Cla.	M 1909 A.B. 1912
—	Phil. Gordon	Pem.	M 1908 A.B. 1911
Ogle,	Phil. Hen. Douglas	Em.	M 1894 A.B. 1897. A.M. 1901
—	Rich. Will. Savile ...	Pem.	M 1901 A.B. 1904
Oglethorpe,	Hen. Clarke	Pem.	M 1904 A.B. 1907
O'Hagan,	Maur. Herb. Ignatius Towneley (*Lord*)	Trin.	M 1900 M. H. T. A.B. 1903. A.M. 1907
Ohashi,	Yeizo	N. C.	M 1907
O'Hea,	Pat. Alf.	N. C.	M 1901
Ohm,	Donald McKay	Joh.	M 1904 A.B. 1907

Oke,	Rob. Will. Leslie ...	Cai.	M 1902 C. C. A.B. 1908. A.M. 1912
O'Keeffe,	Alan Vivian	Sid.	M 1909 A.B. 1912
Okell,	Alf. Will.	Cla.	M 1899 A.B. 1903
—	Cha. Cyril	Joh.	M 1908 A.B. 1911
—	Will.	Cath.	M 1911
Okuma,	Nobutsune	Trin.	L 1906
Okura,	Kishichiro	Trin.	M 1903
Oldfield,	Claude Philip	Trin. H.	M 1908 A.B. 1911
—	Percival Jesse	Qu.	M 1912
—	Rich. Will.	Pem.	M 1910
Oldham,	Eustace Alf. Skinner	Jes.	M 1912
—	John Edw.	Em.	M 1904 A.B. 1907. A.M. 1911
—	John Walt. Hyde ...	Trin.	M 1912
Oliphant,	Fre. Marcus	Qu.	M 1904
—	Granville Rich.	Qu.	M 1908
—	Ja.	Em.	L 1904 A.B. 1906
Olive,	Geo. Will.	Cla.	M 1904 A.B. 1907. A.M. 1911
Oliver,	Dav. Edwin	Trin. H.	M 1912
—	Dav. Tho.	Trin. H.	M 1900 LL.B. 1902. LL.M. 1908
—	Edgar Gale	Down.	M 1898 A.B. 1901. A.M. 1905
—	Edm. Giffard	King's	M 1898 A.B. 1901
—	Fre. Scott	Trin.	M 1883 A.B. 1886. A.M. 1905
—	Geo. Younger	Mag.	M 1908 A.B. 1912
—	Harold Gordon	Cai.	M 1908 A.B. 1911
—	Matth. Will. Baillie	Trin.	M 1900 A.B. 1903. M.B., B.C., A.M. 1909
—	Raymond Edw. Creswick	Pem.	M 1912
—	Tho. Fre.	Trin.	M 1905
—	Tho. Herb.	Cai.	E 1906 A.B. 1909
—	Vere Fane Martin ...	Pem.	M 1907 A.B. 1910
—	Walt. Stanley Victor	Cla.	M 1910
Olivier,	Eric	Trin. H.	M 1907
—	Ockert John	Cla.	M 1905
Ollerenshaw,	Frank	Mag.	M 1910
Ollerhead,	John	H. Sel.	M 1895 A.B. 1901
Ollivant,	Edw.	King's	M 1900 A.B. 1903
—	Rupert Cha.	Trin.	M 1901 A.B. 1904
Olphert,	Wybrants	King's	M 1902 LL.B. 1906
Oman,	John Wood		A.M. 1909
Omar,	Abd-El-Fattah Hamdy	Down.	M 1909
—	Abdel Mageed	Em.	M 1902
Oncken,	Will. Gerhard	Trin.	M 1909
O'Neal,	Tho. Woollcombe Barton	Trin. H.	M 1886 A.B. 1891. A.M.† 1910
Onions,	Ja. Bern.	Trin. H.	M 1902 A.B. 1910
Onslow,	Victor Alex. Herb. Huia	Trin.	M 1908
Ontanon,	Candido	Down.	M 1905 A.B., LL.B. 1908
Onyon,	Rich. Rigby	C. C.	M 1906 A.B. 1909
Openshaw,	Cha. Geoffrey	Trin.	M 1901 A.B. 1904 C. Geofry. A.M. 1909
—	Percy Austin	Em.	M 1902
Opie,	Colin Adams	Cai.	M 1911
—	Philip Adams	Cai.	M 1904 A.B. 1907. B.C. 1911. M.B. 1912
Oppenheim,	Dav. Victor	Chr.	M 1904
—	¹ Lassa Fra. Lawrence		A.M. 1908
Oppenheimer,	Kurt Michael	Jes.	M 1911
Orange,	John Art.	Trin.	M 1905 A.B. 1908. A.M. 1912
Orchard,	Fra. Graham	Em.	M 1894 A.B. 1897. A.M. 1904
Orde,	Cha. Will.	King's	M 1904 A.B. 1907
—	Simon Edwin Hen.	Pem.	M 1912
O'Reilly,	Walt.	C. C.	M 1895 A.B. 1898. A.M. 1907
Orford,	Lewis Alf.	Cla.	M 1883 A.B. 1886. A.M. 1904

¹ Whewell Professor of International Law, 1908.

Orgill,	Harold Will.	N. C.	E 1900 A.B. 1903. A.M. 1907
—	Tyrrell Churton	Trin.	M 1903 A.B. 1906
Oriel,	Geo. Harold	Sid.	M 1912
—	ʼTheodore Hen. Bovington	Trin.	M 1911
O'Riordan,	Pat. Michael	N. C.	M 1901 A.B. 1904. A.M. 1912
Orlebar,	Jeffrey Alex. Amherst	Mag.	M 1897 M.B., B.C. 1905
Orme,	Basil Cross	H. Sel.	M 1911
—	Edm. Stuart	Qu.	M 1911
—	Fra. Reg.	Mag.	M 1911
—	Fra. Steph.	Em.	M 1897 A.B. 1901. A.M. 1905
—	Gilb. Edw.	Cai.	M 1892 A.B. 1896. M.B., B.C., A.M. 1901
Ormerod,	Ern. Will.	Trin.	M 1887 A.B. 1890. M.B., B.C., A.M. 1895.
Ormond,	John Millar	Trin. H.	M 1903 A.B. 1906 [M.D. 1901
Ormrod,	Ja.	Trin. H.	L 1903
—	Will.	Down.	M 1909 A.B. 1912
Ormsby,	Fra. Chatterton	Chr.	M 1900 A.B. 1903. A.M. 1908
Orpen,	Edw. Richards	Trin.	M 1903 A.B. 1906
—	Hen. Fabian	Pem.	M 1908 A.B. 1911
—	Theodore Cecil	Pem.	M 1899 A.B. 1902
—	Walt. Selwyn	H. Sel.	M 1912
Orr,	Art. Wellesley	Chr.	M 1904 A.B. 1907. A.M. 1911
—	Gerald Pet. Layton	Trin.	M 1902
--	John Wellesley	Joh.	L 1898 A.B. 1900. A.M. 1904
Orr-Ewing,	Archib.	Pem.	M 1910
Orr Ewing,	Archib. Ian	Trin.	M 1902
Orrey,	Will. Ern.	Cath.	M 1887 A.B. 1890. A.M. 1903
Orton,	Geo. Harrison	Trin.	M 1892 A.B. 1895. M.B., B.C., A.M. 1901.
—	John Swaffield	Pem.	M 1905 A.B. 1908 [M.D. 1906
—	Will. Hunt	Trin.	M 1897 A.B. 1900. M.B., B.C., A.M. 1906
Osborn,	Alex. Perry	Trin.	M 1905
—	Fre. Hen.	Trin.	M 1911
—	Geo. Steph.	Joh.	M 1891 A.B. 1894. A.M. 1901
—	Hen. Fairfield		*Sc.D.* 1904
—	Hen. Fairfield	Trin.	M 1909
Osborne,	Dav. Rob.	Chr.	M 1901 A.B. 1905
—	Edgar Ja. Phillips ...	N. C.	M 1907 Cath. A.B. 1910
—	Hen. Ja. Reg.	Chr.	M 1910
—	Leslie Hall	Chr.	M 1912
—	Will. Montague	Em.	M 1908 A.B. 1911
Oscroft,	Percy Will.	Sid.	M 1890 A.B. 1893. A.M. 1903
Osman,	Alf. Lancaster	H. Cav.	M 1890 Qu. A.B. 1893. A.M. 1909
Osmaston,	Dudley Fra.	King's	M 1911
—	John Hen.	Em.	M 1902 A.B. 1905
—	Ulric Ern.	Em.	M 1903 A.B. 1906
Osmond,	Tho. Edw.	Em.	M 1903 A.B. 1906
Ostle,	Will. Scott	Jes.	M 1898 A.B. 1901
Ostrehan,	Edw. Alf.	Cla.	M 1906 A.B. 1909
Ostwald,	Wilhelm Friedrich ...		*Sc.D.* 1904
Otter,	Melvil Cha. Woodard	King's	E 1908
—	Will. Hen.	Trin.	M 1898 A.B. 1902
Otter-Barry,	Hugh Van Lynden ...	Trin.	M 1905 A.B. 1908
Ottley,	John Hen. Cyril	Jes.	M 1909 A.B., LL.B. 1912
—	Warner Herb. Taylor	Joh.	M 1908 A.B. 1911
Otto,	Alf. Paul Heinrich ...	Em.	E 1909
Otty,	Harry Ralph	Cath.	M 1908 A.B. 1911
Ough,	Cha.	Em.	M 1899 A.B. 1902. A.M. 1906
—	John	Em.	M 1900 A.B. 1903. A.M. 1907
Oulton,	Ern. Vivian	Chr.	M 1900 A.B. 1903. M.B., B.C. 1909
Ovens,	Adam Beattie	Cla.	M 1910
—	Will. Gilb. Jones ...	Sid.	M 1909 A.B. 1912
Overbury,	Hen. Ralph	Trin.	M 1904

Overy,	Kenneth	Em.	M 1902 A.B. 1905
Owen,	Alb. Harold	Cai.	M 1899 A.B. 1902
—	Art. Ryder Bastard	Trin.	M 1912
—	Cha. Hen.	Jes.	M 1898 A.B. 1901
—	Cha. Maynard	Em.	M 1867 A.B. 1871. LL.M. 1874. A.M.,
—	Dav. Hugh	Joh.	M 1912　　　　　　　　　　[LL.D. 1901
—	Dav. John	Jes.	M 1902 A.B. 1905
—	Edw. Theodore	H. Sel.	M 1898 A.B. 1901
—	Edwin Augustus	Trin.	M 1910 A.B. 1912
—	Fra. Herb. Gordon Tudor	Trin. H.	M 1904 A.B. 1907
—	Gerald Campbell ...	Trin. H.	M 1900 A.B. 1903. LL.B. 1906
—	Gwilym	Chr.	M 1901 A.B. 1904. A.M. 1908
—	Hugh Brindley	Cai.	M 1897 B.C. 1906. M.B. 1908
—	Hywel	Trin.	M 1902 LL.B. 1905
—	John Noel Stowers ...	H. Sel.	M 1907 A.B. 1910
—	Owen	Cai.	M 1908 A.B. 1911
—	Phil. Rich. Tudor ...	Chr.	M 1907
—	Sackville Herb. Edw. Gregg	Pem.	M 1898 A.B. 1902
—	Syd. Art.	Trin.	M 1898 A.B. 1901. B.C. 1905. M.B. 1906.
—	Tho.	Jes.	M 1906　　　　　　　　　　[M.D. 1910
—	Will. Benj.	Cath.	M 1900 A.B. 1903. A.M. 1912
—	Will. Elworthy Montague	H. Sel.	M 1901 A.B. 1905
Owens,	Fra. Hen.	Joh.	M 1912
Owston,	Clifford Scott	Jes.	M 1908 A.B. 1911
Oxberry,	Walt. Geo.	Down.	M 1906 A.B. 1909
Oxley,	Art. Ern.	Trin.	M 1908 A.B. 1911
—	Hor. Finningley	Qu.	M 1902 A.B. 1905

P

Pacey,	Cyril Ja.	Sid.	M 1903 A.B. 1907
Packe,	Geo. Garfield	Trin.	M 1899 A.B. 1902. M.B., B.C., A.M. 1907
Packer,	Geo.	N. C.	E 1902 A.B. 1905. A.M. 1908
—	Geo. Fre. Harold ...	N. C.	E 1902 Down. A.B. 1906. A.M. 1909
Paddison,	Jos. Tonge	H. Sel.	M 1896 A.B. 1899. A.M. 1906
Padfield,	Fra. Jos.	Cai.	M 1903 A.B. 1906. A.M. 1910
—	Will. Herb. Greenland	Em.	M 1893 A.B. 1896. A.M.† 1902
Padget,	Will. Harrap	Qu.	M 1909 A.B. 1912
Padmanabha	Pillai, Kannanthote ⎰ Padmanabhan ⎱	Trin. H.	M 1911
Padwick,	Harold Boultbee	Em.	M 1908 A.B. 1912
Page,	Alf. Hen.	Down.	M 1907 A.B. 1910
—	Art. Shaw	Sid.	M 1889 A.B. 1892. A.M. 1902
—	Cecil Arnold	Qu.	M 1907 A.B. 1910
—	Cecil Grantham	Trin. H.	M 1904 A.B. 1909
—	Cecil Herb. Winter	C. C.	M 1896 A.B. 1899. A.M. 1903. B.C. 1906.
—	Cecil Walt.	Em.	M 1895 A.B. 1898. A.M. 1902 [M.D. 1909
—	Cha. Carew	Cla.	M 1902
—	Dennis Salmon	Cai.	M 1907 A.B. 1910
—	Frank Arundel	Qu.	M 1910
—	Geo. Fre.	Em.	M 1901 A.B. 1904
—	Gerald Fra. Homer	Pem.	M 1901 A.B. 1905
—	John	Cai.	M 1903 A.B. 1906
—	Martin Fountain ...	Cai.	M 1905 A.B. 1908. A.M. 1912

Page,	Syd. Watson	Em.	M 1912
—	Wallace Evans	Em.	M 1910
—	Will. Morton ....*King's	M 1902 A.B. 1905. A.M. 1909
Pageot,	Rene Emile Jos.	Cai.	M 1905
Paget,	Cecil Walt.	Pem.	L 1901
—	Geoffrey Walt.	Cai.	M 1909 A.B. 1912
—	Geo. Norrie	Trin. H.	M 1908
—	Harold Edm. Geo. ...	Chr.	M 1905 A.B. 1908
—	Owen Frank	N. C.	E 1889 Cai. M.B., B.C. 1895. M.D.+ 1906
—	Will. Edm.	Trin.	M 1898 A.B. 1901
Paget-Tomlinson, Edw. Edmondson	Trin. H.	M 1901 A.B. 1904
Pahl,	Carl	Pem.	E 1910
Paige,	John Friend	Cai.	M 1910
Pain,	Art. Wellesley	Cath.	M 1862 A.B. 1866. A.M. 1899. D.D.+ 1903
—	Basil Hewitt	Em.	M 1897 A.B. 1900. M.B., B.C. 1905
—	Cha. And. Wykeham	H. Sel.	M 1906 A.B. 1909
—	Edw. Davy	Pem.	M 1898 A.B. 1901
—	Harold	N. C.	M 1901 A.B. 1904. A.M. 1908
—	John Wyndham	Pem.	M 1905 A.B. 1908
—	Kenneth Wellesley ...	Qu.	M 1910
—	Will.	Jes.	M 1907 A.B. 1910
Paine,	Cha. Alb.	Trin.	M 1891 A.B. 1894. A.M. 1903
—	Hen. Howard	Trin.	M 1905 A.B. 1907. A.M. 1911
—	Walt. Lionel	Sid.	M 1900 A.B. 1903. A.M. 1908
—	Will. Art.	Trin.	M 1909 A.B. 1911
Painter,	Hen. Smith	H. Sel.	M 1911
Paisley,	Fawcett Dodgson ...	Chr.	M 1904 A.B. 1907
Pakeman,	Sid. Arnold	Sid.	M 1910
Palat,	Ramunny Menon ...	Em.	M 1906
Palchoudhuri, Manmatha	Pet.	M 1902
Paley,	Geo. Art.	Trin.	M 1893 A.B. 1896. A.M. 1901
Palles,	Chris.		*LL.D.* 1910
Pallis,	Andreas Alex.	Trin.	M 1907 A.B. 1910
Palliser,	Wray Fre. Cecil	C. C.	M 1911 [1908. M.D. 1911
Palmer,	Alb. Syd. Morton ...	Jes.	M 1897 A.B. 1900. B.C. 1906. M.B., A.M.
—	Basil Hen.	Pem.	M 1900 A.B. 1903. M.B., B.C. 1909
—	Cadwallader Edwards	Cai.	M 1898 A.B. 1901. M.B., B.C., A.M. 1905
—	Clarence Edw. Stanhope	C. C.	M 1902
—	Clayton	Cla.	M 1904
—	Clephan	Sid.	M 1901 A.B. 1904
—	Eric de Sanctis	Cath.	M 1907 A.B. 1910
—	Fre. Will. Morton ...	Jes.	M 1896 A.B. 1899. M.B., B.C. 1905. A.M.
—	Geoffrey Fre. Neill ...	Trin.	M 1912 [1906. M.D. 1909
—	Geo. John Kinloch ...	Trin.	M 1909
—	Harold Godfrey	Trin.	M 1906 A.B. 1909
—	Harry	N. C.	M 1892 A.B. 1896. A.M. 1903
—	Herb. Richmond	Trin. H.	M 1896 A.B. 1899. LL.B. 1900. A.M. 1910
—	John Tho. Edw.	Joh.	M 1900 A.B. 1903
—	Jos. John Beauchamp	Joh.	M 1885 A.B. 1888. A.M. 1903
—	Kenneth Randall ...	Trin.	M 1910
—	Leon. Cha. Ralph ...	N. C.	M 1907
—	Lewis	Trin. H.	M 1879 A.B. 1884 (2). A.M. 1906
—	Michael Geo. Llewellen	Cla.	M 1903
—	Rob.	N. C.	M 1895 Cath. A.B. 1898. A.M. 1903
—	Rob. Cecil	C. C.	M 1889 A.B. 1892. A.M. 1910
—	Roy Hatchard	Pem.	M 1909
—	Tho. Norman Palk ...	Joh.	M 1899 A.B., LL.B. 1904
—	Wilfrid Ern.	Joh.	M 1912
—	Will. Geo.	Joh.	M 1911
—	Will. Harold	Trin. H.	M 1911
Palmer-Douglas, Archib.	Trin.	M 1899 A.B. 1903

M. 27

Palmer Douglas,	Malcolm	Trin.	M 1901
Palmes,	Will. Tevery	Trin.	M 1908 A.B. 1911
Pam,	Eric Art.	Cla.	M 1911
Pandit,	Sadashiva Ramkrishna	N. C.	M 1902 Chr. A.B.1905. LL.B.1906. A.M.†
—	Vasudeo Rāmkrishna	N. C.	M 1895 A.B. 1898. A.M.† 1902 [1912
Pank,	Phil. Esmond Durrell	Cai.	M 1910
Panse,	Damodarrao Ganpatrao	Down.	M 1905
Panter,	Art. Edw.	Cla.	M 1907 A.B. 1910
Panton,	Phil. Noel	Trin.	M 1896 A.B. 1899. M.B., B.C., A.M. 1905
—	Sid. Fraser	Chr.	M 1903 A.B. 1906
Pape,	Alf. Garbutt	Mag.	L 1912
Papp-Szász,	Tho.	Trin.	M 1908
Paramore,	Will. Erasmus	Joh.	M 1896 A.B. 1899. M.B., B.C., A.M. 1905
Paranjpye,	Raghunath Puru-shottam } *Joh.		M 1896 A.B. 1899. A.M.† 1903
Parbury,	Fre. Claud Strachan	Trin.	M 1901 A.B. 1904
Parcell,	Norman Howe	Chr.	M 1904 A.B. 1907. A.M. 1911
Parham,	Hedley John	Trin. H.	M 1911
Parish,	Frank Geo. Woodbine	Trin. H.	M 1908
—	Geo. Woodbine	Cai.	M 1905
—	Will. Oscar	Cath.	M 1912
Parke,	Allan	Jes.	M 1911
Parker,	Fra. Cecil Shirecliffe	Trin. H.	M 1895 A.B. 1898. A.M. 1903
—	Fre. Hen.	Pem.	M 1895 A.B. 1898. M.B., B.C. 1903
—	Geo. Musgrave	Em.	M 1903 A.B. 1906
—	Harold Edm.	Trin.	M 1909 A.B. 1912
—	Hen. Edw.	Pem.	M 1909
—	Hen. Nichols	Cath.	M 1909
—	Herb.	Joh.	M 1907 A.B. 1910
—	Herb. Fra.	Em.	M 1893 A.B. 1896. M.B., B.C. 1899. M.D.
—	Hor. Victor	Jes.	M 1910 [1902
—	Horatio Will.		*Mus.D.* 1902
—	Ja. Douglas	Pem.	M 1906 A.B. 1910
—	John Cartwright	Chr.	M 1904 A.B. 1907
—	(*Hon.*) John Holford	Trin.	M 1904 A.B. 1907
—	John Stanley	Cla.	L 1911
—	John Will.	C. C.	M 1910
—	Leslie Hen.	Trin. H.	M 1909 A.B. 1912
—	Owen Fortrie	Cai.	M 1899 A.B. 1902. A.M.† 1906
—	Percy Herb.	Qu.	M 1911
—	Rich. Gazely	N. C.	L 1876 Chr. A.B. 1879. A.M.† 1912
—	Rob. Derwent	Cai.	M 1890 A.B. 1893. M.B., B.C. 1897. A.M.,
—	Roger	Chr.	M 1900 A.B. 1904 [M.D. 1901
—	Roger Hen.	Trin.	M 1908 A.B. 1911
—	Tho. Will. Lax	Qu.	M 1911
—	Wilfred Hen.	Trin.	M 1908 A.B. 1911
Parker-Jervis,	Evelyn St Vincent	Trin.	M 1902
Parker-Rhodes,	John	Pem.	M 1902
Parker Smith,	Archib. Colin Hamilton }	King's	M 1902 A.B. 1905
—	Rob.	Cath.	M 1900 A.B. 1903
—	Wilmot Babington ...	King's	M 1904 A.B. 1907
Parkes,	Cha. Will.	Trin.	M 1900 A.B. 1903. A.M. 1910
—	Herb. Edgar	Trin.	M 1900 A.B. 1903. A.M. 1907
Parkin,	Reg. Cha.	Cla.	M 1905
Parkinson,	Ern. Alf.	Chr.	M 1907 A.B. 1910
—	Hen. Clifford	Chr.	M 1909
—	John	Joh.	M 1901 A.B. 1903. A.M. 1908
—	Jos. Ern.	King's	M 1903 A.B. 1906. A.M. 1910
—	Louis Coulson	Chr.	M 1888 A.B. 1891. A.M. 1901
—	Percy Rich.	Cai.	M 1898 A.B. 1901. M.B., B.C. 1907

Parkinson,	Wilfrid	Pet.	M 1906 A.B. 1909
—	Will. Gerald	Em.	M 1901 A.B. 1904. B.C. 1908. M.B. 1909.
Parks,	Alb. Leon.	Qu.	M 1911 [A.M. 1910
—	Hub. Tho.	Mag.	M 1895 A.B. 1898. LL.B. 1899. A.M. 1902
Parlby,	Joshua	Trin.	M 1911
Parmenter,	Godwyn Edw. Piper	Jes.	L 1911
Parnell,	Claude Will.	Qu.	M 1892 A.B. 1896. A.M. 1901. Mus.B.
—	Fre. Rich.	Joh.	M 1905 A.B. 1908 [1911
—	Tho.	Joh.	M 1900 A.B. 1903. A.M.† 1908
Parr,	Art. Mountfort	H. Sel.	M 1905
Parrack,	Herb.	Pet.	E 1908 A.B. 1911
Parratt,	Walt.		*Mus.D.* 1910
Parrington,	Noel	Cla.	M 1905 A.B. 1908
—	Will. Ferguson	Cla.	M 1908 A.B. 1911
Parrott,	Jos. Augustine	Chr.	M 1910
Parry,	Art. Haydn	Cla.	M 1910
—	Bern. King	Joh.	M 1911
—	Cha. Bern.	Trin.	M 1903 A.B. 1906
—	Dav. Ja.	Trin.	M 1910 A.B. 1912
—	Edw. Art.	King's	M 1898 A.B. 1902
—	Edw. Gwyn	Chr.	M 1904
—	Fra. Alex.	Trin.	M 1901 A.B. 1904
—	Ja. Hales	Joh.	M 1908 A.B. 1911
—	John Horndon	Pem.	M 1882 A.B. 1885. A.M. 1902
—	Jos.	N. C.	M 1895 Chr. A.B. 1898. A.M. 1904
—	Joshua Powell	Jes.	M 1900 A.B. 1903. A.M. 1907
—	Nevill Edw.	Trin.	M 1906
—	Norman Cecil	Trin.	M 1905 A.B. 1908
—	Raymond Barrington	Trin. H.	M 1912
—	Reg. St John ....*Trin.		M 1876 A.B. 1880. A.M. 1883. B.D. 1903
—	Tho. Hen.	Chr.	M 1900 A.B., LL.B. 1904
—	Tho. Hugh	Em.	M 1908 A.B. 1910
—	Tho. Ja.	Em.	M 1897 A.B. 1900. A.M. 1905
—	Tho. Wilson	Joh.	M 1884 A.B. 1887. A.M. 1891. M.B., B.C.
Parry-Jones,	Montagu Martindale	Trin.	M 1907 A.B. 1910 [1894. M.D. 1905
—	Percival Edw. Holland	Pem.	M 1911
Parsons,	Art. Dav. Clere	Trin.	M 1901 A.B. 1904
—	Basil Geo.	Em.	M 1906 A.B. 1909
—	Cha. Algernon	Joh.	M 1873 A.B. 1877. A.M 1894. *Sc.D.* 1908
—	Cornelius	Pem.	M 1901 A.B. 1904
—	Desmond Clere	Trin.	M 1909 A.B. 1912
—	Harold	Cai.	M 1902 A.B. 1905. M.B., B.C. 1910
—	Herb. John	Qu.	M 1896 A.B. 1899. A.M. 1904
—	John Randal	Trin.	M 1904 A.B. 1907
—	Rich. Edw.	Trin.	M 1907 A.B. 1910
Part,	Gerald Meyrick	Trin.	M 1911
Partington,	John Bertram	Pem.	M 1903 A.B. 1906
Partridge,	Archib. Harry	Em.	M 1905 A.B. 1908. A.M. 1912
—	Arnold	Jes.	M 1888 A.B. 1891. A.M. 1905
—	Cha. Stanley	Chr.	M 1892 A.B. 1895. A.M. 1901
—	Geo. Ja.	Qu.	M 1912
—	Heathfield Walt.	King's	M 1906 A.B. 1909
—	John Wright	Qu.	M 1909 A.B. 1912
—	Rob. Hen.	Pem.	M 1909 A.B., LL.B. 1912
—	Walt. Wright	Qu.	M 1901 A.B. 1904. A.M. 1912
Pascoe,	Art. Percival	Em.	M 1898 A.B. 1901. A.M. 1909
—	Edwin Hall	Joh.	M 1897 A.B. 1900. A.M. 1904
—	Eldred	Jes.	M 1891 A.B. 1894. A.M.† 1909
—	Fre. John	Joh.	M 1912
Pascoe-Williams,	Vernon Gibson	Jes.	M 1906 A.B. 1909
Pashkoff,	Alex. Alexandrovich	Trin.	M 1908 A.B. 1911

Pashkoff,	Basil Alexandrovich	Trin.	M 1908 A.B. 1911
Pask,	Rob.	N. C.	M 1905 A.B. 1908. A.M. 1912
Pask-Hughes, Bern.		Cai.	M 1909
Paskin,	Jesse John	Joh.	M 1912
Pass,	Alf. Douglas	King's	M 1904 A.B. 1907. A.M. 1911
—	Herman Leon.	Joh.	M 1894 A.B. 1898. A.M. 1901
Passant,	Ern. Ja.	Down.	M 1908 A.B. 1911
Passingham, Cha. Will.		Trin.	M 1902
Patchett,	Ern. Will.	Em.	M 1900 A.B. 1903
Pate,	Hen. Reg.	King's	M 1899 A.B. 1902
—	John Alex.	C. C.	M 1899 A.B. 1902. LL.B. 1905. A.M. 1906
Patel,	Jehangir Barjorjee ...	N. C.	M 1907
—	Ranchhodbhai Bhaibabhai	Joh.	M 1899 A.B.1902. LL.B.1904. A.M.†1906
Paternò di Sessa, (Marchese) Emanuele			*Sc.D.* 1912
Paterson,	Alex. Granville	Qu.	M 1881 A.B. 1884 (2). A.M. 1901
—	Archib. Rich.	Em.	M 1890 A.B. 1893. M.B., B.C. 1898. M.D.
—	Cha. Edw.	Pem.	M 1896 A.B. 1899. A.M. 1903　　　[1901
—	Dav. Williamson Stewart	Jes.	M 1908
—	Eric Will.	Trin. H.	M 1907
—	Geo. Art. Reg.	Jes.	M 1911
—	Geo. McLeod	Pem.	M 1909 A.B. 1912
—	Hen.	Sid.	M 1911
—	Herb. John	Trin.	M 1886 A.B. 1889. M.B., B.C., A.M. 1893.
—	Ja.	Cla.	M 1894 A.B. 1897. A.M. 1901 [M.C. 1910
—	Ja. Jardine	Trin.	M 1901
—	John Melvin	Trin. H.	M 1882 A.B., LL.B. 1885. A.M., LL.M.
—	Kenneth	Cla.	M 1912　　　　　　　　　　　[1902
—	Matth. Wallace	Joh.	M 1905 A.B. 1908
—	Reg. Gresham Clive	*Qu.	M 1894 A.B. 1897. A.M. 1901
—	Rob. Denzil	Cla.	M 1911
—	Tho. Will. Staniforth	Cai.	M 1893 A.B. 1896. B.C., A.M. 1901. M.B.
—	Will. Hen.	Mag.	M 1912　　　　　　　　　　　[1902
Paton,	Alf. Maur.	Joh.	E 1899 A.B. 1901
—	Edw. Curphey	Sid.	M 1887 A.B. 1890. A.M. 1903
—	Edw. Richmond	Pem.	M 1907 A.B. 1911
—	Ja. Donald	Trin.	M 1910
—	Leslie Johnston	Cai.	M 1891 A.B. 1895. B.C. 1900. M.B. 1902
—	Roger Clavell	Qu.	M 1895 A.B. 1898. A.M. 1905
—	Walt.	Cla.	M 1911
—	Will. Bern.	Chr.	M 1898 A.B. 1901
Paton Smith, Eric Agar		Trin.	M 1909
Patron,	Fra. Jos.	Trin.	M 1909 A.B. 1912
Pattani,	Anantray Prebhashanker	Down.	M 1905 A.B. 1910
Patten,	Will. Geo.	Sid.	M 1911
Patterson,	Dav. Clarke	Chr.	M 1898 A.B. 1901
—	Eric Ja.	Pet.	M 1910
—	John	N. C.	M 1900 Em. A.B. 1902. A.M. 1907
—	John Rob.	Joh.	M 1911
—	Leon.	Trin.	M 1903 A.B. 1906. A.M. 1912
—	Rich. Ferrar	Joh.	M 1907 A.B. 1910
Patteson,	Cha.	Pem.	M 1911
—	Cyril	C. C.	M 1909
—	John Dossie	Trin.	M 1907 A.B. 1910
Pattinson,	Geo. Norman	Em.	M 1906 A.B. 1909
—	Lawrence Art.	Jes.	M 1909 A.B. 1912
Pattison,	Geo. Hen.	N. C.	L 1899 A.B. 1904
Patton,	Arnold Gordon	Joh.	M 1912
Patuck,	Rustomjee Sorabjee	Joh.	M 1905 A.B. 1908
Patwardhan, Vithalrao Chinta- manrao		Trin.	M 1909 A.B. 1912
Paul,	Art. Blackwell	Chr.	M 1906 A.B. 1909

Paul,	Art. Edw.	Cai.	M 1899 A.B. 1903
—	Hamilton	Cai.	E 1910
—	Jos. Dav. Dallin	Pem.	M 1897 A.B. 1900. A.M. 1904
—	Rob. Joshua	Trin.	M 1902
—	Will. Edm. Jeffrey ...	Trin.	M 1904 LL.B. 1907. A.B. 1908
Paulley,	Harold	Joh.	M 1907 A.B. 1910
—	Will. Minterne	H. Sel.	M 1905 A.B. 1908
Paulson,	John Dickinson	Joh.	M 1899 A.B. 1902
Pauncefort Duncombe,(*Sir*)Everard Philip Digby		Trin.	M 1904 A.B. 1907. A.M. 1911
Pavey-Smith,	Alf. Bern.	Cla.	M 1905 A.B. 1908
Pavlov,	Johannes		*Sc.D.* 1912
Pawar,	Vinayak Madhaorao	Em.	M 1912
Pawle,	Clem. Dawes	Trin.	M 1893 A.B. 1896. A.M. 1901
—	Hanbury	Cai.	M 1904
—	John	Trin.	M 1903
Pawson,	Dav. Owen	Trin. H.	M 1907 A.B., LL.B. 1910
Payn,	Frederic Will.	Trin. H.	M 1891 A.B. 1894. LL.B. 1895. LL.M.
Payne,	Archib. Aldridge ...	C. C.	M 1909 A.B. 1912 [1902
—	Duncan Noel	Em.	M 1902 A.B. 1905. A.M. 1909
—	Frank Reg.	Pet.	M 1899 A.B. 1902
—	Geo. Cha.	N. C.	M 1894 Em. A.B. 1897. A.M. 1902
—	Geo. Herb.	Jes.	M 1911
—	Hen. Carl Fra. Boghurst	N. C.	M 1898 A.B. 1901. LL.B. 1904
—	Herb. Will. Geo. ...	Em.	M 1909
—	Ja. Humphrey Allen	N. C.	M 1895 Trin. H. A.B. 1898. A.M.† 1904
—	Ja. Will.	Em.	M 1911
—·	John Ern.	Pet.	M 1895 A.B. 1898. A.M. 1902. B.C. 1903.
—	Maur. Geo. Jervis ...	H. Sel.	M 1906 A.B. 1909 [M.B. 1904
—	Meyrick Whitmore ...	Trin.	M 1903 A.B. 1906
—	Otto Vaughan	Joh.	M 1897 A.B. 1900. B.C. 1905. M.B. 1907
—	Reg. Merac	C. C.	M 1910
Payne Cook,	Gerald Geo.	C. C.	M 1902 A.B. 1905. A.M. 1909
Payne-Gallwey,	Lowry Philip	Trin.	M 1910
Payton,	Wilfrid Hugh	Trin.	M 1911
Peabody,	Ja. Hen.	N. C.	M 1895 A.B. 1898. A.M. 1906
—	Malcolm Endicott ...	Trin.	M 1910
Peace,	Lister Radcliffe	Qu.	M 1908 A.B. 1911
Peacey,	Capel Coope	Cla.	M 1898 A.B. 1901. A.M. 1906
—	Howard Marriott ...	King's	M 1899 A.B. 1902
Peach,	Will. Stanley	Em.	M 1908 A.B. 1910
Peache,	Rich. Coventry	Trin.	M 1908 A.B. 1911
Peachell,	Fre. Harry	King's	M 1894 A.B. 1897. A.M. 1902
Peacock,	Cha. Ern.	Joh.	M 1895 A.B. 1898. A.M.† 1902
—	Dav. Hen.	Trin.	M 1908 A.B. 1911
—	Geoffrey	Cla.	M 1910
—	Harold Baillie	Cla.	M 1904
—	Ja.	Trin.	M 1903 A.B. 1906
—	Mansel Reg.	Trin.	M 1906 A.B. 1909
—	Nugent Pashley	Trin. H.	M 1910
—	Oswald Raper	Chr.	M 1904
—	Wilfrid Morgan	Jes.	M 1909 A.B. 1912
Peacocke,	Phil. Graeme	C. C.	M 1889 A.B. 1892. A.M. 1901
Peak,	Norman	H. Sel.	M 1908
Peake,	Austin Hen.	Joh.	M 1898 A.B. 1900. A.M. 1905
—	Cecil Gerald Wyatt	Trin. H.	M 1910
—	Edw. Gordon	Cla.	M 1895 A.B. 1898. LL.B. 1905
Pearce,	And. Harman	Cla.	M 1911
—	Bertram Wilson	Joh.	M 1887 A.B. 1890. A.M. 1902
—	Fra. Hen.	Trin.	M 1889 A.B. 1892. M.B., B.C., A.M. 1903
—	Hen.	Qu.	M 1906 A.B. 1910

Pegg,	Harry Geo.	Jes.	M 1909
—	John	Cla.	M 1908 A.B. 1912
—	John Stanton	C. C.	M 1893 A.B. 1899. A.M. 1902
Pegge,	Art. Vernon	Cai.	M 1912
Pegler,	Fra. Egerton	Jes.	M 1909
Peile,	John	Chr.	M 1897 A.B. 1900. A.M. 1904
Peirce,	Edw. Gordon	Jes.	M 1892 A.B. 1895. A.M. 1901
Peiris,	Leon. Ja. Martinus	Joh.	M 1911
Peirson,	Ern. Goodwyn	Pet.	M 1878 A.B. 1882. A.M. 1905
Pelham,	(*Hon.*) Marcus Herb.	Trin.	M 1912
—	Sackville Geo.	Trin.	M 1908
—	Walt. Hen.	Trin.	M 1905 A.B. 1908. A.M. 1912
Pelham Clinton, Guy Edw.		Trin.	M 1912
Pellier,	Cha. de Chanval	Cla.	M 1892 A.B. 1895. A.M. 1899. B.C. 1902
Pelling,	Stewart Breeze	Cla.	M 1904 A.B. 1907. A.M. 1911
Pellow,	John Edwards	Joh.	M 1896 A.B. 1900. M.B., B.C., A.M. 1904
Pelly,	Arnold Claude	Trin.	M 1901 A.B. 1904. A.M. 1910
—	Edm. Godfrey	Trin.	M 1908
—	Evelyn	Pem.	M 1903 A.B. 1907
—	Fra. Brian	Trin.	M 1908
—	Rich. Lawrence	Cla.	M 1905 A.B. 1908. A.M. 1912
—	Rich. Stanley	Pem.	M 1899 A.B. 1902
Peltzer,	Jacques Fernand ...	Trin. H.	M 1909
Pemberton,	Fra. Percy Campbell	Trin.	M 1903
—	John	Cla.	M 1912
—	Will. Harris	Pem.	M 1908 A.B., LL.B. 1911
Pendavis,	Fre. Cha.	Cla.	M 1901
Pendered,	John Hawkes	Cai.	M 1906 A.B. 1909
Penfold,	Harold Lashmar	Joh.	M 1906 A.B. 1909
Penistan,	Edw. Ja.	Cla.	M 1895 A.B. 1898. A.M. 1902
Penman,	Frank Garfield	Jes.	M 1903 A.B. 1906. A.M. 1910
—	Lancelot Tulip	King's	M 1898 A.B. 1901
—	Tho.	Sid.	M 1896 A.B. 1899. LL.B. 1900. A.M. 1904
Penn,	Art. Hor.	Trin.	M 1905 A.B. 1908
—	Geoffrey Mark	Trin.	M 1905 A.B. 1910
Pennell,	Kenneth Eustace Lee	Jes	M 1908 A.B. 1911
—	Vernon Cha.	Pem.	M 1908 A.B. 1911
Penney,	Art. Edwin	Qu.	M 1906 A.B. 1909
Pennington,	Cuthbert Bertram Tho. Pennington }	Cla.	M 1899 A.B. 1902. A.M. 1908
—	Drury	Cai.	M 1893 A.B. 1897. M.B., B.C. 1905
Penny,	Cyril John	Jes.	M 1911
—	Geo. Stephen	Jes.	M 1904 A.B. 1907
—	Will. Maxwell	Jes.	M 1903 A.B. 1906. B.C. 1910. M.B., A.M. [1912
Pennyman,	Ja. Beaumont Worsley	Trin.	M 1902
Penrose,	Edw. John McNeill	Trin.	M 1907 A.B. 1910
—	Joscelyn Denis	Trin. H.	L 1903
Penry,	Ja. Rowland Llewellyn	Qu.	M 1900 A.B. 1903. A.M. 1907
Pentland,	Geo. Cha. Croker ...	Cai.	M 1908 A.B. 1911
Penton,	Cyril Fre.	Trin.	M 1905 A.B. 1908. A.M. 1912
Penzer,	Hen. Art.	N. C.	M 1893 Cath. A.B. 1899. A.M. 1903
—	Norman Mosley	C. C.	M 1911
Pepin,	Art. Raymond	Pem.	M 1912
Pepper,	Geo. Evered	N. C.	M 1906 Cath. A.B. 1909
Percival,	And. Fra.	Cai.	M 1905 A.B. 1908
—	Harold Fez	Trin.	M 1901 A.B. 1904
Percivall,	Cha. Wilhelm	Jes.	M 1898 A.B. 1901. A.M. 1910
Percy,	Hen. Geo. (*Duke of Northumberland*)		LL.D. 1908
Perera,	Galappatti Kankananage Will. }	Chr.	M 1904 A.B. 1907
Perham,	Cecil	Chr.	M 1900 A.B. 1903

Perkin,	Alf. Litton Dix	Trin. H.	M 1911
—	Will. Hen.		*Sc. D.* 1910
Perkins,	Art. Lea	Em.	M 1898 A.B. 1901. A.M. 1906
—	Bertram Mark Nevill	Cai.	L 1907 A.B. 1908
—	Cha. Steele	Joh.	M 1898 A.B. 1901
—	Fra. Art.	Em.	M 1907 A.B. 1910
—	Ja. Stanley	N. C.	M 1912
—	John Shirley Steele	H. Aye.	M 1894 Joh. A.B. 1897. M.B., B.C. 1902
—	Will. Geo.	C. C.	M 1904
Perks,	John Noel Radcliffe	Mag.	M 1911
Perrens,	Cha. Newton Triscott	Trin.	M 1907 A.B. 1910
Perrett,	Geo. Burr	Em.	E 1906 A.B. 1909
Perrier,	Jean Octave Edmond		*Sc. D.* 1909
Perrin,	Eugène Courtenay ...	Pet.	M 1905 A.B. 1908. LL.B. 1909
—	Maur. Nasmith	Pem.	M 1906 A.B. 1909
—	Mich.	King's	M 1908 A.B. 1911
—	Walt. Syd.	Cai.	M 1901 A.B. 1904. A.M. 1908
Perrins,	Cha. Fra. Dyson	Mag.	M 1911
—	Meredith Dyson	Trin.	M 1910
Perrot,	Georges		*Litt. D.* 1904
—	Gordon	Chr.	M 1912
Perry,	Cha. Copland	Trin.	E 1912 A.M. 1912 (Oxf. incorp.)
—	Edw. Will.	Cai.	M 1910
—	Evelyn Walt. Copland	Trin.	M 1908
—	Guy Allan	Qu.	M 1910
—	Hen. Cha.	Qu.	M 1905 A.B. 1908
—	John Cyril	Joh.	M 1907 A.B. 1910
—	John Melbourne	Trin.	M 1904 A.B. 1909. A.M. 1912
—	Lionel Banks	Qu.	M 1903 A.B. 1906. B.C. 1909. M.B. 1910
—	Theodore	Pet.	M 1903 A.B. 1906
—	Walt. Arnold Copland	Trin.	M 1906 A.B. 1909
—	Will. Ja.	H. Sel.	M 1906 A.B. 1909
Pert,	Fre. Ja.	Sid.	M 1885 A.B. 1888. A.M.† 1905
Peshall,	Cha. John Eyre	Pem.	M 1901 A.B. 1904
—	Sam. Fre.	Cai.	M 1902 A.B. 1905
Petch,	Cha. Hen.	C. C.	M 1886 A.B. 1889. A.M. 1909
—	Reg. Walt. Tatton ...	C. C.	M 1890 A.B. 1893. A.M. 1901
Peters,	Art.	Trin.	M 1912
—	August Detlef	Joh.	M 1911
—	Austin Jos.	Chr.	M 1911
—	Benj. Alf. Isaac	Jes.	M 1901 A.B. 1904. B.C. 1908. M.B. 1910
—	Edw. Cha.	Chr.	M 1906 A.B. 1909
—	Marquis	Cath.	M 1909 A.B. 1912
—	Maur. Will.	Chr.	M 1907 A.B. 1910
—	Rudolph Alb.	Cai.	M 1908 A.B. 1911
—	Sid. John	N. C.	M 1904 A.B. 1907. LL.B. 1909
—	Tho. Edw.	Jes.	L 1907 A.B. 1910
—	Will. John	Trin.	M 1903
Petersen,	Will. Sinclair	Trin.	M 1910
Petersmann,	Arnold Ernst Carl ...	Trin. H.	M 1911
Petherbridge,	Fre. Rob.	Sid.	M 1906 A.B. 1909
Petherick,	Geo. Gerald	Trin.	M 1905
—	John Cecil	Trin.	M 1908 A.B. 1911
—	Maur.	Trin.	M 1912
Pethick,	Fra. Noel	Trin.	M 1902
Petman,	Cha. Earle Bevan ...	Trin.	M 1885 A.B. 1888. LL.M.† 1902
Peto,	Hen.	Pem.	M 1908 A.B. 1911
Petrie,	Alex.	Trin.	M 1903 A.B. 1907
Petrocochino,	Paul	Em.	M 1911
Pett,	Fre. Mich.	N. C.	M 1905
Pettigrew,	Alex. Gordon	H. Sel.	M 1903 A.B. 1906

Pettinger,	Ja. Wilson	H. Sel.	M 1892 A.B. 1895. M.B., B.C. 1903
Pettit,	John Rob.	Chr.	M 1912
Pettitt,	Hugh	Cla.	M 1900 A.B. 1903. LL.B. 1904
Pettman,	Harold	Qu.	M 1893 A.B. 1896. A.M. 1906
Petty,	Mich. Jos.	Down.	M 1906 A.B. 1909
—	Will.	C. C.	M 1894 A.B. 1908
Petzing,	John Jacob	Cath.	M 1885 A.B. 1888. A.M. 1905
Pfülf,	Karl	Trin.	E 1905
Phear,	Howard Will.	Cai.	E 1912
Phelps,	Art. Rob.	Trin.	M 1893
—	Eustace Alb.	Em.	M 1899 A.B. 1902
—	Geo. Ingram de Brissac	Cla.	M 1895 A.B. 1898. A.M. 1902
—	Phil. Basil	Down.	M 1908 A.B. 1911
Philbrick,	John Harold	Trin.	M 1893 A.B. 1896. B.C., A.M. 1900. M.B.
Philby,	Harry St John Bridger	Trin.	M 1904 A.B. 1907 [1903
Philip,	Eric Wells	Trin.	M 1911
Philips,	Art. Reg. Trevelyan	C. C.	M 1905
Philipson,	Jos. Will.	H. Sel.	M 1888 A.B. 1891. A.M.† 1907
—	Myles Rowland	Trin.	M 1908 A.B. 1911
Phillimore,	John	Trin.	M 1905 A.B. 1908
Phillipps,	Fre. Alf.	Trin.	M 1910
Phillips,	Alf. Chandos	C. C.	M 1897 A.B. 1900. A.M. 1905
—	Art. Lloyd	Trin.	M 1897 A.B. 1900. A.M. 1908
—	Art. Tho.	Chr.	M 1912
—	Cha. Keith	Cath.	M 1899 A.B. 1902
--	Cha. Stanley	King's	M 1902 A.B. 1905. A.M. 1912
—	Dav.	Trin.	M 1898 A.B. 1901. A.M. 1906
—	Dav. Isaac Washington	Down.	M 1909
—	Douglas Middleton Parnham	Pem.	M 1910
—	Edm. Sixtus	N. C.	L 1904
—	Edw. Stanley	H. Cav.	M 1884 A.B. 1888. Down. A.M. 1901
—	Edw. Stone	Pem.	M 1901 A.B. 1904
—	Edwin Alb.	Cath.	L 1904
—	Ern. Harold	Sid.	M 1900 A.B. 1903
—	Fre.	Em.	M 1903 A.B. 1906
—	Geo. Alick Woodroffe	Jes.	M 1908 A.B. 1911
—	Geo. Wyndham	Trin.	M 1909 A.B. 1912
—	Ja. Osborne	H. Aye.	E 1895 Cath. A.B. 1904. A.M. 1911
—	Jos.	Chr.	M 1903 A.B. 1906
—	Leslie Penhall	Chr.	M 1908 A.B., LL.B. 1911
—	Llewellyn Caractacus⎱ Powell ⎰	Cai.	M 1889 ⎰ A.B. 1892. M.B., B.C. 1895. ⎱ A.M. 1896. M.D. 1903
—	Montagu	Cai.	M 1898 A.B. 1901. A.M. 1908. M.B., B.C.
—	Noel McGregor	Trin. H.	M 1901 [1909. M.D. 1912
—	Oscar Fre.	Cai.	M 1901
—	Percy	Em.	M 1904 A.B. 1906
—	Percy Reg. O'Rourk	Pem.	M 1910
—	Phil. Rich.	Trin.	E 1897 A.B. 1900. A.M. 1904
—	Rich. Lionel	H. Sel.	M 1902 A.B. 1905
—	Rich. Percival	Qu.	M 1906 A.B. 1909
—	Rob. Stowell	Joh.	M 1912
—	Sid. Hill	Joh.	M 1900 A.B. 1903. A.M. 1907
—	Stanley Will.	Em.	M 1904 A.B. 1907. A.M. 1911
—	Tho.	Pem.	M 1894 A.B. 1897. LL.B. 1898. A.M. 1906
—	Tho. Ceredig	Pet.	M 1901 A.B. 1903. A.M. 1907
—	Will. Dav.	Down.	M 1911
—	Will. Mallam	Trin. H.	M 1903 A.B., LL.B. 1906
—	Will. Owen	C. C.	M 1908
—	Will. Rich.	Joh.	M 1908 A.B. 1911. LL.B. 1912
—	Will. Rob.	H. Sel.	M 1907 A.B. 1910
Phillips-Conn,	Tho. Harry Meredeth	Cla.	M 1899 A.B., LL.B. 1902

M.

Phillipson,	Edm.	Pet.	M 1911
Phillp,	John de Riemer	Qu.	M 1907 A.B. 1910
Philp,	Claude Hastings Geo.	Joh.	M 1904 A.B. 1907. M.B., B.C. 1912
Philpot,	Will.	Trin.	M 1898 A.B. 1901. A.M. 1907
Philpots,	Edw. Art.	Trin.	M 1890 A.B. 1893. A.M. 1905
Philpott,	John Maxwell	H. Sel.	M 1910
Phipps,	Cha. Bathurst Hele	Trin. H.	L 1909
—	Walt. Tho.	Em.	M 1901 A.B. 1904. A.M. 1908
Piaggio,	Hen. Tho. Herb. ...	Joh.	M 1903 A.B. 1906. A.M. 1910
Picard,	Cha. Emile		*Sc.D.* 1912
Picciotto,	Cyril Moses	Trin.	M 1907 A.B. 1910
Pickard,	Basil	Trin.	M 1908 A.B. 1911
—	Herb.	N. C.	M 1910
—	Will. Burchell	Qu.	M 1908 A.B. 1911
Picken,	Dav. Kennedy	Jes.	M 1899 A.B. 1902. A.M. 1908
Pickering,	Bern. Milner	Cai.	M 1910
—	Dennison Veitch	Em.	M 1906 A.B. 1909
Pickersgill,	Jos.	Trin. H.	M 1907
Pickett,	Alf. Cleveland	Cai.	M 1903 A.B. 1908
—	Fra. Lionel Adams	Pet.	M 1911
Pickford,	Alf. Garside	Joh.	M 1888 A.B. 1891. A.M. 1903
Pickles,	Art.	Trin.	M 1903
Pickthorn,	Kenneth Will. Murray	Trin.	M 1910
Picton,	Geo. Wilson	Cla.	M 1889 A.B. 1892. A.M. 1908
—	Tho.	Em.	M 1900 A.B. 1902. A.M. 1908
Picton-Evans, Dav.		N. C.	M 1904 Down. A.B. 1907. A.M. 1912
Picton-Warlow, Fra. Temple		Em.	M 1898 A.B. 1901. A.M. 1907
Pienaar,	Lambertus Lochner	King's	L 1911
Piercy,	Hor. Melvill McLeod	H. Sel.	M 1906 A.B. 1909
Pieris,	Paulus Edw.	Trin.	M 1892 A.B. 1895. A.M.† 1899. LL.M.†
Pierson,	Nicolaas Gerard		*Sc.D.* 1904 [1909
Piesse,	Edm. Leolin	King's	M 1901
Pigeon,	Hen. Rich.	Trin.	M 1902
—	John Walt.	Chr.	M 1905 A.B. 1908
Pigg,	Bern. Will.	Jes.	M 1907 A.B. 1910
—	Cha. Herb.	Jes.	M 1906 A.B. 1909
Piggot,	Art. Alf.	Pem.	M 1910
Piggott,	Fre. Stanley Lawrence	Em.	M 1906
—	Harry Edw.	Cla.	M 1897 A.B. 1900. A.M. 1904
—	Julian Ito	Pem.	M 1907 A.B. 1910
Pigott,	Cha. Moreton Digby	Sid.	M 1898 A.B. 1902
—	Dayrell Botry	Mag.	M 1897 A.B. 1901
—	Geo. Godfrey Caledon	Trin. H.	M 1908
Pigou,	[1] Art. Cecil ....*King's		M 1896 A.B. 1899. A.M. 1903
Pike,	Art. John	Cla.	L 1880 A.B. 1883. A.M. 1905
—	Ebenezer	Trin.	M 1904
—	Godfrey	Trin.	M 1905 A.B. 1908
—	Howard Hurstwood	Cai.	M 1909
—	Sam. Aitken	Trin.	M 1908 A.B. 1911
—	Sid. Gilb. Bassett ...	Em.	M 1903 A.B. 1906
—	Will. Bennett	Trin.	M 1892 A.B. 1895. A.M. 1901
Pilcher,	Gonne St Clair	Trin.	M 1909 A.B. 1912
—	Will. Hope	Pem.	M 1904 A.B. 1907
Pilditch,	Phil. Harold	Pem.	M 1909 A.B. 1912
Pilkington,	Archib. Cha.	Joh.	M 1894 A.B. 1897. A.M. 1901
—	Dan. Holme	Pem.	M 1912
—	Denis Fielden	Trin.	M 1912
—	Edw. Fielden	Trin.	M 1904 A.B. 1907
—	Fre. Mervyn Fosbery	Trin.	M 1906 A.B. 1910

[1] Professor of Political Economy, 1908.

Pilkington,	Guy Reg.	Trin.	M 1900 A.B. 1903
—	Hugh Brocklehurst ...	Trin.	M 1905 A.B. 1908
Pillai,	Murgasupillai Valu ...	Down.	L 1908 A.B., LL.B. 1911
Pillay,	Lawrence	Down.	E 1910
Pilling,	Rich. Norman	Trin. H.	M 1910
Pilter,	Alf. Monod	Jes.	M 1900 A.B. 1903
—	Cha.	King's	M 1906 A.B. 1909
—	Rob.	Em.	M 1904 A.B. 1907
Pim,	Herb. Lister	Jes.	M 1910
Pinches,	Hen. Irving	Sid.	L 1897 A.B. 1899. M.B., B.C., A.M. 1904
Pinck,	Rob. Harvey	Em.	M 1907 A.B. 1910
Pinder,	Alb. Humphrey	Qu.	M 1906 A.B. 1909
Pinfold,	Ern. Sheppard	Pet.	M 1907 A.B. 1910
Pingriff,	Geo. Neville	Sid.	M 1904 A.B. 1907
Pink,	Hub. Selwyn	Jes.	M 1906 A.B. 1910
Pinkerton,	John	Em.	M 1909 A.B. 1911
Pinkham,	Cha.	Cai.	M 1908 A.B. 1911
Pinks,	Edwin Dennis Picton	Cla.	M 1906 A.B. 1910
Pinn,	Hen. Geo.	C. C.	M 1910 A.B. 1912
Pinsent,	Dav. Hume	Trin.	M 1910
—	Gerald Hume Saverie	Trin.	M 1907 A.B. 1910
Pinson,	Edw. Tho.	H. Sel.	M 1899 A.B. 1902
Pinto,	Alfonso Mogano	Down.	M 1908
Piper,	John Herb.	Pem.	M 1900 A.B. 1903
Pirbhai,	Rahimtulla Karmali	Down.	M 1905 A.B., LL.B. 1908
Pistorius,	Ernst Heinrich	Trin. H.	M 1903 A.B. 1908
Pite,	Ion Beresford	Trin.	M 1909 A.B. 1912
Pitkin,	Alf. John	Joh.	M 1889 A.B. 1892. LL.B., A.M. 1909
—	Montague Claud Melville	H. Aye.	L 1893 A.B. 1895. N. C. A.M. 1907
Pitt,	Cha. Hen.	C. C.	M 1903 A.B. 1906
—	Frank Art.	Qu.	M 1912
—	Marcus Gysbert	N. C.	M 1897 Pet. A.B. 1900. A.M. 1904
—	Phil. Sept.	Trin.	M 1900 A.B. 1904. A.M. 1908
—	Rob. Brindley	Cla.	M 1907 A.B. 1910
—	Tho. Gordon	Em.	M 1903 A.B. 1907
—	Walt. Ja.	Down.	M 1906 A.B. 1909
—	Will. Octavius	Em.	M 1899 A.B. 1902. M.B., B.C. 1907. M.D. [1910
Pittom,	Will. Wynn Pratt ...	Joh.	M 1908 A.B. 1911
Pitt-Pitts,	Will. Art.	Em.	M 1909 A.B. 1912
Pitts,	Bern. Thursby	Em.	M 1905 A.B. 1909. A.M. 1912
—	Harry Herb.	Cath.	M 1893 A.B. 1896. A.M. 1904
Pitts Tucker,	Geoffrey Somerville	Trin.	M 1905 A.B. 1908
Pixell,	John Vincent	Trin.	M 1901 A.B. 1905. A.M. 1908
Plançon,	Edouard	Mag.	M 1906
Platt,	Art. Hardwicke	Cai.	M 1901 A.B. 1904
—	Edw. Art.	Trin.	M 1907 A.B. 1910
—	Maur. Cedric	Trin.	M 1912
—	Rich. Herb.	Trin.	M 1901 A.B. 1904. A.M. 1908
Platts,	Art. Leslie	Cai.	M 1910
—	Syd. Goodman	Cai.	M 1907 A.B. 1910
—	Will. Hen. John	N. C.	M 1905 Chr. A.B. 1908
Player,	Eric Noel	N. C.	M 1911
Playfair,	Kenneth	Cai.	M 1909 A.B. 1912
—	Pat. Lyon	King's	M 1912
Playne,	Basil Alf.	Pem.	M 1904 A.B. 1907. M.B., B.C. 1912
—	Fre. Southerden	Cath.	M 1896 A.B. 1899. A.M. 1903
—	Harold Fra.	Pem.	M 1904 A.B. 1907
Plessen,	Johann	Trin.	M 1908
—	Ludwig Carl	Trin.	M 1908
—	Magnus Carl August Wilhelm	Trin.	E 1909

Plews,	Art. Gordon	Pem.	M 1902 A.B. 1905
—	Henery Whitfield ...	Cla.	M 1907
Plowden,	Humphrey Roger ...	Cla.	M 1907 A.B. 1910
Plowman,	Clifford Hen. FitzHerbert	Trin.	M 1908 A.B. 1911
Plowright,	Cha. Tertius MacLean	Joh.	M 1897 A.B. 1900. M.B., B.C. 1905
—	Colin Campbell	Joh.	M 1903 A.B. 1906
Plumb,	Harry	Cla.	M 1900 A.B. 1903
Plumptre,	Basil Pemberton	Em.	M 1902 A.B. 1905. A.M. 1911
—	Ern. Aubrey Western	Pem.	M 1907 A.B. 1910
Pluszczewski,	Step.	Chr.	L 1910
Pochin,	Harold	H. Sel.	M 1902 A.B. 1905. A.M. 1909
—	Victor Rob.	Trin.	M 1898 A.B. 1901. A.M. 1906
Pocock,	Archib. Hen.	Trin.	M 1895 A.B. 1898. A.M. 1902
—	Guy Noël	Joh.	M 1899 A.B. 1904
—	Hen. Willmer	Cai.	M 1899 A.B. 1904
—	Phil. Noel	Sid.	M 1902 A.B. 1905
—	Syd. Elsdon	King's	L 1904
—	Will. Agard	Pem.	M 1907 A.B. 1910
Poignand,	Cecil Willoughby ...	Cai.	M 1898 A.B. 1901. A.M. 1907
—	Geo. Clive Irving ...	C. C.	M 1910
—	Ralph Newman	Cai.	M 1897 A.B. 1900. M.B., B.C. 1905
Pointer,	Edw. Harold	Sid.	M 1907 A.B. 1912
—	Ern.	Pem.	M 1900 A.B. 1903
Points,	Walt. Geo.	N. C.	M 1908
Po Jui,	(*The Hon.*)		*A.M.* 1906
Polack,	Alb. Isaac	Joh.	M 1911
—	Benj. Ja.	King's	M 1909
—	Ern. Emanuel	Joh.	M 1912
Pole,	Reg. Will.	C. C.	M 1906 King's A.B. 1910
Polhill,	Cecil Cha.	Trin.	M 1908
—	Douglas Art.	C. C.	M 1909 A.B. 1912
—	Stanley Fredrick Phil.	Jes.	M 1910
Pollak,	Harry	Cai.	M 1904
—	Leslie Alb.	King's	M 1908 A.B. 1911
Pollard,	Armell Rich.	Trin.	M 1900 A.B. 1903
—	Harold Ja. Alex. ...	Cla.	M 1911
—	Sam.	Trin.	M 1912
—	Sid. Pochin	Cai.	M 1891 A.B. 1894. M.B., B.C. 1900. A.M.,
—	Will. Branch	Cla.	M 1898 A.B. 1901 [M.D. 1905
—	Will. Marcus Noël ...	Joh.	M 1909 A.B. 1912
Pollock,	Bertram	Trin.	M 1882 A.B. 1885. A.M. 1890. B.D. 1902.
—	Cha. Tho. Anderdon	Trin.	M 1906 A.B. 1909 [D.D. 1903
—	Fre. John ....*Trin.		M 1897 A.B. 1900. A.M. 1904
—	Hamilton Rivers	Trin.	M 1903 A.B. 1906
—	Humphrey Rivers ...	Trin.	M 1908 A.B. 1911
—	Kenneth	Sid.	M 1895 A.B. 1898. A.M. 1902
—	Martin Viner	Trin.	M 1906 LL.B. 1909
—	Ronald Evelyn	Pem.	M 1910
—	Will. Rivers	Trin.	L 1884 M.B., B.C. 1888. M.D. 1903
Polmeer,	Harold	Down.	M 1912
Polson,	Will.	Pet.	L 1912
Pond,	Leslie Harry	Trin.	M 1901 A.B. 1904. A.M. 1912
—	Ronald Edw.	H. Sel.	M 1909 A.B. 1912
Ponder,	Constant Wells	Em.	M 1898 A.B. 1901. A.M. 1905. M.D. 1909
Ponsonby,	Art. Gordon	Trin.	M 1911
—	(*Hon.*) Bertie Brabazon	Trin.	M 1904 A.B. 1907
—	Cyril Tho.	Pem.	M 1912
—	Vere Brabazon	Trin.	M 1898 A.B. 1901
Pontifex,	Herb. Art.	Pem.	M 1899 A.B. 1902
Poock,	Alf. Graham	Down.	M 1902 A.B. 1905
Pook,	John de Courcy	C. C.	M 1906 A.B. 1909

Poole,	Fra. Stedman	Sid.	M 1901 A.B. 1904
—	Herb.	Sid.	M 1904 A.B. 1907
—	John Twells	Joh.	M 1900 A.B. 1903
—	Nath. John	H. Aye.	M 1895 Cath. A.B. 1898. A.M. 1912
—	Sam. Jos.	Cath.	M 1899 A.B. 1902. A.M. 1906
—	Stanley Paul	H. Sel.	M 1908 A.B. 1911
Pooley,	And. Melville	Cla.	M 1900 A.B. 1903
—	Ern. Hen.	Pem.	M 1895 A.B. 1898. A.M. 1904. LL.B. 1908
—	Geo. Hen.	Cai.	M 1886 A.B. 1907
—	John Sandys	Trin.	M 1908 A.B. 1911
Poore,	Will. Graydon	Trin.	M 1909 A.B. 1912
Pope,	Alf. Rolph	Trin.	M 1890 A.B. 1893. A.M. 1908
—	Cha. Alf. Whiting ...	Trin.	M 1896 A.B. 1899. B.C., A.M. 1904. M.B.
—	Cyril	Trin.	M 1909 A.B. 1912 [1908
—	Frank Montague	Mag.	L 1874 A.B. 1877. M.B. 1881. M.D. 1901
—	Herb. Barrett	Cai.	M 1905 A.B. 1908
—	Lawrence Kelway ...	Sid.	M 1907
—	Norman Chris.	Joh.	M 1901 A.B. 1904. A.M. 1908
—	Phil. Montague	Mag.	M 1910
—	Will. Hen. Conway	Qu.	M 1894 A.B. 1897. A.M. 1902
—	[1] Will. Jackson		A.M. 1908, *Sid.
Popham,	Art. Ewart	King's	M 1908 A.B. 1911
Porritt,	Reg. Norman	Cai.	M 1908 A.B. 1911
Portago,	Antonio	Chr.	M 1910
Porte,	Cedric Cha.	Em.	M 1901 A.B. 1905
Porteous,	Norman Will.	Down.	M 1910
—	Walt. Chadburn	C. C.	M 1903 A.B. 1906
Porter,	Adolphus Reg. Zouch	Trin.	M 1899 A.B. 1902
—	Art. Edw.	Em.	M 1891 A.B. 1894. M.B., B.C. 1898. A.M.,
—	Cedric Ern. Victor ...	Cai.	M 1912 [M.D. 1901
—	Clarence Alb. Pratt	H. Sel.	M 1904 A.B. 1908. A.M. 1911
—	Ern. Ja.	Trin.	M 1909 A.B. 1911
—	Frank	Cai.	M 1896 A.B. 1899. A.M. 1904
—	Graham Hawksworth	Cai.	M 1912
—	Hugh	N. C.	M 1898 A.B. 1902. A.M. 1906
—	Hugh Harold	Chr.	M 1895 A.B. 1898. A.M. 1902
—	John	Em.	M 1912
—	Tho. Hen.	Joh.	M 1900 A.B. 1903
—	Vyvyan Kingsley ...	Chr.	M 1912
—	Will. Tho.	Jes.	M 1899 A.B. 1902
Porterfield,	Tho. Sam.	N. C.	M 1899 Em. A.B. 1902. A.M. 1906
Portway,	Donald	Down.	M 1906 A.B. 1909
Poskitt,	Hen. John	C. C.	M 1907 A.B. 1910
Postance,	Art. Alois	Down.	M 1908
—	Art. Sam.	N. C.	M 1907 Down. A.B. 1910
Postlethwaite,	Cuthbert	Trin.	M 1893 A.B. 1896. A.M. 1905
—	Jos. Marshall	Em.	M 1898 A.B. 1901
—	Rich. Noël	Cla.	M 1903 A.B. 1906
Potbury,	Tho. Rich.	Chr.	M 1885 A.B. 1889. A.M. 1909
Potter,	Alistair Richardson	Em.	M 1901 A.B. 1904. A.M. 1909
—	Ern. Cha.	C. C.	M 1906 A.B. 1909
—	Gerald Peel	Cla.	M 1901 A.B. 1904
—	Hugh Geo.	N. C.	M 1902 A.B. 1905
—	Mich. Cresse	Pet.	M 1877 A.B. 1881. A.M. 1884. Sc.D. 1909
—	Phil. Hen.	Em.	M 1911
—	Reg. Jos. Will. Hen.	King's	M 1900 A.B. 1903. A.M. 1908
—	Will. Ja. Jos.	N. C.	M 1892 A.B. 1895. A.M. 1901
—	Will. Miskin	Cla.	M 1908 A.B. 1912
—	Will. Norman	Pem.	M 1903 A.B. 1906. A.M. 1912

[1] Professor of Chemistry, 1908.

Potts,	Cha. Churton	....	Pem.	M 1890 A.B. 1893. A.M. 1901		
—	Frank Armitage	......*Trin. H.		M 1901 A.B. 1904. A.M. 1908		
—	Harold Gordon	......	Pem.	M 1894 A.B. 1897. A.M. 1903		
—	Will. Alex.	....	Pem.	M 1885 A.B. 1888. A.M. 1911		
Poulett,	Will. John Lydston (*Earl*)		Trin. H.	M 1902		
Pound,	Murray Stuart	......	Pem.	M 1910		
—	Reg. Walt. Geo.	......	N. C.	M 1880 Joh. A.B. 1884. A.M. 1906		
—	Will. Geo. Willoughby		King's	M 1905 A.B. 1908		
Powel Smith,	Leslie John		Cai.	M 1911		
Powell,	Arnold Cecil	....	Trin.	M 1901 A.B. 1904. A.M. 1908		
—	Art. Trevor	....	Trin.	M 1902		
—	Ashley	....	Cai.	M 1910		
—	Edw. Horatio	....	Chr.	M 1911		
—	Edw. John	....	N. C.	M 1900 A.B. 1904		
—	Eric Walt.	....	Trin.	M 1905 A.B. 1908		
—	Evan Caradoc	....	Joh.	M 1911		
—	Frank Aubrey	....	Trin.	M 1904 A.B. 1907		
—	Geo. Gerald	....	Cai.	M 1907 A.B. 1911		
—	Hector Alex.	....	Trin.	M 1896 A.B. 1900. A.M. 1903		
—	John Melton Sparowe		Em.	M 1911		
—	John Roland	....	Qu.	M 1908 A.B. 1911		
—	Kenneth	....	King's	M 1904 A.B. 1907		
—	Leslie	....	King's	M 1902 B.C. 1910. M.B. 1911		
—	Meredith Beckett	...	Pem.	M 1909 A.B. 1912		
—	Nich. Guy	....	Joh.	M 1895 A.B. 1898. A.M. 1905		
—	Percival	....	King's	M 1898 A.B. 1901. A.M. 1905		
—	Reg. Rob.	....	N. C.	E 1903 A.B. 1908		
—	Rhys Campbell Folliot		Trin.	M 1910		
—	Rich. Hen.	....	Trin.	M 1902 A.B. 1905		
—	Ronald Rees	....	Em.	M 1909		
—	Ronald Vanneck	......	Trin.	M 1903		
—	Tho. Folliott	....	Trin.	M 1905 A.B. 1908		
—	Tho. Gilb.	....	Pet.	M 1899 A.B. 1902		
—	Valentine Pryor	......	Trin.	M 1899 A.B. 1903. A.M. 1911		
—	Will. Allan	....	Pem.	M 1905 A.B. 1908		
Powell-Price,	Edw.	....	Cath.	M 1912		
—	John Cadwgan	......	H. Sel.	M 1907 A.B. 1910		
Power,	Ambrose Grattan	...	Em.	M 1905		
—	John Wethered	......	Trin.	M 1912		
Powers,	Carol	....	Trin.	M 1903 A.B. 1906		
Powis	(*Lord*)	....		*See* Herbert, G. C.		
Pownall,	Art. du Terreaux	...	Chr.	M 1900 A.B. 1903. A.M. 1907		
—	Basil Cha.	....	Chr.	M 1899 A.B. 1902. A.M. 1907		
—	John Cecil Glossop		Trin.	M 1909 A.B. 1912		
Powys,	John Cowper	....	C. C.	M 1891 A.B. 1894. A.M. 1901		
—	Littleton Cha.	....	C. C.	M 1893 A.B. 1896. A.M. 1904		
—	Llewelyn	....	C. C.	M 1903 A.B. 1906		
Powys-Jones,	Will. Rich.	....	Cai.	M 1904		
Poynder,	Ern. Geo. Thornton		N. C.	M 1903		
Poyser,	Art. Vernon	....	Mag.	M 1901 A.B. 1904. M.B., B.C. 1909		
Pradit,	Nai	....	Cla.	M 1910		
Prakasa,	Sri	....	Trin.	M 1911		
Prall,	Sam. Reg.	....	Em.	M 1910		
Prance,	Ern. Reg.	....	Cla.	M 1890 A.B. 1897. A.M. 1903		
—	Gerald Lewis	....	Trin.	M 1897 A.B. 1900. A.M. 1904		
Prankerd,	Hor. Art.	....	Qu.	M 1902 A.B. 1905		
—	John	....	H. Sel.	M 1898 A.B. 1901. A.M. 1905		
Prasad,	Bisheshwari	....	Em.	M 1909 A.B. 1911		
—	Ganesh	....	Chr.	M 1899 A.B. 1901		
Pratt,	Cecil John Cha.	......	Cai.	M 1905 A.B. 1908. A.M. 1912		
—	Cha. Edw.	....	N. C.	M 1893 A.B. 1896. A.M. 1911		

Pratt,	Fra. Josiah	Em.	M 1905 A.B. 1908
—	Geoffrey Cheesbrough	Trin. H.	M 1908 A.B., LL.B. 1911
—	Geoffrey Wyatt	Joh.	M 1911
—	Hub. Evans Hills ...	Down.	M 1899 A.B. 1902. A.M. 1910
—	Jermyn Harold	Trin.	M 1902
—	John Hen.	Trin.	M 1900 A.B. 1903. B.C., A.M. 1907. M.B.
—	Ronald Art. Fre. ...	Cai.	M 1906 A.B. 1909 [1909
Preddy,	Edw. Fred Spencer	Cath.	M 1912
Predöhl,	Max Garlieb August	N. C.	E 1904
Preece,	Chris. Tho.	Trin.	M 1898 A.B. 1901. A.M. 1905
Preedy,	Alban	Jes.	M 1911
Preeston,	Ralph Septimus	Cla.	M 1904 A.B. 1907
Prentice,	Tom Noël Rich.	H. Sel.	M 1907 A.B. 1910
Prentis,	Sid. Elvy	C. C.	M 1909 A.B. 1912
Prescott,	Kenneth Loder Cromwell	Trin.	M 1894 A.B. 1897. A.M. 1902
Prest,	Edw. Ern.	N. C.	M 1892 Joh. A.B. 1895. M.B., B.C. 1898.
—	Harold Edw. Westray	Pem.	M 1908 [A.M. 1899. M.D. 1904
Prestige,	Art. Reg.	Cai.	M 1910
—	Syd. Ern.	Cai.	M 1905 A.B. 1908. A.M. 1912
Preston,	Douglas Ja.	Pem.	M 1904 A.B. 1907
—	Eric Watson	Pem.	M 1905
—	Frank Sansome	Pem.	M 1894 A.B. 1897. A.M. 1903
—	(*Sir*) Jacob	Trin.	M 1905 A.B., LL.B. 1908
—	John Edwin	Chr.	M 1904 A.B. 1907
—	Rich. Will. Dades ...	Em.	M 1908 A.B. 1911
—	Tho. Hildebrand	Trin. H.	M 1905
Pretty,	Bern.	Pem.	M 1899 A.B., LL.B. 1902
—	Ivo Alf. Falk	Cai.	M 1911
—	Kenneth	King's	M 1902 A.B. 1905. M.B. 1911
Preuss,	Ernst	Trin.	M 1910
Previté Orton, Cha. Will. ....*Joh.			M 1905 A.B. 1908. A.M. 1912
Prevost,	Pierre Guillaume ...	Down.	L 1902 A.B. 1904. A.M. 1908
Price,	Alf. Franklin Maitland	Down.	M 1901 A.B. 1904
—	Augustine Rhun	Qu.	M 1882 A.B. 1885. A.M. 1908
—	Edwin Jones	Pet.	M 1911
—	Geo. Nowell	Pem.	M 1893 A.B. 1896. A.M. 1904
—	Ja. Art.	Qu.	M 1894 A.B. 1897. A.M. 1901
—	John Dav.	Trin.	M 1900 A.B. 1904
—	John Llewelyn	H. Aye.	E 1891 Qu. A.B. 1894. A.M. 1911
—	Lloyd Owen Lloyd ...	Cai.	M 1903 A.B. 1906
—	Morgan Philips	Trin.	M 1903 A.B. 1906. A.M. 1912
—	Norman Jeredick ...	Joh.	M 1908 A.B. 1911
—	Pet.	N. C.	M 1897 Qu. A.B. 1901
—	Syd. Reg.	Cla.	M 1907 A.B. 1910
—	Tudor Williams	Cla.	M 1912
—	Tudor Yestin	Cath.	M 1908 A.B. 1911
—	Will. John	Qu.	L 1891 A.B. 1893. A.M. 1902
—	Will. Rob.	Trin.	M 1905 A.B. 1908
Prichard,	Art. Abercrombie ...	Cla.	M 1909 A.B. 1912
—	Art. Illtyd	Qu.	M 1899 A.B. 1902
—	Evan Llewellyn	Cla.	M 1905
—	Rich. Edgar Vipan ...	Pet.	M 1899 A.B. 1902. A.M. 1909
—	Rich. Graham	Cla.	M 1907 A.B. 1910
Prickard,	Tho. Fra. Vaughan	King's	M 1898 A.B. 1901
Prideaux,	Hen. Syd.	Joh.	M 1901 A.B. 1907
—	Walt. Reg.	Qu.	M 1884 A.B. 1887. A.M. 1907
Pridham,	Cha. Fortescue	Cai.	M 1885 A.B. 1888. B.C. 1905
Pridmore,	Cha. Atton	Cai.	M 1894 A.B. 1897. A.M. 1901
Priest,	Rob. Cecil	Cai.	M 1901 A.B. 1904. M.B., B.C. 1908
Priestland,	Edw. Andreas	H. Sel.	M 1900 A.B. 1903
—	Jos. Fra. Edwin	H. Sel.	M 1904 A.B. 1907

Priestley,	Douglas Ralph Overend	Pem.	M 1912
—	Gerald Will.	Trin.	M 1906 A.B. 1909
—	Hen. Ja.	Jes.	M 1902 A.B. 1905. 'A.M. 1909
—	Hugh Will.	Trin.	M 1906 A.B. 1909
—	Reg. Fawcett	Cai.	M 1902 A.B. 1905. M.B., B.C. 1909
Prince,	Gerald Webster	Trin. H.	M 1909
—	Herb.	Trin. H.	M 1892 A.B. 1895. A.M. 1902
—	Jos. Fisher	Trin. H.	M 1897 A.B. 1900. A.M. 1904
Pring,	Basil Crompton	Trin.	M 1906
—	John Grattan	Cai.	M 1899 A.B. 1903
Pringle,	John Summers	Cla.	M 1901 A.B. 1904
—	Kenneth Douglas ...	Cai.	M 1901 A.B. 1904. M.B., B.C. 1908
—	Norman Douglas ...	Joh.	M 1902
—	Will. Rennie	Em.	M 1912.
Pringsheim,	Pet.	Trin.	M 1907
Prinsep,	Anth. Leyland	Trin.	M 1907
Prior,	Alf.	C. C.	M 1906 A.B. 1910
—	Asher Carlyle Vincent	King's	M 1899 A.B. 1902. LL.B. 1903. A.M. 1906
—	Basil Cyprian	Em.	M 1902 A.B., LL.B. 1906
—	Carlos Edw.	Pem.	M 1899 A.B. 1902
—	Claude Bern.	Jes.	M 1909 A.B. 1912
—	Clem. Erskine	Em.	M 1901 A.B. 1904. A.M. 1910
—	[1] Edw. Schröder	Cai.	M 1870 A.B. 1874. A.M. 1877
—	Hen. Carlos	King's	M 1909 A.B. 1912
—	Herman Brooke	Cai.	M 1905 A.B. 1908 [ford, R. H.
—	Rich. Hen.	Trin.	M 1888 A.B. 1891. post Prior-Wandes-
Prior-Wandesford, R. H.			*See* Prior, Rich. Hen.
Priston,	Stewart Browne	Joh.	M 1899 A.B. 1902. A.M. 1908
Pritchard,	Dav.	Cai.	M 1905 A.B. 1909
—	Ion Buchanan	Trin.	M 1899 A.B. 1903. A.M. 1906
—	John Edw. Maddock	Trin.	M 1909 A.B. 1912
—	John Laurence	Chr.	M 1904
—	Norman Pallister ...	Trin.	L 1904 A.B. 1907. A.M. 1910
—	Rich.	Cath.	M 1904 A.B. 1911
—	Will. Geo.	Cla.	M 1911
Procter,	John Atkinson	Cla.	M 1900 A.B. 1905
—	Rob. Art. Welsford	Cla.	M 1909 A.B. 1912
—	Rob. FitzHugh	Pem.	M 1898 A.B. 1902
—	Rob. Geo.	Trin.	M 1897 A.B. 1900. A.M. 1904
Protheroe,	Art. Havard	Trin. H.	M 1901
Proudlock,	Robin	Joh.	M 1911
Proudman,	Jos.	Trin.	M 1910
Prout,	Leslie Ern.	Cath.	M 1906 A.B. 1909
Prowde,	Oswald Longstaff ...	Joh.	M 1901 A.B. 1904
Prowse,	Ja. Fre.	H. Sel.	M 1910
—	Rob. Will.	Trin.	M 1909 A.B. 1912
Prust,	Tho. Walt.	N. C.	M 1906
Pryce,	Bern. Vaughan	Trin.	M 1893 A.B. 1896. LL.B. 1897. A.M. 1902
—	Harold Vaughan	Joh.	M 1892 A.B. 1895. M.B., B.C. 1902. A.M.
—	Lewis Hugh Oswald	Pem.	M 1892 A.B. 1895. A.M. 1910 [1903
Pryce-Jones,	Pryce Victor	Jes.	M 1906
Pryde,	Dav.	Mag.	M 1892 A.B. 1896. A.M.† 1912
Prynne,	Edgar Geo. Fellowes	H. Sel.	M 1910
Pryor,	Geo. Hawson Deen	C. C.	M 1912
—	Grafton Deen	Pem.	M 1901 A.B. 1906. A.M. 1911
—	Rich. Coad .	Trin.	M 1885 A.B. 1888. A.M. 1901
—	Walt. Marlborough ...	Trin.	M 1898 A.B. 1901. A.M. 1905
Prytherch,	Dan. Rowland Oswald	Joh.	M 1895 A.B. 1898. A.M. 1902
Przybyszewski-Westrup de Grzy-mala, Zenon Stanisław	}	Pem.	M 1912

[1] Slade Professor of Fine Art, 1912.

Puckle,	Fre. Hale	King's	M 1908 A.B. 1912
Pudumjee,	Nusserwanjee Sorabjee	Cath.	M 1911
Pugh,	Edw. Will. Wynn ...	H. Sel.	L 1894 A.B. 1898. A.M. 1912
—	John Vaughan	Qu.	M 1907 A.B. 1910
Pughe,	Evan Brodribb	Trin.	M 1911
Pulley,	Gerrard Todd	Trin.	M 1907 A.B. 1910
Pulliblank,	Jos.	Cath.	M 1894 A.B. 1897. A.M. 1904
Pullin,	John Henton	Joh.	M 1912
Pulling,	Chris. Rob. Druce ...	Trin.	M 1912
—	John Bernard	Chr.	M 1904 A.B. 1907. B.C. 1911
Pullinger,	Sid. Russell	C. C.	M 1910
Pullman,	Art. Hen.	Chr.	M 1898 A.B. 1902
Pulman,	Will. Prockter	Cla.	M 1907
Pulteney,	Reg. Fra. Osborn ...	Trin.	M 1900 A.B. 1906
Pumphrey,	Cha. Ern.	Chr.	M 1899 A.B. 1902
Punnett,	[1] Reg. Crundall ....*Cai.		M 1894 A.B. 1898. A.M. 1902
Purachatra	of Siam (*Prince*)	Trin.	M 1901
Purcell,	Goodwin	Qu.	M 1900 A.B. 1903. A.M. 1907
Purchas,	Art. Bishop	Pem.	M 1883 A.B. 1886. A.M. 1908
—	Griffiths Tho. Will.	Cath.	M 1879 A.B. 1883. A.M. 1909
Purchase,	Will. Bentley	Sid.	M 1908 A.B. 1911
Puri,	Bhawani Singh	Down.	M 1910
Purser,	Frank Dulcker	Trin.	M 1906 A.B. 1909
—	Geo. Leslie	Trin.	M 1911
—	Will. Cha. Bertrand	Joh.	M 1897 A.B. 1900. A.M.† 1904
Purton,	Gilb. Anth.	Chr.	M 1895 A.B. 1898. A.M. 1902
—	Lionel Pardoe	Qu.	M 1899 A.B. 1902
Purves,	Pat. John Chester } Jervis Laidlaw }	King's	M 1909 A.B. 1912
—	Syd. Octavius	Qu.	M 1881 A.B. 1884 (2). A.M.† 1905
—	Will. Donald Campbell } Laidlaw }	Trin.	M 1907 A.B. 1910
Purvis,	John Stanley	Cath.	M 1909 A.B. 1912
Pusinelli,	Siegfried Jacques	Pem.	M 1908 A.B. 1911
Puttock,	Reg.	Em.	M 1897 A.B. 1900. B.C., A.M. 1905. M.B.
Pye,	Dav. Randall	Trin.	M 1905 A.B. 1908 [1906
—	Edwin Walt.	Trin.	M 1907 A.B. 1910
Pyemont,	Edgar Cha. Hammond	N. C.	M 1895 A.B. 1898. A.M. 1902
Pye-Smith,	Desmond Edw.	Cai.	M 1907 A.B. 1910
—	Talbot Edw. Baines	Cai.	M 1905 A.B. 1908. LL.B. 1909
Pyke,	Geoffrey Nath.	Pem.	M 1912
Pym,	Alex.	King's	M 1906 A.B. 1909
—	Alex. John Will.	H. Sel.	M 1908 A.B. 1911
—	Claude John	Trin.	M 1911
—	Leslie Ruthven	Mag.	M 1903 A.B. 1906
—	Ronald Melville	Trin.	M 1911
—	Tho. Wentworth	Trin.	M 1905 A.B. 1908. A.M. 1912
—	Will. St John	Trin.	M 1908 A.B. 1911
Pyman,	Fre. Cresswell	Cai.	M 1907 A.B. 1910
—	Rob. Frederick	H. Sel.	M 1903 A.B. 1907. A.M. 1910
—	Rob. Lauder	Cla.	M 1900 A.B., LL.B. 1903
—	Ronald Lee	Jes.	M 1905 A.B. 1908
—	Will. Haigh	Chr.	M 1905 A.B. 1908
Pyne,	Fre. Sparke	Pem.	M 1904 A.B. 1907
—	Raymond Walt. John } Wodschow }	King's	M 1910
Pyper,	Jos. Rich.	Jes.	M 1911
Pytches,	Geo. Julian	Cai.	M 1900 A.B. 1912

[1] Professor of Biology, 1910; Arthur Balfour Professor of Genetics, 1912.

Q

Qazi,	Mohammad Husain	Em.	M 1912
Quainton,	Cecil Reg.	Qu.	M 1891 C., A.B. 1894. A.M. 1906
Quarterman,	Ern. Cha. Stilon ...	C. C.	M 1909 A.B. 1912
Quass,	Phineas	Joh.	M 1910
Quentin,	Geo. Augustus Fre.	C. C.	M 1900 A.B. 1903
Quick,	Edw. Keith	Joh.	M 1907 A.B. 1910
Quiggin,	Edm. Crosby ....*Cai.		M 1893 A.B. 1896. A.M. 1901
Quill,	John Jerome	Cla.	M 1902 J. J. Patrick, A.B. 1909
Quiller-Couch,	¹ Art. Tho. ....*Jes.		
Quilter,	Cha. Fre.	King's	M 1903
Quincey,	Tho. Edm. de Quincey	Pem.	M 1912
Quinney,	Harry	N. C.	M 1904 A.B. 1907
Quirk,	John Nath.	Joh.	M 1869 A.B. 1873. A.M. 1876. D.D. 1902
—	Rob.	King's	M 1901 A.B. 1904. A.M. 1912

R

Raad,	Neone Nich. Cha. ...	Joh.	M 1906 A.B. 1910
Raban,	Geo. Fergusson Cockburn	Em.	M 1906 A.B. 1909
Rabinerson,	Raoul Raphael	Cath.	M 1911
Rabinowich,	Myer	C. C.	M 1911
Rabjohns,	Will.	Chr.	M 1905 A.B. 1908
Raby,	And.	N. C.	M 1897 Joh. A.B. 1901. A.M. 1906
—	Frederic Ja. Edw. ...	Trin.	M 1907 A.B. 1910
—	Geo. Hodder	Cai.	M 1912
Race,	Russell Tinniswood	Joh.	M 1898 A.B. 1901. LL.B. 1903
Rackham,	Bern.	Pem.	M 1895 A.B. 1898. A.M. 1907
—	Maur.	Chr.	M 1898 A.B. 1901. A.M. 1907
Radcliffe,	Ashton Gilb.	King's	L 1875 A.B. 1879. A.M. 1910
—	Claude Cha. John ...	Trin.	M 1903 A.B. 1908
—	Clifford Herb.	Trin.	M 1897 A.B. 1902
—	Clifford Walt.	Joh.	M 1907 A.B. 1911
Radclyffe,	Edw. John Dilston ...	Trin.	M 1902 A.B. 1905. A.M. 1910
Radermacher-Schorer, (Jonkheer) Johan		Pem.	M 1911
Radetzky, (*Count*) Josef Franz Johann Theodor Wenzel Maria		Trin. H.	E 1904
Radford,	Archib. Campbell ...	Cai.	M 1901 A.B. 1906
—	Corbet Alex. Freer ...	Trin.	M 1901
—	Lewis Bostock ....*Joh.		M 1887 A.B. 1890. A.M. 1894. B.D. 1908.
—	Rich. Littleton	Cla.	M 1908 A.B. 1911 [D.D. 1909
—	Will. Noel	Sid.	M 1909 A.B. 1912
Radice,	Will. Archib.	Chr.	M 1901 A.B. 1904
Rae,	Art. Jos.	Cai.	M 1900 A.B. 1903
—	Errol Vivian Rochfort	Em.	M 1909 A.B. 1912
—	Will. Norman	C. C.	M 1905 A.B. 1908
Raffle,	Wilfrid	Joh.	M 1909 A.B. 1912

¹ King Edward VII Professor of English Literature, 1912.

Ragg,	Harry Rich.	Joh.	M 1908 A.B. 1911
Rahman,	Ahmed Abd el	Down.	E 1911
Raikes,	Frank Stewart Wad-) dington	Trin.	M 1912
—	Will. Oswell	Cai.	M 1907 A.B. 1910
Raimes,	Alwyn Leslie	King's	M 1904 A.B. 1907
—	Eric Alwyn	Jes.	M 1911
—	Lancelot	Cai.	M 1906 A.B. 1909
Rain,	Will. Hamilton	N. C.	L 1910
Raine,	Reg. Thompson	H. Sel.	M 1909 A.B. 1912
Rainsford,	Will. Ryland·	Qu.	M 1904
Rajan,	Arunachala Tyaga ...	Trin.	M 1904 A.B. 1906
Rake,	Eustace Olpherts ...	Pem.	M 1910
Ralph,	Fre. Hen. Morgan ...	King's	M 1909 A.B. 1912
—	Herb. Walt.	King's	M 1904 A.B. 1907
Ramage,	Hugh	Joh.	M 1899 A.B. 1901. A.M. 1906
Ramamurty,	Sonti Venkata	Trin.	M 1909 A.B. 1912
Ramdas,	Suryakant	Chr.	E 1899 A.B. 1903
Ramsay,	Alex.	Cai.	M 1906 A.B. 1909
—	Allan Beville	King's	M 1891 A.B. 1894. Allen B. A.M. 1901
—	Archib. Hamilton ...	Pem.	M 1904
—	Dav.	Chr.	M 1906 A.B., LL.B. 1909
—	Ja. Hen.		*Litt.D.* 1908
—	Lewis Neil Griffith ...	Chr.	M 1911
—	Malcolm Gordon	Chr.	M 1909 A.B. 1912
—	Rob. Anstruther	Cai.	M 1905 A.B. 1908. B.C., A.M. 1912
—	Will.		*Sc.D.* 1904
Ramsbotham,	Wilfred Hubert ...	Cla.	E 1908
Ramsbottom,	John	Em.	M 1905 A.B. 1908
Ramsden,	Geoffrey Cha. Frescheville	Sid.	M 1912
—	Geo. Taylor	Trin. H.	M 1897 A.B. 1901. A.M. 1904
Ramsey,	Walt. Ja.	Trin. H.	M 1903 A.B. 1906. LL.B. 1907
Rand,	Harold Millward	King's	M 1911
Randall,	Bayard Erle	Trin.	M 1906
—	Gerald Freyne	Trin.	M 1911
—	Hen. Lawrence	Trin.	M 1874 A.B. 1878. A.M. 1908
Randles,	Ja. Gilb. Heighway	Cai.	M 1902 A.B. 1905
Randolph,	John Hugh Granville	Trin.	M 1885 A.B. 1888. A.M. 1893. D.D. 1909
Ranger,	Apsley Sid. Burdett	Pem.	M 1898 A.B. 1901. A.M. 1905
Rankin,	John Kenneth	Qu.	M 1905 A.B. 1908
—	Rob.	Trin.	M 1901
Ranking,	Rob. Maur.	Pem.	M 1895 A.B. 1898. M.B., B.C. 1904
Ranner,	Frank	N. C.	M 1910
—	Sid. Cha.	N. C.	M 1904 A.B. 1907. A.M. 1911
Ransford,	Colin	Em.	M 1901 A.B. 1904
—	Fra. Bolton	King's	M 1904 A.B. 1907
—	Will. Macalister	Chr.	L 1909
Ransom,	John	Pem.	M 1911
—	Pet. Warwick	Pem.	M 1906 A.B. 1909
—	Phil. Lucas	Mag.	M 1911
Rao,	Sarangu Narasimha	N. C.	M 1909
—	Vinayek Ganpat	Joh.	M 1909
Raphael,	Norman Hen.	Trin.	M 1904
Raphaely,	Arnold	Trin. H.	M 1901 A.B. 1904
Rapp,	Tho. Cecil	Sid.	M 1911
Rappis,	Pier Alessandro Giorgio	Chr.	M 1899 A.B. 1902 [Aucher, R. A.
Rappoport,	Rob. Alexis	Chr.	E 1896 A.B. 1899. A.M. 1903. post Fitz-
Rapson,	[1] Edw. Ja. ....*Joh.		M 1879 A.B. 1884. A.M. 1888
Rashid,	Mian Abdul	Chr.	M 1909 A.B. 1911

[1] Professor of Sanskrit, 1906.

Rashleigh,	John Cosmo Stuart	Trin.	M 1890 A.B. 1893. A.M. 1897. B.C. 1901.
—	Will. Stuart	Trin. H.	L 1901 A.B. 1903 [M.D. 1904
Rastall,	Rob. Heron ....*Chr.		M 1899 A.B. 1902. A.M. 1906
Ratcliffe,	Alf. Victor	Sid.	M 1907
—	Cornwallis St Aubyn	H. Sel.	M 1910
Rathbone,	Chris. Greg	Trin.	M 1910
—	Edw. Reynolds	Trin.	M 1911
—	Rich. Reynolds	Trin.	M 1910
Ratib,	Dawood	Trin. H.	M 1909
Rattigan,	Cyril Stanley	Trin.	M 1904
Rattray,	Ian Maxwell	Cai.	M 1910
—	Reg. Campbell	Pem.	M 1908 A.B. 1911
Rau,	Benegal Narasinga ...	Trin.	M 1907 (B. Narsinga) A.B. 1909
—	Benegal Ram	King's	M 1909 A.B. 1911
—	Benegal Sanjiva	Joh.	M 1905 A.B. 1908
—	Kalle Rama Rau Sadashiva	Joh.	M 1903 A.B. 1906
Raven,	Archib. Edw. Tho. ...	Qu.	M 1898 A.B. 1901. A.M. 1906
—	Cha. Earle	Cai.	M 1904 A.B. 1907. *Em. A.M. 1911
—	Edw. Earle	Joh.	M 1909 A.B. 1912
—	Geoffrey Earle	C. C.	M 1912
—	Harry Palgrave	Em.	M 1896 A.B. 1899. A.M. 1903
Ravenscroft,	Pelham Donovan ...	Jes.	M 1908 A.B. 1912
Ravenshear,	Ewart Watson	Cla.	M 1912
Raverat,	Jacques Pierre	Em.	M 1906
Raw,	Rowland	Trin.	M 1903 A.B. 1907
Rawcliffe,	Claude Ramsay	Trin. H.	M 1909
—	Donovan Maclean ...	Cla.	M 1907 A.B. 1910
—	Ja. Hindle	Joh.	M 1894 Cath. A.B. 1899. A.M. 1903
—	Wallace Bern.	H. Sel.	M 1910
Rawes,	Percy Lea	Jes.	M 1902 A.B. 1905
Rawlence,	Art. Raymond	Cla.	M 1907
Rawlings,	Alb. Geo.	Trin.	M 1903 A.B., LL.B. 1906. A.M. 1910
—	Percy Townley	Trin.	M 1906 A.B. 1909
Rawlins,	Art.	King's	M 1908 A.B., LL.B. 1911
—	Evelyn Cha. Donaldson	Trin.	E 1905
—	Frank McCalmont ...	Trin.	M 1911
—	Hen. Guy	Trin.	M 1908 A.B. 1911
Rawlinson,	Art. Rich.	Pem.	M 1912
—	Hugh Augustus	Trin.	M 1897 A.B. 1900. A.M. 1906
—	Hugh Geo.	Em.	M 1899 A.B. 1902. A.M. 1908
—	[1] John Fre. Peel	Trin.	M 1879 LL.B. 1883. LL.M. 1887
—	Rupert Lewis	Trin.	M 1900 A.B. 1903.. B.C. 1912
Rawnsley,	Geo. Tennant	Trin. H.	M 1903 A.B., LL.B. 1906
Rawson,	Hugh Frederic Rawson	Trin.	M 1910
—	Jos. Nadin	Joh.	M 1912
—	Ronald Rawson	Trin.	M 1912
—	Wyatt Trevelyan Rawson	Trin.	M 1912
Rawstorn,	Ja. Oscar	Jes.	M 1910
Ray,	Mervyn Swire	Jes.	M 1910
—	Rich. Cyril	Em.	M 1901 A.B. 1904
—	Sid. Herb.		*A.M.* 1907
Rayleigh	(3rd *Baron*)		*See* Strutt, John Will.
Raymer,	Herb. Ja.	N. C.	M 1895 A.B. 1898. A.M. 1903
Raymond,	Cuthbert	Caj.	M 1900 A.B. 1903. M.B., B.C. 1910
Rayner,	Art. Errington	Cai.	M 1902 A.B. 1905. M.B., B.C., A.M. 1912
—	Edw.	Pem.	M 1905 A.B. 1908. M.B., B.C. 1912
—	Edwin Cromwell	Cai.	M 1904 A.B. 1907
—	Edwin Hartree	Trin.	M 1894 A.B. 1897. A.M. 1903
—	Oliver Crossley	Sid.	M 1911

[1] Commissary, 1900; Representative in Parliament, 1910.

Rayner,	Syd.	Em.	M 1905 A.B. 1908
—	Will. Hartree	Trin.	M 1898 A.B. 1901
Razumovsky,	(*Count*) Leon	Trin.	M 1906
Rea,	John Geo. Grey	Jes.	M 1904
—	John Will. Herb. ...	Em.	M 1901 A.B. 1904. A.M. 1908
—	Tho.	Joh.	L .1902 A.B. 1903. A.M. 1909
Read,	Art. Ja.	Joh.	M 1903 A.B. 1906
—	Eric Oswald	C. C.	M 1909 A.B. 1912
—	Grantly Dick	Joh.	M 1908 A.B. 1911
—	Hen. Cecil	Cai.	M 1909 A.B. 1912
—	Humphrey Mabyn ...	Cla.	M 1911
—	John	Em.	M 1910 A.M. 1912
—	John Walt.	Jes.	M 1912
—	Ralph Irving	Cai.	M 1907 A.B. 1910
—	Ralph Sid.	Sid.	M 1908 A.B. 1910
—	Will. Hen.	Jes.	M 1909 A.B. 1912
—	Willie Ronald	Jes.	M 1905
Reade,	Fra. Vincent	Pem.	M 1894 A.B. 1897. A.M. 1903
—	Geo.	Em.	M 1890 A.B., LL.B. 1893. LL.M. 1901
—	John Alf. Dearden ...	Cla.	M 1893 A.B. 1896. A.M. 1901
—	Reg. Will.	Em.	M 1911
—	Rich. Bancroft Nevil	Cla.	M 1902
—	Will. Parsons	Em.	M 1893 A.B., LL.B. 1896. A.M., LL.M. [1901
Reading,	Eric Will.	King's	M 1911
Readman,	Ja. Forrest Alex. ...	Pem.	M 1906 A.B. 1909
Ready,	Geo. Will.	N. C.	M 1902 A.B. 1905
Ream,	Cha. Fra.	Joh.	M 1903 A.B. 1906. A.M. 1910
Rearden,	Tho. Roche	Trin.	M 1902 A.B. 1906
Reay,	Basil John Mason ...	H. Sel.	M 1891 A.B. 1894. A.M. 1903
—	(*Lord*)		*Litt.D.* 1905
Rebsch,	Rupert Fre. Will. ...	Cla.	M 1901 A.B. 1904
Reckitt,	Alb. Leopold	Trin.	M 1895 A.B. 1898. A.M. 1902
Reddaway,	Harold	Cai.	L 1910 A.B. 1912
Reddy,	Cattamanchi Ramalinga	Joh.	M 1902 A.B. 1905. A.M.† 1909
Redfern,	Edw. North	Sid.	M 1903 A.B. 1906
—	Will. Art. Kennedy	Trin.	M 1900 Down. A.B. 1907
Redlich,	Edwin Basil	Chr.	M 1896 A.B. 1899. A.M.† 1903
Redman,	Cha. Edw.	Pem.	M 1900 A.B. 1903. A.M. 1908. B.C. 1912
—	Geo. Alf.	Trin. H.	M 1900 A.B. 1904. A.M. 1908
—	Geo. Bertram	Jes.	M 1905 A.B. 1908
Redwood,	Fre. Art.	Qu.	M 1909 A.B. 1912
Reece,	Fra. Bertram	Joh.	M 1909 A.B. 1912
—	Morris Geo. Bern. ...	Joh.	M 1901 A.B. 1904
—	Rich. Ja.	Down.	M 1888 A.B. 1891. M.B., B.C. 1892. A.M. [1895. M.D. 1902
Reed,	Bertie	N. C.	M 1912
—	Cha. Hub.	Chr.	M 1900 A.B. 1903
—	Clifford Hugh	Trin.	M 1907 A.B. 1911
—	Edw. Baines	Chr.	M 1902 A.B., LL.B. 1905. A.M. 1911
—	Geo. Hen.	N. C.	M 1904 Down. A.B. 1907. A.M. 1911
—	Harry Leslie	Cla.	M 1903 A.B. 1906. A.M. 1910
—	Hen. Will. Ternent	Trin.	M 1905 A.B. 1908
—	Herb. Saunders	Trin.	M 1905 A.B. 1908. A.M. 1912
—	John	Trin.	M 1909 A.B. 1912
—	Lancelot Geo.	King's	M 1902 A.B. 1906. A.M. 1912
—	Leslie Hen. Brett ...	H. Sel.	M 1911
Reeders,	Wilhelm Johannes Marnitz	N. C.	M 1907
Rees,	Alan Guy Treharne	Cla.	M 1911
—	Alb. Phil.	N. C.	E 1902 Chr. A.B. 1905. A.M. 1909
—	Alf. Will.	Qu.	L 1903 A.B. 1905. A.M. 1910
—	Edw. Lloyd	Chr.	L 1912

Rees,	Geo. Martin Treharne	Cla.	M 1905 A.B. 1908
—	Hub. Leon.	Joh.	M 1909 A.B. 1912
—	John Rawlings	King's	M 1908 A.B. 1911
—	Rob. Athelstane Tait	Down.	M 1904 A.B. 1907. A.M. 1911
—	Tho. Griffith	Qu.	M 1902
—	Tho. John	Chr.	M 1908 A.B. 1910
Rees-Mogg,	Louis Leyson	Sid.	M 1908 A.B. 1911
Reeve,	Adolphus Edm.	Cla.	M 1909 A.B., LL.B. 1912
—	Fre. Palmer	H. Sel.	M 1911
—	Geo. Turner	Em.	M 1906 A.B. 1909
—	Herb.	Joh.	M 1893 A.B. 1896. A.M. 1901
—	Herb. Cha.	Em.	M 1899 A.B. 1902. A.M.† 1906
Reeves,	Frederic Will.	Chr.	M 1895 A.B. 1898. A.M.† 1906
—	Reg. Fre.	H. Sel.	M 1898 A.B. 1901. A.M. 1905
—	Victor Cha. Methuen	Mag.	M 1906
Regan,	Cha. Tate	Qu.	M 1897 A.B. 1900. A.M. 1907
Regnart,	Hor. Griffith	Trin.	M 1893 A.B. 1896. A.M. 1906
Reichert,	Rob. Jacob	Pet.	M 1912
Reid,	Alex. Art.	Cla.	M 1904 A.B. 1908. A.M. 1911
—	Art. Tho.	King's	M 1902 A.B. 1905
—	Cedric Boileau	Cai.	M 1908
—	Cha. Herb.	Jes.	M 1909
—	Douglas Art.	Chr.	M 1905 Trin. H. A.B. 1908
—	Douglas Gavin	Trin.	M 1907 A.B. 1910
—	Edw. Douglas Whitehead	Chr.	M 1902 A.B. 1905. M.B., B.C. 1910
—	Edw. Waymouth ...	N. C.	M 1879 A.B. 1883. H. Cav. M.B. 1885.
—	Forrest	Chr.	M 1905 A.B. 1908 [Down. Sc.D. 1905
—	Fra. Fielding	Mag.	M 1911
—	Gerald Mortimer ...	Pem.	M 1905
—	Ja.	Trin.	M 1909
—	Ja. Scott Cumberland	Jes.	M 1908 A.B., LL.B. 1911
—	Ja. Smith	Trin.	M 1907 A.B. 1910
—	Ja. Whitelaw		*LL.D.* 1902
—	Kenneth Gardner ...	King's	M 1899 A.B. 1902. A.M. 1906
—	Leon. John	Chr.	M 1907 A.B. 1910
—	Rob. Mabean Dickson	Trin.	M 1901 A.B. 1904
Reilly,	Cha. Herb.	Qu.	M 1893 A.B. 1896. A.M. 1901
—	Stanislaus Geo.	Trin.	M 1905
Reindorp,	Hector Will.	N. C.	M 1901 Cath. A.B. 1904. A.M. 1908
Reiner,	Noël And.	Pem.	M 1910
Reinert,	Ernst Leopold	King's.	M 1911
Reiss,	Godfrey Emil	Trin.	M 1891 A.B. 1894. A.M. 1904
Reissmann,	Cha. Hen.	Joh.	E 1892 A.B. 1895. C., M.B., B.C., A.M.
Reitlinger,	Hen. Scipio	King's	L 1906 A.B. 1909 [1899. M.D.† 1903
Remfry,	Fre. Geo. Percy	Cla.	M 1899 A.B. 1902
Rendall,	Fra. Geoffrey	Trin.	M 1909 A.B. 1912
—	Gerald Hen. ....*Trin.		M 1870 A.B. 1874. A.M. 1877. B.D. 1909
Rendle,	Anstruther Cardew ...	N. C.	M 1882 Chr. A.B. 1887. M.B., B.C. 1890.
Rennie,	Donald Williamson	Joh.	M 1904 A.B. 1907 [M.D. 1901
—	Will. ....*Trin.		M 1888 A.B. 1902. A.M. 1905
Rennoldson,	Hen. Fra.	Trin.	M 1906 A.B., LL.B. 1909
Renouf,	Louis Percy Watts ...	Trin.	M 1909 A.B. 1912
Renoy,	René Emile	C. C.	M 1907 A.B. 1910
Renshaw,	Art. Hamilton	Trin.	M 1907 A.B. 1910
—	Howard Wade	Pem.	M 1907 A.B., LL.B. 1910
—	John Harry Thorpe	Cla.	M 1893 A.B. 1896. A.M. 1901
—	Steph. Cha. Bine ...	Trin.	M 1903 A.B. 1907
Renton,	Tho.	Cai.	M 1910
Rentrop,	Carl Hermann	N. C.	E 1910
Renwick,	Hugh Archib.	Pem.	M 1909 (Hugo, A.) A.B. 1912
—	John Ern.	King's	M 1904 A.B. 1907

Renwick,	Tho. Buchanan	King's	M 1912
Resker,	Basil Alf.	C. C.	M 1908 A.B. 1911
—	Herb. Cha.	C. C.	M 1903 A.B. 1906
Retzius,	Magnus Gustaf		*Sc.D.* 1904
Reunert,	Clive	Trin.	M 1906 A.B. 1911
—	John	Pem.	M 1905
Revillon,	Alb. Julian	Trin.	M 1907 A.B. 1910
—	Jos. Whistler	King's	M 1905 A.B. 1908
Rewcastle,	Cuthbert Snowball ...	Trin.	M 1906 A.B. 1909. LL.B. 1910
Rex,	Marcus	Trin.	M 1905 A.B. 1908
Reynard,	Cha. Fre. Pet.	Trin. H.	M 1907 A.B. 1910
Reynolds,	Alf. Rothay	Pem.	M 1892 A.B. 1895. A.M. 1902
—	Cedric Lawton	Cla.	M 1907 A.B. 1910
—	Cha. Edw. White Vincent	H. Sel.	M 1907 A.B. 1910
—	Cha. Harold	Trin.	M 1904 A.B. 1907. A.M. 1912
—	Cha. Percy Herb. ...	C. C.	M 1892 A.B. 1895. A.M. 1910
—	Cha. Will.	Joh.	M 1900 A.B. 1905
—	Duncan Barclay	Cla.	M 1903 A.B. 1906
—	Edw.	Qu.	E 1894 A.B. 1897. A.M. 1901
—	Ern. Art.	Pem.	M 1896 A.B. 1899. A.M. 1903
—	Ern. Percy	Cai.	M 1906 A.B. 1909. LL.B. 1910
—	Geoffrey Howard	Trin.	M 1905 A.B. 1909
—	Hen. Osborne	Em.	M 1902 A.B. 1905
—	Hugh Lewis	Cla.	M 1905
—	John White Vincent	H. Sel.	M 1904 A.B. 1907
—	John Will.	Trin.	M 1905 A.B. 1908. *Sid. A.M. 1912
—	Kenneth	Em.	M 1910
—	Leethem	Trin.	M 1893 A.B. 1896. B.C. 1903. M.B.† 1909
—	Noël Cha. Will.	Trin.	M 1908 A.B. 1911
—	Rich. Percy	N. C.	M 1899 A.B. 1902
—	Ronald Grant	Pem.	M 1901 A.B. 1905
—	Wilfred Tho.	Cai.	M 1907 A.B. 1910
—	Will. Hen. Rob.	Joh.	M 1910
Rhodes,	Edm. Cecil	Trin.	M 1911
—	Edw. Llewellyn Noott	H. Sel.	M 1901 A.B. 1904
—	Herb. Eyton	King's	M 1910
—	Phil. Grafton Mole ...	Pem.	M 1904 A.B. 1907. A.M. 1911
—	Sid. Herb.	Cai.	M 1908 A.B. 1912
—	Timaru Rob.	Mag.	M 1907
—	Walt. Edm.	Pet.	M 1912
—	Wilfred Rhodes	Trin.	*See* Levy, W. R.
—	Will. Atkinson	Cai.	M 1902 A.B. 1905. A.M. 1910
—	Will. Fredrick	H. Sel.	M 1902 A.B. 1905
Rhys,	Walt. Rowland	Em.	M 1898 A.B. 1902. A.M. 1905
Ribeiro,	Geo.	Jes.	M 1907 A.B. 1910
Ricard,	Frank	King's	M 1906 A.B. 1909. LL.B. 1910
Ricardo,	Frank	Trin.	M 1906
—	Harry Ralph	Trin.	M 1903 A.B. 1906
Ricci,	Aldo Antonio	King's	M 1911
Rice,	Cha. Macan	Joh.	M 1889 A.B. 1892. A.M. 1905
—	Fre.	Down.	E 1892 A.B. 1895. A.M. 1903
—	Hen. Goulding	Joh.	M 1903 A.B. 1906. B.C. 1910
—	Leon. Cyril	Joh.	M 1912
—	Mark Napier	H. Sel.	M 1892 A.B. 1895. A.M.† 1908
—	Ronald Miller	Pem.	M 1912
Rice-Jones,	Alf. Theodore	Chr.	M 1909
—	Benj. Rowland	Chr.	M 1907 A.B., LL.B. 1910
Rich,	Clive Noble	Jes.	M 1906 A.B. 1909
—	Herb. Tho.	Pem.	M 1898 A.B. 1901. A.M. 1908
—	Neville Julian	Trin.	M 1911
Richards,	Art. Parry	Pem.	M 1910

Richards,	Claude Willmott	Sid.	M 1912
—	Crosland Smith	Cai.	M 1904 A.B. 1907
—	Cyril Treharne	Chr.	M 1909
—	Dav. Ja.	Trin.	M 1898 A.B. 1901. A.M. 1906
—	Evan Ivor Glasbrook	H. Sel.	M 1908 A.B. 1911
—	Fra. Shakspeare	Cai.	M 1905 A.B. 1908
—	Fre. Maur. Smith ...	Cai.	M 1906 A.B. 1909
—	Hugh Augustine	Cla.	M 1903 A.B. 1906
—	Ivor Armstrong	Mag.	M 1911
—	Percy Art.	Pet.	M 1911
—	Rob.	Joh.	M 1906 A.B. 1908
—	Roger Charnock	Trin.	M 1899 A.B. 1902
—	Theodore Will.		*Sc.D.* 1911
—	Will. Art.	N. C.	M 1902 A.B. 1905
Richardson,	Alf. Hen.	Joh.	M 1903 A.B. 1907. A.M. 1910. M.B., B.C.
—	Archer Stuart	Cai.	M 1912 [1912
—	Art. Vernon	Qu.	M 1905 A.B. 1908. A.M. 1912
—	Cha. Will. Barnard	Cla.	M 1904 A.B. 1908. A.M. 1911
—	Cha. Will. Hen.	Sid.	M 1891 A.B. 1894. A.M. 1904
—	Conrad	Cai.	M 1909
—	Cyril Alb.	Sid.	M 1910
—	Cyril Lacy	Trin.	M 1906 A.B. 1909
—	Daryl Stewart	Trin.	M 1910
—	Dav. Will. Ryder ...	Cai.	M 1912
—	Dudley Ern. Edgar	Cai.	M 1912
—	Edw. Shaw	Trin.	M 1881 A.B. 1885. A.M. 1904
—	Ern. Benbow	Cla.	M 1903 A.B. 1906
—	Fra. Krüger	Cai.	M 1910
—	Frederic Ion	Cla.	M 1902 A.B. 1906
—	Fre.	N. C.	M 1905 A.B. 1908
—	Geo. Stamper	H. Sel.	M 1896 A.B. 1899. A.M. 1903
—	Guy Carleton	Trin.	M 1903
—	Harold Sam. Temple	Trin.	M 1901 A.B. 1904. A.M. 1910
—	Joe Brook	Qu.	M 1901 A.B. 1904. LL.B. 1905. A.M. 1909
—	John Percival Abernethy	Trin.	M 1904 A.B. 1907
—	John Sherbrooke	Trin.	M 1895 A.B. 1898. A.M. 1902
—	John Watson	Trin.	M 1900 A.B. 1903. A.M. 1907
—	Jos. Herb.	Chr.	M 1896 A.B. 1901
—	Lewis Fry	King's	M 1900 A.B. 1903
—	Owen Willans ....*Trin.		M 1897 A.B. 1900. A.M. 1904
—	Percy John	Jes.	M 1910
—	Rob. Scovell	Pem.	M 1911
—	Spencer Will.	Trin.	L 1895 A.B. 1902. A.M. 1907
—	Stansfield Pim	King's	M 1908 A.B., LL.B. 1912
—	Tho.	Cla.	M 1899 A.B., LL.B. 1904
—	Tho. Dow	Trin. H.	M 1905
—	Will. John	H. Sel.	M 1903 A.B. 1906
Richardson Kuhlmann,	Denis	Chr.	M 1908 A.B. 1911
Richings,	Lawrence Walt.	Em.	M 1871 A.B. 1875. A.M. 1910
Richmond,	Fra.	Cla.	M 1892 A.B. 1895. M.B., B.C. 1903
—	Harold Bircham	King's	M 1904 A.B. 1907. B.C., A.M. 1911
—	John Parratts	N. C.	E 1888 A.B. 1892. A.M. 1901
—	Oliffe Legh ....*King's		M 1900 A.B. 1903. A.M. 1907
Richter,	Art. Hen. Louis	Pem.	M 1899 A.B. 1902. LL.B. 1904
Rickards,	John Ayscough	C. C.	L 1902 A.B. 1904. A.M. 1912
Rickett,	Art.	Chr.	M 1889 A.B. 1892. LL.B. 1894. A.M. 1896.
—	Cha. Ern.	King's	M 1903 [LL.M. 1900. LL.D. 1905
—	Gerald Russell	King's	M 1896 A.B. 1899. B.C., A.M. 1903. M.B.
—	Leon. Allen	Trin.	L 1904 [1905. M.D. 1907
Ricketts,	Guy Dunstan	H. Sel.	M 1895 A.B. 1898. A.M. 1902
Rickman,	John	King's	M 1910

Riddell,	Gilb. Bruce	Qu.	M 1910
—	Granville Browne Edmond	C. C.	M 1891 A.B. 1894. A.M. 1901
---	Ja. Alex.	Trin. H.	M 1910
—	Ja. Riddell	Trin.	M 1903 A.B. 1906
—	Will. Edmeston	Cai.	M 1893 A.B. 1896. A.M. 1904
—	Will. Hutton	Trin.	M 1898 A.B. 1901
Riddiford,	Fre. Earle	Cai.	M 1907
Riddiough,	Sid.	King's	M 1910
Riddle,	Hugh Howard	Pet.	M 1895 A.B. 1898. M.B., B.C. 1901. M.D.
Rideal,	Eric Keightley	Trin. H.	M 1908 A.B. 1911 [1912
Ridge,	Basil Art.	Pet.	M 1912
—	Rich.	Chr.	M 1904
Ridge-Jones,	Ivor	Trin. H.	E 1902
Ridgeway,	Cha. John	Trin.	M 1860 A.B. 1864. A.M. 1885. D.D. 1906
—	Jos. West		*LL.D.* 1902
—	[1] Will.	Pet.	L 1877 *Cai. A.B. 1880. A.M. 1883. Sc.D.
Ridgway,	Jos.	Trin.	M 1901 A.B. 1904 [1909
Ridley,	Art. Hilton	Jes.	M 1910
—	Cha. Noel	Jes.	M 1904
—	Douglas Farish	H. Sel.	M 1912
—	Hen. Quentin	Trin.	M 1901
—	Lancelot Edwin	Jes.	M 1910
—	Tho. Dixon	Trin.	M 1901
Ridout,	Edwin Stanley Forsyth	Qu.	M 1904 A.B. 1907. A.M. 1911
—	Gilb. Harry	N. C.	M 1906 A.B. 1909
Riecke,	Eduard		*Sc.D.* 1904
Riesle,	Will. Benj.	Trin. H.	E 1905 A.B., LL.B. 1908
Rieu,	Alf.	Chr.	M 1897 A. Ignatius A.B. 1901
—	Hen.	Cai.	M 1897 A.B. 1900. A.M. 1904
Rigby,	Fra. John	Cai.	M 1906 A.B. 1909. LL.B. 1910
—	Geo.	Cath.	M 1910
—	Ja. Rich. Anderton	Em.	M 1909 A.B. 1912
—	Percy	Chr.	M 1904 A.B. 1907
—	Rich.	N. C.	M 1905 A.B. 1908. A.M. 1912
Rigden,	Cha.	Trin.	M 1908 A.B. 1911
Rigg,	Jos. Harold	Em.	M 1912
—	Theo.	Joh.	M 1912
Riley,	Alex. Walt.	Em.	M 1897 A.B. 1900. A.M. 1912
—	Art.	Chr.	M 1909 A.B. 1912
—	Art. Cecil	Trin.	M 1901 A.B. 1904
—	Cha. Lawrence	Cai.	M 1906 A.B. 1909. LL.B. 1910
—	Chris. John Molesworth	Pem.	M 1912
---	Lambert	Qu.	M 1899 A.B. 1902. A.M. 1906
—	Tho.	Pem.	M 1903 A.B. 1911
—	Will. Nairn	Cath.	M 1911
Riley-Smith,	Will.	Trin.	M 1909
Rintoul,	And. Jeffrey	Cla.	M 1902
Ripley,	Hen. Edw.	Cai.	M 1902 A.B. 1905
—	Hugh Will. Grey ...	Trin.	M 1905 A.B. 1910
Rippmann,	Christian Hugo	King's	M 1898 A.B. 1901. A.M. 1905. B.C. 1907. [M.B. 1908 (2). M.D. 1910
Rischbieth,	Harold	Trin.	M 1895 A.B. 1898. A.M. 1902. B.C. 1904. [M.D. 1909
Ritchie,	Alistair Ferguson ...	Qu.	M 1908 A.B. 1911
—	Alister West	C. C.	M 1907 A.B. 1910
—	Art. Dav.	Trin.	M 1911
—	Art. Gray	Pet.	M 1911
—	Cha. Hen.	Joh.	M 1907 A.B. 1910
—	Geo. Lindsay	Joh.	M 1909
—	John Nevill	Joh.	M 1899 A.B. 1902

[1] Disney Professor of Archæology, 1892, 1898, 1903, 1908.

Ritchie,	Rob. Blackwood	...... Trin.	M 1912
—	Sartoris Cha.	.... Trin.	M 1901 A.B. 1904. Sebastian S. C. A.M.
—	Will. Traill	.... Joh.	M 1901 A.B. 1904 [1908
Ritson,	Art. Stewart	.... Trin.	M 1910
—	Fra.	.... Mag.	M 1909 A.B. 1912
—	John And.	.... Trin.	M 1911
—	Rob.	.... Trin.	M 1906 A.B. 1910
Rittenberg,	Max Mark Lion	...... Cai.	E 1899 A.B. 1902
Rittner,	Geo. Hermann	...... Trin.	M 1894 A.B. 1898. A.M. 1902
Rivers-Smith,	Stanley	.... Cath.	M 1898 A.B. 1901. A.M. 1905
Rives,	Fra. Bayard	.... Trin.	M 1911
Rivett,	Louis Carnac	.... Trin.	M 1906 A.B. 1909
Rivington,	Reg. Thurston	.... Trin.	M 1900 A.B. 1903. LL.B. 1904. A.M. 1910
Rix,	Art. Hen.	.... Trin. H.	M 1900 A.B. 1903
—	Harry Sid.	.... Trin.	M 1890 A.B. 1893. A.M. 1903
—	Reg. Geo. Bertram	... Cai.	M 1903
—	Will. Art.	.... Joh.	M 1895 A.B. 1899. A.M. 1903
Riza,	Ali	.... N. C.	M 1912
Roadhouse,	Ja. Leon.	.... N. C.	M 1906 A.B. 1909
Rob,	Jos. Will.	.... Joh.	M 1895 A.B. 1898. M.B., B.C. 1902. A.M.
Robathan,	Kenneth Minshull	... Cai.	M 1908 A.B. 1911 [1903. M.D. 1905
Robb,	Alf. Art.	.... Joh.	M 1894 A.B. 1897. A.M. 1901
Robbins,	Clifton	.... Qu.	M 1909 A.B. 1912
—	Frank Hub.	.... Pem.	M 1906 A.B. 1909 [1905. M.D. 1908
—	Reg. Hen.	.... Trin.	M 1896 A.B. 1899. B.C., A.M. 1904. M.B.
Roberton,	Ja.	.... Qu.	M 1892 A.B. 1895. A.M. 1907
—	John Art. Wilkie	... Em.	M 1912
Roberts,	Alan Dixon	.... Cai.	M 1907 A.B., LL.B. 1910
—	Alex. Fowler	.... Cla.	M 1901
—	Alf. Adrian	.... Trin. H.	M 1912
—	Alf. Cecil Sam.	...... Trin.	M 1908 A.B. 1911
—	Art. Hallam	.... Jes.	M 1909 A.B. 1911
—	Art. Hen.	.... C. C.	M 1899 A.B. 1902
—	Art. Ja. Rooker	...... Jes.	M 1900 A.B. 1903
—	Art. Will. Rymer	... Trin.	M 1898 A.B. 1901. A.M. 1911
—	Basil Coleby	.... Pem.	M 1906 A.B. 1909
—	Cecil Holmes	.... Trin. H.	M 1912
—	Cecil Quinlan	.... Cla.	M 1910
—	Cha. Cecil Gwynedd	Trin.	M 1899 A.B. 1902
—	Cha. Edw.	.... Joh.	M 1910
—	[1] Ern. Stewart	.........*Cai.	M 1865 A.B. 1869. A.M. 1872
—	Ffrangcon	...............*Cla.	M 1907 A.B. 1910
—	Fra. Bernard	.... Jes.	M 1901 A.B. 1904
—	Fra. Harry	.... Chr.	M 1901
—	Fre. Will.	.... Pem.	M 1904 A.B. 1907
—	Harold Edm. FitzGerald	Pem.	M 1902 A.B. 1905. A.M. 1909
—	Harry Edwin	.... Joh.	M 1894 A.B. 1897. Hen. E. A.M. 1901
—	Hen. John	.... Cla.	M 1901 A.B. 1904. A.M. 1908
—	Herb. Spencer	.... Em.	M 1910 [A.M. 1902
—	Hugh Fra. Bodvel	... Cla.	M 1892 Bodvel-Roberts, H. F., A.B. 1899.
—	Hugh Treharne Llewellyn	Cla.	E 1901 A.B. 1904. A.M. 1910
—	Jesse Haworth	...... Em.	M 1898 A.B. 1901
—	John Ern.	.... Mag.	M 1895 A.B. 1898. A.M. 1909
—	John Haworth	.... Mag.	M 1903 A.B. 1906
—	John Holland	.... Em.	M 1905 A.B. 1908
—	John Rob. Bowden	... Pem.	M 1910
—	John Will. Basil Thornes	Trin.	M 1900 A.B. 1903
—	Llewelyn Caradog	... N. C.	M 1908 Chr. A.B. 1911
—	Raymond Paul Middleton	Qu.	M 1902 [LL.M. 1899. LL.D. 1905
—	Reuben Will.	.... Down.	M 1890 King's A.B., LL.B. 1894. A.M.,

[1] Master of Gonville and Caius College, 1903.

Roberts,	Rich. Bowen	.... Cla.	M 1900 A.B. 1904
—	Rob. Lloyd	.... H. Sel.	M 1895 A.B. 1898. A.M. 1902
—	Rupert Edw.	.... Jes.	M 1900 A.B. 1903
—	Sam.	.... Trin.	M 1900 A.B., LL.B. 1903. A.M. 1907
—	Syd. Castle	.... Pem.	M 1906 A.B. 1909
—	Tho. Junius Sid.	... Chr.	M 1896 A.B. 1899. A.M. 1905
—	Walt. Stewart	.... Cai.	M 1908 A.B. 1911
—	Will. Martyn	.... N. C.	M 1911
Robertshaw,	Jos.	.... Trin.	M 1903 A.B. 1906
Robertson,	Ainslie John	.... Trin.	M 1899 A.B. 1902. A.M. 1906
—	Alex. Gerald	.... Trin.	M 1897 A.B. 1900. A.M. 1909
—	Cha. Donald	.........*Trin.	M 1898 A.B. 1902. A.M. 1905
—	Colin John Trevelyan	Em.	M 1897 A.B. 1900. A.M. 1904
—	Dennis Holme	.... Trin.	M 1908 A.B. 1911
—	Donald Struan	......*Trin.	M 1904 A.B. 1908. A.M. 1911
—	Frank Archib.	.... Down.	M 1909
—	Harold John	.... Trin.	M 1904 A.B. 1907
—	John Art.	.... Down.	M 1910
—	John Kellock	.... Em.	M 1912
—	John Seymour	.... Cla.	M 1901
—	Julius Cha.	.... Trin.	M 1898 A.B. 1901. A.M. 1905
—	Keith Forbes	.... Trin.	M 1908
—	Leo Cayley	.... Qu.	M 1909 A.B. 1912
—	Ludovic Vander Meulen	Qu.	M 1899 A.B. 1902
—	Miles Kenneth	...... Trin.	M 1910
—	Oliver Hope	.... Qu.	M 1908 A.B. 1911
—	Ronald	.... Trin.	M 1905 A.B. 1908
—	Wallace Roderick Duncan	Em.	M 1911
Robertson-Shersby,	Rob.	.... Cai.	M 1909 post Robertson-Shersby-Harvie,
Robertson Smith,	Norman Mitchell	King's	M 1905 A.B. 1908 [R.
Robins,	Gilb. Selwyn	.... Chr.	M 1899 A.B. 1902
—	John Norman	.... Chr.	M 1895 A.B. 1898. A.M. 1902
Robinson,	Alb. Clifford	.... Chr.	M 1903 A.B. 1906. A.M. 1910
—	Alf. Ern.	.... Cath.	M 1900 A.B. 1903
—	Alf. Skirrow	.... Em.	M 1889 A.B. 1892. M.B., B.C. 1896. A.M.
—	Archib. Ja.	.... Chr.	M 1901 [1909
—	Art. Dawes	.... C. C.	M 1911
—	Art. Douglas	.... Down.	M 1895 A.B., LL.B. 1898. A.M. 1902
—	Art. Hugh Rawlins	Cla.	M 1897 A.B.1900. Mus.B.1901. A.M. 1904
—	Art. Mostyn	.... Em.	M 1897 N. C. A.B. 1900. A.M. 1909
—	Art. Will.	.... Jes.	M 1874 A.B. 1878. A.M. 1881. B.D. 1898.
—	Austen Quinton	...... Cai.	M 1904 A.B. 1907 [D.D. 1905
—	Basil Cautley	.... Cath.	M 1908 A.B. 1911
—	Cha. Stanley	.... Em.	M 1907 A.B. 1910
—	Charlie	.... Pem.	M 1901 A.B. 1904
—	Donald Porter	.... Cla.	M 1901 A.B. 1904. A.M. 1908
—	Edgar Vivian	.... Pem.	M 1903 A.B. 1906
—	Edw. Colles	.... Qu.	M 1896 A.B. 1899. A.M. 1903
—	Edw. Forbes	.... Cai.	M 1883 A.B. 1886. A.M. 1905
—	Ern. Harold	.... N. C.	M 1909 Joh. A.B. 1912
—	Fra. Harry	.... Qu.	M 1903 A.B. 1906. M.B., B.C. 1911
—	Fra. John	.... Em.	L 1900 A.B. 1902
—	Fra. Trevor	.... Trin.	M 1899 A.B. 1902. A.M. 1906
—	Fred	.... Pet.	M 1904 A.B. 1907
—	Fre. Percival	.... Pem.	M 1906 A.B. 1909
—	Geo. Michael Moncrieff	Joh.	M 1904
—	Gilb. Wooding	.... Cai.	M 1907 A.B. 1910
—	Harold Claude	...... Trin. H.	M 1901
—	Harold Jos.	.... Joh.	M 1893 A.B. 1898. M.B., B.C. 1904
—	Hen.	.... Trin.	M 1896 A.B. 1899. M.B., B.C., A.M. 1903.
—	Hen. Tho.	.... Cla.	M 1904 A.B. 1907 [M.D. 1908

Robinson,	Hilary Isaac	Joh.	M 1903 A.B. 1906
—	Hugh Douglas	Cai.	M 1907
—	Hugh Methven	Pem.	M 1908 A.B. 1911
—	John Cyril Cha. Hen.	Pet.	M 1906 A.B. 1909
—	John Graham	Trin.	M 1906 A.B. 1909
—	John Harold	Sid.	M 1899 A.B. 1902
—	John Hen.	Qu.	M 1907 A.B. 1910
—	John Stanley	Sid.	M 1907 A.B. 1910
—	Jos. Benj.	Trin.	M 1908
—	Lancelot Roden Claud	Cath.	M 1909
—	Laurence Milner	Pet.	M 1904 A.B. 1907. A.M. 1911
—	Lewis Denham	Cla.	M 1902
—	Louis Fra. Woodward	Joh.	M 1912
—	Theodore Hen.	Joh.	M 1900 A.B. 1903. A.M. 1907
—	Tho.	N. C.	M 1911
—	Walt. de Horne	Pet.	M 1907 A.B. 1910
—	Walt. Syd.	Cath.	M 1911
—	Wilfred Hen.	Trin.	M 1909
—	Will. Edw.	Joh.	M 1897 A.B. 1900. A.M. 1904
—	Will. Harold	Down.	M 1898 A.B. 1901. M.B., B.C. 1906
Robson,	Alan	Sid.	M 1907 A.B. 1910
—	Alf.	Cla.	M 1897 A.B. 1900. A.M. 1904
—	Douglas Rich.	Em.	M 1897 A.B. 1900. A.M. 1905
—	Edgar Iliff	Chr.	M 1892 A.B. 1895. A.M. 1906
—	Edw. Gleadall Uphill	Cla.	M 1901 A.B. 1904
—	Ern.	Trin.	M 1912
—	Gerald Dav.		*See* Rosenberg, G. D.
—	Hen.	Sid.	M 1900 A.B. 1904. A.M. 1911
—	Hen. Renton	Trin.	M 1898 A.B. 1901
—	Herb. Eric	Qu.	M 1897 A.B. 1900. A.M. 1905
—	John Tho.	King's	M 1900 A.B. 1903. A.M. 1907
—	Percy Edw.	Em.	M 1896 A.B. 1899. A.M. 1906
—	Reg. Herb.	N. C.	M 1901 A.B. 1904
—	Tho. Fairfax Uphill	Cla.	M 1894 A.B. 1900. A.M. 1903
—	Will. Newby	Cai.	M 1903 A.B., LL.B. 1906. A.M. 1910
Roby,	Art. Godfrey	Joh.	M 1881 A.B. 1884 (2). A.M. 1903
Rockett,	Frank Addison	Qu.	M 1909 A.B. 1912
Rockwood,	John Marcus Selvaturai	Chr.	M 1907
—	Rajaratnam	Cath.	M 1910
Roden,	Hugh Carlo Bellasys	N. C.	M 1905 A.B. 1908. A.M. 1912
Roderick,	Hen. Buckley	N. C.	M 1891 Em. A.B. 1894. M.B., B.C. 1899.
Rodgers,	Harold Nickinson ...	C. C.	M 1906 A.B. 1909 [A.M. 1901. M.D. 1902
Rodick,	Rob. Lewis	Em.	L 1910 A.B. 1912
Rodney,	(*Hon.*) Ja. Hen. Bertie	Trin. H.	M 1911
Rodocanachi,	Pet.	Trin. H.	M 1909
Roe,	Everard Verdon	Pem.	M 1898 A.B. 1901
—	Rob. Gordon	H. Sel.	M 1907
Roechling,	Godfrey Denne	Qu.	M 1906 A.B. 1909
Roffe,	Cha. Geoffrey	Trin.	M 1903 post Roffe-Silvester, C. G. A.B.
Roffe-Silvester			*See* Roffe, C. G. [1906. A.M. 1910
Rogers,	Alan Leslie	Cla.	M 1900 A.B. 1903
—	Alf. Denys Strickland	Cath.	M 1902 LL.B. 1905
—	Art. Will.	Chr.	M 1891 A.B. 1894. A.M. 1899. Sc.D.† 1908
—	Claude Hugh	Cla.	M 1901
—	Esmond Hallewell ...	Cai.	M 1910
—	Frank	N. C.	M 1902 A.B. 1904
—	Frank St Aubyn ...	Trin.	M 1898 Fra. St A. A.B. 1901
—	Fre. Ern. Woodham	Em.	M 1904 A.B. 1907. B.C. 1910
—	Geo. Swire de Moleyns	Cai.	M 1905 A.B. 1908
—	Gilb. Ashley	Qu.	M 1906 A.B. 1909
—	John Lloyd	Chr.	M 1907 A.B. 1910

Rogers,	Longdon Willmer ...	Trin.	M 1910
— Percy	Walsham Montgomery	Mag.	M 1904 A.B. 1907
—	Reg. Art.	Cla.	M 1904 A.B. 1907
—	Rich. Aubrey	Cai.	M 1894 A.B. 1897. A.M. 1902
—	Rich. Syd. Lloyd ...	Cla.	M 1910
—	Tho. Godfrey	Qu.	M 1905 A.B. 1908
—	Will. Downing	Qu.	M 1908 A.B. 1911
Rogerson,	Sid.	Sid.	M 1912
—	Tho. Scott	H. Sel.	M 1905 A.B. 1908. A.M. 1912
—	Walt. John Lancashire	Joh.	M 1908 A.B. 1911
Rogers-Tillstone,	Hermann Fra. ...	Trin. H.	M 1910
Roget,	Sam. Romilly	Trin.	M 1894 A.B. 1897. A.M. 1901
Rolfe,	Cha.	Cla.	M 1885 A.B. 1888. M.B., B.C. 1891. M.D.
—	Phil.	N. C.	M 1909 A.B. 1912 [1897. A.M. 1905
—	Rich.	Cla.	M 1896 A.B. 1899. M.B., B.C. 1902
Rolls,	Cha. Stuart	Trin.	M 1895 A.B. 1898. C. Stewart A.M. 1902
—	Will. Hereward	Trin.	M 1908 A.B. 1911
Rolston,	Art. Comyn	Cai.	M 1905 A.B. 1909
Romanes,	Ja.	Chr.	M 1905 A.B. 1908. A.M. 1912
Romanis,	Will. Hugh Cowie ...	Trin.	M 1908 A.B. 1911
Romer,	Carrol	Cai.	M 1902 A.B. 1905. A.M. 1909
Romney,	John Edwards Verge	N. C.	E 1909
Ronald,	Alan Bruce	Trin.	M 1897 A.B. 1900. A.M. 1904
—	John Colin	Pem.	M 1909
Ronaldson,	Ja. Bruce	Joh.	M 1903 A.B. 1906. M.B., B.C. 1911
Rönnfeldt,	Frank	Chr.	M 1907 A.B. 1911
Roos,	John Hen. Montagu (*Lord*)	Trin.	M 1905
Roosevelt,	Theodore		*LL.D.* 1910
Rooth,	Alb. Victor	King's	M 1905 A.B. 1908 [1901. Mus.D. 1910
Rootham,	Cyril Bradley	Joh.	M 1894 A.B. 1897. Mus.B. 1900. A.M.
Roper,	Cha.	Cai.	M 1895 A.B. 1898. B.C. 1903. M.B. 1905.
			[M.D. 1911
—	Edgar Stanley	C. C.	L 1900 A.B. 1902. Mus.B. 1903
—	Frank Art.	Trin.	M 1902 A.B. 1905. M.B., B.C. 1910. A.M.
—	Geo.	N. C.	M 1890 A.B. 1893. A.M. 1910 [1911
—	Geo. Hamilton	Qu.	M 1907 A.B. 1910
—	Harold	Sid.	M 1910
Rosbotham,	John	N. C.	M 1909 A.B. 1912
Roscamp,	Alb. Stanley	Joh.	M 1895 A.B. 1898. A.M. 1911
Roscoe,	Art.	King's	M 1909 A.B. 1912
—	John		*A.M.* 1910
—	Norman Keith	Pem.	M 1910
—	Will.	Cai.	M 1907 A.B., LL.B. 1910
Rose,	Alf. Leslie	H. Sel.	M 1908 A.B. 1912
—	Archib.	King's	M 1911
—	Cha. Anderson	Chr.	M 1905
—	Chris. Phil. Godwin	Cath.	M 1905 A.B. 1908
—	Frank Atcherley	Joh.	M 1892 A.B. 1895. M.B., B.C., A.M. 1903
—	Frederic Gardiner ...	Joh.	M 1904 A.B. 1907
—	Geoffrey Keith	King's	M 1908 A.B., LL.B. 1911
—	Harold Emerson	N. C.	M 1905 A.B. 1908
—	Harry Cecil	Joh.	M 1902 A.B., LL.B. 1905. A.M. 1909
—	Hub. Allan	Joh.	M 1905 A.B. 1908
—	John Holland	Chr.	M 1875 A.B. 1879. A.M. 1882. Litt.D. 1903
—	Percy Jesse Gowlett	Joh.	M 1898 A.B. 1901
Rose-Innes,	Geo. Stewart	Pet.	M 1903 A.B. 1906
Rosenberg,	Geo. Fre. Jenner ...	Joh.	M 1889 A.B. 1892. A.M. 1905
—	Gerald Dav.	Trin.	M 1912 post Robson, G. D.
—	Norman E	Joh.	M 1911
Rosenthal,	Curt Arnold Otto ..	Joh.	E 1905
Roseveare,	Hen. Herb.	Joh.	M 1901 A.B. 1904. A.M. 1908

Roseveare,	Walt. Harry	Joh.	M 1898 A.B. 1901. A.M. 1905
Roseway,	Geo. Dav.	Chr.	M 1909 A.B. 1912
Rosher,	John Brenchley	Trin.	M 1907 A.B. 1911. LL.B. 1912
Rosier,	Ja. Erle Radcliff	Sid.	M 1912
Roskill,	Wilfrid Gustav	Trin. H.	M 1908 A.B. 1911
Ross,	Cha. Hackwell	Joh.	M 1893 A.B. 1896. A.M. 1903
—	Colin Macdonald	King's	M 1906 A.B. 1909
—	Edw. Burns	Trin.	M 1902 A.B. 1905
—	Ern. Athole	Trin.	M 1894 M.B., B.C. 1903. M.D. 1906
—	Geo. Alex. Johnston	Chr.	L 1903
—	Ivan Dingley	Cai.	M 1908 A.B. 1911
—	Ja. Alf.	Cla.	M 1900 A.B. 1903. A.M. 1907
—	John Estcourt Cresswell	Joh.	M 1905 A.B. 1908
—	John Stenhouse	Em.	M 1906 A.B. 1909
—	Neville Williams	N. C.	M 1895 Jes. A.B. 1898. A.M. 1907
—	Nigel Douglas Carne	Cai.	M 1902 A.B. 1905
—	Reg. Wellington	H. Sel.	M 1899 A.B. 1902
—	Ronald Deane	Trin.	M 1907 A.B. 1910
—	Tho. Cassels	Em.	M 1901
—	Tho. Harry	Sid.	L 1895 A.B. 1898. A.M. 1901
—	Will. Dallas	King's	M 1905 A.B. 1908
—	Will. Gordon	Trin.	M 1907 A.B. 1910
—	Will. Munro	Pem.	M 1911
—	Will. Stuart	Cath.	M 1911
Rossdale,	Frank Archib.	Mag.	M 1912
Rossi,	Rob.	Trin.	M 1912
Rossiter,	Art. Rawlinson	Pem.	M 1906 A.B. 1909
Rostron,	Syd.	Joh.	M 1902 A.B. 1905. A.M. 1910
Roth,	Georges Jules	Cai.	M 1911
Rothband,	Percy Lionel	Trin.	M 1902
Rothe,	Bayard	Trin.	M 1907
Rothera,	Art. Cecil Hamel ...	Em.	M 1899 A.B. 1902. A.M.† 1908
Rothfield,	Isaac	Down.	M 1911
—	Jacob	N. C.	M 1909 Cath. A.B. 1912
Rothschild,	Nath. Cha.	Trin.	M 1895 A.B. 1898. A.M. 1903
—	Walt. Alf.	Trin.	M 1899 A.B. 1903
Rottenburg,	Harry	King's	M 1895 A.B. 1898. A.M. 1904
Rotton,	Hugh Frederic Art.	C. C.	M 1903 A.B. 1906. A.M. 1910
Roughton,	Fra. Art.	Em.	M 1901 A.B. 1904. A.M. 1909
Roupell,	Art. Norton	Cath.	M 1907 A.B. 1910
Rouquette,	Douglas Geo.	Sid.	M 1910
—	Stewart Hen.	King's	M 1905 A.B. 1908
Rouse,	Percival Will.	Trin.	M 1900 A.B. 1903. A.M. 1907
—	Phil. Graves	Trin.	M 1902 A.B. 1905
—	Will. Hen. Denham	*Chr.	M 1882 A.B. 1885. A.M. 1889. Litt.D. 1903
Routh,	Harold Victor	Pet.	E 1897 A.B. 1900. A.M. 1907
—	Laurence Melville ...	Cai.	M 1902 B.C. 1910. M.B. 1911
—	Rupert John Airy ...	Cai.	M 1898 A.B. 1901
Row,	Vanga Jagannadha ...	Cath.	M 1907
—	Vombatkere Pandrang	Joh.	M 1901 A.B. 1904
Rowan,	Art.	C. C.	M 1905
—	Rob. Wicks	Trin.	M 1898 A.B. 1901
Rowe,	Hen. Price	Jes.	M 1908
—	Will. Hugh Cecil ...	Jes.	M 1902 A.B. 1905
Rowell,	And. Herrick	Joh.	M 1909 A.B. 1912
Rowett,	Fre. Ern.	Joh.	M 1912
Rowland,	Tho. Ja. Semper	Down.	M 1907 A.B. 1910
Rowlands,	John Martin	Em.	M 1903 A.B. 1907
—	Will. Aylmer	Em.	M 1901 A.B. 1904. A.M. 1908
Rowlandson,	Edm. Ja.	H. Sel.	M 1901
—	Tho. Sowerby	Trin. H.	L 1901

Rowlatt,	Art.	King's	M 1912	
Rowley,	Cha. Sam.	Trin.	M 1910	
—	Esmé Norton	Trin. H.	M 1909	
—	Fra. Bern.	Cath.	M 1893	A.B. 1896. A.M. 1906
—	Geo. Rich. Fra.	Trin.	M 1907	
Rowntree,	Jos. Stephenson	King's	M 1894	A.B. 1897. A.M. 1902
—	Malcolm	King's	M 1908	A.B. 1912
Rowse,	Art. Alb.	Down.	M 1907	A.B. 1910
Rowsell,	Herb. Greaves	Jes.	M 1907	A.B. 1910
—	John Bishop	Jes.	M 1904	A.B. 1907
Roxburgh,	Archib. Cathcart	Trin.	M 1905	A.B. 1908
—	John Fergusson	Trin.	M 1907	A.B. 1910
—	Ronald Fra.	Trin.	M 1908	A.B. 1911
—	Tho. Ja. Young	Mag.	M 1910	
Roxby,	Bertram Gordon	Em.	M 1904	A.B. 1907
—	Cyril Leycester Maude	Em.	M 1898	A.B. 1901. A.M. 1905
—	Guy Jocelyn Maude	Qu.	M 1905	A.B. 1908
—	Herb. Suffield Maude	Qu.	M 1898	A.B. 1901. A.M. 1908
—	Ja. Howard Trevelyan Maude	Em.	M 1902	A.B. 1906. post Maude-Roxby, [J. H. T. M. A.M. 1912
—	Osmund Ralph Maude	Em.	M 1901	A.B. 1904. A.M. 1908
Roy,	Donald Whatley	Sid.	M 1899	A.B. 1902. M.B., B.C., A.M. 1908
—	Malcolm Hughes Trevor	Jes.	M 1904	A.B. 1907
—	Poresh Lal	Em.	M 1912	
—	Satyendra Nath	Chr.	M 1907	A.B. 1910
—	Subodh Chandra	N. C.	M 1897	A.B. 1900. LL.B. 1901
Royce,	Ferris Cleveland	Trin.	M 1912	
Royds,	Cha. Cradock Twemlow	Trin.	M 1897	A.B. 1900. A.M. 1904
—	Edric Alban Barrow	Qu.	M 1908	A.B. 1911
—	John Fletcher Twemlow	Trin.	M 1886	A.B. 1889. A.M. 1906
Royeppen,	Jos.	N. C.	M 1901	A.B. 1906
Roylance,	Phil.	C. C.	L 1910	
Royle,	Hub. Turner Peter	Trin. H.	M 1905	A.B. 1909
Royse,	Will. Hen. Harvey ...	Trin.	M 1883	A.B. 1886. A.M. 1910
Royston,	Geo.	Down.	M 1908	A.B. 1911
—	Horace Richmond ...	N. C.	M 1909	A.B. 1912
Rubens,	Heinrich		*Sc.D.* 1912	
Rubie,	Geo. Oswald	H. Sel.	M 1906	A.B. 1909
—	John Gilb.	Jes.	M 1908	A.B. 1911
—	Tho. Art. Cecil	Jes.	M 1911	
Rücker,	Art. Will.		*Sc.D.* 1902	
Ruck-Keene,	Ralph Edgar	Jes.	M 1907	
Rudd,	Cecil Tho.	Cath.	M 1901	A.B. 1904
—	Frank Astin	Trin. H.	M 1903	A.B., LL.B. 1906
—	Noel Bateman	Em.	M 1905	A.B. 1908
—	Will. Art.	Joh.	M 1896	A.B. 1899. A.M. 1907
—	Will. Gilb.	N. C.	M 1900	A.B. 1905
Ruddock,	Dav.	N. C.	M 1900	Cath. A.B. 1903
Rudge,	Will. Art. Douglas ...	Joh.	M 1896	A.B. 1899. A.M. 1903
Rudkins,	Fre. Percy	Chr.	M 1907	A.B. 1910
Rudman,	Fra. Reg. Rider	King's	M 1905	A.B. 1908
Rueff,	Otto	Trin. H.	M 1909	
Ruegg,	Walt. Brian	Jes.	M 1911	
Ruggles-Brise,	Edw. Archib.	Trin.	M 1901	
Rule,	Geo. Simpson	Em.	M 1909	A.B. 1912
Rumsey,	Cecil Frank	Down.	M 1908	A.B. 1911
—	Hen. St John	King's	M 1906	A.B. 1909
Ruscoe,	Reg. Guy	Em.	M 1912	
Rushforth,	Frank Victor	Cai.	M 1907	A.B. 1910
Rushmore,	Fre. Margetson ......*Cath.		M 1895	A.B. 1898. A.M. 1902
Rushton,	Art. Geo. Melville ...	Trin.	M 1893	A.B. 1896. A.M. 1902

Rushton,	Eric Rooksby	Em.	M 1910
—	Harold Lever	Trin.	M 1901 A.B. 1904
—	Will. Frederic	King's	M 1904 Down. A.B. 1907. A.M. 1911
Rushworth,	Art. Norman	Trin.	M 1906
—	John Alb. Victor ...	Down.	M 1906 A.B. 1909
Rusk,	Rob. Robertson	Em.	M 1908 A.B. 1910
Russell,	Alex	Jes.	M 1912
—	Cha. Frank ....*Pem.		M 1901 A.B. 1904. A.M. 1908
—	Edgar Geo.	Trin. H.	M 1910
—	Edm. Neptune	Trin.	M 1903 A.B. 1906. M.B., B.C. 1910
—	Fre. Will.	Trin.	M 1888 A.B. 1891. A.M. 1901
—	Geo. Gray	King's	M 1900 A.B. 1904
—	Harrolde Bedford Geo.	Sid.	M 1905 A.B. 1908. B.C. 1912
—	Hen. Norris	King's	M 1902
—	Ja. Douglas	Trin.	M 1909
—	John	Joh.	M 1878 A.B. 1882. A.M. 1902
—	John	Trin. H.	M 1904
—	John Clem.	Cai.	M 1907
—	Leon. Ja.	Em.	M 1908
—	Phil.	Pem.	M 1903 A.B. 1906
—	Phil. Durham	King's	M 1901 A.B. 1904
—	Tho. Wentworth	Trin.	M 1899 A.B. 1902
—	Wilfred Alan	Em.	M 1905 A.B. 1908
—	Will. Beaumont	Sid.	M 1908 A.B. 1912
Russell-Smith, Alan	....	Joh.	M 1911
—	Hugh Fra. ....*Joh.		M 1906 A.B. 1909
Rust,	Art. Arnold	Chr.	M 1905 A.B. 1908
—	Clarence Alf.	Trin. H.	M 1903 A.B. 1906
—	Cyprian Tho.	Cla.	M 1895 A.B. 1898. A.M. 1903
—	Neville Art.	Pem.	M 1899 A.B. 1902. A.M. 1906
—	Phil. John	Pem.	M 1901 A.B. 1904
Ruston,	Jos. Victor Antony	Trin.	M 1909
Rutherford,	Claud Hamilton	King's	M 1905 A.B. 1908
—	Godfrey Laird	Jes.	M 1910
—	John Douglas	Cla.	M 1908 A.B. 1912
—	Leon. Trevelyan	Cla.	E 1907 A.B. 1910
—	Leslie Douglas	Down.	M 1903 A.B. 1906. A.M. 1910
—	Will. McConnell	Cai.	M 1908 A.B. 1910
Rutherfurd,	Hen. Geo. Gordon ...	Qu.	M 1905 A.B. 1909
Ruthnaswamy,	Mariadas	Down.	L 1908 A.B. 1910
Ruthven,	John	Down.	M 1910
Rutter,	Art. Lionel	N. C.	M 1893 Cath. A.B. 1896. A.M. 1901
Ruttledge,	Hugh	Pem.	M 1903 A.B. 1906
Ryan,	Cha. Diller	Chr.	M 1912
Ryder,	Algernon Fre. Roland Dudley	Trin.	M 1910
Ryffel,	John Hen.	Pet.	M 1896 A.B. 1899. A.M. 1904. B.C. 1908
Rylance,	Art. Cyril	Chr.	M 1902 A.B. 1905. A.M. 1909
Ryland,	Tho. Howard	Trin.	M 1895 A.B. 1898. A.M. 1903
Ryle,	Edw. Hewish	Trin.	M 1904 A.B. 1907
Ryley,	Cha. Meadows	Em.	M 1904
—	Donald Art. Geo. Buchanan	Joh.	M 1912
Ryott,	Tho. Gurney	C. C.	M 1899 A.B., LL.B. 1902

S

Saberton,	Frederic Rupert	Joh.	M 1901 A.B. 1906
Sabin,	John Howard	Cai.	M 1911
Sabit,	Mahmoud	Trin. H.	M 1906
Sabry,	Yousef	Trin. H.	M 1910
Sachs,	Alf. Ludovicus	Pem.	M 1895 A.B. 1898. A.M. 1902. B.C. 1909.
Saddler,	Will.	Joh.	M 1911 [M.D. 1911
Sadek,	Mohamed	N. C.	M 1908
Sadgrove,	Kenneth Hilary O'Reilly	H. Sel.	M 1912
Sadler,	Harold	Jes.	M 1909
—	Will. Arden Crommelin	N. C.	E 1891 Pet. A.B. 1905
Safwat,	Aly Fayek	Down.	M 1910
Sagar,	John Warburton	Jes.	M 1898 A.B. 1901
Sage,	Fre. Stuart	Chr.	M 1902 A.B. 1905. A.M. 1910
Sager,	Judah Levi	N. C.	M 1897 A.B. 1900. A.M. 1904
Saher,	Nanabhai Nasarvanji	Cath.	M 1892 A.B., LL.B. 1896. A.M.†, LL.M.†
Sahni,	Birbal	Em.	M 1911 [1906
Said,	Mohammad	Pem.	M 1911
Sain Das	....	N. C.	M 1909 A.B. 1911
Sainsbury,	Will. Tuke	King's	M 1911
Saint,	Art. Paul	Down.	M 1908 A.B. 1911
—	Percy Johnston	Joh.	M 1904 A.B. 1907
St Aubyn,	Morice Julian	Trin.	M 1910
St Clair Smith, Tho.		Trin. H.	M 1895 A.B. 1898. M.B., B.C. 1903
St George,	Geo. Baker Bligh ...	Trin.	M 1911
St John,	Fleming	Joh.	M 1909 A.B. 1912
St Johnston, Adrian		Trin.	M 1906
Saiyut,	Mom Rajawongse ...	King's	M 1896 A.B. 1899. LL.B. 1900. A.M.†
Sakhalkar,	Chintamani Vinayak	Trin.	M 1912 [1903
Salaman,	Lewis Hen.	Trin.	M 1901 A.B. 1904
—	Redcliffe Nathan	Trin. H.	M 1893 A.B. 1896. M.B., B.C., A.M. 1900.
Salám Khan, Kazi Abdul		Chr.	M 1899 A.B. 1903 [M.D. 1904
Salas,	Adolfo Salvador	Chr.	M 1912
Sale,	Art. Walker	Em.	M 1894 A.B. 1897. A.M. 1904
—	Harold Montague ...	Chr.	M 1909 A.B. 1912
—	Hen. Geo.	Jes.	M 1912
—	John Ford	Em.	M 1903 A.B. 1906. A.M. 1910
Salisbury,	Cha. Edw.	Em.	M 1907 A.B. 1910
—	Fre. Stimpson	Chr.	M 1895 A.B. 1898. A.M. 1903
—	Tho. Hen. Lister ...	Trin.	M 1902
Salmon,	Harold Bryant	Jes.	M 1910
—	Harold Dyster	Qu.	M 1900 A.B. 1904. A.M. 1907
—	Lawrence Hen.	Jes.	M 1901
—	Theodore John Alex.	H. Sel.	M 1906
—	Victor Gabriel	Jes.	M 1899 A.B. 1902
Salmond,	Will. Guthrie	Joh.	M 1912
Salt,	Art. Cecil	H. Sel.	M 1898 A.B. 1901
—	Cha. Edw. Fosbrooke	Pem.	M 1899 A.B. 1902
—	Will. Manning	Pem.	M 1903 A.B. 1906. A.M. 1910
Salter,	Frank Reyner	Trin.	M 1905 A.B. 1908. *Mag. A.M. 1912
—	Rich. Eccleston	Cla.	L 1911
—	Will. Hen.	Trin.	M 1898 A.B. 1901. LL.B. 1902. A.M. 1910
Salusbury,	John Thelwall	Pem.	M 1900 A.B. 1903
Sambrook,	Hen. Fabian	King's	M 1905 A.B. 1908. A.M. 1912
Sample,	Harold Ward	Pet.	M 1882 A.B. 1885. A.M. 1903
Sampson,	Frederic Art.	Trin.	M 1909 A.B. 1912

Sampson,	John	Down.	M 1908	
—	John Fre.	Em.	M 1902	
—	Noël Carleton	Trin.	M 1902	
—	Sam. John Marton ...	Trin.	M 1902 LL.B. 1905	
Sams,	Reuben Alf.	Trin.	M 1906 A.B. 1909	
Samson,	Art. Murray	H. Sel.	M 1910	
Samuel,	Alex. Wenyon	Trin. H.	M 1906	
—	Cecil Harry	Cla.	M 1910	
—	Harry Maurice	Qu.	M 1904 A.B. 1907	
—	John Augustus	H. Sel.	M 1907 A.B., LL.B. 1910	
Samuelson,	Ern. Alex. Gordon ...	King's	M 1903 A.B. 1906	
—	Fra. Hen. Bern.	Trin.	M 1908	
Sanceau,	Reg. Ja.	Joh.	M 1910	
Sanctuary,	Art. Geo. Everard ...	Cai.	M 1910	
—	Campbell Tho.	Cai.	M 1908 A.B. 1911	
Sandall,	Herb. Cecil	Joh.	M 1899 A.B. 1902. A.M. 1906	
Sanday,	Will.		*Litt.D.* 1902	
Sandbach,	Edgar	King's	M 1900 A.B. 1903	
—	Fra. Edw.	King's	M 1899 A.B. 1901. A.M. 1906	
—	John Brown	King's	M 1897 A.B. 1901. A.M. 1905	
Sandberg,	Fre. Clifford	Cath.	M 1906	
—	Will. Burton	Qu.	M 1893 A.B. 1896. A.M. 1906	
Sandeman,	Bern. Stewart	Trin. H.	M 1911	
Sanders,	Hen. Rimer	Trin. H.	M 1902	
—	Ja. Harry	Sid.	M 1901	
—	Leslie Yorath	Trin.	M 1912	
—	Walt. Geo. Percy ...	H. Sel.	M 1905 A.B. 1908	
Sanderson,	Art. Buchanan	Cla.	M 1899 A.B. 1902	
—	Clem. Oliver St John	Pet.	M 1910	
—	Ern. Hen.	Jes.	M 1891 A.B. 1894. A.M. 1903	
—	Fred Borthwick	Cai.	M 1907 A.B. 1910	
—	Geoffrey Euan	Jes.	M 1907 A.B. 1910	
—	Geo. Percy Manners	Trin.	M 1897 A.B. 1902	
—	Hugh Shortreed	Trin.	M 1890 A.B. 1893. A.M.† 1908	
—	Ian Cuthbertson	Trin.	M 1905 LL.B. 1908	
—	Ja. Ross	Trin.	M 1907 A.B. 1910	
—	Phil. MacDonnell ...	H. Sel.	M 1904	
—	Rob. Bruce	Pem.	M 1898 A.B. 1901	
—	Roy Broughton	Qu.	M 1908 A.B. 1911	
—	Tho. Stuart	Trin.	M 1909 A.B. 1912	
—	Will. John	Jes.	M 1902 A.B., LL.B. 1905	
Sandford,	Geo. Ritchie	Qu.	M 1911	
—	Ralph Will. Deshon	Pem.	M 1904 A.B. 1907	
Sandilands,	John Edw.	Trin.	M 1890 A.B. 1893. M.B., B.C., A.M. 1898.	
—	Rob. Bruys	Mag.	M 1912 [M.D. 1903	
Sandison,	Alex.	Trin.	M 1904 A.B. 1907. M.B., B.C. 1911	
Sandon,	Frank	C. C.	M 1909 A.B. 1912	
Sands,	Percy Cooper ....*Joh.		M 1901 A.B. 1904. A.M. 1908	
Sandys,	Alick Cummins Congreve	Chr.	M 1909 A.B. 1912	
Saner,	Fra. Donaldson	Chr.	M 1902 A.B. 1905. M.B., B.C. 1911	
—	John Godfrey.	Cai.	M 1903 A.B. 1909. B.C. 1910	
Sanford,	Dudley Will.	Cai.	M 1909 A.B. 1912	
Sanfuentes,	Vicente Felipe José	Pem.	M 1910	
Sang,	Raghu Nath	Cath.	E 1911 [M.D.† 1906	
Sanger,	Fre.	Joh.	M 1894 A.B. 1897. A.M. 1901. B.C. 1902.	
—	Hub.	Joh.	M 1899 A.B. 1902. A.M. 1906	
—	Percy Morris	Trin.	M 1903 A.B. 1906. A.M. 1912	
Sanger-Davies,	Hugh Jos. Turner	Em.	M 1902 A.B. 1905. A.M. 1909	
—	Llewelyn Herb.	Trin.	M 1912	
Sangster,	Cha. Humphrey	Cla.	M 1906 A.B. 1910	
Sansam,	Alb. Edm. Lane	H. Sel.	M 1907 A.B. 1910	

Sansford,	Fre. Edwin	Qu.	E 1907 A.B. 1910
Sansinena,	Alfredo Gaston	Jes.	M 1910
Santamarina,	Josè Alberto	Chr.	E 1911
Santanan,	Krishnamachari	N. C.	M 1906
Santer,	Art. Gledden	C. C.	M 1903 A.B. 1909
Sapwell,	Baldwin Sparrow ...	King's	M 1908 A.B. 1911
—	Benj. Beckham	C. C.	M 1884 A.B. 1888. LL.B. 1889. M.B., B.C.
Saraoja,	Gustaf Emil	N. C.	M 1911 [1902
Sard,	Harry Sam.	Cath.	M 1910
Sargant Florence,	Phil.	Cai.	M 1909 A.B. 1912
Sargeant,	Hugh	Joh.	M 1903 A.B. 1906
Sargeaunt,	Geo. Montague	Cai.	M 1902 A.B. 1905. A.M. 1910
Sargent,	Douglas Harry Grose	Joh.	M 1897 A.B. 1900. A.M. 1904
—	Edw. Hewlett Gladstone	Joh.	M 1906 A.B. 1909
—	Eric Lancelot Kingsley	Joh.	M 1907 A.B. 1910
Sarkar,	Bimala Kanta	Cla.	M 1911
Sarsby,	Reg. Ambler	Jes.	M 1912
Sasse,	Rossell Harry Jephson	Jes.	M 1905 A.B. 1908
Sassoon,	Dav. Duke	Cath.	M 1910
----	Ellice Victor	Trin.	M 1900 A.B. 1903
—	Hamo Watts	Cla.	M 1905 A.B. 1909
—	Hector Will.	Trin.	M 1906 A.B. 1909
—	Michael Thornycroft	Cla.	M 1904
—	Siegfried Lorraine ...	Cla.	M 1905
Sathe,	Dattatraya Laxmon	N. C.	M 1908 A.B. 1911
—	Jagannath Luxmon	Joh.	M 1905 A.B. 1907
Satow,	Ernest Mason		*LL.D.* 1903
Satterly,	John	N. C.	M 1903 Joh. A.B. 1908. A.M. 1911
Satterthwaite, Maur. Edgar	....	Pem.	M 1900 A.B. 1903
Satthianadhan,	Sam.	C. C.	M 1878 A.B. 1882. LL.B. 1883. A.M.†
Saumarez,	Ja. St Vincent Broke	Trin.	M 1908 [1885. LL.M. 1897. LL.D.† 1903
Saunder,	Douglas Art.	Cai.	M 1910
—	Geo. Bertram	Trin.	M 1912
Saunders,	Alastair Grant	Cla.	M 1908 A.B. 1912
—	Archib. Howard	Chr.	M 1908 A.B. 1911
—	Douglas Mill	Cla.	M 1912
—	Ern. Will. Cotes	King's	M 1895 A.B. 1898. A.M. 1902
—	Fre. Ja.	Chr.	M 1906 A.B. 1909
—	Fre. Page	Cla.	E 1904 F. Joshua P. A.B. 1907
—	Geo. Will.	H. Sel.	M 1899 A.B. 1902. A.M. 1906
—	Granville	Trin.	M 1906 A.B. 1909
—	Hen.	Cai.	M 1879 A.B. 1883. A.M. 1907
—	Howard Fauntleroy	Down.	M 1904 A.B. 1907
—	Hugh Cecil	Qu.	M 1909
—	John Rhys	Em.	M 1906 A.B. 1908
—	John Tennant ....*Chr.		M 1907 A.B. 1910
—	Kenneth Ja.	Em.	M 1902 A.B. 1905
—	Lewis Stephen Shears	Trin. H.	M 1905
—	Lionel Percy	Trin.	M 1905 A.B. 1908
—	Oliver Paley	Trin.	M 1898 A.B. 1901
—	Will. Dan.	N. C.	M 1910 Chr. A.B. 1912
--	Will. Morley	Trin. H.	M 1902
Saunt,	Will. Hen. Gatty ...	Em.	M 1907 A.B. 1910
Savage,	Edw. Graham	Down.	M 1903 A.B. 1906
—	Ern. Urmson	Pem.	M 1897 A.B. 1900. A.M. 1904
—	Hen. Edwin	Chr.	M 1873 A.B. 1877. *C. C. A.M. 1880.
—	Kenric	Qu.	M 1911 [B.D. 1905. D.D. 1910
Savary,	John Tanzia	Trin.	M 1912
Savile,	Eustace Claud	Qu.	M 1898 A.B. 1901
—	Geo. Keith	Em.	M 1909
Savill,	Geo.	N. C.	L 1905 Chr. A.B. 1907. A.M. 1911

Savill,	Herb. Stewart	Cla.	M 1908
—	Phil. Robin Lydall ...	Cai.	M 1903
Saville,	Stanley Herb.	Trin.	M 1910
Savory,	Cha. Harley	Trin.	M 1908 A.B. 1912
—	Donald Stuart	C. C.	M 1904 A.B. 1907
—	Will. Borradaile (*Bart.*)	Trin.	M 1902 A.B. 1908
Savur,	Ramakan Mangesh ...	N. C.	M 1910
Saw,	Hen. Will.	King's	M 1884 A.B. 1887. LL.M. 1898. LL.D.
—	Moung Ba	Down.	M 1909 [1909
Sawday,	Stanley Kessen	Mag.	M 1903 A.B. 1906
Sawhney,	Chooni Lal	Mag.	M 1910
—	Dev Raj	Em.	M 1910
—	Manohar Lall	Down.	M 1910
Sawhny,	Bodh Raj	N. C.	M 1899 Down. A.B., LL.B. 1902
—	Mulk Raj	Down.	E 1903 A.B. 1906. M.B., B.C. 1908
—	Shiv Ram	Down.	M 1910
Sawkins,	Dansie Tho.	Qu.	M 1902 A.B. 1905
Sawtell,	Hor. Dewick	Cla.	M 1909
Sawyer,	Basil Tho. Campion	Pem.	M 1908 A.B. 1911
—	Ernst Fre. Hans ...	Cla.	M 1902 A.B. 1905
—	Will. Ellis	Trin.	M 1897 A.B. 1900. A.M. 1904
Saxton,	Walt. Theodore	Sid.	M 1901 A.B. 1904. A.M.† 1908
—	Will. Isaac	King's	M 1911
Sayer,	Alf. Geo. Walpole ...	Pem.	M 1890 A.B. 1894. A.M. 1898. B.D. 1911
—	Humphrey	Trin.	M 1907 A.B. 1911
—	Michael Wynne	Qu.	M 1905 A.B. 1908
—	Sid. Dan.	N. C.	M 1912
Sayers,	Eldred Frank	Joh.	M 1908 A.B., LL.B. 1911
—	Lawrance Denton ...	Down.	L 1911
Saywack,	Benj.	Chr.	M 1904 A.B. 1907. A.M. 1911
Scales,	Fra. Shillington	Jes.	M 1902 A.B. 1905. M.B., B.C., A.M. 1909
Scallon,	Fra. John	Qu.	M 1906 A.B. 1909
—	Harold Edw.	Qu.	M 1905 A.B. 1908. A.M. 1912
Scanes,	Art. Edwin Leigh ...	Trin.	M 1902 A.B. 1906. A.M. 1909
Scarborough,	Oswald Lowndes	Joh.	M 1896 A.B. 1899. A.M. 1905
—	Will. Hen.	Qu.	M 1896 A.B. 1899. A.M. 1904
Scargill,	Lionel Walt. Kennedy	Trin. H.	L 1905 A.M. Incorp. Oxf. 1905
Scarlett,	Cha. Herb.	Mag.	M 1907 A.B. 1910
Schäfer,	Tho. Syd. Hermann	Cai.	M 1910
Scharff,	Godfrey Edw.	Chr.	M 1909
Schellenberg,	Hans Otto Heinrich } Rudolf	Em.	M 1909
Schiff,	Mortimer Edw. Harold	Jes.	M 1907 A.B., LL.B. 1910
Schipper,	Jacob Marcus		*Litt.D.* 1906
Schlesinger,	Gerald Leon.	Cai.	M 1908 A.B. 1911
Schlosberg,	Solomon Kenneth ...	Trin.	M 1908
Schloss,	Art. Dav.	King's	M 1907 A.B. 1910
—	Walt. Fra. Raphael	Trin.	M 1910
Schlumberger,	André Raoul } Christian	Jes.	M 1907
Schmiechen,	Gerald	Trin.	M 1911 post Merton, G.
—	Wilfred	Trin.	M 1906 „ Merton, W.
Schmitt,	Oscar Phil.	N. C.	M 1902 A.B. 1905
Schmitz,	Geo. de Morla	Cla.	M 1906 A.B. 1912
—	Herman Emil	Joh.	M 1887 A.B. 1890. A.M. 1901
Schniewind,	Georg Emil	N. C.	M 1910
—	Konrad	N. C.	E 1911
Schoell,	Franck Louis	Cai.	M 1910
Schoeller,	Tho. Louis	Joh.	M 1911
Schoener,	Harold August Will.	Chr.	M 1901 A.B. 1904
Schofield,	Augustus Chisholm	Mag.	M 1898 A.B. 1901

Schofield,	Fra. Harold Vaughan	Chr.	M 1900 A.B. 1903
Scholes,	Jos.	Trin.	M 1908 A.B. 1911
—	Walt. Neville	Pem.	M 1908 A.B. 1911
Scholey,	Cha. Harry Norman	Cla.	M 1912
Scholfield,	Alwyn Faber	King's	M 1903 A.B. 1906. A.M. 1910
—	Cha. Noël	Trin.	M 1906 A.B. 1909
—	Ja. Leslie	Mag.	M 1912
—	John Art.	Cai.	M 1907 A.B. 1910
—	Rich. Denham	Joh.	M 1910
—	Will. Farrar	Trin.	M 1903 A.B. 1906
Scholtz,	Claude Justin	Em.	M 1907 A.B. 1910
Schön,	Adolph Heinrich August	C. C.	M 1911
—	Basil	Trin.	M 1901 A.B. 1904. A.M. 1908
Schooling,	Art. John	Sid.	M 1900 A.B. 1903
—	Cecil Herb.	Pem.	M 1903 A.B. 1906. A.M. 1910
—	Leslie Fre.	Qu.	M 1908 A.B. 1911
Schott,	Erich Simon	Chr.	E 1910
—	Rudolf Walther	Chr.	E 1907
Schreiner,	Oliver Deneys	Trin.	M 1911
Schroeder,	Alb. Edw.	Joh.	M 1911
—	Johannes	N. C.	E 1912
Schüddekopf,	Walt. Geo. Adolphus	Em.	M 1910
Schün,	Fre. John Ern.	H. Sel.	M 1905
Schurr,	Chris. Geo.	Cai.	M 1911
Schuster,	Art.		*Sc.D.* 1904
—	Leon. Fra.	Trin.	M 1907
—	Leon. Walton	Trin.	M 1900 A.B. 1903. A.M. 1911
Schwalbe,	Gustav		*Sc.D.* 1909
Schwalm,	Cha. Edw.	Pem.	M 1911
Schwann,	Humphrey	King's	M 1904 A.B. 1907
Schwartz,	Cha.	Qu.	M 1908 A.B. 1911
Schwarz,	Werner	N. C.	M 1908
Schwarzman,	Rudolph Isaac	Qu.	M 1908 A.B. 1911
Scindia,	Madhorao		*LL.D.* 1902
Sclater,	Frank Art.	Cla.	M 1912
—	John Rob. Paterson	Em.	M 1895 A.B. 1898. A.M. 1902
Scoby,	Will. Harrison	Cla.	M 1895 A.B. 1899. A.M. 1902
Scorer,	Norman Veitch	Pem.	M 1899 A.B. 1902
Scorgie,	Norman Gibb	Sid.	M 1903 A.B., LL.B. 1906. Trin. A.M. 1910
Scott,	Alex.	N. C.	L 1876 Trin. A.B. 1879. A.M. 1882. Pet.
—	Art. Pickett	Pet.	M 1904 A.B. 1907 [Sc.D. 1907
—	Bertie Garfield Alma	Trin. H.	M 1901
··	Cha. Martin	Trin. H.	M 1902
—	Cha. Paley	King's	M 1900 A.B. 1903
—	Cha. Tillard	Sid.	M 1896 A.B. 1899. A.M. 1903. B.C. 1906
—	Cha. Wilfred	H. Sel.	M 1898 A.B. 1901
—	Donald Alan	Sid.	M 1912
—	Douglas Art.	Jes.	M 1905 A.B. 1908
—	Edw. Spencer	Pem.	M 1889 A.B. 1892. M.B., B.C. 1903. M.D.
—	Ern.	Trin.	M 1910 [1906
—	Ern. Leopold	Joh.	M 1898 A.B. 1901. A.M. 1905
—	Fra. Errington	Jes.	M 1904 A.B. 1907. A.M. 1912
—	Fra. Will.	Jes.	M 1905 A.B. 1908
—	Fred Purcell	H. Sel.	M 1903 A.B. 1906
—	Geo. Alf.	N. C.	M 1909
—	Geo. Arbuthnot	Em.	M 1898 A.B. 1901. A.M. 1907
—	Geo. Hepburne	Trin.	M 1889 A.B. 1892. M.B., B.C., A.M. 1898.
—	Harold Rich.	Jes.	M 1905 A.B. 1908 [M.D. 1903
—	Hen. Wakeman	Cla.	M 1902 A.B. 1905
—	Hugh	Trin.	M 1903 A.B. 1906. A.M. 1910
—	Hugh Pat. Fowlis ...	Jes.	M 1902 A.B. 1905. A.M. 1909

Scott,	Ja. Harry	Cla.	M 1892 A.B., LL.B. 1896. LL.M. 1899. [LL.D.† 1908
—	Ja. Hen.	Jes.	M 1894 A.B. 1897. A.M. 1901
—	Ja. Humphrey	Chr.	M 1905 A.B. 1908. A.M. 1912
—	John Edw.	Em.	M 1910
—	John Gordon	Pem.	M 1910
—	John Gordon Cameron	Pem.	M 1907 A.B. 1911
—	John Russell	Trin.	M 1898 A.B. 1901
—	John Sebastian	Em.	M 1900 A.B. 1903. A.M. 1909
—	John Todhunter	Qu.	M 1909 A.B. 1912
—	Leon. Bodley	Chr.	M 1894 A.B. 1897. M.B., B.C. 1901. M.D.
—	Mackay Hugh Baillie	Qu.	M 1910 [1906
—	Melville	Chr.	M 1880 A.B. 1884. A.M. 1888. B.D. 1910
—	Percy Dixon	Qu.	M 1907 A.B. 1910
—	Percy Moreton		*LL.D.* 1903
—	Rob. Falcon		*Sc.D.* 1905
—	¹ Rob. Forsyth	*Joh.	M 1871 A.B. 1875. A.M. 1878
—	Rupert Strathmore	Cai.	M 1906 A.B. 1909
—	Sid. Clermont	Jes.	M 1912
—.	Stanley Hen.	Joh.	M 1901 A.B. 1904
—	Stanley Pelham	Em.	M 1896 A.B. 1899. A.M. 1903
—	Tho. Arnold	Chr.	M 1898 A.B. 1901. A.M. 1905
—	Tho. Fraser	N. C.	L 1909 A.B. 1912
—	Tho. Torrance	Joh.	M 1910
--	Walt. Lawrence	Trin.	M 1903
—	Walt. Reg.	Qu.	M 1896 A.B. 1899. A.M. 1910
—	Walt. Tho. Hepburne	Trin.	M 1909 A.B. 1912
—	Warwick Lindsay	Cla.	M 1910
—	Will. Dav.	Em.	M 1912
—	Will. Fra.	Cath.	M 1909 A.B. 1912
—	Will. McDonald	Trin. H.	L 1911
—	Will. Moir	King's	M 1905 A.B. 1908
—	Will. Thurburn	Cla.	M 1895 A.B. 1898. M.B., B.C. 1903
Scott-Davidson,	Walt. Will.	Trin.	M 1909 A.B. 1912 [1907. D.D. 1909
Scott-Moncrieff,	Cha. Elliott	Trin.	M 1881 A.B. 1884 (2). A.M. 1888. B.D.
—	Phil. Dav.	Chr.	M 1900 A.B. 1903. A.M. 1907
Scott Murray,	Austin Edw.	Trin	M 1900 A.B. 1903
—	Ronald Cha.	Trin.	M 1897 A.B. 1901
Scougal,	Harry Ja.	Cai.	M 1900 A.B. 1903
—	Kenneth Hirst	Joh.	M 1906 A.B., LL.B. 1909
Scoular,	Alex. Carlaw	Joh.	M 1893 A.B. 1896. A.M. 1901
—	John Gladstone	Joh.	E 1904 A.B. 1907
Scowcroft,	Hen. Donald	Cla.	M 1912
Scrace,	John	Pet.	M 1911
Scratton,	Edw. Will. Howell Blackburn	Trin. H.	M 1902
Scrimgeour,	Geoffrey Cameron	Cai.	M 1905 A.B. 1908
Scruby,	Frank Sutherland	H. Sel.	M 1899 A.B. 1902. A.M. 1906
Scrutton,	Alex. Will.	Chr.	M 1903 A.B. 1906. A.M. 1910
—	Tom Burton	King's	M 1906 A.B. 1910
Scully,	Vincent Raymond	Down.	M 1905 A.B. 1908
Sculthorpe,	Geo. Walt. Cyril	Cath.	M 1903
Scutt,	Cecil Allison	Cla.	M 1908 A.B. 1911
—	John Alf. Homer	Joh.	M 1910
Seabrooke,	Alex. Stanger	Chr.	M 1903 Alec S. A.B. 1906
Sealy,	Cha. Frederic Noel Prince	Pem.	M 1912
—	Humfrey Newnham	Trin.	M 1905 A.B. 1908
—	Lewis Orr Fern	Down.	E 1903 A.B., LL.B. 1905
—	Philip Temple	Pet.	M 1907 A.B. 1911

¹ Master of St John's College, 1908.

Sealy,	Wilfrid Herb.	Pet.	M 1912
Seaman,	Alf. Jonat.	H. Sel.	M 1906 A.B. 1909
Searle,	Cha. Fre.	Pem.	M 1901 A.B. 1904. B.C. 1909. M.B. 1910
—	Geo. Fre. Cha. ......*Pet.		M 1884 A.B. 1887. A.M. 1891. Sc.D. 1912
---	Geo. Will. von Uslar	King's	M 1879 A.B. 1883. A.M. 1907
---	Gilb. Alf. Hamilton	Chr.	M 1901 A.B. 1904
—	Walt. Reg.	Pem.	M 1909
---	Will. Cavendish	Pem.	M 1908 A.B. 1911. LL.B. 1912
Sears,	John Edw.	Joh.	M 1902 A.B. 1905. A.M. 1910
—	Selwyn Edw.	Joh.	M 1909 A.B. 1912
Seaton,	Alex. Adam ....*Pem.		M 1903 A.B. 1906. A.M. 1911
—	Hugh John Annand	Chr.	M 1901 A.B. 1904
—	Will. Alex.	Qu.	M 1906
Seaver,	Cha.	Em.	M 1912
Sebag-Montefiore,	John	Pem.	M 1910
Sebright,	Ivo Guy	Trin. H.	M 1902
Secondé,	Emile Cha.	King's	M 1902 A.B. 1905. A.M.† 1909
Sedding,	Edm.	H. Sel.	M 1910
Seddon,	Alan Douglas	C. C.	M 1908
—	Art. Ern.	King's	M 1910
—	Geo. Noel	Cla.	M 1912
—	Will. D'Arcy	Cla.	L 1910 A.B. 1912
Sedgefield,	Walt. John	Chr.	M 1896 A.B. 1898. A.M. 1906
Sedgwick,	[1] Adam ....*Trin.		M 1874 A.B. 1878. A.M. 1881
—	Cha. Humphrey	Sid.	M 1895 A.B. 1898. M.B., B.C., A.M. 1902
—	Howard Willmore ...	Em.	M 1893 A.B. 1896. A.M. 1904
—	John Harfield Halifax } Mostyn	Trin.	M 1892 A.B. 1895. A.M. 1902
---	John Steph.	Jes.	M 1895 A.B. 1898. A.M. 1902. LL.M. 1903
---	Leon. John	Pem.	M 1902 A.B. 1905
—	Rich. Ern.	Cai.	M 1893 A.B. 1896. B.C. 1900. M.B. 1901. [M.D. 1907
—	Rich. Romney	Trin.	M 1912
---	Ronald	Em.	M 1900 A.B. 1903
—	Sid. Newman	Em.	M 1891 A.B. 1894. A.M. 1903
—	Walt.	Pem.	M 1896 A.B. 1899. A.M. 1903
Sedwick,	Nath. Asher	Pet.	M 1909 A.B. 1912
See,	Will. Tho.	N. C.	M 1893 A.B. 1900. A.M. 1903
Seebohm,	Frederic		*Litt.D.* 1902
Seekond,	Bishan Singh	Down.	M 1912
Segal,	Mark	Cla.	M 1909 A.B. 1912
Segnitz,	Hermann Ferdinand	Trin.	M 1911
Seiler,	Gerhard Jan Chandler	Cai.	M 1903
Selbie,	Will. Boothby	Trin. H.	L 1903 A.M. Incorp. Oxf. 1903
Selborne,	(*Earl of*)		*LL.D.* 1910
Selby,	Edw. Ja.	Down.	M 1909 A.B. 1912
—	Ronald Walt.	Trin. H.	M 1910
—	Will. Lyle	Trin.	M 1912
Selby-Lowndes,	Geo. Noël	Qu.	M 1905 A.B. 1908
Seligman,	Gerald Abr.	Trin. H.	M 1905 A.B. 1908
Sell,	Wilfrid Hazell	Jes.	M 1900 A.B. 1903
—	Will. Ja.	Chr.	M 1873 A.B. 1877. A.M. 1880. Sc.D. 1906
Sells,	Cha. Claude Vincent } Rodolph	Trin.	M 1904 A.B. 1908
Sellwood,	Frank Greaves	Em.	M 1912
—	Geo. Binford	Em.	M 1909 A.B. 1912
—	Hen. Edgar	H. Sel.	L 1907
Selous,	Gerald Holgate	Pem.	E 1908
Selvam,	Pannir	Pet.	M 1909
Selwood,	Ern. Hen.	N. C.	M 1911

[1] Professor of Zoology and Comparative Anatomy, 1907.

Selwyn,	Edw. Gordon	King's	M 1904 A.B. 1907. *C. C. 1909. A.M. 1911
—	Ern. Will.	Qu.	M 1908 A.B. 1911
—	Geo. Theodore	C. C.	M 1906 A.B. 1909
—	John	C. C.	M 1911
—	Steph. John	Trin.	M 1893 A.B. 1896. A.M. 1902
—	Syd. Fra.	Em.	M 1902 A.B. 1905
—	Will. Marshall	Em.	M 1898 A.B. 1901. A.M. 1906
Semple,	Edgar Geo.	N. C.	M 1909 A.B. 1912
Sen,	Anukul Chandra	N. C.	M 1911
—	Arun	Pet.	M 1908 A.B. 1911
—	Bhupati Mohan	King's	M 1910 A.B. 1912
—	Kshitis Chandra	Trin. H.	M 1910
—	Nirmab Chandra	Cla.	M 1902
—	Prasanta Kumar	Joh.	M 1899 A.B. 1901. LL.B. 1903
—	Sailendra Kumar	Em.	M 1903 Down. A.B. 1906
Senanayeke,	Fred Rich.	Down.	M 1900 A.B., LL.B. 1904
Sen-Gupta,	Jatindra Mohan	N. C.	M 1904 Down. A.B. 1908. LL.B. 1909
Senior,	Alf. Park	Chr.	M 1906 A.B. 1909
—	Cha. Alex. Lorenzo	Joh.	M 1897 A.B. 1900. A.M. 1904
—	Jos.	Cla.	M 1911
—	Sam.	Cath.	M 1909
Seon,	Greville Ewing	Jes.	M 1908
Sephton,	Ralph	Cai.	M 1901 A.B. 1904
Sequeira,	Ern. Rackwitz	H. Sel.	L 1892 A.B. 1894. A.M. 1901
Sessions,	Lionel Frank	Cla.	M 1911
Seth-Smith,	Alex. Garden	Trin.	M 1902 A.B. 1905
—	Douglas Newton	Em.	M 1907 A.B. 1910
—	Gordon	Pem.	M 1906 A.B. 1909
—	Keith John	Cla.	M 1900 A.B. 1904
—	Leslie Moffat	Pem.	M 1898 A.B. 1901
Sett,	Merwanji Kavasji	Down.	M 1910
Severn,	Hew Fergusson	H. Sel.	M 1896 A.B. 1899. A.M. 1908
Severne,	Edm. Cha. Wigley	Trin.	M 1906
Seward,	[1] Alb. Cha.	Joh.	M 1883 A.B. 1886. A.M. 1890. *Em., *Joh.
—	Bertie Hen.	Trin.	M 1899 A.B. 1902. A.M. 1906
—	Rob. Wallis	King's	E 1896 A.B. 1899. LL.B. 1902. A.M. 1903
Sewell,	Algernon Percy	Pem.	M 1898 A.B. 1901
—	Cecil Art. Seymour	Cath.	M 1897 A.B. 1900. A.M. 1909
—	Cha. Will. Hen.	N. C.	M 1898 Em. A.B. 1901. A.M. 1912
—	Clarence John Threlkeld	Trin.	M 1903 A.B. 1906. A.M. 1910
—	Fre. Alex. Seymour	Cath.	M 1899 A.B. 1902. A.M. 1908
—	Herb. Victor	Pet.	M 1907 A.B., LL.B. 1910
—	Horace Dobbs	N. C.	M 1904
—	John Percy Claude	Trin.	M 1909 A.B. 1912
—	Rob. Beresford Seymour	Chr.	M 1899 A.B. 1902
—	Syd. Ewart	Joh.	M 1906 A.B. 1909
—	Tho. Jackson Elliott	Qu.	M 1907 A.B. 1910
—	Will.	N. C.	L 1908 Down. A.B. 1910
Sewill,	John Waterlow	Cla.	M 1908 A.B. 1911
—	Roger Waterlow	Cla.	M 1911
Seymour,	Algernon Giles	Jes.	M 1905 A.B. 1908
—	Art.	Qu.	M 1907 A.B. 1910
—.	Cha.	King's	M 1901 A.B. 1904. A.M. 1909
—	Edw. Hobart		*LL.D.* 1903
—	Fra.	Trin.	M 1904
—	Fre. Will.	Trin.	M 1903 A.B. 1906
—	Horace Ja.	Trin.	M 1903
—	Vere Hugh	Trin. H.	M 1907 A.B. 1910
Seys-Phillips,	Howard	Trin.	M 1911

[1] Professor of Botany, 1906.

Shackel,	Geo. Meredyth	Trin.	M 1912
Shackelford,	Geo. Shuckburgh ...	Jes.	M 1902 A.B. 1905. A.M. 1910
Shackell,	Fra. Theodore	Pem.	M 1901 A.B. 1905
Shackle,	Godfrey Attwood Neild	Em.	M 1908 A.B. 1911
Shackleton,	Cha. Edmond	Trin. H.	M 1900 A.B. 1903. A.M. 1910
Shaen-Carter,	Victor Art. Tilson	Qu.	L 1901
Shah,	Shivlal Panachand ...	Jes.	M 1912
Shahzád,	Ahmad Khán	Pet.	M 1912
Shakespear,	Gilb. Arden	Trin.	M 1897 A.B. 1899. A.M. 1910
Shakespeare,	Geoffrey Hithersay ...	Em.	M 1912
Shamshad,	Ahmad Khan	Pet.	M 1909 A.B., LL.B. 1912
Shand,	Phil. Morton	King's	M 1906 A.B. 1911
Shang Chi-heng,	*His Excellency* ...		*Litt.D.* 1906
Shanks,	Edw. Buxton	Trin.	M 1910
—	Pet. Martin	Chr.	M 1897 A.B. 1900. A.M. 1904
Shankster,	Geo.	Sid.	M 1912
Shanly,	Herb.	Joh.	M 1912
Shann,	Cha. Brodie	Em.	M 1903 A.B. 1906. A.M. 1910
—	Sam. Edw. Thornhill	Cai.	M 1901 A.B. 1904. M.B., B.C. 1909. E. T.
Shannon,	Gerald Cairns	Joh.	M 1902 A.B. 1905 [A.M. 1910
Shapcott,	Will. Hen. Geo.	Down.	E 1898 A.B. 1901
Sharman,	Geo. Hen.	H. Sel.	M 1901 A.B. 1904
Sharp,	Cha. Geo. Gordon ...	Trin. H.	M 1904
—	Clifford Graham	Joh.	M 1903 A.B. 1907. A.M. 1910
—	Cuthbert John	Cla.	M 1909
—	Edm. Colin	Cla.	M 1902 A.B. 1905. A.M. 1909
—	Edw. Mervyn	Cla.	M 1912
—	Everard Will. Lewen	Em.	M 1909
—	Gerald	Joh.	M 1883 A.B. 1886. A.M. 1910
—	Gilb. Granville	N. C.	M 1912
—	Gordon Frank	C. C.	M 1905 A.B. 1908
—	Harold Armstrong ...	Cla.	M 1906
—	Harold Withers	Pem.	M 1907
—	John Edw.	Cai.	M 1907 A.B. 1910
—	John Selwyn	Jes.	M 1901 A.B. 1904. A.M. 1912
—	John Stanley	Trin. H.	L 1911
—	Leon. Ern. Steigenberger	Trin.	M 1908 A.B. 1911
—	Leon. Whittaker	Cai.	M 1901 A.B. 1904. B.C. 1909. M.B., A.M.
—	Milton	Trin. H.	M 1899 A.B. 1902 [1910
—	Sid. Leslie Roy	C. C.	M 1909 A.B. 1912
—	Steph. Oswald	Pem.	M 1909 A.B. 1912
—	Tho. Hicks	Joh.	M 1910
—	Will.	C. C.	M 1908 A.B. 1911
—	Will. Cha. Granville	Em.	M 1893 A.B. 1896. A.M. 1904
—	Will. Hen. Cartwright	Joh.	M 1902 A.B. 1905. LL.B. 1907. A.M. 1909
Sharpe,	Cha. Art.	King's	M 1900 A.B. 1903
—	Edgar	Jes.	M 1906 A.B. 1909
—	Geo. Radford	Chr.	M 1912
—	Gerald Whittaker ...	Trin.	M 1897 A.B. 1901
—	Herb.	Pem.	M 1902 A.B. 1905
—	Rich. Hen.	Trin.	M 1904
—	Will. Hen. Sharpe ...	King's	M 1903 A.B. 1906. A.M. 1910
Sharples,	Frank Deeks	Qu.	L 1908 A.B. 1910
—	Ja. Will.	Sid.	M 1900 A.B. 1903
—	Ovid Edgar Leland	Joh.	M 1895 A.B., LL.B. 1899. A.M. 1902
Sharrer,	Art. Cha. Alb.	Cai.	M 1898 A.B. 1902
Shaughnessy,	Will. Ja.	Trin.	M 1903
Shaw,	Alb.	Trin	M 1910
—	Alb. Norman	Cai.	M 1911
—	Archib.	Em.	M 1897 A.B. 1900. A.M. 1906
—	Cha. Laurence	Sid.	M 1905 A.B. 1908

Shaw,	Clifford	Jes.	M 1910
—	Colin Read	Cla.	L 1899 A.B. 1901
—	Edw. Brian	Trin.	M 1910 [M.D. 1912
—	Ern. Alb.	N. C.	M 1885 King's A.B. 1888. M.B., B.C. 1890.
—	Geoffrey Turton	Cai.	M 1898 A.B. 1901. Mus.B. 1902
—	Gilb. Shuldam	Trin.	M 1905 A.B. 1909
—	Graham Hen.	Cla.	M 1909 A.B. 1912
—	Harold Knox	Trin.	M 1904 A.B. 1907. A.M. 1911
—	John Herb.	Sid.	M 1894 A.B. 1897. A.M. 1901
—	Jos.	Trin.	M 1875 A.B. 1879. A.M. 1904
—	Julius Brinkley	Joh.	M 1901
—	Kenneth Edwin	Em.	M 1902 A.B. 1907. A.M. 1912
—	Pat. Knox	Sid.	M 1912
—	Ralph Reg.	Em.	M 1910
—	Raymond Pugh	Trin.	M 1905 A.B. 1908. A.M. 1912
—	Rob.	C. C.	M 1910
—	Rob. Cyril	Sid.	M 1904 A.B. 1907. A.M. 1911
—	Syd.	Trin. H.	M 1911
—	Tho. Knox	*Sid.	M 1905 A.B. 1908. A.M. 1912
—	Vernon Graham Havergal	Cla.	M 1906 A.B. 1909
—	Will. Napier	*Em.	M 1872 A.B. 1876. A.M. 1879. Sc.D. 1902
Sheaf,	Eric Watson	Down.	M 1897 A.B. 1900. B.C. 1905. M.B., A.M.
			[1906. M.C. 1908
Sheane,	Will. Pakenham Cole	Cath.	M 1898 A.B. 1901. A.M. 1906
Sheard,	Mich. Hen.	Cla.	M 1908
Shearer,	Creswell	Trin.	M 1901 Creswell, A.B. 1906. A.M. 1909
Shearman,	Valentine	Cla.	M 1907
Shearwood,	Geo. Fre. Ferrier	H. Sel.	M 1909 A.B. 1912
Sheehan,	Fre. Rob.	N. C.	M 1894 A.B. 1902
Sheepshanks,	Art. Cha.	Trin.	M 1903 A.B. 1906
—	Cha. John Harcourt	Trin.	M 1904 A.B. 1907. A.M. 1911
—	Edw.	Pem.	M 1903 A.B. 1906
—	Rich. Hasell	Trin.	M 1903 A.B. 1907
—	Will. Ern.	Trin.	M 1900 A.B. 1903
Sheldon,	Fre. Howard	Trin.	M 1905 A.B. 1908
—	Leon. Gordon Melville	Trin.	M 1911
—	Tho. Will.	Em.	M 1907
Shelford,	Rob. Walt. Campbell	Em.	M 1891 A.B. 1894. A.M. 1901
Shell,	Alf.	N. C.	M 1897 Chr. A.B. 1901. A.M. 1908
Shelley,	Geo. Edw.	Trin.	M 1909 A.B. 1912
—	Guy Birkbeck	Trin. H.	M 1909
--	Ja.	N. C.	M 1904 Chr. A.B. 1907
—	John Fre.	Trin.	M 1905
—	Lewis Wilton	Cai.	M 1906 A.B. 1910
—	Malcolm Bond	Chr.	M 1898 A.B. 1901
Shelmerdine,	Tho. Greatorex	Jes.	M 1905 A.B. 1908
Shelton,	Laurence Hugh	Joh.	M 1910
—	Osric Will. Maur.	Jes.	M 1909
—	Ralph Norman	Down.	M 1903 A.B. 1906
Shen,	Cheng Shih	Cath.	M 1909 A.B. 1912
—	Cheng Tung	King's	M 1912
Shennan,	Douglas Fra. Fairfax	Trin.	M 1911
—	Watson Douglas	Chr.	M 1907 A.B. 1912
Shenton,	John Snelson	Jes.	M 1909 A.B. 1912
Shephard,	Will. Hopper	Chr.	M 1908 A.B. 1911
Shepheard,	Edw. Parigi Wallwyn	H. Sel.	M 1901
Shepherd,	Edw. Hoskins	Joh.	M 1909 A.B. 1912
—	Fra. McAndrew	Trin.	M 1910
—	Ja. Sherringham	Trin.	M 1907 A.B. 1910
—	Jos.	N. C.	M 1905
—	Oswald	Qu.	M 1912

Shepherd,	Rob.	N. C.	M 1909 A.B. 1912
—	Tho. Stanley	C. C.	E 1896 A.B. 1901
—	Will. Lisle	Joh.	M 1906 A.B. 1909
Shepley,	Geo. Hen.	Joh.	M 1897 A.B. 1900. A.M. 1906
—	Rob. Guy Shepley ...	Mag.	M 1912
Sheppard,	Bern. Percival	Cath.	M 1910
—	Geoffrey Allan	Trin. H.	M 1910
—	Hugh Rich. Lawrie	Trin. H.	E 1901 A.B. 1904. A.M. 1910
—	John Harding Donald	Pem.	M 1907
—	John Tresidder ......*King's		M 1900 A.B. 1904. A.M. 1907
—	Leslie Alf.	N. C.	M 1909 Cath. A.B. 1912
—	Sam. Edw.	Em.	L 1912
—	Tho. Williams	Cath.	M 1899 A.B. 1902
—	Will. Fleetwood ......*Trin.		M 1881 A.B. 1884 (2). A.M. 1888. LL.M.
—	Will. Geo.	Joh.	M 1906 A.B. 1909 [1889. Sc.D. 1908
Sheppard-Jones			*See* Jones, J. E. S.
Shepperson,	Ern. Whittome	Chr.	M 1898 A.B. 1901. LL.B. 1902. A.M. 1910
Sheppey-Greene,	Ralph Fre.	Cath.	M 1905 A.B. 1908
Shera,	Art. Geoffrey	Em.	M 1908 A.B. 1911
—	Frank Hen.	Jes.	M 1901 A.B. 1904. Mus.B. 1906. A.M.,
Sherburn,	John Clifford	Trin. H.	M 1906 [Mus.M. 1910
Sheriff,	Syed Mohommed ...	Joh.	M 1898 S. Mohammed A.B. 1901. A.M.†
Sheringham,	Hor. Valentine	Cai.	M 1901 [1905
Sherlock,	John Hen.	Em.	M 1912
—	Woodford Wright ...	N. C.	M 1900 A.B. 1906
Sherman,	Reg.	Cai.	M 1906 A.B. 1909
Sherrard,	Geo. Cha.	Trin.	M 1902 A.B. 1905
Sherring,	Cha. Atmore	Trin.	M 1886 A.B. 1889. A.M. 1902
Sherrington,	Cha. Scott	N. C.	M 1879 *Cai. A.B. 1884. M.B. 1885. A.M.
Shervani,	Tasodduq Ahmed Khan	N. C.	L 1910 [1887. M.D. 1893. Sc.D. 1904
Sherwani,	Haroon Khan	Chr.	M 1907
Sherwood,	Ern. Tho. Garton ...	King's	M 1903 A.B. 1905
—	Geo. Douglas	Em.	M 1906 A.B. 1909
—	Harry Purvis	Sid.	M 1912
Shettle,	Phil. Shakespeare ...	Cai.	M 1899 A.B. 1902
Shevade,	Shivaram Vinayak ...	N. C.	M 1905
Shiach,	Art.	N. C.	M 1905 Chr. A.B. 1908
Shields,	Chris. St Barbe	Em.	M 1908
—	Hugh John Sladen ...	Jes.	M 1906 A.B. 1909
Shiells,	Art. Kenward	Trin.	M 1907 A.B. 1910
Shilcock,	John Winton	Chr.	M 1907 A.B. 1910
Shildrick,	Lancelot Rich.	Em.	M 1906 A.B. 1909
Shillington,	John Melville	Trin. H.	M 1896 A.B. 1899. LL.B. 1900. A.M. 1903
Shillito,	Art.	Cai.	M 1891 A.B. 1894. A.M. 1906
—	Norman Wholey	Joh.	M 1912
Shilson,	Donald	C. C.	M 1910
Shimwell,	Humphrey	Trin. H.	M 1903 A.B. 1906
—	Oliver	Trin. H.	M 1904
—	Tho.	Chr.	M 1895 A.B. 1898. A.M. 1902
Shiner,	Oscar Alf.	N. C.	L 1907 A.B. 1910
—	Rupert Phil.	N. C.	M 1902 Chr. A.B. 1906. A.M. 1909
Shingleton Smith,	Fra.	King's	M 1898 A.B. 1901. B.C. 1906
Shingleton-Smith,	Lionel	Joh.	M 1897 A.B. 1901. M.B., B.C. 1908
Shipley,	¹Art. Everett ....*Chr.		M 1880 A.B. 1884 (2). A.M. 1888. Sc.D
—	Jos. Will.	N. C.	M 1912 [1911
Shipman,	Geo. Alf. Cargil	Trin.	M 1894 A.B. 1897. M.B., B.C., A.M. 1901
—	Malcolm Parker	Sid.	M 1896 A.B. 1901
Shipton,	Will.	Em.	M 1902 A.B. 1905. M.B., B.C. 1911

¹ Master of Christ's College, 1910.

Shipway,	Fra. Edw.	Chr.	M 1894 A.B. 1897. A.M. 1901. M.B., B.C.
Shivdasani,	Hassamal Baharmal	Joh.	M 1911 [1902. M.D. 1907
Sholl,	Art. Edw.	Cla.	M 1912
Shone,	Hen. John	Em.	M 1896 A.B. 1899. B.C. 1902. M.B. 1904
Shore,	Harington Offley ...	Em.	M 1889 A.B. 1896. A.M. 1908
—	Lewis Rudall	Joh.	E 1908 A.B. 1911
—	Tho. Hen. Gostwyck	Joh.	M 1906 A.B. 1909
Short,	Hen. Sanderson	Trin.	M 1907 A.B. 1910
—	John Martin	Joh.	M 1906 A.B. 1909
—	Percy Stanley	Trin.	M 1910
Shorter,	Rennie Cha.	Sid.	M 1904 A.B. 1907
Shorting,	Geo. Herb. Cobbold	Qu.	M 1894 A.B. 1897. A.M. 1902
Shout,	Fra. Fre.	Cai.	M 1898 A.B.† 1905
Shove,	Gerald Frank	King's	M 1907 A.B. 1910
—	Ralph Sam.	Trin.	M 1908 A.B. 1911
—	Will. Clive	N. C.	M 1912
Showell-Rogers,	Eric Norman	Cai.	M 1909
Shoyer,	Art. Fre.	Trin. H.	M 1890 A.B. 1893. M.B., B.C. 1897. M.D.
Shrager,	Edwin Herb.	Trin. H.	M 1912 [1901
Shrive,	John Denson	N. C.	M 1893 A.B. 1896. A.M. 1902
Shroff,	Magan Hirabhai	N. C.	M 1912
Shrubbs,	Cha. Art.	Down.	M 1907
—	Edw. Alb.	N. C.	M 1896 A.B. 1899. A.M. 1903
—	Hen.	N. C.	L 1903 A.B. 1907. A.M. 1911
Shrubsall,	Frank Cha.	Cla.	M 1892 A.B. 1895. A.M. 1899. M.B., B.C.
			[1901. M.D. 1903
Shuckburgh,	Evelyn Shirley ......*Em.		M 1862 A.B.1866. A.M. 1869. Litt.D.1903
—	John Evelyn	King's	M 1896 A.B. 1899. A.M. 1906
—	Rob. Shirley	Em.	M 1899 A.B. 1902
Shufflebotham,	Frank	Trin.	M 1893 A.B. 1896. M.B., B.C., A.M. 1900.
Shujauddin,	Khalifa	N. C.	M 1910 A.B., LL.B. 1912 [M.D. 1910
Shurlock,	Fre. Will.	Chr.	M 1911
Shute,	Geoffrey Gay	Cla.	M 1911
Shuter,	Leon. Rob. Allen ...	Pem.	M 1906
—	Rob. Harrison	Jes.	M 1902
Shütze,	Swen Yen	Chr.	M 1906
Shwe,	San	Em.	M 1901 A.B. 1904. A.M. 1910
Siam,	*H.R.H. Prince of* ...		*See* Suriyong, *H.R.H. Prince* (of
—	Chulalongkorn, *H.M. King of*		*LL.D.* 1907 [Siam)
Sibly,	Tho. Mervyn	Joh.	M 1904 A.B. 1907. A.M. 1911
Siciliano,	Paul	Trin. H.	M 1908
Siddle,	Geo.	Cath.	M 1897 A.B. 1900. A.M. 1905
—	Geo. Ludorf	Cai.	M 1901 A.B. 1904
Siddons,	Art. Warry ....*Jes.		M 1895 A.B. 1898. A.M. 1902
Sidebotham,	Cha. Edw.	Joh.	M 1898 A.B. 1902. A.M. 1906
—	Fra. Nasmyth	Cla.	M 1911
—	Fre. Lester	Cai.	M 1912
—	Ja. Nasmyth Wedgwood	Cla.	M 1909
—	John Biddulph	Cai.	M 1911
Sidgwick,	Frank	Trin.	M 1898 A.B. 1901
—	Harry Chris.	Cla.	M 1896 A.B. 1899. M.B. 1904
Sidley,	John	Pet.	M 1879 A.B. 1883. A.M. 1908
Sidney,	Rich. John Hamilton	Mag.	M 1912
Siegert,	Ernst Ludwig Otto	Trin. H.	M 1905
Siffken,	Bern. Cha. de Wiederhold	Mag.	M 1901 A.B. 1904
Silberstein,	Franz Pet.	N. C.	M 1912
Silburn,	Laurence	Cai.	M 1910
Silk,	Frederic Alb.	Qu.	M 1904
Sills,	Tho. Barnard	Joh.	M 1896 A.B. 1899. A.M. 1904
Silvanus,	Eric Miles	King's	M 1899 A.B. 1902
—	Harold Miles	Sid.	M 1893 A.B. 1896. A.M. 1904

Silvertop,	Fra. Somerled	Trin.	M 1901
—	Will. Alex.	Cla.	M 1903 A.B. 1906
Silvester,	Hen.	N. C.	M 1876 A.B. 1880. A.M. 1902
Simcox,	John Lea	Pem.	M 1906 A.B. 1909
—	Will. Martin	Pem.	M 1907 A.B. 1911
Simeon,	John Pole	H. Sel.	M 1896 A.B. 1902. A.M. 1908
—	Leon. Steph. Barrington	Trin.	M 1909 A.B. 1912
Simey,	Athelstane Iliff	King's	M 1892 A.B. 1895. M.B., B.C. 1902. A.M.,
—	Erroll Geo. Tyndall	Qu.	M 1908 A.B. 1911 [M.D. 1906
—	Percy Arnold Tyndall	Qu.	M 1911
Simmonds,	Fra. Mathew	N. C.	L 1906
Simmons,	Branch Ebert	Chr.	M 1911
—	Cha. Edw.	Qu.	M 1908 A.B. 1911
—	Leon. Fre. Geo.	Joh.	M 1912
—	Melton	Mag.	M 1893 A.B. 1897. A.M. 1901
Simms,	Brian	Qu.	M 1910
—	Will.	Qu.	M 1906 A.B. 1909
Simon,	Ern. Darwin	Pem.	M 1898 E. Emil. D. A.B. 1901
—	Heinrich Hellmuth	King's	M 1899 A.B. 1902
Simonds,	Cha. Cabourn Bannister	Cai.	M 1910
Simons,	Art. John	Em.	M 1912
—	Edw.	Down.	M 1904 A.B. 1908
Simpkinson,	Fra. Vaughan	King's	M 1907 A.B. 1910
Simpson,	Adam Ja. Goldie ...	Chr.	M 1906 A.B. 1909
—	Alan Haldane	Trin.	M 1894 A.B. 1897. A.M. 1901
—	Alex. Malcolm	King's	M 1896 A.B. 1899. B.C. 1903. M.B. 1906
—	Art. Goodyear	Trin.	M 1904 A.B. 1907. A.M. 1911
—	Art. Jos. Bradney ...	Trin. H.	M 1905 A.B. 1908
—	Basil Herb. Montagu	Mag.	M 1906 A.B. 1909
—	Clifford Sandford ...	Trin.	M 1910
—	Dav. Annandale	Cath.	M 1901 A.B. 1904
—	Fre. Art. ....*Trin.		M 1911 A.M. 1911 (Oxf. incorp.)
—	Geoffrey Barnsley ...	Trin. H.	M 1909 A.B., LL.B. 1912
—	Geoffrey Hargrave ...	Trin. H.	M 1912
—	Geo. Barré Goldie ...	Chr.	M 1906
—	Geo. Cha. Edw.	Joh.	M 1899 A.B. 1902. B.C. 1906. M.B. 1907
—	Harold Read	Sid.	M 1909 A.B. 1912
—	Ja. Christian	Cai.	M 1898 A.B. 1903. A.M. 1907
—	Ja. Crawford	Em.	M 1907
—	Ja. Gordon	Chr.	L 1908 A.B. 1909
—	Ja. Herb.	Pem.	M 1902 A.B. 1905
—	John Basil	Cai.	M 1899 A.B. 1902. A.M. 1907
—	John Hume	H. Sel.	M 1887 A.B. 1890. A.M. 1906
—	Llewellyn Eardley ...	Em.	M 1898 A.B., LL.B. 1901. A.M. 1905
—	Norman Douglas ...	Trin.	M 1908 A.B. 1911
—	Percy Brumwell	Cai.	M 1894 A.B. 1898. A.M. 1902
—	Roger Cordy	Trin.	M 1902 A.B. 1906
—	Selwyn Geo.	Sid.	M 1900 A.B. 1903. A.M. 1907
—	Tho.	Trin. H.	M 1895 A.B. 1898. A.M. 1902
—	Walt. Anth.	Trin. H.	M 1904 A.B. 1907
Simson,	Colin Cope	Trin.	M 1889 C. Coape, A.B. 1892. A.M. 1896.
—	John	Jes.	M 1910 [M.B., B.C. 1901
Sinclair,	Denis John Oliver ...	Trin.	M 1911
—	Geoffrey Whitfeld ...	King's	M 1908 A.B. 1911
—	Kenneth Duncan Lecky	Trin.	M 1908
—	Rob. Cha. Hamilton	Trin. H.	E 1897 A.B. 1900. A.M. 1904
Sinclair-Loutit,	Will. Hen. Austin	Trin.	M 1901 A.B. 1905
Sing,	Cha. Millington	Chr.	M 1907 A.B. 1910
—	Laurence Millington	Pem.	M 1906 A.B. 1909
—	Martin Millington ...	Chr.	M 1910 [1897. M.D. 1901
—	Wilfrid MacDonald	Chr.	M 1889 A.B. 1892. B.C., A.M. 1896. M.B.

Singer,	Art. Leon.	King's	M 1900 A.B. 1903. B.C. 1910. M.B. 1911
—	Cecil Mortimer	Trin.	M 1908 A.B. 1911
Singh,	Basheshar	Down.	M 1907
—	Bawa Kartar	Down.	M 1904 A.B. 1907
—	Der Indra	Down.	E 1911
—	Dulip	Pem.	M 1903 A.B. 1906
—	Har Kishan	Joh.	M 1900 A.B. 1903. A.M.† 1907
—	Harman	N. C.	M 1908
—	Indarjit	Pem.	M 1902 A.B. 1905. Kanwar I. M.B., B.C.
—	Jatindra	Mag.	M 1912 [1911
—	Labh	Cai.	M 1909 A.B., LL.B. 1911
—	Teja	Down.	L 1907
Singleton,	John Edw.	Pem.	M 1902 A.B., LL.B. 1905
—	Tho. Bayden	Em.	M 1909 A.B. 1912
—	Will. Parkinson	Pem.	M 1900 A.B. 1903. A.M. 1907
Sington,	Alan John Campbell	Trin.	M 1905 A.B. 1908. A.M. 1912
—	Edw. Claude	Trin.	M 1911
Sinha,	Harry Conrod Norbert } Harnath }	Chr.	M 1905
—	Mohim	Down.	M 1909
—	Sisir Kumar	Down.	M 1910
Sinker,	Art.	Pem.	M 1896 A.B. 1899. A.M. 1903
Sisson,	Bern. Harold	Em.	M 1906 A.B. 1909
—	Hen. Arnott	Cla.	M 1904 A.B. 1907. A.M. 1911
Sisterson,	Geo. Edw.	Cai.	M 1899 A.B. 1903. A.M. 1907
Sitwell,	John Knightley	Trin.	M 1893 A.B. 1896. A.M. 1907
Skeen,	Will. Hen.	Sid.	M 1898 A.B. 1901
Skelton,	Norman Art.	Qu.	M 1908 A.B. 1912
Skemp,	Frank Whittingham	Pet.	M 1903
Skene,	Art. Percy	Qu.	M 1901 A.B. 1904
—	Claud Montague Benson	Joh.	M 1903 A.B. 1906
—	Fre. Norman	Joh.	M 1896 A.B. 1900. A.M. 1912
—	Rob. Ern.	N. C.	M 1899 Trin. H. A.B. 1903. A.M. 1907
Skene-Keith,	Pat. Benj. Malcolm	H. Sel.	M 1910
Skey,	Archib. Geo.	King's	M 1899 A.B. 1902
—	Cha. Harland	Qu.	M 1909 A.B. 1912
—	Cyril Oscar	Qu.	M 1911
Skinner,	Cha. Edwin	N. C.	M 1906 A.B. 1909
—	Conrad Art.	Jes.	M 1908 A.B. 1911
—	Cyril Reed	Joh.	M 1908
—	Edw. Fretson	C. C.	M 1899 A.B. 1902. A.M. 1906. M.B., B.C.
—	John		*A.M.* 1903 [1908
—	John Adrian Dudley	Cai.	M 1910
—	John Harding	Em.	M 1896 A.B. 1900. A.M. 1903
—	Rob. Weeding	Jes.	M 1903 A.B. 1906
Skipwith,	(*Sir*) Grey Humberston } D'Estotville }	Trin.	M 1903
Skon,	Mom Chow	Mag.	M 1908 A.B. 1912 [M.B. 1908 (2)
Slack,	Eric	Pem.	M 1893 A.B. 1896. A.M. 1901. B.C. 1908.
Slade,	Geoffrey Rich.	Trin.	M 1890 A.B. 1893. B.C., A.M. 1900. M.D.
—	Gerald Osborne	Trin.	M 1909 A.B. 1912 [1904
—	John Godfrey	Cla.	E 1895 A.B. 1898. A.M. 1903. M.B., B.C.
—	Percival Claude Avery	Mag.	M 1899 A.B. 1902 [1905. M.D. 1907
Slater,	Alf.	Cath.	M 1906 A.B. 1909
—	Bertram Benj.	Trin.	M 1890 A.B. 1893. A.M. 1910
—	John Alan	Em.	M 1903 A.B. 1906. A.M. 1910
Slator,	Frank	Joh.	M 1899 A.B. 1902. A.M. 1906
—	Rich.	Jes.	M 1892 A.B. 1895. A.M. 1901
Slaughter,	Art.	Trin. H.	M 1904 A.B. 1908
Slawson,	Will. Newton	N. C.	M 1912
Sleem,	Mohammed	N. C.	M 1910

Sleeman,	Cyril Montagu	Chr.	M 1902 A.B. 1905. A.M. 1909. *Qu. 1912
—	John Herb. ....*Sid.		M 1898 A.B. 1901. A.M. 1905
Slefrig,	Sam.	Cath.	M 1907 A.B. 1910
Sleigh,	Geo. Basil	Qu.	M 1908 A.B. 1911
—	Gervase Paget	Jes.	M 1912
—	Will. Austin	Mag.	M 1899 A.B. 1902
Sleight,	Alb. Hen.	Joh.	M 1908 A.B. 1911
—	Art. Blomefield	Joh.	M 1900 A.B. 1903
—	Kenneth Rich.	Sid.	M 1910
Slingsby,	Will. Ecroyd	Pem.	M 1904
Sloan,	Eric Barringer	Trin.	M 1911
—	Geo. Fre.	Em.	M 1904 A.B. 1907
—	Lawrence Barringer	Cla.	M 1910
Sloane,	Ja. Renwick	Trin.	M 1903
Sloley,	Rich.	Trin. H.	M 1912
—	Rob. Walt.	Joh.	M 1901 A.B. 1904. A.M. 1908
Sloman,	Art. Eric Penrose ...	Qu.	M 1909 A.B. 1912
Smailes,	Alan	Em.	M 1910
—	Rich.	Em.	M 1897 A.B. 1900. A.M.† 1904
Smale,	Oswald Ridley	Cai.	M 1900 A.B. 1903. M.B., B.C. 1909
Smales,	Reg.	Qu.	M 1906 A.B. 1910
Small,	Walt. Jos. Tombleson	Cai.	M 1901 A.B. 1904. A.M.† 1908
Smalley,	Skelton	Cai.	M 1912
Smallwood,	Art. Edw.	N. C.	L 1900 A.B. 1902. A.M. 1906
Smart,	Fra. Will. Bolton ...	Cath.	M 1890 King's A.B. 1897. A.M. 1901
—	Hen.	N. C.	M 1892 A.B. 1895. A.M. 1901
—	Walt. Alex.	Jes.	M 1903
—	Will. Marshall	Trin.	M 1911
Smedley,	Ralph Davies	Pem.	M 1895 A.B. 1898. A.M. 1903. M.B. 1904.
Smee,	Cyril Walt.	Joh.	M 1911 [M.D. 1908
—	Percival Alf.	N. C.	M 1895 A.B. 1898. A.M. 1907
Smiley,	Hub. Stewart	Trin.	M 1901
Smit,	Barend Jacobus	Chr.	M 1909
—	Jacobus Stephanus ...	Trin. H.	M 1902
Smith,	Alb. Ja.	N. C.	M 1896 Qu. A.B. 1899. A.M. 1904
—	Alb. Malins	Em.	M 1899 A.B. 1902. A.M. 1908
—	Alf. Cecil Denison ...	Chr.	M 1906 A.B. 1909
—	Alf. Ern.	N. C.	M 1905 A.B. 1908
—	Alf. John	Cath.	M 1898 A.B. 1901. A.M. 1905
—	Alf. Will. Exton	Trin. H.	M 1898 A.B. 1901
—	Algernon Cha. Stanley	Trin.	M 1908 A.B. 1911
—	Allison Gould	Mag.	M 1909 A.B. 1912
—	Alton Ewart Clarence	Chr.	M 1906 A.B. 1909
—	Archib. Geo. Edw. ...	N. C.	M 1899 C. C. A.B. 1902. A.M. 1908
—	Arnold John Hugh	Trin.	M 1899 A.B. 1902
—	Art.	N. C.	M 1908 Cath. A.B. 1911
—	Art. Dudley	Pem.	M 1905 A.B. 1908. LL.B. 1909. A.M. 1912
—	Art. Forrester	Jes.	M 1898 A.B. 1903
—	Art. Lionel Hall	Cai.	M 1899 M.B., B.C. 1908
—	Art. Phil. Gordon ...	Sid.	M 1903 A.B. 1906. A.M. 1910
—	Art. Saxon Dennett	Jes.	M 1902 A.B. 1905
—	Bern.	Pet.	M 1896 A.B. 1899. A.M. 1910
—	Bern.	Sid.	M 1900 A.B. 1903. A.M. 1907
—	Bertie Selwyn	Trin.	M 1900 A.B. 1903. A.M. 1908
—	Bertram Tom Dean	N. C.	M 1904 Jes. A.B. 1908. A.M. 1911
—	Brian	Pem.	M 1912
—	Brian Arnold	Trin.	M 1907 A.B. 1910
—	Cecil Furness	Joh.	M 1909 A.B. 1912
—	Cha. Hammond	Sid.	M 1903 A.B. 1906
—	Cha. Home Cecil ...	Trin.	M 1907 A.B. 1910
—	Cha. John	Pem.	M 1899 A.B. 1903. A.M. 1906

Smith,	Cha. Whadcoat ...... Qu.	M 1905 A.B. 1908. A.M. 1912
—	Chris. Will. Winwood Sid.	M 1912
—	Clarence Montague ... Qu.	M 1905 A.B. 1911
—	Claude Soutter ...... Em.	M 1910
—	Clive Le Blanc ...... Pem.	M 1901
—	Cyril Fra. .... Sid.	M 1910
—	Cyril Ja. .... Chr.	M 1907
--	Dav. Barclay Mellis Em.	M 1905 A.B. 1908
—	Douglas .... Em.	M 1901 A.B. 1904
—	Edgar Tho. Goldwin N. C.	M 1897 A.B. 1903
—	Edm. Hastings ..... Qu.	M 1906 A.B. 1909
—	Edw. Boys .... Trin.	M 1893 A.B. 1896. A.M. 1905
—	Edw. Harold .... N. C.	M 1912
—	Edw. Harry .... Joh.	M 1908 A.B. 1911
—	Eric Montague ...... King's	M 1909 A.B. 1912
—	Eric Percival .... Cai.	M 1910
—	Ern. Ja. .... King's	M 1899 A.B., LL.B. 1902. A.M. 1909
—	Ern. Whately .... Cai.	M 1901 A.B. 1904. A.M. 1911
—	Evelyn Fre. .... King's	M 1909 A.B. 1912
—	Everard .... Cai.	M 1904 A.B. 1907. A.M. 1911
—	Fra. Alfonso .... Trin. H.	M 1907
—	Fra. Barry .... Jes.	M 1910
—	Fra. Edwin .... N. C.	M 1909 A.B. 1912
—	Fra. Geo. .... Cla.	M 1898 A.B. 1901
—	Fra. Hen. .... Chr.	M 1901 A.B. 1904
—	Frank .... Em.	M 1910 A.B. 1912
—	Frank Harold .... Pem.	M 1909 A.B. 1912
—	Frederic Ern. .... Cath.	M 1896 A.B. 1899. A.M. 1908
—	Frederic Hen. Hamilton Cla.	M 1906 A.B. 1909. LL.B. 1910
—	Fre. Cha. .... Trin. H.	M 1886 A.B., LL.B. 1889. A.M., LL.M.
		[1893. LL.D. 1902
—	Fre. Sam. .... C. C.	M 1893 A.B. 1896. A.M. 1903
—	Fredric Battinson ... King's	M 1906 A.B. 1909
—	Geoffrey Wilfred Melson Trin.	M 1907 A.B. 1911
—	Geo. Adam	*Litt.D.* 1910
—	Geo. Alf. Cha. ...... Jes.	M 1899 A.B. 1903. A.M. 1912
—	Geo. Cha. Moore ... Joh.	M 1877 A.B.1881. A.M.1884. Litt.D. 1907
—	Geo. Ern. .... Joh.	M 1912
—	Geo. Reg. .... C. C.	M 1902 A.B. 1905
—	Gerald Howard ...... Trin.	M 1899 A.B. 1902
—	Gerald Lionel .... N. C.	M 1906 A.B. 1909
—·	Grafton Elliot ....*Joh.	M 1896 A.B. 1898. A.M.† 1903
—	Graham Burrell ...... King's	M 1899 A.B. 1902. A.M. 1909
—	Graham Udale ...... Joh.	M 1901
—	Hallidie Hen. Montague Pem.	M 1910
—	Harold .... Trin. H.	M 1902 A.B. 1905
—	Harold .... Em.	M 1912
—	Harold Bentley ...... Joh.	M 1898 A.B. 1901
—	Harold Earnshaw ... Chr.	M 1910
—	Harold John .... Sid.	M 1897 A.B. 1900. A.M. 1904
—	Harold Rob. .... Trin.	M 1896 A.B. 1899. A.M. 1908
—	Harry Edgar .... Cai.	M 1910
—	Harry Edw. .... Cai.	M 1883 A.B. 1886. A.M. 1890. M.B., B.C.
—	Harry Percival ...... Qu.	M 1912 [1891. Mus.B. 1911
—	Hen. Leon. Chappell Qu.	M 1910
—	Howard .... Joh.	M 1910
—	Hugh Vandewall ... Trin.	M 1899 A.B. 1902
—	Ian McNaughton ... Qu.	M 1909 A.B. 1912
—	Ja. Fra. Hardy ...... Cla.	M 1906 A.B. 1909
—	Ja. Norman Douglas King's	M 1907
—	Jeffery Pet. Fre. Hanworth Jes.	M 1905 A.B. 1908

Smith,	Jerome Ledward	Pem.	M 1897 A.B. 1900. A.M. 1904
—	Johannes Michel	Chr.	M 1899 A.B. 1902. B.C.† 1906. M.B.†
—	John	H. Sel.	M 1899 A.B. 1903. A.M. 1906 [1912
—	John Alex. Hay	Pem.	M 1909 A.B., LL.B. 1912
—	John Forbes	Joh.	M 1905 A.B. 1908. LL.B. 1909
—	John Gordon	Em.	M 1908 A.B. 1911
—	John Herb. Michael	Trin.	M 1908
—	John Hughes Bennett	Cai.	M 1904
—	John Lister	Sid.	M 1908 A.B. 1911
—	John Stores	Cath.	M 1911
—	John Turner	C. C.	M 1912
—	Jos.	Chr.	M 1912
—	Jos. Frank	H. Sel.	M 1904
—	Jos. Hugh	N. C.	M 1897 Pet. A.B. 1900. A.M. 1904
—	Jos. Stanley	Mag.	M 1900 A.B. 1903. A.M. 1908
—	Kenneth Percival	Cai.	M 1912
—	Lancelot	Em.	M 1904 A.B. 1907
—	Laurence Willoughby	Cai.	M 1899 A.B. 1903
—	Leon. Danvers	Joh.	M 1907 A.B., LL.B. 1910
—	Lucius Palmer	Qu.	M 1897 A.B. 1900. A.M. 1904
—	Matth. Will.	H. Sel.	M 1900 A.B. 1903. A.M. 1910
—	Montague Vivian	Trin. H.	M 1900 A.B. 1903
—	Mowbray	Qu.	M 1898 A.B. 1901. A.M. 1906
—	Neil Campbell	Pem.	M 1906 A.B. 1909
—	Neville Hardcastle	Cla.	M 1908 A.B. 1912
—	Norman Cha.	H. Sel.	M 1907 A.B. 1910
—	Norman Hamilton	Trin. H.	M 1903 A.B., LL.B. 1906
—	Oliver Martin	Trin.	M 1904
—	Oscar Jeffcoat	C. C.	M 1909 A.B. 1912
—	Oswald Carlton	Joh.	M 1906 A.B. 1909
—	Percival Frere	Cai.	M 1899 A.B., LL.B. 1902
—	Percy Hall	Pem.	M 1899 A.B. 1902. post Hall-Smith, P.
—	Pet.	Trin.	M 1912 [A.M. 1907. B.C. 1908. M.D.
—	Rich.	Trin.	M 1910 [1911
—	Rob. Edm.	Em.	M 1899 A.B. 1902
—	Rob. Parker	Cath.	M 1900 Parker Smith, R. A.B. 1903. A.M.
—	Rob. Syd. Steele	Trin.	M 1909 [1907
—	Rob. Workman	Trin.	M 1902 A.B. 1905
—	Robin Snowdon	Chr.	M 1906 A.B. 1909
—	Rocksborough Remington	H. Sel.	M 1896 A.B. 1899. A.M. 1903
—	Roland Audley	Trin.	M 1906 A.B. 1909
—	Roy	Trin. H.	M 1910
—	Sam. Harold	Cai.	M 1907 A.B. 1910. LL.B. 1911
—	Sam. Hood	King's	M 1905 A.B. 1908
—	Sam. Percy	Cai.	M 1907 A.B., LL.B. 1910
—	Sergius	Trin.	M 1910
—	Sid.	Qu.	M 1908 A.B. 1911
—	Sid. Herb. Courtney	Cath.	E 1909
—	Solomon Cha. Kaines	Mag.	M 1895 A.B. 1898. A.M. 1902
—	Stanley	Cla.	M 1910 A.B. 1912
—	Stanley Gordon	Pet.	M 1905 A.B. 1908
—	Stanley Peregrine	Trin.	M 1879 A.B. 1883. A.M. 1902
—	Stanley Tho.	H. Sel.	M 1904 A.B. 1907. A.M. 1911
—	Steph. Berthold	Trin.	M 1909
—	Tho.	N. C.	M 1909 Cai. A.B. 1912
—	Tho.	Qu.	M 1902 A.B. 1905
—	Tho. Alex.	N. C.	M 1903
—	Tho. De	Jes.	M 1894 A.B. 1897. A.M. 1901
—	Tho. Leslie	Cai.	M 1911
—	Tho. Perceval	Pem.	M 1895 A.B. 1898. A.M. 1903
—	Walt.	Cla.	M 1902 A.B. 1905

Smith,	Walt. Austen Neumann	Mag.	M 1912
—	Walt. Campbell	C. C.	M 1906 A.B. 1910
—	Walt. Whately	King's	M 1911
—	Welborn Owston	Trin.	M 1906 A.B. 1909
—	Will. Alf.	Pem.	M 1899 A.B. 1902
—	Will. Art. Worsop ...	Cla.	M 1897 A.B. 1900. A.M. 1904
—	Will. d'Alton	Cai.	M 1903 A.B. 1908
—	Will. Edw.	Cai.	M 1911
—	Will. Faulder	Trin. H.	M 1905
—	Will. Fra.	H. Sel.	M 1899 A.B. 1902
—	Will. Geo.	H. Sel.	M 1894 A.B. 1897. A.M. 1902
—	Will. Gerald Furness	Cla.	M 1907 A.B. 1910
—	Will. Hammond	Sid.	M 1904 A.B. 1907
—	Will. Hen.	Chr.	M 1905
—	Will. Humphrey	Jes.	M 1898 A.B. 1901
—	Will. Ja.	Sid.	M 1906
Smith-Barry,	Rob.	Trin.	M 1904
Smith-Carington,	Art. Eric Conder	Chr.	M 1909 A.B. 1912
—	Michael Conder Harewell	Jes.	M 1905
Smith-Rewse,	Hen. Gilb.	Em.	M 1907
Smith-Sligo,	Ronald Will. Mary } Gerard Jos. }	Trin. H.	M 1911
Smyly,	Alex. Ferguson	Pem.	M 1905 A.B. 1908
—	Cecil Ferguson	Trin. H.	M 1903 A.B. 1906
Smyth,	Austin Edw. Art. Watt *Trin.		M 1896 A.B. 1899. A.M. 1903
—	Basil Broughton	H. Sel.	L 1888 Chr. A.B. 1890. A.M. 1906
—	Hen. Maxwell	Pem.	M 1897 A.B. 1908
—	John Will.	Cla.	M 1899 A.B. 1902
—	John Will. Wallace	C. C.	M 1893 A.B. 1896. A.M. 1901
—	Jos. Haslegrave	Qu.	M 1891 A.B. 1895. A.M. 1906
—	Syd. Sherwood	Jes.	M 1911
—	Will. Hen.	Cla.	M 1906 A.B. 1909
—	Will. Ja. Dobson ...	Pem.	M 1904 A.B. 1907
—	Will. Rowland Beatty	Pem.	M 1912
Smythe,	Dav.	Jes.	M 1910
—	Gerald Art.	Em.	M 1906 A.B. 1909
Smythies,	Evelyn Art.	Chr.	M 1904
Snaith,	Eric Geo.	Mag.	M 1911
Snape,	Harold John	Chr.	M 1894 A.B. 1897. A.M. 1901
—	Rob. Hugh	Em.	M 1905 A.B. 1908. A.M. 1912
—	Will. Rich. Claude ...	Qu.	M 1909 A.B. 1912
Sneath,	Art.	Joh.	M 1903 A.B. 1906
—	Rupert Ern. Fowler	Pem.	M 1911
—	Will.	Joh.	M 1897 A.B. 1901
Snelgrove,	Sid. Hen.	Trin.	M 1910
Snell,	Fra. Saxon	King's	M 1906 A.B. 1909 [1911
—	Hen. Cecil	Cai.	M 1901 A.B. 1904. A.M. 1908. M.B., B.C.
—	Ja. Eric Boobbyer ...	Cai.	M 1895 A.B. 1898. M.B., B.C., A.M. 1902
—	John Aubrey Brooking	Cai.	M 1908 A.B. 1911
Snelling,	Edw. Cha. Colyer ...	Cla.	M 1903
Sneyd-Kynnersley,	Clem. Gerald	Mag.	M 1907
Snow,	John Hen.	Pet.	M 1895 A.B. 1898. A.M. 1909
Snowden,	Art. de Winton	Chr.	M 1891 A.B. 1894. A.M. 1901. M.B., B.C. [1902. M.D. 1905
Soady,	Sid. John	Cla.	M 1876 A.B. 1880. A.M. 1904
Soames,	Art. Lancelot	Trin.	M 1896 A.B. 1899. A.M. 1904
—	Fra. Werner	Chr.	M 1896 A.B. 1899. A.M. 1907
—	John Beecroft	Trin.	M 1902
—	Ralph Martin	Trin.	M 1901 A.B. 1905. M.B., B.C. 1911
—	Will. Noël	Trin. H.	M 1907
Soda,	Küchiro	N. C.	M 1904

Soden,	Wilfred Scovil	Joh.	M 1907 A.B. 1910	
Solms-Laubach, Hermann Graf zu			*Sc.D.* 1909	
Solomon,	Bertie Art.	Pem.	M 1904	
—	Cha. Gordon Ross ...	Trin. H.	E 1904 A.B., LL.B. 1908	
Somers-Clarke, Geoffrey		Cai.	M 1899 A.B. 1902	
Somers Cocks, Reg.		Pem.	M 1912	
Somerset,	Art. Plantagenet Fra. ⎱ Cecil ⎰	Jes.	M 1908	
—	Raglan Horatio Edwyn Hen.	Qu.	M 1904 A.B. 1907	
Somervell,	Arnold Colin	King's	M 1902 A.B. 1905	
—	Art.	N. C.	M 1880 King's A.B. 1884. Mus.D. 1904	
—	Leon. Colin	King's	M 1906 A.B. 1909	
—	Theodore Howard ...	Cai.	M 1909 A.B. 1912	
Somerville,	Cha. Dudley Brooks	Jes.	M 1892 A.B. 1895. A.M. 1901	
—	Kenneth Brooks	Cla.	M 1909	
—	Tho.	Em.	M 1897 A.B. 1900. LL.B. 1901. A.M. 1904	
Sommer,	John Will. Ern.	Cai.	M 1900 A.B. 1903	
Sondhi,	Guru Datt	Trin.	M 1911	
Song Ong Siang		Down.	M 1890 A.B., LL.B. 1893. A.M.†, LL.M.†	
Soni,	Ranbir Chand	Trin.	M 1912	[1901
Sonnenthal,	Hen. Max	Pem.	M 1907	
Soole,	Warwick Bathurst ...	Cath.	M 1898 A.B. 1902. A.M. 1906	
Soothill,	Victor Farrar	Em.	M 1906 A.B. 1909	
—	Will. Edw.		*A.M.* 1911	
Soper,	Ronald Garland	Trin.	M 1906	
Sopwith,	Syd. Shelford	Em.	M 1905 A.B. 1908. A.M. 1912	
Sorabji,	Irach Jehangir	N. C.	M 1911	
Sorby,	Will. Austin	Cla.	M 1912	
Sorley,	Gerald Merson	Cla.	M 1910	
—	¹ Will. Ritchie ....*Trin.		L 1880 A.B. 1883. A.M. 1886. *King's	
Sothers,	Edw. Dudley	Joh.	M 1911	[Litt.D. 1905
Soulby,	Tho. Harding	King's	M 1903 A.B. 1906. A.M. 1910	
Souper,	Adrian Wilfrid Ja. ...	Qu.	M 1907 A.B. 1910	
—	Noel Beaumont	Joh.	M 1899 A.B. 1902	
Soutar,	Alan Ker	Em.	M 1905 A.B. 1909	
South,	Fra. Wilton	Em.	M 1904 A.B. 1907	
Southam,	John Fra. Lovel	Joh.	M 1898 A.B., LL.B. 1901. A.M. 1905	
Southern,	Hugh	Pem.	M 1905 A.B. 1908. A.M.† 1912	
—	Norman	King's	M 1903 A.B. 1906. LL.B. 1908. A.M. 1910	
Southerns,	Leon.	Em.	M 1908 A.B. 1910	
Southgate,	Alb. Will.	N. C.	M 1898 Pet. A.B. 1901	
Southward,	Walt. Chris. Bartlett	Jes.	M 1911	
Southwell,	Fre. Edm. Glanville	Cath.	M 1908 A.B. 1911	
—	Harry Maxwell	Cla.	M 1910	
—	Rich. Vynne ....*Trin.		M 1907 A.B. 1910	
Southworth,	Reg. Edw.	Trin. H.	M 1910	
Sowden,	John Russell	Trin. H.	M 1906 A.B., LL.B. 1910	
Sowels,	Frank	Chr.	M 1895 A.B. 1898. A.M. 1902	
Sowerbutts,	Rich.	N. C.	M 1909 Cath. A.B. 1912	
Sowter,	Art. Cha.	Qu.	M 1907 A.B. 1910	
Spackman,	Eric Dickins	Qu.	M 1912	
—	Harold Cha.	Cai.	M 1907 A.B. 1910	
—	Harry Maurice	Joh.	M 1911	
Spalding,	Percy John	Jes.	M 1896 A.B. 1899. LL.M. 1903	
Spanton,	Alf. Temple	Trin.	M 1894 A.B. 1897. A.M. 1902	
Spargo,	Fre. Wilson	Joh.	M 1907 A.B. 1910	
Spark,	Durbin Sanderson ...	Em.	M 1911	
Sparke,	Ja. Berthon	Cla.	M 1904 A.B. 1907. LL.B. 1908. A.M. 1911	
Sparks,	Cedric Harold	Joh.	M 1911	

¹ Knightbridge Professor of Moral Philosophy, 1900.

Sparling,	Hart Phil.	Qu.	M 1908 A.B. 1911
—	Wilfred Hugh	Qu.	M 1910
Sparrow,	Edw. Cyril	Trin.	M 1897 A.B. 1900. M.B., B.C., A.M. 1908
—	Geoffrey	Cai.	M 1905 A.B. 1908
—	Hen. Edw.	Chr.	M 1892 A.B. 1895. A.M. 1903
Sparrow Simpson,	Will. John	Trin.	M 1878 A.B. 1882. A.M. 1885. B.D. 1909.
Sparshatt,	Wyndham Hen.	H. Sel.	M 1902 A.B. 1905 [D.D. 1911
Spartali,	Cyril	Trin.	M 1907
Späth,	Hellmut Ludwig	Trin.	M 1907
Speakman,	Laurence Art.	Cai.	M 1903 A.B. 1906. A.M. 1910
Spear,	Geo. Fre.	Qu.	M 1898 A.B. 1901. LL.B. 1902. A.M. 1905
Spearing,	Edw.	Em.	M 1908 A.B. 1911. LL.B. 1912 [1907
Spearman,	Barugh	Cai.	M 1896 A.B. 1899. M.B., B.C. 1902. A.M.
—	Rob.	Cai.	M 1895 A.B. 1898. M.B., B.C. 1902. A.M.
—	Will.	Cai.	M 1900 A.B. 1903. A.M. 1907 [1903
Specht,	Johannes Karl August Herrmann }	Trin. H.	E 1906
Speer,	Will. Hen.	Trin.	M 1883 A.B. 1886. Mus.B., A.M. 1890.
Speir,	Kenneth Rob. Napier	Pem.	M 1901 [Mus.D. 1906
Spence,	Cha. Bennett	Pem.	M 1907 A.B. 1910
—	Douglas Leigh	H. Sel.	M 1905 A.B. 1908
—	Kenneth Graham Lionel Brooke }	Em.	M 1906 A.B. 1909
—	Rich. Bennett	Cai.	M 1901
Spencer,	Beckwith Alex.	King's	M 1897 A.B. 1901. A.M. 1908
—	Cha. Hen.	Qu.	M 1894 A.B. 1897. A.M. 1901
—	Gerald Theodosius Leigh	Trin.	M 1902 A.B., LL.B. 1905
—	Gordon Winstanley	Joh.	M 1907 A.B. 1910
—	Herb.	Qu.	M 1911
—	Hub.	Cath.	M 1907 A.B. 1910
—	Lawrence Douglas Winstanley }	Chr.	M 1896 A.B. 1899. A.M. 1903
—	Rob.	Cla.	M 1901 A.B. 1912
—	Tho. Barton Winstanley	Jes.	M 1902 A.B. 1905
—	Tho. Dever	Trin.	M 1909 A.B. 1912
Spencer-Hogbin, Fre.		Em.	M 1908 A.B. 1911
Spencer-Smith, Arnold Pat.		Qu.	M 1903 A.B. 1907
—	Phil.	Qu.	M 1901 A.B. 1904. A.M. 1909
Spens,	Hugh Baird	King's	M 1904 A.B. 1907
—	Will.	King's	M 1901 A.B. 1905. *C.C. 1907. A.M. 1908
Spero,	Leopold	Sid.	M 1907 A.B. 1910
Spicer,	Douglas	Trin.	M 1901 A.B. 1904. A.M. 1908
—	Eric Evan	Trin.	M 1912
—	Gerald Evan	Trin.	M 1909 A.B. 1912
—	Hen. Wallis	Jes.	M 1909
—	John Evan	Trin.	M 1894 A.B. 1897. M.B., B.C., A.M. 1903.
—	Lancelot Dykes	Trin.	M 1912 [M.D. 1908
—	Malcolm	Trin. H.	M 1902 A.B. 1905
—	Norman	Trin. H.	M 1899 A.B. 1903
—	Ronald	Trin.	M 1904 A.B. 1907. A.M. 1911
Spielmann,	Claude Meyer	King's	M 1907 A.B. 1910
—	Harold Lionel Isidore	Pem.	M 1911
Spiers,	Archib. Lionel Clive	Trin.	M 1903 A.B. 1906
—	Ern. Isidore	Qu.	M 1902 A.B. 1906
—	Hen. Michael	Cai.	M 1911
Spikes,	Walt. Herb.	C. C.	M 1909 A.B. 1912
Spiller,	Leon.	Qu.	M 1909 A.B. 1912
Spilsbury,	Leon. Joy	Em.	M 1903 A.B. 1906
Spink,	Cecil Cooper	Sid.	M 1910
—	Jos. Fenner	Joh.	M 1901 A.B. 1904. A.M. 1908
Spinks,	Geo. Tuke	Trin. H.	M 1907 A.B. 1910

Spinney,	Montague Herb.	H. Sel.	M 1906 A.B., Mus.B. 1909
Spiritus,	Friedrich August Paul	Chr.	E 1904
Spittall,	Alex. Buchanan	Chr.	M 1901 A.B. 1904. A.M. 1908
Spittle,	John Trevor ....*Pem.		M 1905 A.B. 1908. A.M. 1912
—	Tho. Stanley	Cla.	M 1903 A.B. 1906. A.M. 1912
Spong,	Ja. Leon.	Sid.	M 1898 A.B. 1902
Spooner,	Will.	N. C.	M 1911
—	Will. Wycliffe	Trin.	M 1899 A.B. 1902
Spoor,	Art. Twynham	Em.	M 1912
Spowart,	Will. Carl	Qu.	M 1908
Spragg,	Cha. Edw. Wright ...	Trin.	M 1911
Spragge,	Fra. Basil Brook ...	Trin.	M 1911
Sprake,	Leslie Cecil	Trin. H.	M 1904 A.B. 1907
Spranger,	John Alf.	Trin.	M 1908 A.B. 1911
Spratt,	Herb. Ja.	Sid.	M 1893 A.B. 1896. Trin. H. A.M. 1907
Sprigg,	Hen. Aldwin Guildford	Trin.	M 1901 A.B. 1904
Sprigge,	Sam. Squire	Cai.	M 1878 A.B. 1882. M.B., B.C. 1887. M.D.,
Spring,	Alb.	Pet.	M 1906 A.B. 1909　　　[A.M. 1904
—	Eric	Sid.	M 1910
Springmann,	John Blanchard	Trin.	M 1910
Spring Rice,	Cha.	Trin.	M 1906
—	Edw. Dominick	King's	M 1909 A.B. 1912
Sprott,	Maur. Will. Campbell	Pet.	M 1906 A.B. 1909
Sproule,	Fre.	Trin. H.	M 1911
Sproxton,	Cha.	Pet.	M 1909 A.B. 1912
Spry,	Cha. Gordon	Cath.	M 1899 A.B. 1902. A.M. 1906
—	Hen. Ern.	Sid.	M 1899 A.B. 1902
Spurgin,	Rob. Geo. Lancelot	C. C.	M 1901 A.B. 1907
Spurrier,	Harry	Cai.	M 1894 A.B. 1897. M.B., B.C. 1905
Squire,	Alf. Morgan	Chr.	M 1901 A.B. 1904
—	Cha. Edw.	Trin.	M 1908 A.B. 1911
—	Hen. Fremlin	Cai.	M 1912
—	John Collings	Joh.	M 1903 A.B. 1906
—	Sam. Gimson	Chr.	M 1898 A.B. 1901. A.M. 1905
—	Will. Barclay	Pem.	M 1875 A.B. 1879. A.M. 1902
Squires,	Cha. Stephenson	Cai.	M 1907 LL.B. 1910　　[1903. D.D. 1908
Srawley,	Ja. Herb.	Cai.	M 1888 A.B. 1891. A.M. 1895. H.Sel. B.D.
Stable,	Jerem. Jos.	Em.	M 1902 A.B. 1905. A.M. 1910
Stackard,	Steph. Frank Cyril	King's	M 1911
Stackhouse,	John Hall	Pet.	M 1908
Staerker,	Hermann Edw.	Pem.	M 1912
Stafford,	Geo. Brabazon	Jes.	M 1908 A.B. 1912
—	Harry Neville	Cai.	M 1909 A.B. 1912
—	John Hugh	Cath.	M 1895 A.B. 1898. A.M. 1902. LL.B. 1905
—	Ronald Seymour Sempill Howard	Jes.	M 1909 A.B. 1912
Staffurth,	Alan Edw.	Sid.	M 1906
—	Sam. Fra.	Pem.	M 1891 A.B. 1894. A.M. 1903
Stagg,	Cecil	Cai.	M 1901 A.B. 1904. A.M. 1908
Staines,	Ja. Howard	Sid.	M 1884 A.B. 1887. A.M. 1906
Stainsby,	Herb. Hen.	H. Sel.	M 1908 A.B. 1911
Staley,	Hen. Samble	Em.	M 1905 A.B. 1908. A.M. 1912
—	Ja. Edwin	N. C.	M 1904 A.B. 1907. A.M. 1911
Stallard,	Geo. Victor	Cai.	M 1906 A.B. 1909
—	Hugh Kitson	Pem.	M 1894 A.B. 1897. A.M. 1901
—	Phil. Lechmere	Cai.	M 1899 A.B. 1902. A.M. 1909
Stammers,	Fre. Dighton	C. C.	M 1896 A.B. 1899. A.M. 1903
Stamper,	Edwin Poulden Fenton	Jes.	M 1905
Stancomb,	John Mortimer Duniam	Em.	M 1908 A.B. 1911
Standfast,	Cecil	C. C.	M 1900 A.B. 1904
Standidge,	Cecil	H. Sel.	M 1898 A.B. 1901

Standish,	Geoffrey Norton	......	H. Sel.	M 1899 A.B. 1902
—	Harold	....	H. Sel.	M 1902 A.B. 1905
Stanfield,	Alf. Vivian	....	Cla.	M 1903 A.B. 1906. A.M. 1911
Stanford,	Herb. Claude	....	Joh.	M 1904 A.B. 1907
Stanford-Szewlinski, John Hen.	...	N. C.	E 1901
Stanham,	Cha. Taylor	....	Joh.	M 1910
Stanhope,	Rob. Melodew	....	Sid.	M 1905 A.B. 1908
Stanier,	Harold	....	Joh.	M 1912
Stanley,	Alan Wroughton ⎱ Wentworth ⎰		Trin.	M 1909
—	Cha. Milner	....	H. Sel.	M 1904 A.B. 1907
—	Edm. Stewart	....	King's	M 1910
—	Edw. John	....	Trin.	M 1897 A.B. 1902. A.M.† 1906
—	Percival	....	Cath.	M 1896 A.B. 1903. A.M. 1907
—	Will.	....	Qu.	M 1894 A.B. 1897. A.M. 1901
Stanley-Clarke, Crispian	....	Cai.	M 1898 A.B. 1901. M.B., B.C. 1908
Stanners,	Rob. Whitfield	......	Cai.	M 1911
Stanning,	Cha. Gordon	....	Trin.	M 1903
Stansbury,	Chris. Geoffrey	......	Trin. H.	M 1903 A.B. 1906. A.M. 1911
Stansfeld,	Alf. Ellington	....	Joh.	M 1902 A.B. 1905. B.C. 1909. M.B., A.M.
—	Cecil Alf.	....	Jes.	M 1910 [1911
—	Geo. Reg.	....	Trin.	M 1889 A.B., LL.B. 1893. A.M. 1901
—	Rex	....	Joh.	M 1907 A.B. 1910
Stansfield,	John	....	Em.	M 1904 A.B. 1907
—	Wilfrid Willard Hartley	Chr.	M 1902
Stanton,	Ja. Vincent	....	Joh.	M 1902
Stapledon,	Gerald	....	Em.	M 1896 A.B., LL.B. 1899. A.M. 1903
—	Reg. Geo.	....	Em.	M 1901 A.B. 1904. A.M. 1908
Stapler,	Ja. Beverley	....	Chr.	M 1908 A.B. 1911
Staples-Browne, Rich. Cha.	....	Em.	M 1899 A.B. 1902. A.M. 1906
Stapleton,	Edw. Parker	....	Pem.	M 1908 A.B. 1911
Starck,	Herb. Phil.	....	N. C.	M 1912
Starey,	Augustin Helps	......	H. Sel.	M 1904 A.B. 1907
—	Leon.	....	Cla.	M 1900 A.B. 1903. A.M. 1909
Starkey,	Hen. Sam. Crichton	Down.	M 1904 A.B. 1907. M.B. 1910
Starkie,	Rich. Pat. Aloysius	Trin.	M 1908 A.B. 1911
Starling, Edwin Cyril Widmerpoole	Jes.	M 1907 A.B. 1910
—	Geo.	....	N. C.	L 1908
Starte,	Horace Wilderspin	...	Cla.	M 1907
—	Oliver Harold Baptist	Cla.	M 1901 A.B. 1904
Statham,	Heathcote Dicken	...	Cai.	M 1908 Mus.B. 1911
—	Herb. Purefoy	....	King's	M 1899 A.B. 1902. A.M. 1907
—	Hugh	....	Chr.	M 1895 A.B. 1898. B.C. 1903. M.B. 1905
—	Noel Horner	....	Trin. H.	M 1912
—	Randulph Meverell	...	Pet.	M 1909 A.B. 1912
Stathers,	Geo. Syd.	....	Trin.	M 1907
—	Gerald Nicholson	...	Trin.	M 1904
Staveley,	Claude Harold	....	Cla.	M 1907 A.B. 1911
—	Herb. Will.	....	Pem.	M 1904 A.B. 1907
—	Hugh Sheardown	...	Jes.	M 1907 A.B., LL.B. 1910
—	Leslie Hodder Barrett	Qu.	M 1910
Stavers,	Will. Mackey	....	Chr.	M 1911
Stead,	Gilb.	....	Cla.	M 1906 A.B. 1909
—	Herb. Alf.	....	Em.	M 1897 A.B. 1901. A.M. 1904
—	John	....	King's	M 1903 A.B. 1906. A.M. 1911
—	Will. Ja. Victor	......	Joh.	M 1904 A.B. 1907. A.M. 1911
Steane,	Sam. Will.	....	Trin.	M 1904 A.B. 1908
Stearn,	Alf. John Steed	......	N. C.	M 1908 A.B. 1911
—	Clem. Hodgson	......	Qu.	M 1907 A.B. 1910
Steavenson,	Archib. Graham	......	Pem.	M 1905 A.B. 1908. A.M. 1912
Stebbing,	Cha. Ferdinand	......	Jes.	M 1899 A.B. 1902. A.M. 1906

Stebbing,	Fra. Augustine	Qu.	M 1899 A.B. 1902. A.M. 1910
—	Tho. Hen. Langdale	Qu.	M 1909 A.B. 1912
Stedall,	Geoffrey St George ...	Jes.	M 1911
Steed,	Fre. Augustus	N. C.	M 1899 A. F. Trin. H. A.B. 1905. A.M.
Steedman,	Mackenzie Thwaites } Wills	Cla.	M 1907 A.B. 1910 [1909
Steel,	Harry Fra.	Qu.	M 1902 A.B. 1905. A.M. 1909
—	Jos.	Trin.	M 1904
—	Owen Will. Dyne ...	Em.	M 1905
—	Sam. Strang	Trin.	M 1900 A.B. 1903. A.M. 1908
Steele,	John Wheatley	Trin. H.	M 1901 A.B. 1904
—	Rob. Balfour	King's	M 1909
Steen,	Will. Peile	N. C.	M 1896 Chr. A.B. 1899. A.M. 1903
Steichen,	Adolf	N. C.	M 1904
Steimann,	Bern. Benj.	Joh.	M 1910
Stein,	Mark Aurel		*Sc.D.* 1910
—	Phil.	Cai.	M 1910
Steinfeld,	István	Trin.	M 1909
Steinmetz,	John Baptist	N. C.	M 1911
Stenhouse,	John Maitland	Sid.	M 1897 A.B. 1900. B.C. 1903. M.B. 1904
Stenning,	Ern. Hen.	H. Sel.	M 1896 A.B. 1903. A.M. 1907
—	Ern. Hen.	Down.	M 1906 A.B. 1909
Stephan,	Hen. John Cha.	Trin. H.	M 1903
Stephen,	Adrian Leslie	Trin.	M 1902 A.B. 1905
—	Alex. Murray	King's	M 1911
—	Allan Farquhar	Cla.	M 1907 A.B., LL.B. 1910
—	Dan. Rushton	Pem.	M 1904 A.B. 1907. A.M. 1911
—	Fre. Cha.	Em.	M 1909 A.B. 1912
—	Harry Leslie	Trin.	M 1878 LL.B. 1882. LL.M.† 1904
—	Julian Thoby	Trin.	M 1899 A.B. 1902
Stephens,	Art. Ralph	C. C.	M 1897 A.B. 1902. A.M. 1905
—	Dav.	N. C.	M 1906 A.B. 1909
—	Edw. Cha.	Qu.	L 1898 A.B. 1902. A.M. 1906
—	Ern. Aitken	N. C.	M 1899 C. C. A.B. 1903. A.M. 1907
—	John Frė. Douglas ...	Pem.	M 1885 A.B. 1888. A.M. 1902
—	John Oliver	N. C.	M 1909
—	John Phillips	N. C.	M 1908 A.B. 1912
—	John Sturge	Joh.	M 1910
—	Pet. Stuart	Trin.	M 1898 A.B. 1901
Stephenson,	Art. John	C. C.	M 1900 A.B. 1903
—	Cyril Heath	Cla.	M 1907 A.B. 1910
—	Denys Geo.	Trin.	M 1901 A.B. 1905
—	Herb.	N. C.	M 1909 A.B. 1912
—	Humphrey Meigh ...	Cai.	M 1906 A.B. 1909
—	Rob.	Pem.	M 1894 A.B. 1897. A.M. 1901
—	Rob.		*A.M.* 1905
—	Tho. Grange	Sid.	M 1904
Sterckeman,	Pierre	Down.	M 1909
Sterling,	Tho. Smith	Down.	M 1905 A.B. 1908. A.M.† 1912
Stern,	Geo.	N. C.	L 1911
—	John	C. C.	M 1898 A.B. 1901. A.M. 1905
—	Leon. Herman	Mag.	M 1910
—	Nathan	Joh.	M 1901
Sternberg,	Edgar Adolphus Josef	Trin. H.	M 1908
—	Rupert Oswald	Cla.	M 1911
Sterndale-Bennett,	Ja. Bury	Joh.	M 1907
—	John	Joh.	M 1897 A.B. 1906
—	Rob.	Joh.	M 1901 A.B. 1904. A.M. 1908
Stevens,	Cecil Ja. Duff	Trin.	M 1911
—	Cha. Geoffrey Buckland	Em.	M 1908 A.B. 1911
—	Frank Bentham	Chr.	M 1899 A.B. 1902. LL.B. 1903

Stevens,	Gilb. Hen.	Cai.	M 1908 A.B. 1911
—	Harry Hastings	Cla.	M 1909 A.B. 1912
—	Herb. Lawrence	Down.	M 1911
—	Hor. Will. Petit	Down.	M 1871 A.B. 1875. A.M. 1878. LL.M. 1896.
—	Hugh Leslie	Qu.	M 1907 A.B. 1910 [LL.D. 1902
—	John Kelland	Joh.	M 1911
—	Leicester Bradney ...	Cai.	M 1904 A.B. 1907. A.M. 1911
—	Rutland Duel	Cai.	M 1904 A.B. 1907. R. Duell A.M. 1911
—	Sid. Herb.	C. C.	M 1906 A.B. 1910 [LL.M. 1901
—	Silas Will.	Joh.	M 1881 A.B., LL.B. 1884 (2). A.M. 1892.
—	Tho.	Mag.	M 1859 A.B. 1863. A.M. 1867. D.D. 1901
—	Will. Geoffrey	Down.	M 1905 A.B. 1908
—	Will. Geo.	Cath.	M 1907 A.B. 1911
Stevenson,	Claude Maberly	Joh.	E 1898 B.C. 1905. M.B. 1907. M.D. 1910
—	Fra. Phil.	Sid.	M 1902 A.B. 1905. A.M. 1910
—	Ja. Kenneth Hewlett	Mag.	M 1911
—	Ronald Will.	Pem.	M 1912
—	Sam. Delano	Trin.	M 1905 A.B. 1908
—	Will. Hen.	N. C.	M 1906
Steward,	Sid. John '..............	Down.	M 1897 M.B., B.C. 1904. M.D. 1910
Stewart,	Alex. Cha.	Pet.	M 1911
—	Alex. Gordon	Em.	M 1907 A.B. 1910
—	Art. Dudley	Trin.	M 1896 A.B. 1900. A.M. 1904
—	Bern. Halley	Jes.	M 1893 A.B. 1896. B.C. 1904. M.B., A.M.
—	Caleb And.	Trin.	M 1909 A.B. 1912 [1908. M.D. 1911
—	Cha. Rob.	H. Sel.	M 1897 A.B. 1900. A.M. 1905
—	Douglas Martin	Joh.	M 1904 A.B. 1907. LL.B. 1908. A.M. 1912
—	Eric Will. Hylton ...	Sid.	M 1905 A.B. 1908. A.M. 1912
—	Fra. Will.	Trin.	M 1904 A.B. 1907
—	Hen. Elliot	Qu.	M 1886 A.B. 1889. A.M. 1904
—	Hugh	Trin.	M 1904 A.B. 1907
—	Hugh Fraser	Trin.	M 1883 A.B. 1886. A.M. 1891. B.D. 1906.
—	Ja. Alex. Logan	Trin.	M 1911 [*Joh. 1907
—	Ja. Will.	N. C.	M 1898 Chr. A.B. 1901
—	Martin	C. C.	M 1904 A.B. 1907
—	Ninian Bannatyne ...	Pem.	M 1910
—	Ronald Ja.	Trin.	M 1911
—	Will. Howard Edwin	Cai.	M 1893 A.B. 1898. A.M. 1902
Stickland,	John Reynolds	Pem.	M 1906 A.B. 1909
Stidston,	Percy Harcourt	Pem.	M 1905 A.B. 1910
Stiebel,	Cha.	Trin. H.	M 1894 M.B. 1904
Stiff,	Harold Hen.	Cai.	M 1892 M.B., B.C. 1902
Stigand,	Ivan Ascanio	Trin.	M 1899 A.B. 1902. A.M. 1907
Stileman,	Cecil Everard Cheere	Qu.	M 1911
—	Cecil Herb.	Pem.	M 1912
—	Douglas Cha. Gibbard	Qu.	M 1908 A.B. 1911
—	Frederic Will. Cheere	Pem.	M 1905 A.B. 1908
Stiles,	Walt.	Em.	M 1905 A.B. 1908. A.M. 1912
Still,	Harold Norman	Chr.	M 1912
—	Will. Herb.	Chr.	M 1910
Stimson,	Cha. Casson	Em.	M 1908 A.B. 1911
—	John Perrott	Pet.	M 1909 A.B. 1912
—	Will. Benj.	Em.	M 1912
Stinson,	Hen. John Edwin ...	Em.	M 1905 A.B., LL.B. 1908. A.M. 1912
Stirling,	Edw. Cha.	Trin.	M 1866 A.B. 1870. A.M. 1873. M.B. 1874.
—	Ern. Morgan	Cai.	M 1901 A.B. 1904 [M.D. 1880. Sc.D.†1910
—	Fra. Purser Holbrooke	Em.	M 1900 A.B. 1903
—	Gordon Sheffield	Cla.	M 1905 A.B., LL.B. 1908
Stirling-Hamilton,	John	Jes.	M 1892 A.B. 1896. M.B., B.C., A.M. 1904
Stiven,	Harold Edw. Sutherland	Trin.	M 1902 A.B. 1905. B.C., A.M. 1909. M.B.
Stobart,	John Clarke	Trin.	M 1897 A.B. 1901. A.M. 1904 [1911

Stobart,	John Geoffrey	Pem.	M 1910
—	Will.	Jes.	M 1912
Stock,	Clarence Sid.	Cla.	M 1910
—	Geo. Steph; August	Pem.	M 1902
—	Will. Lievesley	H. Cav.	E 1885 Pet. A.B. 1888. A.M. 1908
Stockdale,	Frank Art.	Mag.	M 1901 A.B. 1904. A.M. 1912
Stocker,	Cha. Ja.	Trin.	M 1904 A.B. 1907. M.B., B.C. 1911
—	Hub. Goodman	Trin.	M 1901 A.B. 1906
Stocks,	Art. Vernon	Joh.	M 1907 A.B. 1910
—	Percy	King's	L 1908 A.B. 1910
Stockwell,	Geo. Ephraim St Clair	King's	M 1895 A.B. 1898. B.C. 1902. M.B. 1904
Stockwood,	Illtyd Hen.	Joh.	M 1911
Stoddard,	John Wilkie	Jes.	M 1902 A.B. 1907
Stoddart,	Ja. Roylance	Joh.	M 1907
—	Will.	N. C.	M 1871 A.B. 1876. A.M. 1904
Stoffel,	Charley	Sid.	M 1911
Stogdon,	Fra. Roe	Cla.	M 1897 A.B. 1901
Stokes,	Art. Barnard	Qu.	M 1893 A.B. 1896. A.M.† 1902
—	Cosby Hudleston ...	Joh.	M 1899 A.B. 1902. A.M. 1910
—	Evan Fraser	King's	M 1911
—	Frederic Frank	Trin.	M 1899 A.B. 1902
—	Fre. Will.	Chr.	M 1898 A.B. 1901
—	Geo. Fre.	Cath.	M 1909 A.B. 1912
—	[1] Geo. Gabriel ....*Pem.		M 1837 A.B. 1841. A.M. 1844. *LL.D.*,
—	Hugh Gabriel	Pem.	M 1905 A.B. 1908 [*Sc.D.* 1888
—	John Laurence	Pem.	M 1899 A.B. 1902
—	John Whitley Gabriel	Joh.	M 1905 A.B. 1908
—	Josiah	Joh.	M 1901 A.B. 1905
—	Leon.	H. Sel.	M 1910
—	Phil. Folliott	Jes.	M 1905
—	Rob. John	Cath.	M 1907 A.B. 1910
—	Will. Alb.	Em.	M 1905 A.B. 1908
—	Will. Hen.	N. C.	M 1910
Stokoe,	Frank Woodyer	Cai.	M 1910
Stone,	Art.	King's	M 1896 A.B. 1899. A.M. 1903
—	Bertram John Vivian	Em.	M 1912
—	Ern. Rich.	Em.	M 1901 A.B. 1904. B.C. 1910
—	Gilb.	Cai.	M 1906 A.B., LL.B. 1909
—	Hen. Brassington ...	King's	M 1909 A.B. 1912
—	Reg. Jos.	Jes.	M 1898 A.B. 1902
—	Theodore Handley ...	Sid.	M 1909 A.B. 1912
—	Walt. Napleton	Pem.	M 1910
—	Will. Bayford	King's	M 1897 A.B. 1900. A.M. 1904
Stoneham,	Ralph Thompson ...	Pet.	M 1906
Stonehouse,	Geo. Hen.	Sid.	M 1903 A.B. 1906. A.M. 1910
Stoneley,	Rob.	Joh.	M 1912
Stoney,	Tho. Ramsay	Pem.	M 1901 A.B. 1904
Stoodley,	Percy Ballard	Cla.	M 1912
Stooks,	Gerald Sumner	Sid.	M 1899 A.B. 1902. A.M.† 1910
Stopford,	John	Joh.	M 1910
Storer,	Rich. Sam.	Cla.	M 1908 A.B. 1912
Storey,	Cha. Ambrose	Trin.	M 1907 A.B. 1910
—	Gilb.	Qu.	M 1909 A.B. 1912
—	Kenneth Lushington	Trin.	M 1905 A.B. 1908
—	Lewis Hen. Tutill ...	Cai.	M 1907 A.B. 1910
—	Ronald Alex.	Trin.	M 1907 A.B. 1910
Storr,	Edw. Cha.	Pem.	M 1899 A.B. 1902. A.M. 1907
Storrar,	Art. Percival Wynne	Sid.	M 1902
Storrs,	Bern. St John	King's	M 1903 A.B. 1906

[1] Master of Pembroke College, 1902.

Storrs,	Chris. Evelyn	Pem.	M 1907 A.B. 1910
—	Fra. Edm.	Jes.	M 1902 A.B. 1905
—	Ja. Parker	Cla.	M 1908 A.B. 1911
—	Ronald Hen. Amherst	Pem.	M 1900 A.B. 1903
Stote,	Art. Will.	N. C.	M 1895 Cai. A.B. 1898. A.M. 1903
Stott,	Arnold Walmsley ...	Trin.	M 1904 A.B. 1907. A.M. 1911
—	Cecil Ainsworth	Trin.	M 1912
—	Edgar Shirley	Trin.	M 1905
—	Ja. Pilkington	Cai.	M 1895 A.B. 1898. A.M. 1907
—	Millie Dow	Trin.	M 1905 A.B. 1908
—	Raymond	Trin.	M 1908
—	Verney	Pet.	M 1909 A.B. 1912
Stoughton,	John Wilberforce ...	Joh.	M 1893 A.B. 1901
Stout,	Olaf Eirik	Jes.	M 1908 A.B., LL.B. 1912
Stowe,	Harold Steed	Down.	M 1893 A.B. 1898. A.M. 1902
Stowell,	Edgar la Mothe	C. C.	M 1912
—	Reg.	Joh.	M 1890 A.B. 1893. A.M. 1905
Stower,	Bertram Herb. Russel	Qu.	M 1905 B. H. Russell A.B. 1908. A.M.
Strachan,	Ja.	Cla.	M 1899 A.B. 1902. A.M. 1909 [1912
—	Leslie Franklin	Cath.	M 1901
—	Rob. Harvey	Chr.	E 1911
Strachey,	Giles Lytton	Trin.	M 1899 A.B. 1903
—	Ja. Beaumont	Trin.	M 1905 A.B. 1908
Stradling,	Art. Renny	Cai.	M 1905 A.B. 1908
—	Will.	Joh.	M 1898 A.B. 1901. A.M. 1907
Strahan,	Aubrey	Joh.	M 1871 A.B. 1875. A.M. 1878. Sc.D. 1907
—	Will. Roscoe	Em.	M 1909 A.B. 1912
Strain,	Tho. Greer	Joh.	M 1902 A.B. 1905. A.M. 1912
Straker,	Art. Coppin	Jes.	M 1911
—	Edw. Cha.	Jes.	M 1909
—	Guy Herb.	Jes.	M 1910
—	Hen. Gilman	Pem.	M 1908 A.B. 1911
—	Ian Allgood	Trin.	M 1908 A.B. 1911
—	Lawrence Seton	Jes.	M 1910
Strang,	Ja. Howard	Trin. H.	M 1911
Strange,	Edw. Howard	Pet.	M 1908 A.B. 1910
—	Harry St John Bland	Pem.	M 1910
Stratton,	Fre. John Marrian ...*Cai.		M 1901 A.B. 1904. A.M. 1908
—	Sam. Wesley		*Sc.D.* 1908
Straughan,	Tho. Art.	H. Sel.	M 1910
Straus,	Ralph Sid. Alb.	Pem.	M 1901 A.B. 1904
Straw,	Rob. Will.	Cla.	M 1900 A.B. 1903. A.M. 1907
Strawson,	Hen.	Em.	M 1911
Stream,	Ern. John	N. C.	M 1891 A.B. 1895. A.M. 1902
Street,	Ja. Hen.	Joh.	M 1869 A.B. 1874. A.M. 1908
—	Reg. Owen	Joh.	M 1908 A.B. 1911
Streeten,	Art. Herb.	Em.	M 1904 A.B. 1907. A.M. 1912
—	Basil Rob.	Joh.	M 1908 A.B. 1911
—	Edgar Rob.	King's	M 1901 A.B. 1904. A.M. 1910
Stretton,	John Weston	Cai.	M 1906 A.B. 1910
Strickland,	Alan Faulkner	Cai.	M 1905 A.B. 1908
—	Cyril	Cai.	M 1899 A.B. 1902. B.C., A.M. 1911
—	Noël	Sid.	M 1899 A.B. 1902. A.M. 1906
Stringer,	Cha. Edw. Woodcock	Em.	M 1902 A.B. 1906
—	Cuthbert Hen.	Cla.	M 1905 A.B. 1908
—	Gerald Moffatt	Down.	M 1911
—	Harold	Cai.	M 1905 A.B. 1908
Strong,	Eustace Mordaunt ...	Pem.	M 1901 A.B. 1904. A.M. 1909
—	Rupert Stanley Kitteridge	C. C.	M 1898 A.B. 1901. A.M. 1905
—	Walt. Mersh	Trin.	M 1892 A.B. 1895. A.M. 1899. B.C., M.D.
Strover,	Ern. Ja.	H. Sel.	M 1904 A.B. 1907 [1903

Stroyan,	John Rob. Anderson	Jes.	M 1909 A.B. 1912
Strugnell,	Evelyn Herb.	Trin.	M 1903 A.B. 1906
Struthers,	Duncan Gordon	Trin.	M 1907 A.B. 1910
Strutt,	Algernon Hen.	Trin.	M 1902
—	John Will. ....*Trin.		M 1861 A.B. 1865. A.M. 1868. *Sc.D.* 1888
—	Rob. John ....*Trin.		M 1894 A.B. 1897. A.M. 1901
Stuart,	Art.	Trin.	M 1908 A.B. 1911
—	Cha. Erskine ....*Trin.		M 1901 A.B. 1905. A.M. 1908
—	Cha. Pat.	Pem.	M 1911
—	Colin Montague	Trin. H.	M 1908
—	Cyril Edgar	Joh.	M 1911
—	Douglas Cecil Rees	Trin. H.	M 1905 A.B., LL.B. 1909
—	Eric Alex. Gordon ...	Em.	M 1904 A.B. 1907
—	Fra. Art. Knox	Cai.	M 1893 A.B. 1905
—	Herb.	Joh.	M 1909 A.B. 1912
—	Herb. Edw.	Joh.	M 1905 A.B. 1908
—	Rob. Spurrell Dacre	Cai.	M 1910
—	Rob. Will. Hall	H. Aye.	M 1884 Cath. A.B. 1887. A.M.† 1910
—	Tho.	Joh.	L 1901 A.B. 1902
—	Whitewright Ruthven	Trin.	M 1902
Stubbs,	Noel Howard	Qu.	M 1905 A.B. 1908
Stuckenschmidt, Freidrich Geo. ...		Cla.	M 1905 A.B. 1908
Studd,	Eric Fairfax	King's	M 1908
—	John Edw. Kynaston	Trin.	M 1880 A.B. 1884. A.M. 1911
—	Lionel Fairfax	Trin.	M 1909 A.B. 1912
—	Vivian Mortlock	Trin.	M 1909
Sturdee,	Rob. Ja.	N. C.	M 1899 A.B. 1902. Jes. A.M. 1906
Sturdy,	Art. Carlile	Pem.	M 1902 A.B. 1906
—	Edwin Carlile	Pem.	M 1909 A.B. 1912
Sturge,	Paul Dudley	Cai.	M 1910
Sturges,	Edw. Laurence	Em.	M 1903 A.B. 1906
Sturgess,	John	Cai.	M 1908 A.B. 1911
Sturgis,	Roland Joceline Russell	Mag.	M 1907
Sturton,	Keith Mansfield	Em.	M 1905 A.B. 1908
Stutfield,	Jack Gregory	Down.	M 1902 John G. A.B. 1905. LL.B. 1907.
Stutter,	Will. Orridge	Cai.	M 1886 A.B. 1890. A.M. 1905 [A.M. 1912
Style,	Art. Hurrell	Em.	M 1893 A.B. 1897. M.B., B.C., A.M. 1901.
Suan,	Tan Seng	Chr.	M 1902 A.B. 1905 [M.D. 1908
Subbarao,	Nanjangud Subbarao	Joh.	M 1905 A.B. 1908. A.M.† 1912
Suchier,	Gerhard Hugo Otto	N. C.	E 1909
Suddard,	Ebenezer Fra. Edw.	Cai.	M 1912
Sudhasi,	Mom Chow	Trin.	M 1901
Suffern,	Canning	Em.	M 1911
Sugden,	Guy Hatton	Pem.	M 1907 A.B. 1910 [B.C. 1908
Suhr,	Alf. Chris. Hermann	Cai.	M 1899 A.B. 1902. A. C. Herman, M.B.,
Sukthankar,	Vishnu Sitaram	Joh.	M 1903 A.B. 1906. A.M.† 1912
Sulaiman,	Shah Muhammad ...	Chr.	M 1906 A.B. 1909. LL.B. 1910
Sulieman,	Ahmed Awad	Chr.	M 1909
Sulivan,	Eugene Gilb.	Trin.	M 1911
Sullivan,	Arnold Moon	Chr.	M 1897 A.B. 1900. A.M. 1904
—	Jos. Hub. Baron	Chr.	M 1909
—	Tho. Archdeacon ...	N. C.	M 1909 A.B. 1912
Sully,	Clifford	King's	M 1901 A.B.† 1907
Sultan Ahmad Khan, Sáhibzádá		Chr.	M 1891 A.B., LL.B. 1894. A.M., LL.M.
Summerhayes, Julius Ja.		Em.	M 1890 A.B. 1893. A.M. 1902 [1909
Summers,	Alf. Spencer Mason	Trin.	M 1905 A.B. 1908
—	Edw. Sam.	Trin. H.	M 1872 A.B. 1876. A.M. 1906
—	Geoffrey	Cai.	M 1910
—	Will. Edgar	Trin.	M 1895 A.B. 1898. A.M. 1902

Summerson,	Will.	Sid.	M 1912
Sunderland,	Geoffrey	H. Sel.	M 1910
Sunderland-Taylor, Guy Edw. ...		Em.	M 1897 A.B. 1900. A.M. 1908
Sunter,	Ja.	N. C.	M 1908
Suriyong,	*H.R.H. Prince* (of Siam)	Trin.	M 1903
Surrage,	Harold Ja. Rocke ...	Pem.	M 1912
Surridge,	Brewster Jos.	Down.	M 1912
Surtees,	John Clark	Cla.	E 1907
—	Will. Fre.	King's	M 1890 A.B. 1893. A.M. 1903
Susmann,	Walt. Ja.	Cai.	M 1893 A.B. 1896. M.B., B.C., A.M. 1903
Susskind,	Manfred Julius	Pem.	M 1909 A.B. 1912
Sutcliffe,	Alan Lee	Sid.	M 1906 A.B. 1909
—	Art.	Em.	M 1905 A.B. 1908
—	Jos. Hedley	Cai.	M 1904 A.B., LL.B. 1907. A.M. 1911
Sutherland,	Alex. Geo.	Trin.	M 1907 A.B. 1910
—	Donald Geo.	Joh.	M 1899 A.B. 1901. A.M. 1908
—	Fre. Bertram	Cai.	M 1912
—	Geo. Art.	Joh.	E 1911
—	Ja. Fleming	Cai.	M 1906 A.B. 1909
Sutton,	Art. Rob. Pym	Cla.	M 1901
—	Cha. John	Em.	M 1905 A.B., LL.B. 1908
—	Edw. Will.	Cath.	M 1897 A.B. 1901. A.M. 1904
—	Fra. Jos.	Em.	M 1898 A.B. 1901. A.M.† 1905
—	Geo. Gerhard	Em.	M 1899 LL.B. 1902
—	Gordon Bower	Pem.	M 1903 A.B. 1906
—	Hub. Joscelin	Trin.	M 1905 A.B. 1908
—	John Rich.	Sid.	M 1886 A.B. 1889. A.M.† 1901. Sc.D.†
—	Kenneth Herb. Moxhay	Pem.	M 1910 [1908
—	Leon. Jos.	H. Sel.	M 1911
—	Leon. Noel	Trin.	M 1912
—	Rob. Nihön Drummond	Cath.	M 1902 A.B. 1905. A.M.† 1912
—·	Will. Hub. Reitz ...	Down.	M 1900 A.B. 1903. M.B., B.C. 1907
Svensson,	Rob.	Cai.	M 1900 A.B. 1903. M.B., B.C. 1910
Swaffield,	Alf. Ronald Otway ...	Cai.	M 1908
Swain,	Herb. John	Em.	M 1909 A.B. 1911
Swaine,	John Kenneth	Trin.	M 1903 A.B. 1906
Swainson,	Alf. Cyril	H. Sel.	M 1903 A.B. 1906
—	Archib. Douglas	Sid.	M 1909 A.B. 1912
—	Will. Goad	C. C.	M 1897 A.B. 1900. A.M. 1904
Swallow,	John Reg.	N. C.	M 1907 A.B. 1911
Swan,	Cecil Will. Edwin ...	H. Sel.	M 1909 A.B. 1912
—	Fre.	Trin.	M 1906 A.B. 1909
—	Fre. Geo.	Pem.	M 1906 A.B. 1909
—	Hen. Newton	Pem.	M 1908
—	Percival	King's	M 1899 A.B. 1902
—	Warren Alex.	H. Sel.	M 1907 A.B. 1909
Swann,	Alf.	Trin. H.	M 1911
—	Cecil Gordon Aldersey	Cath.	M 1907 A.B. 1910
—	Clem. Herb.	N. C.	M 1902 Chr. A.B. 1905. A.M. 1909
—	John Geo. Langhorn	N. C.	M 1901 Chr. A.B. 1904
—	Meredith Blake Robson	Cai.	M 1912
—	Sam. Ern.	Em.	M 1898 A.B. 1901. A.M. 1905
—	Sid. Ern.	Trin. H.	M 1909 A.B. 1912
Swann-Mason, Rich. Swann			*See* Mason, S.
Swanston,	Cha. Bertram	Trin.	M 1901
—	Eric Romilly	C. C.	M 1911
—	Hen. Eric	Jes.	M 1906
Swanwick,	Fre. Bertrand	Trin.	M 1905 A.B., LL.B. 1908
—	Russell Kenneth	Trin.	M 1903 A.B. 1906
Swayne,	Ja. Colin	Mag.	M 1904 A.B. 1907
Swe,	Maung Chit	Down.	M 1911

Swears,	Hugh Miller	....	Jes.	M 1912
Sweet,	John Laxon Leslie	...	Trin. H.	M 1906
Sweeting,	Hen. Carol	....	Trin. H.	M 1904
—	Hen. Ravenhill	......	Jes.	M 1894 A.B. 1897. A.M. 1901
Swift,	Brian Herb.	....	Cai.	M 1911
—	Claude Theodore	......	King's	M 1905 A.B. 1909
—	Edgar Russell	....	N. C.	M 1889 Cath. A.B. 1895. A.M. 1903
—	John McIntosh	......	Joh.	M 1905 A.B. 1908. A.M. 1912
Swinburne,	Wynford Percy	......	Pem.	M 1903
Swindlehurst,	Jos. Eric	....	Cai.	M 1908 A.B. 1911
Swinstead,	Norman Hillyard	...	Cla.	M 1911
Sword,	Art. Nicholson	......	Cai.	M 1908 A.B. 1911
Swords,	Will. Fra.	....	N. C.	M 1905 Joh. A.B., LL.B. 1908
Sydenham,	Herb. Cecil	....	Em.	M 1896 A.B. 1899. A.M. 1904
Sydney,	Hen.	....	Trin.	M 1906
Sydney-Turner,	Saxon Arnoll	......	Trin.	M 1899 A.B. 1903
Sykes,	Art. Hovey Charlesworth		Jes.	M 1911
—	Carrington	....	Cai.	M 1906
—	Cha. Edw.	....	Pem.	M 1893 A.B. 1896. A.M. 1903
—	Frank Morris	....	H. Sel.	M 1897 A.B. 1900. A.M. 1908
—	John Newton	....	Qu.	M 1906 A.B. 1909
—	Maur. Gaskell	....	Joh.	M 1902
—	Ronald	....	Cai.	M 1908 A.B. 1911. LL.B. 1912
—	Stanley Will.	....	Cai.	M 1903 A.B. 1906. A.M. 1910
—	Will. Dodgson	....	Joh.	M 1908 A.B. 1911
Sylvester,	Harry Art.	....	Sid.	M 1911
Syme,	Gordon Wemyss	......	Cai.	M 1908 A.B. 1912
Symes,	Edgar Cha.	....	Pem.	M 1894 A.B. 1897. A.M. 1902
—	Reg.	....	Pem.	M 1900 A.B., LL.B. 1903
Symes-Thompson,	Hen. Edm.	......	Chr.	M 1891 A.B. 1894. A.M. 1898. B.C., M.D.
Syme Thomson,	Fraser	......	Cla.	M 1906 A.B. 1909 [1903
Symington,	Archib. Will.	....	Cla.	M 1911
Symns,	Archib. Art. Montfort		Pem.	M 1905 A.B. 1908
—	Ja. Llewellyn Montfort		Cai.	M 1904 A.B. 1907
—	John Montfort	......	Cai.	M 1898 A.B. 1901. A.M. 1905
Symonds,	Edw.	....	King's	M 1908 A.M. (incorp.) 1908
—	Frederic Cotton	......	Cai.	M 1906 A.B. 1909
—	John Ashby	....	Cai.	M 1899 A.B. 1903. A.M. 1906
—	Nath. Hen.	....	Qu.	M 1869 A.B. 1880. A.M. 1906
Symons,	Cha. Douglas	....	Trin.	M 1905 A.B. 1908. A.M. 1912
—	Will. John Fra.	......	Sid.	M 1907 A.B. 1910
Sympson,	Tho. Mansel	....	Trin.	M 1908
Szumowski,	Herb. Vladimir Maximilian	}	Joh.	M 1885 A.B. 1888. A.M. 1902

T

Tabberer,	Cecil Osmond	....	Em.	M 1908 A.B. 1911
Tabor,	Britton Stone	....	C. C.	M 1904
—	Fra. Levinge	....	Trin.	M 1900 A.B. 1903
—	Fre. Alf. Megerlin	...	C. C.	M 1909 A.B. 1912.
Tacey,	Dalton Will.	....	Chr.	M 1896 A.B. 1899. A.M. 1904
Tacon,	Dudley Geo. Tomline		Trin. H.	M 1907 A.B. 1912
—	Rich. Cha.	....	Trin.	M 1901 A.B. 1905. A.M. 1912
Tadman,	Gerard Rich.	....	H. Sel.	M 1901 A.B. 1904

Taffs,	Leslie Hugh	Down.	M 1904 A.B. 1907
Taggart,	Art. Watson	N. C.	M 1905 A.B. 1908. A.M. 1912
—	Will. Quayle	Em.	M 1911
Tait,	Archib. Campbell ...	Sid.	M 1901 A.B. 1906
—	Art. Ja.	Joh.	M 1891 A.B. 1894. A.M. 1898. B.D. 1910
—	Greville Brend	King's	M 1911
—	Hugh Nimmo	Joh.	M 1907 A.B. 1910
Tajima,	Tan	N. C.	M 1898 Pem., post Hamaguchi, Tan A.B.
Talbot,	Alb. Edw.	Em.	L 1902 A.B. 1904. A.M. 1908 [1902
—	Art. Tho. Surman ...	Pem.	M 1897 A.B. 1900. A.M. 1904
—	Edw. Stuart		*LL.D.* 1908
—	Eustace	Trin.	M 1892 A.B. 1895. A.M. 1899. M.B., B.C.
—	Gerald Fra.	Cai.	M 1901 [1901
—	John	Trin.	M 1895 A.B. 1898. A.M. 1902
—	Rich.	Em.	L 1897 A.B. 1899. A.M. 1903
—	Tho. Will. Livesey ...	N. C.	M 1900 Cath. A.B. 1904. A.M. 1911
Tall,	John Jeffery	Cath.	M 1912
Tallents,	Ern. Fra.	H. Sel.	M 1894 A.B. 1897. A.M. 1901
Talpur,	Gholom Ali	Down.	M 1910
També,	Vaman Gopal	Cath.	M 1912
Tampoe,	Alf. McGowan Coomarasamy }	Cla.	M 1899 A.B. 1902
Tampoe-Philips, Edw. Matthew ...		Cai.	M 1912
Tancock,	Ern. Osborne	H. Sel.	M 1905 A.B. 1908
Tanfield,	John Fre.	Chr.	M 1896 A.B. 1899. A.M. 1903
Tanner,	Edw. Victor	Em.	M 1905 A.B. 1908. A.M. 1912
—	Evelyn Lloyd	Cla.	M 1900 A.B. 1903
—	Humphrey Russell ...	Chr.	M 1911
—	Jos. Robson ....*Joh.		M 1879 A.B. 1883. A.M. 1886. Litt.D. 1905
—	Laurance Edgar	Joh.	M 1910
—	Lawrence Edw.	Pem.	M 1909 A.B. 1912
Tannett-Walker, Art. Randall		Trin.	M 1902
Tanqueray,	Truman	Mag.	M 1907 A.B. 1910
Tansley,	Leon. Beaumont	Trin.	M 1912
Tapp,	Theodore Art.	Cai.	M 1902
Tarbet,	Claud Edw.	Cla.	M 1898 A.B. 1901
Tarrant,	Walt. Noel Haden ...	Sid.	M 1910
Tasker,	Claude Lee	Cath.	M 1909
—	Hub. Sanderson	Em.	M 1905 A.B. 1908
—	Morris Bennet	Sid.	M 1899 A.B. 1902. A.M. 1906
—	Theodore Ja.	Trin.	M 1903 A.B. 1906
Tatchell,	Frank	Trin.	M 1891 A.B. 1898. A.M. 1901
Tate,	Alf. Leon.	Down.	M 1908
—	Art. Wignall	Trin.	M 1906
—	Ja. Elford	Jes.	M 1911
Tatham,	Cecil Fra.	Cla.	M 1906 A.B. 1909. LL.B. 1911
—	Chris. Kemplay	Trin.	M 1900 A.B. 1903. A.M. 1907
—	Geoffrey Bulmer ......*Trin.		M 1902 A.B. 1905. A.M. 1909
—	Lancelot Reeve	Qu.	M 1912
Tattersall,	Fra. Redmayne	N. C.	M 1911
—	Oswald Eric	Cath.	M 1899 A.B. 1902
Taunton,	Ivon Hope	Cla.	M 1909 A.B. 1912
Taylor,	Alb. Will. Ferris ...	Pet.	M 1897 A.B. 1901. A.M. 1908
—	Alf. Jesse	King's	M 1912
—	Alf. Rickard	Cai.	M 1900 A.B. 1904
—	Alf. Rob.	King's	M 1911
—	Arnold Douglas	Joh.	M 1904 A.B. 1907
—	Art. Ainsworth	Qu.	M 1902 [A.M.† 1905. M.D.† 1908
—	Art. Ern.	N. C.	E 1895 Down. A.B. 1898. M.B., B.C. 1902
—	Art. Lombe	Trin.	M 1900 A.B. 1903. LL.B. 1904. A.M. 1907
—	Benj. West	Cath.	M 1905 A.B. 1908

Taylor,	Bertram Cha.	Cath.	M 1896 A.B. 1899. A.M. 1903
—	Cecil Fra.	Em.	M 1905 A.B. 1908
—	Cedric Rowland	Cai.	M 1906 A.B. 1909
—	Chapman Carey And.	Pem.	M 1884 A.B. 1887. A.M. 1911
—	Cha. Edgar	Cla.	M 1904
—	Cha. Hen. Shinglewood	Cai.	M 1901 A.B. 1904. M.B., B.C., A.M. 1910
—	Cha. Paul	Cla.	M 1900 A.B. 1903
- -	Cha. Somers	Em.	M 1901 A.B. 1905
—	Cha. Tyerman	Pet.	M 1909 A.B. 1912
—	Chris. Cha.	Cath.	M 1909 A.B. 1912
—	Cuthbert Tuke	Trin.	M 1904 A.B. 1907
—	Cyril Eustace	Trin. H.	M 1912
—.	Dav. Gladstone	Joh.	M 1901 A.B. 1904. A.M. 1908
—	Dav. Robertson	Chr.	M 1898 A.B. 1901
—	Edw. Archib. Thornton	C. C.	M 1904 A.B. 1907
—	Edw. Ja. Davis	Cai.	M 1892 A.B. 1898. M.B., B.C. 1905
—	Eric Fra. Howard ...	Jes.	M 1909
—	Eric Stuart	King's	M 1907 A.B. 1910
—	Frank Costou	Pem.	M 1895 A.B. 1898. A.M. 1903
—	Fre. Burleigh	Trin.	M 1910
—	Fre. Lewis	Joh.	M 1911
- -	Geoffrey Cha. Rimington	Mag.	M 1899 A.B. 1902
—	Geoffrey Ingram ......*Trin.		M 1905 A.B. 1908. A.M. 1912
—	Geo. Hebb	Cai.	M 1910
—	Geo. Stuart	Sid.	M 1911
—	Geo. Will.	Trin.	M 1910 [1897. M.D. 1902
—	Gerard Cha.	Chr.	M 1887 A.B. 1890. B.C., A.M. 1894. M.B.
—	Godfrey Midgley Chassereau	Joh.	M 1904 A.B. 1907. A.M. 1911
—	Guy Art.	C. C.	M 1909 A.B. 1912
—	Harold Cha. Norman	Joh.	M 1911
—	Harold Milman Strickland	Trin.	M 1909 A.B. 1912
—	Hen.	Cai.	M 1894 A.B. 1897. A.M. 1901
—	Hen. Douglas	Trin.	M 1899 A.B. 1902
—	Hen. Edw. Irving ...	Pem.	M 1894 A.B. 1897. A.M. 1905
—	Herb. Geo.	Trin.	M 1900 A.B. 1903
—	Herb. Hampden	Pem.	M 1900 A.B. 1903. B.C. 1908. M.B. 1908 (2)
—	Ja. Edw. John	Qu.	M 1904 A.B. 1907
—	Ja. Geo.	King's	M 1893 A.B. 1896. M.B., B.C. 1900. M.D.,
—	John Dudley	N. C.	M 1909 [A.M. 1903
—	John Frank	H. Sel.	M 1905 A.B. 1908
—	John Holman	Pem.	M 1896 A.B. 1899. post Holman, J. H.
			[Taylor A.M. 1903
—	John Norman	Joh.	M 1902 A.B., LL.B. 1905. A.M. 1909
—	John Ralph Strickland	Pem.	M 1903 A.B. 1906. A.M. 1910
—	John Reg.	King's	M 1899 A.B. 1902. A.M. 1906
—	John Rowland	Trin.	M 1889 A.B. 1892. A.M. 1903
—	Lawson	N. C.	L 1906
—	Leon. Fre.	H. Sel.	M 1908 A.B. 1911
—	Leon. Mainwaring ...	Pem.	M 1901 A.B. 1904. A.M. 1908
—	Leslie Fernandes ...	Cla.	M 1909 A.B. 1912
—	Lewis Enfield	Trin.	M 1901
—	Maur. Llewellyn	Pem.	M 1897 A.B. 1901
—	Phil. Mountford	Trin.	M 1906 A.B. 1909
—	Raymond	Qu.	M 1909 A.B. 1912
—	Reg. Cha.	Em.	M 1901 A.B. 1904
—	Rob. Emery	Pem.	M 1899 A.B. 1903
—	Rob. Oswald Pat. ...	Joh.	M 1892 A.B. 1899. A.M. 1907
—	Rob. Stanley	Down.	M 1899 A.B. 1902. M.B., B.C. 1907
—	Ronald Fra.	Pem.	M 1907 A.B. 1910
—	Rupert Burleigh	Cla.	M 1902
—	Sam.	Chr.	M 1898 A.B. 1901

Taylor,	Sam.	Trin.	M 1903 A.B. 1906
—	Steph. John	Qu.	M 1896 A.B. 1899. A.M. 1904
—	Tho. Fra. Gawan ...	Sid.	M 1912
—	Tho. Griffith	Em.	M 1907 A.B. 1909
—	Tho. Morisey	Cla.	M 1904
—	Walt. Mark	N. C.	M 1893 Cai. A.B. 1896. A.M. 1902
—	Wilfrid Reynell	Jes.	M 1910
—	Will. Edw.	Trin. H.	M 1899 A.B. 1902
—	Will. Okey Lamond	Chr.	M 1893 A.B. 1896. A.M. 1903
Teague,	John Jessop	Em.	M 1875 A.B. 1879. A.M. 1910
Teakle,	Steph. Goddard	Joh.	M 1899 A.B. 1902. A.M. 1910
Teale,	Edwin	N. C.	E 1900 A.B. 1903
—	Kenneth Will. Pridgin	Em.	M 1894 A.B. 1901. A.M. 1904
Teall,	Frederic Hathaway ...	Sid.	M 1902 A.B. 1905
—	Jethro Justinian Harris *Joh.		M 1869 A.B. 1873. A.M. 1876. Sc.D. 1905
Tear,	Fre. John	Sid.	M 1905
Tebbs,	Basil Nelson	Qu.	E 1892 A.B. 1895. A.M. 1899. B.C., M.D.
—	John Archib.	C. C.	M 1910 [1904
Tebbutt,	Roger Jos.	King's	M 1912
Tedder,	Art. Will.	Mag.	M 1909 A.B. 1912
Teichmann,	Erik	Cai.	M 1901 A.B. 1904
—	Oskar	Cai.	M 1898 A.B. 1901. A.M. 1907
Telfer,	Andr. Cecil	H. Sel.	M 1912
—	Leigh Patteson	Sid.	M 1909 A.B. 1912
—	Will.	Cla.	M 1905 A.B. 1908
Telford,	Evelyn Davison	Cai.	M 1894 A.B. 1897. A.M. 1902. B.C. 1903
Temperley,	Art. Ridley	Cla.	M 1907 A.B. 1910
—	Clive Errington	Trin.	M 1912
—	Ern. Walt. Pyemont	King's	M 1894 A.B. 1897. A.M. 1901
—	Eustace Ern. Vazeille	Sid.	M 1908 A.B. 1911
—	Harold Will. Vazeille	King's	M 1898 A.B. 1901. *Pet. A.M. 1906
Tempest,	Fra. Lewis	H. Sel.	M 1912
—	Roger Ern.	H. Sel.	M 1909 A.B. 1912
Temple,	Edwin	Pem.	M 1886 A.B. 1889. A.M. 1911
—	Montagu	Trin.	M 1901 A.B. 1904
Templeman,	Will. Hen.	Joh.	M 1902 A.B. 1906. LL.B. 1908
Templer,	John Fra. Harvey ...	Trin.	M 1904 LL.B. 1907
ten Bosch,	Geo.	Trin.	M 1899 A.B. 1903
Tendall,	Claude Stanford	Mag.	M 1906
Tennant,	Bern. Victor Ashlin	Pem.	M 1909 A.B. 1912
—	Cha. Grant	Trin.	M 1901 A.B. 1904
—	Fre. Rob.	Cai.	M 1885 A.B. 1888. A.M. 1894. B.D. 1903.
—	Hugh Vincent	Trin.	M 1910 [D.D. 1907
—	Noel Roy Dalcour ...	Pem.	M 1902 A.B. 1905
—	Will. Galbraith	Trin.	M 1897 A.B. 1900. A.M. 1904
Tennyson,	(*Hon.*) Alf. Aubrey	Trin.	M 1910
—	Cha. Bruce Locker ...	King's	M 1899 A.B. 1902
—	Lionel Hallam	Trin.	M 1908
Terrell,	Edw. Banfield	King's	M 1901
—	Frank Will.	C. C.	M 1912
Terry,	Fre. Stirling	Joh.	M 1896 A.B. 1899. A.M. 1906
—	Jos. Edw. Harold ...	Pem.	M 1903
Tetley,	Cha. Harold	Trin.	M 1895 A.B. 1898. A.M. 1904
—	Michael Hub.	Trin.	M 1906 A.B. 1909
—	Rob. Fra.	Pem.	M 1907 A.B. 1910
Teuten,	Leon. Montague	Em.	M 1907 A.B. 1910
Tew,	Gilb. Cha.	Em.	M 1903 A.B. 1906
te Water,	Cha. Theodore	Chr.	M 1905 A.B. 1908. LL.B. 1909
Tewfik,	Ahmed	Trin. H.	M 1907
Tewson,	Edw. Geo.	Cai.	M 1905
Tha,	Htoon Oo	Cla.	M 1905

Tha,	Maung Chan	....	Down.	M 1908
Thacker,	Cecil Rob. Allen	...	Down.	M 1908 A.B. 1911
—	Clarence Cha. à Becket		H. Sel.	M 1910
Thackeray,	Jos. Makepeace	......	Pem.	M 1907 A.B. 1910
Thackrah,	Matth. Will.	....	Qu.	M 1897 A.B. 1901. A.M. 1905
Thadani,	Nenumal Pohoomal		Qu.	M 1912
Tha Din,	Moung	....	Cath.	M 1907
Thakor,	Ramnikrai Jadavrai		Down.	M 1908
Tharp,	Phil. Anth.	....	Qu.	M 1909 A.B. 1912
Thatcher,	Frank	....	N. C.	M 1909 A.B. 1912
—	Will. Sutherland	......	N. C.	M 1907 A.B. 1911
Theobald,	Walt. Gordon	....	Trin.	M 1898 A.B. 1901
Theodor,	Gustav Hans Will.	...	Em.	M 1905
Theophilus,	Reg. Art.	....	Joh.	M 1900 A.B. 1903
—	Stanley Cecil	....	Chr.	M 1903 A.B., LL.B. 1906
Thew,	Vivian Gordon	......	Trin. H.	M 1906 A.B. 1909
Thickett,	Jos. Hedley	....	Cath.	M 1900 A.B. 1903. A.M. 1907
Thicknesse,	Raymond Sam.	......	Pem.	M 1909
Thin,	Myat	....	Trin.	M 1905
Thirkill,	Hen.	....	*Cla.	M 1905 A.B. 1908. A.M. 1912
Thiselton-Dyer,	Geo. Hen.	....	Trin.	M 1897 A.B. 1900. A.M. 1909
—	Will. Turner	....		Sc.D. 1904
Thoday,	Dav.	....	Trin.	M 1902 A.B. 1905. A.M. 1909
—	Fra. Alb.	....	Down.	M 1907 A.B. 1910
Thom,	Art. Murray	....	Chr.	M 1898 A.B. 1901. A.M. 1905
Thomas,	Archib. Allen	....	Chr.	M 1911
—	Art. Hen. Leopold	...	Em.	M 1902
—	Art. Hermann	....	Cath.	M 1896 A.B. 1899. A.M. 1906
—	Art. Nutter	....	Pem.	M 1888 A.B. 1891. A.M. 1895. D.D. 1906
—	Basil Parker	....	Qu.	M 1909 A.B. 1912
—	Bern. Hen.	....	Pem.	M 1902 A.B. 1905
—	Cecil Strangward	...	Em.	M 1883 N. C. A.B. 1896. A.M. 1903
—	Cha. Rowley	....	Qu.	M 1905
—	Dan. Octavius	....	Pet.	M 1908 A.B. 1910
—	Dav. Basil	....	Cath.	M 1905
—	Dav. Edw.	....	Sid.	M 1904 A.B. 1907. A.M. 1911
—	Dav. Vivian Dudley		Trin.	M 1907
—	Duncan Collisson Willey		Cai.	M 1908
—	Ebenezer Rees	......	Em.	M 1911
—	Edw. Aubrey	....	Cath.	L 1911
—	Edw. Foreshew	......	Em.	M 1912
—	Edw. Jos.	....	Em.	M 1903 A.B. 1905. A.M. 1910
—	Elliott Crewdson	......	Chr.	M 1894 A.B., LL.B. 1897. A.M. 1901
—	Evan Meredyth	......	Pem.	M 1902 A.B. 1905
—	Geo. Rob. Seager	...	Down.	M 1906 A.B. 1909
—	Gwilym Ewart Aerom		Cai.	M 1904 Aeron, A.B. 1907. LL.B. 1908
—	Gwilym Ungoed	......	Trin.	M 1900 post Ungoed, Gwilym Tho. A.B.
—	Harold	....	Pet.	M 1912 [1903. A.M. 1912
—	Harold Augustus	...	N. C.	M 1904 Joh. A.B., LL.B. 1907
—	Hen. Evan Eric	......	H. Sel.	M 1909
—	Herb. Hen.	....	Sid.	M 1894 A.B. 1897. A.M. 1904
—	Herb. Ja.	....	N. C.	M 1903 Cla. A.B. 1907. A.M. 1911
—	Hor. Wyndham	......	King's	L 1910 A.B. 1912
—	Hugh	....	N. C.	M 1889 Cath. A.B. 1894. A.M. 1905
—	Hugh Hamshaw	......	Down.	M 1904 A.B. 1907. A.M. 1911
—	Hugh Whitelegge	...	Jes.	M 1906 A.B. 1909
—	John	....	Trin.	M 1908 A.B. 1910
—	John Dav.	....	Joh.	M 1896 A.B. 1899. A.M. 1903
—	John Fleetwood	......	Cath.	M 1902 A.B. 1905
—	John Glyndor Treharne		Cai.	M 1910
—	John Llewelyn	......	Trin.	M 1899 A.B. 1902. A.M. 1906

Thomas,	Kenneth Galbraith ...	Pet.	M 1907 A.B., LL.B. 1910
—	Matthew Gilb. Thornley	Jes.	M 1907 A.B. 1911
—	Norman Llewellyn ...	Down.	M 1911
—	Oscar Clifford	Trin. H.	M 1907 A.B. 1911
—	Otho Vincent	Trin.	M 1908 A.B. 1911
—	Owen Vincent	Jes.	M 1912
—	Percy Goronwy	N. C.	M 1897 Cai. A.B. 1900. A.M. 1904
—	Pet. Haig	Trin.	M 1901
—	Russell Eric	N. C.	M 1908 A.B. 1911
—	Sam. Hen.	Pem.	M 1909 A.B. 1912
—	Tannikkil Itty	Down.	M 1904
—	Terry	N. C.	M 1911
—	Tho. John	Chr.	M 1902
—	Tho. Price	Cai.	M 1893 A.B. 1896. A.M. 1903
—	Tho. Shenton Whitelegge	Qu.	M 1898 A.B. 1901
—	Tudor Aneurin Talbot	Sid.	M 1912
—	Tudor Gordon	N. C.	M 1902
—	Walt. Edison	Trin.	M 1909 A.B., LL.B. 1912
—	Wilfrid Savage	Pem.	M 1897 A.B. 1900. A.M. 1904
—	Will. John	Sid.	M 1909 A.B., LL.B. 1912
—	Will. Jolliffe	H. Sel.	M 1890 A.B. 1893. A.M. 1901
Thomas-Peter,	Geo. Franklen	Cla.	M 1901
Thom-Postlethwaite,	Andr. Cecil Scott	Pem.	M 1908 A.B. 1912
Thompson,	Alan Brodrick	Em.	M 1907 A.B. 1910
—	Alb. Ern.	Chr.	M 1898 A.B. 1901. A.M. 1905
—	Alex. Challis	Joh.	M 1904 A.B. 1911
—	Alex. Hamilton	Joh.	M 1892 A.B. 1895. A.M. 1903
—	Alf.	Chr.	M 1902 A.B. 1905. A.M. 1909
—	Alf. Ross	Joh.	M 1906 A.B. 1909
—	Ansle Will. Haughton	Trin.	M 1906 A.B. 1909
—	Art.	Qu.	M 1886 A.B. 1889. A.M. 1901
—	Art. Brereton	Sid.	M 1912
—	Art. Pat.	Chr.	M 1912
—	Ashley Geo. Gyton	Pem.	M 1908 A.B. 1911
—	Augustus Perronet ...	Pem.	M 1898 A.B. 1901
—	Barry Cort	Pem.	M 1895 A.B. 1898. A.M. 1902
—	Basil	Pem.	M 1887 A.B. 1890. A.M. 1904
—	Bern. Woolcott	King's	M 1911
—	Cecil Hen. Farrer ...	Trin.	M 1901 A.B. 1904
—	Cha. Brodrick	Joh.	M 1908 A.B. 1911
—	Cha. Broughton	C. C.	M 1904 A.B. 1907. A.M. 1911
—	Cyril Newton	Joh.	M 1911
—	D'Arcy Wentworth ...	Trin.	M 1880 A.B. 1884. A.M. 1893. Litt.D. 1912
—	Douglas Errol Hay	Trin.	M 1908 A.B. 1911
—	Douglas Hildebrand	Mag.	M 1905 A.B. 1908
—	Edw.	Pem.	M 1899 A.B. 1902
—	Edw. Vincent	King's	M 1899 A.B. 1903
—	Ern. Edw.	Joh.	M 1903 A.B. 1906. A.M. 1910
—	Fra. Clem.	Trin.	M 1907 A.B. 1910
—	Fra. D'Arcy	Qu.	M 1886 A.B. 1889. A.M. 1909
—	Fra. Dixon	C. C.	M 1905 A.B. 1908
—	Fra. Will.	Pem.	M 1905 A.B. 1908
—	Frank Wilfrid	Sid.	M 1896 A.B. 1899. A.M. 1903
—	Geo. Hen. Main	Chr.	M 1910
—	Gordon	Qu.	M 1907 A.B. 1910
—	Harold Sigston	Trin.	M 1903 A.B., LL.B. 1906 [M.D. 1906
—	Harold Theodore ...	Chr.	M 1896 A.B. 1899. M.B., B.C., A.M. 1903.
—	Harrison	Joh.	M 1887 A.B. 1890. A.M.† 1902
—	Harry Kayss	Joh.	M 1902 A.B. 1905
—	Haselden	King's	M 1908 A.B. 1911

Thompson,	Herb. John	Qu.	M 1910
—	Horace Brockbank ...	Qu.	M 1909 A.B. 1912
—	Hugh Cecil	Em.	M 1908 A.B. 1911
—	Hugh Vernon	Trin.	M 1907 A.B. 1910
—	Ja. Denton	N. C.	M 1879 C. C. A.B. 1883. A.M. 1887. D.D.
—	John Barwick	Pem.	M 1901 A.B. 1904 [1912
—	John Cecil Caster ...	Pem.	M 1900 A.B. 1903
—	John Percival	Jes.	M 1910
—	Joshua Clibborn	C. C.	M 1899 A.B. 1902
—	Kenneth Furnivall ...	Cath.	M 1900 A.B. 1903
—	Mark	Qu.	M 1910
—	Merrick Arnold Bardsley	Em.	M 1907 A.B. 1910
—	Norcliffe Fourness ...	Pem.	M 1902 A.B. 1905
—	Oswald Stuart	Cai.	M 1910
—	Percy Ja.	Chr.	M 1912
—	Reg. Campbell	Cai.	M 1895 A.B. 1898. A.M. 1902
—	Reg. Dudley	Em.	M 1902 A.B. 1905. A.M. 1909
—	Rowland Guy	Pem.	M 1910
—	Sid. Lionel	Joh.	M 1907 A.B. 1910
—	Stewart Wyvol	Cla.	M 1911
—	Tho. Coates	Jes.	M 1900 A.B. 1903
—	Tho. Will.	Cai.	M 1899 A.B. 1902. A.M. 1906
—	Tho. Will.	Jes.	M 1906 A.B. 1909
—	Tom	Cai.	M 1899 A.B. 1902. A.M. 1906
—	Walt. Stuart	Qu.	M 1910
—	Will. Cyril	Joh.	M 1904 A.B. 1907
—	Will. Farrer	Pem.	M 1905 A.B. 1908
—	Will. Frank	King's	M 1906 A.B. 1909
—	Will. Grainger	Down.	M 1909 A.B. 1912
—	Will. Hugh	Jes.	M 1904 A.B. 1907
—	Will. Jameson	Trin.	M 1904 A.B. 1907
—	Willie Benj.	Cath.	M 1909 A.B. 1912
Thompson-Smith,	Edw.	Em.	M 1905 A.B. 1908
Thoms,	Alex. Hepburn	Chr.	M 1907 A.B. 1910
Thomson,	Bertram Will.	Cath.	M 1888 A.B. 1891. A.M. 1902
—	Cha. Herb.	Cla.	M 1909 A.B. 1912
—	Claude Lindsay	Mag.	M 1907 A.B. 1910
—	Dav. Halton	Pem.	M 1903 A.B. 1906. A.M. 1911
—	Douglas Gordon	Pem.	M 1908 A.B. 1911
—	Fre. Geo.	Sid.	M 1892 A.B. 1895. A.M. 1911
—	Geo. Paget	Trin.	M 1910
—	Gordon Duncan	Cai.	M 1912
—	Gordon Lindsay	Trin. H.	M 1906
—	Herb. Archer	Pem.	M 1887 A.B. 1890. A.M. 1909
—	Ja. Geo. Orr	Trin. H.	M 1900 A.B. 1903. A.M. 1908
—	Ja. Oliver	Trin.	M 1911
—	John	Trin. H.	M 1905 A.B. 1908
—	John Bathurst	Trin.	M 1907 A.B. 1910
—	Kenneth Sinclair ...	Joh.	M 1906 A.B. 1909
—	Moffat Scott	Cla.	M 1908 A.B. 1911
—	Sam. Pestell Donald	Pem.	M 1907
—	Will.	N. C.	E 1909
Thorburn,	John Melland	Trin.	M 1907 A.B. 1911
—	Malcolm Murray	Pem.	M 1907 A.B. 1910
—	Tho. Ja.	Chr.	M 1875 A.B. 1879. A.M. 1882. B.D. 1908.
Thoresby-Jones,	Mervyn	Trin.	M 1909 A.B. 1912 [D.D. 1911
Thorman,	Fre. Pelham	Qu.	M 1906 A.B. 1910
—	John Leslie	Pem.	M 1911
—	Will. Spencer Pelham	Qu.	M 1905
Thornborrow,	Wilfrid Crone	Pem.	M 1901
Thornburgh,	Fra. Thornburgh ...	Qu.	M 1901 A.B. 1904

Thorne,	Art. Henty	Em.	M 1902
—	Cornelius	Cla.	M 1911
—	Fre. John	Jes.	M 1904 A.B. 1907
—	Herb. Stanley	Chr.	M 1911
—	Hub. Prangley	Jes.	M 1899 A.B. 1902
—	Percy Cyril Lesley ...	C. C.	M 1909 A.B. 1912
—	Rich. Squire	Em.	M 1903 A.B. 1907
—	Will. Roy Prangley	Pet.	M 1901 A.B. 1904
Thornely,	Percival Ern. Wilfrid	Trin. H.	M 1898 A.B., LL.B. 1901. A.M. 1905
—	Ronald Roscoe	Trin. H.	M 1908 A.B. 1911
Thorne Waite,	Arnold	Joh.	M 1905 A.B. 1908. A.M. 1912
Thornewill,	Cha. Clive	Trin. H.	M 1904
Thorneycroft,	Kenneth Harman ...	H. Sel.	M 1912
Thornhill,	Alb.	N. C.	E 1899 A.B. 1902. A.M. 1906
—	Geo. Rob.	Trin.	M 1910
—	Noel	King's	M 1901 A.B. 1904
Thorns,	Frank Art.	C. C.	L 1891 A.B. 1896. A.M.† 1904
Thornton,	Archib. Clem.	Cla.	M 1904
—	Bern. Giles	Cla.	M 1904
—	Cedric Grosvenor ...	Em.	M 1907
—	Claude Cyprian	Trin.	M 1897 A.B. 1900. A.M. 1904
—	Douglas Montagu ...	Trin.	M 1892 A.B. 1895. A.M. 1903
—	Edw.	Trin.	M 1912
—	Fra. John	Cai.	M 1899 A.B. 1902. M.B., B.C., A.M. 1906
—	Fra. Ruthven	Trin.	M 1902 A.B. 1905. M.B., B.C., A.M. 1910
—	Frank	Trin.	M 1912
—	Geo. Lestock	Trin.	M 1890 A.B. 1893. A.M. 1902
—	Geo. Pet.	Qu.	L 1911
—	Geo. Ruthven	Trin.	M 1901 A.B. 1904. A.M. 1908
—	Harold	Pet.	M 1899 A.B. 1904
—	Herb. Parry	Trin.	M 1874 A.B. 1878. A.M. 1901
—	John Gordon	Trin.	M 1904 A.B. 1907. A.M. 1911
—	Leslie Heber	N. C.	E 1893 *A.M.* 1911
—	Lewis Hen. Douglas	Em.	M 1907 A.B. 1910
—	Lionel Spencer	Em.	M 1904 A.B. 1907. A.M. 1911
—	Noel Shipley	Trin.	M 1902 A.B. 1905
—	Percy Melville	Jes.	M 1860 LL.B. 1865. LL.M. 1909
—	Rob. Hill	Pet.	M 1896 A.B. 1899. A.M. 1906
—	Victor Stuart	Em.	M 1908 A.B. 1911
—	Will. Hen. Jelf	Jes.	M 1907 A.B. 1910
Thornycroft,	Oliver	Cla.	M 1903 A.B. 1906
Thorp,	Bertram Leland	Trin.	M 1900 A.B. 1903
—	Colingwood Foster ...	Em.	M 1898 Collingwood F., A.B. 1901
—	Edgar Brayshaw	Trin.	M 1904 A.B. 1907. A.M. 1911
—	Mark Leon.	Cla.	M 1893 A.B. 1899. A.M. 1904
—	Rob. Oakeley Vavasour	King's	M 1897 A.B. 1900. A.M. 1907
Thorpe,	Archib. Fra.	Jes.	M 1907 A.B. 1911
—	Chun	Joh.	M 1906
—	Edgar Rich.	Mag.	M 1906 A.B. 1909
—	Geo. Kelson	Cla.	M 1900 A.B. 1903
—	John Hobbs	Em.	M 1904
Thoseby,	Alb. Edw. Victor ...	Cai.	M 1891 A.B. 1894. A.M. 1910
Thouless,	Rob. Hen.	C. C.	M 1912
Thrash,	Walt. Ern.	Chr.	M 1903 A.B. 1906
Threlfall,	Cuthbert Raymond Forster }	Cai.	M 1912
—	Hen. Cha.	N. C.	M 1907 Qu. A.B. 1910
—	Rich. Evelyn	Cai.	M 1910
Thresher,	Will. Harrison	Cai.	M 1896 A.B. 1899. B.C., A.M. 1905. M.B.
Thrift,	Jos.	N. C.	M 1901 A.B. 1904. A.M. 1911 [1906
Thring,	Leon. Godfrey Pinney	Trin.	M 1891 A.B. 1894. A.M. 1911

Thurlow,	Art. Geoffrey	Cai.	M 1911
—	Art. Rob.	Cath.	M 1899 A.B. 1902
—	Basil Lyons	Cai.	M 1896 A.B. 1899. M.B., B.C. 1902. M.D.
Thurneysen,	Eduard Rudolf		*Litt.D.* 1911 [1906
Thursby,	Walt.	Qu.	M 1909
Thursfield,	Gerald Art. Rich. ...	Joh.	M 1905 A.B. 1908. A.M. 1912
—	Rich. Mortimer Rowland	H. Sel.	M 1903 A.B. 1906. B.C. 1911
Thurston,	Edgar Hugh	Cai.	M 1907
—	Edw. Tho.	Chr.	M 1908 A.B. 1911
Thwaites,	Gerald Evans	Cla.	M 1901
Thynne,	Leon. Wilks	Trin. H.	M 1904 A.B. 1908
Ticehurst,	Claud Buchanan	Joh.	M 1900 A.B. 1903. B.C., A.M. 1908
—	Gerald Augustus	Joh.	M 1897 A.B. 1900. M.B., B.C., A.M. 1906
—	Norman Frederic ...	Cla.	M 1892 A.B. 1895. A.M. 1899. B.C. 1901.
Tiddy,	Claude Winstanley Elliott	Joh.	M 1901 A.B. 1904 [M.B. 1903
Tidman,	Oscar Paul	Cai.	M 1902 A.B. 1906. A.M. 1912
Tijou,	Cha. Kiddy	Trin.	M 1896 A.B. 1900. A.M. 1903. post Alton,
			[C. K. Tijou
Tilbury,	Hub. Fra.	H. Sel.	M 1895 A.B. 1898. A.M. 1912
Till,	Will. Slade	Trin. H.	M 1912
Tillard,	Laurence Berkeley ...	Joh.	M 1906 A.B. 1909
—	Phil. John Berkley	Cai.	M 1903 P. J. Berkeley, A.B. 1906
—	Tho. Atkinson	Trin.	M 1902 A.B. 1905
Tillbrook,	Herb. John Ja.	Jes.	M 1906
Tilleke,	Will. Guna	N. C.	L 1912
Tilly,	John	Pem.	M 1905 A.B. 1908
—	Reynolds Leiton	Em.	M 1912
Tillyard,	Eustace Mandeville ⎫ Wetenhall ⎬	Jes.	M 1908 A.B. 1911
—	Hen. Julius Wetenhall	Cai.	M 1900 A.B. 1904. A.M. 1910
—	Rob. John	Qu.	M 1900 A.B. 1903. A.M.† 1907
Tilston,	Harold Einion	H. Sel.	M 1901 A.B. 1904. A.M. 1908
Timacheff,	Geo.	Trin.	M 1911
Times,	Wilberforce Onslow	Trin.	M 1907 A.B., LL.B. 1910
Timins,	Douglas Theodore ...	Jes.	M 1889 A.B. 1893. A.M. 1905
Timiriazeff,	Clem.		*Sc.D.* 1909
Timmins,	John Lewes	Em.	M 1893 A.B. 1896. B.C., A.M. 1901. M.B.
—	Jos. Child Buckley	Pet.	M 1911 [1902. M.D. 1906
Timmis,	Rob. Berks	Trin.	M 1899 A.B. 1902
Timms,	Herb. Phil.	Trin.	M 1891 A.B. 1902
Tims,	Hen. Will. Marett ...	King's	M 1899 A.B. 1901. A.M. 1906
Tin,	Maung	Down.	M 1905
—	Maung Ba	Chr.	M 1909 A.B. 1912
Tindal,	John Humphrey	Pet.	M 1908 A.B. 1911
Tindall,	Cha. Godfrey	Pem.	M 1912
—	Cuthbert	Chr.	M 1902 A.B. 1906
—	Cyril Ryan Williford	Qu.	M 1911
—	Howard Simson	Pem.	M 1903 A.B. 1906. A.M. 1910
—	Oswald	Qu.	M 1910
—	Rich. Fre.	Pem.	M 1909 A.B. 1912
Ting,	Ven Kian	Chr.	M 1906
Tingey,	Will. Harold	Trin. H.	M 1887 A.B. 1891. A.M. 1905
Tinker,	Brian	Mag.	M 1910
—	Frank Stanley	Pem.	M 1905 A.B. 1908
—	Hen. Will. Cossart ...	Trin.	M 1903 A.B. 1906
Tinling,	Ja. Forbes Bisset ...	Joh.	M 1860 A.B. 1864. A.M. 1901
Tinn,	Nai	King's	M 1901 A.B., LL.B. 1904. A.M.† 1908
Tinsley,	Rob. Percival	Qu.	M 1911
—	Rupert Lawies	Trin.	M 1912
Tinto,	John Ferguson	Trin.	M 1906 A.B. 1909
Tipper,	Frank	Down.	M 1905 A.B. 1909

Tipper,	Geo. Howlett	Cla.	M 1900 A.B. 1903. A.M. 1908
Tipping,	Ernest John	Chr.	M 1905 A.B. 1908
—	Llewellyn	N. C.	M 1892 Jes. A.B. 1895. A.M. 1912
Tirard,	Nestor Seppings	Trin.	M 1909
Tisdall,	Alf.	Trin.	M 1896 A.B. 1899. A.M. 1910
—	Art. Walderne St Clair	Trin.	M 1909 A.B. 1912
Tisza,	Stefan	Cai.	M 1907
Titley,	Lionel Gardner	Pem.	M 1895 A.B. 1898. A.M. 1903
Titterington,	Edw. John Goodall	Joh.	M 1903 A.B. 1906. A.M. 1910
Titterton,	Sid. John	Cai.	M 1907 A.B. 1910
Tizzard,	Fre. Geo.	N. C.	L 1906 A.B. 1908. A.M. 1912
Toase,	Edw. Ja.	Joh.	M 1908 A.B. 1911
—	Fre. Godfrey	Qu.	L 1901 A.B. 1903. A.M. 1908
Tobias,	Geo. Wolfe Rob.	Sid.	M 1904 A.B. 1906. A.M. 1910
Tobin,	Tho. Cha.	Joh.	M 1894 A.B. 1897. A.M. 1905
Tobitt,	Art.	Qu.	M 1896 A.B. 1899. A.M. 1903
Tod,	And. Keith	Pem.	M 1909 [1897. M.D. 1908
—	Hunter Finlay	Trin.	M 1889 A.B. 1892. B.C., A.M. 1896. M.B.
Todd,	Cha.	Cla.	M 1888 A.B. 1891. M.B., B.C. 1895. M.D.
—	Edgar Will.	Trin.	M 1908 A.B. 1911 [1898. A.M.† 1907
—	Geo. Will.	Em.	M 1909 A.B. 1911
—	Horace	Pem.	M 1912
—	Hugh Wilfrid	Joh.	M 1908 A.B. 1911
—	Ja.	Trin.	M 1910
—	John Geo.	Jes.	M 1901 A.B., LL.B. 1904
—	Killingworth Art. Utten	Trin.	M 1901 A.B. 1904. A.M. 1910
—	Leon.	King's	M 1894 A.B. 1897. A.M. 1902
—	Leslie Alder	N. C.	M 1905
—	Marshall	Chr.	M 1908 A.B. 1912
Todhunter,	Herb. Will.	Trin.	M 1892 A.B. 1895. A.M.† 1902
—	John Reg. Art. Digby	Cai.	M 1904 A.B. 1907
Toft,	Cha.	Pet.	M 1910
—	Ja. Hen.	Em.	M 1902 A.B. 1905. A.M. 1909
Tolhurst,	Fre.	Em.	M 1902 A.B. 1905. A.M. 1909
—	Geo. Alb.	Sid.	M 1907 A.B. 1911
Tollemache,	Art. Hen. Will.	Trin.	M 1912
—	John Eadred	Mag.	M 1911
Toller,	Tho. Eric	Cla.	M 1904
Tolley,	Frank Gordon	Trin. H.	M 1886 A.B., LL.B. 1889. LL.M. 1901.
Tollit,	Reg. Ja.	N. C.	M 1909 [A.M.† 1906
Tolmie,	Will. Lester	Trin.	M 1906 A.B. 1909
Tom,	Gee Fong	Down.	M 1906
—	Nai	King's	M 1906 A.B. 1909. LL.B. 1910
Tomblings,	Douglas Griffith	H. Sel.	M 1908 A.B. 1911
Tomkins,	Leopold Cha. Fellows	N. C.	M 1912
Tomkinson,	Cyril Edric	Sid.	M 1905 A.B. 1908. A.M. 1912
—	Geoffrey Stuart	King's	M 1902 A.B. 1905
—	Herb. Fre.	Sid.	M 1901 A.B. 1904. A.M. 1909
Tomkins-Russell,	Will. Howard	C. C.	M 1907 A.B. 1910
Tomlin,	Cha. Geoffrey	Jes.	M 1910
—	John Read le Brockton	Pem.	M 1883 A.B. 1886. A.M. 1902
Tomlins,	Art. Gladstone	Qu.	M 1904
Tomlinson,	Alb. Ern.	Em.	M 1912
—	Cecil Fra.	Em.	M 1898 A.B. 1901. A.M. 1905
—	Fre. Roger John	Trin.	M 1910
—	Geo. Art.	Joh.	M 1906
—	Harold	H. Sel.	M 1906
—	Hen. Rich.	Em.	M 1897 A.B. 1900. A.M. 1905
—	Percy Rob.	H. Sel.	M 1903 A.B., Mus.B. 1906. A.M. 1911
Tompson,	Alan Hawtin	Trin.	M 1899 A.B. 1902
—	Alf. Edw.	Trin.	M 1895 A.B. 1898. A.M. 1903

Tompson,	Cecil	Pem.	M 1901 A.B., LL.B. 1905
—	Frank Gordon	Joh.	M 1900 A.B. 1903. A.M. 1907
Tomson,	Douglas Vernon	Pet.	M 1902 A.B. 1905
Tonge,	Geo. Preston	Em.	M 1896 A.B. 1899. A.M. 1903
—	Rich. Dacre	Pem.	M 1910
Tongtor,	Mom Chow	Pet.	M 1912
Tongue,	Eric Dauncey	Em.	M 1910
Tonkin,	Reg. Sebert	Pem.	M 1911
Tonking,	Dav. Wilson	Mag.	M 1909
Tonks,	John Wilson	Cai.	M 1906 A.B. 1909
Toolis,	Ja. Hollingworth	Cla.	M 1912
Toone,	Cha. Gilb.	Joh.	M 1903 A.B. 1906. A.M. 1910
Tootal,	Reg. Mervyn	Trin.	M 1910
Tootell,	Raymond	Chr.	M 1911
Topham,	Denis Bevan	Cai.	M 1910
—	Hen. Angrave Cecil	Cla.	M 1910
Topley,	Will. Whiteman Carlton	Joh.	M 1904 A.B. 1907. M.B., B.C. 1911
Toplis,	Art. Rob.	Pet.	M 1904 A.B. 1907
—	Hen. Fre.	Cla.	M 1899 A.B. 1902. A.M. 1906
Topping,	Alex. Ross	Pem.	M 1911
Torbitt,	Ja. Hen.	N. C.	M 1897 A.B. 1900. A.M. 1912
—	Will. Stansfield	N. C.	M 1896 Pet. A.B. 1899. A.M. 1903. LL.B.
Torr,	John Herb. Graham	Trin.	M 1911 [1908. LL.M. 1910
Torrance,	Geo. Hammond	Em.	M 1894 A.B. 1897. A.M. 1902
Torrey,	Cecil Eric	Trin.	M 1908 A.B. 1911
—	Gerald Everett Franklin	Trin.	M 1902 A.B. 1905
Torry,	Art. Ja. Dashwood	Joh.	M 1905 A.B. 1908
Tosswill,	Cha. Gibson	Trin.	M 1894 A.B. 1897. A.M. 1901
Tottenham,	Cha. Edw. Loftus	Cai.	M 1906
Tottie,	Hen. Will.		*LL.D.* 1910
Toulmin,	Eric Humphrey	King's	M 1912
—	Geoffrey Edelston	King's	M 1907 A.B. 1911
Toulmin-Smith,	Alf. Kendal	Em.	M 1899 A.B. 1902
Tower,	Geoffrey Egerton	Trin.	M 1910
—	Hen. Bern.	Cath.	M 1901 A.B. 1904
Towers,	Will. Geo.	Trin.	M 1895 A.B. 1898. A.M. 1907
Towle,	John Howard	Joh.	M 1897 A.B. 1900. A.M. 1905
Town,	Art. Hen.	H.Cav.	M 1883 C. C. A.B. 1888. A.M. 1903
—	Cha. Aubrey	Jes.	M 1903 A.B., LL.B. 1906. A.M. 1910
Towndrow,	Edwin Ja.	N. C.	E 1907 A.B. 1910
Townend,	Harry Douglas	Qu.	M 1910
—	Merton Vincent	Joh.	M 1905
—	Roy Duncan Morrow	Sid.	M 1907 A.B. 1910
Townley,	Alex. Peregrine	Trin. H.	L 1892 A.B. 1902. A.M. 1908
—	Cha. Evelyn	Trin.	M 1906 A.B. 1909
Townsend,	Aubrey Lewis Hume	Cai.	M 1904 A.B. 1907
—	Ja.	N. C.	M 1904 Cath. A.B. 1907
—	Ja. Hen.	Pem.	M 1898 A.B. 1901. A.M. 1908
—	John Sealy Edw.	*Trin.	M 1895 A.B. 1897. A.M. 1903
—	Phil. Cha.	Trin. H.	M 1907
—	Rob. Wilfred	Joh.	M 1910
Townshend,	Hugh	Trin.	M 1909 A.B. 1912
Townson,	Benj. Arnold	Chr.	M 1911
Towsey,	Art. Stanley	Trin.	M 1907 A.B. 1910
Toye,	John Fra.	Trin.	M 1904
Toyne,	Fra. Digby	Qu.	M 1895 A.B. 1904. A.M. 1908
Tozer,	Ern. Fra.	Joh.	M 1905 A.B. 1908
Trachtenberg,	Hen. Lyon	Trin.	M 1901 A.B. 1904
—	Mendel Isidore	Joh.	M 1901 A.B. 1904
Tracy,	Geo. Dillon Croil	Em.	M 1912
Trafford,	Cecil Edw.	Trin.	M 1901

Trafford,	Lionel Guy	Jes.	M 1906
Traidos,	Mom Chow	Trin.	M 1901 A.B. 1904
Traill,	Ralph Rob.	Trin.	M 1911
Trapnell,	Fra. Cyril	King's	M 1898 A.B. 1901. M.B., B.C. 1909
—	John Graham	King's	M 1899 A.B., LL.B. 1903
Trasenster,	Will. Augustus	Trin.	M 1909 A.B. 1912
Trautmann,	Harry Fre.	Em.	M 1911 [M.B. 1909. M.D. 1911
Treadgold,	Cecil Hallworth	Cla.	M 1899 A.B. 1903. A.M. 1907. B.C. 1908.
—	Harry	Cai.	M 1905 A.B. 1908. A.M. 1912
—	Hen. Ashbourne	Down.	M 1903 A.B. 1906
Trechmann,	Otto Leopold	Cla.	M 1902
Tredcroft,	John Lennox	Trin.	M 1908
Tredennick,	John Nesbitt Ern. ...	Trin. H.	M 1911
Tree,	Cha. Ja.	Pem.	M 1909 A.B. 1912
Treffry,	Tho. Justin	Cai.	M 1906 A.B. 1910
Tregelles,	Geoffrey Phil.	Cai.	M 1911
Tregenza,	Cha. Wilfrid	Down.	M 1909 A.B. 1912
Treglown,	Claude Jesse Helby	Qu.	M 1911
Tregoning,	Art. Langford	Trin.	M 1893 A.B. 1896. A.M. 1911
—	Edgar Avery	Trin.	M 1902 A.B. 1905. A.M. 1912
—	Geoffrey Norris	Trin.	M 1900 A.B. 1903
—	Wynn Harold	Trin.	M 1894 A.B. 1897. A.M. 1907
Trehern,	Ern. Cha.	N. C.	L 1897 Joh., E. C. Meldon, A.B. 1899.
Treherne,	Fre. Geo. Will.	N. C.	M 1905 [LL.B. 1900. LL.M. 1905
Treleaven,	Woodman	Joh.	M 1906 A.B. 1909
Tremearne,	Allen Riddle	N. C.	E 1905 Joh. A.B. 1908
—	Art. John Newman	Chr.	L 1906 A.B. 1910
—	Tho. Fitzalan	Cai.	M 1903
—	Will. Crew	Chr.	L 1910
Trench,	Alf. Saward Chenevix	Trin.	M 1905 A.B. 1908
—	Claud Will.	Trin.	M 1900 A.B. 1903. LL.B. 1904. A.M. 1911
—	Clive Newcome	Trin.	M 1902 A.B. 1906
—	Edw. Cosby	Trin.	M 1899 A.B. 1902
—	Fre. Cha.	Trin.	M 1896 A.B. 1900. A.M.† 1910
—	Geo. Fre.	H. Sel.	M 1899 A.B. 1902. A.M. 1908
—	Hub. Roland	Trin.	M 1905 A.B. 1908
—	John Hen.	Trin.	M 1897 A.B. 1901. A.M. 1907. M.B., B.C.
—	Rob. Hamilton	Trin.	M 1899 A.B. 1902 [1908
—	Will. Langton	Trin.	M 1899 A.B. 1902
Trenchard,	Fre. Alf.	Trin. H.	M 1906 A.B. 1909
Trend,	John Brande	Chr.	M 1906 A.B. 1909
Trendell,	Claude Cha. Wollaston	Cla.	M 1911 [B.C. 1907
Tresawna,	Will. Samson	Sid.	M 1898 A.B. 1901. W. Sampson M.B.,
Trestrail,	Alf. Ern. Yates	Chr.	E 1894 A.B. 1897. A.M.† 1906
Treumann,	Heinrich Hermann ...	Em.	M 1895 A.B. 1898. A.M.† 1906
Trevaskis,	Hugh Kennedy	King's	M 1901 A.B. 1904
Trevelyan,	Geo. Otto	Trin.	M 1857 A.B. 1861. A.M. 1864. *Litt.D.* 1908
Treves,	Fre. Boileau	Cai.	M 1898 A.B. 1901. M.B., B.C., A.M. 1909
—	Wilfrid Warwick ...	Cai.	M 1901 A.B. 1904. M.B., B.C. 1909
Trevitt,	Will. Reg.	N. C.	M 1904 A.B. 1907. A.M. 1911
Trevor-Roper,	Cha. Cadwaladr ...	Cla.	M 1904
Trew,	Maur. Fre.	Pem.	M 1911
Trewby,	Art.	Pem.	M 1899 A.B. 1902. A.M. 1907
Trewhella,	Cha. Bern.	Pem.	M 1912
Tribe,	Keith Wilberforce ...	Em.	M 1909 A.B. 1912
Trickett,	Wilfrid Rich.	C. C.	M 1898 A.B., LL.B. 1901. A.M. 1905.
Trier,	Norman Ern.	Cla.	M 1907 A.B. 1911 [LL.M. 1906
Trikha,	Karam Chand	N. C.	L 1911
Trill,	Harold Durham	Trin. H.	M 1905 A.B. 1908. LL.B. 1909
Trimble,	Cha. John Agnew ...	Trin.	M 1902 A.B. 1905
Trinder,	Arnold Anderson ...	Cla.	M 1898 A.B. 1901

Tringham,	Harold Rob. Parnell	Cla.	M 1894 A.B. 1897. A.M. 1901
Tripp,	Noel Fra.	Em.	M 1911
Trist,	Leslie Hamilton	Cath.	M 1902 A.B. 1905. A.M. 1909
Trollope,	Cha. Hen. Bathurst	Trin.	M 1895 A.B. 1898. A.M. 1902
—	Tho. Anth.	Cai.	M 1912
—	Tho. Cha. Stapleton	Trin. H.	M 1912
Trotman,	Frank Fiennes	Sid.	E 1899 A.B. 1903
Trott,	Fra. Will.	Joh.	M 1912
Trotter,	Colin Liddell	Trin.	M 1909
—	Frowyke	Cla.	M 1905
—	Ja. Maitland Yorke	King's	M 1907 A.B. 1910
—	John	Trin.	M 1872 A.B. 1876. A.M. 1907
—	John Fre. Art.	Trin. H.	M 1906
—	John Lonsdale	Cla.	M 1912
—	Kenneth Stuart	Trin.	M 1911
—	Leslie Batten Currie	Cla.	M 1902 A.B. 1905. B.C. 1909. A.M. 1910
—	Rich. Durant	Trin.	M 1905 A.B. 1908
—	Will. Finlayson	Trin.	M 1892 A.B. 1896. A.M., LL.M. 1902
Troubridge,	Ja. Lewis	Joh.	M 1905 A.B. 1908
Trought,	Trevor	Joh.	M 1910
Trouton,	Edm. Art.	Trin.	M 1910
—	Fre. Tho.	Trin.	M 1910
Trower,	Geoffrey Say	King's	M 1909 A.B. 1912
Trubshaw,	Cha. Smith	Cla.	M 1908 A.B. 1911
—	Harold Ern.	Cla.	M 1901 A.B. 1906. A.M. 1910
Truell,	Rob. Holt Stuart ...	Trin.	M 1894 A.B. 1897. A.M. 1901
—	Will. Hen. Stuart ...	Jes.	M 1910
Truman,	Marcus Geo.	H. Sel.	M 1909 A.B. 1912
Trumper,	John Hen. Walwyn	Joh.	M 1904 A.B. 1907
Truscott,	Fra. Geo.	Trin.	M 1912
—	Roy Fra.	King's	M 1899 A.B. 1904. A.M. 1909
Trusted,	Harry Herb.	Trin. H.	M 1909
Tryon,	Geo. Art.	Pem.	M 1905 A.B. 1908. A.M. 1912
Tsai Tse,	*H.I.H.* Fung En Chen Ko (*Duke*)		*LL.D.* 1906
Tsan,	Yu Huan	Trin.	M 1904 A.B. 1909. A.M. 1912
Tseng,	Tsung Kieng	Pem.	M 1904
Tso,	Cheng-Yi	Chr.	M 1905
Tubbs,	Leon.	Cai.	M 1889 A.B. 1892. A.M. 1902
—	Norman Hen.	Cai.	M 1898 A.B. 1902. A.M. 1905
Tuck,	Cha. Herb.	Cath.	M 1911
—	Desmond Adolph ...	King's	M 1907
—	Gerald Louis Johnson	King's	M 1909 A.B. 1912
—	Gilb. Bern. Owen ...	Pem.	M 1900 A.B. 1903
—	Gnoh Lean	Em.	M 1896 A.B. 1899. M.B., B.C. 1902. A.M.
—	Noel Johnson	Trin.	M 1911 [1903. M.D.† 1905
Tucker,	Alf. Rob.		*LL.D.* 1908
—	Ern. Edwin Geo. ...	Cai.	M 1904 A.B. 1907
—	Geo. Dean Raffles ...	Mag.	M 1897 A.B. 1901. A.M. 1910
—	Lewis Gordon	Qu.	M 1907 A.B. 1910
—	Rich. Will. Ethelbert	H. Sel.	M 1911
—	Will. Eldon	Cai.	M 1891 A.B., M.B., B.C. 1902
Tuckett,	Ivor Lloyd ....*Trin.		M 1890 A.B. 1893. A.M. 1897. M.D. 1910
Tuckey,	Cha. Orpen	Trin.	M 1894 A.B. 1897. A.M. 1903
Tudor,	Oswald Campbell Owen	H. Sel.	M 1905 A.B. 1909. A.M. 1912
—	Roland Grimston ...	H. Sel.	M 1910
Tudsbery,	Fra. Cannon Tudsbery	King's	M 1906 A.B., LL.B. 1909
Tufnell,	Neville Charsley	Trin.	M 1907
Tufnell-Klug,	Maur. Will.	Cla.	M 1903
Tugwell,	Herb.	C. C.	M 1877 A.B. 1881. D.D.† 1906
Tulloch,	Herb. Maur.	Qu.	M 1911
Tunmer,	Edwin Ja. Eastlake	Em.	M 1902 A.B. 1905. A.M. 1909

Turcan,	Ja. Somerville	Cai.	M 1909 A.B. 1912
Turkington,	Ja. Stewart	Chr.	M 1912
Turkovich,	(*Baron*) Velimir	Trin. H.	M 1912
Turnbull,	Art. Peveril	Trin.	M 1903 A.B. 1906. A.M. 1910
—	Edwin Laurence	Chr.	M 1907 A.B. 1910. LL.B. 1912
—	Herb. Westren	Trin.	M 1904 A.B. 1907. A.M. 1911
—	Ja. Geo. Stuart	Trin.	M 1900 A.B. 1903
—	Peveril Hayes	Qu.	M 1908 A.B. 1912
—	Phil. Corbett	Trin.	M 1898 A.B. 1901. A.M. 1905
—	Roger Will.	Trin.	M 1901 A.B. 1904. A.M., LL.B. 1908
—	Tho. Lancelot Gawain	Trin.	M 1911
—	Valentine Mounsey	Trin.	M 1888 A.B. 1891. A.M. 1906
—	Will. Art.	Em.	M 1912
—	Will. Elliot	King's	M 1907 A.B. 1910
Turnell,	Cyril Mee	Joh.	M 1899 A.B. 1902. A.M. 1906
Turner,	Alf. Cha.	Em.	M 1911
—	Alf. Geoffrey	Trin.	M 1905
—	Anth. Whitelock	Trin.	M 1908 A.B. 1911
—	Archer	Qu.	M 1906 A.B. 1909
—	Art. Charlewood	*Trin.	M 1900 A.B. 1903. A.M. 1907
—	Art. Ja.	Cai.	M 1908 A.B. 1911
—	Edw. Percy	Chr.	M 1911
—	Edwin Muncaster	N. C.	M 1899 A.B. 1902
—	Eric Mark	Cath.	M 1908
—	Ern. Geo.	Joh.	M 1893 A.B. 1896. A.M. 1902
—	Ern. Hen.	Trin. H.	M 1901 A.B. 1904
—	Fra. Gordon	Trin.	M 1908 A.B. 1911
—	Frank John	Down.	M 1895 A.B. 1898. A.M. 1904
—	Geo. Ja.	Joh.	M 1886 A.B. 1889. A.M. 1901
—	Geo. MacDougall	Cath.	M 1909 A.B. 1911
—	Harold Agnew	Pem.	M 1911
—	Harold Wilton	N. C.	M 1905 Chr. A.B. 1908. A.M. 1912
—	Hen. Charlewood	Em.	M 1898 A.B. 1901. A.M. 1908
—	Hen. Hawkins	Trin.	M 1891 A.B. 1894. A.M. 1910
—	Hen. Ja.	Down.	M 1906 A.B. 1910
—	Ja. Will. Cecil	Qu.	M 1906 A.B. 1909. LL.B. 1910
—	John Cross	Chr.	M 1900 A.B. 1903. A.M. 1907
—	John Pater	H. Sel.	M 1911
—	John Reg.	King's	L 1902 A.B. 1905
—	John Sid.	H. Sel.	M 1903 A.B. 1906
—	John Trench	Cla.	M 1899 A.B. 1902. A.M.† 1906
—	Jos. Will.	N. C.	M 1903 A.B. 1906
—	Laurence Beddome	King's	M 1904 A.B. 1907. A.M. 1912
—	Percy Reg.	Pem.	M 1895 A.B. 1898. A.M. 1902
—	Ralph Charlewood	Trin.	M 1898 A.B. 1901. A.M. 1905
—	Ralph Lilley	*Chr.	M 1907 A.B. 1910
—	Roland	Joh.	M 1902 A.B. 1906
—	Ronald	Qu.	M 1904 A.B. 1907
—	Sid.	Cai.	M 1901 A.B. 1904
—	Will. Art. Scales	Trin.	M 1908 A.B. 1911
—	Will. Hovell	Chr.	M 1912
—	Will. Leslie	Joh.	M 1909 A.B. 1912
Turpin,	Ja. Knowles	Chr.	M 1911
Turrall,	Rupert Guy	Trin. H.	M 1912
Turton,	Willie Jack Trevor	Trin. H.	M 1892 A.B. 1895. A.M. 1911
Tuson,	Alan Art. Lancelot	Jes.	M 1909 A.B. 1912
Tuttle,	Dan. Sylvester		LL.D. 1908
Twamley,	Cyril Ern.	H. Sel.	M 1903 A.B. 1907
Tweddell,	John Ruthven Marshall	Cla.	M 1899 A.B. 1902
Tweedale,	Frank	Down.	M 1903
Tweedie,	Gershom Ivan Fra.	Cai.	M 1911

Tweedie,	Harley Alex.	Trin.	M 1906
—	Ja: Moore	Cai.	M 1903 A.B. 1906
—	Leslie Kinloch	Cai.	M 1908 A.B. 1912
Tweedy,	Owen Meredith	Cai.	M 1908 A.B. 1911
—	Roger John	Cai.	M 1907 A.B. 1910
—	Wharton Rich.	Trin.	M 1907
Tween,	Alf. Stuart	Cai.	M 1910
Twells,	John	Jes.	M 1904 A.B. 1907
Twentyman,	Denzil Clive Tate ...	Joh.	M 1909
—	Geo.	N. C.	E 1897 A.B. 1900. A.M. 1904
—	John Musgrave	Chr.	M 1888 A.B. 1891. M.B., B.C. 1903
—	Wilfrid Price	Chr.	M 1897 A.B. 1900. A.M. 1904
Twigg,	Garnet Wolsley	Cai.	M 1901 A.B. 1904. M.B., B.C. 1910
Twinn,	Frank Cha. Geo.	Joh.	M 1904 A.B. 1907
Tyabji,	Husain Budroodin ...	Down.	M 1891 A.B. 1895. LL.B. 1896. A.M.,
Tyágarája,	Jagannathan	Chr.	M 1912 [LL.M.† 1909
Tyau,	Phil. King Chin	Chr.	M 1902 A.B. 1905. A.M., LL.B. 1909
Tye,	Will.	Chr.	M 1910
Tyer,	Austin Arnold	King's	M 1906 A.B. 1909
Tyers,	Fre. Geo.	Pem.	M 1899 A.B. 1902. A.M.† 1910
Tyler,	Cha. Hen.	Pem.	M 1886 A.B. 1889. A.M. 1909
—	Ern. Alb.	Joh.	M 1893 A.B. 1897. A.M. 1909
—	Hector Granville } Sutherland }	Trin.	M 1890 A.B. 1893. A.M. 1901
Tylor,	Chris.	Cai.	M 1898 A.B. 1902. B.C., A.M. 1907. M.B.
—	Edw. Burnett		*Sc.D.* 1905 [1910. M.D. 1911
—	Geo. Cunningham ...	Pem.	M 1908 A.B. 1911
Tyndale-Biscoe,	Harold L'Estrange	Jes.	M 1911
Tyrrell,	Cuthbert Frank	Joh.	M 1898 A.B. 1903. A.M. 1906
Tyrwhitt-Drake,	Barnard Halsey	Pem.	M 1901 A.B. 1904. A.M. 1908
Tyrwhitt Drake,	Cha. Will.	Trin.	M 1898 A.B. 1901 [1900. M.D. 1912
Tyson,	Wilson	Cai.	M 1889 A.B. 1892. B.C. 1896. M.B., A.M.

U

Uesugi,	Noriaki	N. C.	E 1904
Uhthoff,	Roland King	Cai.	M 1906 A.B. 1909
Uloth,	Alex. Wilmot	Pem.	M 1908 A.B. 1911
Ulyat,	Edw. Stewart	Trin.	M 1906 A.B. 1909
Underdown,	Herb. Will.	Pem.	M 1882 A.B. 1886. LL.M. 1901
Underwood,	Hen. Laurence	Cla.	M 1894 A.B. 1897. LL.B. 1898. A.M. 1906
Ungoed,	G. T.		*See* Thomas, G. U.
Unstead,	John Fre.	N. C.	M 1895 A.B. 1898. A.M. 1906
Unthank,	Herb. Will.	King's	M 1911
—	John Baxter	H. Sel.	L 1905 A.B. 1907. A.M. 1911
Unwin,	Ern. Frederic	Cath.	M 1900 A.B. 1903
—	Harold Art. Rob. Edmond	H. Sel.	M 1899 A.B. 1902. M.B., B.C., A.M. 1907
—	Phil. Hen.	H. Sel.	M 1904 A.B. 1907
—	Steph. Ralph	H. Sel.	M 1895 A.B. 1899. A.M. 1906
—	Wilfrid Norman	Cla.	M 1897 A.B. 1901. A.M. 1904
Upcher,	Edw. Cyrill Sparke	Trin.	M 1891 A.B. 1894. A.M. 1905
—	Nich.	Trin.	M 1905 A.B. 1908
Upjohn,	Dudley Fra.	Trin.	M 1901
—	Will. Moon	Trin.	M 1903

Upsdell,	Geo. Edgar Skynner	N. C.	M 1907 A.B. 1910
Upton,	Geo. Frazier	Em.	M 1900 A.B. 1903. A.M. 1907
—	Rich.	Jes.	M 1899 A.B. 1903
—	Will. Edwin	Sid.	M 1902 A.B. 1905. A.M. 1909
Upward,	Harold Art.	Chr.	M 1892 A.B. 1895. M.B., B.C. 1901
—	Leslie Vaughan	Qu.	M 1909 A.B. 1912
Ure,	Colin McGregor	Pem.	M 1911
—	Percy Neville	Cai.	M 1898 A.B. 1901. A.M. 1911
Urquhart,	Ja. Lawrence	Em.	M 1910
—	John	Jes.	M 1906 A.B. 1909
Urwick,	Reg. Hen.	Trin.	M 1894 A.B. 1897. M.B., B.C., A.M. 1901.
Usher,	Herb. Brough	Trin. H.	M 1912　　　　　　　[M.D. 1905
—	Reg. Nevile	Cai.	M 1903 A.B. 1906. A.M. 1910
—	Tho.	Trin. H.	M 1902 A.B. 1905. LL.B. 1907
Usherwood,	Edw. Cuthbert	King's	M 1896 A.B. 1899. A.M. 1904
Uzielli,	Clive Fre.	Trin.	M 1902
—	Herb. Rex	Pem.	M 1909 A.B. 1912

V

Vachell,	Eustace Tanfield	King's	M 1912
—	Frank	Trin. H.	M 1908 A.B. 1912
Vachha,	Fardunji Bejanji	N. C.	E 1910 Chr. A.B. 1912
Vaidya,	Shridhar Balkrishna	Joh.	M 1908 A.B. 1911
Vaish,	Nehal Chand	N. C.	M 1911
Vaizey,	Reg. Bromley	Cath.	M 1910
Valassopoulo,	Geo.	King's	M 1908 A.B. 1911
Vale,	Hen. Edm. Theodoric	Joh.	M 1909
Valentine,	Cha. Wilfrid	Down.	M 1905 A.B. 1908
Valpy,	John Herb. Julius ...	Trin.	M 1888 A.B. 1891. A.M. 1903
van Beneden, Édouard			Sc.D. 1909
van Breda,	Will.	Cla.	L 1904 A.B., LL.B. 1907
Vance,	John Gabriel	N. C.	M 1907 A.B. 1910
van Cuylenburg, Carl Willhem Fre.		Chr.	M 1905
Van der Byl, Alb. Myburgh		Pem.	M 1900 A.B. 1903
—	Alex. Hen.	Pem.	M 1905 A.B. 1908
—	Pieter Voltelyn Graham	Pem.	M 1907 A.B. 1910
van Druten, Hen. John		Joh.	M 1911
Van Duzer,	Selah Reeve	Trin.	M 1899 A.B. 1902
Vane,	(Hon.) Chris. Will. ...	Trin.	M 1907 A.B. 1910
—	Ralph Frederic	Trin.	M 1909
Vane-Tempest, Ern. Cha. Will. ...		Trin.	M 1912
Van Hamen, Howard		Down.	M 1902
van Hees,	Alb. Strancham Marsh	Joh.	E 1903 A.B., LL.B. 1906. A.M.† 1910
Vann,	Art. Harrison Allard	Jes.	M 1909
—	Bern. Will.	Jes.	M 1907 A.B. 1910
van Pallandt, Hugh Hope Alex. (Baron)		Joh.	L 1911
van Raalte, Noel Marcus		Trin.	M 1907
van Schalkwijk, Johannes		Cai.	M 1904 A.B. 1906. B.C., A.M. 1911
van Soelen, Cha. Bernardus Schraüdt		Trin. H.	E 1904 A.B. 1907

van Soelen,	Johannes Gerhardus } Verstolck {	Trin. H.	M 1902 A.B., LL.B. 1905
van Someren,	Hen. Arnold Avenel	Pem.	M 1903
van Verschuer,	(Baron) Wolter } Frans Frederik {	Chr.	M 1909
Van Vestraut, Leon.		Pet.	M 1908 A.B. 1911
van Zijl,	Hendrik Stephanus	Joh.	M 1898 LL.B. 1901
Varain,	Adolf Josef	Chr.	M 1908
Vardy,	Alb. Theodore	Pem.	M 1907 A.B. 1910
Varley,	Gilb.	Chr.	M 1893 A.B. 1896. A.M.† 1911
—	Harold	Qu.	M 1908 A.B. 1911
—	Leon.	Trin.	M 1911
—	Will. Mansergh	N. C.	M 1901 Em. A.B. 1903. A.M. 1908
Varma,	Lala Sarada Prasad	Down.	M 1910
Varvill,	John Kenneth	Mag.	M 1910
Varwell,	Ralph Peter	Joh.	M 1901 A.B. 1906
Vatcher,	Hen. Monckton	Cla.	M 1905 A.B. 1908
Vaudrey,	Will. Edm.	Cai.	M 1912
Vaughan,	Art.	Trin.	M 1887 A.B. 1890. A.M. 1911
—	Eric Will. Bowman	Trin.	M 1907 A.B. 1910
—	John Hen.	C. C.	M 1911
—	Reg. Bowman	Trin.	M 1904 A.B. 1908
Vaughan-Williams,	Ralph	Trin.	M 1892 Mus.B. 1894. A.B. 1895. Mus.D.
Vause,	Tho. Chris.	Joh.	M 1904 A.B. 1907. A.M. 1911 [1901
Vaux,	Reg. Worship	Cla.	L 1910
Veevers,	Will.	Joh.	M 1905 A.B., LL.B. 1908
Veitch,	Alex. Gordon	Qu.	M 1907 A.B. 1910
Vejdovský,	František		Sc.D. 1909
Vellacott,	Humphrey Doidge ...	N. C.	M 1912
—	Paul Cairn	Pet.	M 1910
Venables,	Art. John	Pem.	M 1903
—	Frank Leslie	C. C.	M 1899 A.B. 1902
Venn,	Art. Dennis	Pem.	M 1899 A.B. 1903. A.M. 1907
—	John Archib.	Trin.	M 1902 A.B. 1905. A.M. 1909
Venning,	Ja. Art.	Trin.	M 1899 A.B. 1902. M.B., B.C., A.M. 1907
Vercoe,	Rich. Herb.	Joh.	M 1903 A.B. 1906
Verdon,	Egbert Sumner	Jes.	M 1887 A.B. 1891. A.M. 1896. M.B., B.C.
—	Phil.	Jes.	M 1905 A.B. 1908 [1897. M.D.† 1901
Vereker,	Geo. Gordon Medlicott	Trin.	M 1907 A.B. 1910
—	(Hon.) Standish Rob.	Trin.	M 1907
Vere-Walwyn,	Algernon Edw.	Pet.	M 1907 A.B. 1910
Verey,	Hen. Edw.	Trin.	M 1896 A.B., LL.B. 1899. A.M. 1906
—	Lewis	Trin. H.	M 1893 A.B. 1897. A.M. 1902
Verma,	Hiralal	Chr.	L 1900 A.B. 1903
Vernon,	Cecil Heygate	Joh.	M 1911
—	John Campion	Trin.	M 1904
—	Rob. Douglass	Em.	M 1909 A.B. 1911
—	Rupert John	Cai.	M 1899 A.B. 1903. M.B., B.C., A.M. 1911
Vernon-Jones			See Jones, Vernon S.
Verrall,	¹Art. Woollgar ....*Trin.		M 1869 A.B. 1873. A.M. 1876. Litt.D. 1888
—	Chris. Fra.	Trin.	M 1907 A.B. 1911
—	Fre. Herb.	Em.	M 1902 A.B. 1905. LL.B. 1906
—	Paul Jenner	Trin.	M 1902 A.B. 1905. M.B., B.C. 1908
Verry,	Bertrand Tyrrell	Pem.	M 1902 A.B. 1905
Verworn,	Max		Sc.D. 1909
Vestey,	Frank	Cla.	M 1911
—	Percy Cha.	Cla.	M 1911
Vey,	Dav. Chris. Leslie ...	Cla.	M 1908 A.B. 1911
—	Frank Hamilton	Cla.	M 1907 A.B. 1910

¹ King Edward VII Professor of English Literature, 1911.

Veysey,	Will. Burdett	Qu.	M 1903 A.B. 1906. A.M. 1912
Vicary,	Ronald Herb.	Cai.	M 1902
Vick,	Godfrey Russell	Jes.	M 1910
—	Reg. Martin	Jes.	M 1902 A.B. 1905. B.C., A.M. 1909
Vickers,	Rob.	Trin.	M 1912
—	Stansfeld	Cai.	M 1900 A.B. 1903
—	Vernon Cha. Whitby	Em.	M 1907
Vigers,	Edgar Hall	Joh.	M 1896 A.B. 1900. A.M. 1903
Viggars,	Spencer Hollins	C. C.	M 1909 A.B. 1912
Vigo,	Ja. Dav.	Pem.	M 1912
Villar,	Rob.	Pem.	M 1904 A.B. 1907
Vincent,	Harold Graham	Jes.	M 1911
—	Jos. Herb.	Joh.	M 1897 A.B. 1899. A.M. 1904
—	Leslie Jack	N. C.	M 1910
—	Rich. Beaumont	Trin.	M 1911
Vine,	Bernard Theodore ...	Joh.	M 1906 A.B. 1910
Vines,	Howard Will. Copland	Chr.	M 1911
—	Neville Boultbee	N. C.	L 1900 Cath. A.B. 1902. A.M. 1908
Viney,	Fra. Hen.	Cai.	M 1901 A.B. 1904. A.M. 1909
Vining,	Leslie Gordon	Em.	M 1907 A.B. 1910
Vinning,	Harold Syd.	Qu.	M 1902 A.B. 1905. A.M. 1909
Vinogradoff,	Paul		*LL.D.* 1905
Vint,	Morley Dyson	Chr.	M 1912
Vinter,	Ern.	N. C.	M 1896 A.B., LL.B. 1900. A.M. 1912
—	Eustace Art. Fitz-gerald	Em.	M 1903 A.B. 1906
Vinycomb,	Tho. Bern.	Joh.	M 1903
Vipond,	Harry Ja.	Pem.	M 1904 A.B. 1907
Vischer,	Hanns	Em.	M 1896 A.B. 1899. A.M. 1903
—	Marcus Matthaeus ...	Em.	M 1898 A.B. 1901. A.M. 1905
Vivian,	Cha. St Aubyn	Cai.	M 1901 A.B. 1904
—	Cha. Treble Vivian	Trin.	M 1903
—	Graham Linsell	H. Sel.	M 1906 A.B. 1909
Volterra,	Vito		*Sc.D.* 1904
von Achenbach, Gyso		Trin.	M 1910
von Biedermann, Rob. Hans Simon Ritter		Trin.	M 1901
von Blücher, Friedrich Jobst August Otto Alex.		Chr.	E 1902
von Dietze, Friedrich Carl Nicolaus Constantin		Trin.	E 1909
von Friedenthal-Falkenhausen, (*Freiherr*) Ernst Carl Rudolf Friedrich		King's	E 1904
von Glehn,	Louis Camille	King's	M 1888 A.B. 1892. A.M. 1904
von Goebel,	Karl Eberhard		*Sc.D.* 1909
von Graff,	Ludwig		*Sc.D.* 1909
von Groth,	Paul Heinrich		*Sc.D.* 1904
von Heeringen, Moritz		N. C.	E 1909
von Herkomer, Hubert			*LL.D.* 1908
von Kaufmann, Geo.		Chr.	M 1912
—	Gunther Jacob Ferdinand Rob.	Cai.	M 1902
von Klitzing, Dietrich Wilhelm Leopold		Trin.	M 1908
von Latinovits, Johann		Mag.	M 1912
von Lübtow, Wilhelm August Julius Gustav		Chr.	M 1911
von Oldenburg-Beisleiden, Curt Claus Botho Bernhard Gottvertrau Elard		N. C.	E 1901
von Plener, (*Baron*) Ern. Jos. ...		Trin.	M 1907

von Pongratz, Guido	Trin. H.	L 1912	
von Pretis-Cagnodo, (*Baron*) Sisinio	Trin.	M 1910	
von Schmidt-Pauli, Fiath Florentin Rich. Edgar	Pet.	M 1901	
von Schoenburg-Waldenburg, Günther Alexander Johann Wilhelm	Trin.	E 1905	
von Schröder, Rudolf Ernst Karl Helmuth	Trin.	M 1911	
von Strasser, Erwin Andreas	Trin.	L 1912	
von Tarnóczy, Friedrich Aloys Ludwig	Trin.	E 1907	
von Taussig, Felix Ritter	Pet.	L 1909	
— Georg Ritter	Pet.	L 1909	
von Tiedemann, Heinrich Erich Helmut Egid	King's	E 1904	
von Tobel, Clem. Ambrose	Jes.	M 1907	
von Ullmann, Francis	Trin.	L 1912	
— Georg Maria	Trin.	M 1908	
von Vöchting, Hermann		*Sc.D.* 1909	
von Voss, Agathon Carl Wilhelm Fritz	Chr.	E 1902	
von Weiss, Alfons Benno	Trin.	M 1908	A.B. 1911
von Wilamowitz-Moellendorff, Ulrich		*LL.D.* 1908	
Vos, Phil.	Cai.	M 1909	
— Solomon	Trin.	M 1907	
Vulliamy, Edw. Owen	King's	M 1895	A.B. 1898. A.M. 1910
Vyvyan			*See* Warschawski, R. R. V.
— Edw. Courteney Ferrars	Pem.	M 1905	A.B. 1908
— Maur. Courtenay	Cai.	M 1910	
— Wilmot Lushington	Trin.	M 1880	A.B. 1884. A.M. 1896. D.D. 1908

W

Wace,	Alan John Bayard ...*Pem.	M 1898	A.B. 1901. A.M. 1906
—	Gerald Art.	Qu.	M 1905 A.B. 1909
—	Hen. Edw.	Pem.	M 1908
Wacher,	Harold	Joh.	M 1894 A.B. 1897. M.B., B.C. 1903
Wada,	Jumpei	N. C.	L 1912
Waddington,	Alb. Edw. John	Jes.	M 1901
Waddy,	Art. Cyril	Cai.	M 1911
—	John Raymond	Pem.	M 1906 A.B. 1909
Wade,	Art. Nugent	C. C.	M 1903 A.B. 1906
—	Ern. Aughtry	H. Sel.	M 1906 A.B. 1909
—	Hugh Blake	Pem.	M 1902
—	John Roland	Qu.	M 1909 A.B. 1912
—	Ralph Porter	Chr.	M 1902 A.B. 1905. A.M. 1909
—	Ruben	Chr.	M 1898 A.B. 1901
Wadely,	Fre. Will.	H. Sel.	M 1900 A.B., Mus.B. 1903. A.M. 1907
Wadham,	Sam. MacMahon	Chr.	M 1910
Wadia,	Ardeshir Ruttonji	N. C.	M 1912
—.	Hirjibhoy Hormusji	N. C.	L 1896 A.B. 1897. A.M.† 1910
—	Nowrojee Jehangir	Joh.	M 1904 Nowroji, J. A.B. 1907
—	Siavax Hirji	Joh.	M 1910
Wadley,	Geo. Fra.	King's	M 1901
—	Harold Walt. Attwood	H. Sel.	M 1901 A.B. 1904. A.M. 1908

Wadsworth,	Sid.	Jes.	M 1908 A.B. 1911
Wagg,	Fre. John	Qu.	L 1908 A.B. 1910
Waggett,	Phil. Napier	Trin.	M 1909 A.M. Incorp. Oxf. 1910
Wagle,	Balvant Krishnarao	Sid.	M 1908 A.B. 1911
Wagner,	Karl Wilhelm Rob.	Em.	M 1909 A.B. 1912
—	Rich. Harry	Chr.	M 1910
Wagstaff,	Cha. John Leon.	Em.	M 1894 A.B. 1897. A.M. 1901
—	John Edw. Pretty ...	Joh.	M 1911
Wahlen,	Adolf	Chr.	M 1910
Wailes,	Fra. Geo.	Em.	M 1906 A.B. 1909
Wailes-Fairbairn, Neville Will. ⎰ Fairbairn ⎱		Jes.	M 1911
Wainwright, Cha. Barron		Cai.	M 1905 A.B. 1908. M.B., B.C. 1912
—	Ern. Harry	Joh.	M 1894 A.B. 1897. A.M. 1902
—	Geo. Bertram	Trin.	M 1899 A.B. 1902. M.B., B.C. 1910
—	Leon. Austin	Qu.	L 1909
—	Ronald Cha.	Trin.	M 1908 A.B. 1911
Wait,	Roland Ja.	Jes.	M 1912
Waite,	Wilfrid Fabian	Down.	M 1904
Waite-Browne, Hen. Franklyn ...		Joh.	M 1900 A.B. 1903
Wajid Ali,	Sheikh	Chr.	M 1910 A.B. 1912
Wakefield,	Archib. Hamlyn	Cath.	M 1912
—	Art. Will.	Trin.	M 1895 A.B. 1898. M.B., B.C., A.M. 1906.
—	Hen. Russell	Cath.	M 1910 [M.D. 1909
—	John Hylbert	Trin.	M 1905 A.B. 1908
—	Roger Will.	Trin.	M 1883 A.B. 1886. A.M. 1894. B.C. 1897.
—	Will. Vivian	Jes.	M 1910 [M.B. 1903
Wakeford,	Edw. Kingsley	Trin.	M 1912
Wakelam,	Henry Blythe Thornhill	Pem.	M 1911
Wakely,	Ern. Hedley	N. C.	M 1896 A.B. 1899. A.M. 1903
—	Herb. Denning	Joh.	M 1901 A.B. 1904
—	Leon. Day	Joh.	M 1898 A.B. 1901
Walcot,	Tho. Bielby	N. C.	M 1898 A.B. 1901. A.M. 1905
Walcott,	Cha. Doolittle		*Sc.D.* 1909
Waldegrave,	Geo. Turner	Em.	M 1908 A.B. 1911
—	Sam. Cha.	Em.	M 1907 A.B. 1910
Walden-Vincent, Alf. Coplestone		Pem.	M 1908 A.B., LL.B. 1911
—	Cha. Lorraine	Pem.	M 1903 A.B. 1906
Walder,	Ern.	Cai.	M 1891 A.B. 1894. A.M. 1907
Waldeyer,	Wilhelm		*Sc.D.* 1904
Waldram,	Horace Geo.	Sid.	M 1908 A.B. 1911
Wale,	Eric Harry	Trin.	M 1910
Wales,	Edw. Garneys	Down.	M 1895 A.B. 1898. M.B., B.C., A.M. 1902
—	Herb.	Sid.	M 1896 A.B. 1899. B.C., A.M. 1903. M.B.
Waley,	Frank Raphael	King's	M 1912 [1905
Walford,	Hen. Howard	Cai.	M 1906 A.B. 1909. LL.B. 1910
Wali-Mohammad, Choudhri		Pet.	M 1908 A.B. 1910
Walker,	Alf. Holloway	Trin.	M 1901 A.B. 1904. A.M. 1908
—	Alf. Ja.	Joh.	M 1892 A.B. 1895. A.M. 1904
—	Angus Campbell	Cai.	M 1911
—	Archib. Edw. John	Jes.	M 1908
—	Archib. Galbraith ...	Joh.	M 1900 A.B. 1903
—	Art.	Em.	M 1897 A.B. 1900. M.B., B.C. 1907
—	Art. Nimmo	Qu.	M 1892 A.B. 1895. M.B., B.C. 1899. M.D.
—	Art. Rob.	Em.	M 1911 [1910
—	Basil Scarisbrick	King's	M 1908 A.B., LL.B. 1911
—	Cecil Edw.	Cla.	M 1904 A.B. 1907
—	Cha. Aug. Percival ...	Cai.	M 1912
—	Cha. Valentine	Cla.	M 1905 A.B. 1908
—	Denham	Pem.	M 1907 A.B. 1910
—	Edm. Basil	Em.	M 1907 A.B. 1910

Walker,	Edw. Melville	Pet.	L 1912
—	Edw. Rich. Zouche	Cath.	M 1901 A.B. 1904
—	Ern. Elliot	Trin.	M 1902 A.B. 1905
—	Fra. Gerald	Trin.	M 1901 A.B. 1904
—	Fre. Carrington	Chr.	M 1909 A.B. 1912
—.	Fre. Geo.	Jes.	L 1909 A.M. Incorp. Dubl. 1909
—	Garrett Alex. Cooper	Cla.	M 1912
—	Geo. Dav.	Em.	M 1907
—	Geo. Stafford	Mag.	M 1910
—	Geo. Walker ....*Trin.		M 1894 A.B. 1897. A.M. 1901 [M.B. 1911
—	Gerald	Trin.	M 1901 A.B. 1904. A.M. 1908. B.C. 1909.
—	Gilb. Tho. ....*Trin.		M 1886 A.B. 1889. A.M. 1893. Sc.D.† 1904
—	Harold	King's	M 1893 A.B. 1896. M.B., B.C., A.M. 1902
—	Hen.	Em.	M 1898 A.B. 1901. A.M. 1905
—	Hen. Colin	King's	M 1899 A.B. 1902. A.M. 1909
—	Herb.	Jes.	M 1905 A.B. 1908
—	Humphrey Bevis Meredith	Cath.	M 1911
—	John Art.	Trin. H.	M 1911
—	John Eric	Joh.	M 1905 A.B. 1910
—	John Fra. Edw. Gelson	Sid.	M 1902 A.B. 1906. A.M. 1910
—	John Osborne	Cai.	M 1898 A.B. 1901
—	John Percy Ern. ...	Trin.	M 1911
—	Jos. Gordon	Jes.	M 1903 A.B. 1906. A.M. 1910
—	Josiah	Cla.	M 1902 A.B. 1905. M.B., B.C. 1910
—	Kenneth McFarlane	Cai.	M 1901 A.B. 1904. M.B., B.C., A.M. 1909
—·	Kenrick Prescott ...	Trin.	M 1905 A.B. 1908
—	Lawrence Cecil	Chr.	M 1904 A.B. 1907
—	Lewis	Qu.	M 1886 A.B. 1889. A.M. 1901
—	Lionel Prescott	Em.	M 1900 A.B. 1903
—	Louis Will. Lancelot	Em.	M 1893 A.B. 1896. A.M. 1907
—	Maur. Ashley	Trin.	M 1903 A.B. 1906
—	Maur. John Lea	Pem.	M 1911
—	Miles	Joh.	M 1896 A.B. 1899. A.M. 1911
—	Norman	Sid.	M 1901 A.B. 1904
—	Norman Duguid	Trin.	M 1899 A.B. 1902. LL.B. 1903
—	Oscar Rob.	Trin. H.	M 1902 A.B., LL.B. 1905
—	Reg.	Down.	M 1908
—	Rob. Alex.	Cla.	M 1893 A.B. 1896. M.B., B.C. 1901
—	Rob. Ern.	Pet.	M 1894 A.B. 1897. A.M. 1901
—	Rob. Ja. Milo	Trin.	M 1908 A.B. 1911
—	Rob. Oborne	N. C.	L 1902 A.B. 1904. A.M. 1908
—	Rob. Wynne Stanley	Trin.	M 1901 A.B. 1904. A.M. 1908. B.C. 1909. [M.D.† 1912
—	Ronald Ralph	Joh.	M 1900 A.B. 1903. B.C., A.M. 1907
—	Rupert Eden	Mag.	M 1908
—	Spencer Lewis	Sid.	M 1900 A.B. 1903. B.C. 1907. M.B. 1908
—	Syd. Watkin	Em.	M 1911
—	Tho. Rich.	Pet.	M 1909 A.B. 1912
—	Victor Art.	Cla.	M 1901 A.B. 1904
—	Will. Maitland	Cai.	M 1911
Walkerdine,	Wilfred Ern.	C. C.	M 1896 A.B. 1899. A.M. 1908
Walkey,	Ja. Rowland	Chr.	M 1899 A.B. 1902. A.M. 1906
Wallace,	Alex. Ross	C. C.	M 1910
—	Art. Gordon	Down.	M 1906
—	Art. Will. Watson ...	Trin.	M 1907 A.B. 1910
—	Cha. Roland Pedley	Sid.	M 1912
—	Fre. Will.	Em.	M 1909 A.B. 1912
—	Ja. Montague	Down.	M 1904 A.B. 1907. A.M. 1912
—	John Alf. Victor ...	Trin.	M 1910
—	John Cameron	Em.	M 1909 A.B. 1912
—	Pet. Brown	Trin. H.	M 1900 A.B. 1904

Wallace,	Rob. Will. Joshua ...	Cai.	M 1908 A.B.† 1911
—	Will. Ern.	Trin.	M 1907 A.B. 1910
—	Will. Middleton	King's	M 1912
Waller,	Alf. Hamilton	Qu.	M 1886 A.B. 1889. A.M. 1902
—	Alf. Rayney		*A.M.* 1905
—	Bertram Pretyman ...	Joh.	M 1898 A.B. 1901. A.M. 1905
—	Cha. Cameron	Joh.	M 1887 A.B. 1890. A.M. 1902
—	Fre.	Sid.	L 1903 A.B. 1905
—	Gerald Lea	Sid.	M 1909 A.B. 1912
—	John Claude	King's	M 1910
—	Noel Huxley	Em.	M 1899 A.B. 1902. A.M. 1906
—	Robin Daniel	Joh.	M 1902
Walley,	Geoffrey Steph.	Cla.	M 1911
Wallice,	Percy	King's	M 1908 A.B. 1911
Walling,	Tho.	Em.	M 1903 A.B. 1906. A.M. 1910
Wallis,	Anth.	King's	M 1898 A.B. 1901. A.M. 1906
—	Art. Bertram Ridley	Down.	M 1903
—	Basil	Trin.	M 1899 A.B. 1902. M.B., B.C. 1910
—	Duncan Boyd	Pem.	M 1910
—	Edw. Percy	Cla.	M 1912
—	Frank Arnold	Pem.	M 1906 A.B. 1909
—	Frederic Cyril	Cla.	M 1894 A.B. 1897. A.M. 1901
—	Geo. Dudley	Pem.	M 1901 A.B. 1905. A.M. 1911
—	Herb. Hen.	Chr.	M 1905 A.B. 1908. A.M. 1912
—	Hub. Edgar	Down.	M 1907 Qu. A.B. 1910
—	Ja.	Chr.	L 1900 A.B. 1902. A.M. 1906
—	Owen Bern.	Em.	M 1907 A.B., LL.B. 1910
—	Percy Boyd	Pem.	M 1903 A.B. 1906
—	Rob. Lauder Mackenzie	Down.	M 1904 A.B. 1907
—	Will. Evershed	Cla.	M 1902 A.B. 1905. M.B., B.C. 1911
Walls,	Frederic Ritchie	King's	M 1910
Walmesley,	Rich.	Mag.	M 1908
Walmsley,	Alf. Moss	N. C.	M 1903 Joh. A.B. 1906. A.M.† 1910
—	Cha.	King's	M 1910
—	Ja.	Trin.	M 1905 A.B. 1908
Walpole,	Cha. Archib.	Trin.	M 1901
—	Hugh Seymour	Em.	M 1903 A.B. 1906
—	Rob. Hen.	Mag.	M 1911
Walrond,	Edw. Dalrymple	Cai.	M 1880 A.B. 1884. A.M. 1903
—	Victor	Trin.	M 1908
Walsh,	Alan Dudley	Trin.	M 1909 A.B. 1912
—	Art. St George	Trin. H.	M 1912
—	Maur. Fra. Xavier ...	Pet.	M 1909
Walter,	Cha. Edw. Herb. } Lethbridge	Trin. H.	M 1907
—	Gerald Lewis	Mag.	M 1909
—	Hub. Conrad	Pet.	M 1911
—	Louis Heathcote	Trin.	M 1894 A.B. 1897. A.M. 1901
—	Will. Louis	N. C.	M 1895 Joh. A.B. 1898. A.M. 1902
Walters,	Cha. Barrington	Em.	M 1878 A.B. 1884. A.M. 1903
—	Frank Ern.	Qu.	M 1895 A.B. 1900. A.M. 1904
—	John Radley	Sid.	M 1907 A.B. 1910
—	Tho. Will.	N. C.	M 1901 Qu. A.B. 1904. A.M. 1908
—	Wilfred Leon.	Trin.	M 1907 A.B. 1910
—	Will. Ja.	Cla.	M 1909 A.B. 1912
Walther,	Dav. Rodolph Philippe	Pem.	M 1900 D. Rodolphe P. A.B. 1903. A.M.
Walton,	Geo. Warren	Cai.	M 1907 A.B. 1910 [1909
—	John Erskine Hedderwich	Trin. H.	L 1905 A.B. 1909
—	John Hugh	King's	M 1909 A.B. 1912
—	John Humphrey	Cai.	M 1907
—	Jos.	Trin.	M 1901 A.B., LL.B. 1904

Walton,	Richmond	Cai.	M 1907 A.B. 1910
—	Tho. Art.	N. C.	M 1905 A.B. 1908. A.M. 1912
—	Tho. Harold	Joh.	M 1895 A.B. 1898. A.M. 1905
—	Will. Heward Murray	Pem.	M 1909 A.B. 1912
Walworth,	Geo.	Joh.	M 1911
Wan,	Yik-Shing	Joh.	M 1912
Wandesforde, Syd. Alb.		King's	M 1902
Wane,	Frank Innes	Cla.	M 1907 A.B. 1910
—	Horace Basil	Cla.	M 1909 A.B. 1912
—	John Skilbeck	Qu.	M 1912
Wang,	Kyi Hsii	Chr.	M 1909 A.B. 1912
Wang Tahsieh, *His Excellency*			*LL.D.* 1906
Wanklyn,	Kenneth	Pem.	M 1911
Wankowicz,	Witold	Down.	L 1908 A.B. 1911
Wanless,	Geo. Lee	Cla.	M 1906 A.B., LL.B. 1909
Warburg,	Edgar John	Chr.	E 1911
—	Emil Gabriel		*Sc.D.* 1908
—	Oscar Emanuel	Trin.	M 1895 A.B. 1898. A.M. 1902
Ward,	Archib. Gordon	Trin.	M 1887 A.B. 1890. A.M. 1901
—	Archib. Hen. Montgomery	Pem.	M 1898 A.B. 1901. A.M. 1905
—	Clarence Edwin	Qu.	M 1891 A.B. 1894. A.M. 1901
—	Dudley Cuthbert Leslie	C. C.	M 1910
—	Dudley Will.	*Joh.	M 1904 A.B. 1907. A.M. 1911
—	Edw. Fra. Campbell	Sid.	M 1888 A.B. 1891. A.M. 1905
—	Eric Harrison	Sid.	M 1907 A.B. 1910
—	Ern.	Cla.	M 1896 A.B. 1899. A.M. 1903. B.C. 1904.
—	Fra. Kingdon	Chr.	M 1904 A.B. 1912 [M.B. 1905. M.D. 1908
—	Fra. Leigh	Sid.	M 1888 A.B. 1891. A.M. 1906
—	Fra. Will.	Cla.	L 1904 A.B. 1906
—	Geo. Humphrey	Cai.	M 1911
—	Harold Matthias Art.	Cla.	M 1903 A.B. 1906. A.M. 1910
—	Harry	N. C.	M 1898 Cath. A.B. 1902. A.M. 1906
—	Herb. Lipson	Trin. H.	M 1900 A.B., LL.B. 1904
—	Ivor Fanshawe	Trin.	M 1905 A.B. 1908
—	John Sebastian Marlow	Trin. H.	M 1905 A.B. 1908
—	John Whewell	Em.	M 1912
—	Jos. Geo.	H. Sel.	M 1908
—	(*Sir*) Jos. Geo.		*LL.D.* 1911
—	Jos. Harry	N. C.	M 1907 A.B. 1910
—	Kenneth Martin	Em.	M 1906 A.B. 1910
—	Lancelot Bangor	Trin.	M 1901 A.B. 1904
—	Leon. Sumner	Qu.	M 1911
—	Octavius Whittard	Pem.	M 1901 A.B. 1904
—	Owen Sumner	Em.	M 1901 A.B. 1904. A.M. 1908
—	Reg. Somerset	Pem.	M 1900 A.B. 1903. A.M. 1911
—	Reg. Will. Alf.	N. C.	M 1910
—	Rob.	N. C.	L 1906 Chr. A.B. 1909. A.M. .1912
—	Rob. Oscar Cyril	Trin.	M 1900 A.B. 1904
—	Ronald Fra. Campbell	Joh.	M 1894 A.B. 1897. M.B., B.C. 1900. A.M.
—	Tho. Fra.	Em.	M 1898 A.B. 1901 [1902. M.D. 1903
—	Vincent Sumner	Qu.	M 1899 A.B. 1902. A.M. 1906
—	Walt. Delay	Sid.	M 1901 A.B. 1904
—	Wilbraham Danson	Joh.	M 1894 A.B. 1897. A.M. 1906
—	Will. Dudley	Trin.	M 1896 A.B. 1903
—	Will. Jos.	Trin.	M 1906 A.B. 1909
—	Yeo	N. C.	M 1898 Cath. A.B. 1901. A.M. 1906
Warde-Aldam, Will. St Andrew		Trin.	M 1900 A.B. 1903
Wardell,	John Meredith	Trin.	M 1904 A.B. 1907
Wardell-Yerburgh, Geoffrey Basset		Trin.	M 1912
Warden,	Art. Reg. Stuart	Cai.	M 1906 A.B. 1911
—	Horace Fre. Will.	Pem.	M 1906 A.B. 1909

Ward-Jackson,	Rob.	Trin.	M 1910
Wardle,	Will. Lansdell	Cai.	M 1895 A.B. 1898. A.M. 1902
Wardley,	Donald Joule	H. Sel.	M 1912
—	Geoffrey Cha. Norton	Trin.	M 1910
Ward-Price,	Geo.	Cath.	M 1906 A.B. 1909
—	Hen. Lewis	Cath.	M 1909 A.B. 1912
—	Leon. Stanley	Cath.	M 1912
Ware,	Art. Maitland	Pem.	M 1892 A.B. 1895. M.B., B.C., A.M. 1899.
—	Ja. Geo. Wyndham	Trin.	M 1902 [M.D. 1903
Waring,	Cuthbert Leon.	N. C.	M 1910
—	Norman Harold	Trin. H.	M 1912
Warming,	Eugenius		*Sc.D.* 1912
Warmington,	Edw. Steph.	Trin.	M 1900 A.B. 1903
Warner,	Alb. Cyril	C. C.	M 1898 A.B. 1901
—	Archib.	Qu.	M 1902 A.B. 1905
—	Cuthbert	Pem.	M 1906 A.B. 1909
—	Hen. Brooks	Trin.	M 1898 A.B. 1901
—	Hen. Geo. Phil.	N. C.	M 1905
—	Marmaduke	Cai.	M 1897 A.B. 1902. A.M. 1905
Warnes,	Geo. Gerald	Cai.	M 1911
Warre Cornish,	Gerald Warre	King's	M 1894 A.B. 1897. A.M. 1912
Warre-Dymond,	Godfrey	Trin.	M 1909
Warren,	Alf. Castle	Em.	M 1894 A.B. 1897. A.M. 1905. B.C., M.D.
—	Cha. Herb.	N. C.	L 1895 A.B. 1898. A.M. 1904 [1909
—	Cha. Kenneth Wolton	Jes.	M 1912
—	Geo. Maxwell	Pem.	M 1911
—	Hor. Geo.	C. C.	M 1889 A.B. 1892. A.M. 1904
—	John Howard	Cai.	M 1898 A.B. 1901
—	Leslie Alec	Jes.	M 1906 A.B. 1909
Warrington,	John Carlisle	Trin.	M 1905 A.B. 1908
—	Tho.	Trin.	E 1907 Em. A.B. 1911
Warschawski,	Rich. Rawlinson } Vyvyan {	C. C.	E 1882 A.B. 1886, Vyvyan R. R. A.M.† [1902
Warters,	Reg. Art.	Joh.	M 1908 A.B. 1911
Warwick,	Art. Ja.	Cla.	M 1870 A.B. 1874. A.M. 1903
—	Cha. Ralph	Pem.	M 1909
—	Guy Ransom	Pem.	M 1902 A.B. 1905. A.M. 1909
—	Will. Tom	Em.	M 1906 A.B. 1909
Wasbrough,	Cha. Hen. Sid.	Trin. H.	M 1897 H. C. S. A.B. 1903
—	Will. Lewis	Trin.	M 1910
Wasim,	Mohammad	Mag.	M 1904 A.B., LL.B. 1907
Wasson,	Ja. Craig	Trin.	M 1910
Waterall,	Leon. Saxton	Jes.	M 1904 A.B. 1907. A.M. 1911
Waterer,	Clarence Roy	Em.	M 1906 A.B., LL.B. 1909
Waterfall,	Cha. Fra.	Qu.	M 1906 A.B. 1909
Waterhouse,	Gilb.	Joh.	M 1907 A.B. 1910
Waterlow,	Guy Walleron	Trin.	M 1902
—	Syd. Phil. Perigal ...	Trin.	M 1897 A.B. 1900. A.M. 1905
Watermeyer,	Ern. Fre.	Cai.	M 1899 A.B. 1902. LL.B. 1903
—	Herb. Arnold	Cai.	M 1906 A.B. 1912
Waters,	Cha.	Down.	M 1887 A.B., LL.B. 1890. LL.M. 1894.
—	Claud Dallinger	Down.	M 1905 A.B. 1909 [A.M. 1909
—	Clifton Dav. Frank	N. C.	M 1903 A.B. 1906
—	Jos. Bow	Pem.	M 1901 A.B. 1904
—	Kenneth Selby	Joh.	M 1909 A.B. 1912
Waterworth,	Hilary	Chr.	M 1909 A.B. 1912
—	Sid.	Cai.	M 1912
Wathen,	Gerard Anstruther ...	Pet.	M 1898 A.B. 1902. A.M. 1905
Watkin,	Ern. Lucas	Joh.	M 1895 A.B. 1898. A.M. 1902
Watkin-Jones,	Nath. Tho. Howard	Cai.	M 1907 A.B. 1910
Watkins,	Allen	Joh.	M 1908 A.B. 1912

Watkins,	Cha. Rowlatt	Em.	M 1901 A.B. 1904
—	Cuthbert John	Em.	M 1901 A.B. 1904. A.M. 1908
—	Edw. Vincent	Sid.	M 1901 A.B. 1904. A.M. 1911
--	Eric Leopold Cha. ...	Em.	M 1910
—	Iltyd Edwin Maitland	King's	M 1908 A.B., LL.B. 1911
—	John Ja.	Chr.	M 1899 A.B. 1902
—	Lawrence Theodore	C. C.	M 1906 A.B. 1909
—	Will. Bertram	Cai.	M 1910
—	Will. Fred	Em.	M 1906 A.B. 1909
—	Will. Strugnell	Trin. H.	M 1909 A.B., LL.B. 1912
Watkinson,	Hugh Leslie	Qu.	M 1911
Watkyn-Thomas, Alwyn		Trin.	M 1910
—	Frederic Will.	Trin.	M 1906 A.B. 1909
Watmough,	Geo. Will.	N. C.	M 1903 Down. A.B. 1908
—	Will. Hen.	N. C.	M 1894 Cath. A.B. 1897. A.M. 1903
Watney,	Gerard Norman	Trin.	M 1897 A.B. 1900. A.M. 1904
—	Martyn Herb.	Trin.	M 1906 A.B. 1909
—	Will. Herb.	Trin.	M 1898 A.B. 1901. A.M. 1906
Watson,	Ainslie Hen.	Pem.	M 1911
—	Alf. Joyce	H. Sel.	M 1903 A.B. 1906. A.M. 1911
—	Arnold Petrie	King's	M 1898 A.B. 1903. A.M. 1906
—	Art. Lockhart	Joh.	M 1901 A.B. 1904
—	Aubrey Wentworth Harrison	Cla.	M 1911
—	Basil Lockhart	Joh.	M 1908 A.B. 1911
—	Cecil Lilliott	Em.	M 1898 A.B. 1901. A.M. 1905
—	Cha. Art.	King's	M 1901 A.B. 1904
—	Cha. Challinor	King's	M 1908 A.B. 1911
—	Cha. Edw.	Sid.	M 1899 A.B. 1902
—	Douglas Hamilton ...	Cla.	M 1912
—	Douglas John	Cla.	M 1909 A.B. 1912
—·	Edwin Roy	Jes.	M 1899 A.B. 1903. A.M.† 1906
—	Elliot Lovegood Grant	Trin.	M 1906 A.B. 1909
—	Fra. Herb.	Cai.	M 1904 A.B. 1907. B.C. 1911. M.B. 1912
—	Fra. Will.	King's	M 1911
—	Fre.	Qu.	M 1899 A.B. 1902
—	Fre. Bainbridge	Trin.	M 1898 A.B. 1901
—	Fre. Will.	Em.	M 1903 A.B. 1907
—	Geo. Carr	King's	M 1906 A.B. 1909
—	Geo. Neville ....*Trin.		M 1904 A.B. 1907. A.M. 1911
—	Harold Argyll	Qu.	M 1903 A.B. 1906
—	Harold Newall	Trin. H.	M 1907
—	Herb.	Chr.	M 1894 A.B. 1897. A.M. 1901
—	Herb. Armstrong ...	Pet.	M 1878 A.B. 1882. A.M. 1885. B.D. 1909.
—	Herb. Edmeston	N. C.	M 1910 [D.D. 1912
—	Hugh	Trin.	M 1907 A.B. 1910
—	John		*A.M.* 1911
—	John Alex. Percy ...	Jes.	M 1910
—	John Edw.	Sid.	M 1891 A.B. 1894. A.M. 1905
—	Kenneth Falshaw ...	Mag.	L 1912
—	Norman Wace	Qu.	M 1911
—	Nowell Lake	Jes.	M 1902 A.B. 1905
—	Rob. Hamilton Lindsay	Trin.	M 1905
—	Roger Alan	Trin.	M 1911
—	Roger Wentworth ...	King's	M 1912
—	Ronald Bannatyne ...	Trin.	M 1901 A.B. 1904
—	Tertius Tho. Boswall	Chr.	M 1908 A.B. 1911
—	Tho. Clifford	Jes.	M 1906 A.B. 1909
—	Tho. Haughton	Trin. H.	M 1900 A.B. 1904
—	Tho. Herman	Pem.	M 1900 A.B. 1910
—	Tho. Palmer	Sid.	M 1910
—	Tho. Will.	Joh.	M 1908 A.B. 1911

Watson,	Walt. Geoffrey	Cai.	M 1905 A.B. 1909
—	Will. Bern.	H. Sel.	M 1895 A.B. 1899. A.M. 1905
Watson-Armstrong, (*Hon.*) Will. ⎱ John Montagu ⎰		Trin.	M 1911
Watson Scott, Clive Harry		Pem.	M 1909 A.B. 1912
Watson-Taylor, Art. Simon		Trin.	M 1902 A.B. 1905
Watson Taylor, Cyril Alf.		Trin.	M 1904 A.B. 1907
Watson Williams, Eric		Cai.	M 1909 A.B. 1912
Watson-Williams, Eubulus Ja. ...		Pem.	M 1895 A.B. 1898. A.M. 1902. B.D. 1912
Watt,	Ern. Alex. Stuart ...	King's	M 1893 A.B. 1896. A.M. 1901
—	Ern. Loraine	Trin. H.	M 1898 A.B. 1901. A.M. 1905
—	Geo. Robertson	Em.	L 1903 A.B. 1905
—	Geo. Townshend Candy	Cai.	M 1905 A.B. 1908
—	Sam. Mackey	N. C.	M 1906
—	Walt. Oswald	Trin.	M 1896 A.B. 1899. A.M. 1904
Watts,	Alb. Everett	Trin.	M 1907 A.B. 1910
—	Art. Edw.	Down.	M 1909 A.B. 1912
—	Art. Tomlinson	Pet.	M 1890 A.B. 1893. A.M. 1904
—	Bertram Tom	Joh.	M 1902 A.B. 1905
—	Chris. Cha.	C. C.	M 1896 A.B. 1899. A.M. 1904
—	Edgar Marshall	Cai.	M 1912
—	Hamilton	King's	M 1892 A.B. 1895. A.M. 1903
—	Hen. Leon.	Cath.	M 1903 A.B. 1906
—	Herb. Art.	N. C.	L 1905 Chr. A.B. 1907
—	Herb. Paris	Sid.	M 1905 A.B. 1908
—	Nevile Hunter	Pet.	M 1904 A.B. 1907
—	Percy Reg.	Cath.	E 1907 A.B. 1910
—	Ronald Will. Ailsa ...	Qu.	M 1912 [A.M. 1903
—	Sam. Harvard	Cla.	M 1886 Harvard-Watts, S. H., A.B. 1897.
—	Sid. Johnson	Trin. H.	M 1902 [1894. A.M. 1900. B.C. 1904
—	Tho. Hen. Evered ...	Cai.	M 1891 Watts-Silvester, T. H. E., A.B.
—	Tho. John	Cai.	M 1886 A.B. 1891. A.M. 1910
—	Will. Whitehead ......*Sid.		M 1878 A.B. 1882. A.M. 1885. Sc.D. 1909
Waugh,	Archib. Douglas	Mag.	M 1908 A.B. 1911
—	Art. John	Pem.	M 1905 A.B. 1908
Wauton,	Algernon Douglas ⎱ Brenton ⎰	Cla.	M 1903 A.B. 1906
—	Cha. Art. Neville ...	Cla.	M 1895 A.B. 1899. A.M. 1902
—	Eric Astell	Trin.	M 1910
Way,	Cha. Cecil Lewis ...	Mag.	M 1892 A.B. 1895. A.M. 1901
—	Cha. Parry	Joh.	M 1889 A.B. 1892. A.M. 1901
Wayet,	John Wyndham Field	Em.	M 1901 A.B. 1904
Waylen,	Donald Campbell ...	Jes.	M 1911
—	Geo. Hen. Hitchcock	King's	M 1899 A.B. 1902. B.C., A.M. 1910
Wayne,	St John	Mag.	M 1895 A.B. 1899. A.M. 1902
Weatherburn, Cha. Ern.		Trin.	M 1906 A.B. 1908
Weatherell, Rob. Kingsley		Em.	M 1905 A.B. 1908
Weatherhead, Ern.		Trin.	M 1892 Joh. M.B. 1904
—	Hen. Walt.	Trin.	M 1889 A.B. 1892. A.M.† 1909
—	Herb. Tho. Candy ...	Em.	M 1894 A.B. 1897. A.M. 1911
Weatherly, Lionel Ja.		Trin. H.	M 1901 A.B.1904.A.M.1908 [LL.M. 1901
Weaver,	Alf. Berry	Trin.	M 1893 A.B. 1896. LL.B. 1897. A.M.,
—	Fre. Kearsley	Trin.	M 1890 A.B. 1893. M.B., B.C., A.M. 1902
—	Fre. Will. Herron ...	Cla.	M 1898 A.B., LL.B. 1902. A.M. 1905
—	Geo. Cherry	C. C.	L 1894 A.B. 1896. A.M. 1901
—	Ja.	N. C.	M 1908 A.B. 1911
Webb,	Alf. Henderson	Chr.	M 1912
—	Art. Hen.	C. C.	M 1911
—	Cha. Morgan	Joh.	M 1891 A.B. 1894. A.M.† 1906
—	Conrade Leslie	N. C.	M 1912
—	Edmondson	N. C.	M 1901 A.B. 1904. A.M. 1908

Webb,	Edw. Oliver	Chr.	M 1911
—	Frank Hardy	Down.	M 1912
—	Frank Sam.	Joh.	M 1898 A.B. 1901
—	Fre. Edw. Apthorpe	Down.	M 1895 A.B. 1911
—	Geo. Herb.	C. C.	M 1894 A.B. 1897. A.M. 1902
—	Gilb. Lowell	Cai.	M 1899 A.B. 1902. B.C. 1906. M.B. 1907
—	Hen. Bertram Law	Cath.	M 1904 A.B. 1907
—	Hen. Carlyle	Chr.	M 1911
—	Hen. John	Cai.	M 1910
—	Herb. Anth. ....*Trin.		M 1899 A.B. 1902. A.M. 1906
—	Herb. Cha.	Chr.	M 1902 A.B. 1905. LL.B. 1906. A.M. 1910
—	John Clifford	Jes.	M 1912
—	Maur. Everett	Pem.	M 1898 A.B. 1902. A.M. 1905
—	Tho. Langley	Cai.	M 1903 A.B. 1906
—	Will. Redginald Valentine	Trin. H.	M 1903
Webb-Benton,	Ja.	Sid.	M 1911
Webbe,	Will. Harold	Qu.	M 1904 A.B. 1907
Webber,	Alf. Hen.	Mag.	M 1895 A.B. 1898. A.M. 1902
—	Harald Norris	Joh.	M 1900 A.B. 1903
Weber,	Douglas McRae	Cla.	M 1906 A.B. 1909
—	Harold Ern.	Pem.	M 1904 A.B. 1907. A.M. 1912
—	Hen. Guy	Cla.	M 1903 A.B. 1906. LL.B. 1907
—	Reg. Evelyn	Pem.	M 1902 A.B. 1905
—	Will. Edwin	H. Sel.	M 1896 A.B. 1899. A.M. 1903
Webster,	Art. Harold	Trin.	M 1893 A.B. 1896. A.M. 1901
—	Cha. Kingsley ....*King's		M 1904 A.B. 1907. A.M. 1911
—	Geo. Godfrey	Jes.	M 1911
—	Harold Colin	Trin.	M 1897 A.B. 1900. A.M. 1904
—	Hen.	Cath.	M 1912
—	John Fre.	H. Sel.	M 1910
—	John Rich.	Cla.	M 1899 A.B. 1902
—	Jos. Frain	Trin.	M 1912
—	Rowland Burdon	Trin. H.	M 1908
—	Vivian Tho. Pearce	Em.	M 1901 A.B. 1904
—	Will. Gordon	Trin. H.	M 1909
Wedd,	Edw. Parker Wallman	Cai.	M 1902 A.B. 1906
Weddell,	John Murray	Chr.	M 1903 A.B. 1906
Wedderburn,	Cha. Carmichael ...	Pem.	M 1900 A.B. 1903
Wedel,	Hans Albrecht	Cai.	M 1908
Wedgwood,	Allen	Cai.	M 1911
—	Cha. Hen.	Cla.	L 1902 A.B. 1904
Weekes,	Carey Rich. Hampton	Trin.	M 1912
—	Cha. Davey	Sid.	M 1894 A.B. 1897. A.M. 1906
—	Christian Will. Hampton	Trin.	M 1899 A.B. 1903. A.M. 1907
Weekley,	Ern.	Trin.	M 1893 A.B. 1896. A.M. 1901
Weeks,	Cha. Alb.	H. Sel.	M 1894 A.B. 1897. A.M. 1903
—	Llewellyn McIntyre	Cai.	M 1905 A.B. 1908. M.B., B.C. 1912
—	Rich. Ja.	Pem.	M 1902 A.B. 1905. A.M. 1909
—	Ronald Morce	Cai.	M 1909 A.B. 1912
Wegg,	Hugh Neville	Cai.	M 1900 A.B. 1904
Wegg-Prosser,	Cecil Fra. Jos.	Trin.	M 1911
Weguelin,	Tho. Noel	Trin.	M 1906
Weightman,	Will. Hen.	Joh.	M 1906 A.B. 1909. LL.B. 1910 [1910
Weir,	Hen. Bright	Trin.	M 1899 A.B. 1902. A.M. 1908. M.B., B.C.
—	Hugh Heywood	Trin.	M 1894 A.B. 1897. A.M. 1902. M.B. 1904
—	Napier	Pet.	M 1908 A.B. 1911
—	Will. Mortimer	C. C.	M 1898 A.B. 1899. A.M. 1904
Weisberg,	Hyman	Chr.	M 1910
Welbourne,	Edw.	Em.	M 1912
Welch,	Douglas	Jes.	M 1905 A.B. 1909
—	Ja. Johnson	Trin.	M 1907 A.B. 1910

Welch,　　　　John .... Trin.　M 1903 A.B., LL.B. 1906. A.M. 1910
—　　　　　　John Hen. .... Trin. H. M 1904 A.B. 1907
Welchman,　Rich. Herb. .... Qu.　M 1889 A.B. 1892. A.M. 1906
Welcker,　　Cha. .... Em.　M 1907
Weld,　　　Cha. Geo. .... Em.　M 1896 A.B. 1900. A.M. 1906
Weller,　　Cha. Alex. .... Cla.　M 1907 A.B. 1910
—　　　　　Chris. Harold .... H. Sel.　M 1898 A.B. 1901. A.M. 1911
—　　　　　John Reg. .... H. Sel.　M 1910
—　　　　　Rich. Dudley .... H. Sel.　M 1906 A.B. 1909
Wellesley,　Rich. .... King's　M 1902 R. Alf., A.B. 1905
Welling Laurie, John .... C. C.　M 1908
Wellington,　Alban Hen. .... Sid.　M 1905 A.B. 1908
—　　　　　Hen. Martyn .... Sid.　M 1869 A.B. 1873. A.M. 1905
—　　　　　Wilfrid Orford ...... Sid.　M 1901 A.B. 1904
Wellisch,　Edw. Montagu ...... Em.　M 1907 A.B. 1909
Wells,　　　Alf. Percy .... H. Sel.　M 1906 A.B. 1909
—　　　　　Art. Manfred Wintle Cla.　M 1894 A.B., LL.B. 1897. A.M. 1901
—　　　　　Cha. Alex. .... Em.　M 1900 A.B. 1903. A.M. 1907
—　　　　　Edw. .... Pem.　M 1899 A.B. 1902. A.M. 1909
—　　　　　Ern. .... Chr.　M 1899 A.B. 1902. A.M 1911
—　　　　　Gerald Will. .... Pet.　M 1905 A.B. 1908
—　　　　　Harold Marty .... N. C.　M 1911
—　　　　　Leslie Howard Elliott Qu.　M 1904 A.B. 1908
—　　　　　Norman Lancaster ... Cai.　M 1906 A.B. 1909
—　　　　　Randolph Cecil ...... Em.　M 1904 A.B. 1907
—　　　　　Rob. Douglas .... Trin.　M 1893 A.B. 1896. A.M. 1907
—　　　　　Walt. Douglas .... Joh.　M 1908 A.B. 1911
Wells-Cole,　Gervas Cha. .... Cai.　M 1908 A.B. 1911
Welsby,　　Syd. Walt. Humfrey Trin. H. M 1910
Welsh,　　　Anth. Reg. .... Trin.　M 1902 A.B. 1906. A.M. 1910
—　　　　　Augustus Seymour ... Pem.　M 1910
Wenden,　　Geo. .... Pem.　M 1911
Wenham,　Cha. Hugh .... Trin.　M 1910
—　　　　　Eric Heseltine .... Trin.　M 1912
—　　　　　John Hen. .... Trin.　M 1909 A.B. 1912
Wenley,　　Ja. Adams Seton ... Jes.　M 1911
Went,　　　Rich. Douglas .... N. C.　L 1896 Down A.B. 1900. A.M. 1903
Wentworth-Fitzwilliam, Geo. Ja.⎱
　　　　　　Cha.　　　　　　⎰ Trin.　M 1907
Wentworth-Stanley, Cha. Sid. Bowen Trin.　M 1910
Werner,　　Cha. Augustus ...... King's　M 1896 A.B. 1900. A.M. 1904
—　　　　　Cha. Hen. .... Cla.　M 1894 A.B. 1897. A.M. 1901
Wernicke,　Wilfred Graham ...... Em.　M 1911
Wesley Smith, Harry .... Trin.　M 1911
Wessels,　　Alf. Bertrand .... King's　M 1905
—　　　　　Cornelis Hermanus Trin. H. E 1903
West,　　　Cha. Skeffington ...... Trin.　M 1908 A.B. 1911
—　　　　　Edw. Brooks .... Trin.　M 1911
—　　　　　Frank Revell .... Cai.　M 1912
—　　　　　Geo. Steph. .... Joh.　M 1895 A.B. 1898. A.M. 1902
—　　　　　Herb. .... C. C.　M 1884 A.B. 1887. A.M. 1905
—　　　　　Herb. Kenelm .... Cla.　M 1911
—　　　　　John Ja. .... Qu.　M 1894 A.B. 1897. A.M. 1912
—　　　　　Lionel Geo. Aubrey Joh.　M 1896 A.B. 1899. A.M. 1903
—　　　　　Roger Rolleston Fick King's　M 1910
Westall,　　Bern. Clem. .... Qu.　M 1912
—　　　　　Douglas Cameron ... Mag.　M 1909 A.B. 1912
—　　　　　Lancelot McAlpine ... Qu.　M 1892 A.B. 1896. A.M. 1910
Westbrook,　Herb. Wotton .... Em.　M 1899 A.B. 1903
Westby,　　Fre. Will. .... N. C.　M 1910
—　　　　　Perceval St George Cha. Trin.　M 1908 A.B. 1911

Westcott,	Fre. Brooke ....*Trin.	M 1877 A.B. 1881. A.M. 1884. B.D. 1910
—	Geo. Foss .... Qu.	M 1912
Western,	Alf. Edw. .... Trin.	M 1892 A.B. 1895. A.M. 1899. Sc.D. 1910
—	Fre. Ja. .... Trin.	M 1898 A.B. 1901. A.M.† 1905
—	Geo. Trench .... Pem.	M 1896 A.B. 1899. A.M. 1903. M.B., B.C.
—	Oswald .... Trin.	M 1907 A.B. 1910 [1905. M.D. 1907
Westley,	Herb. Geo. .... Em.	M 1893 A.B. LL.B., 1896. A.M. 1910
Westoll,	Ja. .... Trin.	M 1908 A.B. 1911
Weston,	Cecil Edw. .... Jes.	M 1884 A.B. 1889. A.M. 1901
—	Eric .... Joh.	M 1911
—	Ern. Art. .... Joh.	M 1899 A.B. 1902
—	Geoffrey .... Trin.	M 1903 A.B. 1907
—	Geo. Edw. .... Mag.	M 1906 A.B. 1909
—	Geo. Elgar .... C. C.	M 1902 A.B. 1905. A.M. 1909
—	Hen. Plantagenet ... Em.	M 1907 A.B. 1910
—	John Cecil .... King's	M 1901 A.B. 1904
—	Tho. Alex. .... Joh.	M 1902 A.B. 1905. M.B., B.C. 1910
West Watson,	Campbell ....*Em.	M 1896 A.B. 1899. A.M. 1903. D.D. 1910
Westwell,	Art. .... Cla.	M 1903 A.B. 1906
—	Chris. .... N. C.	M 1900 Pet. A.B. 1903. A.M. 1907
Westwood,	Alf. Herb. .... Chr.	M 1910
Wetenhall,	Will. Thornton ...... Cai.	M 1907 A.B., LL.B. 1910
Wethered,	Ern. .... Pem.	M 1896 E. Handel Cossham, A.B., LL.B.
—	Hugh Ellison .... Trin.	M 1907 A.B. 1910 [1899. A.M. 1908
Wetherell,	Alf. Will. Seymour C. C.	M 1900 A.B. 1903
Whale,	Art. .... Pem.	M 1907 A.B. 1910
—	Geo. .... Pem.	M 1905 A.B. 1908
—	Geo. Harold Lawson Jes.	E 1895 A.B. 1898. M.B., B.C. 1902. M.D.
—	Hugh Stansell .... H. Sel.	M 1903 A.B. 1906 [1907
Whaley,	Oswald Stanley ...... Chr.	M 1908 A.B. 1911
Whalley,	Cuthbert Will. Hen. Pet.	M 1894 A.B. 1897. A.M. 1901
Wharam,	Harold Neville ...... Chr.	M 1903 A.B. 1909
Wharton,	Cha. Harold Lewis ... H. Sel.	M 1905 A.B., LL.B. 1909
—	Frank Hammond ... Trin. H.	M 1909 A.B., LL.B. 1912
—	John .... Joh.	M 1895 A.B. 1898. B.C. 1902. M.B. 1903.
—	John Rob. .... Trin.	M 1900 A.B. 1903 [A.M., M.D. 1907
Whatham,	Alan .... Cla.	M 1910
Whatley,	Will. Hughes .... Trin.	M 1894 A.B. 1903
Wheat,	Ern. Godfrey .... Chr.	M 1897 A.B. 1900. A.M. 1904. B.C. 1908.
Wheatcroft,	Geo. Hanson .... Trin.	M 1907 A.B. 1910 [M.B. 1909
—	Kenneth Douglas ... Trin.	M 1901
—	Will. Hen. .... N. C.	M 1889 Down. A.B. 1892. LL.M. 1896.
Wheeler,	Alb. Martin .... Sid.	M 1906 A.B. 1909 [LL.D. 1902
—	Art. Wain .... Qu.	M 1907 A.B. 1910
—	Harold Will. .... Qu.	M 1906 A.B. 1909
—	Ja. Norman .... Chr.	M 1901 A.B. 1904. M.B., B.C. 1910
—	Leon. .... Trin. H.	M 1897 A.B. 1903
—	Montague .... Trin. H.	M 1895 A.B. 1898. A.M. 1903
—	Russell Mervyn ...... N. C.	M 1907 A.B. 1910
—	Stanley Mortimer ... Chr.	M 1905 A.B. 1908. A.M. 1912
Wheldon,	Emrys John .... Cai.	M 1907 A.B. 1910
—	Wynn Powell .... Joh.	M 1900 A.B., LL.B. 1903
Whelon,	Cha. Eric .... King's	M 1906 A.B. 1910
Whelpton,	Hen. Edw. .... Chr.	M 1909 A.B. 1912
—	Leon. Gould .... Jes.	M 1910
—	Marsden .... Pem.	M 1912
Whewell,	Herb. .... Joh.	M 1906 A.B. 1909
—	Will. Edw. .... Mag.	M 1910
Whibley,	Cha. .... Jes.	M 1879 A.B. 1884. A.M. 1912
Whidborne,	Bertram Seymour ... Trin.	M 1912
—	Geo. Ferris .... Trin.	M 1909

Whiddington,	Rich.	*Joh.	M 1905 A.B. 1908. A.M. 1912
Whigham,	Kenneth Gilb.	Trin.	M 1899 A.B. 1902
Whipple,	Fra. John Welsh ...	Trin.	M 1894 A.B. 1897. A.M. 1901
Whitaker,	Alex. Kerr	Joh.	M 1896 A.B. 1902
—	Art. Lionel	H. Sel.	M 1895 A.B. 1898. A.M. 1902
—	Cha.	Em.	M 1899 A.B. 1902
—	Frank	Pem.	M 1911
—	Fre.	Trin.	M 1893 A.B. 1896. B.C., A.M. 1903
—	Geo. Halstead	Cla.	M 1908 A.B. 1911
—	John Richardson ...	Sid.	M 1905 A.B. 1908
—	Tho. Savile	Cai.	M 1911
—	Victor	Trin.	M 1905 A.B. 1908
Whitby,	Ja. Hornby	Cai.	M 1912
Whitcombe,	Leon.	Trin. H.	M 1905 A.B. 1908. A.M. 1912
—	Rich. Cuthbert Percival	King's	M 1911
White,	Alf. Hale	King's	M 1906 A.B. 1909
—	Arnold Sinclair	King's	M 1902 A.B. 1905
—	Aubrey Hunt Searle	Trin.	M 1906 A.B. 1909
—	Bern.	Pem.	M 1907 A.B. 1910
—	Clem.	Chr.	M 1892 A.B. 1895. M.B., B.C. 1898. M.D.
—	Edw. John	C. C.	M 1905 A.B. 1908　　　　　　　[1903
—	Fra. Alf.	Joh.	M 1903
—	Fra. de Lacy	Sid.	M 1864 A.B. 1868. A.M. 1907
—	Fra. Geo.	Em.	M 1901 A.B. 1906
—	Fra. Puryer	Joh.	M 1912
—	Fra. Reg.	Cath.	M 1911
—	Frank	Em.	M 1912
—	Frank Saxon	Pem.	M 1905
—	Fre. Vernon	N. C.	M 1900 Chr. A.B. 1903
—	Geo. Fraser	Cai.	M 1894 A.B. 1899. A.M. 1908
—	Geo. Gilmour	Jes.	M 1911
—	Geo. Stewart		*LL.D.* 1903
—	Gilb. Clement Whit	H. Sel.	M 1912
—	Gilb. Edw.	Cath.	M 1907 A.B. 1910
—	Harman Maul	Pem.	M 1898 A.B. 1901. A.M. 1905
—	Harold Edw.	Trin.	M 1904 A.B. 1907
—	Harry Bernard Wingate	Trin.	M 1905
—	Harry Lawrence	Sid.	M 1899 A.B. 1902. A.M. 1906
—	Hen. Coxwell	Qu.	M 1910
—	Hen. Cracroft	Pem.	M 1912
—	Hen. John	N. C.	M 1899 A.B. 1902. A.M. 1907
—	Herb.	Em.	M 1902
—	Hor. Claude Aubrey	Trin.	M 1900 A.B. 1903. A.M. 1907
—	Jack	Jes.	M 1912　　　[LL.M. 1894. LL.D. 1901
—	Ja. Dundas	Trin.	M 1885 A.B., LL.B. 1888. A.M. 1892.
—	John Banwell	N. C.	M 1900 A.B. 1903
—	John Douglas Campbell	Trin.	M 1891 A.B. 1894. A.M. 1899. M.D. 1905
—	John Lawrence	N. C.	M 1907 A.B. 1910
—	Kenneth Hamilton ...	Sid.	M 1905
—	Leon. Twisdale	Cla.	M 1907 A.B. 1911
—	Lionel	N. C.	M 1912
—	Lynton Woolmer ...	Trin.	M 1905 A.B. 1908
—	Malcolm Graham ...	King's	M 1905 A.B. 1908
—	Norman Cecil	Trin.	M 1909 A.B. 1912
—	Reg. de Lacy	H. Sel.	M 1895 A.B. 1898. A.M.† 1911
—	Reg. Julius	Trin. H.	M 1898 A.B., LL.B. 1901
—	Ronald Edwin	Trin.	M 1909 A.B. 1912
—	Roy Mordaunt	Trin. H.	M 1899 A.B. 1902
—	Rudolph Dymoke ...	Trin.	M 1906 A.B. 1910
—	Sam. Deane Gordon	Cla.	M 1895 A.B. 1900. A.M. 1906
—	Tho. Mutlow	Down.	M 1909

White,	Will. Ern. Crabtree	Cla.	M 1890 A.B. 1893. A.M., LL.M. 1897.
			[LL.D. 1903
—	Will. Herb.	Trin.	M 1898 A.B. 1901. A.M. 1907
—	Will. Verner Gordon	Em.	M 1897 A.B. 1901. A.M. 1906
Whitefield,	Caleb Gordon	Mag.	M 1910
Whitehead,	Alf. Gordon	Cai.	M 1911
—	Alf. North ....*Trin.		M 1880 A.B. 1884. A.M. 1887. Sc.D. 1905
—	Brian	Cla.	M 1907 A.B. 1911
—	Cha. Ern.	Cai.	M 1901 A.B. 1904. M.B., B.C. 1911
—	Frank	Trin.	M 1908
—	Herb.	Down.	M 1908
—	John Rob. Gobertus	Trin.	M 1908
—	Percy Neil	Cla.	M 1907
—	Reg. Binyon	Chr.	M 1908 A.B. 1912
—	Reg. Hen. Hughes ...	Cla.	M 1899 A.B. 1902
—	Reg. Willoughby	Trin.	M 1907 A.B. 1910
—	Rob. Fra.	Em.	M 1900 A.B. 1903
—	Tho. North	Trin.	M 1910
Whitehorn,	Roger Herb.	Em.	M 1905 A.B. 1908
—	Roy Drummond	Trin.	M 1910
Whitehouse,	Alf.	Joh.	M 1902 A.B. 1905. A.M. 1909
—	Arnold Art. Gray ...	Qu.	M 1897 A.B. 1900. A.M. 1904
—	Bertram Reg.	Joh.	M 1910
—	John Ja.	Joh.	M 1900 A.B. 1903. A.M.† 1908
—	Owen Cha.		A.M. 1909
Whitelegge,	Maur. Horsley	Pem.	M 1908 A.B. 1911
Whiteley,	Edw. Pulleyn	Em.	M 1903 A.B. 1906. A.M. 1910
—	Geo. Cecil	King's	M 1894 A.B. 1897. A.M. 1901
—	Ronald Ern.	Trin. H.	M 1899 A.B. 1903
—	Tho.	Em.	M 1903 A.B. 1906. A.M. 1910
Whiteman,	Reg. John Nelson ...	Chr.	L 1907
Whiteside,	Cecil Frank Winton	H. Sel.	M 1906 A.B. 1909
Whiteway,	Leon. Luscombe	N. C.	M 1895 A.B. 1901
Whitfeld,	Nigel Bern.	Trin. H.	M 1909
Whitfield,	Edw. Hilliard Day ...	Joh.	M 1910
—	Ern. Oswald	Cai.	M 1912
—	Ern. Salisbury Butler	C. C.	L 1892 A.B. 1894. A.M. 1905
—	Ja. Gibson	Cla.	M 1895 A.B. 1898. A.M. 1902
—	John Burrows	Qu.	M 1908 A.B. 1911
—	John Osborn	Pem.	M 1904 A.B. 1907. A.M. 1911
—	Jos. Louis	N. C.	M 1897 A.B. 1900. A.M. 1905
—	Syd. Phil.	Trin.	M 1909
Whitham,	Alb.	Cath.	M 1910
—	John Wilkinson	Trin.	M 1911
Whiting,	Edw. Rob. Stuart-Menteith }	Cai.	M 1912
—	Maur. Hen.	Down.	M 1904 A.B. 1907. B.C. 1910. M.B. 1911
—	Ralph Oakley	Trin.	M 1911
—	Will. Rob. Gerald ...	Qu.	M 1903 A.B. 1906. A.M. 1910
—	Wykeham Herb.	Joh.	M 1880 A.B. 1884. A.M. 1912
Whitlark,	John Howard	Trin.	M 1908
Whitley,	Ern. Bennett	C. C.	M 1905 A.B. 1908. A.M. 1912
—	Geo.	Joh.	M 1900 A.B. 1904
—	Herb.	Cai.	M 1905
—	Norman Hen. Pownall	Em.	M 1901 A.B. 1904
Whitlock,	Percy Oddie	Joh.	M 1907 A.B. 1910
Whitmore,	Alf.	Cai.	M 1894 A.B. 1897. B.C. 1900. M.B. 1903
—	Cha. Ja. Rich.	Down.	M 1907 A.B. 1910
—	Geo. Fre.		A.M. 1901
—	Herb. Searle	Sid.	M 1909 A.B. 1912
Whitney,	Ja. Pounder	King's	M 1877 A.B. 1881. A.M. 1884. B.D. 1906

Whittaker,	Cha. Dav.	N. C.	M 1881 Sid. A.B.1884(2).A.M.1888.LL.M.
—	Geo.	Pet.	M 1908 A.B. 1911 [1898. LL.D. 1904
Whittall,	Hen. Cecil	Cai.	M 1907 A.B. 1910
—	Norman Reg. La Fontaine	Pem.	M 1909
Whittam,	Matth. John Goldsborough	C. C.	M 1912
Whittard,	Courtenay Lancelot	Trin.	M 1906
Whittick,	Tho.	Jes.	M 1910
Whitting,	Art. Gregory	King's	M 1891 A.B. 1894. A.M. 1901
—	Rob. Everard	King's	M 1897 A.B. 1900. B.C. 1904. M.B., A.M.
			[1905. M.D. 1908
Whittingham, Walt. Godfrey		N. C.	L 1884 Pet. A.B. 1886. A.M. 1909
Whittingstall, Geo. Herb. Fearnley		Qu.	M 1910
Whittington, Theodore		Trin.	M 1909
Whittle,	Dennis	Trin.	M 1908 A.B. 1911
Whittles,	Cyril Leon.	Down.	M 1907
Whitton,	Tho.	Cla.	M 1895 A.B. 1898. A.M. 1902
Whitty,	Hamlin Nowell	Cai.	M 1901 A.B. 1904. A.M. 1908
—	Lewellin Wallingford	Qu.	M 1907 A.B. 1910
Whitwell,	Raymond	Chr.	M 1905 A.B. 1908. A.M. 1912
Whitwill,	Tho. Norman	Em.	M 1912
Whitworth,	Cyril Clinton Allen	Trin.	M 1909 A.B. 1912
—	Eric Edw. Allen	Trin.	M 1908 A.B. 1911
—	Geo. Elwes Allen ...	Trin.	M 1906 A.B. 1909
—	John	Cai.	M 1902
—	Will. Hervey Allen	Trin.	M 1905 A.B. 1908
Whye,	John Will.	N. C.	M 1902 Joh. A.B. 1905
Whyley,	Gregory John Morrah	Em.	M 1898 A.B. 1901. LL.B. 1902. A.M. 1906
Whyte,	Hen. Edw.	H. Aye.	M 1889 A.B. 1892. N. C. A.M. 1906
—	Will. John Arnold ...	Cai.	M 1912
Whytehead, Hen. Layard		H. Sel.	M 1897 A.B. 1904. A.M. 1910
Whyte-Venables, Harold Art.		Qu.	M 1910
Wicks,	Cha. Alf.	Cai.	M 1896 A.B. 1903. A.M. 1906
Widgery,	Alban Gregory	Cath.	M 1905 A.B. 1908. A.M. 1912
—	Gilb. Hen.	King's	M 1908 A.B. 1911
Wiener,	Harold Marcus	Cai.	M 1894 A.B. 1897. LL.B. 1898. A.M. 1901
Wiggin,	Cha. Rich. Hen.	Trin.	M 1903 A.B. 1907
—	Geo. Rob.	Trin.	M 1907
—	Will. Hen.	Trin.	M 1906 A.B. 1909
Wiggins,	Rob. Hen.	Pet.	M 1894 A.B. 1897. A.M. 1901
Wight,	Rob. Burt	C. C.	M 1895 A.B. 1898. A.M. 1906
Wightman,	Will. Crewe	H. Sel.	L 1912
Wightwick,	Claude	Pem.	M 1900 A.B. 1903
Wigley,	Hugh Middleton	Mag.	M 1909 A.B. 1912
—	Tho.	N. C.	M 1909 A.B. 1912
—	Wilfrid Cyril Sprye	Em.	M 1909 A.B. 1912
Wigmore,	Ja. Buckley Aquilla	Cai.	M 1905 J. B. Aquila, A.B. 1908
Wigram,	Cha. Knox	Trin.	M 1908 A.B. 1911
—	Gerrard Edm.	Jes.	M 1895 A.B. 1898. A.M. 1906
—	Loftus Edw.	Trin.	M 1896 A.B. 1899. M.B., B.C., A.M. 1903
—	Marcus Edw.	Trin.	M 1894 A.B. 1897. A.M. 1901
—	Percy Solly	Down.	L 1896 Trin. A.B. 1899. A.M. 1904
—	Will. Ainger	Trin. H.	M 1891 A.B. 1894. A.M. 1907
Wijewardene, Don Edm.		Pet.	M 1911
—	Tudugalage Don Rich.	Pet.	M 1907 A.B. 1910
Wilberforce, Harold Hartley		C. C.	M 1900 A.B. 1903. LL.B. 1904. A.M. 1909
Wilcock,	John	Chr.	M 1911
—	John Arnold	Down.	M 1911
Wilcockson, Will. Howson		Cai.	M 1910
Wilcox,	Alf. Geo.	N. C.	M 1879 Cla. A.B. 1883. A.M. 1906
—	Art. John	Em.	M 1909 A.B. 1912

Wilcox,	Hen.	Joh.	M 1888 A.B. 1892. A.M. 1907
—	John Cha.	N. C.	M 1883 Joh. A.B. 1886. A.M. 1912
—	Stanley Murray	Em.	M 1906 A.B. 1909
Wild,	Art. Edwin	Qu.	M 1909 A.B. 1912
—	Ja. Anstey Preston	Jes.	M 1901
—	Tho. Napier	Chr.	M 1903 A.B. 1906
Wilde,	Cecil Arden Graham	Jes.	M 1911
—	Edw. Hugh Norris ...	King's	M 1898 A.B. 1901. A.M. 1905
Wilderspin,	Bertram Cha.	Down.	M 1908 A.B. 1912
Wilding,	Anth. Fre.	Trin.	M 1902 A.B. 1905
--	Will. Hen.	N. C.	M 1894 Em. A.B. 1897. A.M. 1901
Wileman,	Gerald Watkins Brett	Cai.	M 1909 A.B. 1912
Wiles,	Clem. Chris.	Joh.	M 1897 A.B. 1901. A.M.† 1904
—	Gilb.	Cath.	M 1898 A.B. 1901
—	Harold Herb.	Chr.	M 1911
—	Ja. Will.	N. C.	E 1900 A.B. 1904
—	Jos. John	Cla.	M 1909 A.B. 1912
Wilgress,	John Hen. Farquhar	H. Sel.	M 1894 A.B. 1897. B.C. 1903. M.B. 1905
Wilkes,	John Fiske	Trin.	M 1898 A.B. 1901. A.M. 1905
Wilkin,	Art.	King's	M 1898 A.B. 1901. B.C. 1908
—	Lancelot	Pem.	M 1890 A.B. 1893. A.M. 1898. B.C. 1901
—	Walt. Harold	Pem.	M 1895 A.B. 1898. A.M. 1903
—	Walt. Reg.	Trin.	M 1904 A.B. 1907
Wilkins,	Art. Norman	Joh.	M 1890 A.B. 1893. A.M. 1901
—	Walt. Gordon	Joh.	M 1902
Wilkinson,	Alan Fre. Lawder ...	Trin.	M 1911
—	Cha. Fra. Wellesley	Qu.	M 1904 A.B. 1907
—	Clennell Anstruther	Sid.	M 1902 A.B. 1905
—	Edw.	Cath.	M 1912
—	Edw. Fra.	Qu.	M 1912
—	Edw. Nevile	Joh.	M 1907
—	Ern. Roland	Joh.	M 1901 A.B. 1904. A.M. 1909
—	Fra. Alf. Wilmot ...	Mag.	M 1900 A.B. 1903
—	Frank Campbell	Jes.	M 1906
—	Frank Cooper	Sid.	M 1902 A.B. 1905
—	Geo. Jerrard	Cai.	M 1905 A.B. 1908
—	Geo. Rob.	Trin.	M 1894 A.B. 1897. A.M. 1912
—	Gordon Austin Wilmot	Qu.	M 1906 A.B. 1909
—	Harold Mayfield	Joh.	M 1894 A.B. 1897. A.M. 1901
—	Herb. Augustus	Pem.	M 1910
—	Hubert Cooper	Pem.	M 1904 A.B. 1908
—	Ja. Reg.	Qu.	M 1912
—	Ja. Shakespeare	Cath.	M 1908 A.B. 1911
—	Kenneth	Pem.	M 1910
—	Loughton Astling ...	N. C.	L 1911
—	Louis Umfreville ...	Joh.	M 1902 A.B. 1905. A.M. 1909
—	Noël	Cai.	M 1909 A.B. 1912
—	Rich. Ja.	Trin.	M 1886 A.B. 1901
—	Syd.	Cla.	M 1910
—	Syd. John	Chr.	M 1907 A.B. 1910
—	Valentine	Chr.	M 1911
—	Will. Reg.	Mag.	M 1912
Wilks,	Edw. Leslie	Down.	M 1912
—	Ja. Elwyn	Cla.	M 1910
—	Will. Art. Reg. ......*Cai.		M 1904 A.B. 1907. A.M. 1911
Will,	John Geo.	Down.	M 1911
Willan,	Art. Conrad	Trin.	M 1907
—	Gerald Ralph	Pem.	M 1899 A.B. 1903
Willans,	Esmond Tetley	Em.	M 1903 A.B. 1906
—	Gordon Jeune	Joh.	M 1904 A.B. 1908
Willbourn,	Eric Stewart	Sid.	M 1908 A.B. 1911

Willcocks,	Anth. Brodrick	C. C.	M 1911
—	Rob. Waller	Cai.	M 1905 A.B. 1908
—	Roger Hussey	King's	M 1907 A.B., LL.B. 1910
Willcox,	Ja. Mark	Trin.	M 1906 A.B. 1909
Wille,	Geo.	Chr.	M 1899 A.B. 1902. LL.B. 1903
Willett,	Everard Will.	Joh.	M 1905 A.B., LL.B. 1908. A.M. 1912
—	Rob. Norman	Trin. H.	M 1902
—	Wilfred Leslie	Trin.	M 1909
Willey,	Harold	King's	M 1899 A.B. 1902
—	Rupert Harold	Cai.	M 1905 A.B. 1908
Williams,	Alan Copland	Chr.	L 1908 A.B. 1911
—	Alf. Gregson	Cai.	M 1907
—	Art. Alf. Strover ...	Trin. H.	M 1902
— Art.	Donald John Bedward	Cai.	M 1902 A.B. 1905
—	Art. John	Cai.	M 1902 A.B. 1905
—	Art. Lawrence	Jes.	M 1911 [D.D. 1911
—	Art. Lukyn	Jes.	M 1871 A.B. 1875. A.M. 1878. B.D. 1906.
—	Art. Oswald	Jes.	M 1902 A.B. 1905. A.M. 1909. post Lukyn-
—	Art. Sam.	H. Sel.	M 1904 A.B. 1907 [Williams, A. O.
—	Carrington Bonsor ...	Cla.	M 1908 A.B. 1911
—	Caryl Bransby	Cai.	M 1903
—	Cecil	Cai.	M 1900 A.B. 1903. A.M. 1907
—	Cha.	Trin.	M 1905 A.B. 1908
—	Cha. Art.	Qu.	M 1898 A.B. 1901. A.M. 1909
—	Cha. Edw.	Cai.	E 1884 A.B. 1887. M.B., B.C. 1890. A.M.
—	Cha. Harold	Em.	M 1906 A.B. 1909 [1904. M.D. 1905
—	Cha. Ja.	Cla.	M 1906 A.B. 1909. LL.B. 1912
—	Cha. Mollan	N. C.	M 1896 Chr. A.B. 1899. A.M. 1905
—	Cha. Willoughby ...	Sid.	M 1877 A.B. 1881. LL.M. 1908
—	Claude St Maur	H. Sel.	M 1903 A.B. 1906
—	Colin Ern.	Trin.	M 1900 A.B. 1903
—	Dav. Esaiah	Mag.	M 1894 A.B. 1897. A.M. 1901
—	Dav. Geoffrey	Chr.	M 1912
—	Dav. Lewis	Joh.	M 1898 A.B. 1901. A.M. 1907
—	Dav. Rich. Art.	Qu.	M 1898 A.B. 1905
—	Edw.	Trin.	M 1909 A.B. 1912
—	Edw. Gordon	Trin.	M 1907
—	Edw. Hen. Yate	Cla.	M 1902 A.B. 1905
—	Ern. Trevor Morgan	Sid.	M 1892 N.C. A.B. 1902 E.M.T., A.M. 1905
—	Frank Hiram	Em.	M 1907 A.B. 1910
—	Frank Lukyn	Chr.	M 1910
—	Frank Silvers	Trin.	M 1897 LL.B. 1900. post Williams-Tho-
—	Geoffrey Commeline	Cai.	M 1910 [mas, F. S. A.B., LL.M. 1904
—	Geo. Conway	Trin.	M 1903 A.B. 1906. A.M. 1911
—	Geo. Trevor	Trin.	M 1911
—	Gerald Hen.	Trin.	M 1910
—	Gerald Vernon	Pet.	M 1912
—	Gordon	Trin.	M 1908 A.B. 1911
—	Græme Douglas .....:	C. C.	M 1901
—	Guy Gurney	C. C.	M 1902 A.B. 1905. A.M. 1911
—	Gwilym	Em.	M 1912
—	Harold Austin	Em.	M 1904 A.B. 1908
—	Harold Herb.	Chr.	M 1900 A.B. 1903. A.M. 1909
—	Harry Geo. Everard	King's	M 1911
—	Harvey	Pem.	E 1902 A.B. 1904. A.M. 1908
—	Hen. Currer	Pem.	M 1893 A.B. 1896. M.B., B.C., A.M. 1903
—	Hen. Frank Fulford	Cla.	M 1904 A.B. 1907
—	Hen. Morrison	H. Sel.	M 1896 A.B. 1899. A.M. 1906
—	Herb. John	H. Sel.	M 1906 A.B. 1909
—	Hor. Ern.	N. C.	M 1903 Down. A.B. 1906
—	Hugh	Qu.	M 1898 A.B. 1901. A.M. 1905

Williams,	Hugh Owen	King's	M 1912
—	Hugh Pat. Will. Bedward	Em.	M 1906 A.B. 1909
—	Iolo Aneurin	King's	M 1910
—	Ja. Evan	N. C.	M 1887 Chr. A.B. 1890. A.M. 1901
—	John Alex.	N. C.	M 1891 A.B. 1897. A.M. 1904
—	John Clifford	Pem.	M 1906 A.B. 1909
—	John Evan	N. C.	L 1910 Cath. A.B. 1912
—	John Foster	Qu.	M 1897 A.B. 1900. A.M. 1904
—	John Herb.	Trin.	M 1876 LL.B. 1880. LL.M. 1909
—	John Lias Cecil	Cai.	M 1910
—	John Rich.	N. C.	M 1901
—	Jos. Coryton Stanley	Cai.	M 1902
—	Jos. Ern.	N. C.	M 1908 Chr. A.B. 1911
—	Joshua Appleyard ...	Cla.	M 1896 A.B., LL.B. 1899. A.M. 1903
—	Keith Gaster	Chr.	E 1906 A.B. 1909
—	Milbourne Bransby	Cai.	M 1899 A.B. 1903
—	Moses Awoonor	Joh.	M 1894 A.B. 1897. A.M.† 1910
—	Neville Scott	Cla.	M 1904 A.B. 1907. B.C. 1910
—	Noel Dyson	Trin.	M 1908
—	Osborne St Maur ...	Em.	M 1902 A.B. 1905
—	Oswald Hub.	Qu.	M 1911
—	Oswald Temple	Cai.	M 1909 A.B. 1912
—	Penry Malcolm Wykeham	Joh.	M 1908 A.B. 1911
—	Phil.	Trin.	M 1903 A.B. 1906
—	Phil. Stanhope	Cai.	M 1908 A.B. 1911
—	Rainald Fra.	H. Sel.	M 1900 A.B. 1903
—	Raymond Burke	Cai.	M 1905 A.B. 1908
—	Reg. Fowke	Cai.	M 1894 A.B. 1897. B.C. 1901. M.B. 1903
—	Rich.	H. Aye.	M 1895 Joh. A.B. 1899. A.M. 1904
—	Rich. Gregson	Cai.	M 1902 A.B. 1905
—	Rich. Lloyd	Joh.	M 1910
—	Rich. Myrddin	Mag.	M 1909 A.B. 1912
—	Rob.	Mag.	L 1909
—	Robin Art. Walton	King's	M 1912
—	Ronald Cha. Lambert	Pet.	M 1900 A.B. 1904
—	Rowland Art.	H. Sel.	M 1898 A.B. 1901
—	Roy Bruce	Pem.	M 1906
—	Sam. Leslie	Trin. H.	M 1909
—	Sam. Roy	Cai.	M 1912
—	Selwyn Coldham	Cai.	M 1912
—	Syd. Cecil	Em.	M 1912
—	Syd. Ern.	Jes.	E 1889 A.B. 1894. A.M. 1902
—	Theophilus	N. C.	M 1904 Pet. A.B. 1908
—	Tho. Bowen	Cai.	M 1905 A.B. 1908
—	Tho. Cuthbert Leighton	N. C.	M 1900 A.B. 1903. A.M. 1909
—	Tho. Llewelyn	N. C.	M 1887 Pet. A.B. 1890. A.M. 1903
—	Tho. Reinallt	Pem.	M 1909 A.B., LL.B. 1912
—	Tho. Taliesin	N. C.	M 1907 Pet. A.B. 1910
—	Trevor Mathias Owen	Chr.	M 1901 A.B. 1905
—	Ulric Gaster	Cai.	M 1910
—	Walt. Nalder	Trin.	M 1899 A.B. 1902. LL.B. 1903. A.M. 1906
—	Walt. Stanley	Cath.	M 1911
—	Will.	Qu.	L 1900 A.B. 1902. A.M. 1907
—	Will. Cha. Banford	Pem.	M 1904 W. C. Bamford, A.B. 1907
—	Will. Ern.	H. Sel.	M 1906 A.B. 1909
—	Will. Fre.	Cla.	M 1903 A.B. 1906. A.M. 1910
—	Will. Hen.	N. C.	M 1909
—	Will. Humphry	Cai.	M 1898 W. Humphrey, A.B. 1903
—	Will. Percy	Down.	M 1899 W. Percival, A.B. 1902. M.B. 1906
—	Will. Roland	Qu.	M 1911
—	Will. Troth	Joh.	M 1911

Williams-Ellis,	Bertram Clough ...	Trin.	M 1902
Williams Ellis,	Rupert Greaves ...	Sid.	M 1896 A.B. 1901
Williams-Green,	Will. Tho.	Trin.	M 1911
Williamson,	Alex. John Neeve ...	Pem.	M 1907 A.B. 1910
—	Art. Geo.	C. C.	M 1908 A.B. 1911
—	Cecil Gordon	Mag.	M 1908 A.B. 1911
—	Dorian Adair	Trin.	M 1912
—	Fra. Lorrimer	C. C.	M 1900 A.B. 1903. A.M. 1909
—	Frc.	Em.	M 1909 A.B. 1912
—	Fre. Arnold	Qu.	M 1908 A.B. 1911
—	Geo. Evans	Trin.	M 1905 A.B., LL.B. 1908. A.M. 1912
—	Geo. Hamilton	Em.	M 1910
—	Hen. Cecil Roxburgh	Trin.	M 1898 A.B. 1901
—	Ja. Bruce	Trin.	M 1911
—	John Maur.	Cai.	M 1908 A.B., LL.B. 1911
—	Kenneth Bertram Franklin	Joh.	M 1894 A.B. 1897. A.M. 1903
—	Oliver Key	Trin.	M 1886 A.B. 1890. A.M. 1895. M.B., B.C.
—	Ralph	Chr.	M 1906 A.B. 1909 [1896. M.D. 1902
—	Ralph Stanley	Chr.	M 1901 A.B. 1904
—	Reg. Montague	Pem.	M 1906 A.B. 1909
—	Rob. Howard Wallace	King's	M 1911
—	Steph. Kenneth Guthrie	Trin.	M 1906 A.B. 1909
—	Tho. Ranald Macalister	Cla.	M 1906
—	Tho. Roy	Qu.	M 1912
Williams-Thomas			*See* Williams, F. S.
Williams Wynn,	Watkin	Trin.	M 1909
Willink,	Art. Cha. Eric	Em.	M 1900 A.B. 1903
—	Art. Ja. Wakefield ...	King's	M 1909 A.B. 1912
—	Hen. Urmston	Trin.	M 1912
—	Herman Ja. Lindale	Cai.	M 1903 A.B. 1906
Willis,	Alex. Galbraith Fleming	Chr.	M 1909 A.B. 1912 [1905
—	John Chris.	N. C.	M 1886 A.B. 1889. Cai. A.M. 1893. Sc.D.†
—	John Jamieson	Pem.	M 1891 A.B. 1894. A.M. 1898. D.D. 1912
—	John Keith	Qu.	M 1898 A.B. 1901. M.B. 1907
—	Reg. Elgar	Down.	M 1906 A.B. 1909
—	Rob.	Cai.	M 1887 A.B. 1907
—	Zwinglius Frank	King's	M 1909 A.B. 1912
Willock,	Guy Cha. Boileau ...	King's	M 1910
Willoughby,	Fra. Geo. Godfrey ...	Trin.	M 1908 A.B. 1911
—	Tho. Oborne	H. Sel.	M 1894 A.B. 1897. A.M. 1901
—·	Willoughby Mason ...	Cai.	M 1894 A.B. 1897. M.B., B.C. 1900. M.D.
Willows,	Rich. Smith	Trin.	L 1898 A.B. 1899. A.M. 1904 [1904
Willox,	Alex. Geo.	Cla.	M 1910
Wills,	Alf. Gordon	King's	M 1910
—	Art. Gerald Phillips	C. C.	M 1910
—	Eric Foulger	Joh.	M 1908 A.B. 1911
—	John Pearce	Em.	M 1909
—	Leon. Johnston ......*King's		M 1903 A.B. 1906. A.M. 1910
—	Oliver Byerley Walters	Trin.	M 1911
—	Rob. Bruce Melville	Trin.	M 1908 A.B. 1911 [1905
—	Rob. Glover	N. C.	M 1897 Joh. A.B. 1900. M.B., B.C., A.M.
—	Rob. Lyne	N. C.	M 1898 Joh. A.B. 1900. A.M. ⁿ07
—	Ronald Dewhurst ...	Trin.	M 1910
—	Sydenham Waldie ...	Trin.	M 1907 A.B. 1910
—	Walt. Douglas Melville	Trin.	M 1906 A.B. 1909
Willson,	Cecil Hen. Hyde Salter	Em.	M 1893 A.B. 1897. A.M. 1901
—	Fre. Ja.	Em.	M 1907 A.B. 1910
—·	Howard Sam.	Em.	M 1887 A.B. 1890. M.B., B.C. 1893. M.D.
Wilmore,	Alb. Nelson	Joh.	M 1908 [1905
Wilmott,	Alf. Ja.	Joh.	M 1906 A.B. 1909
--	Alf. John	Em.	M 1894 A.B. 1897. A.M. 1901

Wilson,	Alan Hood	Pem.	M 1911
—	Alan Plumpton	Pem.	M 1908 A.B. 1911
—	Alex. Garrick	Cai.	M 1892 A.B. 1895. M.B. 1899. B.C. 1901.
—	Alf. John	Sid.	M 1909 [M.C. 1907
—	Angus Bewley	Pem.	M 1895 A.B. 1904. M.B. 1907
—	Arnold	Cla.	M 1903 A.B. 1906. A.M. 1910
—	Art. Edw.	Cla.	M 1908 A.B. 1911
--	Art. Lewis	Pem.	M 1899 A.B. 1902
—	Aubyn Harold Raymond	Trin.	M 1908 A.B. 1911
—	Basil Hugh Campbell	Trin.	M 1904
—	Bassett FitzGerald ...	Trin.	M 1907 A.B. 1910
—	Bern.	Sid.	M 1908 A.B. 1911
—	Bicton Clemence	Qu.	M 1901 A.B. 1904. A.M. 1908
—	Cecil	Jes.	M 1879 A.B. 1883. A.M. 1886. D.D. 1908
—	Cecil Wilfred	C. C.	M 1894 A.B. 1897. A.M. 1901
—	Chris. Ja.	Chr.	M 1898 A.B. 1901. M.B., B.C., A.M. 1906
—	Claude Bawden	Pem.	M 1910
—	Clem. Eustace Macro	Trin.	M 1894 A.B. 1899. A.M. 1903
—	Clyde Tabor	Trin.	M 1907 A.B., LL.B. 1911
—	Cornelius Eric	Trin.	M 1911
—	Dav. Art. Calder ...	Joh.	M 1901
--	Dav. Rex	Jes.	L 1910 A.B. 1912
—	Edm. Beecher		*Sc.D.* 1909
—	Edw. Rowland	Trin. H.	M 1907 A.B. 1910
—	Edwin John	Em.	M 1910 A.B. 1912
—	Ern. John	Mag.	M 1898 A.B. 1901. A.M. 1907
—	Evelyn Rockley	Trin.	M 1898 A.B. 1901. A.M. 1905
—	Fred Warren	N. C.	M 1912
—	Frederic Bonhôte ...	Trin.	M 1900 A.B. 1903
—	Fre. Arnold	Chr.	M 1912
—	Gardiner	Joh.	M 1901 A.B. 1904. A.M. 1908
—	Geoffrey Remington	Trin.	M 1893 A.B. 1896. B.C., A.M. 1902. M.B.
—	Geo. Balfour	Trin.	M 1906 A.B. 1909 [1903
—	Geo. Ja.	Joh.	M 1903
—	Geo. Murray	Pem.	M 1897 A.B. 1900. A.M. 1911
—	Geo. Noël	Jes.	M 1907 A.B. 1910
—	Harold Alb. ....*Trin.		M 1897 A.B. 1899. A.M. 1904
—	Harold Crewdson ...	Cai.	M 1904 A.B. 1907
—	Harold Fra.	Trin.	E 1907
—	Harold Graham	Em.	M 1901 A.B. 1904
—	Harold Hen.	N. C.	M 1895 A.B. 1898. A.M. 1905
—	Harold Remington ...	Trin. H.	M 1894 A.B. 1897. A.M. 1908
—	Harry	Em.	M 1912
—	Harry Montefiore ...	Trin. H.	M 1895 A.B. 1898. B.C. 1902. M.B.† 1906
—	Hen. Alb.	C. C.	M 1895 A.B. 1898. A.M. 1903
—	Hen. Lydiard	H. Sel.	M 1895 A.B. 1898. B.C. 1904. M.B. 1905.
—	Hen. Olaf Selwyn ...	Sid.	M 1912 [M.D. 1910
—	Herb. Noel Stanley	Trin.	M 1903 A.B. 1907. A.M. 1911
—	Hub. Fra.	Chr.	M 1904 A.B. 1907. B.C. 1912
—	Hugh Stanley	King's	M 1904 A.B. 1907. A.M. 1912
—	Humphrey Bowstead	Pem.	M 1902 A.B. 1905. M.B., B.C. 1910
—	Ja. Maur. ....*Joh.		M 1855 A.B. 1859. A.M. 1862. B.D., D.D.
—	Ja. Rob. Menzies ...	Pem.	M 1910 [1903
—	Ja. Steuart	King's	M 1908 A.B. 1911
—	Ja. Vernon	Cai.	M 1900 A.B. 1903. A.M. 1907
—	John	N. C.	L 1901 Cath. A.B. 1903. A.M. 1907
—	John	N. C.	M 1912
—	John Chris.	Trin.	M 1910
—	John Dover	Cai.	M 1900 A.B. 1903. A.M. 1908
—	John Granville	Trin.	M 1905
—	John Kenneth	C. C.	M 1908 A.B. 1911

Wilson,	John Phil.	Pem.	M 1909
—	John Stanley	H. Sel.	L 1906 A.B. 1911
—	Kenneth Hen.	Trin.	M 1903
—	Kevin Fitzjames	Cla.	M 1906 A.B. 1910
—	Lionel Gathorne	Trin.	M 1895 A.B. 1898. A.M. 1908
—	Norman	Pem.	M 1897 A.B. 1900. B.C., A.M. 1907. M.D.
—	Percy Macdonald ...	Pem.	M 1909 A.B. 1912 [1911
—	Pet. McCandlish	Cla.	M 1899 A.B. 1902. A.M. 1909
—	Phil. Fre.	Cai.	M 1902 A.B. 1905. M.B., B.C. 1911
—	Ralph Edwyn	Trin.	M 1911
—	Raymond Will.	H. Sel.	M 1903 A.B. 1907
—	Ronald Edw.	C. C.	M 1904 A.B. 1907
—	Stanley	N. C.	L 1905
—	Tho.	Em.	M 1898 A.B. 1901. A.M. 1905
—	Tho.	C. C.	M 1912
—	Tho. Bowstead	Pem.	M 1901 A.B. 1904. A.M. 1908
—	Tho. Erskine	Cai.	M 1894 A.B. 1897. A.M. 1904
—	Tho. Irving Ward ...	King's	M 1901 A.B. 1904. A.M. 1908
—	Tho. Martin	Pet.	M 1912
—	Tom Bonhote	Pem.	M 1911
—	Walt. Edw.	Pem.	M 1901 A.B. 1904
—	Walton Ronald	Em.	M 1909 A.B. 1912
—	Will.	Cai.	M 1910 A.B. 1912
—	Will. Arbuthnot	Pem.	M 1912
Wilson-Barkworth, Kenneth Art.		Jes.	M 1902 A.B. 1905. A.M. 1909
Wilson-Todd, Ja. Hen.		Trin. H.	M 1911
Wilton,	Ja. Percy	Jes.	M 1902 A.B. 1905. A.M. 1911
—	John Raymond	Trin.	M 1904 A.B. 1907. A.M. 1911
—	Sam. Brammer	Down.	M 1911
—	Tho. Ryder	Jes.	M 1897 A.B. 1900. A.M. 1910
—	Will. Parker	Sid.	M 1893 A.B. 1896. A.M. 1908
Wiltshire,	Fre.	N. C.	M 1892 Cai. A.B. 1895. A.M. 1912
—	Harold Waterlow ...	Cla.	M 1897 A.B. 1900. A.M. 1904. M.B., B.C.
—	Hen. Goodwill	Em.	M 1908 A.B. 1911 [1907. M.D. 1910
Wimbush,	Geo. Barnes	Trin.	M 1895 A.B. 1899. A.M. 1902
—	Gordon Stewart	Cai.	M 1908
—	Hector Geo.	Pem.	M 1912
—	Ronald	Cai.	M 1905 A.B. 1908. A.M. 1912
Wimperis,	Harry Egerton	Cai.	M 1898 A.B. 1900. A.M. 1908
Win,	Maung San	Pet.	E 1908
Winans,	Tho. Geo.	Mag.	M 1905
Winby,	Lewis Phillips	Trin.	M 1894 A.B. 1897. A.M. 1902
Winch,	Gordon Bluett	Trin.	M 1895 A.B. 1899. A.M. 1902
—	Stanley Brooke	Trin.	M 1903
—	Will. Hen.	Joh.	M 1895 A.B. 1898. A.M. 1902
Winder,	Norman Hathornthwaite	Pem.	M 1907 A.B. 1910
—	Reg. McDonnell	Joh.	M 1908 A.B. 1911
Windley,	Fra. Morse	Jes.	M 1908 A.B. 1911
—	Tho. Noble	Chr.	M 1900 A.B., LL.B. 1903
Windsor,	Ja. Fre.	H. Sel.	M 1899 A.B. 1902. B.C. 1908. M.B. 1908 (2).
Windsor Clive, (*Hon.*) Archer ...		Trin.	M 1909 A.B. 1912 [M.D. 1912
Windsor-Clive, (*Hon.*) Ivor Miles		Trin.	M 1907 (*Lord*) Windsor, A.B. 1910
Windsor Clive, (*Hon.*) Other Rob.		Trin.	M 1903
Windust,	Will. Hufton	Sid.	M 1890 A.B. 1893. A.M. 1902
Winfield,	Art.	Down.	M 1905 A.B. 1908
—	Fre. Butwell	Down.	M 1909 A.B. 1912
—	Geo.	Down.	M 1905 A.B. 1908. A.M. 1912
—	Leon.	Trin.	M 1911
—	Percy Hen.	Joh.	M 1896 A.B., LL.B. 1899. LL.M. 1906
Wing,	Tycho	H. Sel.	M 1897 A.B. 1900. A.M. 1904
Wingate,	Geo. Ronald Lauderdale	Jes.	M 1907

Wolff,	Lucien	Cai.	M 1906 A.B. 1910
Wolff-Metternich, *(Count)* Paul ...			*LL.D.* 1912
Wolffson,	Johannes Julius Ferdinand }	Chr.	M 1908
Wollaston,	Alex. Fre. Richmond	King's	M 1893 A.B. 1896. A.M. 1906
—	Herb. Cha.	Trin.	M 1908 A.B. 1911
Wolryche-Whitmore, John Eric Alex.		Trin.	M 1902 A.B. 1905
—	Phil. Malcolm	Jes.	M 1910
Wolstencroft, Alf. Stratten		Joh.	M 1912
Wolton,	St John Fleming ...	Trin.	M 1905
Womersley,	Sinclair Patteson ...	King's	M 1910
—	Will. Dobson	Em.	M 1912
—	Will. Edw.	Cath.	M 1910
Wong,	Siew Qui	Jes.	M 1906
Wontner,	Tho. Sewell	H. Sel.	M 1896 A.B. 1900. A.M. 1904
Woo,	Ching Sung	Joh.	M 1906
Wood,	Alex. ....*Em.		M 1902 A.B. 1904. A.M. 1909
—	Alf. Will. Maitland	Trin.	M 1907 A.B. 1912
—	Ardern Relf	Trin.	M 1908 A.B. 1911
—	Art. Edw. Frances ...	Trin.	M 1908
—	Art. John	Cath.	M 1911
—	Bern. Reader	Sid.	M 1909 A.B. 1912
—	Cecil John	Pet.	M 1893 A.B. 1896. A.M. 1901. D.D. 1912
—	Cecil Shuckburgh ...	Cai.	M 1907 A.B. 1910
—	Cha. Travers	Pem.	M 1894 A.B. 1897. *Qu. A.M. 1901
—	Chris. Fra.	Chr.	M 1903 A.B. 1906
—	Claud Tho. Thellusson	Trin.	M 1903 A.B. 1906
—	Denys Embrey Cecil	Em.	M 1904
—	Edgar Will.	Jes.	M 1911
—	Edm. Baddeley	Trin. H.	M 1902 A.B. 1905. A.M. 1909
—	Edw. Fra.	Pem.	M 1894 A.B. 1897. A.M. 1903
—	Edw. Reg.	Trin.	M 1904 A.B. 1907
—	Eric Horace	Cai.	M 1908 A.B. 1911
—	Eric Rawlinson	Cath.	M 1912
—	Ern.	Joh.	M 1900 A.B. 1903
—	Fra. Ern.	Down.	M 1895 A.B. 1899. M.B., B.C. 1902
—	Frank	Trin.	M 1908
—	Franklin Garrett ...	Jes.	M 1910
—	Fre. Bower	Cath.	M 1910
—	Fre. Erskine	Em.	M 1909 A.B. 1912
—	Fre. Gordon	Jes.	M 1907 A.B. 1910
—	Geo. Edw. Cha.	Pem.	M 1912
—	Geo. Rob. Harding ...	Chr.	M 1906 A.B. 1909
—	Hen. Geo. Westmorland	Pet.	M 1909 A.B. 1912
—	Herb. Geo. ....*Jes.		M 1899 A.B. 1902. A.M. 1906
—	Ja.	Jes.	M 1908 A.B. 1911
—	Ja. Edw. Hathorn ...	Joh.	M 1910
—	John Alf.	N. C.	M 1899 Em. A.B. 1902. A.M. 1906
—	John Lawrence	Trin.	M 1899 A.B. 1902
—	Jos. Art.	Joh.	M 1893 A.B. 1896. A.M. 1901. M.B., B.C.
—	Leslie Will.	Qu.	M 1909 A.B. 1912 [1903
—	Lynton Beddingfield Thayer	Cla.	M 1909 A.B. 1912
—	Nevil Preesall	Sid.	L 1902 A.B. 1904. A.M. 1912
—	Norris Ramsden	Cai.	M 1902
—	Paul Bern.	Cla.	M 1904 A.B., LL.B. 1907. A.M. 1911
—	Phil. Worsley ....*Em.		M 1899 A.B. 1902. A.M. 1906
—	Ravenshaw Will. Bodkin Cecil }	Cai.	M 1900 A.B. 1903
—	Reg. Syd. Carruthers Hathorn }	Joh.	M 1897 A.B. 1900. A.M. 1908
—	Rob. Stanford	Jes.	M 1905 A.B. 1908

Wood,	Ronald McKinnon ...	Pem.	M 1911
—	Sam. Rutter	Cla.	M 1905 A.B. 1908
—	Stanley	Chr.	M 1901 A.B. 1904
—	Tho.	Cai.	M 1893 A.B. 1896. M.B., B.C. 1901
—	Tho. Alb. Victor ...	Joh.	M 1912
—	Tho. Eugène	Joh.	M 1905 A.B., LL.B. 1908. A.M.† 1912
—	Tho. John	H. Sel.	M 1910
—	Tho. Percival	Pet.	M 1901 A.B. 1904
—	Tom Nevill	Pem.	M 1900 A.B. 1903. B.C. 1909
—	Trevor Ley Codner	Trin.	M 1898 LL.B. 1901. A.B. 1905
—	Wilfrid Burton	Jes.	M 1902 A.B. 1905. A.M. 1909. B.C. 1911.
—	Will.	Down.	M 1910 [M.B. 1912
—	Will. Levi	Joh.	M 1905
—	Will. Lyon	Chr.	M 1903 A.B. 1906
Woodall,	Frank Ewart	Joh.	M 1908 A.B. 1911
—	John Corbet	Trin.	M 1902 A.B. 1905
Woodard,	Alf. Lambert	Trin.	M 1899 A.B. 1902. A.M. 1906
—	Egbert Askew	Chr.	M 1905 A.B. 1908. A.M. 1912
—	Fra. Alwyne	Jes.	M 1908 A.B. 1911
Woodburn,	Will. Harrison	Chr.	M 1898 A.B. 1901
Woodcock,	Fra. Percy	Cla.	M 1898 A.B. 1901. A.M. 1905
—	Frank	Pem.	M 1897 A.B. 1900. A.M. 1905
—	Geo.	Cath.	M 1912
Woode,	Alf. Ferdinand	C. C.	M 1903
—	Cha. Edw.	C. C.	M 1898 A.B. 1901
Woodfield,	Sam. Percy	H. Sel.	M 1912
Woodhead,	Herb. Milne	Chr.	M 1912
—	John Ackroyd	Cla.	M 1900 A.B. 1903
Woodhouse,	Cecil	King's	M 1889 A.B. 1892. M.B., B.C. 1896. M.D.
—	Cha. Hall	Mag.	M 1909 A.B. 1912 [1901
—	Coventry Ernest	Pem.	M 1905 A.B. 1908
—	Disney Cha.	Cla.	M 1902 A.B. 1905. A.M. 1909
—	Douglas Edmonstone	Trin.	M 1901
—	Edw. John	Trin.	M 1903 A.B. 1906. A.M.† 1911
—	Edw. Livesey	H. Sel.	M 1895 A.B. 1899. A.M. 1910
—	Fra. Cyprian	Em.	M 1899 A.B. 1903. A.M. 1906
—	Geo. Fraser	Cai.	M 1893 A.B. 1897. A.M. 1901
—	Gerald Herb.	Trin.H.	M 1908 A.B. 1911
—	Guy Walker	Cla.	M 1909 A.B. 1912
—	Rob. Arnold	Down.	M 1911
—	Walt. Edw.	Mag.	M 1910
—	Will. Geo.	Joh.	M 1886 A.B. 1889. G. W. A.M. 1910
Woodland,	Clem. Art.	Trin.	M 1904 A.B. 1907
—	Vincent Reynolds ...	Trin.H.	M 1898 A.B. 1901. A.M. 1906
Woodman,	Cyril Herb.	Qu.	M 1899 A.B. 1902
—	Guy Stanley	Jes.	M 1905 A.B. 1908
Woodmansey,	Geoffrey Erskine ...	Joh.	M 1910
Woodroffe,	Kenneth Herb. Clayton	Pem.	M 1912
—	Neville Leslie	Trin.	M 1911
—	Walt. Gordon	Pem.	M 1912
Woodruff,	Geo. Gould	Cai.	M 1905 A.B. 1908
—	John Shedden	Trin.H.	M 1906 A.B. 1909
Woods,	Bertie Fountain	Joh.	M 1899 A.B. 1902. A.M.† 1908
—	Edw. Syd.	Trin.	M 1896 A.B. 1899. A.M. 1903
—	Fre. Art.	H. Sel.	M 1906 A.B. 1910
—	Fre. John	Trin.	M 1908 A.B. 1911
—	Fre. Lindsay	Cai.	M 1897 A.B. 1900. M.B., B.C. 1905
—	Geo. Constantine ...	Pem.	M 1904 A.B. 1907
—	John	C. C.	M 1900 A.B. 1905. A.M. 1908
—	John Murray	Trin.	M 1906
—	Matth. Grosvenor ...	Trin.	M 1897 A.B 1900. A.M. 1904

Woods,	Matth. May	Cla.	M 1901
—	Norman Cha.	H. Sel.	M 1903 A.B., Mus.B. 1906. A.M. 1910
—	Reg. Salisbury	Down.	M 1911
—	Sandford	H. Aye.	L 1892 Cath. A.B. 1894. A.M. 1911
—	Tho. Hen.	H. Sel.	M 1910
—	Will. Ashburnham ...	N. C.	M 1912
—	Will. Hen. Ogle	H. Sel.	M 1894 A.B. 1897. M.B., B.C. 1901
Woodsend,	Phil. Duncan	Cai.	M 1910
Woodward,	Frank Ja.	Cai.	M 1903 A.B. 1906
—	Frank Lee	Sid.	M 1890 A.B. 1893. A.M. 1902
—	Herb. Croker Sperling	H. Sel.	M 1887 Down. A.B. 1891. A.M. 1896. B.C. [1903. M.B. 1905
—	Herb. Niel	Down.	M 1892 A.B. 1896. A.M. 1902
--	Will. Edw.	Trin.	M 1907 A.B. 1910
Woodwark,	Harold Brodrick	Joh.	M 1898 A.B. 1901
Wooldridge,	Duncan Wakeman ...	Joh.	M 1908 A.B. 1911
Wooler,	Cyril Upton	Joh.	M 1905 A.B. 1908
—	Herb. Sykes	Joh.	M 1911
Woolf,	Alb. Edw.	Em.	M 1902 A. E. Mortimer, A.B. 1905. B.C.
—	Cecil Nathan Sid. ...*Trin.		M 1906 A.B. 1909 [1909. M.B. 1911
–	Edgar Sid.	Sid.	M 1902 A.B. 1905
—	Hen. Mortimer Alb.	Cai.	M 1907
—	Leon. Sid.	Trin.	M 1899 A.B. 1902
—	Phil. Sid.	Sid.	M 1908
—	Walt. Rich. Mortimer	Chr.	M 1904 A.B., LL.B. 1907
Woollcombe,	John Vivian	C. C.	M 1900 A.B. 1903. A.M. 1911
Woollcombe-Boyce,	Kenneth Woollcombe }	Cai.	M 1907 A.B. 1910
Woollen,	Wilfrid Hen.	Joh.	M 1906 A.B. 1909
Woollett,	Geo. Hen.	N. C.	M 1892 Joh. A.B. 1895. A.M. 1905
Woolley,	Cha. Austin Lawrence	Trin.	M 1910
--	Edw. John	Cai.	M 1890 A.B. 1893. M.B., B.C. 1898. M.D.
—	Erik Christensen ...	Trin.	M 1907 Chr. A.B. 1910 [1907
—	Jasper Maxwell	Chr.	M 1890 A.B. 1893. M.B. 1896. M.D.† 1912
—	Reg. Maxwell	N. C.	E 1896 Joh. A.B. 1899. A.M. 1903. B.D. [1910
—	Victor Ja. ....*King's		M 1896 A.B. 1899. A.M. 1903. M.D. 1912
Woolliscroft,	Fre. Harold	H. Sel.	M 1912
Woolls,	Geo. Harman	Cai.	M 1909
Woolrich,	Will. Grant	Joh.	M 1912
Woolston,	Ja. Hawthorn	Pem.	M 1893 A.B. 1896. A.M.† 1908
—	Walt. Keep	Jes.	M 1895 A.B. 1898. A.M. 1902
Woolward,	Art. Trevor	Cai.	M 1909 A.B. 1912
Woosnam,	Cha. Tho.	Down.	M 1905 A.B. 1908
—	Maxwell	Trin.	M 1911
Wooster,	Fre. Richards	Trin. H.	M 1902
Wootton,	Hub. Art.	Cla.	M 1902 A.B. 1905. A.M. 1909
—	John Wesley	Trin.	M 1910
Wordie,	Ja. Mann	Joh.	M 1910 A.B. 1912
Wordley,	Eric	Em.	M 1905 A.B. 1908
Wordsworth,	And. Gordon	Qu.	M 1905
—	Cha. Will.	Trin.	M 1899 A.B. 1902
—	John		*LL.D.* 1908
—	John Craufurd	Trin.	M 1904 A.B. 1908
—	John Lionel	Cai.	M 1901
—	Osmund Bartle	Trin.	M 1906 A.B. 1909
—	Will. Art.	Pem.	M 1900 A.B. 1903. A.M. 1907
Workman,	Edw.	Trin.	M 1905 A.B. 1908
—	Eric Woodside	Trin.	M 1908
—	Herb. Will.	Pem.	M 1897 A.B. 1900. A.M. 1907
—	Rob.	Cla.	M 1902

Worley,	Newnham Art.	Em.	M 1910
Wormald,	Drury Percy	Trin.	M 1904
—	Guy	Trin.	M 1902 LL.B. 1905
—	Hugh	Trin.	M 1903 A.B. 1906
—	Oliver Edw.	Cath.	M 1911
Worman,	Ern. Ja.	N. C.	L 1896 A.B. 1898. A.M. 1902
Wormell,	Cha. Octavius Rich.	N. C.	E 1899 A.B. 1903. A.M. 1908
—	Rob. Leon.	N. C.	M 1906 Cath. A.B. 1909
—	Rowland	N. C.	M 1897 Qu. A.B. 1900. A.M. 1904
Worrall,	Newton	Joh.	M 1903 A.B. 1906
—	Phil.	Trin.	M 1899 A.B. 1902
Worsley,	Fre. Will.	Cla.	M 1910
—	Hen. Meyer	Trin.	M 1905 A.B. 1908. A.M. 1912
Worsley-Worswick, Chris. Fra. } Aloysius }		Cai.	M 1904 A.B. 1907
Worster-Drought, Cha.		Down.	M 1906 A.B. 1909
Worters,	Syd. Rob.	Trin.	M 1897 A.B. 1900. A.M. 1905
Wortham,	Hugh Evelyn	N. C.	M 1903 King's A.B. 1906
Worthington, Art. Fra. Bennett ...		N. C.	M 1899 Qu. A.B. 1902. A.M. 1910
—	Art. Furley	Sid.	M 1893 A.B. 1896. A.M. 1910
—	Cha. Rob.	Cai.	M 1895 A.B. 1899. B.C. 1903
—	Edw. Hen. Burdett	Em.	M 1890 A.B. 1893. A.M. 1911
—	Frank	Joh.	M 1898 A.B. 1901. B.C. 1906. M.B. 1909
—	Rich. Fitzpatrick ...	Em.	M 1900 A.B. 1903
—	Rich. Till	Trin.	M 1893 A.B. 1896. M.B., B.C., A.M. 1904
—	Rob. Alf.	Cla.	E 1897 A.B. 1900. B.C. 1904. M.B. 1905
—	Warwick	Pem.	M 1907 Nicholas W. Dennis, A.B. 1910
Wortley,	Harry Almond Saville	Down.	M 1904 A.B. 1907
—	John Dixon	Trin. H.	M 1889 A.B. 1894. A.M. 1909
Wragg,	Ern.	Trin. H.	M 1897 A.B. 1901
—	John Hobson	Qu.	M 1911
—	Norman John	Cla.	M 1909 A.B. 1912
Wray,	Kenneth Chris. Geo.	Jes.	M 1910
—	Rob. Bury	H. Sel.	M 1907 A.B. 1910
Wren,	Tho. Lancaster	Joh.	M 1908 A.B. 1911
Wrenford,	Hugh John Wollaston	Joh.	M 1899 A.B. 1902. A.M. 1912
Wright,	Alan	Jes.	M 1909
—	Alb. John	Cla.	M 1909 A.B. 1912
—	Alf. Gordon	H. Sel.	M 1909 A.B. 1912
—	Alf. Leopold	N. C.	M 1908 Cath. A.B. 1911
—	Art. ....*Qu.		M 1863 A.B. 1867. A.M. 1870. B.D. 1903.
—	Art. Basil	Trin.	M 1899 A.B. 1902 [D.D. 1904
—	Art. Ja.	Jes.	M 1908 A.B. 1911
—	Cha. Alban	Joh.	L 1902 A.B. 1904
—	Cha. Harold	Sid.	M 1899 A.B. 1902
—	Cha. Sam. Eric	Em.	M 1902 A.B. 1905. M.B., B.C. 1911
—	Cha. Seymour	Cai.	M 1908
—	Claude Reg.	Chr.	M 1905 A.B. 1908. B.C. 1912
—	Clem. Vernon	Pem.	M 1906 A.B. 1910
—	Cuthbert Edw.	Em.	M 1897 A.B. 1900. A.M. 1910
—	Cyril Carne Glenton	Pem.	M 1906 A.B. 1909
—	Edw. Gordon Dundas	Qu.	M 1903 A.B. 1906
—	Edw. Martin	King's	M 1910
—	Eric Alf.	H. Sel.	M 1896 A.B. 1899. M.B., B.C. 1904
—	Eric Ja. Howard ...	Trin.	M 1899 A.B. 1902
—	Ern. Hugh	Qu.	M 1891 A.B. 1896. A.M. 1908
—	Fra. Tho.	Cla.	M 1909 A.B. 1912
—	Fra. Whitworth	King's	M 1901 A.B. 1904
—	Frank Trueman Wynyard	Em.	M 1904 A.B. 1908
—	Fre. Hornsby	Trin.	M 1907
—	Geo. Angus	Chr.	M 1894 B.C. 1903. M.B. 1904

Wright,	Geo. Augustus Art.	Qu.	M 1896 A.B. 1899. A.M. 1904
—	Geo. Sid.	King's	M 1901 A.B. 1904
—	Guy Jefferys Hornsby	Em.	M 1893 A.B. 1897. A.M. 1901
—	Harold	Pem.	M 1908 A.B. 1912
—	Hen. Dixon	C. C.	M 1889 A.B. 1892. A.M. 1904
—	Herb. Lawrence	Sid.	M 1905
—	Herb. Middleton	Cai.	M 1906 A.B. 1910
—	Herb. Russell	H. Sel.	M 1893 A.B. 1896. A.M. 1903
—	Ja. Eric	C. C.	M 1907 A.B. 1910 [A.M., M.D. 1902, Sid.
—	John Aldren	N. C.	M 1887 A.B. 1890. M.B. 1894. B.C. 1896.
—	John Moncrieff	Jes.	M 1903 A.B. 1906
—	Jos. Edm. ....*Trin.		M 1897 A.B. 1900. A.M.† 1904
—	Jos. Marshall McCaldin	Pem.	M 1912
—	Leon. Almroth Wilson	Trin.	M 1908 A.B. 1911
—	Lionel Bache Hornsby	Em.	M 1893 A.B. 1897. A.M. 1903
—	Maur. Edw. Art. ...	Cai.	M 1912
—	Oswald Kentish	Chr.	M 1900 A.B. 1903. M.B., B.C. 1910
—	Reg. Montague	Trin.	M 1909 A.B. 1912
—	Reg. Will.	Qu.	M 1909
—	Rich. Gane	Qu.	M 1899 A.B. 1902
—	Rob.	Trin.	M 1901 A.B. 1904
—	Rob. John Despard	Sid.	M 1911
—	Theodore	Joh.	M 1912
—	Will. John	C. C.	M 1903 A.B. 1906
—	Will. Roland Hen. ...	N. C.	M 1906 Joh. A.B. 1911
Wright-Ingle,	Cecil Hubert	Pem.	M 1903 A.B. 1906. A.M. 1910
Wrightson,	Wilfrid Ingram	Trin.	M 1894 A.B. 1898. A.M. 1902
Wrigley,	Alf.	Chr.	M 1908 A.B. 1911
—	Ja. Cecil	King's	M 1894 A.B. 1897. LL.B. 1898. A.M. 1901
—	John Crompton	C. C.	M 1907 A.B. 1910
—	Ruric Whitehead ...	Em.	M 1902 A.B. 1905
Wroth,	Edw. Cha.	Pem.	M 1902 A.B. 1905. A.M. 1912
Wurtzburg,	Cha. Edw.	Em.	M 1910
Wyatt,	Cha. Hen.		*A.M.* 1907
—	Rendel Hammond ...	N. C.	M 1912
—	Rob. Geo. Frederic ...	Qu.	M 1904 A.B. 1907
—	Travers Carey	Chr.	M 1906 A.B. 1909
Wyche,	Cha. Kenneth Hatherell	Sid.	M 1911
Wycliffe-Jones,	Walt. Edmond ...	Qu.	M 1912
Wyer,	Fre. Fra.	Cla.	M 1910
—	John Fra. Wilcox ..:	Em.	E 1902 A.B. 1905
Wyeth,	Frank John	Joh.	M 1897 A.B. 1900. A.M.† 1908
Wyley,	Donald Hen. Fitz-Thomas	Jes.	M 1906 A.B., LL.B. 1909
Wylie,	Angus	Pem.	M 1895 A.B. 1898. B.C., A.M. 1904. M.B.
—	Geo. Munro	Qu.	M 1909 A.B. 1912 [1905
Wyman,	Alf. Bern.	Pem.	M 1903
—	Bern.	Cai.	M 1902 A.B. 1905
—	Hen. Norman	Cai.	M 1899 A.B. 1902
—	Rob. Alex.	Sid.	M 1895 A.B. 1898. A.M. 1902
Wyndham,	Geo. Herimon	Mag.	M 1912
Wynn,	Alf. Norman	Pem.	M 1895 A.B. 1898. A.M. 1902
—	Harold Edw.	Trin. H.	M 1907 A.B. 1910
Wynne,	Art. Meredyth	Trin.	M 1910
—	Rich. Owen	Cla.	M 1912
Wynne-Edwards,	John Copner ...	Sid.	M 1909 A.B. 1912
Wynne-Jones,	Morys	Trin.	M 1905 A.B. 1908
Wynne-Yorke,	Bulkeley Aneurin } Yorke	Cai.	M 1907

Y

Young,	Hen. Will. Pennyfather	Cai.	M 1890 A.B. 1893. M.B., B.C. 1897. M.D.
—	Ja. Vincent	H. Sel.	M 1911 [1902
—	John	Chr.	M 1897 A.B. 1900. A.M. 1904
—	John Douglas	Pem.	M 1902 A.B. 1907
—	John Geo. Coleman	Sid.	M 1911
—	John Gordon	Chr.	M 1910
—	John Villiers	Em.	M 1905
—	Mark Aitchison	King's	M 1905 A.B. 1908
—	Norman Campbell ...	Chr.	M 1904
—	Pat. Cha.	Chr.	M 1899 A.B. 1902. A.M. 1907
—	Phil. Mortlock	Cla.	M 1911
—	Phil. Norton Frushard	Joh.	M 1903 A.B. 1906. A.M. 1910
—	Rich. Alf.	King's	M 1904 A.B. 1908
—	Rob. Frew	Chr.	M 1898 A.B. 1901. B.C. 1907. M.B. 1909
—	Rob. Keith	Mag.	M 1910
—	Sam. Leggate Orford	Chr.	M 1896 A.B. 1899. A.M. 1903. M.B., B.C.
—	Tho. Lowbridge	C. C.	M 1903 A.B. 1907 [1904. M.D. 1907
—	Tho. Pallister	Cla.	M 1901 A.B. 1904. LL.B. 1905. A.M. 1908
—	Walt. Roy Hartridge	Jes.	M 1903 A.B., LL.B. 1906
—	Walt. Stuart	Chr.	M 1899 A.B., LL.B. 1902. A.M. 1906
—	Will.	Cath.	M 1908
—	Will. Dinsdale	Jes.	M 1909 A.B. 1912
—	Will. Hen. ....*Pet.		M 1881 A.B. 1884 (2). A.M. 1888. Sc.D.
Younghusband,	Fra. Edw.		Sc.D. 1905 [1904
—	Leigh Norman	Pem.	M 1912
Yugala,	(*Prince* of Siam)	Trin.	M 1902 A.B. 1906
Yusuf,	Mohamed	Down.	M 1910
—	Zain Maur.	Em.	M 1911 [A.M.†, LL.M.† 1901
Yusuf-Ali, Abdullah Khan Bahadur		Joh.	M 1891 A. ibn K. B., A.B., LL.B. 1895.

Z

Zabriskie,	Geo. Gray	Trin.	M 1910
Zaidi,	Syed Mohammed } Mustahsin }	Cath.	M 1910
Zaiman,	Barnet Abr.	Pem.	M 1911
Zair,	John Art.	Em.	M 1898 A.B. 1901. A.M. 1905
Zambra,	Nelson	Trin.	M 1900 A.B. 1903. A.M. 1908
Zamora,	Alberto Medardo ...	Chr.	M 1906 A.B. 1912
Zan,	Maung Bah	Down.	M 1908
Zehme,	Eugen Edgar	Trin.	E 1903
Zeiller,	Cha. René		Sc.D. 1909
Ziar,	Yoong-Sung	N. C.	M 1907 Yung-Sung, Cla. A.B. 1911
Ziegler,	Cha. Hugo	N. C.	M 1909 Pem. A.B., LL.B. 1912
Zoolcadur (*Beg*),	Mirza Mohammed	Chr.	M 1894 A.B. 1897. Zoolcadur Jung, M. M.
			[A.M.† 1903

TABLE OF MATRICULATIONS AND DEGREES, 1901—1912

Year	Matriculations	D.D.	LL.D.	M.D.	Litt.D.	Sc.D.	Mus.D.	B.D.	A.M.	LL.M.	M.C.	Mus.M.	M.B.	B.C.	A.B.	LL.B.	Mus.B.	A.M. incorp.	A.B. incorp.	Total Degrees	Titular	Year
1901	896	2	4	20	1		1	3	427	16	1		50	61	695	38	2			1321	1	1901
1902	909	3	10	21	2	3		1	420	13			62	69	739	40	2			1385	13	1902
1903	929	8	5	23	5			6	420	5			59	83	720	38	4	1		1377	12	1903
1904	935	5	6	19		4	1	5	369	4	3		75	77	718	43		3		1332	31	1904
1905	1047	6	6	30	3	6	2		397	7	2		62	59	691	59	2	1		1333	12	1905
1906	1079	10		22	1	5	2	6	395	8	3		62	67	752	61	4	1	1	1400	13	1906
1907	1162	5	2	28	1	4		7	382	4	4		56	63	731	45	4	1	1	1338	25	1907
1908	1181	6	3	25	1	9		7	381	4	3		{47, 13*}	{62, 7*}	835	56	4			1459	32	1908
1909	1207	7	1	27	3	5		4	339	7	2		48	57	817	56	3	2		1378	26	1909
1910	1191	9		35	2	4	1	5	394	3	4	1	66	70	971	63	2	2		1632	15	1910
1911	1160	8	3	24	1	4			361				54	60	916	59	5	1		1496	18	1911
1912	1201	6	1	22	2	5		3	389	4	2		50	52	933	55	2	2	1	1529	10	1912

* Inaugurated 19 Dec. 1908.

For EU product safety concerns, contact us at Calle de José Abascal, 56–1°,
28003 Madrid, Spain or eugpsr@cambridge.org.

www.ingramcontent.com/pod-product-compliance
Ingram Content Group UK Ltd.
Pitfield, Milton Keynes, MK11 3LW, UK
UKHW042149130625
459647UK00011B/1256